Nursing Times

Why read Nursing Times?

Nursing Times is the leading nursing journal in Britain, offering each week an unrivalled range of medical features on all aspects of health care and first class news coverage of the people and events that shape today's health service.

Nursing Times provides a fund of invaluable information for nurses at every stage of their careers and in every nursing speciality.

Nursing Times' regular features and special supplements provide the best nursing journalism and offer an absorbing challenge to the nurse who wants to be involved in her work.

PERSONAL INFORMATION

NAME JENNIE GRIER.

ADDRESS 21 LAURELBANK AVE Tel. No. 3291

GREENHILL
BONNYBRIDGE
STIRLINGSHIRE
SCOTLAND

Training School

Date of entry ________ Date of leaving ________

General Nursing Council Index No. ________

State Examination ________

Date passed ________

State Registration No. ________ Date ________

Additional training at ________

Examinations passed ________ **Date**

Appointments held ________ **From** ________ **To**

1.________

2.________

3.________

BAILLIÈRE'S NURSES' DICTIONARY

Eighteenth Edition

BARBARA F. CAPE
S.R.N., S.C.M., D.N.(LOND.)
Formerly Tutor,
Saint Bartholomew's Hospital, London

AND

PAMELA DOBSON
S.R.N., S.C.M., R.N.T.
Principal Nursing Officer, Education Division,
United Cambridge Hospitals (Addenbrooke's)

BAILLIÈRE TINDALL
LONDON

Baillière Tindall
7 & 8 Henrietta Street, London WC2E 8QE

Cassell & Collier Macmillan Publishers Ltd, London
35 Red Lion Square, London WC1R 4SG
Sydney, Auckland, Toronto, Johannesburg

The Macmillan Publishing Company Inc.
New York

First edition 1912
Seventeenth edition 1968
Reprinted 1969, 1971, 1972 (twice), 1973
ELBS edition 1974
Reprinted 1975
Spanish edition (Elicien, Barcelona) 1970
Eighteenth edition 1974
Reprinted 1975, 1976, 1977

ISBN 0 7020 0518 5

Made and printed in Great Britain by
William Clowes & Sons, Limited,
London, Beccles and Colchester, for Baillière Tindall

PREFACE

When Miss Cape suggested to me that I might take over from her the revision of the *Nurses' Dictionary*, for successive editions of which she had been responsible over the last fifteen years, I felt deeply honoured, for this little book has been in existence now for more than sixty years—the first edition appeared in 1912—and during that time, I am told, more than a million and a half copies have been sold to nurses all over the English-speaking world.

Keeping this dictionary abreast of rapidly expanding medical knowledge is a heavy responsibility for both the author and the publisher, as it plays such an important part in the education of the student nurses' training in all parts of the world where the English language is used. Nothing is more valuable to the student than a dictionary and an understanding of how to use it as a guide to knowledge. *Baillière's Nurses' Dictionary* not only defines the meaning of each word and shows how it is pronounced, but often gives an explanation of it as well. The number of medical words used increases continually and once again in this revision many new definitions have been added. The larger size of page which has now been adopted has, however, resulted in the definitions, though more numerous, occupying fewer pages than in the last edition.

Certain information, with which student and pupil nurse should be familiar but which cannot be dealt with

in dictionary form, is presented in the form of appendices. The purpose of these appendices, which make up about a quarter of the contents of the book, is to put at the disposal of nurses a wide variety of factual knowledge. For this edition the appendices have been rearranged and brought up to date and some of them have been radically revised, notably those dealing with Dietetics, the Legal Control of Drugs, Legal Aspects of Nursing, and Professional Organizations and Statutory Bodies. The usefulness of these appendices for reference purposes has been generally accepted and they now cover many of the subjects most likely to be of practical importance in day-to-day work in the ward. Once again a series of whole page photographic illustrations has been included between the dictionary section and the appendices.

I would like to thank all my friends and colleagues who have offered advice and help, and particularly Miss Cape for her assistance in the preparation of this new edition, and Miss Lace, Chief Dietician at St Bartholomew's Hospital, who helped with the revision of Appendix 10. I should also like to thank my publishers for their constant help and guidance.

PAMELA DOBSON

Addenbrooke's Hospital, Cambridge
January 1974

CONTENTS

LIST OF PLATES

Plates are bound in between pages 238 *and* 239

A

a- or an- Prefix denoting 'lacking' or 'without'.

ab- Prefix denoting 'from'.

abarticulation (*ab-ar-tik-u-la'-shun*). (1) Dislocation. (2) Diathrosis (*q.v.*).

abdomen (*ab-do'-men*). The belly. The cavity between the diaphragm and the pelvis, lined by a serous membrane, the peritoneum, and containing the stomach, intestines, liver, gall-bladder, spleen, pancreas, kidneys, suprarenal glands, ureters and bladder.

For descriptive purposes, its area can be divided into nine regions:

1. *Right hypochondriac*
2. *Epigastric*
3. *Left hypochondriac*

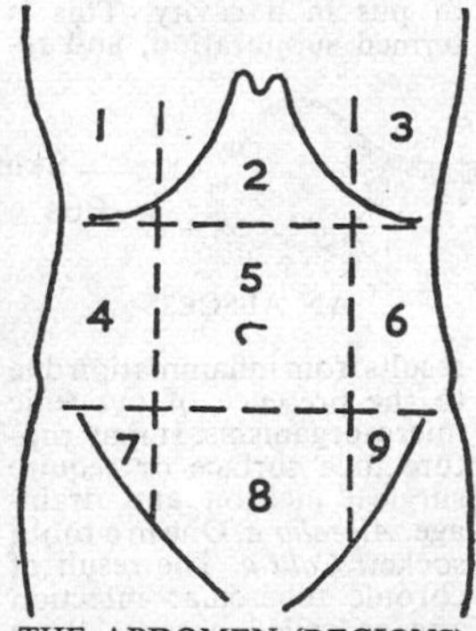

THE ABDOMEN (REGIONS)

4. *Right lumbar*
5. *Umbilical*
6. *Left lumbar*
7. *Right iliac*
8. *Hypogastric*
9. *Left iliac*

abdominal (*ab-dom'-in-al*). Pertaining to the abdomen. *A. aneurysm*. A dilatation of the abdominal aorta. *A. aorta*. That part of the aorta below the diaphragm. *A. bandage*. A many-tailed bandage. *A. breathing*. Deep breathing—hyperpnoea (*q.v.*). *A. reflex*. Reflex contraction of abdominal wall muscles observed when skin is lightly stroked. *A. section*. Incision through the abdominal wall.

abdomino-perineal excision (*ab-dom'-in-o per-in-e'-al*). An operation for excision of the rectum by means of two incisions, an abdominal and a perineal. Often done as a combined synchronized operation by two surgeons, one working at each approach. A colostomy is performed.

abducens (*ab-du'-sens*). Drawing away. Hence: *a. muscle*, the external rectus muscle of the eye, rotating it outward; *a. nerve*, the sixth cranial nerve, supplying this muscle.

abduct (*ab-dukt'*). To draw away from the midline, e.g. of the body.

abductor muscle (*ab-duk'-tor*). One which abducts.

aberrant (*ab-er'-ant*). Taking an unusual course. Said of blood vessels and nerves that are not following their usual course.

aberration (*ab-er-a'-shun*). Deviation from the normal. In optics, failure to focus rays of light. *Mental a.* Mental disorder of an unspecified kind.

ability (*a-bil'-it-e*). The power to perform an act either mental or physical, with or without training. *Innate a.* The ability with which a person is born.

abiosis (*a-bi-o'-sis*). Lifelessness.

abiotrophy (*a-be-ot'-tro-fe*). A nutritional defect, causing a loss of vitality and diminished resistance.

ablation (*ab-la'-shun*). Taking away from, as in amputation or excision of a growth or part of the body.

abnormal (*ab-nor'-mal*). Varying from what is regular or usual

abort (*ab-ort'*). (1) To give birth to a fetus earlier than the twenty-eighth week of pregnancy. (2) To terminate a process or disease before it has run its normal course.

abortifacient (*ab-or-te-fa'-shent*). A drug which produces abortion.

abortion (*ab-or'-shun*). (1) Premature cessation of a normal process. (2) Emptying of the pregnant uterus before the end of the seventh month. *Complete a.* The contents of the uterus are expelled intact. *Criminal a.* The termination of pregnancy for reasons other than those stated in The Abortion Bill 1967 (danger to mental or physical health of mother or child or family), carried out without the approval of two registered medical practitioners and by persons other than registered medical practitioners. *Incomplete a.* Some part of the fetus or placenta is retained in the uterus. *Induced a.* The uterus is emptied intentionally. *Inevitable a.* Bleeding is more profuse accompanied by pains, the cervix is dilated and the contents of the uterus can be felt. *Missed a.* All signs of pregnancy disappear and later the uterus discharges a blood clot surrounding a shrivelled fetus, i.e. a carneous mole (*q.v.*). *Septic a.* One associated with infection. *Therapeutic a.* One induced on medical advice because of danger to the mother's health. *Threatened a.* Bleeding is slight, the cervix is closed.

abrasion (*ab-ra'-zhun*). A superficial injury, where the skin is rubbed or torn.

abreaction (*ab-re-ak'-shun*). A form of psychotherapy in which a patient relives a past painful experience, with the release of repressed emotion.

abscess (*ab'-sess*). A collection of pus in a cavity. This is termed suppuration, and re-

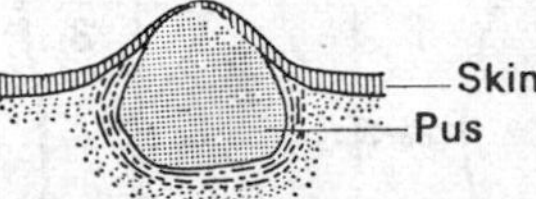

AN ABSCESS

results from inflammation due to the presence of pyogenic micro-organisms. It may rupture to a surface or require surgical incision and drainage. *Alveolar a.* One in a tooth socket. *Cold a.* The result of chronic tubercular infection and so called because there are few, if any, signs of inflammation. *Psoas a.* A cold abscess that has tracked down the psoas muscle from caries of the lumbar vertebrae. *Subphrenic a.* One situated under the diaphragm.

absorbent (*ab-sor'-bent*). (1) Taking up by suction. (2) Any agent that does this.

abulia (*a-bu'-le-ah*). Deficient will-power.

acapnia (*a-kap'-ne-ah*). Deficient carbonic acid content of the blood.

acatalasia (*a-kat-al-a'-ze-ah*). A condition in which there is absence of the enzyme catalase in the patient's cells. Many of these patients may suffer from oral sepsis.

acatalepsy (*a-kat-a-lep'-se*). Lack of understanding.

acataphasia (*a-kat-a-fa'-ze-ah*). Lack of power to express connected thought. Associated with a cerebral lesion.

accidental haemorrhage. *See under* Haemorrhage.

accommodation. The process which, on contraction of the ciliary muscles of the eye, renders the lens more convex, so enabling better focus of the rays of light for near vision, e.g. for reading.

accouchement (*ak-koosh-mon'*). Childbirth.

accoucheur (*ak-koosh-ur'*). An obstetrician.

accoucheuse (*ak-koosh-urz'*). A female obstetrician.

accretion (*ak-re'-shun*). Accumulation of deposits, e.g. of salts to form a calculus in the bladder.

accumulator (*ak-ku'-mu-la-tor*). An apparatus for the collection and storage of electricity.

acephalous (*a-kef'-al-us*). Without a head.

acetabuloplasty (*as-et-ab'-u-lo-plas-te*). An operation performed to improve the depth and shape of the hip socket in correcting congential dislocation of the hip or in treating osteo-arthritis of the hip.

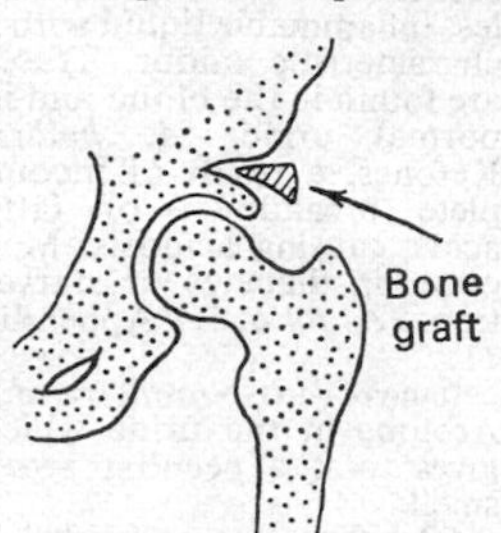

ACETABULOPLASTY

acetabulum (*as-et-ab'-u-lum*). The cup-like socket in the innominate bone, receiving the head of the femur.

acetazolamide (*as-et-a-zol'-am-ide*). A sulphonamide compound which is an oral diuretic and has proved of great benefit in treating glaucoma by reducing the formation of aqueous humour and encouraging its drainage from the anterior chamber. Diamox is a proprietary preparation.

acetic acid (*as-e'-tik as'-id*). The acid of vinegar. It may be used as an antidote to alkaline poisons or as a reagent in urine testing. *See* Appendix 11.

aceto-acetic acid (*as-e'-to as-e'-tik as'-id*). Diacetic acid. A product of fat metabolism. It occurs in excessive amounts in diabetes and starvation giving rise to acetone bodies in the urine.

acetonaemia (*as-e-to-ne'-me-*

ah). Acetone bodies in the blood.

acetone (*as'-e-tone*). A colourless inflammable liquid with a characteristic odour. Traces are found in the blood and in normal urine. *A. bodies*. Ketones, a result of incomplete breakdown of fatty acids, causing acidosis. May occur in diabetes or starvation. *Test for a. See* Appendix 11.

acetonuria (*as-e-to-nu'-re-ah*). Acetone in the urine which gives to it a peculiar sweet smell.

acetylcholine (*as-et-il-ko'-lin*). A chemical transmitter that is released by some nerve endings at the synapse between one neurone and the next or between a nerve ending and the effector organ it supplies. These nerves are said to be cholinergic, e.g. the parasympathetic nerves and the lower motor neurones to skeletal muscles. It is rapidly destroyed in the body by cholinesterase (*q.v.*).

acetylsalicylic acid (*as-e'-til-sal-e-sil'-ik*). The same as aspirin (*q.v.*). An analgesic and antipyretic.

achalasia (*a-kal-a'-ze-ah*). Failure of relaxation of a muscle sphincter causing dilation of the part above, e.g. of the oesophagus above the cardiac sphincter.

Achilles tendon (*ak-il'-eez*). That which inserts the gastrocnemius and soleus muscles into the calcaneum (os calcis).

achillorrhaphy (*ak-il-or'-raf-e*). Repair of the Achilles tendon after it has been torn.

achillotomy (*ak-il-ot'-o-me*). The subcutaneous division of the Achilles tendon.

achlorhydria (*a-klor-hi'-dre-ah*). Absence of HCl in the stomach. A condition found in pernicious anaemia and gastric cancer.

acholia (*a-ko'-le-ah*). A lack of secretion of bile.

acholuria (*a-ko-lu'-re-ah*). Absence of bile from the urine.

acholuric jaundice (*a-ko-lu'-rik*). *See* Jaundice.

achondroplasia (*a-kon-dro-pla'-ze-ah*). The early union of the epiphysis and diaphysis of long bones. Growth is arrested and dwarfism is the result.

achromatopsia (*a-kro-mat-op'-se-ah*). Colour-blindness. It is most often a partial colour deficiency. The subject has cones that are sensitive to only two of the three primary colours (red, blue and green), and the missing colour is interpreted as a mixture of the other two.

achylia (*a-ki'-le-ah*). Literally, absence of chyle. *A. gastrica*. A condition in which gastric secretion is reduced or absent.

acid (*as'-id*). A substance which, when combined with an alkali, will form a salt. Any acid substance will turn blue litmus red. Individual acids may be found under their proper names.

acidaemia (*as-id-e'-me-ah*). Acidity of the blood. The normal reaction is just on the alkaline side of neutrality.

acid–base balance. The normal ratio between the acid ions and the basic or alkaline ions required to maintain the pH of the blood and body fluids. *See* Appendix 2.

acid-fast A bacteriological term to describe those micro-organisms not easily decolorized when once stained.

acid–alcohol-fast. Stained bacteria that are resistant to decolorization by both acid and alcohol.

acidity (*as-id'-it-e*). The quality of being acid.

acidosis (*as-id-o'-sis*). The relation of alkalinity to acidity of the blood is very delicately balanced. A diminution of alkali content or increase of acid will cause a condition termed acidosis. It is characterized by vomiting, drowsiness, hyperpnoea, acetone odour of breath (of 'new-mown hay'), and acetone bodies in urine. It may occur in diabetes mellitus owing to incomplete metabolism of fat. May also be termed ketosis.

acidotic (*as-e-dot'-ik*). A term applied to one suffering from acidosis.

acid phosphatase (*as-id-fos'-fa-taze*). An enzyme secreted by the prostate gland. Higher levels than normal in the blood serum are indicative of carcinoma of the gland or of secondary deposits from the same cause.

acini (*as'-in-i*). Minute saccules or alveoli lined by secreting cells, e.g. the secreting portion of the mammary gland.

acme (*ak'-me*). The highest part of a fever when the symptoms are fully developed.

acne (*ak'-ne*). A term denoting an inflammatory condition of the sebaceous glands. *A. rosacea.* A redness of the forehead, nose and cheeks due to chronic dilatation of the subcutaneous capillaries, which becomes permanent with the formation of pustules in the affected areas. *A. vulgaris.* Occurs commonly in adolescents and young adults on the face, chest and back with the formation of comedones and then pustules. It is thought to be due to androgenic stimulation.

acoustic (*ak-koos'-tik*). Relatting to sound, or the sense of hearing.

acquired. Term applied to disease, habits or immunity developed after birth; not congenital.

acriflavine (*ak-re-fla'-veen*). A powerful antiseptic derived from coal tar used in an aqueous solution 1:1000.

acro- (*ak'-ro*). Prefix meaning extremity.

acrocephalia (*ak-ro-kef-a'-le-ah*). Malformation of the head, in which the top is pointed.

acrocyanosis (*ak-ro-si-an-o'-sis*). A blue appearance of the hands and feet often associated with a vasomotor defect.

acrodynia (*ak-ro-din'-e-ah*). Neuritic pains in the fingers and toes with erythema.

acromegaly (*ak-ro-meg'-al-e*). Marked bony overgrowth especially of the jaw, hands and feet. Associated with over-activity of the anterior lobe of the pituitary gland in adults.

acromioclavicular (*ak-ro'-me-o-klav-ik'-u-lah*). Refers to the joint between the acromion process of the scapula and the lateral aspect of the clavicle.

acromion (*ak-ro'-me-on*). The outward projection of the spine of the scapula, forming the point of the shoulder.

acronyx (*ak'-ro-niks*). Ingrowing of the toe or finger nail.

acroparaesthesia (*ak-ro-par-es-the'-ze-ah*). An orthopaedic condition in which pressure on the nerves of the brachial plexus causes numbness, pain and tingling of the hand and forearm.

acrophobia (*ak-ro-fo'-be-ah*). Morbid terror of being on a height.

acrylics (*ak-ril'-iks*). Synthetic plastic materials derived from acrylic acid, from which dental and medical prostheses may be made.

ACTH. Adrenocorticotrophic hormone. Corticotrophin (*q.v.*).

actinism (*ak'-tin-izm*). The chemical action of rays of light.

actinodermatitis (*ak'-tin-o-derm-at-i'-tis*). Inflammation of the skin, due to the action of Röntgen rays, sun rays or ultraviolet light.

Actinomyces (*ak-tin-o-mi'-seez*). A genus of branching, spore-forming, vegetable parasites, which may give rise to a chronic infective disease, actinomycosis, and from which many antibiotic drugs are produced, e.g. streptomycin.

actinomycin (*ak-tin-o-mi'-sin*). A group of cytotoxic drugs used in the treatment of malignant disease. Have produced encouraging results in Wilm's tumour.

actinotherapy (*ak'-tin-o ther'-ap-e*). Treatment of disease by rays of light, e.g. artificial sunlight.

activate (*ak'-te-vate*). To render active. (1) Yeast is the activator in the process by which sugar is converted into alcohol. (2) The digestive secretions are activated by hormones to carry out normal digestion. *See* Gastrin, *and* Secretin.

activator (*ak'-te-va-tor*). A substance, hormone or enzyme, that stimulates a chemical change though it may not take part in the change.

active movements. Refers to movement or effort to move, by the patient as distinct from 'passive movements' (*q.v.*).

active immunity. An immunity in which the individual has been stimulated to produce his own antibodies.

active principle. Applied to drugs it is the potent part of the drug responsible for its action. *See* Alkaloid.

acupuncture (*ak'-u-punkt-chur*). Puncture of any part by needles in order to carry off fluid.

acuity (*ak-u'-e-te*). Sharpness. *A. of hearing*. An acute perception of sound. *A. of vision*. Clear focussing ability.

acus (*a'-kus*). A needle. (Latin.)

acute (*ak-ute'*). A term applied to a disease in which the attack is sudden, severe and of short duration.

acystia (*a-sis'-te-ah*). Absence of bladder.

ad- Prefix meaning 'next' or 'near'.

Adam's apple. The prominentia laryngea, a protrusion on the front of the neck caused by the thyroid cartilage.

adaptation (*ad-ap-ta'-shun*). The ability to overcome difficulties and to adjust oneself to changing circumstances. Neuroses and psychoses are often associated with failures of adaptation.

addiction (*ad-dik'-shun*). The habitual taking of drugs or alcohol, for which a craving develops that is beyond the will of the person addicted to control and excessive quantities are consumed. *See* Drug dependence.

Addison's anaemia (*ad'-dis-on*). Pernicious anaemia. *See* Anaemia.

Addison's disease. Deficiency disease of the suprarenal cortex; often tuberculous. There is wasting, brown pigmentation of the skin and extreme debility. Treated by deoxycortone acetate DOCA), cortisone and sodium chloride.

adducens (*ad-du'-sens*). Leading toward the midline. Hence, *a. oculi*, the internal rectus muscle of the eye, turning it inward.

adduct (*ad-dukt'*). To draw towards the midline of the body.

adductor (*ad-dukt'-or*). Any muscle which adducts. The opposite of abductor.

adenectomy (*ad-en-ek'-to-me*). Excision of a gland.

adentitis (*ad-en-i'-tis*). Inflammation of a gland.

adenocarcinoma (*ad'-en-o-kar-sin-o'-mah*). A malignant new growth of glandular epithelial tissue.

adenoid (*ad'-en-oid*). Resembling a gland. Generally applied to abnormal lymphoid growth in the nasopharynx.

adenoidectomy (*ad-en-oid-ek'-to-me*). The removal of adenoid tissue from the nasopharynx by curettage.

adenoma (*ad-en-o'-mah*). An innocent tumour of glandular tissue, often containing fibrous tissue when it is, strictly, a *fibro-adenoma*, e.g. of the breast or thyroid.

adenomatome (*ad-en-o'-mat-ome*). An instrument for the removal of adenoids.

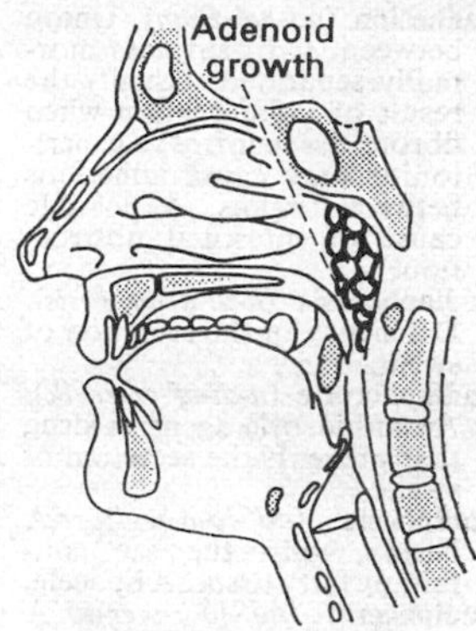

SECTION THROUGH PHARYNX SHOWING ADENOID GROWTH

adenomyoma (*ad-en-o-mi-o'-mah*). An innocent new growth involving both glandular and muscle tissue, usually applied to benign growths of the uterus.

adenopathy (*ad-en-op'-ath-e*). Any disease of a gland, particularly of a lymphatic gland.

adenosclerosis (*ad-en-o-skler-o'-sis*). Hardening of a gland usually the result of calcification.

adenovirus (*ad-en-o-vi'-rus*). A variety of virus. Many types have been isolated, some of which cause respiratory tract infections, while others are associated with conjunctivitis or epidemic keratoconjunctivitis.

adeps (*ad'-eps*). Lard. (Latin.) a foundation fat for ointments. *A. lanoe hydrosus* is lanolin (*q.v.*).

ADH. Antidiuretic hormone (*q.v.*).

adhesion (*ad-he'-zhun*). Union between two surfaces normally separated. Usually the result of inflammation when fibrous tissue forms: e.g. peritonitis may cause adhesions between organs. A possible cause of intestinal obstruction.

adiaphoresis (*a-di-af-or-e'-sis*). Deficiency in the secretion of sweat.

adiaphoretic (*a-di-af-or-et'-ik*). An anhidrotic agent. A drug that prevents the secretion of sweat.

adipocele (*ad'-ip-o-seel*). A hernia, with the sac containing fatty tissue. A lipocele.

adipocere (*ad'-ip-o-seer*). A waxy substance formed in dead bodies when decomposing in water.

adipose (*ad'-ip-ose*). Of the nature of fat. Fatty.

adiposuria (*ad-ip-o-su'-re-ah*). Fat in the urine. Lipuria.

aditus (*ad'-it-us*). An opening or passageway, often applied to that between the middle ear and the mastoid antrum.

adjustment (*ad-just'-ment*). In psychology the ability of a person to adapt to changing circumstances or environment.

adjuvant (*ad'-ju-vant*). A secondary remedy, assisting the action of another.

Adler's theory. (*Alfred Adler, Austrian psychiatrist 1870–1937*). The theory that neuroses develop as a compensation for feelings of inferiority either social or physical.

adnexa (*ad-neks'-ah*). Appendages. *Uterine a.* The ovaries and Fallopian tubes.

adolescence (*ad-o-les'-ense*). The period between puberty and maturity. In the male—14 to 21 years. In the female—12 to 19 years.

adrenal (*ad-re'-nal*). The suprarenal gland, an endocrine gland placed on top of each kidney.

adrenalectomy (*ad-ren-a-lek'-to-me*). Surgical removal of the adrenal glands. Replacement therapy by giving cortisone is essential.

adrenaline (*ad-ren'-a-lin*). A hormone secreted by the medulla of the adrenal gland. Has an action similar to normal stimulation of the sympathetic nervous system: (1) causing dilatation of bronchioles; (2) raising of the blood pressure by constriction of surface vessels and stimulation of the cardiac output; (3) releasing glycogen from the liver. It is therefore used to treat such conditions as asthma, collapse and hypoglycaemia. It acts as a haemostat in local anaesthetics.

adrenergic (*ad-ren-er'-jik*). A term applied to nerves that release the chemical transmitter noradrenaline in order to stimulate the muscles and glands they supply.

adrenogenital (*ad-re-no-jen'-it-al*). Relating to both the adrenal glands and the gonads. *A. syndrome.* A condition of masculinization in women caused by over-activity of the adrenal cortex.

adrenolytic (*ad-re-no-lit'-ik*). Drugs that inhibit the stimulation of the sympathetic nerves and the activity of adrenaline.

adsorbent (*ad-sorb'-ent*). A substance that has the power of attracting gas or fluid to itself.

adrenocorticotrophic hormone. Corticotrophin (*q.v.*).

adsorption (*ad-sorp'-shun*). The power of certain substances to attach other gases or substances in solution to their surface and so concentrate them there. This is made use of in chromatography (*q.v.*).

advancement (*ad-vans'-ment*). An operation to detach a tendon or muscle and reattach it further forward.

adventitia (*ad-ven-tish'-e-ah*). The outer coat of an artery or vein.

Aëdes aegypti mosquito (*ah-e'-deese-gip'-ti-mos-ke'-to*). The intermediate host of the germ of yellow fever.

aegophony (*e-goff'-o-ne*). A sound heard in the chest on auscultation, when the patient speaks. Compared to the 'bleat of a goat'.

aeration (*air-a'-shun*). Supplying with air. Describes the oxygenation of blood which takes place in the lungs.

aerobe (*air'-obe*). An organism that can live and thrive only in the presence of oxygen.

aerogenous (*air-oj'-en-us*). Applied to micro-organisms that give rise to the formation of gas, usually by the fermentation of lactose or other carbohydrate.

aerophagy (*air-off'-aj-e*). Swallowing of air.

aerosol (*air'-o-sol*). Finely divided particles or droplets. *A. sprays* are used in medicine to humidify air or oxygen or for the administration of drugs by inhalation.

aetas (*e'-tas*). Age. (Latin.)

aetiology (*e-te-ol'-o-je*). The science of the cause of disease.

afebrile (*a-feb'-ril*). Absence of fever.

affect (*af-fekt'*). The feeling experienced in connection with an emotion or mood. A term used in psychiatry.

affective (*af-fekt'-if*). Pertaining to the emotions or moods. *A. psychoses.* Major mental disorders in which there is grave disturbance of the emotions. *See* Psychoses.

afferent (*af'-er-ent*). Conveying towards the centre. *A. nerves.* The sensory nerve fibres which convey impulses from the periphery towards the brain. *A. paths or tracts.* The course of the sensory nerves up the spinal cord and through the brain. *A. vessels.* Arterioles entering the glomerulus of the kidney, or lymphatics entering a lymph gland. *See also* Efferent.

affiliation (*af-fil-e-a'-shun*). The judicial decision of paternity of a child with a view to a maintenance order.

affinity (*af-fin'-it-te*). Chemically, the attraction of two substances for each other, e.g. carbon monoxide has a greater affinity for haemoglobin than has oxygen.

affusion (*af-fu'-zhun*). Pouring of hot or cold water over the body.

after-birth. The placenta, cord and membranes, expelled after childbirth.

after-care. The term applied to social, medical or nursing care following a period of hospital treatment.

after-image. A visual impression that remains briefly following the cessation of sensory stimulation.

after-pains. Pains due to uterine contraction, after childbirth.

agalactia (*a-gal-ak'-te-ah*). Absence of the milk secretion after childbirth.

agammaglobulinaemia (*a-gam-*

mah-glob-u-lin-e'-me-ah). A condition found in children in which there is no gamma-globulin (*q.v.*) in the blood. They are therefore susceptible to infections because of an inability to form antibodies.

agar-agar (*a'-gah a'-gah*). A gelatinous substance prepared from seaweed. Used (a) as a culture-medium for bacteria. (b) As a laxative because it absorbs liquid from the digestive tract and swells, so stimulating peristalsis.

agenesia (*a-jen-e'-ze-ah*). Failure of a structure to develop properly. Often applied to the reproductive organs where *A*. may lead to impotence or sterility.

agglutination (*ag-glu-tin-a'-shun*). Collecting into clumps. *Cross a.* A simple test to decide the group to which a given blood belongs. (*See* Blood grouping.) A drop of serum of known classification is put on a microscope slide, to this is added a drop of the blood to be tested. An even admixture indicates compatibility. A flaky, spotted appearance, incompatibility—as the corpuscles have clumped together. *A. test.* A means of aiding diagnosis and identification of bacteria. If serum containing known agglutinins comes into contact with the specific bacteria clumping will take place. *See* Widal reaction.

agglutinative (*ag-glu'-tin-a-tiv*). (1) Adherent or glueing together. (2). A term applied to serum which causes clumping of bacteria, e.g. in the Widal reaction.

agglutinins (*ag-glu'-tin-ins*). Antibodies formed in blood which cause clumping together of bacteria, so that they are more readily destroyed by phagocytes.

agglutinogen (*ag-glu'-tin-o-jen*). Any substance that, when present in the blood stream, can cause the production of specific antibodies or agglutinins.

aglutition (*a-glu-ti'-shun*). Difficulty in the act of swallowing Dysphagia (*q.v.*).

aggressin (*ag-gres'-sin*). A substance said to be produced by some bacteria which increases their effect upon the host.

aggression (*a-gre'-shun*). Animosity or hostility shown towards another person or object, as a response to opposition or frustration.

aglossia (*a-glos'-e-ah*). Absense of the tongue

agnathia (*ag-na'-the-ah*). Absence, or defective development of the jaw.

agnosia (*ag-nos'-e-ah*). An inability to recognize objects as the sensory stimulus cannot be interpreted in spite of a normal sense organ.

agoraphobia (*ag-or-af-fo'-be-ah*). A fear of open spaces.

agranulocyte (*a-gran'-u-lo-site*). A white blood cell without granules in the cytoplasm. Includes monocytes and lymphocytes.

agranulocytosis (*a-gran'-u-lo-si-to'-sis*). A condition in which there is a marked decrease or complete absence of granular leucocytes in the blood. May result from: (1) the use of drugs, e.g. gold salts, sulphonamides, thiouracil and benzol preparations; (2) excessive irradiation of the bone marrow. Characterized by sore throat, ulceration of the mouth and pyrexia. It may result in severe prostration and death.

agraphia (*a-graf'-e-ah*). Loss of the power of expressing thought in writing.

ague (*a'-gu*). Malaria. Intermittent fever, accompanied by recurring fits of shivering and sweating. *See* Malaria.

AHG. Antihaemophilic globulin (*q.v.*).

A.I.D. Artificial insemination with donor semen.

A.I.H. Artificial insemination of a woman by her husband's semen.

air. A mixture of gases surrounding the earth. It consists of: non-active nitrogen 79 per cent, oxygen 21 per cent which supports life and combustion; traces of neon, argon, hydrogen, etc., and carbon dioxide 0·04 per cent except in expired air when 4 per cent is exhaled, due to diffusion which has taken place in the lungs. Air has weight and exerts pressure. The latter aids in syphonage from body cavities. *Complemental a.* Additional air which can be inhaled with inspiratory effort. *Residual a.* That remaining in the lungs after deep expiration. *Stationary a.* That remaining in the lungs after normal expiration. *Supplemental a.* The extra air forced out of the lungs with expiratory effort. *Tidal a.* That which passes in and out of the lungs in normal respiratory action.

air-bed. A rubber mattress inflated with air.

air-hunger. A form of dyspnoea in which there are deep sighing respirations, characteristic of severe haemorrhage or acidosis.

akinesia (*a-kin-e'-ze-ah*). Loss of muscle power. This may be the result of a brain or spinal cord lesion or temporarily due to anaesthesia.

akinetic (*a-kin-et'-ik*). An adjective applying to states or conditions where there is lack of movement.

alalia (*al-a'-le-ah*). Loss or impairment of the power of speech due to muscle paralysis or cerebral lesion.

alastrim (*a-las'-trim*). A contagious eruptive fever probably a mild form of smallpox. *See* Variola.

Albee's operation (*al'-be*). A bone graft from the tibia is placed along affected vertebrae to secure immobilization. The spinous processes are split and the graft inserted.

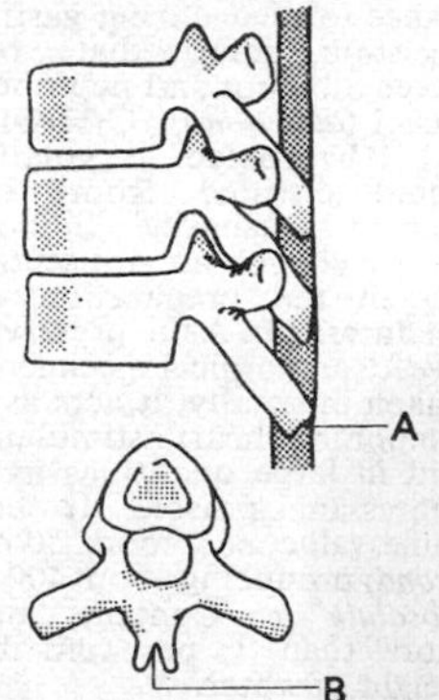

ALBEE'S OPERATION
A and B, site of graft.

albinism (*al'-bin-izm*). A condition in which there is congenital absence of pigment in the skin, hair and eyes. It may be partial or complete.

albino (*al-be'-no*). A person affected with albinism.

albumin (*al-bu'-min*). A protein present in most animal tissues. It is soluble in water and coagulates on heating, e.g. white of egg. *Tests for a. See* Appendix 11.

albuminuria (*al-bu-min-u'-re-ah*). The presence of albumin in the urine, occuring e.g. in renal disease, in most feverish conditions and sometimes in pregnancy. *Orthostatic* or *postural a.* A non-pathological form which affects some individuals after prolonged standing.

albumose (*al'-bu-mose*). A substance formed during gastric digestion, intermediate between albumin and peptone.

alcohol (*al'-ko-hol*). C_3H_5OH. Ethyl hydroxide. A volatile liquid distilled from fermented saccharine liquids. Used: (1) As an antiseptic. (2) In the preparation of tinctures. (3) As a preservative for anatomical specimens. Taken internally, it acts as a temporary heart stimulant, and in large quantities as a depressant poison. It has some value as a food. 30 ml *brandy* producing about 400 J. *Absolute a.* Contains not more than 1 per cent by weight of water.

alcohol-fast. A term used of bacteria that having once been stained are resistant to decolorization by alcohol.

alcoholism (*al'-ko-hol-izm*). The state of poisoning by excessive consumption of alcohol.

alcoholic (*al-ko-hol'-ik*). A person addicted to excessive, uncontrolled alcohol cosumption. This results in loss of appetite and vitamin B deficiency, leading to peripheral neuritis with eye changes and cirrhosis of the liver and to progressive deterioration in the personality. *A. delirium. See* Delirium.

alcoholuria (*al-ko-hol-u-re'-ah*). The presence of alcohol in the urine. This may be estimated when excess blood levels of alcohol are suspected.

aldosterone (*al-dos'-ter-one*). A hormone, isolated from the adrenal cortex, that aids the retention of sodium and the excretion of potassium in the body and by so doing aids in maintaining the electrolyte balance.

aldosteronism (*al-dos'-ter-on-izm*). An excess secretion of aldosterone caused by an adrenal neoplasm. The serum potassium is low and the patient has hypertension.

aleukaemia (*a-lu-ke'-me-ah*). Diminished numbers of white cells in the blood. Leucopenia (*q.v.*).

alexia (*a-leks'-e-ah*). A form of aphasia, when there is inability to recognize written or printed words. Word-blindness.

algae (*al'-je*). Simple forms of plant life. These form a slimy film on sand filter beds and aid purification of water.

algesia (*al-je'-ze-ah*). Sensitiveness to pain.

algesimeter (*al-jes-im'-et-er*). An instrument which indicates the degree of sensitiveness of the skin.

algid (*al'-jid*). Chilly and cold. *A. state.* One of severe collapse and prostration which may occur in certain types of malaria and in cholera.

algorithm (*al'-gor-rithm*). A rule of procedure for solving problems by breaking down a process of learning or decision taking into simple stages.

aliment (*al'-e-ment*). Food or nourishment.

alimentary (*al-e-ment'-ar-e*). Relating to the system of nutrition. *A. canal.* The passage through which the food passes, from mouth to anus. *A. system.* The alimentary tract together with the liver and other organs concerned in digestion and absorption. *A. glycosuria.* The temporary presence of sugar in the urine following a meal. Causes: (1) An excessive amount of this taken in the diet. (2) When there is a lower renal threshold (*q.v.*) than is normal.

alimentation (*al-e-ment-ta'-shun*). Supplying the patient's need for nutrition.

aliquot (*al'-e-kwot*). One of a number of equal parts forming a compound or solution.

alkalaemia (*al-kal-e'-me-ah*). An increase in the alkali content of blood. The pH is above 7·40. Alkalosis (*q.v.*).

alkali (*al'-kal-i*). A substance capable of uniting with acids to form salts, and with fats to form soaps. It turns red litmus paper blue. *Sodium*, *potassium* and *ammonia* are the chief ones used in medicine. *A. reserve.* An estimation of the plasma bicarbonate. The normal is about 0·2 per cent of carbon dioxide. In acidosis there is a fall, and in alkalosis a rise in this figure.

alkaloid (*al'-kal-oid*). Active nitrogenous compounds that are alkaline in solution and have a bitter taste. The active principles in many medicinal plants and now many can be synthesized.

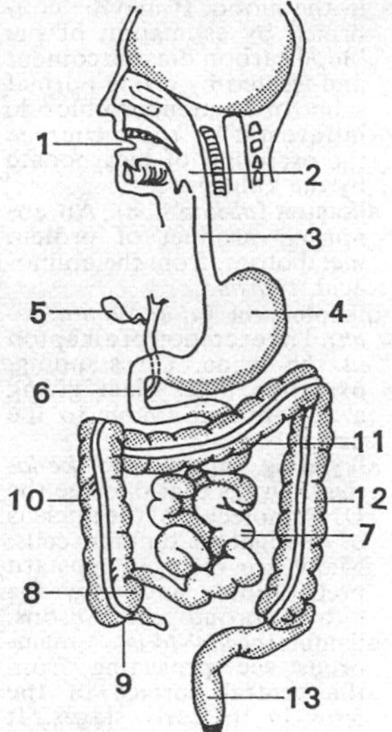

ALIMENTARY CANAL

1. Mouth.
2. Pharynx.
3. Oesophagus.
4. Stomach.
5. Gall bladder.
6. Duodenum.
7. Small intestine.
8. Ileo-caecal valve.
9. Caecum and vermiform appendix
10. Ascending colon.
11. Transverse colon.
12. Descending colon.
13. Rectum and anus.

alkalosis (*al-kal-o'-sis*). An increase in the alkali reserve in the blood. It may be confirmed by estimation of the blood carbon dioxide content and treated by giving normal saline or ammonium chloride intravenously to encourage the excretion of bicarbonate by the kidneys.

alkapton (*al-kap'-ton*). An abnormal product of protein metabolism, from the amino-acid, *tyrosine*.

alkaptonuria (*al-kap-ton-u'-re-ah*). The excretion of alkapton in the urine. On standing, oxidation takes place giving a dark-brown colour to the urine.

alkylating agents (*al'-ke-la-ting*). Drugs that damage the DNA molecule of the nucleus of malignant tumour cells. Many are nitrogen mustard preparations and may be termed chromosome poisons.

allantois (*al-lan'-to-is*). A membrous sac projecting from the ventral surface of the fetus in its early stages. It eventually helps to form the placenta.

allergen (*al'-er-jen*). A substance that stimulates an altered reaction in the body known as an allergy.

allergy (*al'-er-je*). A hypersensitiveness to some foreign protein, small doses of which produce a violent reaction in the patient. Asthma, hay fever, angioneurotic oedema, migraine, and some types of urticaria and eczema are allergic states. *See also* Anaphylaxis.

allocheiria (*al-o-sher'-e-ah*). A response or sensation felt on (referred to) the opposite side from that to which a stimulus is applied.

allopurinol (*al-o-pu'-rin-ol*). A drug which reduces the formation of uric acid. Used in the long term treatment of gout to lessen the frequency and severity of attacks. Zyloric is a proprietary preparation.

allograft (*al'-o-graft*). Tissue transplanted from one person to another. *Non-viable a.* Skin taken from a cadaver that cannot regenerate. *See* Lyophilized skin. *Viable a.* Living tissue transplanted.

almoner (*ah'-mon-er*). A medical social worker (*q.v.*).

aloes (*al'-oze*). Extract from the leaves of the aloe. An irritant purgative likely to cause griping. It is contra-indicated in pregnancy.

alopecia (*al-o-pe'-she-ah*). Baldness.

alternating current. An electrical current that runs alternately from the negative and positive poles, as in the ordinary Faradic coils.

altruism (*al'-tru-izm*). A regard for the well-being of other people.

alum (*al'-um*). A powerful astringent and styptic, composed of aluminium and potassium sulphate. *A. precipitated toxoid:* APT (*q.v.*).

aluminium (*al-u-min'-e-um*). A silver-white metal with a low specific gravity, compounds of which are astringent and antiseptic. *A. hydroxide.* Used in the treatment of gastric cases as an antacid. *A. paste.* Combined with zinc oxide and liquid paraffin it forms a good skin protective against ileostomy discharge. *A. silicate.* Kaolin, used as a dusting powder or as a poultice. Refined kaolin may be given orally to check diarrhoea.

alveoli (*al-ve-o'-li*). (1) The sockets of the teeth. (2) The air sacs of the lungs. (3) The acini of glands.

alveolitis (*al-ve-o-li'-tis*). Inflammation of the alveoli. *Extrinsic allergic a.* Inflammation of the alveoli of the lung caused by inhalation of an antigen such as pollen.

Alzheimer's disease (*alts'-hi-mer*). Presenile dementia with cerebral atrophy and characteristic histological changes.

amalgam (*am-al'-gam*). A compound of mercury and other metals. *Dental a.*: used for filling teeth.

amastia (*a-mas'-te-ah*). Congenital absence of breast tissue.

amaurosis (*am-aw-ro'-sis*). Blindness in which there are no discernible changes in the structures of the eye. Often temporary, it may be present in hysteria, nephritis, uraemia or may be due to a sudden change of posture.

amaurotic familial idiocy (*am-aw-rot'-ik.*) Tay-Sachs disease. A familial metabolic disorder commencing in infancy or childhood. Characterized by progressive mental deterioration, blindness and spastic paralysis.

ambidextrous (*am-be-deks'-trus*). Equally skilful with either hand.

ambivalence (*am-biv'-al-ense*). The existence of contradictory emotional feelings towards an object, commonly of love and hate for another person. If these feelings occur to a marked degree they lead to psychological disturbance.

amblyopia (*am-ble-o'-pe-ah*). Dimness of vision.

amblyoscope (*am'-ble-o-skope*). An instrument used in orthoptic treatment to aid the correction of strabismus and develop binocular vision.

amboceptor (*am'-bo-sep-tor*). A substance present in blood after immunization. *Syn.*, immune body.

ambulant (*am'-bu-lant*). One who is able to walk.

ambulatory (*am'-bu-la-tor-e*). The capacity to walk.

amelia (*a-me'-le-ah*). The complete absence of an extremity at the shoulder or pelvic girdle.

amelioration (*a-me-le-or-a'-shun*). Improvement of the patient's symptoms; a lessening of the severity of a disease.

amenorrhoea (*a-men-or-e'-ah*). Absence of menstruation. *Primary a.* when menses have never occurred. *Secondary a.* The menses cease after they have been established owing to disease or pregnancy.

amentia (*a-men'-she-ah*). Mental subnormality. The result of heredity, failure of development of the embryo or birth trauma.

amethocaine (*a-meth'-o-kane*). A local anaesthetic for mucous membranes. *A. pastille*. This, slowly dissolved in the mouth, will aid the passage of a bronchoscope or gastroscope.

ametria (*a-me'-tre-ah*). Congenital absence of the uterus.

ametropia (*a-me-tro'-pe-ah*). Defective vision. A general word applied to incorrect refraction.

amidone (*am'-e-do-n*). Methadone, a powerful analgesic which is included in the Misuse of Drugs Act list. Physeptone is a proprietary preparation of the drug.

amino acids (*am'-in-o as'-ids*). Chemical compounds containing the radical NH_2. The end-products of protein digestion. *Essential a a.* Those required for replacement and growth, which cannot be synthesized in the body in sufficient amounts. *Non-essential a a.* Are necessary for proper growth but can be synthesized in the body.

aminophylline (*am-in-off'-il-in*). An alkaloid from camellia, it relaxes plain muscle spasm of the bronchioles and coronary arteries. It may be given by mouth, intravenously or as a suppository, and is useful in treating asthma and heart failure.

aminosalicyclic acid. *See* Para-aminosalicylic acid.

amiphenazole (*am-e-fen'-a-zol*). A drug that stimulates the central nervous system and respiratory centre. Daptazole is a proprietary preparation of it.

amitosis (*a-mi-to'-sis*). Multiplication of cells by simple division or fission.

amitriptyline (*am-e-trip'-tel-een*). An antidepressant drug that is chemically related to chlorpromazine. It is useful in relieving tension and anxiety but may cause dizziness and hypotension.

ammonia (*am-mo'-ne-ah*). NH_3. A colourless pungent liquid. Used as a cardiac stimulant, a diuretic and an expectorant.

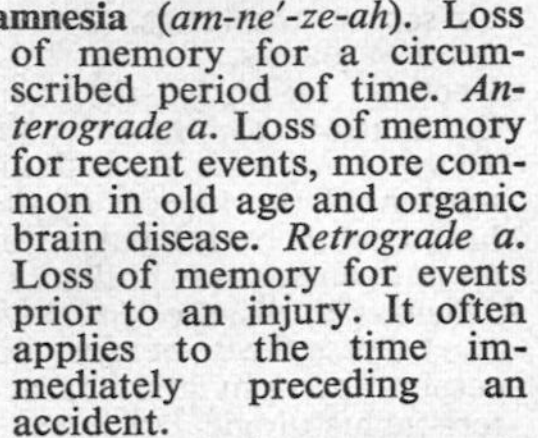

amnesia (*am-ne'-ze-ah*). Loss of memory for a circumscribed period of time. *Anterograde a.* Loss of memory for recent events, more common in old age and organic brain disease. *Retrograde a.* Loss of memory for events prior to an injury. It often applies to the time immediately preceding an accident.

amniocentesis (*am-ne-o-sen-te'-sis*). The withdrawal of fluid from the uterus through the abdominal wall by means of syringe and needle in cases of hydramnios.

amnion (*am'-ne-on*). The innermost membrane enveloping the fetus and enclosing the liquor amnii.

amnioscopy (*am-ne-os'-ko-pe*). Inspection of the amniotic sac using an amnioscope.

amniotomy (*am-ne-ot'-o-me*). The surgical rupture of the amniotic sac via the cervical os. *A. forceps* are used.

Amoeba (*am-e'-bah*). A family of one-celled protozoans. One type is the cause of dysentry. *See* *Entamoeba histolytica*.

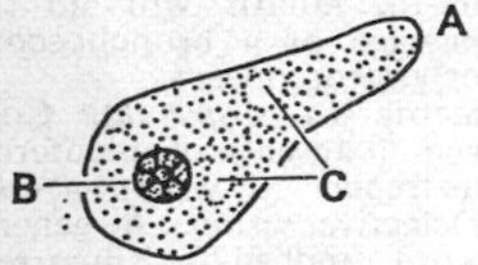

In motion

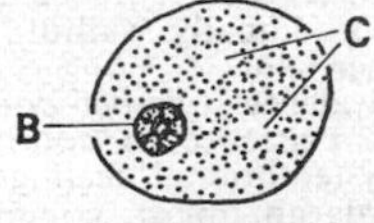

Resting stage

AMOEBA

A. Pseudopodia; B. Nucleus; C. Vacuoles.

amoebiasis (*am-e-bi'-a-sis*). An ulcerative colitis due to the *Entamoeba histolytica*, with special tendency to formation of liver abscess.

amoeboid (*am-e'-boid*). Referring to structure or movement like that of the amoeba.

amorphous (*a-mor'-fus*). Without definite shape, The term may be applied to fine powdery particles, as opposed to crystals.

ampère (*am'-pair*). The unit of intensity of an electrical current.

amphetamine (*am-fet'-a-meen*). A synthetic drug which stimulates the higher nerve centres, so increasing mental alertness and abolishing fatigue. It is a Controlled Drug and may give rise to addiction, so should be used with care.

amphiarthrosis (*am-fe-ar-thro'-sis*). A form of joint in which the bones are joined together by fibrocartilage, e.g. the junctions of the vertebrae.

amphoric (*am-for'-ik*). Pertaining to a bottle. The term is used to describe the sound, sometimes heard on auscultation over cavities in the lungs. It resembles that produced by blowing across the mouth of a bottle.

ampicillin (*am-pe-sil'-in*). An oral penicillin with a wide range of antibacterial action. It may be given orally or by intramuscular injection.

ampoule (*am'-pool*). A small glass vessel in which drugs of specified dose for injection are sealed.

ampulla (*am-pull'-ah*). The dilated end of a canal, e.g. of a uterine tube.

amputation (*am-pu-ta'-shun*). Surgical removal of a limb or part of the body, e.g. the breast.

amputee (*am-pu-tee'*). A person who has had a limb amputated.

amyl (*am'-il*). C_5H_{11}. *A. nitrite* is prescribed for inhalation in cases of angina pectoris. It is a vasodilator and heart stimulant. In capsules which are broken into a handkerchief and the fumes inhaled.

amylase (*am'-il-ase*). An enzyme that reduces starch to maltose. Found in saliva (ptyalin) and pancreatic juice (amylopsin).

amylobarbitone (*am-il-o-bar'-be-tone*). A barbiturate hypnotic. Amytal is a proprietary preparation.

amyloid (*am'-il-oid*). Resembling starch. *A. degeneration.* A degenerative change in tissues, with formation of an abnormal, white, waxy substance.

amyloidosis (*am-il-oid-o'-sis*). Degenerative changes in the tissues in which amyloid tissue is formed. It may be a primary condition or secondary to prolonged infection.

amylopsin (*am-il-op'-sin*). Amylase (*q.v.*).

amylum (*am'-il-um*). Starch.

anabolic (*an-ab-ol'-ik*). Referring to a substance that aids in the repair of body tissue, particularly protein. Androgens may be used in this way.

anabolism (*an-ab'-ol-izm*). The building up or synthesis of cell structure from digested food materials. *See* Metabolism.

anacidity (*an-as-id'-it-e*). Decrease in normal acidity.

anacrotic (*an-a-krot'-ik*). An abnormal curve in the ascending line of a pulse tracing by sphygmograph. Typical of aortic stenosis.

anaemia (*an-e'-me-ah*). Deficiency in either quality or quantity of red corpuscles in the blood, giving rise especially to symptoms of anoxaemia (*q.v.*). There is pallor, breathlesness on exertion with palpitations, slight oedema of ankles, lassitude, headache, giddiness, albuminuria, indigestion, constipation and amenorrhoea. Anaemia may be due to many different causes. *Addison's a.* or *pernicious a.* Due to the inability of the stomach to secrete the intrinsic factor necessary for the absorption of vitamin B_{12} from the diet. *Aplastic a.* The bone marrow is unable to produce red blood corpuscles. A rare condition of unknown cause in most cases, but it may arise from the administration to susceptible persons of certain drugs or from their injudicious use, e.g. benzol preparations or chloramphenicol. *Deficiency a.* Any type which is due to a lack of the necessary factors for cell formation, e.g.: *Iron deficiency a.* The commonest anaemia in Great Britain, due to a lack of iron in the diet. It may also be due to excessive blood loss. *Haemolytic a.* A variety in which there is excessive destruction of red blood corpuscles caused by antibody formation in the blood (*see* Rhesus factor) by drugs or by severe toxaemia, as in extensive burns. *Macrocytic a.* A type in which the cells are larger than normal; present in pernicious a. *Microcytic a.* A variety in which the cells are smaller than normal, as in iron deficiency. *Splenic a.* A congenital, familial disease in which the red blood corpuscles are fragile and easily broken down.

anaerobe (*an'-er-obe*). Micro-organisms which derive their oxygen from the media in which they grow and not from the air, e.g. the bacilli of tetanus and gas gangrene.

anaesthesia (*an-es-the'-ze-ah*). (1) Insensibility to touch or pain. Loss of sensation in a part or in the whole of the body, induced by drugs. (2) *Basal a.* One in which consciousness is lost, but supplemental drugs have to be given to ensure complete anaesthesia. (3) *Hysterical a.* A common symptom in hysteria, in which the insensibility to touch or pain has a local distribution unrelated to the nerve supply. (4) *Inhalation a.* The drugs or gas used are administered by a face mask or endotracheal tube to cause general anaesthesia. (5) *Intravenous a.* To produce unconsciousness by introduction of a drug, e.g. hexobarbitone, into a vein. (6) *Rectal a.* A barbiturate or paraldehyde may be given per rectum. (7) *Regional*, *block* or *local a.* Either by infiltration of the operation field with injections of procaine (*field block*); or by injecting it near main nerve trunks (*nerve block*). (8) *Spinal a.* Injection of procaine or Nupercaine into the spinal canal to anaesthetize the lower half of the body. (9) *Splanchnic a.* A cocaine preparation is injected into the splanchnic ganglion which causes complete relaxation of abdominal viscera. A preliminary local skin anaethesia is needed to make the incision.

anaesthetic (*an-es-thet'-ik*). A drug causing anaethesia, either local or general.

anaesthetist (*an-ees'-thet-ist*).

One who administers an anaesthetic.

anal (*a'-nal*). Pertaining to the anus. *A. eroticism*. Sexual pleasure derived from anal functions. *A. fissure*. Fissure in ano. *See* Fissure. *A. fistula*. Fistula in ano. *See* Fistula.

analeptic (*an-a-lep'-tik*). A drug that stimulates the central nervous system and is an antagonist to drugs causing depression.

analgesia (*an-al-je'-ze-ah*). Insensibility to pain.

analgesic (*an-al-je'-sik*). A remedy which relieves pain.

analogous (*an-al'-o-gus*). Having the same function but different in structure and origin.

analogue (*an'-a-log*). (1) An organ with different structure and origin but the same function. (2) A compound with similar structure but differs in respect of a particular element.

anamnestic reaction (*an-am-nes'-tik*). When antibodies from one type of an organism previously encountered are stimulated during the response to another type.

anaphylaxis (*an-a-fil-ak'-sis*). Often termed anaphylactic shock. It is the name given to a severe reaction, often fatal, occurring when a second injection of a particular foreign protein is given, e.g. horse serum. The symptoms are severe dyspnoea, rapid pulse, profuse sweating and collapse. The condition may be avoided by giving a test dose before all serum injections. If the patient has any reaction he may be desensitized by giving repeated small doses.

anaplasia (*an-a-pla'-se-ah*). Without form, or a reversion of cells to a more primitive form.

anasarca (*an-a-sar'-kah*). Fluid in the cellular tissues. Generalized oedema. *See also* Ascites.

anastomosis (*an-as-to-mo'-sis*). In *surgery*, any artificial connection of two hollow structures, e.g. gastro-enterostomy (*q.v.*) *Porta-caval a*. The operation of choice in portal hypertension. The portal vein is joined to the inferior vena cava. In *anatomy*, the joining of the branches of two blood vessels.

anatomy (*an-at'-o-me*). The science of the structure of the body.

anconeus (*an-ko'-ne-us*). An extensor muscle of the forearm.

androgens (*an'-dro-jens*). Hormones secreted by the testes and adrenal cortex. They are steroids which can be synthesized and produce the secondary male characteristics and the building up of protein tissue.

anencephalous (*an-en-kef'-al-us*). Having no brain. A form of congenital monstrosity.

anergic (*an-er'-jik*). Sluggish, inactive.

aneurine hydrochloride (*an'-u-rin hi-dro-klor'-ide*). Vitamin B_2; thiamine. *See* Appendix 10.

aneurysm (*an'-u-rizm*). A local dilatation of an artery. It may start as a congenital weakness, be due to chronic inflammation or be caused by trauma. The pressure of blood causes it to increase in size and rupture is likely. Sometimes excision of the aneurysm or ligation of the artery is possible. *Dissecting a*. A

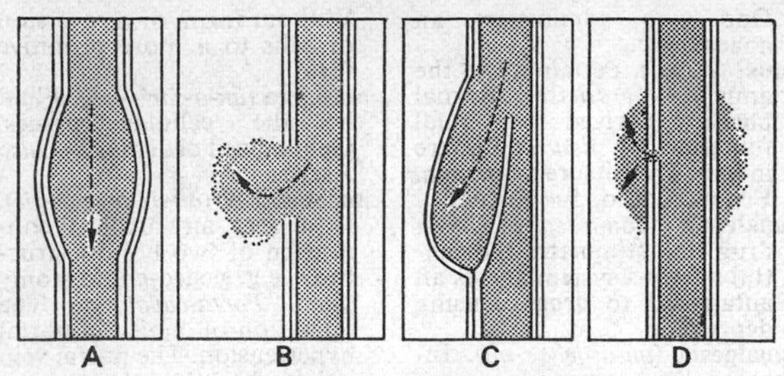

TYPES OF ANEURYSM

A. Fusiform; B. Saccular; C. Dissecting; D. False.

condition in which a tear occurs in the aortic lining where the middle coat is necrosed and blood gets between the layers stripping them apart. Death usually occurs from rupture of the vessel.

angiectasis (*an-je-ek′-tas-is*). Abnormal enlargement of capillaries.

angiitis (*an-je-i′-tis*). Inflammation of a blood or lymph vessel.

angina (*an-ji′-nah*). (1) A tight strangling sensation or pain. *A. of effort* or *A. pectoris.* Cardiac pain which occurs, on exertion, owing to insufficient blood supply to the heart muscle. It can be relieved by a vasodilatant drug, glyceryl trinitrate. (2) An inflammation of the throat causing pain on swallowing. *Lugwig's a.* Acute pharyngitis with swelling and abscess formation. *Vincent's a.* Infection and ulceration of the gums, fauces and tonsils by a spirochaete, *Borrelia vincenti*, and a rod-like bacillus, *Fusiformis.*

angiocardiography (*an-je-o-kar-de-og′-raf-e*). The radiological examination of the heart and large blood vessels by means of cardiac catheterization and a radio-opaque dye.

angiogram (*an′-je-o-gram*). A radiological picture of blood vessels.

angioma (*an-je-o′-mah*). An innocent tumour composed of dilated blood vessels. *See also* Lymphangioma.

angioneurotic oedema (*an-je-o-nu-rot′-ik e-de′-mah*). An allergic reaction causing increased permeability of the capillary walls, with often sudden marked oedema. There is danger of asphyxia if the larynx is involved. It may be treated by adrenaline, antihistamine drugs, or corticosteroids.

angioplasty (*an′-je-o-plas-te*). Plastic surgery of a blood vessel.

angiosarcoma (*an-je-o-sar-ko′-mah*). A malignant vascular growth.

angiospasm (*an′-je-o-spazm*). A spasmodic contraction of an artery. This may be caused by a clot within the vessel, by trauma or by impairment to nerve supply.

angiotensin (*an-je-o-ten'-sin*). A pressor substance that raises the blood pressure. It is a polypeptide produced by the action of renin on plasma globulins.

Ångström unit (*ang'-strom*). A measure of wavelength. One unit is one ten-thousand millionth of a metre.

anhidrosis (*an-hi-dro'-sis*). Marked deficiency in the secretion of sweat.

anhidrotic (*an-hi-drot'-ik*). An agent that diminishes the secretion of sweat. An adiaphoretic.

anhydraemia (*an-hi-dre'-me-ah*). Deficiency of fluid in the blood.

anhydrous (*an-hi'-drus*). Containing no water.

aniline (*an'-il-een*). A chemical compound derived from coal tar, used for the making of dyes, e.g. methylene blue. It is a strong antiseptic.

anion (*an'-i-on*). An electronegative ion which travels against (or up) the current towards the anode. *See also* Cation.

aniridia (*an-i-rid'-e-ah*). Lack or defect of the iris.

anisocoria (*an-i-so-ko'-re-ah*). Inequality of diameter of the pupils.

anisocytosis (*an-i'-so-si-to'-sis*). Inequality in the size of cells, especially applied to red blood cells.

anisomelia (*an-i-so-me'-le-ah*). A congenital condition in which one of a pair of limbs is longer than the other.

ankle (*an'-kl*). The joint between the leg and the foot formed by the tibia and fibula articulating with the talus (*astragalus*).

ankyloblepharon (*an-ki-lo-blef'-ar-on*). Adhesions and scar tissue on the ciliary borders of the eyelids, giving the eye a distorted appearance. This may result from burns or from chronic blepharitis (*q.v.*).

ankylosis (*an-ki-lo'-sis*). Abnormal consolidation and immobility of the bones of a joint.

Ankylostoma duodenale (*an-ki-lo-sto'-mah du-o-den-a'-le*). A genus of hookworm which may inhabit the duodenum and cause extreme anaemia.

annular (*an'-nu-lah*). Ring-shaped. *A. ligament*. That surrounding the wrist or ankle.

anoci-association (*an-o'-se as-so-se-a'-shun*). The exclusion of pain, fear and shock in surgical operations, brought about by means of local anaesthesia and basal narcosis (*q.v.*).

anode (*an'-ode*). The positive pole of an electric battery or accumulator.

anodyne (*an'-o-dine*). A drug which relieves pain.

anomaly (*a-nom'-al-e*). Considerable variation from the normal.

anomie (*an'-om-e*). A sociological term denoting a person who no longer identifies himself with other people. He is lonely and cannot project his own personality.

anonychia (*an-o-nik'-e-ah*). Having no nails.

Anopheles (*an-off'-el-eez*). A genus of mosquito. Many are carriers of the malarial parasite and by their bite infect human beings. Other species transmit filariasis.

anorchism (*an-or'-kizm*). Absence of testicles.

anorexia (*an-or-rek'-se-ah*). Loss of appetite. *A. nervosa*. A symptom occurring in

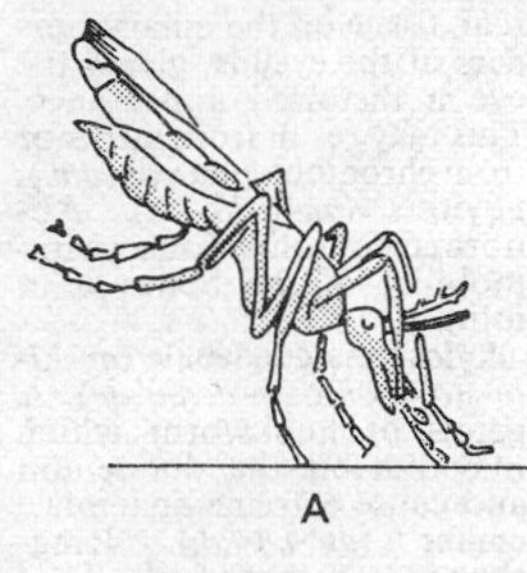

ANOPHELES MOSQUITO (A) SHOWING TYPICAL STANCE COMPARED WITH THAT OF CULEX (THE GNAT) (B)

hysteria, in which there is complete lack of appetite with extreme emaciation.

anosmia (*an-oz'-me-ah*). Loss of the sense of smell.

anovular (*an-ov'-u-lah*). In the absence of ovulation, usually referring to uterine bleeding or the menstrual cycle when drugs have been taken to inhibit ovulation.

anoxaemia (*an-oks-e'-me-ah*). Lack of oxygen in the blood.

anoxia (*an-oks'-e-ah*). Lack of oxygen to an organ or tissue. *Cerebral a.* Lack of sufficient oxygen to the brain. *See* Hypoxia.

antacid (*ant-as'-id*). A substance neutralizing acid.

antagonism (*an-tag'-on-izm*). Applied to drugs, the impairment of efficacy of one or of each drug in the presence of the other.

antagonist (*an-tag'-on-ist*). One that has an opposite action to another, e.g. the biceps muscle to the triceps or one drug neutralizing another.

ante- Prefix meaning 'before'.

anteflexion (*an-te-flek'-shun*). A bending forward, as of the body of the uterus. *See also* Retroflexion.

ante mortem (*an-te mort'-em*). Before death.

antenatal (*an-te-na'-tal*). Before birth.

antepartum (*an-te-par'-tum*). An event that occurs before birth. *A. haemorrhage*. Bleeding occurring before birth. *See* Placenta praevia.

anterior poliomyelitis (*po-le-o-mi-el-i'-tis*). *See* Poliomyelitis.

anteversion (*an-te-ver'-shun*). The state of tilting forward, e.g. the normal position of the uterus. *See also* Retroversion.

anthelmintic (*an-thel-min'-tik*). Destructive to worms. A vermifuge.

anthracene purgatives (*an'-thra-seen purg'-at-ivs*). Vegetable drugs which stimulate peristalsis and increase secretion, e.g. senna, rhubarb, cascara, etc.

anthracosis (*an-thra-ko'-sis*). A disease of the lungs, caused by inhalation of coal dust. 'Miner's lung'.

anthrax (*an'-thraks*). A contagious disease of cattle, transmitted to man by direct contact or by wool or hide infected with the *Bacillus anthracis*, causing malignant pustules of the skin or woolsorter's pneumonia if inhaled. It is treated by penicillin.

anthropoid (*an'-thro-poid*). (1)

Resembling a man, e.g. a species of ape. (2) Applied to a pelvis that is narrowed from side to side. A form of contracted pelvis.

anti- Prefix which means 'against'.

antibiotic (*an-te-bi-ot'-ic*). A drug derived from living matter, which prevents the growth of, or destroys bacteria, e.g. penicillin.

antibodies (*an'-te-bod-ees*). Specific protein substances or globulins formed in the body which counteract the effects of bacterial antigens or toxins.

anticholinergic (*an-te-ko-lin-er'-jik*). Drugs that inhibit the action of acetylcholine, the chemical transmitter by which the vagus nerve stimulates the stomach and intestines.

anticholinesterase (*an-te-ko-lin-est'-er-aze*). A substance that will inhibit cholinesterase and thereby block the nerve impulse transmitted by the latter.

anticoagulant (*an-te-ko-ag'-u-lant*). A substance which prevents blood from clotting, e.g. sodium citrate or heparin.

anticonvulsants (*an-te-kon-vuls'-ants*). A group of drugs which arrest or prevent convulsions and are used in epilepsy and other conditions in which convulsions arise. The drugs include phenobarbitone and Epanutin.

antidepressants (*an-te-de-press'-ants*). Drugs that are used in the treatment of depression. There are three groups: (1) Stimulants such as amphetamine of only limited use; (2) Monoamine oxidase inhibitors (*q.v.*); (3) Imipramine group, chemically related to chlorpromazine.

antidiabetic (*an-te-di-a-bet'-ik*). Drugs that aid in controlling diabetes by lowering the blood sugar. *See* Tolbutamide. *A. hormone.* Insulin is the naturally occurring agent secreted by the pancreas.

antidiuretic (*an-te-di-u-ret'-ik*). Against diuresis, i.e. reducing the volume of urine. *A. hormone*. Secreted by the posterior pituitary gland, its function is to regulate the reabsorption of water by the kidney tubules.

antidote (*an'-te-dote*). An agent which counteracts the effect of a poison, e.g. alkalis neutralize acids.

antiemetic (*an-te-e-met'-ik*). Drugs that prevent or overcome nausea and vomiting.

antifibrinolytic (*an-te-fib-rin-o-lit'-ik*). Drugs that neutralize or block the action of the enzyme that causes fibrinolysis. Fibrinolysis may be a cause of haemorrhage.

antigen (*an'-te-jen*). Any substance, bacterial or otherwise, which stimulates the production of an antibody. *Pollen a.* Extract of the pollen of plants used for diagnosis and treatment in hay fever.

antihaemophilic globulin (*an-te-hem-o-fil'-ik*). One of the factors (Factor VIII) present in plasma, necessary for blood clotting. There is a deficiency of it in haemophilia (*q.v.*).

antihistamine (*an-te-hist'-a-min*). Any one of a group of drugs, which block the tissue receptors for histamine. They are used to treat allergic conditions, e.g. drug rashes, hay-fever, serum sickness, etc. They include promethazine and mepyramine.

antihypertensive (*an-te-hi-per-ten'-siv*). Drugs that lower raised blood pressure.

antimalarial (*an-te-ma-lair'-e-al*). Drugs that suppress or cure malaria.

antimetabolites (*an-te-met-ab'-ol-ites*). Chemical compounds which prevent the effective utilization of the corresponding metabolite, so that the action is selective and interferes with normal growth or cell mitosis if the process requires that metabolite. They are used in treating malignant disease.

antimitotic (*an-te-mi-tot'-ik*). Preventing mitosis in the cells. *A. drugs*. Those drugs that prevent malignant cell multiplication. Cytotoxic drugs.

antimony (*an'-tim-on-e*). A metallic drug poisonous to protozoa now mainly used in the treatment of tropical parasitic infestation, e.g. schistosomiasis.

antimycotic (*an-te-mi-kot'-ik*). Preparations that are effective in treating fungal infections.

antineoplastic (*an-te-ne-o-plast'-ik*). A term applied to drugs that are effective against the multiplication of malignant cells. *See* Cytotoxic *and* Antimitotic.

antiperistalsis (*an-te-per-e-stal'-sis*). A movement reversing that of peristalsis (*q.v.*). It may cause vomiting.

antipruritic (*an-te-pru-rit'-ik*). An external application or drug that relieves itching.

antipyretic (*an-te-pi-ret'-ik*). An agent which reduces fever.

anti-rhesus serum (*an-te-re'-sus seer'-um*). A substance containing rhesus agglutinins produced in the blood of those who are rhesus-negative if the rhesus-positive antigen obtains access to it, e.g. by blood transfusion. Haemolysis and jaundice are the result. *See* Rhesus factor.

antisepsis (*an-te-sep'-sis*). The use of antiseptic methods.

antiseptic (*an-te-sep'-tik*). Preventing infection. An agent which tends to prevent the growth of organisms causing sepsis in wounds.

antiserum (*an-te-seer'-um*). A serum prepared against a specific disease by immunizing an animal so that antibodies are formed These can then be used to create a passive immunity or to treat the infection in man.

antisocial (*an-te-so'-shal*). Against society. *A. behaviour*. A term used in psychiatry to describe the refusal of an individual to accept the normal obligations and restraints imposed by the community upon its members.

antispasmodic (*an-te-spas-mod'-ik*). Preventing spasm, especially by drugs, such as atropine or chloroform. *A. enema*. *See* Enema.

antistatic (*an-te-stat'-ik*). The term applied to measures taken to prevent the build up of static electricity. *See* Appendix 5.

antitoxin (*an-te-toks'-in*). A substance produced by the body cells as a reaction to invasion by bacteria, which neutralizes their toxins. Serum from immunized animals contains these antitoxins, and is used in the treatment of specific diseases, e.g. diphtheria, tetanus, etc. *See* Immunity.

antivenin (*an-te-ven'-een*). An antitoxic serum to neutralize the poison injected by the bite of a snake, especially the cobra.

antrostomy (*an-tros'-to-me*). Opening the maxillary antrum, usually for drainage purposes.

antrum (*an'-trum*). A cavity in a bone. *A. of Highmore* or *maxillary a.* is the air-containing hollow in the upper jawbone (maxilla). *Mastoid a.* That in the mastoid bone.

anuria (*an-u'-re-ah*). Suppression of urine.

anus (*a'-nus*). The extremity of the alimentary canal, through which the faeces are discharged. *Imperforate a.* One which is not patent. Usually due to congenital defect.

anxiety (*ang-zi'-et-e*). A chronic state of tension which affects both mind and body. *A. neurosis*. *See* Neurosis.

aorta (*a-ort'-ah*). The large artery rising out of the left ventricle of the heart. *Abdominal a.* That part of the vessel in the abdomen. *Arch of the a.* The curve of the tube over the heart. *Thoracic a.* That part which passes through the chest.

aortic (*a-or'tik*). Pertaining to the aorta. *A. incompetence.* Due to previous inflammation the aortic valve has become fibrosed and unable to close completely, thus allowing backward flow of blood (*a. regurgitation*) into the left ventricle during diastole. *A. stenosis.* Scar tissue has caused narrowing of the aortic valve.

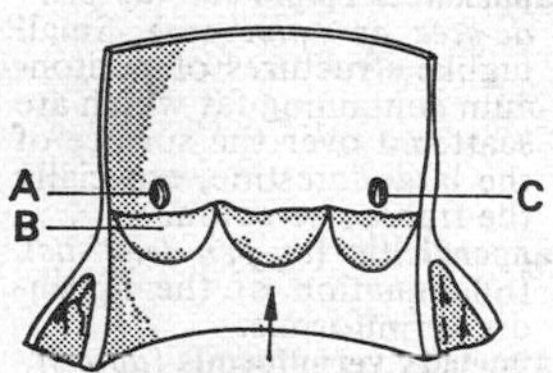

THE AORTIC VALVE
A. Right coronary orifice.
B. Semilunar pocket.
C. Left coronary orifice.

aortitis (*a-or-ti'tis*). Inflammation of the aorta.

aortography (*a-or-tog'-raf-e*). A radio-opaque dye is inserted into the aorta to render visible lesions of the aorta or its main branches. The insertion may be translumbar or by passing a catheter up the femoral or brachial artery.

apathy (*ap'-ath-e*). An appearance of indifference, with no response to stimuli or display of emotion.

apepsia (*a-pep'-se-ah*). Impairment or absence of gastric digestion.

aperient (*a-peer'-e-ent*). A drug which produces an action of the bowels.

aperistalsis (*a-per-e-stal'-sis*). Lack of peristaltic movement of the intestines.

apex (*a'-peks*). The top or pointed end of a cone-shaped structure. *A. of the heart.* the blunt end enclosing the left ventricle. *A. beat.* the beat of the heart against the chest wall which can be felt during systole. *A. of lung.* the extreme upper part of the organ.

Apgar score (*Ap'-gah*). A numerical expression used in the assessment of the new born; values are given for heart rate, respiratory effort, muscle tone, reflex irritability and colour.

aphagia (*a-fa'-je-ah*). Loss of the power to swallow.

aphasia (*a-fa'-ze-ah*). Loss of the power of speech or of understanding the written or spoken word. The cause may be disease, or haemorrhage affecting the speech centre in the brain. *Motor a.* Inability to speak. *Sensory a.* Inability to understand the written or spoken word.

aphonia (*a-fo'-ne-ah*). Inability to produce sound. The cause may be organic disease of the larynx, or be purely functional.

aphrodisiac (*af-ro-dis'-e-ak*). A drug which excites sexual desire.

aphthae (*af'-the*). Thrush. Small greyish-white vesicles, which form ulcers on the tongue and inside the mouth (*aphthous stomatitis*). It is likely to occur in infants with fever or digestive disorders, but can be prevented by careful regard to mouth hygiene.

apicectomy (*a-pe-sek'-to-me*). Excision of the root of a tooth.

apicolysis (*a-pe-kol'-is-is*). A treatment to ensure collapse of the apex of a tuberculous lung by stripping off the parietal pleura.

aplasia (*a-pla'-ze-ah*). Defective development of tissue.

aplastic (*a-plas'-tik*). Without power of development. *A. anaemia. See* Anaemia.

apnoea (*ap-ne'-ah*). Cessation of respiration due to temporary reduction of the CO_2 content in the blood. *See* Cheyne–Stokes respiration.

apocrine (*ap'-o-krin*). Sweat glands that develop in hair follicles, mainly found in the axilla and pubic and perineal areas.

apomorphine (*ap-o-mor'-fin*). A derivative of morphine which produces vomiting.

aponeurosis (*ap-o-nu-ro'-sis*). A tendinous expansion on broad muscles to give attachment usually to bone.

apophysis (*ap-off'-is-is*). A bony prominence or excrescence.

apoplexy (*ap'-o-pleks-e*). A sudden fit of insensibility, usually caused by rupture of a cerebral blood vessel. The symptoms are coma, accompanied by stertorous breathing, and a varying degree of paralysis of the opposite side of the body to the lesion. *Embolic a.* Due to the blocking of a blood vessel in the brain; e.g. by a fragment of clot carried by the blood from a diseased heart valve.

apothecaries' weight and fluid measure (*a-poth'-e-kair-eez*). The English system of weights and measures. Now being replaced by the metric system. *See* Appendix 14.

apothecary (*a-poth'-e-kair-e*). One who prepares and sells drugs.

appendectomy (*ap-pen-dek'-to-me*). *See* Appendicectomy.

appendicectomy (*ap-pen-de-sek'-to-me*). Removal of the appendix vermiformis (*q.v.*).

appendices epiploicae (*ap-pen'-de-seez ep-e-ploi'-see*). Small taglike structures of peritoneum containing fat which are scattered over the surface of the large intestine, especially the transverse colon.

appendicitis (*ap-pen-de-si'-tis*). Inflammation of the appendix vermiformis.

appendix vermiformis (*ap-pen'-diks ver - me - for' - mis*). A worm-like tube with a blind end, projecting from the caecum in the right iliac region. It may be from 2·5 to 15 cm (1 to 6 in.).

apperception (*ap-per-sep'-shun*). Conscious reception and recognition of a sensory stimulus.

applicator (*ap'-lik-a-tor*). An instrument for setting in place such local remedies as radium.

apposition (*ap-po-sish'-un*). To fix together correctly, e.g. fragments of bone in setting a fracture.

apprehension (*ap-re-hen'-shun*). A feeling of dread or fear.

apraxia (*a-praks'-e-ah*). The inability to perform correct movements because of a brain lesion and not because of sensory impairment or loss of muscle power in the limbs. It may result from cerebral arteriosclerosis.

APT (alum precipitated toxoid). A special preparation used for diphtheria immunization. *See* Toxoid.

aptitude (*ap'-te-tude*). The natural ability or capacity to acquire mental and physical skills.

apyrexia (*a-pi-reks'-e-ah*). The absence of fever.

aqua (*ak'-wah*). Water. *Aqua bulliens* (*aq. bull.*) = boiling water. *A. destillata* (*aq. dest.*) = distilled water. *A. fontana* (*aq. font.*) = tap water. *A. fortis* (*aq. fort.*) = nitric acid. *A. marina* (*aq. mar.*) = seawater.

aqueduct (*ak'-we-duct*). A canal for the passage of fluid. *A. of Sylvius* connects the third and fourth ventricles of the brain.

aqueous humour (*ak'-we-us hu'-mor*). The fluid filling the anterior and posterior chambers of the eye.

arachis oil (*ar'-ak-is*). Peanut oil; used as a substitute for olive oil.

arachnodactyly (*ar-ak-no-dakt'-il-e*). Spider fingers. A congenital condition.

arachnoid (*ar-ak'-noid*). A web-like membrane covering the central nervous system between the dura and pia mater.

arborization (*ar-bor-i-za'-shun*). The branching terminations of many nerve fibres and processes.

arboviruses (*ar-bo-vi'-rus-ez*). Viruses transmitted by insect vectors (arthropod-borne), e.g. mosquitoes, sandflies or ticks. The diseases caused include many types of encephalitis, also yellow, dengue, sandfly and rift valley fevers.

arcus senilis (*ar'-kus sen-il'-is*). An opaque circle appearing round the edge of the cornea in old age.

areola (*a-re-o'-lah*). A ring of pigmentation, e.g. that surrounding the nipple.

areolar tissue. *See* Tissue.

argentum (*ar-jen'-tum*). Silver.

arginine (*ar'-jen-een*). A basic amino acid which is necessary for urea formation and creatine synthesis.

argon (*ar'-gon*). An inert gaseous element in the atmosphere.

Argyll Robertson pupil (*ar-gile' rob'-ert-son*). *See* Pupil.

arrector pili (*ar-rek'-tor pi-li*). Arrectores pilorum (pl.). Small muscle attached to the hair follicle in the skin. When contracted causes the hair follicle to become more erect.

arrhenoblastoma (*ar-en-o-blast-o'-mah*). A rare ovarian tumour which causes masculinization in the woman, with male distribution of hair and coarsening of the skin.

arrhythmia (*a - rith' - me - ah*). Lack of rhythm, e.g. in the heart's action. *Sinus a.* An abnormal pulse rhythm due to disturbance of the sino-atrial node (*see* Node), causing quickening of the heart on inspiration and slowing on expiration. It seems to be normal in some children.

arsenic (*ar-sen-ik*). A soft grey metal, organic preparations of which are used in medicine.

artefact (*ar'-te-fakt*). Something that is man made or introduced artificially.

arteriectomy (*ar-te-re-ek'-to-me*). The removal of a portion of artery wall usually followed by anastomosis or a replacement graft. *See* Arterioplasty.

arteriography (*ar-te-re-og'-raf-e*). Radiography of arteries.

arteriole (*ar-te'-re-ole*). A small artery.

arterioplasty (*ar-te-re-o-plas'-te*). The reconstruction of an artery by means of replacement surgery. Now most often achieved by using a portion of vein from the patient or a tube made from plastic cloth.

arteriorraphy (*ar-te-re-or'-raf-e*). Ligature of an artery.

arteriosclerosis (*ar - te' - re - o - skler-o'-sis*). A gradual loss of elasticity in the walls of arteries due to thickening and calcification. It is accompanied by high blood pressure, and precedes the degeneration of internal organs associated with old age or chronic disease.

arteriotomy (*ar-te-re-ot'-o-me*). An incision into an artery. This may be done for removal of an embolus.

arteritis (*ar-ter-ri'-tis*). Inflammation of an artery. *Giant-cell a.* A variety of polyarteritis resulting in partial or complete occlusion of a number of arteries. The carotid arteries are often involved. Corticosteroids may result in complete resolution.

artery (*ar'-ter-e*). A tube of muscle and elastic fibres lined with endothelium which distributes blood from the heart to the capillaries.

arthralgia (*ar - thral' - je - ah*). Neuralgic pains in a joint.

arthrectomy (*ar-threk'-to-me*). Excision of a joint.

arthritis (*ar-thri'-tis*). Inflammation of a joint. *Osteo-a.* A degenerative condition attacking the articular cartilage and is aggravated by an impaired blood supply, previous injury, or overweight. *Pyogenic a.* An infection of a joint by pyogenic organisms. These may be gonococci, staphylococci, or streptococci. *Rheumatoid a.* A chronic inflammation, usually of unknown origin. The disease is progressive and incapacitating, owing to the ankylosis resulting.

arthro- (*ar'-thro-*). A prefix meaning relating to a joint.

arthroclasia (*ar-thro-kla'-ze-ah*). The breaking down of adhesions in a joint to produce freer movement.

arthrodesis (*ar - throd' - e - sis*). The fixation of a movable joint by surgical operation. *Compression a.* The two bone ends are held together by clamps. *See* Charnley.

arthrodynia (*ar-thro-din'-e-ah*). Painful joints. *See* Arthralgia.

arthrogram (*arth'-ro-gram*). An X-ray film taken after a joint has been injected with a radio-opaque substance to outline the bone and cartilage.

arthrography (*arth-rog'-raf-e*). The examination of a joint by means of X-rays. A contrast or opaque medium may be used.

arthroplasty (*ar'-thro-plas-te*). Plastic surgery for the reorganization of a joint, frequently the hip joint. *Cup a.* The articular surface may be reconstructed and covered by a vitallium cup. *Replacement a.* The head of the femur may be partially removed and replaced by a metal prosthesis. *Excision a.* The affected joint surfaces are excised and the gap fills with fibrous tissue or muscle. *Girdlestone a.* An excision arthroplasty of the hip. *McKee Farrar a.* Both the head of the femur and the socket are replaced, the latter being cemented into the prepared acetabulum.

arthrotomy (*ar-throt'-o-me*). An incision into a joint.

articulation. (1) A junction point of two or more bones. (2) The enunciation of words.

articulo mortis (*ar-tik'-u-lo mor'-tis*). In the act of dying.

artificial feeding. The giving of food by orifices other than the mouth. (1) *Nasal route*, by introducing nutritive fluids into the stomach, through a fine tube via the nostril. (2) *Via the mouth*, by means of an oesophageal or Ryle's tube. (3) *Rectal route*, by catheter and funnel. Only

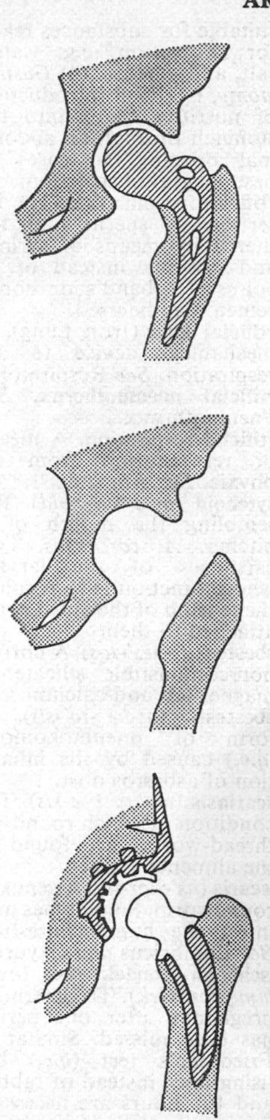

McKEE FARRAR ARTHROPLASTY

The stainless steel ball and cup are embedded in plastic cement. A screw is driven into the bone, through the cement, above the joint.

suitable for substances ready for absorption, e.g. water, salt, and glucose. (4) *Gastrostomy*, by direct introduction of nutritive fluids into the stomach through an abdominal opening, in cases of oesophageal obstruction.

artificial insemination. The insertion of sperm into the uterus by means of syringe and cannula instead of by coitus. Husband's or donor semen may be used.

artificial lung (Iron Lung). A mechanical device to aid respiration. *See* Respirator.

artificial pneumothorax. *See* Pneumothorax.

artificial respiration. A means of resuscitation from asphyxia. *See* Appendix 1.

arytenoid (*ar-e-tee'-noid*). Resembling the mouth of a pitcher. *A. cartilages*. Two cartilages of the larynx, whose function is to regulate the tension of the vocal cords attached to them.

asbestos (*as-bes'-tos*). A fibrous non-combustible silicate of magnesium and calcium.

asbestosis (*as-bes-to'-sis*). A form of pneumokoniosis (*q.v.*) caused by the inhalation of asbestos dust.

ascariasis (*as-kar-i'-a-sis*). The condition in which round- or thread-worms are found in the alimentary tract.

Ascaris (*as'-kar-is*). A genus of roundworm. Some types may infest the human intestine. *See* Lumbricus *and* Oxyuris.

Aschheim–Zondek test (*ash'-hime zon'-dek*). To determine pregnancy after one period has been missed. Similar to Friedman's test (*q.v.*) but using mice instead of rabbits and 100 hours are necessary for its completion.

Aschoff's nodules or **bodies** (*ash'-hoff*). The nodules present in heart muscle in rheumatic myocarditis.

ascites (*as-si'-teez*). Free fluid in the peritoneal cavity. It may be the result of local inflammation, of venous obstruction, or part of a generalized oedema.

ascorbic acid (*as-kor'-bik*). Vitamin C. This acid promotes healing and should therefore be given pre- and post-operatively especially when nutrition is below normal, e.g. in gastric disease. *See* Appendix 10.

asemia (*a-se'-me-ah*). Inability to understand or to use speech or signs. A symptom of cerebral lesion.

asepsis (*a-sep'-sis*). Free from pathogenic micro-organisms.

aseptic technique (*a-sep'-tik tek-neek'*). A method of carrying out sterile procedures so that there is the minimum risk of introducing infection. Achieved by the sterility of equipment and a non-touch method. *See* Appendix 6.

asexual (*a-seks'-u-al*). Without sex. *A. reproduction*. The production of new individuals without sexual union, e.g. by cell division or budding.

aspergillosis (*as-per-jil-o'sis*). A bronchopulmonary disease in which the mucous membrane is attacked by the fungus, Aspergillus. Most likely to occur in patients with leukaemia or those being treated with corticosteroids or cytotoxic drugs.

Aspergillus (*as-per-jil'-us*). A genus of moulds. *A. fumigatus* may infect the nose, antrum, etc.

asphyxia (*as-fiks'-e-ah*). Suffocation. Treatment is by artificial respiration. *See* Appendix 1.

aspiration (*as-pi-ra'-shun*). The drawing off of fluid from a cavity by means of suction.

aspirator (*as'-pi-ra-tor*). Any apparatus for withdrawing air or fluid from a cavity of the body.

aspirin (*as'-pi-rin*). A compound of acetylsalicylic acid which reduces temperature and relieves pain. *A. in mucilage* is prescribed for tonsillitis, following tonsillectomy, and for other conditions when the throat is painful. *Soluble a.* Is combined with citric acid and calcium carbonate which renders it less irritating to the gastric mucosa.

assimilation (*as-sim-il-a'-shun*). The process of transforming food, so that it can be absorbed into the circulatory system and utilized as nourishment for the tissues of the body.

association (*as-so-se-a'-shun*). Co-ordination of function of similar parts. *A. fibres.* Nerve fibres linking different areas of the brain. *A. of ideas.* In which a thought or any sensory impulse will call to mind another object or idea connected in some way with the former. *Free a.* A method employed in psychoanalysis in which the patient is encouraged to express freely whatever comes into his mind. By this method material that is in the unconscious can be recalled. *See* Psychoanalysis.

astasia (*as-ta'-ze-ah*). Inability to stand or walk normally, due to inco-ordination of muscles.

asteatosis (*as - te - a - to' - sis*). Lack of sebaceous secretion. There is a dry and scaly skin in which fissures may occur.

astereognosis (*as-ter-e-og-no'-sis*). Inability to recognize the shape of objects by feeling or touch.

asthenia (*as-the'-ne-ah*). Want of strength. Loss of tone.

asthenopia (*as-then-o'-pe-ah*). Eye strain giving rise to aching, burning sensation, and headache. Likely to arise in long-sighted people when continual effort of accommodation is required for close work in artificial light.

asthenic (*as-then'-ik*). A term used to describe a type of body build. A pale, lean, narrowly built person with poor muscle development.

asthma (*asth'-mah*). Paroxysmal dyspnoea. *Bronchial a.* Attacks of dyspnoea in which there is wheezing and difficulty in expiration due to muscular spasm of the bronchi. The attacks may be precipitated by hypersensitivity to foreign substances or associated with emotional upsets. There is often a family history of asthma or other allergic condition. Attacks may accompany chronic bronchitis. They can be relieved by adrenaline or isoprenaline and between attacks the cause should be sought and removed if possible and breathing exercises instituted. *Cardiac a.* Attacks of dyspnoea and palpitation arising most often at night, associated with left-sided heart failure and pulmonary congestion. *Renal a.* Dyspnoea occurring in kidney disease, which may be a sign of developing uraemia (*q.v.*).

astigmatism (*as-tig'-mat-izm*). Inequality of the refractive power of an eye, due to defective curvature of its corneal meridians. The curve across the front of the eye from side to side is not quite the same as the curve from above downwards. The focus on the retina is then not a point, but a diffuse and indistinct area.

astragalus (*as-trag'-al-us*). The talus or ankle-bone which articulates with the tibia.

astringent (*as-trin'-jent*). An agent causing contraction of organic tissues, so checking secretions, e.g. silver nitrate, tannic acid.

astrocytoma (*as-tro-si-to'-mah*). A slow growing infiltrating cerebral or cerebellar tumour, relatively benign. A glioma.

asymmetry (*a-sim'-et-re*). Inequality in size or shape of two structures normally the same.

asymptomatic (*a-simp-to-mat'-ik*). Without symptoms.

atavism (*at'-av-izm*). The reappearance of some hereditary peculiarity which has missed a few generations.

ataxia, ataxy (*a-taks'-e-ah, a-taks'-e*). Failure of muscle co-ordination. *Locomotor a.* or *tabes dorsalis*. A degenerative disease of the spinal cord; a manifestation of tertiary syphilis allied to general paralysis of the insane (*q.v.*). Among signs and symptoms are: incoordinated movements of the legs in walking, absence of reflexes, and loss of sphincter control. The disease is chronic and progressive, but can be controlled by antisyphilitic treatment.

atelectasis (*a-tel-ek'-ta-sis*). Partial collapse of the air vesicles of the lungs: (1) From imperfect expansion at birth. (2) As the result of disease when small air passages are constricted and air cannot reach the alveoli. *See also* Emphysema.

atherogenic (*ath-er-o-jen'-ik*). Predisposing factors to the formation of atheroma. Animal fat and mental stress have been named.

atheroma (*ath-er-o'-mah*). (1) A sebaceous cyst. (2) Patchy degeneration of the walls of large arteries in which fat-like plaques appear.

atherosclerosis (*ath-er-o-skler-o'-sis*). A condition in which the fatty degenerative plaques of atheroma are accompanied by arteriosclerosis, a narrowing and hardening of the vessels.

athetosis (*ath-et-o'-sis*). A recurring series of abnormal movements of the hands and feet usually due to a cerebral lesion, and most often seen in children.

athlete's foot (*ath'-leetz*). A fungal infection between the toes which is easily transmitted to others. *See* Tinea.

atlas (*at'-las*). The first cervical vertebra, articulating with the occipital bone of the skull.

atmosphere (*at'-mos-feer*). *See* Air.

atmospheric pressure (*at-mos-fer'-ik*). The term given to the pressure exerted by the air in all directions. At sea level it is about 101 kN/m^2 (15 lbf/in^2), depending on the humidity. Dry air exerts more pressure than moist air.

atom (*at'-om*). A minute particle of matter made up of a central nucleus positively charged and, moving around it in an orbit, negatively charged electrons.

atomizer (*at'-om-i-zer*). An instrument by which a liquid is very finely divided to form a spray.

atony (*at'-o-ne*). Lack of tone.

atopen (*at'-o-pen*). An antigen responsible for causing atopy.

atopic (*a-top'-ik*). Out of place or misplaced.

atopy (*at'-o-pe*). A state of hypersensitivity to certain antigens. There is an inherited tendency and it includes asthma, eczema and hay-fever.

atresia (*a-tre'-ze-ah*). Absence of a natural opening, e.g. of the anus or vagina; usually a congenital malformation.

atrial (*a'-tre-al*). Relating to the atrium or auricle. *A. fibrillation*. When there is over-stimulation of the atrial walls and many areas of excitation arise so that the atrio-ventricular node is bombarded with impulses many of which it cannot transmit. *A. flutter*. Rapid regular action of atria, the atrio-ventricular node transmits alternate impulses or one in three or four. *A. septal defect*. The non-closure of the foramen ovale at the time of birth giving rise to a congenital heart defect.

atrio-ventricular (*a'-tre-o-ven-trik'-u-lah*). Pertaining to the atrium and ventricle. *A-V. node*. A node of neurogenic tissue situated between the two and transmitting impulses. *A-V. valves*. The bicuspid and tricuspid valve on the left and right sides of the heart respectively.

atrium (*a'-tre-um*). One of the two upper chambers of the heart. *Plur. atria*. Also called auricle.

atrophy (*at'-ro-fe*). Wasting of any part of the body, due to degeneration of the cells from disuse, lack of nourishment, or of nerve supply. *Acute yellow a.* Massive necrosis of liver cells. A rare condition that may follow acute hepatitis or eclampsia or be precipitated by certain drugs, e.g. cinchophen, mepacrine, or phosphorus. *Muscular a.* Wasting of muscle tissue. Myopathy (*q.v.*).

atropine (*at'-ro-pin*). The active principle of belladonna. An alkaloid which inhibits respiratory and gastric secretions, relaxes muscle spasm and dilates the pupil. Used pre-operatively, and to relieve renal and biliary colic and as drops to aid examination of the eye.

attenuation (*at-ten-u-a'-shun*). A bacteriological process by which organisms are rendered less virulent by culture in artificial media through many generations, exposure to light, air, etc. Used for vaccine preparations.

atypical (*a-tip'-ik-al*). Not conforming to type, e.g. *a. pneumonia*.

audiogram (*aw'-de-o-gram*). A tracing of the intensity of hearing which is helpful in deciding the type of deafness present.

audiometer (*aw-de-om'-e-ter*). An instrument for measuring hearing.

auditory (*aw'-de-tor-e*). Pertaining to the sense of hearing.

Auerbach's plexus (*aw'-er-barks plex'-us*). The ganglionic neurones of the vagus nerve that supply the muscle fibres of the intestine.

aura (*aw'-rah*). The premonition peculiar to individuals which often precedes an epileptic fit.

aural (*aw'-ral*). Referring to the ear.

auricle (*aw'-rik-l*). (1) appendage to the cardiac atrium; (2) the external portion of the ear.

auricular fibrillation (*aw-rik'-u-lar fib-ril-la'-shun*). *See* Atrial fibrillation.

auricular flutter (*aw-rik'-u-lar flut'-ter*). *See* Atrial flutter.

auriculo-ventricular bundle (*aw-rik'-u-lo ven-trik'-u-lar bun'-dl*). Atrio-ventricular bundle. *See* Bundle of His.

auriscope (*aw'-ris-kope*). An instrument for examining the drum of the ear.

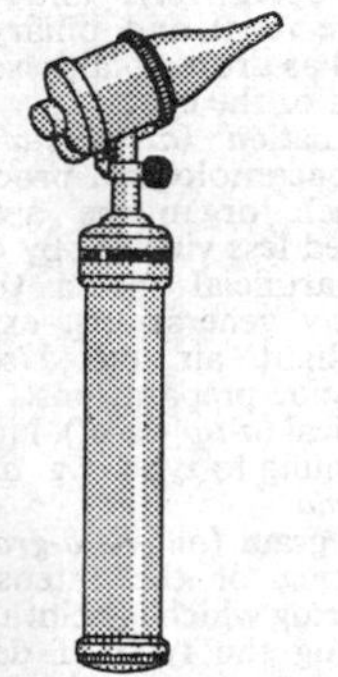

AURISCOPE

auscultation (*aws-kul-ta'-shun*). A method of examining the internal organs by listening to the sounds which they give out. *Immediate a.* The ear is placed directly against the body. *Mediate a.* A stethoscope is used.

autism (*aw'-tizm*). Self absorption.

autistic (*aw-tis'-tik*). A term used to describe a withdrawn personality; the patient is apathetic and appears absorbed in his own thoughts or daydreams, showing little awareness of his surroundings. A condition occurring in schizophrenia.

autoclave (*aw'-to-klave*). A steam-heated sterilizing apparatus in which the temperature is raised by reducing the atmospheric pressure and then injecting steam under pressure, so bringing about efficient sterilization. The aim of newer patterns is to raise the pressure and shorten the time, so that the capacity of the machines is increased and they can be used to replace water boilers for many articles.

auto-eroticism (*aw-to-e-rot'-is-izm*). Sexual pleasure derived from self stimulation of erotogenous zones, the mouth, the anus, the genitals and the skin.

autogenous (*aw - toj' - en - us*). Generated within the body and not acquired from external sources. *A. vaccine.* Made from the patient's serum.

autograft (*aw'-to-graft*). The transfer of skin or other tissue from one part of the patient's body to another to repair some deficiency.

auto-immune diseases (*aw-to-im-mune'*). Those caused by auto-immunization. *See* Hashimoto.

auto-immunization (*aw-to-im-*

mu-ni-za'-shun). The formation of antibodies against the individual's own tissue proteins.

auto-infection (*aw-to-in-fek'-shun*). Self-infection, i.e. transferred from one part of the body to another by fingers, towels, etc.

auto-intoxication (*aw - to - in - toks-e-ka'-shun*). Poisoning by toxins generated within the body itself.

autolysis (*aw-tol'-is-is*). A breaking up or digestion of living tissues as may occur, e.g. if pancreatic ferments escape into surrounding tissues.

automatic (*aw-to-mat'-ik*). Performed without the influence of the will.

automatism (*aw-tom'-at-izm*). Performance of acts without apparent volition, and of which there is no memory afterwards. *Post-epileptic a.* Automatic acts following an epileptic fit of which the patient has no knowledge.

autonomic (*aw - to - nom' - ik*). Self-governing. *A. nervous system.* Consists of the sympathetic and parasympathetic nerves which control involuntary muscles and glandular secretion over which there is no conscious control.

autoplasty (*aw'-to-plas-te*). Replacement of missing tissue by grafting a healthy section from another part of the body.

autopsy (*aw'-top-se*). Post-mortem examination.

autosome (*aw'-to-soh-m*). Any chromosome other than the sex chromosomes. In man there are 22 pairs of autosomes and 1 pair of sex chromosomes.

autotransfusion (*aw-to-trans-fu'-shun*). The reinjection of blood taken from one part of the body, into another.

avascular (*a-vas'-ku-lah*). Not vascular. Bloodless. *A. necrosis.* Death of bone owing to deficient blood supply, usually following an injury.

aversion (*a-ver'-shun*). Intense dislike. *A. therapy.* A method of treating alcoholism and other addictions by associating the desired article with painful or unpleasant stimuli.

avitaminosis (*a-vit-a-min-o'-sis*). The result of insufficiency of vitamins in the diet. Also known as *deficiency disease*.

avulsion (*a-vul'-shun*). Tearing away. *Phrenic a.* A crushing or separation of the phrenic nerve: it will paralyse the diaphragm on the affected side.

axilla (*aks-il'-ah*). The armpit.

axis (*aks'-is*). The second cervical vertebra.

axis cylinder (*aks'-is cil'-in-der*). *See* Axon.

axon (*aks'-on*). The nerve fibre which extends from a nerve cell to its termination in an organ, or its arborization with the dendrites of other nerve cells. *Syn.*, Axis cylinder.

azoospermia (*a-zo-o-sperm'-e-ah*). Absence of spermatozoa in the semen. Tests for this are carried out following vasectomy.

azotaemia (*a-zot-e'-me-ah*). The accumulation of urea in the blood.

azote (*a'-zo-te*). Nitrogen gas.

azoturia (*az-o-tu'-re-ah*). Increase of urea in the urine.

azygos (*az'-e-gos*). An unpaired vein that ascends the posterior mediastinum and enters the superior vena cava.

B

Babinski's reflex *or* **sign** (*bab-in'-ske*). Present in disease or injury to the upper motor neurone. On stroking the sole of the foot, the great toe bends upwards instead of downwards (*dorsal* instead of *plantar* flexion). Babies who have not walked react in the same way, but normal flexion develops later.

bacillaemia (*bas-il-e'-me-ah*). The presence of bacilli in the blood.

Bacille Calmette-Guérin (*bas-eel' kal-met'-ga-ran'*). A vaccine prepared from living tubercle bacilli which through prolonged culture have lost their virulence. It is used to produce active immunity against tuberculosis in children and young adults, particularly those liable to become infected. Also called BCG vaccine.

bacilluria (*bas-il-u'-re-ah*). The presence of bacilli in the urine.

bacillus (*bas-il'-us*) *Pl.* bacilli. A rod-shaped bacterium. Bacilli may be divided into: (1) those which form spores (*q.v.*) and require oxygen (*aerobic*), e.g. *B. anthracis*, the cause of anthrax. (2) those that form spores and need the exclusion of oxygen (*anaerobic*), e.g. *Clostridium botulinum*, the cause of botulism; *Cl. tetani*, the cause of tetanus and *Cl. welchii* (*Cl. perfringens*) a cause of gas gangrene. (3) non-spore-bearing bacilli, e.g. *Escherichia coli*. A normal inhabitant of the bowel but a common cause of urinary infection. *Klebs-Löffler b.* (*Corynebacterium diphtheriae*). The cause of diphtheria. *Döderlein's b.* A lactic acid-forming organism normally found in the vagina, which destroys other bacteria. *Flexner, Shiga and Sonne b.* The causative organisms of bacillary dysentery. The salmonellas are a food-poisoning group which includes *Salmonella typhimurium* and *S. enteritidis* (*Gärtner's bacillus*). *Bordet-Gengou b.* (*Haemophilus pertussis*). The cause of whooping cough or pertussis. *Smegma b.* A type found in urine, closely resembling the tubercle bacillus, which make diagnosis by identification unreliable.

bacitracin (*bas-e-tra'-sin*). An antibiotic drug derived from *Bacillus subtilis*. Used for surface application.

back pressure. Describes the damming back of the blood through the pulmonary circulation and into the veins as the result of organic heart disease. A cause of many of the symptoms in advanced mitral stenosis.

bacteraemia (*bak-ter-e'-me-ah*). The presence of bacteria in the blood stream.

bacteria (*bak-te'-re-ah*). *Sing.* bacterium. A general name given to minute vegetable organisms which live on organic matter. Each consists of a single cell and, given favourable conditions, multiplies by subdivision. Bacteria are classified, according to their shape into:

1. *Bacilli*, rod-shaped.
2. *Cocci*, spherical:
(*a*) streptococci—in chains;
(*b*) staphylococci—in groups;

(*c*) diplococci—in pairs.
3. *Spirilla*, spiral-shaped.

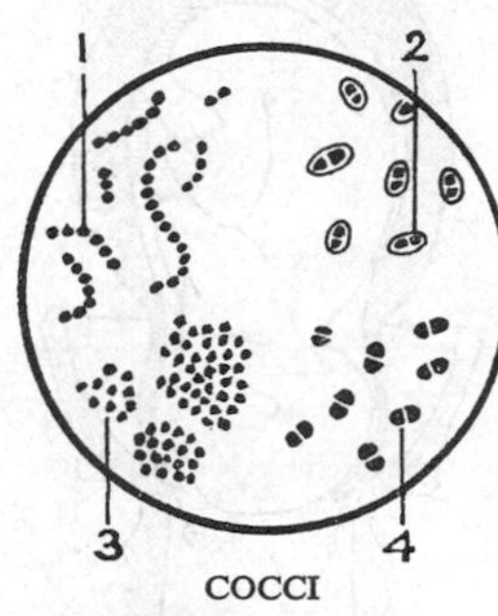

COCCI

1. Streptococci.
2. Diplococci (encapsuled).
3. Staphylococci.
4. Diplococci.

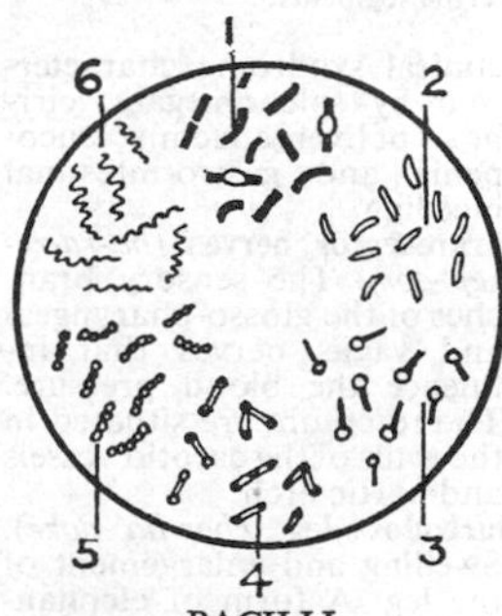

BACILLI

1. Anthrax bacilli showing spores.
2. Coliform bacilli.
3. Tetanus bacilli showing terminal spores.
4. Klebs-Löffler bacilli (diphtheroids).
5. Tubercle bacilli showing beading.
6. Spirochaetes.

Pathogenic b. Those whose growth in the body gives rise to disease, either by destruction of tissue, or by formation of toxins which circulate in the blood. They thrive on organic matter in the presence of warmth and moisture.

bactericidal (*bak-te-re-si′-dal*). Capable of killing bacteria, e.g. disinfectants, great heat, intense cold or sunlight.

bactericide (*bak′-te-re-side*). An agent that kills bacteria.

bacteriologist (*bak-te-re-ol′-oj-ist*). One who has studied and is skilled in the science of bacteria.

bacteriology (*bak-te-re-ol′-o-je*). The science which treats of bacteria.

bacteriolysin (*bak-te-re-ol′-i-sin*). An antibody (*q.v.*) produced in blood to assist in the destruction of bacteria. The action is specific.

bacteriolysis (*bak-te-re-o-li′-sis*). The dissolution of bacteria by a bacteriolytic agent.

bacteriolytic (*bak-te-re-o-lit′-ik*). Capable of destroying or dissolving bacteria.

bacteriophage (*bak-te′-re-o-faj*). A virus parasite on bacteria. Many strains exist, some of which are used for typing staphylococci and organisms of the typhoid group.

bacteriostatic (*bak-te-re-o-stat′-ik*). Inhibiting the growth of bacteria.

bacteriotherapy (*bak-te-re-o-ther′-ap-e*). Treatment of disease by the injection of bacteria into the blood, e.g. malaria therapy in the treatment of neurosyphilis.

bacteriuria (*bak-te-re-u′-re-ah*). The presence of bacteria in urine.

baker's itch *or* **eczema.** *See* Itch.

balanitis (*bal-an-i'-tis*). Balanoposthitis. Inflammation of the glans penis and of the prepuce.

Balkan frame. A framework fitted over a bed to carry pulleys and slings or splints for the support of a limb undergoing surgical treatment. Used chiefly in fracture or osteo-arthritic cases or to aid physiotherapy.

ballotement (*bal-ot-mon'*). A method of testing pregnancy from the fourth month. The uterus is pushed upward by a finger in the vagina, and if a fetus is present it will fall back again like a heavy body in water.

balneotherapy (*bal-ne-o-ther'-ap-e*). The treatment of disease by baths.

balsam (*bawl'-sam*). An aromatic vegetable juice. *Friar's b.* A compound containing tincture of benzoin. Used for steam inhalations, and as an antiseptic for ulcers. *B. of Peru.* Used externally as an antiseptic ointment or in tulle gras (*q.v.*). *B. of Tolu.* Used as an expectorant.

bandage (*band-'aj*). An appliance to give support or apply pressure to a part or for fixing a dressing in position.

Bandl's ring (*band'-l*). A ridge appearing between the upper retracted segment of the uterus and the lower dilated segment, occurring during an obstructed labour. It suggests that rupture of the uterus is likely.

Bankhart's operation (*bank'-hart*). An operation carried out to repair the defect in the glenoid cavity when there is repeated dislocation of the shoulder joint.

Banti's disease (*ban'-te*). A clinical syndrome characterized by splenomegaly, cirrhosis of liver, anaemia, leucopenia and gastro-intestinal bleeding.

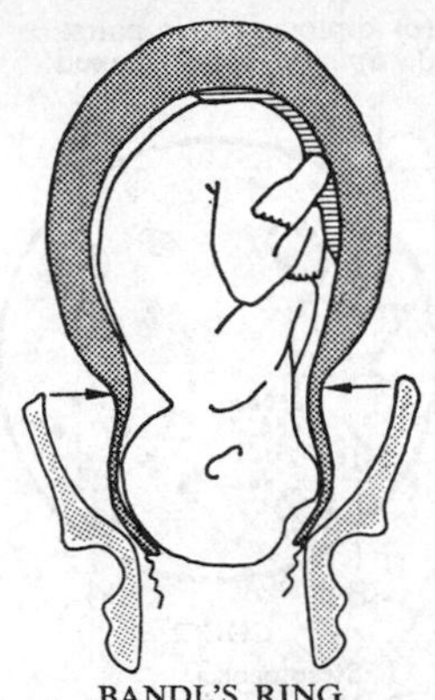

BANDL'S RING

Arrows show marked difference in thickness of the upper and lower uterine segments.

barareceptor nerves (*ba-ra-re-sep'-tor*). The sensory branches of the glosso-pharyngeal and vagus nerves that influence the blood pressure. The receptors are situated in the walls of the carotid vessels and aortic arch.

Barbados leg (*bar-ba'-doze*). Swelling and enlargement of the leg. A form of elephantiasis (*q.v.*).

barber's rash. Sycosis (*q.v.*).

barbiturates (*bar-bit'-u-rates*). A large group of hypnotic drugs derived from urea, e.g. phenobarbitone, butobarbitone, etc. Their action is potentiated by alcohol.

barbotage (*bar-bo-taj'*). A method of spinal anaesthesia by which some of the anaesthetic is injected followed by partial withdrawal and then reinjected with more of the drug. This process is repeated until the full amount has been given, allowing dilution and mixing with the cerebrospinal fluid.

barium sulphate (*bair'-e-um sul'-fate*). A heavy mineral salt that is comparatively impermeable to X-rays. The chief ingredient of opaque meals or given as an enema. Used therefore to demonstrate abnormality in the stomach or intestines, and to show peristaltic movement. Bismuth is used similarly.

barium sulphide (*bair'-e-um sul'-fide*). The chief constituent of depilatory preparations, i.e. those which remove hair.

Barlow's disease (*bar'-lo*). Infantile scurvy. A deficiency disease due to lack of vitamin C.

barrier-nursing. A method of bed isolation which enables a patient suffering from an infectious disease to be nursed amongst those not so infected.

Bartholin's glands (*bart'-o-lin*). Two glands situated in the labia majora, with ducts opening inside the vulva.

basal ganglia (*ba'-sal gang'-le-ah*). The collections of nerve cells or grey matter in the base of the cerebrum. They consist of the caudate nucleus and putamen forming the corpus striatum and the globus pallidus. Parkinson's disease is associated with degenerative changes in these structures.

basal metabolic rate (BMR) (*ba'-sal met-a-bol'-ik*). An indirect method of estimating the rate of metabolism in the body by measuring the O_2 intake and CO_2 output on breathing. For this to be done, the patient must be quiet in bed and have had no food for 12 hr. The age, weight and size of the patient have to be taken into account.

basal narcosis (*ba'-sal nar-ko'-sis*). *See under* Narcosis.

base. (1) The lowest part or foundation. (2) An alkali, or substance which can unite with an acid to form a salt.

basement membrane. A thin layer of modified connective tissue supporting layers of cells. Found at the base of the epidermis and underlying mucous membranes.

basilar (*bas'-il-ar*). Situated at the base. *B. artery*, at the base of the skull, formed by the junction of the vertebral arteries.

basilic (*bas-il'-ik*). Prominent. *B. vein*. A large vein on the inner side of the arm.

basophile (*ba'-zo-fil*). Leucocytes or white cells of the blood having an affinity for basic dyes.

basophilia (*ba-zo-fil'-e-ah*). Increase of basophiles in the blood.

Batchelor plaster (*bat'-shel-or*). A plaster of Paris splint which corrects congenital dislocation of the hip. *See* Plaster.

Bateman's needle (*bate'-man*). A special type used for intravenous injection in infants. It has two cannulas which fit into each other.

bath. Used for cleansing and to stimulate the circulation. Suggested temperatures for: a *cold b.* 18°C (65°F); *tepid b.* 29°C (85°F); *warm b.* 38°C (100°F); *hot b.*

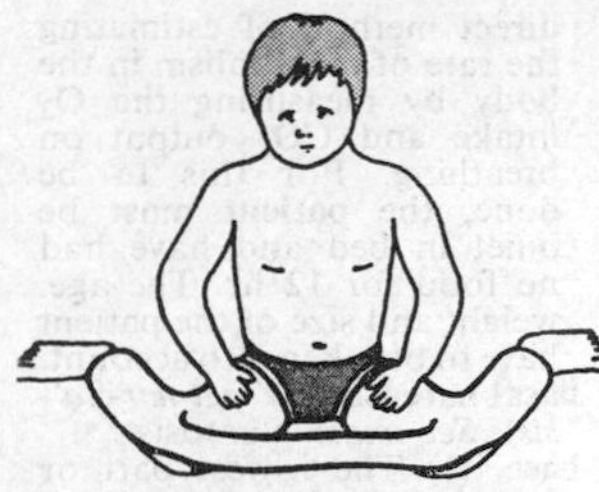
BATCHELOR PLASTER

40°C (105°F). Baths containing *bran*, *oatmeal*, *starch*, or *sodium bicarbonate* are soothing and may be ordered in skin diseases. *Electric b.* One in which a current is passed through the water may be used to treat peripheral nerve or vascular conditions of the limbs. *Saline b.* May be used in the treatment of burns. *Wax b.* Used to increase the circulation to the small joints of the hands and feet and relax the muscles.

battered baby syndrome. A clinical condition in which an infant or young child is found to have soft tissue injuries, e.g. bruises, and radiological evidence of fractures either new or at different stages of healing. It usually results from serious physical abuse by parents or foster parents, who may admit injuring the child or whose explanation of the injury may be at variance with the medical evidence.

battery (*bat'-ter-e*). An apparatus for generating electricity by chemical means. *Faradic b.* One which produces a Faradic or induced current. *Galvanic b.* Produces a continuous electric current from chemicals.

battledore placenta (*bat'-tl-dor pla-sen'-tah*). In which the umbilical cord is attached to the margin of the placenta and not the centre.

BCG Bacille (Bacillus) Calmett-Guérin (*q.v.*).

'bearing down' (1) The expulsive pains in the second stage of labour. (2) A feeling of heaviness and downward strain in the pelvis present with some uterine growths or displacements.

'Beaver Breather' (*bee'-ver*). An electro-motor respirator particularly useful in bulbospinal poliomyelitis in which the respiratory and swallowing reflexes are lost.

bed-bug. *Cimex lectularius.* A blood-sucking parasite which lives in cracks of woodwork and furniture and can survive for up to 12 months without food.

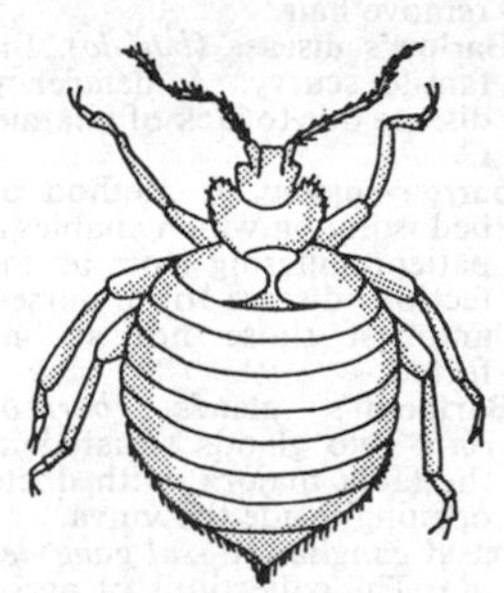
BED BUG

bed-sore. Better termed a pressure sore. Decubitus ulcer. A wound caused by constant pressure of the bed on any part of the body and a consequently diminished blood-supply. The chief pressure points are the buttocks, shoulders, hips, heels, and elbows. The best preventive measures are cleanliness of the part, a good diet with ample fluid and vitamins, and a frequent change of position.

Beer's knife. One with a triangular blade used in cataract operations, for incising the cornea preparatory to removal of the lens.

beeswax. Yellow wax secreted by bees, and used in the manufacture of ointments.

behaviour (*be-ha'-vyor*). The way in which an organism reacts to an internal or external stimulus. *Incongruous b.* Behaviour that is out of keeping with the person's normal reaction or has the opposite effect to that consciously desired. *B. disorders.* May take many forms, such as truancy, stealing, temper, tantrums, bed wetting, or thumb sucking. For example, they may occur when a child is put under stress in his home or school environment.

behaviourism (*be-ha'-vyor-izm*). A psychological term describing the purely objective study and observation of the behaviour of individuals.

bejel (*be'-jel*). A non-venereal but infectious skin disease caused by a treponema, indistinguishable from that causing syphilis.

Belcroy feeder (*bel'-croy*). A bottle for baby feeding whereby a weak sucking action may be assisted by light pressure on a rubber bulb at the opposite end from the teat.

Bell's palsy. Facial paralysis.

belladonna (*bel-ah-don'-ah*). A drug from the deadly nightshade plant. Used as an antispasmodic in colic, and to check secretions. Atropine is its active principle.

belle indifference (*bell in-dif'-er-ance*). A sign in conversion hysteria. The patient describes his symptoms, appearing not to be distressed by them.

Bellocq's sound *or* **cannula** (*bel'-ok*). A curved tube for the arrest of nasal bleeding by passing it with plugging attached into the nose.

bellringer's wrist. Tendinitis or tenosynovitis of the wrist which may result from chronic mechanical strain or from trauma.

Bence-Jones's protein (*bense-jones pro'-teen*). That present in the urine in cases of bone-marrow diseases — particularly if malignant. It coagulates at a lower temperature than does albumin, and is redissolved on boiling.

bendrofluazide (*ben-dro-flu'-a-zide*). An oral diuretic of the thiazide group. Apinox and Neo-Naclex are proprietary preparations.

bends. A colloquial term for caisson disease (*see under* Decompression sickness) in which there is severe abdominal cramp.

Benedict's solution (*ben'-e-dikts sol-u'-shun*). A solution of copper sulphate used as a test for sugar in urine. *See* Appendix 11.

benethamine penicillin (*ben-eth'-a-meen*). An antibiotic. *See* Penicillin.

benign (*be-nine'*). The opposite to malignant (*q.v.*). *B. tumour. See* Tumour. *B. tertian fever* is due to a malarial parasite, more tractable to treatment than that which causes malignant tertian fever.

Bentley's suspension apparatus (*bent'-le*). An apparatus for treating torticollis (*q.v.*) by suspending the patient by the head for 10 to 15 min twice daily.

benzathine penicillin (*benz'-ath-een*). A long-acting antibiotic. *See* Penicillin.

benzene (*ben-zeen'*). Benzol. A coal-tar derivative used externally as a parasiticide.

benzhexol (*benz'-hex-ol*). An antispasmodic drug which helps to overcome the tremors and rigidity of Parkinson's disease. Artane and Pipanol are proprietary preparations.

benzoin (*ben'-zo-in*). An aromatic resin. *Compound Tincture of B. See* Friar's balsam *under* Balsam.

benzyl benzoate (*ben'-zil ben'-zo-ate*. An emulsion used in the treatment of scabies. A hot bath is taken and then a 25 per cent emulsion is applied carefully over the whole body except the face and scalp and left on for 24 hr. In 99 per cent of cases one application is sufficient and it must never be applied more than twice.

benzylpenicillin (*benz-il-pen-e-sill'-in*). A soluble penicillin, quickly absorbed, by which high blood levels can be obtained but need frequent injections.

beri beri (*ber'-e ber'-e*). A deficiency disease due to insufficiency of vitamin B_1 in the diet. It is a form of neuritis, with pain, paralysis and oedema of the extremities.

berylliosis (*ber-il-e-o'-sis*). An industrial lung disease in which the inhalant is beryllium. Interstitial fibrosis arises impairing lung function. Steroids may improve the condition.

Besnier's prurigo (*bes'-ne-a-s pru-ri'-go*). An inherited neurodermatitis with impaired peripheral circulation and dry thickened epidermis with outbreaks of eczema. The atopic syndrome.

betamethazone (*be-ta-meth'-a-zone*). A derivative of prednisolone but seven times more active. It may be used in eye drops, creams, ointments or as tablets. It is the chief ingredient in Betnovate.

Betz cells (*bets*). The pyramidal cells in the pre-Rolandic area of the cerebrum.

bi-. A prefix meaning 'two'.

bicarbonate (*bi-kar'-bon-ate*). A compound containing two equivalents of carbonic acid with one of an alkali or base.

biceps (*bi'-seps*). Having two heads. *B. muscles*. (*a*) A flexor of the arm. (*b*) One of the hamstring muscles of the thigh.

biconcave (*bi'-kon-kave*). A lens or structure with a

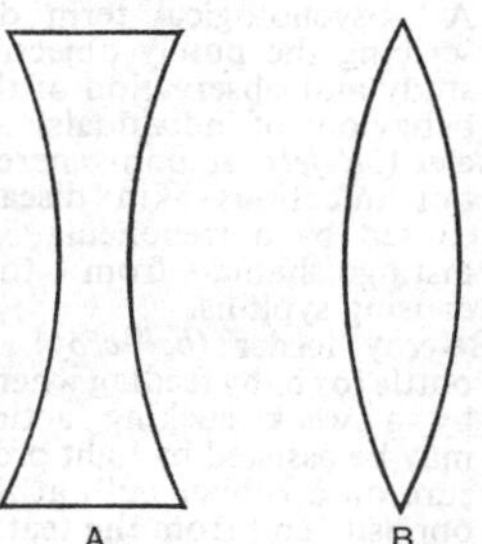

BICONCAVE (A) AND BICONVEX (B) LENSES

hollow or depression on each surface.

biconvex (*bi'-kon-vex*). A lens or structure that protrudes on both surfaces.

bicornuate (*bi - korn' - u - ate*). Having two horns. *B. uterus.* A congenital malformation in which there is a partial or complete vertical division of the body of the uterus.

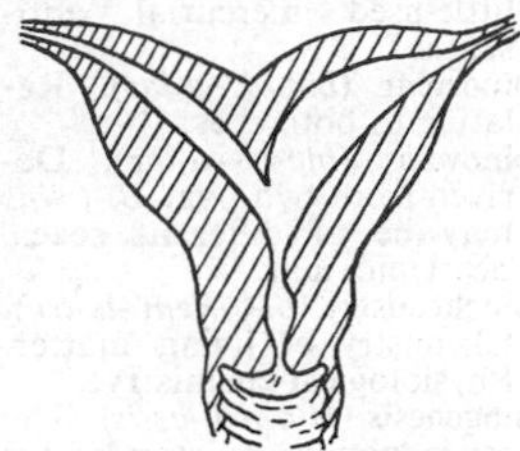

BICORNUATE UTERUS

bicuspid (*bi-kus'-pid*). Having two cusps. *B. teeth.* The premolars. *B. valve.* The mitral valve of the heart, between the left atrium and ventricle.

bidet (*bid-ay'*). A sitz-bath. It can also be used for vaginal and rectal injections.

bifid (*bi'-fid*). A division or cleft into two parts.

bifocal spectacles (*bi-fo'-kal*). Those in which the lens has two different foci, the lower for close work and the upper for distant vision.

bifurcate (*bi'-fur-kate*). To divide into two; arteries bifurcate frequently, thereby getting smaller.

bifurcation (*bi-fur-ka'-shun*). The junction where a vessel divides into two halves, e.g. where the aorta divides into the right and left iliac vessels.

bigeminus (*bi - jem' - in - us*). Double. *Pulsus b.* When two pulse beats occur together, regular in time and force—the third beat being missed. A regular irregularity.

Bigelow's evacuator (*big'-e-lo*). Similar to Freyer's evacuator. *See* Evacuator.

biguanides (*big-u-an'-ides*). Oral hypoglycaemic drugs for treating diabetes. They aid the entry of glucose into the cells so that metabolism of sugar can take place.

bilateral (*bi-lat'-er-al*). Pertaining to both sides.

bile. A secretion of the liver, golden - brown in colour, which has a bitter taste and is slightly antiseptic. It passes into the intestine, where it assists digestion by emulsifying fats and stimulates peristalsis. *B. pigments.* Bilirubin and biliverdin produced by haemolysis in the spleen. Normally these colour the faeces, but in jaundice cause the coloration of the skin and urine. *B. salts.* Sodium taurocholate and sodium glycocholate which cause the emulsification of fats. They are the constituents responsible for irritation of the skin and the slow pulse in jaundice. *Urine tests for b. See* Appendix 11.

Bilharzia (*bil-har'-ze-ah*). The type of fluke, now called *Schistosoma*, which causes schistosomiasis (*q.v.*).

bilharziasis (*bil-har-zi'-a-sis*). A parasitic infection of the intestinal or urinary tract, now termed schistosomiasis.

biliary (*bil'-e-ar-e*). Pertaining to bile. *B. ducts.* The tubes through which the bile passes from the liver and gall-bladder to the intestine. *B. colic.* Spasm of muscle walls of the duct causing excruciating pain when gall-stones are blocking the tube. Pain is in the right upper quadrant of the abdomen and referred to the shoulder. *B. fistula*. An abnormal opening between the gall-bladder and the surface of the body or some internal portion of the gastro-intestinal tract. It may be a complication of operation on the gall-bladder, especially if there has been drainage of the ducts.

bilious (*bil'-e-us*). A condition caused by an excessive secretion of bile, and its regurgitation into the stomach with catarrh of that organ.

bilirubin (*bil-e-ru'-bin*). A bile pigment. *See* Bile.

biliuria (*bil-e-yu'-re-ah*). Bile or bile salts in the urine.

biliverdin (*bil-e-ver'-din*). A bile pigment, derived from haemolysis of red blood cells and quickly converted to bilirubin. *See* Bile.

Billroth's operation (*bil'-ro-t*). *See* Gastrectomy.

bimanual (*bi-man'-u-al*). Using both hands. *B. examination*. Examination with both hands. Used chiefly in gynaecology, when the internal genital organs are examined between one hand on the abdomen, and the other hand or finger within the vagina.

binary fission (*bi'-nar-e*). The multiplication of cells by division into two equal parts.

binaural (*bin-aw'-ral*). Pertaining to both ears. *B. stethoscope*. *See* Stethoscope.

binder (*bine'-der*). An abdominal bandage which can be used: (1) for support after childbirth or abdominal operation; (2) for support when ascitic fluid is removed by tapping.

Binet's test (*Be'-na*). A method of ascertaining the mental age of children or young persons by using a series of questions standardized on the capacity of normal children at various ages.

biniodide of mercury (*bin-i'-o-dide*). Mercuric iodide. A little-used mercurial antiseptic.

binocular (*bin-ok'-u-lar*). Relating to both eyes.

binovular (*bin-o'-vu-lar*). Derived from two ova. *B. twins* may be of different sexes. *See* Uniovular.

biochemistry (*bi-o-kem'-is-tre*). Chemistry of living matter. Physiological chemistry.

biogenesis (*bi-o-jen'-es-is*). The reproduction of living beings from those already living.

biology (*bi-ol'-o-je*). The science of living forms, dealing with their structure, function and organization.

biomicroscopy (*bi-o-mi-cros'-ko-pe*). A microscopic examination of the structures of the anterior of the eye during life. *See* Slit lamp.

bioplasm (*bi'-o-plazm*). Protoplasm. The active principle in matter which produces living organisms.

biopsy (*bi-op'-se*). Observation of the living. Used to describe the removal of some tissue or organ of the body, e.g. a lymph gland, for examination to establish a diagnosis.

Biot's respiration (*be-o'*). Periods of hyperpnoea occurring in normal respiration. It is sometimes seen in meningitis. *Also called* Grouped breathing.

biotin (*bi'-ot-in*). Formerly termed vitamin H, now part of vitamin B complex and present in all normal diets.

biparous (*bi'-par-us*). Giving birth to twins or two at a time.

bipolar (*bi-po'-lah*). With two poles. *B. nerve cells*. Having two nerve fibres, e.g. ganglionic cells.

BIPP. An antiseptic paste composed of bismuth, iodoform, and paraffin.

birth. The act of being born. *B. control*. Limiting the size of the family by abstention or the use of contraceptives. *B. mark*. A haemangioma (*q.v.*) present from birth. *Premature b*. One taking place after 28 weeks of pregnancy but before term. Now all infants under 2500 g (5½ lb.) weight are considered premature.

bisacodyl (*bis-a-ko'-dil*). A laxative that acts directly on the rectum. Used most frequently in the form of suppositories.

bisexual (*bi-seks'-u-al*). Possessing characteristics of both sexes; hermaphroditic.

bismuth (*biz'-muth*). A greyish metal. Used in medicine as a gastric sedative; by injection for the treatment of syphilis; and as an antiseptic in skin diseases. Taken internally it causes a greyish-black coloration of the stools.

bistoury (*bis'-too-re*). A slender surgical knife: sometimes curved.

Bitot's spots (*be-to'*). Collections of dried epithelium, micro-organisms, etc., forming shiny, greyish spots on the cornea. A sign of vitamin A deficiency. *See* Appendix 10.

bitters. Drugs characterized by bitter taste; used to stimulate the appetite.

bivalve (*bi'-valv*). Consisting of two halves. Cutting a plaster cast into an anterior and posterior section. *B. speculum*. A vaginal one having two blades that can be adjusted for easy insertion.

blackhead. *See* Comedones.

blackwater fever. A rare complication of malaria in which severe haemolysis causes a dark discoloration of the urine.

bladder. A membraneous sac. *B. worm*. A cysticercus (*q.v.*). *Atonic b*. Lack of tone in the bladder wall, which may be the result of over dilatation. *Gall-b*. The reservoir for bile. *Ileal b*. One made by detaching a portion of ileum and inserting the ureters. It necessitates wearing an ileostomy appliance. *Irritable b*. Causing frequent desire to micturate. *Urinary b*. The reservoir for urine.

bland fluids. Those mild and non-irritating, such as barley water and milk.

blastocyst (*blas'-to-sist*). Blastula (*q.v.*).

blastocyte (*blas'-to-site*). An embryonic cell that has not yet become differentiated into its specific type.

blastoderm (*blas'-to-derm*). The germinal cells of the embryo consisting of three layers, the ectoderm, mesoderm, and entoderm.

blastomycosis (*blas-to-mi-ko'-sis*). A fungal infection which after invasion of the skin may cause granulomatous lesions in the mouth, pharynx and lungs.

blastolysis (*blas-tol'-is-is*). The destruction of germ substance.

blastula (*blas'-tu-la*). Biastocyst. An early stage in the development of the fertilized ovum when the morula becomes cystic and later infolds to become the gastrula.

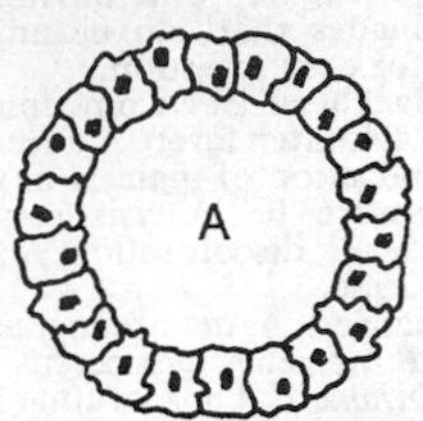

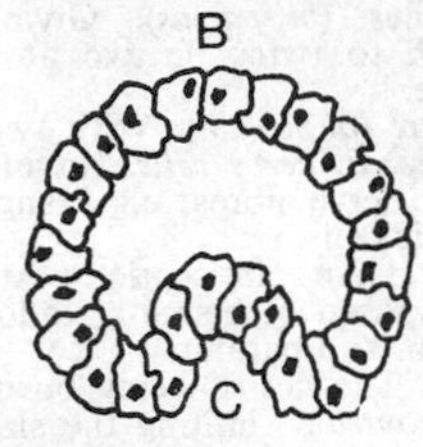

BLASTULA
A. Sphere of cells; B. Ectoderm; C. Endoderm.

bleaching powder. Chlorinated lime, which is a powerful disinfectant.

bleb. A blister (*q.v.*).

bleeders. A popular name for those who suffer from haemophilia (*q.v.*).

'bleeding time'. The time taken for oozing to cease from a sharp single finger prick. The normal is 3 to 4 min. It is influenced by the retraction of the blood vessel wall as well as by the clotting power of blood. *See* Clotting time.

blennophthalmia (*blen - off - thal'-me-ah*). Catarrhal conjunctivitis.

blennorrhagia (*blen-or-a'-je-ah*). An excessive discharge of mucus, e.g. leucorrhoea (*q.v.*).

blepharitis (*blef-ar-i'-tis*). Inflammation of the eyelids.

blepharon (*blef'-ar-on*). The eyelid.

blepharoptosis (*blef-ar-op-to'-sis*). Drooping of the upper eyelid.

blepharospasm (*blef'-ar-o-spazm*). Prolonged spasm of both orbicularis muscles around the eye.

blind. Without sight. *B. spot.* The point where the optic nerve leaves the retina, which is insensitive to light.

blind loop syndrome. A condition of stasis in the small intestine which aids bacterial multiplication leading to diarrhoea and salt deficiencies. The cause may be intestinal obstruction or surgical anastomosis.

blister. A bleb or vesicle. A collection of serum between the epidermis and the true skin.

blood. The fluid that circulates through the heart and blood vessels, supplying nutritive material to all parts of the body, and carrying off waste products. It is a colourless fluid (*plasma*) in which float myriads of minute bodies (*corpuscles*). These are of three kinds; *red* and *white* (in the proportion of about 500:1), and *platelets*. (1) The red corpuscles or *erythrocytes,* contain haemoglobin which combines with oxygen in passing through the lungs. This oxygen is released into the tissues from the capillaries and oxidation (*q.v.*) takes place. (2) The white corpuscles, or *leucocytes*, defend

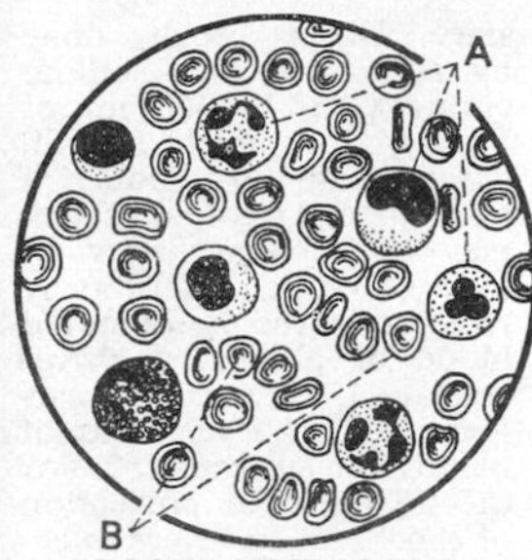

BLOOD—MICROSCOPIC APPEARANCE

A. White blood cells.
B. Red blood cells.

against invading micro-organisms, which they have power to destroy. (3) Blood platelets, or *thrombocytes*, are concerned with the clotting of blood. *See* Normal Values, Appendix 12. Injury to the wall of a blood vessel activates the formation of clot, which is nature's method of sealing a wound, so preventing prolonged haemorrhage. For this process, *see under* Thrombin.

blood–brain barrier. A hypothetical bar dividing the blood from the parenchyma of the central nervous system. Some substances will pass from the blood stream into the cerebro-spinal fluid and some will not do so; streptomycin, for instance, will not pass the *b.–b. barrier*.

blood casts. Minute filaments of coagulated blood found in the urine in some cases of kidney disease.

blood count. Calculation of the number of red and white corpuscles in one cubic millimetre of blood, as seen through the microscope. *Differential b. c.* One which gives the relative number of the different types of white cells. *See* Leucocytes *and* Normal Values, Appendix 12.

blood culture. The cultivation of bacteria present in blood in order that a disease may be diagnosed or sensitivity tests carried out.

blood grouping. All human blood belongs to one of four groups. If two which are incompatible are mixed, agglutination of corpuscles results. Therefore, in blood transfusion the donor's and recipient's blood must be of the same or a compatible group. Introduction of incompatible blood produces a severe reaction which may be fatal. Theoretically, Group O (universal donors) can give to anyone but this is not invariably so and it is imperative that direct cross-matching should precede

Donor (cells)	Recipient (serum) AB	A	B	O
AB	O	X	X	X
A	O	O	X	X
B	O	X	O	X
O	O	O	O	O

TABLE OF BLOOD TYPES SHOWING COMPATIBILITY

O, compatible; X, incompatible
Group AB: Incompatible with all other types.
Group O: Compatible with all (universal donor).

blood transfusion. *See* Rhesus factor.

blood plasma. The fluid portion of blood that contains proteins, salts, hormones, and the end products of digestion, together with waste and toxic substances for excretion.

blood pressure. The tension of the blood in the arteries measured in millimetres of mercury by the sphygmomanometer (*q.v.*). It depends on the force of the heart beat, the condition of the arterial walls, and the peripheral resistance. *See* Arteriosclerosis *and* Hypertension, in which the pressure is raised. In weakness of the heart's action, shock, etc., the pressure is low (*hypotension*). The average systolic pressure in a young adult is 100 to 120; in middle age 130 to 150 mm. Over 160 mm is considered high. *Diastolic b. p.* The lowest point registered on the apparatus corresponding to the resting stage of the heart. *Systolic b. p.* The highest point registered when the arteries are fullest following cardiac contraction.

blood serum (*seer'-um*). Plasma without the clotting agents. It may be used: (1) for intravenous infusion, (2) as a bacteriological culture medium.

blood sugar. The normal is 0·08 to 0·12 per cent (80 to 120 mg/100 ml of blood). 0·18 per cent is the normal renal threshold (*q.v.*). The amount rises in diabetes mellitus.

blood transfusion (*trans-fu'-zhun*). Introduction of blood from the vein of one person (*donor*) to the vein of another (*recipient*). Clotting must be prevented in the transition stage. This is usually done by admixture with sodium citrate (1 g to 450 ml of blood). Too much sodium citrate tends to produce a reaction, and rigor and shock may occur. Transfusion of fresh blood has been largely replaced by the use of stored blood or plasma. *See* Appendix 3. Used as treatment: (1) In severe loss of blood from any cause. (2) For the treatment or prevention of shock. (3) In severe infections, to supply healthy blood to fight the infection.

blood urea (*u-re'-ah*). The normal is 0·015 to 0·04 per cent (15 to 40 mg/100 ml of blood). Renal failure causes retention of urea in the blood and signs of *uraemia* are likely to develop.

'blue baby'. A child born with a very blue colour. It may be due to a defect in the heart, in consequence of which arterial and venous blood become mixed. *See* Fallot's tetralogy.

blue paint. An antiseptic made from aniline dyes. It consists of 1 per cent *brilliant green* and 1 per cent *gentian violet* in 25 per cent *spirit*. Both skin and linen are badly stained by it. Bonney's blue.

blue pus. The coloured discharge from a wound infected with *Pseudomonas pyocyanea*.

blue stone. Copper sulphate.

bluxism (*blux'-izm*). Teeth clenching. This occurs in persons under tension and due to muscle fatigue may cause headaches.

BMR. Basal metabolic rate. *See* Basal.

Boeck's disease (*Bek*). A form of sarcoidosis, *q.v.*

Bohn's nodules (*bone*). Small white nodules on the palate of the newly born.

boil. An acute staphylococcal inflammation of the skin and subcutaneous tissues round a hair follicle. It causes a painful swelling with a central core of dead tissue (*slough*), which is eventually discharged. A furuncle.

bolus (*bo'-lus*). (1) A large pill. (2) A rounded mass of masticated food immediately before being swallowed.

bone. The dense connective tissue forming the skeleton. It is composed of cartilage or membrane impregnated with mineral salts, chiefly calcium phosphate and calcium carbonate. This is arranged as an outer hard *compact* tissue and an inner network of cells as *cancellous* tissue, in the spaces of which is red bone marrow. In the shaft of long bones is a medullary cavity containing white marrow. Microscopically, the bone tissue is perforated with minute (Haversian) canals containing blood vessels and lymphatics for the maintenance and repair of the cells. Bone is covered by a fibrous membrane—the *periosteum*—containing blood vessels and by which the bone grows in girth.

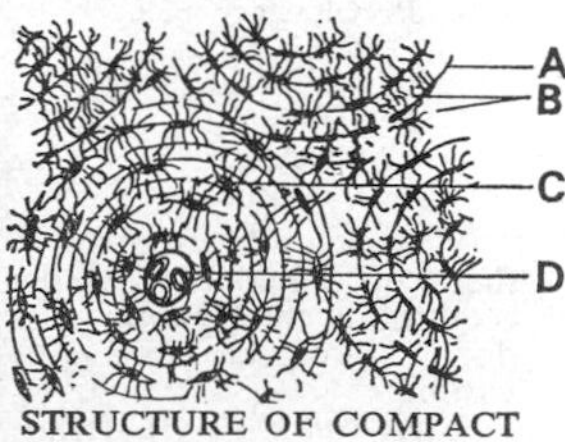

STRUCTURE OF COMPACT BONE

A. Lamellae.
B. Canaliculi.
C. Lacunae containing bone cells.
D. Haversian canal.

bone-graft. Transplantation of healthy bone to replace missing or defective bone.

boracic acid (*bor-as'-ik as'-id*). Boric acid. A mild antiseptic prepared from borax and used mainly for the irrigation of mucous or delicate surfaces, e.g. the eyes.

borax (*bor'-aks*). A compound of soda and boric acid. Used as a mild antiseptic, and to allay irritation of the mouth and skin.

borborygmus (*bor-bor-ig'-mus*). A rumbling sound caused by gas in the intestines.

Bordet-Gengou bacillus (*bor-da djon'-goo bas-il'-us*). *Haemophilus pertussis. See under* Bacillus.

Bornholm disease (*born'-holm*). An epidemic myalgia with pleural pain due to the Coxsackie virus infection. It receives its name from the Danish island of Bornholm.

Bothriocephalus (*both-re-o-kef'-al-us*). A genus of tapeworm. *B. latus*, the broad tapeworm. It may measure 7·5 m (25 ft) in length and 18 mm (¾ in.) in breadth. *See* Tapeworm.

botulism (*bot'-u-lizm*). A rare form of food poisoning in which the central nervous system is affected by the toxins from the *Clostridium botulinum*. It is an anaerobic spore-forming organism from the soil and survives in imperfectly canned vegetables and in meat and fish preparations. These may be normal in taste and appearance.

bougie (*boo'-je*). A flexible instrument used to dilate a stricture, as in the oesophagus or urethra. *Medicated b.* A soluble form impregnated with a medicinal substance. Used for urethral treatment. *Whip b.* Has a fine whip-like commencement, but gradually enlarges.

Bourneville's disease. Tuberous sclerosis. *See* Epiloia.

bovine (*bo'-vine*). Relating to the cow or ox. *B. tuberculosis.* That caused by infection from infected cow's milk, usually affecting glands and bones.

bowel (*bow'-el*). The intestine (*q.v.*).

Bowman's capsule. The commencement of the kidney tubule, which surrounds a tuft of renal capillaries—the *glomerulus.* Filtration takes place from the blood into the tubule.

Bozemann's catheter (*bo'-ze-mans kath'-e-ter*). For uterine irrigation, grooved on one side to allow back flow, and to avoid danger of forcing fluid into the Fallopian tubes.

brachial (*brak'-e-al*). Relating to the arm. *B. artery.* The continuation of the axillary artery along the inner side of the upper arm. *B. plexus.* A network of nerves, situated at the root of the neck, supplying the upper limb.

brachium (*brak'-e-um*). The arm, from the shoulder to the elbow.

Bradford frame (*brad'-ford*). A metal and canvas frame which immobilizes the bones, and is used in the treatment of spinal tuberculosis.

bradycardia (*bra-de-kar'-de-ah*). Abnormally low rate of heart contractions and consequent slow pulse.

Bragg-Paul respirator. A type of cuirass respirator. *See under* Respirator.

brain. That part of the central nervous system contained in the skull. It consists of the cerebrum, cerebellum, medulla oblongata, and pons varolii.

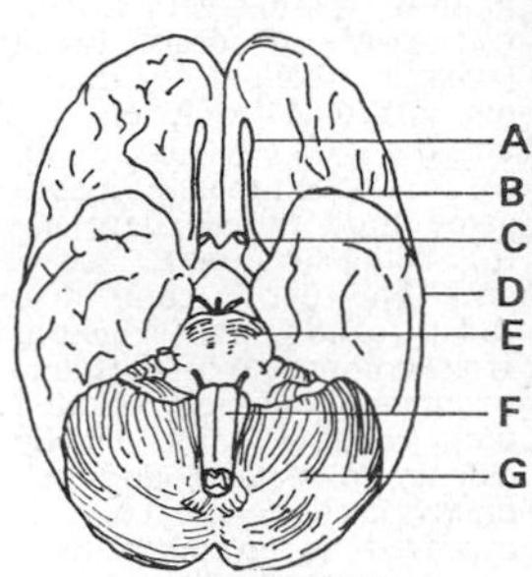

THE BRAIN

A. Olfactory bulb.
B. Olfactory tract.
C. Optic nerve.
D. Cerebrum.
E. Pons.
F. Medulla.
G. Cerebellum.

branchial (*bran'-ke-al*). Relating to the clefts that are present in the neck and pharynx in the developing embryo. Normally they disappear. *B. cyst.* A cystic swelling may arise if there is failure of closure of a cleft. *B. sinus* or lateral cervical sinus. A track leading from the posterior cervical region to open in the lower neck in front of the sternomastoid muscle.

Braun's splint. A metal splint

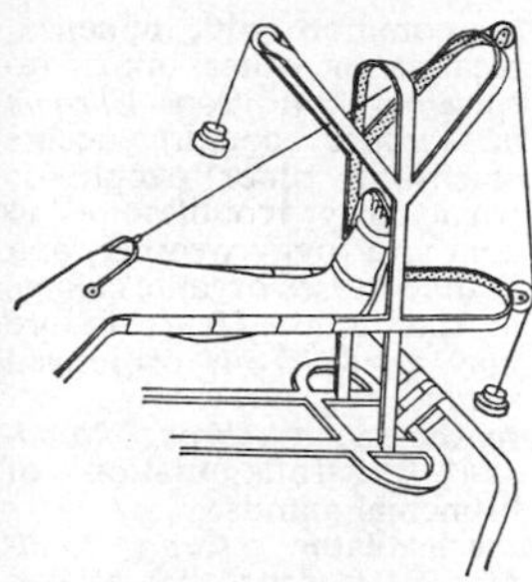
BRAUN'S SPLINT

which incorporates one or more pulleys and is used chiefly to elevate the lower limb and to apply skeletal traction for a compound fracture of tibia and fibula.

Braunula (*brawn'-u-lah*). A plastic disposable cannula fitted with a metal needle for ease of insertion. It is used for intravenous therapy.

breast. (1) The anterior or front region of the chest. (2) The mammary gland. *B. abscess.* Formation of pus in the mammary gland, a possible complication from infection in nursing mothers. *B. bone.* The sternum. *Pigeon b.* Prominent sternum, a deformity resulting from rickets. *B. pump.* An apparatus for removal of milk from the breast.

breech. The buttocks. *B. presentation.* The position of the fetus in the uterus is such that the buttocks are the presenting part.

bregma (*breg'-mah*). The anterior fontanelle. The membranous junction between the coronal, frontal and sagittal sutures.

bretylium tosylate (*bret-il'e-um tos'-il-ate*). A vasodilatant drug that affects the peripheral blood vessels supplied by the sympathetic nervous system. It is used in the treatment of hypertension. Darenthin is a proprietary preparation of it.

Bright's disease. An inflammation of the kidneys. *See* Nephritis.

brilliant green. An aniline dye used as an antiseptic.

brittle (*brit'-tl*). A term applied to diabetes when the patient's blood, sugar and glycosuria appear to vary from day to day or hour to hour, and so make his diabetes difficult to control.

broad ligaments. Folds of peritoneum extending from the uterus to the sides of the pelvis, and supporting the blood vessels to the uterus and uterine tubes.

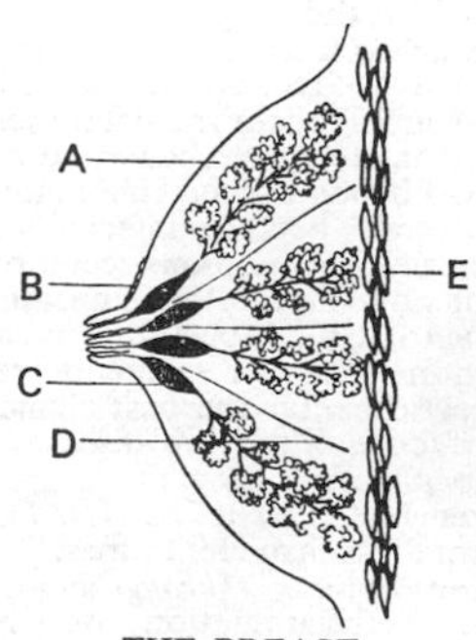

THE BREAST

A. Fat.
B. Areola.
C. Ampulla.
D. Fibrous septum.
E. Muscle.

Broca's area of speech (*Bro'-kah*). Nerve cells in the left cerebral hemisphere which have some control over speech.

Brodie's abscess (*bro'-dees ab'-sess*). Abscess of the head of the tibia or other long bone. A form of chronic tuberculous or staphylococcal osteomyelitis.

bromide (*bro'-mide*). A compound of bromine. *Potassium b.*, *sodium b.*, and *ammonium b.* can be prescribed as hypnotics, but they are strongly depressant and cumulative in action.

bromidrosis (*bro-mid-ro'-sis*). Offensive and foetid sweat, especially associated with the feet.

bronchi (*brong'-ki*). The two branches into which the trachea divides, before entering the lungs. *Sing*. bronchus.

bronchial tubes (*brong'-ke-al*). Subdivisions of the bronchi within the lungs.

bronchiectasis (*brong-ke-ek'-tas-is*). Dilatation of the bronchi or bronchial tubes, associated with the formation of fibrous tissue. The dilated bronchi become infected resulting in a copious secretion of pus. Treatment is unsatisfactory, but lobectomy, pneumonectomy or segmental resection offer the best chance of cure when the disease is localized.

bronchiole (*brong'-ke-ole*). The smallest bronchial tubes.

bronchiolitis (*brong-ke-o-li'-tis*). Inflammation of the bronchioles.

bronchitis (*brong-ki'-tis*). Inflammation of the bronchi. *Acute b.* Common in young children and the elderly. It is a descending infection from the common cold, influenza, measles or other upper respiratory condition. *Chronic b.* (winter cough) occurs chiefly in older people, is particularly troublesome in cold and foggy weather, and in time causes organic change in the lungs. Heart failure may result from prolonged strain.

broncho-adenitis (*brong'-ko aden-i'-tis*). Inflammation of bronchial glands.

bronchodilator (*brong-ko-di-la'-tor*). A drug that relaxes the plain muscle of the bronchi and bronchioles and so increases the lumen.

bronchogram (*brong'-ko-gram*). The X-ray film of the lungs after radio-opaque dye has been inserted.

bronchography (*brong-ko'-graf-e*). X-ray photography of the bronchial tree after introduction of an iodized oil opaque to the rays.

bronchomycosis (*brong-ko-mi-ko'-sis*). An industrial disease affecting agricultural workers stablemen, etc., and due to inhalation of microfungi which infect the air-passages. Causes can be the *Actinomyces*, or *Aspergillus* species. Symptoms are similar to those of pulmonary tuberculosis.

bronchophony (*brong-koff'-on-e*). Resonance of the voice as heard in the chest over the bronchi, on auscultation.

bronchopleural fistula (*brong-ko-plu'-ral*). An opening between the pleural space and one of the bronchi.

bronchopneumonia (*brong-ko-nu-mo'-ne-ah*). *See* Pneumonia.

bronchopulmonary (*brong-ko-pul'-mon-ar-e*). Relating to the lungs, bronchi and bronchioles.

bronchorrhoea (*brong-kor-re'-ah*). Copious expectoration from the bronchi.

bronchoscope (*brong' - ko - skope*). An instrument which enables the operator to see inside the bronchi; to remove foreign bodies or to take a biopsy.

bronchoscopy (*brong-kos'-ko-pe*). Examination of the bronchi by means of a bronchoscope.

bronchospasm (*brong'-ko-spazm*). Difficulty in breathing caused by the sudden constriction of plain muscle in the walls of the bronchi. This may arise in asthma, whooping cough, or pneumoconiosis.

bronchospirometer (*brong-ko-spi-rom'-e-ter*). An instrument used to measure the capacity of one lung or of one lobe of a lung.

bronchotracheal (*brong-ko-trak'-e-al*). Relating to both the trachea and the bronchi. *B. suction.* A term applied to the removing of mucus with the aid of suction, using an electrical or foot operated sucker.

brow. The forehead. *B. presentation.* When the brow of the child is presented first in labour.

Brucella abortus (*bru-sel'-lah ab-or'-tus*). An organism which produces abortion in cattle and undulant fever in man.

Brucella melitensis (*bru-sel'-lah mel-e-ten'-sis*). An organism in infected goats' milk that causes brucellosis or Malta fever in man.

brucellosis (*bru-sel-o'-sis*). Undulant fever. An intermittent fever caused by organisms transmitted in infected milk from cattle or goats.

Brudzinski's signs (*Brud-zin'-ske*). (1) When passive flexion of one thigh causes spontaneous flexion of the opposite thigh. (2) When flexion of the neck causes bilateral flexion of the hips and knees. These signs are indicative of meningeal irritation.

bruise (*brooz*). A superficial injury to tissues produced by sudden impact, in which the skin is unbroken. A contusion.

bruit (*bru'-e*). An abnormal sound or murmur heard on auscultation of the heart and large vessels. It occurs in disease of the heart and in anaemia.

Brunner's glands (*Broo'-ner*). Small compound tubular glands in the mucous membrane of the duodenum.

bubo (*bu'-bo*). A term applied to inflammation of the lymphatic glands of the axilla or groin. Typical of bubonic plague (*see* Plague) and venereal infections.

bubonocele (*bu-bon'-o-seel*). An early stage of inguinal hernia resembling a bubo.

buccal (*buk'-kal*). (1) Pertaining to the cheek. (2) Pertaining to the mouth.

buccinator (*buk'-sin-a-tor*). A muscle of the cheek.

Buerger's disease (*ber'-ger*). Thrombo-angeitis obliterans (*q.v.*).

buffer (*buff'-er*). A chemical substance which, when present in a solution, will allow only a very slight change in reaction when an acid (or alkali) is added to it. Sodium bicarbonate is the chief buffer of the blood and tissue fluids.

bulbar (*bul'-bah*). Pertaining to the medula oblongata. *B. paralysis*. *See* Paralysis.

bulbo-urethral (*bul-bo-u-re'-thral*). A term applied to small glands opening into the male urethra. Cowper's glands.

bulimia (*bu-lim'-e-ah*). Excessive appetite.

bulla (*bul'-lah*). A large blister. *Pl.* bullae.

Buller's shield. A type of protection placed over one eye when the other is infected. A watch glass placed over the eye and fixed with adhesive strapping or cellotape is a simple substitute.

bundle of His. The special band of neuromuscular fibres which passing through the septum of the heart divides at the apex into two parts, these being distributed into the wall of the ventricles. The impulse of contraction is conducted through this structure. Disease of it causes heart block (*q.v.*).

bunion (*bun'-yon*). A prominence on the head of the metatarsal bone at its junction with the great toe, caused by inflammation and swelling of the bursa at that joint. Usually due to shoes which distort the natural shape of the foot. The bone itself is much enlarged from chronic irritation.

Burkitt's tumour (*Bur'-kit*). African lymphoma. A lymphosarcoma occurring almost exclusively in children living in low lying moist areas of Central Africa. It may attack the jaw, lymph nodes, kidneys or thyroid gland.

burn. An injury to tissues caused by: (a) physical agent, the sun, excess heat or cold, (b) chemical agents, acids or caustic alkalis, (c) electrical current in which part of the body is placed in the circuit and the damage to tissue may be more extensive than is immediately apparent. Burns are now divided into partial thickness or full thickness according to the depth of skin destroyed. The former will heal from the germinal cells below but the latter require grafting. The treatment of shock and prevention of infection need special attention. For First Aid treatment, *see* Appendix 1.

bursa (*bur'-sah*). A small sac of fibrous tissue, lined with synovial membrane and containing synovial fluid. It is situated between parts that move upon one another at a joint, to reduce friction.

bursitis (*bur-si'-tis*). Inflammation of a bursa. *Prepatella b.* Housemaid's knee (*q.v.*).

busulphan (*bu-sul'-fan*). A cytotoxic drug that depresses the bone marrow and may be used to treat myeloid leukaemia. A trade name is Myleran.

butacaine (*bu'-ta-kane*). A local anaesthetic used in ophthalmology. Butyn is a proprietary preparation.

butobarbitone (*bu-to-bar'-be-tone*). A widely used barbiturate drug whose sedative action lasts from 4 to 8 hr and is unlikely to cause drowsiness on the following morning. Soneryl is a proprietary preparation of it.

buttock (*but'-ok*). The flesh-covered gluteal muscles at either side of the lower spine.

byssinosis (*bis-in-o'-sis*). An industrial disease caused by inhalation of cotton dust in factories. A type of pneumokoniosis (*q.v.*).

C

C. (1) The chemical symbol for *carbon*. (2) The abbreviation of *centigrade*. (3) The abbreviation for *calorie*.

cacao butter (*kak-a'-o*). A solid fat obtained from the seeds of *Theobroma cacao*, used as a base for suppositories.

cachet (*kash'-a*). Two pieces of wafer, joined in the form of a capsule to contain an unpalatable medicine.

cachexia (*ka-keks'-e-ah*). A condition of extreme debility. The patient is emaciated, the skin loose and wrinkled from rapid wasting, but shiny and tense over bone. The eyes are sunken, the skin yellowish, and there is a grey 'muddy' complexion. The mucous membranes are pale and anaemia is extreme. The condition is typical of the late stages of cancer.

cadaver (*kad-av'-er*). A corpse. The dead body used for dissection.

caecostomy (*se-kos'-to-me*). The making of an opening into the caecum by incision through the abdominal wall.

caecum (*se'-kum*). The commencement of the large intestine, to which the vermiform appendix is attached.

Caesarean section (*se-zair'-e-an sek'-shun*). Delivery of a fetus by an incision through the abdominal wall and uterus. Tradition has it that Julius Caesar was born in this way.

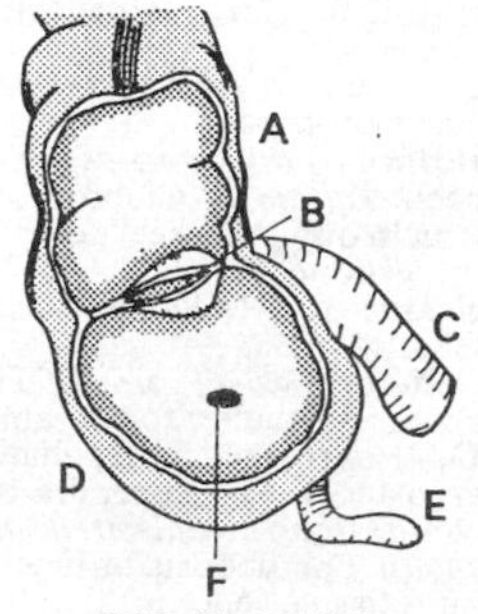

THE CAECUM

A. Ascending colon.
B. Ileo-caecal valve.
C. Ileum.
D. Caecum.
E. Appendix.
F. Orifice of appendix.

caesium 137 (*se'-se-um*). *Radioactive C.* An element that is a fission product from uranium. Sealed in a suitable container it can be used for beam therapy instead of cobalt, or sealed in needles or tubes it can be used for local application instead of radium.

caffeine (*kaf'-een*). An alkaloid of tea and coffee, used as a nerve stimulant and diuretic.

caisson disease (*ka'-son*). Decompression sickness (*q.v.*).

Calabar bean (*kal'-ab-ah*). The seed of the *Physostigma venenosum*. The alkaloid (*eserine* or *physostigmine*) is stimulative to involuntary muscle and is used as a miotic.

calamine (*kal'-a-mine*). Prepared from zinc carbonate. It is an astringent and antipruritic used in lotion or ointment form for skin diseases.

calcaneum (*kal-ka'-ne-um*). The heel-bone.

calcaneus (*kal-ka'-ne-us*). The heel. *Talipes c.* Clubfoot, in which only the heel touches the ground.

calcareous (*kal-kar'-e-us*). Chalky.

calciferol (*kal-sif'-er-ol*). The chemical name for vitamin D. It is formed in irradiated ergosterol. *See* Appendix 10.

calcification (*kal-sif-ik-a'-shun*). The deposit of lime in any tissue, e.g. in the formation of callus (*q.v.*).

calcium (*kal'-se-um*). A silver-white metal, the base of lime. *C. carbonate*, chalk. *C. chloride* is a disinfectant. *C. gluconate* is easily absorbed and can be given by intramuscular or intravenous route to raise the blood calcium. *C. hydroxide*, slaked lime. *C. lactate* increases coagulability of blood. *C. mandelate* is a urinary antiseptic.

calculoid (*kal'-ku-loid*). Like a calculus.

calculus (*kal'-ku-lus*). A stony concretion which may be formed in any of the secreting organs of the body or their ducts. *Arthritic c.* Gouty deposits in or near joints. *Biliary c.* Gall-stone (*q.v.*). *Mulberry c.* One made of calcium oxalate and shaped like a mulberry. *Renal c.* One formed in the kidney. *Salivary c.* Stone in a salivary duct. *Staghorn c.* A many branched stone sometimes found in the renal pelvis. *Urinary c.* One found anywhere in the urinary tract. *Vesical c.* Stone formed in the urinary bladder.

Caldwell–Luc operation (*kald'-well-luk*). An antrostomy operation to drain the maxillary sinus. The incision is made above the upper canine tooth.

calibrator (*kal'-e-bra-tor*). An instrument for measuring the size of openings.

caliper (*kal'-ip-er*). A two-pronged instrument that may be used to exert traction on a part. *Walking c.* An appliance fitted to a boot or shoe to give support to the lower limb. It may be used when the muscles are paralysed or in the repair stage of fractures.

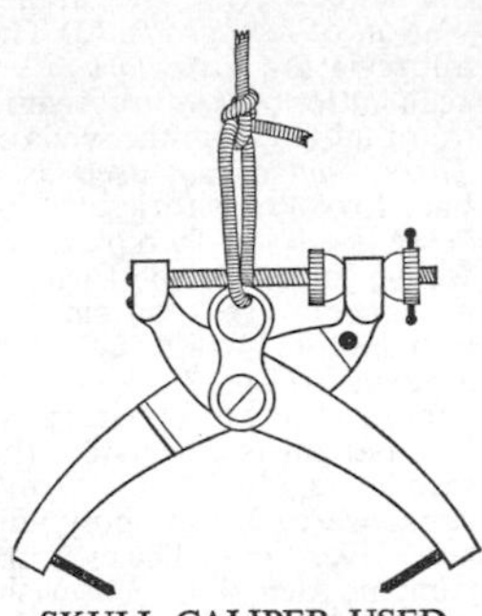

SKULL CALIPER USED FOR TRACTION

calipers (*kal'-ip-ers*). Compasses for measuring diameters and curved surfaces. *See* Pelvimeter.

callisthenics (*kal-is-the'-niks*). Mild gymnastics for developing the muscles and producing a graceful carriage.

callosity (*kal-os'-it-e*). The plaques of thickened skin often seen on the soles of the feet or the palms of the hand.

callous (*kal'-us*). Hard and thickened.

callus (*kal'-us*). The tissue which grows round fractured ends of bone and develops into new bone to repair the injury.

calyx (*ka'-lix*). Any cup-shaped vessel or part. *C. of kidney*. The cup-like terminations of the ureter in the renal pelvis surrounding the pyramids of the kidney. *Pl.* Calyces.

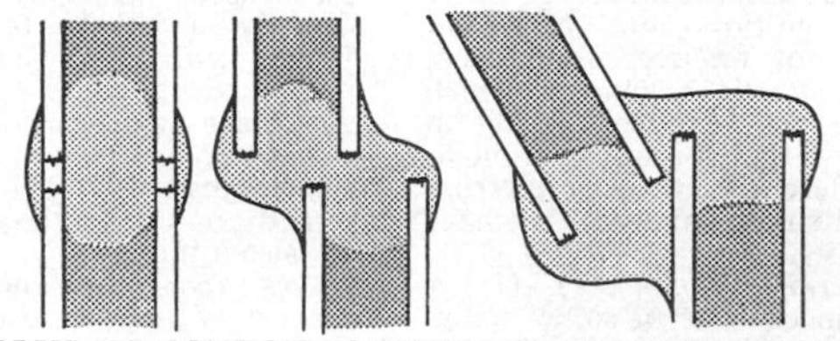

CALLUS FORMATION IN THREE TYPES OF FRACTURE

caloric test (*ka-lor'-ik*). A method of estimating vestibular disease of the ear by using warm or cool irrigations.

calorie (*kal'-or-e*). A standard unit of heat. Used to denote physiological values of various food substances, estimated according to the amount of heat they produce on being oxidized in the body. *See* Oxidation. A *calorie* represents the heat required in raising 1 kg (1000 g or 2·2 lb) 1°C. A *small calorie* = the heat produced in raising 1 g of water 1°C. For calorie value of foods, *see* Appendix 10.

calorific (*kal-or-if'ik*). Heat producing.

calorimeter (*kal-or-im'-e-ter*). An apparatus for measuring the heat that is produced by combustion.

calvities (*kal-vish'-e-ez*). Baldness.

calx (*kalks*). Calcium oxide or lime. The basis of slaked lime, bleaching powder, and quick lime. Used in making eusol (*q.v.*).

camphor (*kam'-for*). A crystalline substance prepared from the camphor laurel. It is used internally as a carminative. *Camphorated oil* is 1 part camphor to 4 parts oil prepared for external application as a rubefacient.

canaliculus (*kan-al-ik'-ul-us*). A small channel or canal. *See* Bone.

cancellous (*kan-sel'-us*). The spongy or honeycomb type of bone tissue in the ends of long bones and in flat and irregular bones. *See* Tissue.

cancer (*kan'-ser*). A general term to describe malignant growths in tissues, of which *carcinoma* (*q.v.*) is of epithelial, and *sarcoma* (*q.v.*) of connective tissue origin, as in bone and muscle. A cancerous growth is one which is not encapsulated, but infiltrates into surrounding tissues, the cells of which it replaces by its own. It is spread by the lymph and blood vessels and causes metastases (*q.v.*) in other parts of the body. Death is caused by destruction of organs to a degree imcompatible with life; to extreme debility and anaemia; or to haemorrhage. The importance of early recognition and treatment cannot be over-emphasized. *Anaplastic c.* One in which the cells are so lacking in form that it is not possible to differentiate them or tell from which type of tissue they have arisen.

cancroid (*kan'-kroid*). (1) A skin tumour of some malignancy. (2) Resembling cancer.

cancrum oris (*kan'-krum aw'-ris*). Gangrenous stomatitis. An ulceration of the mouth, which is a rare complication of measles in debilitated children. Penicillin lessens the severity of this condition. *Syn.*, Noma.

Candida (*kan'-did-ah*). A genus of small fungi, formerly called Monilia. *C. albicans.* The variety which causes moniliasis.

canine teeth (*kan'-ine*). Four in number. Two in each jaw between the incisors and molars, commonly known as 'eye teeth'.

canker (*kan'-ker*). Ulceration, usually of the mouth.

cannabis indica (*kan'-na-bis in'-dik-ah*). An Indian hemp (*hashish*), antispasmodic and narcotic. Large doses cause intoxication and delirium. A drug of addiction controlled by the Misuse of Drugs Act.

cannula (*kan'-u-lah*). A metal tube for insertion into the body by which fluids are introduced or removed. Usually a trocar (*q.v.*) is fitted into it to facilitate introduction.

cantharides (*kan-thar'-id-eez*). An extract from the body of the Spanish fly, applied externally as a counter-irritant to raise a blister.

canthus (*kan'-thus*). The angle formed by the junction of the upper and lower eyelids.

capillarity (*kap-il-lar'-it-e*). The action by which a liquid will rise upwards in a fibrous substance or in a fine tube.

capillary (*kap-il'-ar-e*). Hair-like. (1) Minute vessels connecting an artery and vein. (2) Minute vessels of the lymphatic system.

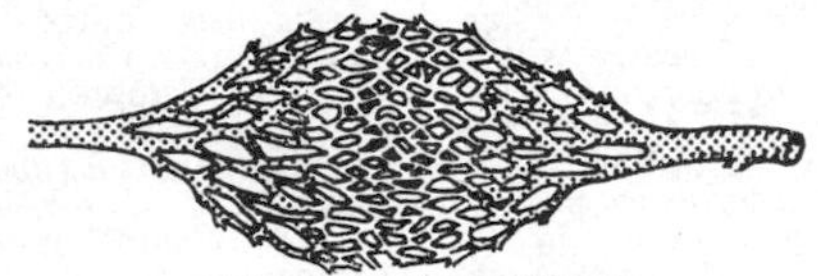

CAPILLARY NETWORK

capitellum (*kap-it-el'-um*). (a) The small rounded head at the elbow end of the humerus. (b) The bulb of a hair.

capsular ligaments (*kap'-su-lah lig'-a-ments*). The ligaments which completely envelop a joint. This capsule loosely encloses the bones, and is lined with synovial membrane which secretes a fluid for lubrication of the articular surfaces. Known also as *articular capsule*.

capsule (*kap'-sule*). (1) A fibrous or membranous sac

enclosing an organ. (2) A small soluble case of gelatin in which a nauseous medicine may be enclosed. (3) The gelatinous envelope which surrounds and protects some bacteria.

capsulotomy (*kap-sul-ot'-o-me*). The tearing of a hole in the remaining lens capsule after an extracapsular cataract extraction. Needling.

caput (*kap'-ut*). Head. *C. succedaneum*, a soft swelling on an infant's head, due to pressure during labour.

carbachol (*kar'-ba-kol*). A drug related to and acting like acetylcholine (*q.v.*), but more stable. It causes contraction of plain muscle and relaxation of the voluntary sphincter, so relieving post-operative retention of urine.

carbimazole (*kar-bim'-a-zol*). An antithyroid drug that is used to stabilize a patient with thyrotoxicosis.

carbaminohaemoglobin (*karb'-am-in-o-he-mo-glo'-bin*). The combination of carbon dioxide with haemoglobin. This takes place most readily with reduced haemoglobin.

carbenoxolone (*kar-ben-oks'-o-lone*). A derivative of liquorice that increases the healing rate of gastric ulcers. Biogastrone is a proprietary preparation.

carbohydrate (*kar-bo-hi'-drate*). That class of food represented by the starches and sugars—they are energy and heat-producing substances. *See* Appendix 10.

carbol fuchsin (*kar-bol fook'-sin*). A mixture of carbolic acid and fuchsin used for staining purposes in bacteriology.

carbolic acid (*kar-bol'-ik*). Phenol. A powerful disinfectant and poison derived from coal tar. In its pure form it can be used as a caustic. Diluted, used to disinfect linen and excreta. Lotion containing 1 per cent has an anaesthetic action.

carbo ligni. Wood charcoal. Used for the relief of digestive disorders and diarrhoea.

carbon dioxide (CO_2) (*kar'-bon di-oks'-ide*). A gas which, dissolved in water, forms weak carbonic acid. As a product of metabolism by the oxidation of carbon, it leaves the body by the lungs. It can be compressed till it freezes, and then forms a solid—*carbon dioxide* snow, used to destroy superficial naevi. Inhalations of CO_2 (5 per cent) are useful to stimulate the depth of respiration. *See* Appendix 4.

carbon monoxide (CO) (*kar'-bon mon-oks'-ide*). A colourless gas produced by incomplete combustion of coal. It is a major constituent of coal gas. In poisoning there is vertigo, flushed face with very red lips, loss of consciousness, and convulsions. The blood is bright red, from carboxyhaemoglobin.

carbon tetrachloride (*kar'-bon tet-ra-klor'-ide*). A powerful anthelmintic used in treating hookworm and whipworm but in certain individuals can lead to severe necrosis of liver cells. A high carbohydrate and high protein diet are good preventive measures The drug must not be given to alcoholics.

carboxyhaemoglobin (*kar-boks'-e-he-mo-glo'-bin*). The combination of carbon monoxide with haemoglobin in the blood in carbon monoxide poisoning.

carboxyhaemoglobinaemia (*kar-boks' - e - he - mo - glo - bin - e'-me-ah*). The condition of carbon monoxide in the blood.

carbromal (*kar'-brom-al*). A drug of the barbiturate group combined with bromine. A useful sedative with no unpleasant after effects.

carbuncle (*kar'-bung-kl*). An acute staphylococcal inflammation of subcutaneous tissues, which causes local thrombosis in the veins and death of tissue. In appearance it resembles a collection of boils.

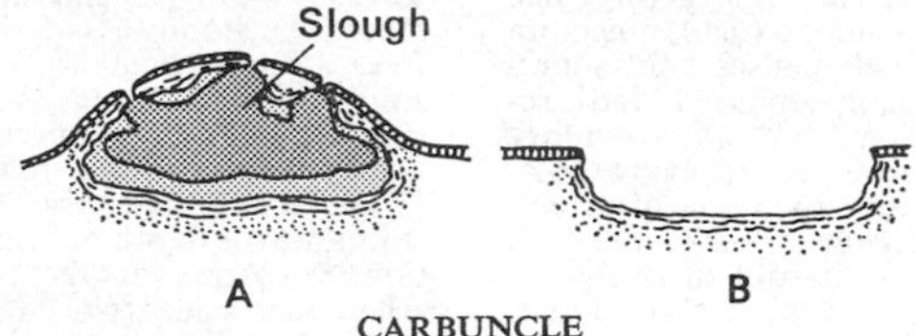

CARBUNCLE
Before (A) and after (B) separation, showing tissue destruction.

carcinogen (*kar'-sin-o-jen*). Any substance which can produce a cancer.

carcinogenic (*kar-sin-o-jen'-ik*). A term applied to agents which produce or predispose to cancer. Crude oils are said to contain a *c. factor*.

carcinoma (*kar-sin-o'-mah*). A malignant growth of epithelial tissue. Microscopically the cells resemble those of the tissue in which the growth has arisen. (1) Squamous-celled, like the outer layers of the skin (*epithelioma*). (2) Spheroidal-celled arising from glandular tissue, e.g. the breast. (3) Columnar-celled, e.g. from the intestinal tract.

carcinomatosis (*kar-sin-o-mat-o'-sis*). The condition when a carcinoma has given rise to widespread metastasis.

cardia (*kar'-de-ah*). (1) The cardiac orifice of the stomach. (2) The heart.

cardiac (*kar'-de-ak*). Pertaining to the heart. *C. asthma. See* Asthma. *C. atrophy.* Fatty degeneration of the heart-muscle. *C. bed.* One which can be manipulated to form a chair shape for those heart cases who are comfortable only when sitting up. The head can be raised to form a back rest, and the foot lowered. An angle to flex the knees prevents slipping. *C. catheterization.* A radio-opaque catheter is passed from an arm vein to the heart. Its passage through the heart can be watched on a screen. Also blood pressure readings and specimens can be taken, thus aiding diagnosis of heart abnormalities. *C. compensation.* Hypertrophy of the muscle of the heart by which valvular defects are compensated, and the circulation is effectively maintained.

cardialgia (*kar-de-al'-je-ah*). Pain in the region of the heart.

cardiogenic (*kar-de-o-jen′-ik*). Originating in the heart. *C. shock*. A term applied to shock caused by disease or failure of heart action.

cardiogram (*kar′-de-o-gram*). A tracing made by the cardiograph.

cardiograph (*kar′-de-o-graf*). An instrument for registering the movements of the heart.

cardiologist (*kar-de-ol′-o-jist*). One who has made a particular study of the diagnosis and treatment of heart disease.

cardiology (*kar-de-ol′-o-je*). The study of the heart and how it works.

cardiolysis (*kar-de-ol′-is-is*). The breaking down of adhesions between the pericardium and chest wall, by operation.

cardiomyopathy (*kar-de-o-mi-op′-ath-e*). A myocarditis that may accompany an acute fever and require prolonged rest even after the original condition is cured.

cardiomyotomy (*kar-de-o-mi-ot′-o-me*). An operation to divide the circular muscle fibres at the cardiac end of the stomach to relieve cardiospasm.

cardiopathy (*kar-de-op′-ath-e*). Any disease of the heart.

cardiopulmonary (*kar-de-o-pul′-mon-ar-e*). Relating to the heart and lungs. *C. bypass*. The use of the heart lung machine to oxygenate and pump the blood round the body while the surgeon operates on the heart.

cardiospasm (*kar′-de-o-spazm*). Spasm of the sphincter muscle at the cardiac end of the stomach, it may result in dilation of the oesophagus.

cardiotocography (*kar-de-o-to-kog′-raf-e*). The instantaneous recording of the fetal heart rate, fetal movements and the uterine contractions; in order to discover possible lack of oxygen (hypoxia) to the fetus. Fetal monitoring.

cardiotomy syndrome (*kar-de-ot′-o-me sin′-drome*). An inflammatory reaction following heart surgery. There is pyrexia, pericarditis, and pleural effusion.

cardiovascular (*kar-de-o-vas′-ku-lar*). Concerning the heart and blood vessels.

cardioversion (*kar-de-o-ver′-shun*). A method of terminating abnormal heart rhythm as in atrial fibrillation by means of electrodes and an electrical discharge.

carditis (*kar-di′-tis*). Inflammation of the heart.

caries (*kair′-re-eez*). Suppuration and subsequent decay of bone, corresponding to ulceration in soft tissues. In *caries*, the bone dissolves; in *necrosis* it separates in large pieces and is thrown off. *Dental c*. Decay of the teeth due to penetration of bacteria through the enamel to the dentine. *Spinal c*. Pott's disease (*q.v.*).

carina (*kar′-een-ah*). The term applied to the bifurcation of the trachea into the bronchi as the terminal cartilage is keel-shaped.

carminative (*kar′-min-a-tiv*). An aromatic which relieves flatulence. Cloves, ginger, cardamon, and peppermint are examples.

carneous mole (*kar′-ne-us*). A tumour of organized blood clot surrounding a dead fetus in the uterus. *See* Abortion.

carotene (*kar′-o-tin*). The colouring matter in carrots, tomatoes, and other yellow foods and fats. It is a provitamin capable of conversion into vitamin A in the liver. *See* Appendix 10.

carotid (*ka-rot'-id*). The principal artery on each side of the neck.

carphology (*kar-fol'-o-je*). Constant picking at the bedclothes, occurring in cases of serious illness, especially in the typhoid state (*q.v.*).

carpopedal spasm (*kar'-po-pe'-dal*). Spasm of the hands and feet as occurs in tetany.

carpus (*kar'-pus*). The eight bones forming the wrist and arranged in two rows: (1) Scaphoid, lunate, triquetral, pisiform. (2) Trapezium, trapezoid, capitate, hamate.

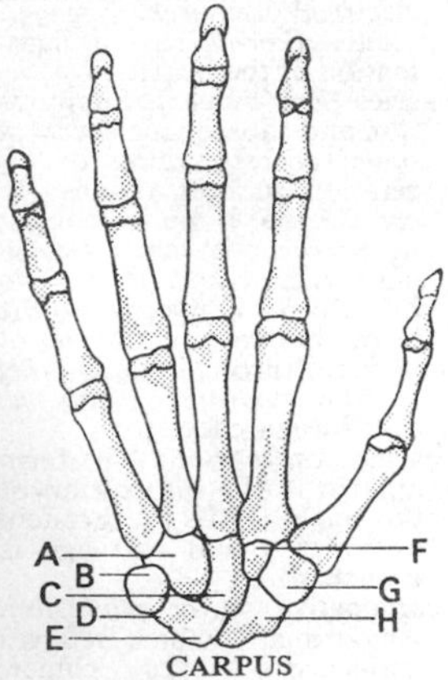

CARPUS
A. Hamate.
B. Pisiform.
C. Capitate.
D. Triquetral.
E. Lunate.
F. Trapezoid.
G. Trapezium.
H. Scaphoid.

carrier. A person who harbours the micro-organisms of a disease, but is not necessarily affected by it; e.g. *meningococci* and *diphtheria bacilli* can be harboured in the throat of a healthy person who may infect others by direct contact. *Typhoid c.* One who harbours the organism, as a rule in the gall-bladder, by which the faeces are infected. This may be the origin of an epidemic, especially if the water supply be contaminated from such a source.

cartilage (*kar'-til-aj*). Gristle. A tough connective tissue of three varieties: (1) *Hyaline c.* A dense groundwork containing cartilaginous cells, forming the embryonic bones before ossification and covering the articular surfaces of bone. (2) *Fibro-c.* In which bundles of white fibres predominate, forming the intervertebral discs and costal cartilages. (3) *Elastic c.* Containing elastic fibres and forming the pinna of the ear, the epiglottis and part of the nasal septum. *Costal c.* Joins the ribs to the sternum. *Ensiform c.* (xiphoid process). The cartilaginous termination to the sternum.

cartilaginous (*kar-til-aj'-in-us*). Of the nature of cartilage.

caruncle (*kar-ung'-kl*). (1) A small reddish body situated at the medial junction of the eyelids. (2) A small fleshy growth, occurring chiefly at the urinary orifice in females, and giving rise to great pain on micturition.

cascara (*kas-kar'-ah*). A laxative prepared from the bark of the Californian buckthorn. It may be prepared as an elixir or as tablets.

caseation (*ka-se-a'-shun*). Degeneration in tuberculous infection, forming a cheesy mass.

casein (*ka'-se-in*). The chief protein of milk. It forms a curd, from which cheese is made. *C. hydrolysate*. A predigested concentrated protein; a useful supplement for a high protein diet.

caseinogen (*ka-se-in'-o-jen*). The precursor of casein—activated by rennin.

Casilan (*kas'-e-lan*). A proprietary preparation of calcium caseinate. A fine powder containing 90 per cent protein. A useful aid where a high protein diet is required.

castor oil (*kah'-stor*). Internally it is a purgative. Least nauseous when given with lemon or brandy. Externally it is protective and soothing and may be used in ointments or in eye drops.

castration (*kas-tra'-shun*). Removal of the testicles or, in a female, the ovaries.

casts (*kahsts*). Plastic material thrown off in various diseases, and moulded to the shape of that part in which it has accumulated. *Renal c.* or *hyaline c.* are degenerating cells cast off into the urine in some cases of chronic kidney disease.

catabolism (*kat-ab'-ol-izm*). Katabolism. The breaking down process in tissue structure.

catalase (*kat'-al-aze*). An enzyme found in many body cells.

catalepsy (*kat'-a-lep-se*). (1) A nervous state characterized by trance-like sleep with passive rigidity of the muscles. During an attack the limbs will remain in any position in which they are placed. (2) A stage of hypnosis where the limbs remain rigid, and in any position suggested.

catalyst (*kat'-a-list*). A substance which hastens or brings about a chemical change without itself undergoing alteration; e.g. enzyme action during digestion.

catamenia (*kat-a-me'-ne-ah*). The menses, or monthly discharge of blood from the uterus.

cataphoresis (*kat-a-for-e'-sis*). A method of introducing drugs through the skin. *See* Ionization.

cataplasm (*kat'-a-plazm*). A poultice. It acts as a counterirritant. Materials of which it can be made are: *linseed*, *bread* and *bran*. Kaolin is more frequently used.

cataract (*kat'-a-rakt*). Opacity of the crystalline lens of the eye causing blindness. It may be congenital, senile, or due to diabetes.

catarrh (*kat-ar'*). Simple inflammation of a mucous membrane accompanied by an excessive discharge of mucus. It is usually a chronic condition of the nose or nasopharynx with few signs of inflammation.

catatonia (*kat-a-to'-ne-ah*). A symptom occurring in schizophrenia, but less commonly in organic cerebral disease, characterized by stupor (*q.v.*), the adoption of strange postures, or outbursts of excitement and overactivity. The patient may change suddenly from one of these states to another.

catecholamines (*kat-e-kol-a'-meens*). A group of compounds that have the effect of sympathetic nerve stimulation. They have an aromatic and an amine portion and include dopamine, adrenaline and noradrenaline.

catechu (*kat'-e-choo*). A powerfully astringent extract of the leaves and young shoots of Acacia. It may be given to check diarrhoea but refined kaolin is more effective.

catgut (*kat'-gut*). A substance prepared from the intestines of sheep and used in surgery for sutures and ligatures. It becomes gradually absorbed in the body. Careful and thorough sterilization is needed, as it cannot be subjected to high temperatures.

catharsis (*kath-ar'-sis*). (1) Purgation. (2) Abreaction (*q.v.*).

cathartic (*kath-ar'-tik*). Purgative.

catheter (*kath'-e-ter*). A fine hollow tube for removing or inserting fluid into a body cavity or viscus. Most commonly associated with the urinary bladder and made of plastic material or rubber. *Cardiac c.* A plastic one used in investigation of heart abnormalities. *See* Cardiac. *Eustachian c.* A silver one used to open up the pharynotympanic tube. *Self-retaining c.* is so made that after introduction the blind end expands so that it can remain in the bladder. Useful for continuous or intermittent drainage or where frequent specimens are required. *Ureteric c.* A fine catheter passed up the ureter to the renal pelvis and used to insert a dye in retrograde pyleography. For sterilization and illustrations of varieties of urinary catheters *see* Appendices 7 and 20.

catheterization (*kath'-et-er-i-za'-shun*). The use of a catheter.

cathode (*kath'-ode*). The negative electrode which is joined to the negative pole of a battery.

cation (*kat'-i-on*). A positively charged ion which moves towards the cathode when an electric current is passed through an electrolytic solution. *See also* Anion.

cauda (*kaw'-dah*). A tail. *C. equina.* The bundle of sacral and lumbar nerves with which the spinal cord terminates.

caudal (*kaw'-dal*). Referring to the cauda. *C. block.* An anaesthetic agent injected into the sacral canal, so that operations may be carried out in the perineal area without the risk of a general anaesthetic.

caul (*kawl*). The amnion, which occasionally does not rupture, but envelopes the infant's head at birth.

causalgia (*caws-al'-je-ah*). An intense burning pain which persists after nerve injuries.

caustic (*kaws'-tik*). A substance capable of burning organic tissue. Silver nitrate (*lunar c.*), carbolic acid, and carbon dioxide snow are those most commonly used in surgery.

cautery (*kaw'-ter-e*). The means of applying a caustic substance. *Actual c.* Cauterizing by direct heat. *Electric c.* A wire heated to red or white heat by means of electricity.

cavernous (*kav'-er-nus*). Having caverns or hollows. *C. breathing* Sounds heard on auscultation over a pulmonary cavity. *C. sinus*. A venous channel lying on either side of the body of the sphenoid bone through which pass the internal carotid artery and several nerves. *C. sinus thrombosis* is a very serious complication of any infection of the face, the veins from the orbit draining into this and carrying the infection into the cranium.

cavitation (*kav-e-ta'-shun*). The formation of cavities, e.g. in the lung in tuberculosis.

cavity (*kav'-et-e*). A confined space or hollow with containing walls.

cells (*sels*). Microscopic masses of protoplasm of which all organic tissues are made.

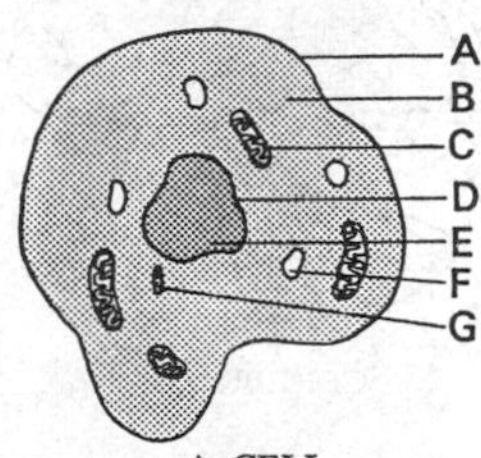

A CELL

A. Thin, elastic cell membrane.
B. Cytoplasm.
C. Mitochondrion.
D. Nuclear membrane.
E. Nucleoplasm.
F. Vacuole.
G. Centrosome.

cellulitis (*sel-u-li'-tis*). Streptococcal inflammation of cellular tissue which causes a typical brawny, oedematous appearance of the part, but local abscess formation is not common.

cellulose (*sel'-u-loze*). (1) A carbohydrate forming the covering of vegetable cells. i.e. vegetable fibres. Not digestible in the alimentary tract of man, but gives bulk, and as 'roughage' stimulates peristalsis. (2) Specially prepared cellulose tissue is a cheap form of absorbent dressing for wounds.

censor (*sen'-sor*). According to Freud, the psychic phenomenon which normally prevents impressions from the unconscious mind reaching the consciousness.

centi- A prefix meaning a hundredth part of. Used in the metric system of weights and measures. *See* Appendix 14.

centigrade (*sen'-te-grade*). The scale of heat measurement used in those countries where the metric system is employed. It is now usually called the Celsius scale. The thermometer registers 100°, as the boiling-point of water, and 0° (zero) as the freezing-point. *See also* Fahrenheit. *See* Appendix 15.

centrifugal (*sen-trif'-u-gal*). Conveyance away from a centre, such as from the brain to the periphery. Efferent.

centrifuge (*sen'-trif-uj*). An apparatus which will hold a test-tube, and permits of rotation at great speed. If the tube is filled with fluid, e.g. blood or urine, any bacteria, cells, or other solids in it are precipitated by such rotation.

centripetal (*sen-trip'-et-al*). The reverse of centrifugal. Conveyance from the periphery to the centre. Afferent.

centrosome (*sen-tro'-som*). A body in the cytoplasm of most animal cells, close to the nucleus. It divides during mitosis, and half migrates to each daughter cell.

cephalalgia (*kef-al-al'-je-ah*). Pain in the head.

cephalhaematoma (*kef-al-he-mat-o'-mah*). A subcutaneous swelling containing blood, which may be present on the head of a newborn infant.

cephalic version (*kef-al'-ik ver'-shun*). The method used to convert a transverse into a head presentation to facilitate labour, i.e. turning an abnormal into a normal presentation.

cephalocele (*kef'-al-o-seel*). Cerebral hernia. *See* Hernia.

cephalometry (*kef-al-om'-et-re*). The measurement of the fetal head by radiography.

cephaloridine (*kef-al-or'-e-din*). An antibiotic that is effective against a wide range of organisms and useful against penicillin-resistant strains and for urinary infection.

cerebellum (*ser-e-bel'-um*). The portion of the brain below the cerebrum and above the medulla oblongata. The hind-brain.

cerebral (*ser'-e-bral*). Relating to the cerebrum. *C. haemorrhage*. Rupture of a cerebral blood vessel. Likely causes are aneurysm and hypertension. *See* Apoplexy. *C. hernia*. *See* Hernia. *C. irritation*. A condition of general nervous irritability and abnormality, often with photophobia, which may be an early sign of meningitis, tumour of the brain, etc. It is also associated with trauma, as concussion or contusion. *C. palsy*. Impairment of development of the nervous system due to birth injury. *See* Spastics.

cerebration (*ser-e-bra'-shun*). Mental activity.

cerebritis (*ser-e-bri'-tis*). Inflammation of the brain.

cerebrospinal (*ser'-e-bro-spi'-nal*). Relating to the brain and spinal cord. *C. fever*. A meningitis caused by the meningococcus. *C. fluid*. The fluid made in the choroid plexus of the ventricles of the brain and circulating from them into the subarachnoid space around the brain and spinal cord.

cerebrum (*ser'-e-brum*). The largest part of the brain, occupying the greater portion of the cranium and consisting

Cerebrum

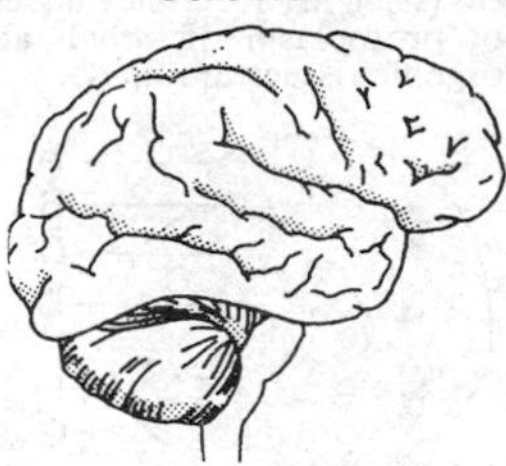

CEREBRUM

of the right and left hemispheres. The centre of the higher functions of the brain.

cerumen (*ser-u'-men*). A waxy substance secreted by the ceruminous glands of the auditory canal.

cervical (*sur-vi'-kal*). Pertaining to the neck. *C. rib*. A short, extra rib, often bilateral, which sometimes occurs on the seventh cervical vertebra and may cause pressure on an artery or nerve.

cervix (*sur'-viks*). A constricted portion or neck. *C. uteri*. The neck of the uterus;

it is about 2 cm long and opens into the vagina.

cestode (*ses'-tode*). Tapeworm (*q.v.*).

cetrimide (*set'-re-mide*). Cetyltrimethylammonium bromide (CTAB). A detergent and antiseptic widely used for pre-operative skin preparation and the cleansing of wounds. Strength 1 per cent. Cetavlon is a proprietary preparation of it.

cevitamic acid (*se-vit-am'-ik*). Ascorbic acid (*q.v.*).

chalazion (*kal-a'-ze-on*). A Meibomian or tarsal cyst. A sebaceous cyst in the eyelid.

chalicosis (*kal-ik-o'-sis*). A condition resembling silicosis (*q.v.*) but found mainly among stone-cutters, and due to the inhalation of stone dust.

chancre (*shan'-ker*). The initial lesion of syphilis (*q.v.*) developing at the site of inoculation.

chancroid (*shang'-kroid*). Soft chancre. A venereal ulceration, due to Ducrey's bacillus, accompanied by inflammation and suppuration of the local glands.

charcoal (*char'-kole*). Carbon, obtained by burning animal or vegetable tissue. Vegetable charcoal is sometimes given in the form of biscuits or tabloids, in cases of dyspepsia.

Charcot's joint (*shar'-ko*). A disease of the head of bones with effusion of fluid into the joints, occurring in locomotor ataxia. *C.'s triad* (nystagmus, intention tremor and scanning speech). An early sign of disseminated sclerosis.

Charnley's clamps (*charn'-lee*). These consist of two horizontal bars connected by two screw clamps and are used to exert tension on two bone ends following arthrodesis.

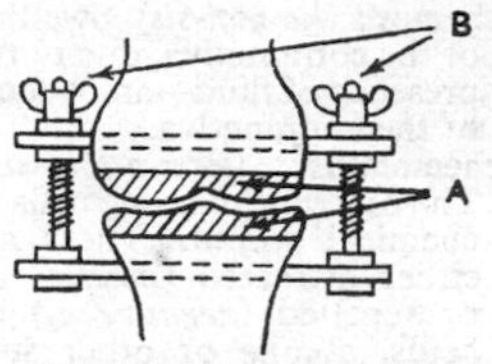

CHARNLEY'S CLAMPS

A. Excised area of bone.
B. Wing nuts for tightening.

cheilitis (*ki-li'-tis*). Inflammation of the lip.

cheiloplasty (*ki'-lo-plas-te*). Any plastic operation on the lip.

cheilorrhaphy (*ki-lor'-raf-e*). A suturing or repair of a harelip.

cheiloschisis (*ki-los'-kis-is*). Hare-lip (*q.v.*).

cheiropompholyx (*ki-ro-pom'-fo-liks*). A skin disease characterized by vesicles on the palms and soles.

chelate (*ke'-late*). A chemical organized into a fixed ring structure.

chelating agent (*ke'-lat-ing*). A drug that has the power of combining with certain metals and so aiding excretion to prevent or overcome poisoning. *See* Dimercaprol *and* Penicillamine.

chemopallidectomy (*ke'-mo-pal-le-dek-to-me*). The insertion of a chemical to limit activity of the globus pallidum. A treatment for paralysis agitans.

chemoreceptor (*ke-mo-re-sep'-tor*). A sensory nerve ending or group of cells that are excited by chemical stimuli, often those present in the blood stream.

chemosis (*ke-mo'-sis*). Swelling of the conjunctiva, due to the presence of fluid—an oedema of the conjunctiva.

chemotaxis (*kem-o-tak'-sis*). The reaction of living cells to chemical stimuli. These are either attracted (*positive c.*) or repelled (*negative c.*) by acids, alkalis or other substances.

chemotherapy (*ke-mo-ther'-ap-e*). The specific treatment of disease by the administration of chemical compounds. A term commonly applied to the sulphonamide group of drugs.

Cheyne – Stokes respiration (*chain-stoke-s res-pir-a'-shun*). Tidal respiration. A form of irregular but rhythmic breathing caused by increase in acidity in the blood (e.g. of carbonic acid). There are alternating periods of *hyperpnoea* and *apnoea*. It is likely to be present in advanced cases of arteriosclerosis, uraemia, etc.

chickenpox (*chik'-en-poks*). Varicella (*q.v.*).

chilblain (*chil'-blain*). A condition resulting from defective circulation when exposure to cold causes localized swelling and inflammation of the hands or feet, with severe itching and burning sensations.

chiniofon (*kin'-e-o-fon*). A quinine compound used in treating amoebic dysentery. Quinoxyl is a proprietary preparation.

chiropodist (*ki-rop'-o-dist*). One who treats the feet, particularly regarding corns and conditions of the nails.

chiropody (*ki-rop'-o-de*). The treatment of corns, callosities, and other foot conditions.

chloasma (*klo-az'-mah*). A condition in which there is brown, blotchy discoloration of the skin, appearing on the face, especially during pregnancy.

chloral hydrate (*klor'-al hi'-drate*). A drug used as a hypnotic which does not cause respiratory depression and is well tolerated by children.

chlorambucil (*klor-am-bu'-sil*). A nitrogen mustard preparation used in treating chronic myeloid leukaemia. A cytoxic drug. Leukeran is a trade preparation.

chloramine (*klor'-a-min*). An antiseptic which owes its power to its chlorine content (used in 3 per cent solution). A special preparation of it is *chloramine T*.

chloramphenicol (*klor-am-fen'-e-kol*). An oral antibiotic which may give rise to agranulocytosis. The drug of choice for treating typhoid fever. Used in drops and ointment for eye infections. Chloromycetin is a proprietary preparation of it.

chloroquine (*klor'-o-kwin*). An antimalarial drug that has a strong suppressant action and may also be used in the treatment of amoebic hepatitis and rheumatoid arthritis.

chlorbutol (*klor-bu'-tol*). Chloretone. A mild sedative; used to prevent sea-sickness or overcome vomiting due to radiotherapy.

chlordiazepoxide (*klor-di-az-e-poks'-ide*). A drug that depresses the central nervous system and so relieves anxiety and tension. Librium is a proprietary preparation.

chlorhexidine (*klor-heks'-e-din*). An antiseptic derived from coal tar that has a wide anti-bacterial action and is used as a skin antiseptic and as a disinfectant solution for instruments. Hibitane is a proprietary preparation of it.

chloride of lime (*klor'-ide*). A powerful disinfectant and bleaching agent, composed of lime and chlorine.

chlorine (*klor'-in*). A yellow, irritating poisonous gas. A well-known poison gas. The chief element in Dakin's solution and eusol (*q.v.*).

chloro-acetone (*klor'-o as'-e-tone*). Tear gas.

chlorocresol (*klor-o-kre'-sol*). A coal tar product with a bacteriocidal action more powerful than phenol and a lower toxicity. Used as an antiseptic and as a preservative in injection fluids.

chlorodyne (*klor'-o-deen*). A carminative mixture used for treating diarrhoea containing chloroform and morphine.

chloroform (*klor'-o-form*). A colourless volatile liquid, administered through inhalation as a general anaesthetic. *C. liniment*. Equal parts of chloroform and camphor liniment. *C. water*. Used in pharmacy to disguise the taste of nauseous drugs.

chloroma (*klor-o'-mah*). A sarcoma having a greenish colour, usually found in skull bones. It is accompanied by symptoms resembling leukaemia.

chlorophyll (*klor'-o-fill*). The green pigment of plants, closely related to the pigment in haemoglobin. An ingredient in many deodorants.

chlorothiazide (*klor-o-thi'-a-zide*). An oral diuretic which is rapidly excreted. If used for long periods potassium chloride should be administered as there is a loss of chloride and potassium in the diuresis. This may be supplied as Chlorothiazide K. Saluric is a proprietary preparation of it.

chloroxylenol (*klor-ok-zi'-le-nol*). An antiseptic which is less irritating to the skin and mucous membranes than cresol and has a powerful disinfectant action. Roxenol is a proprietary preparation of it and Dettol is very similar.

chlorpheniramine maleate (*klor-fen-ir'-a-meen mal'-e-ate*). An antihistamine drug that has no sedative action but is useful in combating or preventing allergic reactions to blood transfusions and to other drugs. Piriton is a proprietary preparation of it.

chlorpromazine (*klor-pro'-maz-een*). A sedative anti-emetic drug, used in psychiatry. It is also hypotensive and enhances the effect of analgesics and anaesthetics. It may cause skin sensitization, jaundice and Parkinsonism. Largactil is a proprietary preparation of it.

chlorpropamide (*klor-pro'-pam-ide*). An hypoglycaemic agent used in the treatment of mild diabetes. Diabinese is a proprietary preparation.

chlortetracycline (*klor-tet-ra-si'-kleen*). A wide-range antibiotic effective in treating many pathogenic infections that do not respond to penicillin. Aureomycin.

chocolate cyst. *See under* Cyst.

cholaemia (*ko-le'-me-ah*). The presence of bile in the blood, causing jaundice.

cholagogue (*ko'-la-gog*). A drug which increases the flow of bile, e.g. magnesium sulphate.

cholangiogram (*ko-lan'-je-o-gram*). A radiological film of the hepatic, cystic and bile ducts after the insertion of a dye.

cholangitis (*ko-lan-ji'-tis*). Inflammation of the bile ducts.

cholecystangiogram (*ko-le-sis-tan'-je-o-gram*). A radiological film of the gall bladder, and the cystic and common bile ducts.

cholecystduodenostomy (*ko-le-sist-du-o-den-os'-to-me*). An anastomosis between the gall-bladder and the duodenum.

cholecystectomy (*ko-le-sis-tek'-to-me*). Excision of the gall-bladder.

cholecystenterostomy (*ko-le-sis-ten-ter-os'-to-me*). The formation of an artificial opening from the gall-bladder into the intestine. An operation performed in cases of obstruction of the bile duct, e.g. due to a growth of the head of the pancreas.

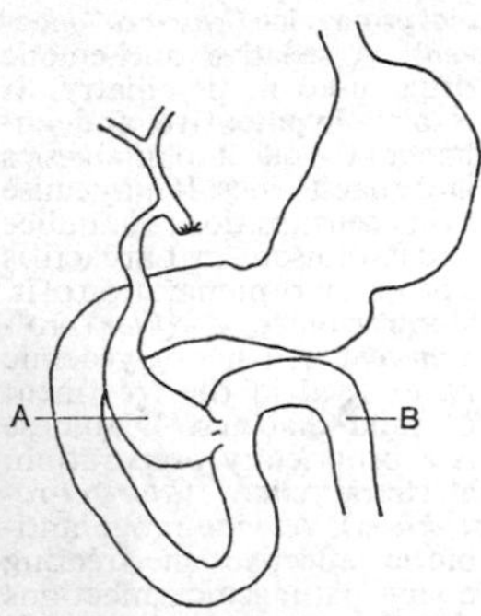

CHOLECYSTENTEROSTOMY
A. Gall bladder
B. Jejunum.

cholecystitis (*ko-le-sis-ti'-tis*). Inflammation of the gall-bladder.

cholecystogastrostomy (*ko-le-sis-to-gas-tros'-to-me*). An operation by which the gall-bladder is made to open into the stomach.

cholecystography (*ko-le-sis-tog'-raf-e*). X-ray photography of the gall-bladder after it has been made opaque by administration of a radio-opaque dye.

cholecystokinin (*ko-le-sis-to-kin'-in*). A hormone released by the presence of fat in the duodenum which causes contraction of the gall-bladder.

cholecystolithiasis (*ko-le-sis-to-lith-i'-as-is*). Stones in the gall-bladder.

cholecystotomy (*ko-le-sis-tot'-o-me*). An incision into the gall-bladder.

choledocholithotomy (*ko-le-dok-o-lith-ot'-o-me*). Incision into the bile ducts to remove stones.

choledochostomy (*ko-le-dok-os'-to-me*). Opening and draining the common bile duct.

cholelithiasis (*ko-le-lith-i'-as-is*). Presence of gall-stones in gall-bladder or bile ducts.

cholera (*kol'-er-ah*). An acute infectious disease caused by the *Spirillum cholerae asiaticae* from infected water. It is marked by profuse diarrhoea, muscle cramp, suppression of urine and severe prostration.

cholestasis (*ko-le-sta'-sis*). Arrest of the flow of bile.

cholesteatoma (*kol-es-te-at-o'-mah*). (1) A small tumour of dermal tissue which may occur in the middle ear. (2) A type of cerebral tumour.

cholesterol (*ko-les'-ter-ol*). A

sterol found in nervous tissue, red blood corpuscles, animal fat and bile. Excess in the bile can lead to gall-stone formation.

cholesterolosis (*ko-les-ter-ol-o'-sis*). A condition of the gall-bladder when the mucosa is studded with deposits of cholesterol.

choline (*ko'-leen*). A vitamin of the B group that exists in the colon and in many plants. It aids fat metabolism and deficiency leads to fatty degeneration and cirrhosis of the liver.

cholinergic (*ko-lin-er'-jik*). Applied to nerves that release acetylcholine at their nerve endings as the chemical stimulator. *C. drugs* inhibit cholinesterase and so prevent the destruction of acetylcholine.

choline theophyllinate (*ko'-leen the-of'-il-in-ate*). An antispasmodic drug used in respiratory conditions. Choledyl is the proprietary preparation.

cholinesterase (*ko-lin-est'-er-ase*). An enzyme which rapidly destroys the chemical transmitter acetylcholine (*q.v.*).

choluria (*ko-lu'-re-ah*). The presence of bile in the urine.

chondritis (*kon-dri'-tis*). Inflammation of cartilage.

chondroblast (*kon'-dro-blast*). An embryonic cell which forms cartilage.

chondrocyte (*kon'-dro-site*). A cartilage cell.

chondroma (*kon-dro'-mah*). An innocent new growth arising in cartilage.

chondromalacia (*kon'-dro-mal-a'-she-ah*). A condition of abnormal softening of cartilage.

chondrosarcoma (*kon'-dro-sar-ko'-mah*). A malignant new growth arising from cartilaginous tissue.

chordee (*kor-de'*). Painful erection of the penis, usually due to gonorrhoeal inflammation.

chorditis (*kor-di'-tis*). Inflammation of a vocal cord.

chordotomy (*kor-dot'-o-me*). An operation on the spinal cord to divide the antero-lateral nerve pathways for relief of intractable pain. Also cordotomy.

chorea (*ko-re'-ah*). St Vitus's dance. A nervous disease of rheumatic origin characterized by irregular and involuntary contraction of muscles. *Huntington's C.* The adult form, with cerebral degenerative changes, leading to dementia. A familial disease.

choreic (*ko'-re-ik*). Involuntary movements of an irregular jerky nature.

choreo-athetotic (*ko'-re-o-ath-e-tot'-ik*). A combination of the jerky movements with the writhing action of athetosis. Seen in some cerebral lesions, most often in children.

chorion (*kor'-e-on*). The outer membrane enveloping the fetus. The placenta (*q.v.*).

choriocarcinoma (*kor-e-o-kar-sin-o'-mah*). A malignant growth originating from chorionic tissue. *See* Chorion epithelioma.

chorion epithelioma (*kor'-e-on ep-e-the-le-o'-mah*). A malignant growth of the uterus which may develop after an abortion or evacuation of a hydatidiform mole, when the uterus was not completely emptied. Metastases usually develop rapidly.

chorionic villi (*kor-e-on'-ik vil'-li*). Structures of the chorion which give it a shaggy appearance, and from which

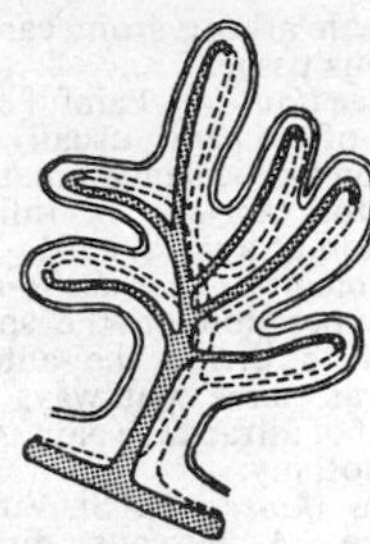

CHORIONIC VILLI

the placenta is formed. They are in close association with the maternal blood, and by diffusion interchange of nutriment, oxygen, and waste matters is effected between it and the fetal blood.

chorioretinitis (*kor'-e-o-ret-in-i'-tis*). Inflammation affecting both the choroid coat and the retina of the eye.

choroid (*kor'-oid*). The pigmented and vascular coat of the eyeball, continuous with the iris and situated between the sclera and retina.

choroiditis (*kor-oid-i'-tis*). Inflammation of the choroid.

choroidocyclitis (*kor-oid-o-sik-li'-tis*). Inflammation of the choroid and ciliary body.

choroidoretinitis (*kor-oid-o-ret-in-i'-tis*). An inflammatory condition of both the choroid and retina of the eye. May be termed chorioretinitis.

Christmas disease (*crist'-mas*). A form of haemophilia in which the blood is defective in clotting Factor IX.

chromatogram (*kro'-ma-to-gram*). The tracing produced by chromatography.

chromatography (*kro-ma-tog'-raf-e*). A method of chemical analysis by which substances in solution can be separated as they percolate down a column of powdered absorbent or ascend an absorbent paper by capillary traction. A definite pattern is produced and substances may be recognized by the use of appropriate colour reagents. Amino acids can be separated in this way and the anti-anaemic factor isolated from liver extract.

chromatosis (*kro-ma-to'-sis*). A condition of abnormal pigmentation of the skin. *See* Addison's disease.

chromic acid (*kro'-mik as'-id*). A strong caustic sometimes used for removal of warts.

chromicize (*kro'-mis-ize*). To impregnate with chromic acid, e.g. chromicized catgut.

chromophil adenoma (*kro'-mo-fil ad-en-o'-mah*). The tumour of the pituitary gland that gives rise to gigantism and acromegaly.

chromophobe adenoma (*kro'-mo-fobe*). The commonest of the pituitary tumours giving rise to hypopituitarism.

chromosomes (*kro'-mo-somes*). The filaments into which the nucleus of a cell divides during mitosis (*q.v.*). Each chromosome consists of hundreds of molecules of nucleoprotein called genes (*q.v.*).

chronic (*kron'-ik*). Of long duration, the opposite to acute.

chrysarobin (*kris-ar-o'-bin*). A derivative of Goa powder, used in ointment form, especially in the treatment of psoriasis. As it is irritant to the eyes, it must be used with care and not applied to the face. It stains linen a yellow colour, therefore special sheets should be kept for these cases. Benzole will remove the stains. *See* Dithranol.

chyle (*kile*). Digested fats which, as a milky fluid, are absorbed into the lymphatic capillaries (*lacteals*) in the villi of the small intestine.

chyluria (*ki-lu'-re-ah*). The presence of chyle in the urine. Possibly due to a lymphatic vessel communicating with the urinary tract, as may occur in filariasis.

chyme (*kime*). The semi-liquid, acid mass of food which passes from the stomach to the intestines.

chymotrypsin (*ki-mo-trip'-sin*). An enzyme from the pancreatic-secretion. It is activated by trypsin and aids in the breakdown of proteins.

cicatrix (*sik'-a-triks*). The scar of a healed wound.

cilia (*sil'-e-ah*). (1) Eyelashes. (2) Slender microscopic filaments projecting from some epithelial cells, e.g. in the bronchi, which wave the secretion upwards.

ciliary (*sil'-e-ar-e*). Hair-like. *C. body*. Structure just behind the corneo-scleral margin composed of the ciliary muscle and processes. *C. muscle*. The circular muscle surrounding the lens of the eye. *C. processes*. The fringed part of the choroid coat arranged in a circle in front of the lens.

Cimex (*si'-meks*). A genus of blood-sucking bugs. *C. lectularius*. The common bed-bug.

cinchocaine (*sin'-ko-kane*). A local anaesthetic agent. It may be used in the form of a solution, eye drops, lozenges, or rectal suppositories.

cinchona (*sin-ko'-nah*). Peruvian bark, from which quinine is obtained.

cinchonism (*sin'-ko-nizm*). Poisonous effect of cinchona and its alkaloids, i.e. tinnitus, deafness, headache and giddiness, and weakness of heart muscle. Quininism.

cineangiocardiography (*sin-e-an-je-o-kar-de-og'-raf-e*). The photographic record of fluoroscopic images of the heart and blood vessels, by which the movements of the organs may be seen.

cinnamon (*sin'-nam-on*). An extract from the bark of an East Indian laurel, used in medicine as a digestive and carminative.

circinate (*sur'-sin-ate*). Having a circular outline. Ringworm of the body is *tinea circinata*.

circle of Willis. An anastomosis of arteries at the base of the brain, formed by the branches of the internal carotids and the branches of the basilar artery.

circulation. A circular course, as of the blood. *Collateral c.* Small vessels enlarge, establishing adequate blood supply when the main vessel to the part has been occluded. *Coronary c.* The system of vessels which supply the heart muscle itself. *Extracorporeal c.* The blood is removed by intravenous cannulae, passed through a machine to oxygenate it and then pumped back into circulation. Termed the 'heart lung' machine or pump respirator, it is used in cardiac surgery. *Lymph c.* The flow of lymph through lymph vessels and glands. *Portal c.* collects the blood from the alimentary tract, pancreas, and spleen, and carries it via the portal vein and its branches through the liver and into the hepatic veins. *Pulmonary c.* is that of the blood from the right ventricle via the pulmonary artery through the lungs and back to the heart by the pulmonary veins. *Systemic c.* That of the blood throughout the body. The direction of flow is from the left atrium to the left ventricle and through the aorta with its branches and capillaries. Veins then carry it back to the right atrium, and so into the right ventricle.

circumcision (*sur-kum-siz'-shun*). Excision of a circular portion of the prepuce. An operation usually performed on young boys to allow the prepuce to be drawn back over the glans penis to facilitate urination and cleansing of the penis.

circumduction (*sur-kum-duk'-shun*). Moving in a circle, e.g. the circular movement of the upper limb.

circumoral (*sur-kum-or'-al*). Around the mouth. *C. pallor.* A pale area round the mouth contrasting with the flushed cheeks in scarlet fever.

circumvallate (*sur-kum-val'-ate*). Surrounded by a wall. *C. papilla. See* Papilla.

cirrhosis (*sir-o'-sis*). A degenerative change which can occur in any organ, but especially in the liver, caused by various poisons bacterial or otherwise. Fibrosis results, and this interferes with the working of the organ. In the liver it causes portal obstruction, with consequent ascites. *Alcoholic c.* affects the liver and is a result of chronic alcoholism and nutritional deficiency.

cisterna (*sis-ter'-nah*). A space or cavity containing fluid. *C. chyli.* The dilated portion of the thoracic duct containing chyle. *C. magna.* The subarachnoid space between the cerebellum and medulla oblongata.

cisternal (*sis-ter'-nal*). Concerning the cisterna. *C. puncture.* Insertion of a hollow needle into the cisterna magna, to withdraw cerebrospinal fluid as an alternative to lumbar puncture.

citric acid (*sit'-rik as'-id*). The juice of lemons, limes, etc. An antiscorbutic.

clamp. A metal surgical instrument used to compress any part of the body, e.g. to prevent or arrest haemorrhage.

claudication (*klaw-dik-a'-shun*). Lameness. *Intermittent c.* Limping, accompanied by severe pain in the legs on walking, which disappears with rest. Associated with spasm of arteries.

claustrophobia (*klaw-stro-fo'-be-ah*). Fear of confined spaces like small rooms.

clavicle (*klav'-ikl*). The collar-bone.

clavus (*kla'-vus*). A corn. *C. hystericus.* A pain near the midline on top of the skull associated with hysteria.

cleft palate. A congenital defect in the roof of the mouth, due to failure of the medial plates of the palate to meet. Speech is indistinct, words being blurred. A plastic operation may be performed, or a plate fitted over the gap. Hare-lip is often present at the same time.

climacteric (*kli-mak'-ter-ik*). The period of the menopause in women. *C. psychoses.* Mental disorders occurring at this time.

clinical (*klin'-ik-al*). Relating to bedside observation and treatment of patients.

clinicopathological (*klin-e-ko-path-o-loj'-ik-al*). Relating to both the symptoms and pathology of disease.

clinicoradiological (*klin-e-ko-ra-de-o-loj'-ik-al*). Relating the bedside observations to the results of radiological investigations.

clitoridectomy (*kli-tor-id-ek'-to-me*). Excision of the clitoris.

clitoris (*klit'-or-is*). A small organ, formed of erectile tissue, in front of the urethra in the female. The homologue of the penis.

cloaca (*klo-a'-kah*). An opening to the exterior for the purpose of discharge of waste: (a) an anus; (b) opening through newly formed bone from a diseased area so that pus may escape. *See* Involucrum.

clofibrate (*klo-fib'-rate*). A drug used to lower the blood cholesterol. Atromid-S is a proprietary preparation.

clonic (*klon'-ik*). Having the character of clonus.

clonus (*klo'-nus*). Muscle rigidity and relaxation which occurs spasmodically. *Ankle c.* Spasmodic movements of the calf muscles when the foot is suddenly pushed upwards, the leg being extended. A reaction which may be an indication of spinal cord disease.

Clostridium (*klos-trid'-e-um*). A genus of anaerobic spore-forming bacilli, found as commensals of the gut of animals and man and as saprophytes of the soil. Pathogenic species include *Cl. tetani* (tetanus) *Cl. welchii* (gas gangrene) *Cl. botulinum* (botulism).

clotting or coagulation time. The length of time taken for shed blood to coagulate. The normal is 4 to 8 min.

clove hitch. A knot. A simple sling formed by making two similar loops with a length of bandage and placing the first behind the second.

Clover's crutch. An apparatus for supporting a patient in the lithotomy position. *See* Positions.

cloxacillin (*kloks'-a-sil-in*). A form of penicillin effective against penicillin-resistant staphylococci for the treatment of which it should be reserved. Orbenin is a trade name.

clubfoot. Talipes (*q.v.*).

clubbed fingers. Broadening and thickening of the tips of the fingers (and toes), due to bad circulation. It occurs in chronic diseases of the heart and respiratory system, e.g. congenital cardiac defect, tuberculosis, etc.

clumping. Describes the action of bacteria and blood cells when agglutination (*q.v.*) occurs.

Clutton's joint (*klut'-ton*). A painless synovial swelling of joints, which may occur in congenital syphilis.

coagulase (*ko-ag'-u-laze*). An enzyme formed by pathogenic staphylococci that causes coagulation of plasma. Such bacteria are termed *C. positive*.

coagulum (*ko-ag'-u-lum*). The mass of fibrin and cells when blood clots or the mass formed when other substances coagulate, e.g. milk curd.

coalesce (*ko-al-ess'*). To come

together or to converge.

coal tar. A viscid fluid obtained from coal and petroleum, from which many germicides are derived, e.g. benzole, phenol, aniline dyes, etc.

coarctation (*ko-ark-ta'-shun*). A condition of contraction or stricture. *C. of aorta.* Usually a congenital defect which

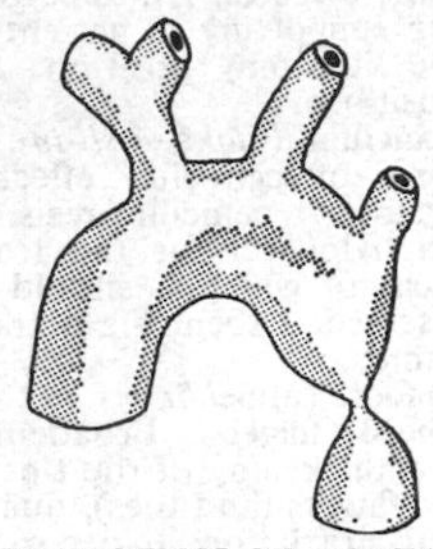

COARCTION OF AORTA

may be incompatible with life, but in many cases a compensating collateral circulation is established. Surgical resection of the stricture may be performed.

cobalt (*ko-balt*). A hard metal. *Radioactive c.* Cobalt 60 used as a source of gamma irradiation in radiotherapy.

cocaine (*ko-kane'*). A colourless alkaloid obtained from coca leaves, used as a local anaesthetic applied to mucous membranes for nose and throat treatments. For local anaesthesia it is increasingly being replaced by less toxic synthetic preparations like procaine, lignocaine and amethocaine. Cocaine is a drug of addiction.

cocainism (*ko-kane'-izm*). The condition following continued use of cocaine, when the initial stimulation and feeling of well-being is followed by mental and physical deterioration. Danger of cardiac failure.

coccus (*kok'-µs*). A micro-organism of spheroidal shape.

coccydynia (*kok-se-din'-e-ah*). Persistent pain in the region of the coccyx usually following trauma.

coccygodynia (*koks-e-go-din'-e-ah*). Coccydynia (*q.v.*).

coccyx (*kok'-siks*). The terminal bone of the spinal column, in which four rudimentary vertebrae are fused together.

cochlea (*kok'-le-ah*). The spiral canal of the internal ear.

codeine (*ko'-deen*). An alkaloid of opium said to be less depressant to the respiratory centre than other forms, and particularly favoured for persistent cough in bronchitis, etc. An analgesic and hypnotic.

cod-liver oil. Purified oil from the liver of the cod-fish particularly valuable for its vitamin A and D content.

coeliac disease (*se'-le-ak*). A condition of early childhood, characterized by steatorrhoea (*q.v.*), distended abdomen and failure to grow. The failure of carbohydrate and fat metabolism appears to be due to the gluten in wheat flour. It is treated by giving a gluten-free diet. *See* Appendix 10.

co-enzyme (*ko-en-zime'*). Small non-protein molecules that are accessory to the larger protein enzyme and necessary for its function.

cognition (*kog'-nish-un*). Action of knowing. Cognitive function of the conscious mind in contrast to the affective (feeling) and conative (willing).

coitus (*ko'-it-us*). Sexual intercourse. Copulation.

colchicum (*kol'-chik-um*). A drug obtained from the seeds of *Colchicum autumnale*. Used in treating gout.

colectomy (*ko-lek'-to-me*). The excision of a portion or all of the colon.

colic (*kol'-ik*). Severe pain due to spasmodic contraction of the involuntary muscle of tubes. *Biliary c.* Due to presence of a gall-stone in a bile duct. *Intestinal c.* Severe griping abdominal pain which may be a symptom of food poisoning or of intestinal obstruction. *Painter's c.* A sign of chronic lead poisoning to which painters are especially prone. *Renal c.* Due to presence of a stone in the ureter. *Uterine c.* Dysmenorrhoea (*q.v.*).

coliform (*ko'-li-form*). Resembling the bacillus *Escherichia coli*.

colitis (*ko-li'-tis*). A condition of inflammation of the colon. It may be due to a specific organism, as in dysentery, but the term *ulcerative c.* denotes a chronic disease often of unknown cause in which there are attacks of diarrhoea with the passage of blood and mucus.

collagen (*kol'-a-gen*). A protein constituent of fibrous tissue. *C. diseases*. Those in which there is a typical fibrinoid degeneration of collagen, e.g. rheumatic fever, rheumatoid arthritis and scleroderma (*q.v.*).

collapse (*kol-laps'*). (1) A state of extreme prostration due to defective action of the heart, severe shock, or haemorrhage. (2) Falling in of a structure. *C. of lung*. A condition due to alteration of air pressure between the inside of the lung and the pleural cavity. *See* Pneumothorax. *Lobar c.* One or more lobes of the lung collapse due to blockage of a bronchus.

collateral (*kol-lat'-er-al*). Accessory to. *C. circulation* is an alternative to the direct route.

Colles's fracture (*kol'-lees*).

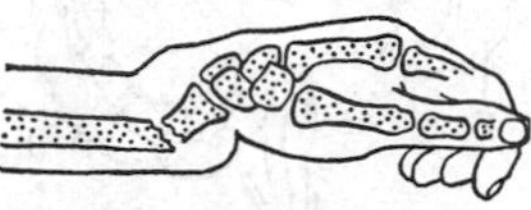

DEFORMITY IN COLLES'S FRACTURE

Of the radius at the wrist. It is usually impacted and the styloid process of the ulna may be torn off. Typically, it produces the 'dinner fork' deformity.

collodion (*kol-lo'-de-on*). A solution of *pyroxylin* (guncotton) in alcohol and ether, which, when exposed to the air, becomes solid by evaporation of the solvents. It is used in surgery as a protective covering for small clean wounds. *C. flexile* contains oils which prevent it cracking.

colloid (*kol'-loid*). A gelatinous fluid made by substances suspended in a medium but not forming a sediment.

colloidal gold test (*kol-loid'-al*). *See under* Test.

coloboma (*kol-o-bo'-mah*). A congenital fissure of the eye affecting the choroid coat and the retina.

colon (*ko'-lon*). The large intestine from the caecum to the rectum. *Ascending c.* That part to the right of the abdomen to the liver. *Descending c.* From the spleen to the

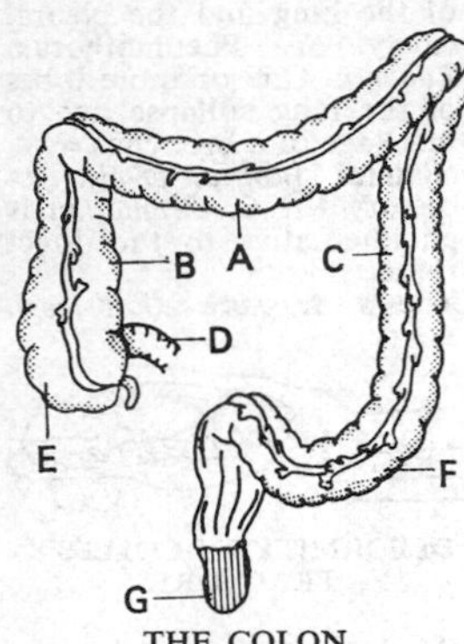

THE COLON

A. Transverse colon.
B. Ascending colon.
C. Descending colon.
D. Ileum.
E. Caecum.
F. Pelvic colon.
G. Anus.

rectum. *Giant c.* Megacolon (*q.v.*), *Irritable c.* A nervous type, associated with abdominal pain and distension. *Pelvic c.* That part in the pelvis. *Transverse c.* That across the upper abdomen connecting the ascending and descending portions.

colonic lavage (*ko-lon'-ik lav'-aj*). *See* Lavage.

colony (*kol'-on-e*). A mass of bacteria formed by multiplication of cells when bacteria are incubated under favourable conditions.

colostomy (*ko-los'-to-me*). The surgical formation of a permanent opening into the colon. This acts as an abdominal artificial anus.

colostrum (*kol-os'-trum*). The first fluid from the mother's breasts after childbirth. It contains more protein but less fat and sugar than true milk.

colour blindness. Achromatopsia (*q.v.*).

colour index. Estimated in examination of the blood by finding the ratio between the percentage of haemoglobin present to the number of red blood cells. Normal is taken to = 1. *See* Blood.

colpitis (*kol-pi'-tis*). Inflammation of the vagina.

colpocele (*kol'-po-seel*). A hernia into the vagina.

colpocleisis (*kol-po-kli'-sis*). Closure of the vagina by surgical means.

colpohysterectomy (*kol-po-his-ter-ek'-to-me*). Removal of the uterus through the vagina, usually for prolapse of uterus.

colpoperineorrhaphy (*kol-po-per-in-e-or'-af-e*). The repair by suturing, of an injured vagina and torn perineum.

colporrhaphy (*kol-por'-af-e*). Repair of the vagina. *Anterior c.* for cystocele (*q.v.*). *Posterior c.* for rectocele (*q.v.*).

colpos (*kol'-pos*). The vaginal canal leading from the vulva to the cervix.

colposcope (*kol'-po-skope*). A binocular instrument with magnification, used to study the vagina and cervix uteri. Benign and malignant changes may be seen and selective biopsy taken, so aiding early diagnosis of malignant disease.

colpotomy (*kol-pot'-o-me*). Incision of the vaginal wall. *Posterior c.* To drain a pelvic or parametric abscess.

coma (*ko'-mah*). Complete unconsciousness, in which all reflexes are absent. *Diabetic c.* Due to ketosis which occurs in diabetes mellitus. Treated by immediate administration of insulin and intravenous saline. *Hypoglycaemic c.* (*insulin c.*) results from too much insulin or too little food taken. Treated by giving sugar. *Uraemic c. See* Uraemia.

comatose (*ko'-ma-toze*). The condition of coma.

comedone (*kom'-e-done*). A blackhead. Formed of epithelial cells enclosing dried sebum blocking the entrance to the sebaceous gland. Caused by hyperkeratosis of the neck of the follicle and blackened by melanin. Common during adolescence.

commensal (*kom-en'-sal*). An organism which normally lives in or on a part of the body without detriment to it. Some are potentially pathogenic.

communicable disease (*kom-mu'-nik-abl*). One that can be transmitted from one person to another.

comminuted fracture (*kom'-in-u-ted*). *See under* Fracture.

commutator (*kom'-mu-ta-tor*). A device by which the direction of an electrical current can be interrupted or reversed.

compact tissue. *See* Bone.

compatibility (*kom-pat-ib-il'-it-e*). Mixing together of two substances without chemical change, or loss of power. *See* Blood grouping.

compensation (*kom-pen-sa'-shun*). (1) To make good a functional or structural defect. (2) Mental mechanism (unconscious) by which a person covers up a weakness by exaggerating a lesser or more desirable characteristic. *Cardiac c. See under* Cardiac.

Complan (*kom'-plan*). A proprietary hydrolysed preparation containing protein, carbohydrate and fat and all the necessary mineral salts and vitamins for maintaining health, useful for tube feeds and to supplement the diet, particularly where a high protein diet is required.

complement (*kom'-ple-ment*). In bacteriology, a substance present in blood which aids the destruction of bacteria invading the body.

complemental air (*kom-ple-men'-tal*). *See under* Air.

complex (*kom'-pleks*). A grouping of ideas of emotional origin which are completely or partially repressed in the unconscious mind. A possible cause of mental illness. *Inferiority c.* A compensation by assertiveness or aggression to cover a feeling of inadequacy. *See* Electra *and* Oedipus.

complication (*kom-ple-ka'-shun*). Another disease process arising during the course of or following the primary condition. Many diseases have their particular hazards and close observation should be kept for early signs.

complicated fracture. *See under* Fracture.

compos mentis (*kom'-pos men'-tis*). Of sound mind.

comprehension (*kom-pre-hen'-shun*). Mental grasp of the meaning of a situation.

compound fracture. *See under* Fracture.

compress (*kom'-press*). Folded material, e.g. lint, wet or dry, applied to a part of the body. (1) For the relief of swelling and pain. (2) To produce localized pressure. *Lead lotion c.* Applied to bruised areas, or to relieve pain in a strained muscle.

compression (*kom-presh'-un*). Pressing together. *C. bandage.* One in which there are alternate layers of wool and bandage to exert a firm pressure without constriction of the blood supply. *C. of brain.* May be due to pressure of tumour, blood clot, etc.

compulsion (*kom-pul'-shun*). An urge to perform some action that the patient recognizes to be irrational but resistance leads to mounting anxiety which is only relieved by the performance of the act. The term may also be applied to compulsive words, thoughts, and fears.

conation (*ko-na'-shun*). A striving in a certain direction.

concept (*kon'-sept*). A group of abstract ideas.

conception (*kon-sep'-shun*). The act of becoming pregnant by the fertilization of an ovum.

concha (*kon'-shah*). A shell. Applied in anatomy to shell-like structures; e.g. *c. auriculae*, the hollow part of the external ear.

concordance (*kon-cord'-ance*). Running a parallel course. In medicine may be applied to both twins developing the same disease, e.g. diabetes.

concretion (*kon-kre'-shun*). A calculus or other hardened material. *Faecal c.* One of faecal material, a faecalith (*q.v.*).

concussion (*kon-kush'-un*). A violent jarring shock. *C. of the brain* is produced by a fall or blow on the head, and is characterized by unconsciousness, prostration, pallor, feeble pulse, and shallow breathing. Return of consciousness is often heralded by sudden drawing up of the knees and by vomiting. Rest, quietness, and protection of the eyes from light, aid recovery.

condenser (*kon-den'-ser*). (1) An apparatus for collecting charges of electricity in which two conducting surfaces are separated by some insulating material, such as glass. (2) An arrangement for condensing light on to a microscope slide.

conditioning (*kon-dish'-un-ing*). The process by which a response is obtained to a stimulus by repetition of a situation until it becomes automatic.

condom (*kon'-dom*). A contraceptive sheath to be worn by the male.

conductor (*kon-duk'-tor*). (1) The portion of an electric battery which transmits the current. (2) Any part of the nervous system which conveys impulses. (3) A means of transmitting heat: *good c.*—copper, silver, cotton materials; *bad c.*—a vacuum, air, wool, etc.

condyle (*kon'-dile*). A rounded eminence occurring at the end of some bones.

condyloma (*kon-dil-o'-mah*). A wart-like growth of syphilitic origin occurring during the secondary stage, at the junction of skin and mucous membrane, e.g. the anal or vulval margins. It is covered with a moist epithelium and the discharge teems with spirochaetes, so is highly infectious.

cones (*kones*). Receptor end organs in the retina of the eye, used for the most acute and colour vision.

confabulation (*kon-fab-u-la'-shun*). The production of fictitious memories, and the relating of experiences which have no relation to truth to fill in the gaps due to loss of memory. A symptom of Korsakoff's syndrome.

confection (*kon-fek'-shun*). A preparation of sugar or honey containing drugs, e.g. senna.

conflict (*kon'-flict*). When two opposing wishes or impulses cause emotional tension and often cannot be resolved without repressing one of the impulses into the unconscious. Conflict situations may be associated with an anxiety neurosis (*q.v.*).

confluent (*kon'-flu-ent*). Running together. *C. smallpox.* A variety in which the pustules coalesce.

confusion (*kon-fu'-zhun*). A clouding of consciousness so that the capacity to think is impaired, perception is dulled and response to stimuli is less acute.

congenital (*kon-jen'-it-al*). Applied to conditions existing at or before birth. *C. dislocation of hip.* Failure in position of the head of the femur and development of the acetabulum. *C. heart disease.* Abnormalities in development or failure to adjust to extra-uterine life. *See* Fallot.

congestion (*kon-jest'-shun*). Hyperaemia (*q.v.*). *C. of lungs* Pneumonia.

conization (*ko-ni-za'-shun*). A method of treating erosion of the cervix by removing a cone-shaped piece of tissue by diathermy.

conjugate (*kon'-ju-gate*). (1) United in pairs or couples. (2) The distance between two parts. *True c.* The distance between the symphysis pubis and the sacral prominence. (3) To inactivate by a change in solubility.

conjunctiva (*kon-junk-ti'-vah*). The mucous membrane covering the eyeball and lining the eyelids.

conjunctivitis (*kon-junk-tiv-i'-tis*). Inflammation of the conjunctiva. Ophthalmia (*q.v.*). *Catarrhal c.* A mild form, usually due to cold or irritation. *Granular c.* Trachoma (*q.v.*). *Phlyctenular c.* Marked by small vesicles or ulcers on the membrane. *Purulent c.* There is discharge of pus.

connective (*kon-ek'-tiv*). Joining together. *C. tissues.* Those that develop from the mesenchyme and are formed of a matrix containing fibres and cells. Areolar tissue, cartilage, and bone are examples.

consanguinity (*kon-san-gwin'-it-e*). Blood relationship.

conservative treatment. *See under* Treatment.

consolidation (*kon-sol-e-da'-shun*). A state of becoming solid. *C. of lung.* In pneumococcal pneumonia the infected lobe becomes solid and congested with blood—known as red hepatization (*q.v.*).

constipation (*kon-stip-a'-shun*). Incomplete or infrequent action of the bowels. *Atonic c.* Due to lack of muscle tone in the bowel wall. *Spastic c.* When spasm of part of the bowel wall narrows the canal.

consumption (*kon-sump'-shun*).

The popular name for phthisis (*q.v.*) or advanced pulmonary tuberculosis.

contact (*kon'-tact*). A person who has been exposed to a contagious disease. *C. lens.* A glass or plastic lens worn under the eyelids close to the cornea. It may be worn for therapeutic or cosmetic reasons.

contagion (*kon-ta'-jun*). Communication of disease from one person to another by direct contact.

contraceptive (*kon-trah-sep'-tiv*). An agent used to prevent conception, e.g. male sheath, cap that occludes the cervix, spermaticidal pessary or cream, intra-uterine device, i.e. IUD (*q.v.*) and the oral pill (steroid hormones).

contracted pelvis. *See under* Pelvis.

contraction (*kon-trak'-shun*). A shortening or drawing together. Applied to muscle action and the healing process in scar tissue.

contracture (*kon-trak'-chur*). Fibrosis causing deformity, *Dupuytren's c.* One of the palmar fascia. *Volkmann's ischaemic c.* One of the hand and forearm due to lack of blood to the muscles.

contrecoup (*kon'-tre-coo*). An injury occurring on the opposite side or at a distance from the site of the blow, e.g. fracture or haemorrhage on the opposite side of the skull.

contusion (*kon-tu'-zhun*). A bruise.

convection (*kon-vek'-shun*). A method of transmission of heat by the circulation of warmed molecules of a liquid or a gas.

conversion (*kon-ver'-shun*). In psychology, the mechanism whereby repressed mental conflicts manifest themselves by physical symptoms.

convolutions (*kon-vo-lu'-shuns*). Folds or coils, e.g. of the cerebrum, or renal tubules.

convulsions (*kon-vul'-shuns*). Spasmodic contractions of muscles. They may herald the onset of an infectious disease but may be a symptom of a more serious underlying cause and all cases should be fully investigated. *See* Fits *and* Epilepsy. *Localized c.* Tetany (*q.v.*) is an example of this type.

Cooley's anaemia (*koo'-leez*). A rare progressive anaemia confined to children of the Mediterranean races.

Coomb's test (*kooms*). A quantitative test carried out on the mother's blood for the formation of antibodies to the Rhesus factor where there is likelihood of incompatibility.

copper (*kop'-per*). Cuprum. An irritant poison. *C. sulphate.* In solid form (*blue stone*) it is used as a caustic for granulating surfaces. It is also the reagent in tests for the presence of sugar in urine. *See* Appendix 11.

coprolalia (*kop-ro-la'-le-ah*). Uncontrolled obscene speech.

coprolith (*kop'-ro-lith*). A faecalith (*q.v.*).

coprostasis (*kop-ro-sta'-sis*). The accumulation of faecal matter in the intestines, causing obstruction.

copulation (*kop-u-la'-shun*). Coitus. Sexual intercourse.

coracoid (*kor'-ak-oid*). (1) Shaped like a raven's beak. (2) The coracoid process of the scapula.

cord. A rope, a long flexible body. *Spermatic c.* That

UMBILICAL CORD

which suspends the testicle in the scrotum, and contains the spermatic artery and vein, and vas deferens. *Spinal c.* The part of the central nervous system enclosed in the spinal column. *Umbilical c.* The connection between the fetus and its mother by which it receives nourishment. *Vocal cords.* Structures in the larynx which vibrate to produce the voice.

cordotomy (*kord-ot′-o-me*). *See* Chordotomy.

corium (*kor′-e-um*). The true skin. *See* Dermis.

corn. A local hardening and thickening of the skin, from pressure or friction, occurring usually on the toes.

cornea (*kor′-ne-ah*). The transparent portion of the anterior surface of the eyeball, continuous with the sclerotic coat.

corneal graft. A means of restoring sight by grafting healthy transparent cornea in place of tissue opaque from scarring, following corneal ulceration.

corneoscleral (*kor-ne-o-scler′-al*). Relating to both the cornea and sclera. *C. junction.* Where these two join the limbus.

cornify (*kor-ne′-fi*). To harden. The laying down of keratin.

cornu (*kor′-nu*). Hornlike. *C. of uterus.* The area where the fallopian tubes join the uterus at the upper pole on either side.

corona (*ko-ro′-nah*). A crown. *C. dentis.* The crown of a tooth.

coronal suture (*kor′-o-nal suchur*). The junction of the frontal and parietal bones.

coronary (*kor′-on-ar-e*). Encircling. *C. arteries.* The vessels which supply the heart. *C. circulation. See* Circulation. *C. embolism.* Obstruction of a coronary artery—usually by a clot. *C. sinus. See* Sinus. *C. thrombosis. See* Thrombosis.

coronoid (*kor′-o-noid*). Shaped like a crow's beak. A bony process of the mandible and ulna.

cor pulmonale (*kor pul-mon-ah′-le*). Heart failure secondary to disease of the lungs or pulmonary circulation.

corpus (*kor′-pus*). Body. *C. callosum.* The mass of white matter which joins the two cerebral hemispheres together. *C. luteum.* The yellow body left on the surface of the ovary and formed of the remains of the Graafian follicle after the discharge of the ovum. If it retrogresses menstruation occurs, but it persists for several months if pregnancy supervenes. *C. striatum.* A mass of grey and white matter in the base of each cerebral hemisphere.

corpuscle (*kor-pus′-l*). A small protoplasmic body or cell, as of blood or connective tissue. *See* Blood cells.

correctives (*kor-rek'-tivs*). Drugs which modify the action of other drugs.

Corrigan's pulse (*kor'-ig-an*). Water-hammer pulse. *See* Pulse.

corrosive (*kor-o'-siv*). Destroying, eating into. *C. sublimate*. Perchloride of mercury. An antiseptic.

cortex (*kor'-teks*). The external layer of an organ, e.g. of the cerebrum.

corticosteroids (*kor-te-ko-ster'-oids*). Hormones produced by the adrenal cortex or their synthetic substitutes.

corticotrophin (*kor-te-ko-tro'-fin*). ACTH. Adrenocorticotrophic hormone, secreted by the anterior lobe of the pituitary body. Stimulates the adrenal cortex to produce cortisol. If lacking, it can be given by injection.

cortisol (*kor'-te-zol*). The naturally occurring hormone of the adrenal cortex. Hydrocortisone (*q.v.*).

cortisone (*kor'-te-zone*). A synthetic preparation of cortisol. It is of most value and least likely to cause side effects if given where there is lack of secretion, e.g. in Addison's disease and following adrenalectomy or hypophysectomy.

Corynebacterium (*kor-i'-ne-bak-ter'-e-um*). A genus of slender, rod-shaped, Gram-positive and non-motile bacteria.

coryza (*ko-ri'-zah*). Cold in the head, with headache, nasal catarrh, and purulent discharge.

costal (*kos'-tal*). Relating to the ribs. *C. cartilages*. Those which connect the ribs to the sternum directly or indirectly.

cotyledon (*kot-e-le'-don*). A cup-shaped depression. A term applied to the subdivisions of the placenta.

counter extension (*kown'-ter ex-ten'-shun*). (1) Holding back the upper fragment of a fractured bone while the lower is pulled into position. (2) Raising the foot of the bed in such a way, that the weight of the body counteracts the pull of the extension apparatus on the lower part of the limb. Used especially for fracture of the femur.

counter-irritants (*kown'-ter ir'-rit-ants*). Applications to the skin which relieve deep-seated pain, now applied in the form of heat.

Cowper's glands (*kow'-per*). Two small glands situated close to the bulb of the urethra in the male.

cowpox. An eruption occurring on the cow, considered to correspond to smallpox in man.

coxa (*koks'-ah*). The hip. *C. valga*. A deformity of the hip causing increased abduction of the femur, and marked external rotation. *C. vara*. The angle of the neck and shaft of the femur is less acute.

coxalgia (*koks-al'-je-ah*). Pain in the hip joint.

coxitis (*koks-i'-tis*). Inflammation of the hip joint.

Coxsackie viruses (*koks'-sac-e*). A group of enteroviruses that may give rise to a variety of illnesses including meningitis, pleurodynia, and the common cold.

crab louse. *Pediculus pubis*. *See* Louse.

cracked nipples. A split on the outer surface of the nipple. Organisms entering are a common cause of abscess of the breast.

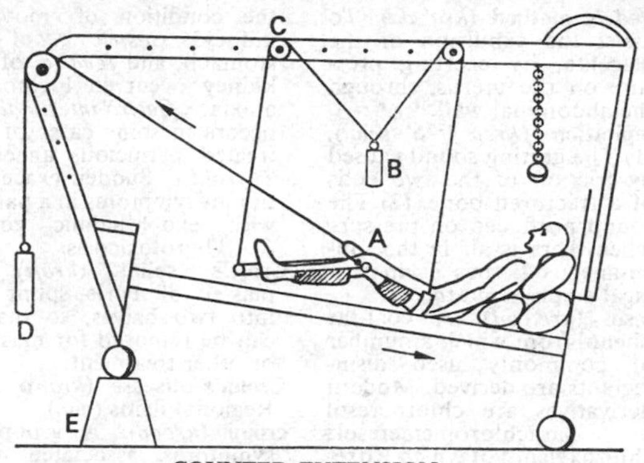

COUNTER EXTENSION

A. Thomas's splint with flexion iron.
B. Weight to aid knee movement.
C. Support for splint.
D. Weight pulling on the Steinmann's pin through the tibial tubercle.
E. Blocks.

cramp. Involuntary, slow, forcible, and painful contraction of a muscle. Associated with muscle fatigue, salt loss through dehydration; also to poisons of various kinds affecting either the muscles or the nerves which control them.

craniopharyngioma (*kra'-ne-o-far-in-je-o'-mah*). A cerebral tumour arising in the craniopharyngeal pouch just above the sella turcica.

craniostenosis (*kra-ne-o-sten-o'-sis*). Premature closure of the suture lines of the skull in an infant. If this leads to raised intracranial pressure surgery is indicated.

craniotabes (*kra-ne-o-ta'-beez*). A patchy thinning of the bones of the vault of the skull. Seen in rickets (*q.v.*).

craniotomy (*kra-ne-ot'-o-me*). A surgical opening of the skull made to relieve pressure, arrest haemorrhage, or remove a tumour.

cranium (*kra'-ne-um*). The bony cavity which contains the brain.

creatine (*kre'-at-in*). A nitrogenous compound found in muscle, and present in urine in conditions in which muscle is rapidly broken down, e.g. acute fevers, starvation, etc.

creatinine (*kre-at'-in-een*). A normal constituent of urine—a product of protein metabolism.

creatorrhoea (*kre-at-or-re'-ah*). The presence of muscle fibres in the faeces. It occurs if trypsin is absent from the intestine, or in acute diarrhoea.

Credé's method (*kra'-da*). To assist the expulsion of the placenta, by exerting pressure on the uterus, through the abdominal wall.

crepitation (*krep-it-a'-shun*). (1) The grating sound caused by friction of the two ends of a fractured bone. (2) The sound produced on pressure when there is air in the subcutaneous tissues as in surgical emphysema (*q.v.*).

cresol (*kre'-sol*). A coal-tar phenol from which a number of commonly used disinfectants are derived. Modern derivatives are chlorocresol or parachlorometacresol; chloroxylenol of which Roxenol and Dettol are proprietary preparations.

cretinism (*kret'-in-izm*). A congenital disease due to lack of thyroid secretion, characterized by thickness of neck, stunted growth, and imperfect mental development. Myxoedema (*q.v.*) is the acquired form.

cribriform (*krib'-rif-orm*). Perforated like a sieve. *C. plate.* Part of the ethmoid bone.

cricoid cartilage (*kri'-koid*). The ring-shaped cartilage at the lower end of the larynx.

crises (*kri'-seez*). Plural of crisis. Especially recurrent attacks of the varieties listed below.

crisis (*kri'-sis*). A decisive point in acute disease; the turning-point towards (a) recovery; (b) death. *Cf.* Lysis. Sudden, violent attacks of pain affecting certain of the viscera. *Dietl's c.* Attack of severe pain in the loins, with nausea and vomiting, and the passing of a small amount of blood-stained urine. Probably due to kinking of a ureter in the condition of 'movable kidney'. *Gastric c.* of the stomach, and *renal c.* of the kidney occur in locomotor ataxia. *Gastro-intestinal c.* occurs in some cases of untreated pernicious anaemia. *Thyroid c.* Sudden exacerbation of symptoms in a patient with exophthalmic goitre. *See* Thyrotoxicosis.

Croft's splint (*kroft*). A plaster of Paris splint cut into two halves, so that it can be removed for massage or other treatment.

Crohn's disease (*kron*). *Syn.* Regional ileitis (*q.v.*).

croup (*kroop*). A group of symptoms associated with inflammation or spasm of the larynx. There is spasmodic dyspnoea, a harsh cough, and stridor. *See* Laryngismus stridulus. *Membranous c.* Laryngeal diphtheria.

crucial (*kru'-shal*). Resembling a cross. *C. ligament. See under* Ligament.

crural (*kru'-ral*). Relating to the thigh.

'crush' syndrome. Occurs when large areas of muscle tissue are damaged by crushing accidents. There is severe shock with local necrosis and oedema and scanty output of urine leading to acute uraemia.

cryoextractor (*kri-o-eks-trak'-tor*). An instrument in which intense cold coagulates the lens to the needle for removal in cataract extraction.

crutch palsy. *See under* Palsy.

cryptogenic (*krip-to-jen'-ik*). Of unknown or obscure origin.

cryptomenorrhoea (*krip-to-men-o-re'-ah*). Menstruation is occurring but the loss fails to escape from the vagina due to an obstruction such as imperforate hymen or vaginal atresia. *Syn.* Haematocolpos.

cryptorchism (*kript-or'-kizm*). Failure of the testicles to descend into the scrotum.

crystalline lens (*kris'-tal-line lens*). The lens of the eye. *See* Lens.

cubitis (*ku'-bit-us*). The forearm.

cuirass respirator (*kui-rass'*). A mechanical device that fits round the chest to aid respiration.

culdocentesis (*kul-do-sen-te'-sis*). The aspiration of fluid from the pouch of Douglas via the posterior fornix of the vagina.

culdoscope (*kul'-do-skope*). An instrument consisting of a trocar, cannula and lighted telescope for viewing the pelvic cavity by passing it through the posterior vaginal wall.

culture. The development of micro-organisms on artificial media.

cumulative action (*ku'-mu-la-tiv*). The toxic effects produced by prolonged use of a drug, given in comparatively small doses.

cuneiform (*ku'-ne-form*). Three of the tarsal bones of the feet.

cuprum (*ku'-prum*). Copper (*q.v.*).

curare (*ku-rah'-re*). Arrow poison. An extract from a South American plant. Now used in surgery to produce complete muscle relaxation. It is given intravenously as Intocostrin or tubocurarine.

curettage (*ku-ret-ahj'*). Treatment by the use of a curette.

curette (*ku-ret'*). A spoon-shaped instrument used for the removal of unhealthy tissues by scraping. Curetting may be performed on membranous surfaces, e.g. of the uterus; on tuberculous and other chronic ulcers, or to remove dead bone.

Cushing's disease (*koosh'-ing*). A condition of oversecretion of the adrenal cortex due to an adenoma of the pituitary gland.

Cushing's syndrome. A group of symptoms including adiposity, abnormal distribution of hair, and atrophy of the genital organs due to a tumour of the adrenal cortex.

cusp. (1) The projections on the crown of a molar tooth. (2) One of the sections of the heart valves, formed of fibrous tissue and endocardium.

cutaneous (*ku-ta'-ne-us*). Pertaining to the skin. *C. ureterostomy.* The ureters are transplanted to open on to the skin of the abdominal wall.

cuticle (*ku'-tikl*). The epidermis or external layer of skin.

cutis (*ku'-tis*). The derma, or true skin.

cyanocobalamin (*si-an-o-ko-bal'-a-meen*). A preparation of vitamin B_{12} administered by injection in the treatment of pernicious anaemia. Cytamen is a proprietary preparation.

cyanosis (*si-an-o'-sis*). A bluish appearance of the skin and mucous membranes, caused by imperfect oxygenation of the blood. It indicates circulatory failure, and is also common in respiratory diseases. Constriction of veins from any cause will result in localized blueness.

cyclical syndrome (*si'-klik-al*). Applied to the emotional and physical changes occurring in women, not only in the premenstrual period but also before puberty and after the menopause. During the menstrual cycle referred to as premenstrual syndrome or tension.

cyclical vomiting (*si'-klik-al*). *See under* Vomiting.

cyclitis (*si-kli'-tis*). Inflammation of the ciliary body of the eye.

cyclizine (*si'-kli-zeen*). An antihistamine drug and mild sedative. Useful to prevent travel sickness. Marzine is a proprietary preparation.

cyclobarbitone (*si-klo-bar'-be-tone*). A short-acting barbiturate drug. Phanodorm is a proprietary preparation of it.

cyclodialysis (*si-klo-di-al'-is-is*). An operation to improve drainage from the anterior chamber of the eye at the corneoscleral junction.

cyclodiathermy (*si-klo-di-a-ther'-me*). A treatment for glaucoma without opening the eye. Diathermy is applied to the sclera to cause fibrosis around the ciliary body, so decreasing the amount of aqueous humour made.

cyclopenthiazide (*si-klo-pen-thi'-az-ide*). A thiazide diuretic. Navidrex is a proprietary preparation.

cyclopentolate (*si-klo-pent'-o-late*). Mydriatic eye drops that dilate the pupil. Cyclogyl is a proprietary preparation.

cyclophosphamide (*si-klo-foss'-fa-mide*). A cytotoxic drug that can be given by mouth or intravenously. Endoxana is a trade preparation.

cycloplegia (*si-klo-ple'-je-ah*). Paralysis of the ciliary muscle of the eye.

cyclopropane (*si-klo-pro'-pane*). A gas used for general anaesthesia. It is not irritating to the respiratory tract but must be used with a high oxygen concentration and is therefore potentially dangerous. Diathermy must not be used in the theatre at the same time.

cyclothymia (*si-klo-thi'-me-ah*). A term used to describe the mood swings in manic-depressive psychosis (*q.v.*).

cyclotomy (*si-klot'-o-me*). An operation to relieve glaucoma, by incision of the ciliary muscle.

cyclotron (*si'-klo-tron*). A machine, for imparting high velocities to atomic particles, by means of which radioactive isotopes can be prepared.

cyesis (*si-e'-sis*). Pregnancy. *Pseudo-c.* Signs and symptoms suggestive of pregnancy arising when no fertilization has taken place.

cyst (*sist*). A tumour with membranous capsule and containing fluid. *Branchial c.* One formed in the neck due to non-closure of the branchial cleft during development. *Chocolate c.* of the ovary. Endometrial cells are present so bleeding occurs during each menstrual period, causing enlargement and congestion. It is associated with endometriosis (*q.v.*). *Corpus luteal c.* One which develops from a corpus luteum. *Daughter c.* A small one which develops from a larger. *Dermoid c.* A congenital type containing skin, hair, teeth, etc. It is due to abnormal development of embryonic tissue. *Hydatid c.* Contains the larval form of the tapeworm. *Meibomian c.* A chalazion (*q.v.*). *Multilocular c.* of the ovary. Divided into compartments or locules. *Papilliferous c.* of ovary. It is lined with papillae which may grow through the cyst wall and on to the peritoneum and other organs, giving rise to ascites. *Pseudomucinous c.* of ovary, containing fluid similar to mucin. *Retention c.* One caused by blockage of a duct, e.g. ranula (*q.v.*). *Sebaceous c.* Due to blockage of a duct from a sebaceous gland so that the sebum collects. *Thyroglossal c.* One in the thyroglossal tract near the hyoid bone at the base of the tongue. *Unilocular c.* One containing only one cavity.

cystadenoma (*sist-ad-en-o'-mah*). An innocent new growth of glandular tissue, e.g. *c. of breast.*

cystalgia (*sist-al'-je-ah*). Pain in the bladder.

cystectomy (*sist-ek'-to-me*). Usually refers to complete or partial removal of the urinary bladder.

cystic disease of lung (*sist'-ik*). A congenital condition in which there is an abnormal amount of thick viscid secretion starting in the pancreas and later involving the lung with widespread bronchiectasis and emphysema.

cysticercus (*sist-e-ser'-kus*). The cystic or larval form of the tapeworm, causing hydatid cysts. *See* Echinococcus *and* Hydatid.

cystine (*sist'-in*). An amino-acid. Sometimes excreted in urine in the form of minute crystals.

cystitis (*sist-i'-tis*). Inflammation of the bladder.

cystitome (*sist'-e-tome*). A surgical knife used in cataract operations.

cysto- (*sist'-o*). A prefix relating to the bladder.

cystocele (*sist'-o-seel*). A hernia of the bladder, usually into the vagina, as the result of over-stretching of the wall during childbirth. *See* Colporraphy.

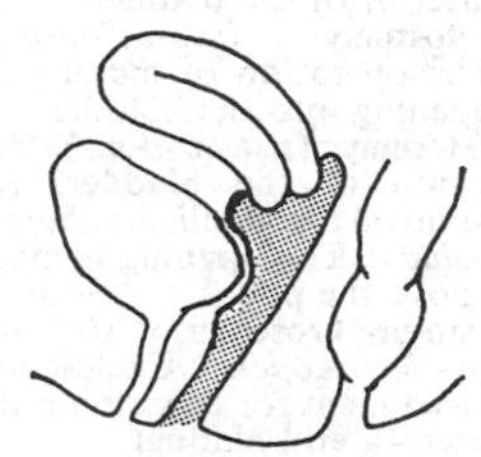

CYSTOCELE

cystodiathermy (*sist-o-di-a-ther'-me*). The application of a high-frequency electric current to the bladder mucosa usually for the removal of papilloma.

cystogram (*sist'-o-gram*). A radiological film demonstrating the urinary bladder. *Micturating c.* taken during the act of passing urine.

cystography (*sist-og'-raf-e*). The X-ray examination of the bladder by the aid of radio-opaque dye.

cystolithiasis (*sist-o-lith-i'-as-is*). Stone in the urinary bladder.

cystoma (*sist-o'-mah*). A term applied to a tumour containing cysts. Most usual in the ovary.

cystometry (*sist-om'-e-tre*). A method of ascertaining the tone of the urinary bladder wall.

cystonephrosis (*sist-o-nef-ro'-sis*). A cystic condition of the kidney.

cystopexy (*sist′-o-peks-e*). An operation for stress incontinence in which the bladder neck is slung to the fascia at the back of the symphysis pubis.

cystoscope (*sist′-o-skope*). An instrument for examining the interior of the bladder.

cystostomy (*sist-os′-to-me*). The operation of making an opening into the bladder.

cystotomy (*sist-ot′-o-me*). Incision of the bladder, for removal of calculi, etc. *Suprapubic c.* The opening is made above the pubes.

cysto-urethroscope (*sist′-o-u-re′-thro-skope*). A telescopic instrument for examining the urethra and bladder.

cytogenetics (*si-to-jen-et′-iks*). The study of cells during mitosis to examine the chromosomes and the relationship between chromosome abnormality and disease.

cytology (*si-tol′-o-je*). The microscopic study of the cells of the body. *Exfoliative c.* An aid to the early diagnosis of malignant disease. Secretions or surface cells are examined for pre-malignant changes. *See* Papanicolaou *under* Test.

cytolysis (*si-tol′-is-is*). The property of certain substances to dissolve cells. *See* Bacteriolysin *and* Haemolysin.

cytoplasm (*si′-to-plazm*). The protoplasmic part of the cell surrounding the nucleus.

cytotoxic (*si-to-toks′-ik*). Damaging to cell structure and division. *C. drugs.* Those that influence the course of malignant disease by their action on cells, the aim being the destruction of malignant cells without harming normal tissues.

cytotoxin (*si-to-toks′-in*). A toxin or antibody that prevents the normal function of a cell.

D

Dacron (*dak′-ron*). A synthetic fibre used widely in replacement surgery of the heart and blood vessels.

dacryo-adenectomy (*dak-re-o-ad-en-ek′-to-me*). Removal of the lacrimal gland.

dacryo-adenitis (*dak-re-o-ad-en-i′-tis*). Inflammation of a lacrimal gland.

dacryo-adenotomy (*dak-re-o-ad-en-ot′-o-me*). An incision into a lacrimal gland to drain pus.

dacryocystitis (*dak-re-o-sist-i′-tis*). Inflammation of a lacrimal sac.

dacryocystorhinostomy (*dak′-re-o-sist′-o-ri-nos′-to-me*). An operation to establish drainage from the lacrimal sac to the middle meatus of the nasal cavity.

dacryocystotomy (*dak-re-o-sist-ot′-o-me*). Incision of a lacrimal sac to remove pus from an abscess.

dacryolith (*dak′-re-o-lith*). Calculus in a lacrimal duct.

dactyl (*dak′-til*). A finger or toe. A digit.

dactylion (*dak-til′-e-on*). Webbed fingers. *See* Syndactylism.

dactylitis (*dak-til-i′-tis*). Inflammation of one or more fingers or toes. The bone and subcutaneous tissue is affected.

dactylology (*dak-til-ol′-o-je*). Deaf and dumb language. Talking by signs made with the fingers.

Dakin's solution (*da'-kin*). An antiseptic (*sodium hypochlorite*) which liberates chlorine gas in the presence of septic material.

Daltonism (*dal'-ton-ism*). Colour blindness.

dandruff (*dan'-druff*). White scales shed from the scalp. If moist from serous exudate they have a greasy appearance. Scurf.

Dangerous Drugs Act. *See* The Legal Control of Drugs. *See* Appendix 8.

dapsone (*dap'-zone*). A sulphone drug used in the treatment of leprosy.

daughter cyst. *See under* Cyst.

day dreams. Ideas drifting through the mind that do not lead to action.

DDT (dichlor-diphenyl-trichlorethane). Dicophane. A synthetic insecticide of great value.

deafness (*def'-ness*). The inability to hear. *Conduction* or *Middle ear d.* When there is obstruction to the sound waves reaching the cochlea. *Nerve d.* There is disease of the cochlea or auditory nerve.

deamination (*de-am-in-a'-shun*). A process of hydrolysis taking place in the liver by which amino acids are broken down and urea formed.

debility (*de-bil'-it-e*). A condition of feebleness, weakness, and lack of physical tone.

débridement (*da-breed-mon'*). The removal of foreign substances and injured tissues from a traumatic wound. Part of the immediate treatment to promote healing.

decalcification (*de-kal-sif-ik-a'-shun*). Removal of lime salts, e.g. from bone in some disorders of calcium metabolism.

decapitation (*de-kap-it-a'-shun*). Severing the head from the body.

decapsulation (*de-kaps-u-la'-shun*). Removal of a fibrous capsule. *Renal d.* Freeing and removing the capsule of the kidney.

decidua (*de-sid'-u-ah*). The thickened lining of the uterus for the reception of the fertilized ovum to protect the developing embryo. It is shed when pregnancy terminates. *D. basalis.* That part which becomes the maternal placenta. *D. capsularis.* That part which covers the embryo. *D. parietalis* lines the rest of the uterine cavity.

deciduoma malignum (*de-sid-u-o'-mah mal-ig'-num*). Chorion epithelioma (*q.v.*).

decannulation (*de-kan-u-la'-shun*). A term applied to the introduction of decreasingly smaller tubes to wean an infant from a tracheostomy and still ensure adequate lung ventilation.

decompensation (*de-kom-pen-sa'-shun*). Failure of the heart to overcome disability or increased work load.

decomposition (*de-komp-o-zish'-un*). (1) Resolving into original elements, as decomposition of water into hydrogen and oxygen by electrolysis. (2) Decay or putrefaction (*q.v.*).

decompression (*de-kom-presh'-un*). To remove internal pressure. *D. of brain.* A trephining operation to relieve pressure, e.g. of fluid on the brain. *D. chamber.* One to bring about a gradual lowering of atmospheric pressure to normal. *D. sickness.* A condition caused by too-rapid return from high to normal pressure environments, affecting caisson workers, deep sea divers, high altitude fliers, etc. Symptoms include severe abdominal and joint pain, cramps, vomiting and asphyxia. Treatment is to recompress the patient urgently, and return him slowly to normal environmental pressure.

decongestion (*de-kon-jest'-shun*). The overcoming of congestion, e.g. the use of ephedrine for inflammation and swelling of the nasal mucosa.

decortication (*de-kort-e-ka'-shun*). Removal of the cortex. (1) *D. of lung:* the removal of fibrosed pleura surrounding the lung, following chronic empyema, to allow expansion of the lung. (2) *Renal d.* Removal of the capsule of the kidney.

decubitus (*de-ku'-bit-us*). In a recumbent position. *D. ulcer.* A bedsore.

decussation (*de-kus-a'-shun*). A crossing. *Pyramidal d.* The crossing of the pyramidal nerve fibres in the medulla oblongata.

defaecation (*de-fe-ka'-shun*). Evacuation of the bowels.

defervescence (*de-fer-ves'-ense*). Falling of a raised temperature to normal.

defibrillation (*de-fib-ril-a'-shun*). The restoration of normal rhythm to the heart in ventricular fibrillation by means of a high voltage electric shock applied to the heart or the chest wall.

defibrillator (*de-fib-ril-a'-tor*). An instrument by which normal rhythm is restored in ventricular fibrillation.

defibrinate (*de-fib'-rin-ate*). The removal of fibrin from blood plasma. Used in the preparation of sera.

deficiency disease (*de-fish'-en-se dis-eez'*). *See under* Disease.

degeneration (*de-jen-er-a'-shun*). A structural change which lowers the vitality of the tissue in which it takes place. *Amyloid d.* A waxy starch-like substance occurring in tissues in chronic wasting diseases. *Calcareous d.* Tissues become impregnated with lime salts. *Fatty d.* Fat is deposited in tissues. *Fibroid d.* Fibrous tissue is laid down. *See* Fibrosis. *Red d. See* Necrobiosis. *Subacute combined d.* of the spinal cord is a complication of untreated pernicious anaemia due to vitamin B_{12} deficiency.

deglutition (*de-gloo-tish'-un*). The act of swallowing.

dehydration (*de-hi-dra'-shun*). Excessive loss of fluid from the body by persistent vomiting, diarrhoea or sweating or from the lack of intake. A cause of the loss of weight in diabetes mellitus owing to polyuria.

déjà vu. A disturbance of memory where a new experience or situation is experienced as if it has happened before.

deleterious (*del-e-te'-re-us*). Harmful; injurious.

delinquency (*de-lin'-kwen-se*). Usually applied to asocial and antisocial acts committed during youth, e.g. stealing and truancy.

delirium (*de-lir'-e-um*). Mental excitement. A common condition in high fever. It is marked by an irregular expenditure of nervous energy, incoherent talk, and delusions. *Chronic alcoholic d.* Korsakoff's syndrome (*q.v.*). *D. tremens.* Is a form common in alcoholics. *Traumatic d.* May occur following severe head injury. There is much confusion and disorientation.

delouse (*de-lows'-*). To free from lice.

deltoid (*del'-toid*). Triangular. *D. muscle.* The triangular muscle of the shoulder, arising from the clavicle and scapula, with insertion into the humerus. Frequently the site for intramuscular injections.

delusion (*de-lu'-zhun*). A false idea or belief held by the patient which cannot be corrected by reasoning. *D. of grandeur.* The patient has an erroneous belief in his own greatness, wealth or position.

demarcation (*de-mar-ka'-shun*). To define the bounds of. *Line of d.* The limit of a gangrenous area shown by a red or black line.

dementia (*de-men'-she-ah*). A condition of permanent mental deterioration as a result of organic cerebral disease. *Arteriosclerotic d.* Dementia occurring due to insufficient blood supply to the brain caused by arteriosclerosis. *D. praecox.* The old term for schizophrenia, implying the early onset of dementia. *Organic d.* Dementia occurring in the course of damage to the brain produced by infections, neoplasms or senile changes, etc. *Presenile d.* A group of conditions may produce dementia before the age of sixty. These show cerebral atrophy aad histological changes of a distinct nature. *Senile d.* Dementia occurring after the age of sixty-five due to cerebral atrophy of unknown cause.

demography (*de-mog'-raf-e*). The social study of persons viewed collectively in regard to race, occupation or conditions. Concerned with vital statistics.

demulcents (*de-mul'-sents*). Agents which soothe and allay irritation, especially of sensitive mucous membranes.

demyelinization (*de-mi-el-in-i-za'-shun*). Destruction of the medullary or myelin sheaths of nerve fibres as occurs in disseminated sclerosis (*q.v.*).

dendrite (*den'-drite*). One of the protoplasmic filaments of a nerve cell by which impulses are transmitted from one neurone to another. *Syn.,* dendron.

dendritic ulcer (*den-drit'-ik*). A corneal ulcer caused by the virus of herpes simplex during the course of a febrile illness. It has a branching appearance on straining.

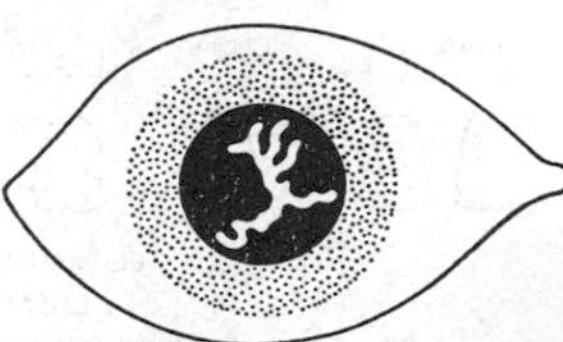

DENDRITIC ULCER

denervation (*de-nerv-a'-shun*). To sever or remove the nerve supply to a part.

dengue (*deng'-ga*). A mild infectious fever lasting about seven days, occurring in the tropics and conveyed by mosquitoes. The symptoms are headache, an eruptive rash and pains in the muscles and joints—especially the knee-joints—causing a peculiar or 'dandy' gait.

denitrify (*de-ni'-tre-fi*). To remove nitrogen.

Dennis Browne splints. Metal splints for the treatment of club foot in infancy, so designed that the more the baby kicks the more he corrects the deformity.

dentalgia (*den-tal'-je-ah*). Toothache.

dentine (*den'-teen*). The substance forming the bulk of a tooth beneath the enamel.

dentition (*den-tish'-un*). The process of teething. *Primary* molars or 'wisdom teeth'. There are thirty-two permanent teeth—eight incisors, four canines, eight premolars or bicuspids and twelve molars.

dentoid (*den'-toid*). Tooth-like.

deodorant (*de-o'-dor-ant*). A substance which destroys an odour.

deoxycorticosterone (*de-oks-e-kor-te-kos'-ter-one*). A naturally occuring adrenal steroid.

deoxycortone acetate (*de-oks-e-kor'-tone as'-e-tate*). A synthetic preparation of cortisol (*q.v.*), used mainly in the

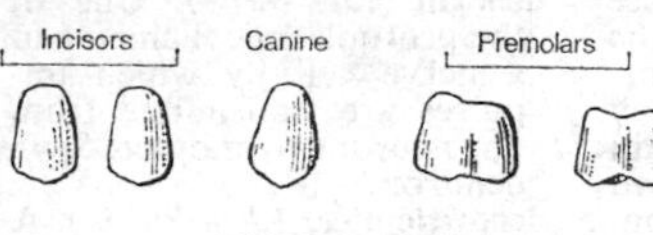

TEMPORARY TEETH

PERMANENT TEETH

DENTITION

The above teeth are present in each quarter of the jaw.

d. Cutting of the temporary or milk teeth, beginning at the age of 6 or 7 months and continuing until the end of the second year. A full set consists of eight incisors, four canines, and eight premolars; twenty in all. *Secondary d.*, or appearance of the permanent teeth, begins in the sixth or seventh year, and is complete by the twelfth to fifteenth year except for the posterior

treatment of Addison's disease. DOCA and Percorten are proprietary preparations of it.

deoxygenated (*de-oks'-e-jen-a-ted*). Deprived of oxygen. *D. blood.* That which has lost much of its oxygen in the tissues, and returns to the lungs for a fresh supply.

deoxyribonucleic acid (*de-oks'-e-ri-bo-nu'-kle-ik*). DNA. The nucleic acid molecule consists of long chains of atoms in a particular order. Variation in the structure may lead to congenital defects.

depersonalization (*de-per-son-al-iz-a'-shun*). A condition in which the patient feels his personality to have changed. It may occur in almost any mental illness.

depilatory (*de-pil'-at-or-e*). An agent which will destroy hair.

depolarization (*de-po-la-i-za'-shun*). The neutralization of an electrical charge at the neuro-muscular junction.

depression (*de-pres'-shun*). A lowering of psycho-physical activity. A mood change experienced as sadness, melancholy or suicidal thoughts. *Endogenous d.* occurs in the course of manic-depressive psychosis. The mood change is associated with slowing of thought and action and feelings of guilt. *Involutional d.* Occurs for the first time between 45 and 64 years of age. *Reactive d.* Depression occurring as a result of some event, such as illness, loss of money, bereavement.

depressant (*de-pres'-ant*). A drug which reduces functional activity of an organ.

Derbyshire neck (*dar'-be-sher*). Goitre (*q.v.*).

derealization (*de-re-al-iz-a'-shun*). A symptom in which the surroundings appear to have lost their reality.

dermatitis (*der-mat-i'-tis*). Inflammation of the skin. *Contact d.* That arising from touching a substance to which the person is sensitive. *Secondary exfoliative d.* May arise during treatment by drugs, e.g. arsenic, bismuth, gold and mercury. *Sensitization d.* May be due to contact or be endogenous from the ingestion of certain foods to which there is sensitivity. *Traumatic d.* Inflammation due to exposure to irritants or physical agents, e.g. the sun or X-rays. *Varicose d.* usually of the lower portion of the leg due to varicosities of the smaller veins.

dermatology (*der-mat-ol'-o-je*). The science of skin diseases.

dermatome (*der'-mat-ome*). An instrument for cutting thin slices of skin for skin grafting.

dermatosis (*der-mat-o'-sis*). Any skin disease.

dermis (*der'-mis*). The skin, especially the layer under the epidermis.

dermatographia (*der-mat-o-graf'-e-ah*). A condition in which urticarial wheals occur on the skin if a blunt instrument or finger-nail is lightly drawn over it.

dermatomycosis (*der-mat-o-mi-ko'-sis*). A fungal infection of the skin.

dermatomyositis (*der'-mat-o-mi-o-si'-tis*). An inflammation of the voluntary muscles and skin with oedema.

dermoid cyst (*der'-moid sist*). *See* under Cyst.

Descemet's membrane (*des-e-mayz' mem'-brain*). The elastic membrane lining the posterior surface of the cornea.

desentization (*de-sen-sit-i-za'-shun*). To lessen sensitivity to foreign protein. This process is used to prevent reaction in those likely to be susceptible, by frequent small doses of the protein. *See* Anaphylaxis.

desoxycorticosterone (*des-oks-e-kor-te-kos'-ter-one*). Deoxycortone acetate (*q.v.*).

desquamation (*des-kwa-ma'-shun*). The peeling of the superficial layer of the skin either in flakes or in powdery form.

detergent (*de-ter'-jent*). A cleansing and antiseptic agent. It is present in many domestic cleansers and skin applications.

deterioration (*de-te-re-or-a'-shun*). Progressive impairment of function. Worsening.

detoxication (*de-toks-e-ka'-shun*). The process of neutralizing toxic substances. A function of the liver.

detumescence (*de-tu-mes'-ense*). The subsidence of a swelling.

devitalized (*de-vi'-tal-ized*). Without vitality. Used especially to describe tissues which are deprived of their nerve supply and therefore of their recuperative powers.

dexamphetamine (*deks-am-fet'-a-meen*). A stimulant to the central nervous system. Used in depressive states, narcolepsy, post-encephalitic Parkinsonism and to control appetite in obesity. Dexedrine is a proprietary preparation of it.

dexter (*deks'-ter*). Upon the right side.

dextran (*deks'-tran*). A plasma substitute formed of large glucose molecules which given intravenously increase the osmotic pressure of blood and can be used to treat shock.

dextrin (*deks'-trin*). A soluble carbohydrate which is the first stage in the breakdown of starch and glycogen to sugar.

dextrocardia (*deks-tro-kar'-de-ah*). Situation of the heart in the right side of the thorax.

dextrose (*deks'-troze*). Grape sugar or glucose ($C_6H_{12}O_6$). The chief end-product of carbohydrate digestion.

dhobie itch (*do'-be*). A term used for tropical ringworm. *See* Tinea cruris.

diabetes (*di-a-be'-teez*). A disease characterized by excessive excretion of urine. (1) *D. insipidus*. Marked by an increased flow of urine of low specific gravity, accompanied by great thirst. This disease is rare, and some cases can be controlled by daily injections of pituitary extract. *D. mellitus* is due to deficiency or ineffectiveness of the endocrine secretion of the pancreas—*insulin*. There is polyuria and sugar present in the urine, which makes it of high specific gravity. (For urine tests, *see* Appendix 11.) Other signs are lassitude and debility, loss of weight, pruritis and a lowered resistance to infection. It is especially serious in young people, coma and death resulting from acidosis in untreated or inefficiently treated cases. Treatment is by (1) a properly regulated diet, to maintain the nutrition of the patient; (2) to keep the blood sugar normal by injections of insulin if an adequate carbohydrate intake cannot be taken without. (For diet, *see* Appendix 10.) *Bronze d.* A special type marked by pigmentation of the skin, and in which there is liver and pancreatic disease.

diabetic (*di-a-bet'-ik*). Relating to diabetes. *D. coma*, a severe acidosis (*q.v.*) occurring in diabetes mellitus. It is treated by immediate administration of insulin and intravenous fluids. *D. gangrene* and *d. cataract* are complications of diabetes mellitus.

diabetogenic (*di-a-bet-o-jen'-

ik). Inducing diabetes. Some drugs precipitate the symptoms of diabetes in those prone to the disease.

diacetic acid (*di-a-se'-tik*). Aceto-acetic acid (*q.v.*).

diagnosis (*di-ag-no'-sis*). Determination of the nature of a disease. *Clinical d.* is made by study of actual symptoms. *Differential d.* The patient's symptoms are compared and contrasted with those of other diseases. *Tentative d.* A provisional one—judged by apparent facts and observations.

dialyser (*di'-al-i-zer*). (1) The membrane used in dialysis. (2) The machine or 'artificial kidney' used to remove waste products from the blood in cases of renal failure.

dialysis (*di-al'-is-is*). The process by which crystalline substances will pass through animal membrane, while colloids cannot.

diamorphine hydrochloride (*di-a-mor'-feen hi-dro-klor'-ide*). Heroin. A powerful analgesic and drug of addiction. *See* Appendix 8.

diapedesis (*di-ap-e-de'-sis*). The passage of white blood cells through the walls of blood capillaries.

diaphoresis (*di-af-or-e'-sis*). Visible perspiration.

diaphoretics (*di-af-or-et'-iks*). Agents which increase perspiration.

diaphragm (*di'-af-ram*). The muscular dome-shaped partition separating the thorax from the abdomen. *D. needle.* One that can be left in a vein for further injections through a rubber seal. Gordh needle.

diaphragmatocele (*di-af-rag-mat'-o-seel*). Hernia of the diaphragm.

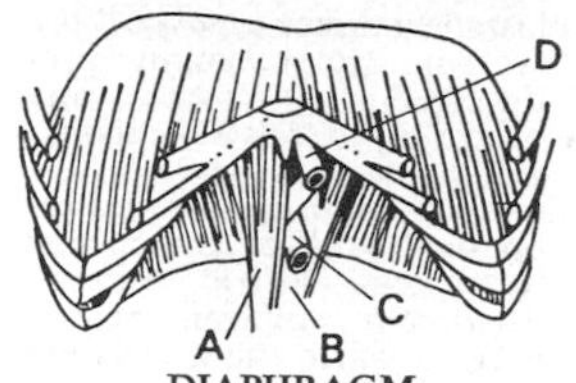

DIAPHRAGM

A. Right crus.
B. Left crus.
C. Aorta.
D. Oesophagus.

diaphysis (*di-af'-is-is*). The shaft of a long bone.

diarrhoea (*di-ar-e'-ah*). Frequent discharge of loose faecal matter from the bowels. Some of the causes are: (1) Incorrect diet. (2) Bacterial infections. (3) Poisons, e.g. arsenic. (4) Nervous influences. *Summer d.* Gastro-enteritis (*q.v.*) of infants.

diarthrosis (*di-ar-thro'-sis*). A freely moving articulation, e.g. ball and socket joint.

diastase (*di'-as-tase*). (1) An enzyme formed during germination of seeds, which converts starch into sugar. (2) One of the pancreatic enzymes, which is excreted in the urine. *D. test.* Used to estimate the excretion of diastase and therefore the pancreatic function in pancreatitis.

diastole (*di-as'-tol-e*). The resting stage of heart muscle, during which the chambers fill with blood, followed by systole or contraction. These stages occur simultaneously in both atria, and then in both ventricles, followed by a period during which all chambers rest, thus completing the cardiac cycle.

diastolic murmur (*di-as-tol'-ik*). An abnormal sound produced during diastole, and occurring in valvular disease of the heart.

diathermy (*di-a-ther'-me*). Production of heat by a high frequency electric current. *Medical d.* Sufficient heat is used to warm the tissues but not to harm them. *Short wave d.* Used in physiotherapy to relieve pain or treat infection. *Surgical d.* Of very high frequency, used to coagulate blood vessels or to dissect tissues.

diathesis (*di-ath'-es-is*). A constitutional predisposition to certain diseases.

dichloralphenazone (*di-klor-al-fen'-a-zone*). A mild hypnotic drug, well suited to the elderly. Welldorm is a proprietary preparation.

dichlorophen (*di-klor'-o-fen*). An anthelmintic against tapeworms. There is no preliminary starvation and one dose can cause the worm to disintegrate. Anthiphen is a proprietary preparation.

dichotomy (*di-kot'-o-me*). Division into two parts.

dichromatic (*di-kro-mat'-ik*). A term applied to colour blindness when there is ability to see only two of the three primary colours.

dicrotic (*di-krot'-ik*). Having a double beat. *D. pulse.* A small wave of distension following the normal pulse beat; occurring at the closure of the aortic valve. It occurs when the output from the heart is forceful and the tension of the pulse is low as in fever.

didymitis (*did-e-mi'itis*). Orchitis. Inflammation of the testicle.

diet (*di'-et*). A regularly ordered system of nourishment, according to the requirements of the body. Hospital diets are usually graded as: (1) *Full or ordinary d.* (2) *Light, or convalescent d.* of especially nutritive but easily digested foods of good calorie value. (3) *Fluid or milk d.* which may mean milk only, or include other fluids. Special diets usually consist of a reduction of, or increased quantities of, one or more of the food factors. *Diabetic d. See* Appendix 10. *High calorie d.* A diet of 4000 calories (16750 J) daily for those underweight. *Low calorie d.* A diet reduced to 1000 calories (4200 J) daily for weight reduction. *Lawrence's Line Ration d.* A diabetic diet. *Low fat d.* A diet used in conditions of the gall-bladder and jaundice. *High protein d.* Used in all cases where there has been much protein loss or excess breakdown as in subacute nephritis or severe burns. *Low protein d.* Suitable for cases of acute nephritis, hypertension and uraemia. *High residue d.* One containing much roughage for the treatment of constipation. *Low residue d.* One with a restricted fibre or roughage content, suitable for inflammation of, or operations on, the intestinal tract. *Low salt d.* May consist of no table salt and salt-free cooking or may require special low salt bread and butter. Used particularly where there is tissue oedema.

dietetics (*di-et-et'-iks*). The science of regulating diet.

dietitian (*di-et-ish'-an*). One who specializes in dietetics.

Dietl's crises (*De'-tl*). *See under* Crises.

differential (*dif-er-en'-she-al*). Making a difference. *D. blood count*. Comparison of the numbers of the different cells present in the blood. *See* Blood count. *D. diagnosis*. *See* Diagnosis.

diffuse (*dif-fu'z*). Scattered or widespread, as opposed to localized.

diffusion (*dif-fu'-shun*). The intermixing of molecules of liquid or gas so they are equally distributed in the containing structure or vessel.

digestion. The process performed in the alimentary system, by which food is broken up, for the purpose of absorption and use by the body tissues.

digit (*dij'-it*). A finger or toe.

digitalis (*dij-it-a'-lis*). Comprises a group of drugs used extensively for their action on the heart. They strengthen the heart beat and slow down the conducting power of the bundle of His, thereby enabling the ventricles to beat more slowly and more effectively. Particularly valuable in treating atrial fibrillation (*q.v.*). Prepared digitalis tablets are formed from the powdered leaves of the purple foxglove. Its chief glycosides are *digitalin* and *digitoxin*. *Digoxin* is the chief glycoside from the white foxglove. The effects of digitalis are cumulative, indicated by a very slow pulse and coupling of the beats.

digitalization (*dij-it-al-i-za'-shun*). Large doses of digitalis are given within a short period of time, so that a powerful effect is produced quickly. Sometimes called *Rapid* or *Intensive d.*

diguanides (*di-gwu'-an-ides*). Hypoglycaemic drugs. Biguanides (*q.v.*).

dihydrocodeine bitartrate (*di-hi-dro-ko'-deen bi-tar'-trate*). An analgesic derived from codeine. It has greater analgesic powers but also greater risk of addiction. D.F. 118 is a trade preparation.

dihydromorphone (*di-hi-dro-mor'-fone*). An analgesic derived from morphine. Dilaudid is a proprietary preparation.

Dihydrotachysterol (*di-hi-dro-tak-e-ster'-ol*). A preparation closely related to vitamin D that promotes calcium absorption.

dilatation (*di-la-ta'-shun*). (1) The operation of stretching a constricted passage, as in stricture of the urethra. (2) Stretching of a hollow organ. *D. of heart* when the muscle is overstrained; *d. of stomach* may be: (a) acute, following an anaesthetic when vomiting is persistent: (b) chronic, from scar tissue or growth obstructing the pylorus. Profuse vomiting at intervals is typical.

dilator (*di-la'-tor*). An instrument used for enlarging an opening, such as the rectum, cervix etc., by dilatation.

dill water. A weak carminative given for flatulence in infants.

dimenhydrinate (*di-men-hi'-drin-ate*). An antihistamine drug, useful for motion sickness. Dramamine is a proprietary preparation.

dimercaprol (*di-mer-kap'-rol*). A drug which combines with heavy metals to form a stable compound, which is rapidly excreted. Used when adverse effects are felt during treatment with gold or mercurial salts, or poisoning by arsenic, antimony or bismuth. Also called British anti-Lewisite or BAL.

dimethyl phthalate (*di'-meth-il-thal'-ate*). DIMP. An insecticide in liquid or ointment form that is effective for several hours when applied to the skin.

diodone (*di'-o-done*). A contrast medium similar to iodoxyl used in radiology, especially for arthrography.

diodoquin (*di-od'-o-kwin*). A quinoline preparation used in treatment of amoebic dysentery, especially useful for ambulant cases.

dioptre (*di-op'-ter*). The unit used in measuring lenses for spectacles. Normally, parallel light entering a lens, focuses at a distance of 1 metre, i.e. the refractive power of the lens is one dioptre, and from this basis abnormalities are reckoned.

diphenhydramine (*di-fen-hi'-dra-meen*). An antihistamine drug, used in treating hay fever and urticaria. Benadryl is a proprietary preparation of this substance.

diphtheria (*dif-the'-re-ah*). A specific infectious disease, caused by the *Corynebacterium diphtheriae* or Klebs-Löffler bacillus, which most often infects the fauces and tonsils, causing a greyish white membrane to form. Powerful exotoxins are produced that cause severe toxaemia and attack the heart muscle. It is a preventable disease by using a toxoid (*q.v.*). *D. immunization* should be carried out in infancy and booster doses given at intervals.

diphtheroid (*dif'-ther-oid*). Resembling diphtheria. A general term applied to organisms or membranes apparently similar to true diphtheria types.

diplegia (*di-plee'-je-ah*). Paralysis of similar parts on either side of the body. *Spastic d.* Little's disease (*q.v.*).

diplococci (*dip-lo-kok'-i*). Cocci found always in pairs. They may be encapsulated, e.g. pneumococci. *See* Bacteria.

diploë (*dip'-lo-e*). The cancellous tissue between the outer and inner surfaces of the skull.

diplopia (*dip-lo'-pe-ah*). Double vision in which two images are seen in place of one due to lack of co-ordination of the external muscles of the eye.

dipsomania (*dip-so-ma'-ne-ah*). A morbid craving for alcohol, which occurs in bouts.

director (*di-rek'-tor*). The grooved instrument for directing the knife in surgical operations.

Disablement Resettlement Officer. One appointed by the Ministry of Labour and Social Security to advise and organize the retraining and placing of handicapped persons in suitable employment.

disaccharide (*di-sak'-ar-ide*). A sugar yielding two monosaccharides on hydrolysis.

disarticulation (*dis-ar-tik-u-la' shun*). Amputation at a joint.

disc (*disk*). A flattened circular structure. *Intervertebral d.* A fibrocartilaginous pad that separates the bodies of two adjacent vertebrae. *Optic d.* A white spot in the retina. It is the point of entrance of the optic nerve.

discission (*dis-sis'-shun*). Dividing. In cataract operations, the cutting of the capsule of the lens.

discrete (*dis-kreet'*). The opposite of confluent (*q.v.*). Separate.

disease (*dis-eez'*). Any departure from normal health. It may be congenital; that which has been present from birth, or acquired, and it may come under one of the following headings. *Degenerative d.*, when the tissues regress, commoner in older people. *Deficiency d.* Due to lack of vitamins or glandular secretion. *Functional d.* One which affects the working of an organ but in which no structural change can be found. *Infectious d.* One due to a specific organism which can be transmitted to others. *Malignant d.* One which is severe, progressive and likely to prove fatal. *Metabolic d.* One in which there is improper digestion and absorption of food or improper cell function. *Secondary d.* A condition resulting from another, e.g. bronchopneumonia consequent upon measles. (For separate diseases, see under individual names.)

disimpaction (*dis-im-pak'-shun*). Reduction of an impacted fracture.

disinfectant (*dis-in-fek'-tant*). An agent which is capable of destroying germs of disease; such as sunlight, heat and various chemicals.

disinfestation (*dis-in-fest-a'-shun*). Getting rid of animal parasites and pests.

diskography (*disk-og'-raf-e*). X-ray following the injection of a radio-opaque dye into an intervertebral disc. Degeneractive changes or herniation may be seen.

dislocation (*dis-lo-ka'-shun*). The displacement of a bone from its natural position.

disobliteration (*dis-ob-lit-er-a'-shun*). A method of recanalizing a blocked blood vessel by coring out the obstruction with the inner wall.

disorientation (*dis-or-e-en-ta'-shun*). Inability to appreciate surroundings, time or personal identity.

dissect (*dis-ekt'*). (1) To cut carefully in the study of anatomy. (2) During operation to separate according to natural lines of structure.

disseminated (*dis-sem'-in-a-ted*). Scattered, or dispersed. *D. sclerosis*. *See* Sclerosis.

dissociation (*dis-so-se-a'-shun*). Separation. The splitting up of molecules of matter into their component parts, e.g. by heat or electrolysis. *Medically*. Anaesthesia to pain and other sensations as may occur in spinal cord lesions. *Psychologically*. The separation of ideas, emotions or experiences from the rest of the mind, giving rise to a lack of unity of which the patient is not aware.

distal (*dis'-tal*). Situated away from the centre of the body or point of origin. *See also* Proximal.

distension (*dis-ten'-shun*). Enlargement. *Abdominal d.* The abdomen is distended by gas in the intestines or fluid in the abdominal cavity.

distichiasis (*dis-tik-i'-as-is*). A double row of eyelashes, the inner one causing irritation to the globe of the eye.

distillation (*dis-til-a'-shun*). Evaporization by heat of the volatile parts of a compound, and subsequent condensation of the vapour.

dithranol (*dith'-ra-nol*). A synthetic preparation used as a substitute for chrysarobin in the treatment of psoriasis. It is more effective and less dangerous and only stains the linen slightly.

diuresis (*di-u-re'-sis*). Increased secretion of urine.

diuretic (*di-u-ret'-ik*). An agent which increases the flow of urine. Most act by preventing reabsorption in the renal tubule.

divaricator (*di-var'-ik-a-tor*). A metal or wooden splint for the treatment of congenital dislocation of the hip. Putti's splint is one variety.

diverticulitis (*di-ver-tik-u-li'-tis*). Inflammation of a diverticulum. It is commonest in the colon, and signs and symptoms similar to those of appendicitis may occur. With the formation of scar tissue there is narrowing of the tube. Colostomy is sometimes necessary.

diverticulosis (*di-ver-tik-u-lo'-sis*). The condition when many diverticula are present in the colon. They can be seen on barium X-ray.

diverticulum (*di-ver-tik'-u-lum*). A pouch or pocket in the lining of a hollow organ, as in the bladder, oesophagus or large intestine.

dizziness (*diz'-e-ness*). A feeling of unsteadiness or haziness, accompanied by anxiety.

DNA. Deoxyribonucleic acid, a complex molecule, part of the chromosome which is thought to be the carrier of the genetic code to the offspring.

Döderlein's bacillus (*de'-der-lin*). A lactobacillus occurring normally in vaginal secretions.

dolor (*dol'-or*). Pain.

dominant genes. Factors present in the chromosomes. *See* Genes.

donor (*do'-nor*). One who gives (1) Blood to another. *See* Blood grouping. (2) An organ, e.g. kidney to another.

dopamine (*dop'-a-meen*). A compound that is an intermediate product in the synthesis of noradrenaline.

dorsal (*dor'-sal*). Relating to the back or posterior part of an organ.

dorsiflexion (*dor-se-flek'-shun*). Bending backwards. In the foot and toes upwards. *See also* Plantar flexion.

dorsum (*dor'-sum*). The upper or posterior surface.

douche (*doosh*). A stream of water directed to flush out a cavity of the body.

Down's syndrome. *See* Mongolism.

Douglas's pouch (*dug'-las*). *See under* Pouch.

drachm (*dram*). Sixty grains by weight. Sixty minims by fluid measurement. *See* Appendix 14.

Drinker respirator (*drink'-er res'-pir-a-tor*). *See under* Respirator.

dropsy (*drop'-se*). A popular term used to describe excess fluid in the tissues (*oedema*) or in the peritoneal cavity (*ascites*).

drug. Any substance used as a medicine.

drug dependence. When drugs are taken repeatedly and the patient is unable to do without them either emotionally or physically. *D. d.* is now used in preference to the term drug addiction.

duck bill speculum. Sims's speculum.

Ducrey's bacillus (*du-kray'*). The organism causing soft chancre. *See* Chancroid.

duct (*dukt*). A tube or channel for conveying away the secretion of a gland.

ductless glands (*dukt'-less*). The endocrine glands, the secretion passes directly into the blood stream, e.g. the thyroid gland.

ductus arteriosus (*duk'-tus-ar-ter-e-o'-sus*). A passage connecting the pulmonary artery and aorta in intra-uterine life, which normally closes at birth. In some cases it

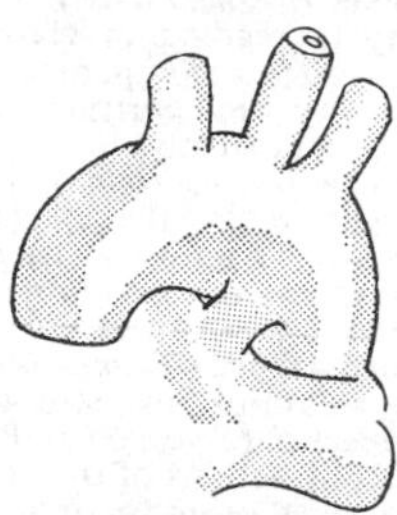

DUCTUS ARTERIOSUS

remains patent, and seems to predispose to the development of septic endocarditis. Operation to close the duct has benefited many cases.

Duke's apparatus. Used for continuous or intermittent bladder irrigation.

'dumping syndrome'. May occur after meals, following the operation of subtotal gastrectomy. The symptoms are: a feeling of fullness, weakness, sweating, dizziness and palpitations.

duodenal (*du-o-de'-nal*). Pertaining to the duodenum. *D. intubation.* The use of a special tube having a metal end which is passed via the mouth and stomach into the duodenum. Used for withdrawal of duodenal contents for pathological examination. *D. ulcer* is one in the first inch of the small intestine.

duodenitis (*du-o-den-i'-tis*). Inflammation of the duodenum.

duodenopancreatectomy (*du-o-den-o-pan-kre-a-tek'-to-me*). Surgical removal of the duodenum and much of the pancreas. Usually accompanied by anastomosis of the bile ducts and tail of the pancreas to the jejunum.

duodenostomy (*du-o-den-os'-to-me*). The formation of an artificial opening into the duodenum, through the abdominal wall, for purposes of feeding in cases of gastric disease.

duodenum (*du-o-de'-num*). The first 23 or 25 cm (9 or 10 in.) of the small intestine, from the pyloric opening of the stomach to the jejunum. The pancreatic and common bile ducts open into it.

Dupuytren's contraction (*du'-pwe-trens kon-trak'-shun*).

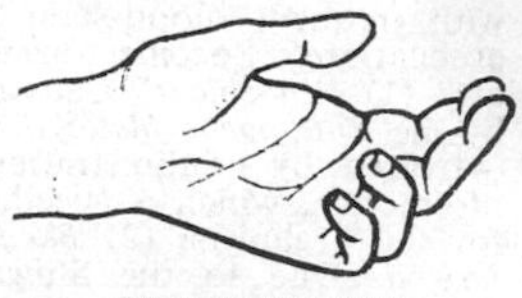

DUPUYTREN'S CONTRACTION

Contracture of the palmar fascia, causing permanent bending and fixation of one or more fingers.

dura mater (*du'-rah ma'-ter*). A strong fibrous membrane, forming the outer covering of the brain and spinal cord. It lines the inner surface of the protecting bones.

dwarfism (*dwarf'-izm*). Arrest of growth, e.g. due to renal rickets, cretinism or deficient pituitary function.

dynamometer (*di-nam-om'-e-ter*). An instrument by which the strength of the grip can be measured.

dys- Greek prefix meaning 'difficult'.

dysaesthesia (*dis-es-the'-ze-ah*). Impaired sense of touch.

dysarthrosis (*dis-ar-thro'-sis*). Deformed, dislocated or false joint.

dyschezia (*dis-che'-ze-ah*). Difficult defaecation. A form of constipation due to delay in the passage of faeces from the pelvic colon into the rectum for evacuation.

dyscoria (*dis-kor'-e-ah*). Abnormal formation of the pupil.

dyscrasia (*dis-kra'-ze-ah*). Disorder of development. *Blood d.* A developmental disorder of the blood.

dysentery (*dis'-en-ter-e*). A tropical or subtropical infectious disease, characterized by inflammation and ulceration of the large intestine, with frequent blood-stained evacuations. Specific forms are: (1) *Amoebic d.* Caused by the *Entamoeba histolytica* —treated by administration of emetine, which is specific for the organism. (2) *Bacillary d.* Due to the Shiga, Flexner or Sonne bacillus. Treatment by maintenance of the salt and water intake and the giving of Neomycin or tetracycline.

dysfunction (*dis-funk'-shun*). Impairment of function.

dysgenesis (*dis-jen'-e-sis*). Defective development or loss of fertility.

dysgerminoma (*dis-jer-min-o'-mah*). A solid embryological tumour derived from germinal cells that have not been differentiated to either sex, occurring in either the ovary or testis.

dyshidrosis (*dis-hi-dro'-sis*). A disturbance of the sweat mechanism, in which an itching vescicular rash may be present.

dyslalia (*dis-la'-le-ah*). Impairment of articulation.

dyslexia (*dis-leks'-e-ah*). Difficulty in reading or learning to read; accompanied by difficulty in writing and spelling correctly.

dysmelia (*dis-me'-le-ah*). Malformation in the development of the limbs. There may be excessive or impaired growth. *See* Amelia.

dysmenorrhoea (*dis-men-or-re'-ah*). Painful menstruation. *Primary d.* (*Spasmodic*). Painful contractions of the uterus arise just prior to or at the time of menstruation for the first few hours and then subside. *Secondary d.* (Congestive). Most often owing to endometriosis (*q.v.*) and gets progressively worse as the local congestion increases.

dysostosis (*dis-os-to'-sis*). Abnormal development of bone.

dyspareunia (*dis-par-yu'-ne-ah*). Difficult coitus.

dyspepsia (*dis-pep'-se-ah*). A term used to describe symptoms associated with the upper digestive tract. A feeling of fullness, discomfort, nausea and anorexia. *Nervous d.* Anxiety and tension aggravate the symptoms.

dysphagia (*dis-fa'-je-ah*). Difficulty in swallowing.

dysphasia (*dis-fa'-ze-ah*). Difficulty in speaking, due to a brain lesion.

dysplasia (*dis-pla'-ze-ah*). Abnormal development of tissue.

dyspnoea (*disp-ne'-ah*). Difficult or laboured breathing. *Inspiratory d.* Difficulty in intake of air. *Expiratory d.* Difficulty in expelling air.

dysrhythmia (*dis-rith'-me-ah*). Disturbance of a regular occurring pattern. Often applied to abnormality of rhythm of the cardiac cycle or of brain waves as shown on the electroencephalogram (*q.v.*).

dystaxia (*dis-taks'-e-ah*). Difficulty in controlling movements.

dystocia (*dis-to'-se-ah*). Difficult or slow labour. *Maternal d.* When the cause is with the mother. *Fetal d.* Due to abnormal size or position of the child.

dystonia (*dis-to'-ne-ah*). A lack of tonicity in a tissue often referring to the muscles.

dystrophia (*dis-tro'-fe-ah*). Abnormal growth or deposition of tissue due to defective nutrition. *D. myotonica.* An hereditary disease of early adult life in which there is progressive muscle wasting and gonodal atrophy.

dystrophy (*dis'-tro-fe*). Muscular weakness. *Muscular d.* A group of hereditary diseases in which there is progressive muscular weakness.

dysuria (*dis-u'-re-ah*). Difficult or painful micturition.

E

ear. The organ of hearing. It consists of three parts: (1) The *external e.* is made up of the expanded portion, or pinna, and the auditory

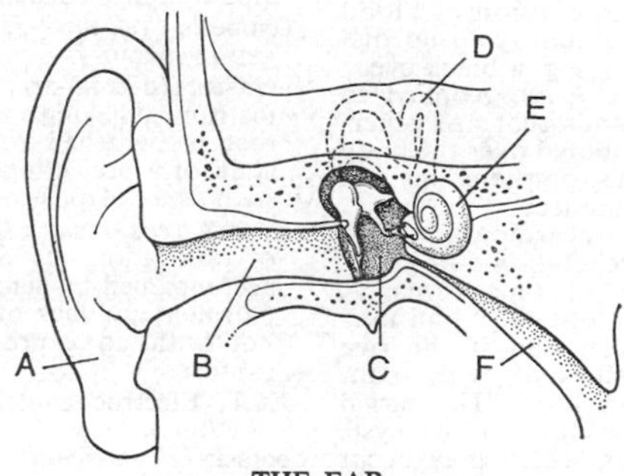

THE EAR

A. Pinna
B. Auditory canal } External ear.
C. Middle ear.
D. Semicircular canals
E. Cochlea } Internal ear.
F. Eustachian tube

canal separated from the middle ear by the drum or tympanum. (2) The *middle e.* is an irregular cavity containing the three small bones of the ear (*incus*, *malleus* and *stapes*) which link the tympanic membrane to the internal ear. It also communicates with the Eustachian tube and the mastoid cells. (3) The *internal e.* consists of a bony and a membranous labyrinth (the *cochlea* and *semicircular canals*). *E. syringe*. A special metal type.

Eberth's bacillus (*a'-bairt*). The *Salmonella typhosa.*

eburnation (*e-burn-a'-shun*). Increased density of bone, following inflammation.

ecbolic (*ek-bol'-ik*). A type of drug which stimulates uterine contractions and so may be used to induce abortion.

ecchondroma (*ek-kon-dro'-mah*). An innocent cartilaginous tumour arising as an outgrowth to cartilage or bone.

ecchymosis (*ek-ke-mo'-sis*). A bruise. An effusion of blood under the skin, causing discoloration, e.g. a black eye.

eccrine (*ek'-krin*). Applied to sweat glands that are generally distributed over the body but densest on the palms and soles of the feet.

ECG. Electrocardiogram (*q.v.*).

Echinococcus (*ek-in-o-kok'-us*). A genus of tapeworms. A species infests dogs and may also infect man if the ova are swallowed with contaminated food. The larval form develops into cysts (*hydatids*), which may occur in the liver, lung, brain or other organ, being carried by the blood or lymph stream from the intestine.

echo-encephalography (*ek'-ko-en-kef-al-og'-raf-e*). A simple method of brain investigation by means of reflecting sound waves, using a probe fitted to a portable apparatus and mains electricity.

echolalia (*ek-o-la'-le-ah*). The repetition of phrases or words overheard.

echophony (*e-kof'-on-e*). The echo of the voice heard in the chest on auscultation.

echopraxia (*ek-o-praks'-e-ah*). The automatic repetition by a patient of acts he has seen performed by others. These are carried out without expression or emotion.

eclampsia (*ek-lamp'-se-ah*). The fits which may occur in untreated cases of toxaemia of pregnancy. Now considered preventable, as toxaemia should be diagnosed early by good antenatal care. This includes regular weighing, recording of the blood pressure and testing of the urine for albumin. *See* Toxaemia.

ecmnesia (*ek-mne'-ze-ah*). A gap in memory.

ecraseur (*a-krah'-zer*). An in-instrument having a wire loop that is tightened round the stalk of a projecting growth, such as a polypus to sever it.

ecstasy (*eks'-tas-e*). A feeling of exaltation. It may be accompanied by sensory impairment and lack of activity but with an expression of rapture.

ECT. Electroconvulsive therapy (*q.v.*).

ectasia (*ek'-ta-ze-ah*). Dilation of a canal or organ. *Alveolar e.* Distension of the air sacs of the lung. *Corneal e.* Bulging and thinning of the cornea due to disease or raised intraocular pressure.

ectasis (*ek'-ta-sis*). A dilatation or over-stretching. *See* Bronchiectasis.

ecthyma (*ek-thi'-mah*). An inflammatory skin disease, with an eruption of pustules, usually with a hardened base. A pigmented scar remains after healing takes place.

ecto- (*ek'-to*). A prefix meaning 'outside'.

ectoderm (*ek'-to-derm*). The outer germinal layer of the developing embryo from which the skin and nervous system are derived.

ectogenous *ek-toj'-en-us*). Produced outside the organism. *See also* Endogenous.

-ectomy (*ek'-to-me*). A suffix denoting excision. *See also* '*-stomy*'.

ectoparasite (*ek-to-par'-ah-site*). One that lives on the external surface of its host.

ectopia (*ek-to'-pe-ah*). Displacement, or abnormal position of any part. *E. vesicae*. A congenital defect of the abdominal wall in which the bladder is exposed.

ectopic gestation (*ek-top'-ik jes-ta'-shun*). *See* Gestation.

ectozoon (*ek-to-zo'-on*). An external animal parasite.

ectrodactylia (*ek-tro-dak-til'-e-ah*). Congenital absence of one or more fingers or toes.

ectropion (*ek-tro'-pe-on*). Eversion of an eyelid, often due to contraction of the skin, or to paralysis.

eczema (*ek'-ze-mah*). An acute or chronic inflammatory condition of the skin, non-contagious although secondary infection is common. The eruption appears first as papules which become moist and finally form scabs. There is great irritation of the affected part and constitutional disturbances may also be present. Many forms are allergic in origin. *Baker's e*. A type due to the irritating effect of flour. *Dry e*. The affected area is dry and scaly. *Infantile e*. An allergic form commoner in babies fed on cow's milk. *Washer-woman's e*. Due to the irritation of soda in soaps. *Weeping e*. A serous exudation from the affected area, which precedes drying up and healing.

eczematous (*ek-zem'-at-us*). Affected with, or resembling eczema.

edentulous (*ed-ent'-ul-us*). The absence of teeth especially applied to the elderly.

EEG. Electro-encephalogram (*q.v.*).

effector (*e-fek'-tor*). A motor or sensory nerve ending in a muscle, gland or organ.

efferent (*ef'-er-ent*). Conveying from the centre to the periphery. *E. nerves*. Motor nerves coming from the brain to supply the muscles and glands. *E. tracts*. The pathway of the motor nerves from the cerebral cortex and descending the spinal cord. *See also* Afferent.

effervescent (*ef-er-ves'-sent*). Foaming, or giving off gas bubbles.

effluent (*ef'-lu-ent*). The fluid portion of sewage. The sludge or more solid portion may have been separated from it.

effluvium (*e'-flu'-ve-um*). The subtle odour which may be given off by a substance or person, usually unpleasant.

effort syndrome (*ef'-fort sin'-drome*). A condition characterized by breathlessness palpitations, chest pain and fatigue, a form of anxiety neurosis.

effusion (*e-fu′-zhun*). The escape of blood or serum into surrounding tissues or cavities.

ego (*eg′-o*). A term used in psychology of that part of the mind that the individual experiences as his 'self' and is concerned with satisfying the unconscious primitive demands of the 'id' in a socially acceptable form.

Ehrlich's side chain theory (*air′-lik*). An explanation of the phenomena of immunity, in which protoplasmic cells are said to possess certain chemical attachments or side chains, which are capable of uniting with bacterial toxins and in so doing render them harmless.

ejaculation (*e-jak-u-la′-shun*). The act of ejecting semen.

elastic (*e-las′-tik*). Capable of stretching. *E. bandage*. One that will stretch lengthways. *E. stocking*. A woven rubber stocking usually worn for varicose veins. *E. tissue*. Connective tissue containing yellow elastic fibres.

Elastoplast (*e-las′-to-plast*). A proprietary brand of adhesive elastic bandage useful to give support to a part or as a fixative for small dressings. *Extension E.* This stretches crossways instead of lengthwise and so moulds easily to the limb and allows a steady pull.

elation (*e-la′-shun*). In psychiatry a feeling of well-being or a state of excitement which may vary considerably in degree. A lesser degree may be termed euphoria, while it occurs in marked degree in hypomania and in intense degree in mania.

Electra complex (*e-lek′-trah*). From Greek mythology. The excessive attachment of a daughter for her father, with antagonism towards the mother.

electric (*e-lek′-trik*). Pertaining to electricity. *E. cautery*. *See* Cautery.

electricity (*e-lek-tris′-it-e*). A natural force and fundamental form of energy. *Static e.* The building up of an electric charge by friction between two different surfaces. *See* Appendix 5.

electrocardiogram (*e-lek-tro-kar′-de-o-gram*). A tracing made of the various phases of the heart's action by means of an electrocardiograph.

NORMAL ELECTRO-CARDIOGRAM

P, atrial contraction.
QRST, due to ventricular activity.

electrocardiograph (*e-lek′-tro-kar′-de-o-graf*). A machine for recording the potential of electrical currents that traverse the heart muscle and initiate contraction.

electrocardiophonography (*e-lek′-tro-kar-de-o-fon-og′-raf-e*). The recording of the heart sounds by means of a phonocardiogram.

electrocoagulation (*e-lek-tro-ko-ag-u-la′-shun*). A method of coagulation using a high frequency current. A form of surgical diathermy (*q.v.*).

electroconvulsive therapy (*e-lek-tro-kon-vul'-siv ther'-a-pe*). The passage of an electric current through the frontal lobes of the brain in the treatment of mental disease. ECT. With the aid of relaxant drugs this no longer causes a convulsion and is now termed electroplexy.

electrocorticography (*e-lek-tro-kor-te-kog'-raf-e*). Electro-encephalography with the electrodes applied directly to the cortex of the brain. Performed in the operating theatre to locate a small lesion, e.g. a scar.

electrode (*e-lek'-trode*). The terminal of the conducting coils of a battery, through which electricity is applied to the body.

electro-encephalogram (*e-lek'-tro en-kef'-al-o-gram*). A tracing of the electrical activity of the brain. Abnormal rhythm is an aid to diagnosis in epilepsy and cerebral tumour.

electro-encephalography (*e-lek'-tro en-kef-al-og'-raf-e*). A machine for recording the electrical activity of the cortex of the brain.

electrolysis (*e-lek-trol'-is-is*). Chemical decomposition by means of electricity: e.g. an electric current passed through water decomposes it into oxygen and hydrogen.

electrolyte (*e-lek'-tro-lite*). A substance which can be decomposed by electrolysis. *E. balance*. The maintenance of the correct balance between the different elements in the body tissues and fluids. *See* Appendix 2.

electromotive force (EMF). The measure of the force by which the current of electricity will flow from one point to another. The unit of EMF is the volt.

electromyography (*e-lek-tro-mi-og'-raf-e*). Recording of electrical currents generated in active muscle.

electronarcosis (*e-lek-tro-nar-ko'-sis*). A state of sleep or unconsciousness induced by placing electrodes on the temple and passing an electric current through the brain.

electron (*e-lek'-tron*). The unit of negative electricity revolving round a nucleus of positive electricity, of which the atom consists.

electro-oculargraph. *See* Electroretinography.

electroplexy (*e-lek'-tro-pleks-e*). *See* Electroconvulsive therapy.

electroretinogram (*e-lek-tro-re-tin'-o-gram*). Records the tracings produced by electroretinography.

electroretinography (*e-lek-tro-re-tin-og'-raf-e*). A method of examining the retina of the eye by means of electrodes and light stimulation for assessment of retinal damage.

electrotherapy (*e-lek-tro-ther'-ap-e*). The treatment of disease by use of electricity.

element (*el'-e-ment*). The simplest form into which matter can be divided. It must consist of identical atoms. Iron oxide consists of the elements iron and oxygen.

elephantiasis (*el-ef-an-ti'-as-is*). A chronic disease of the lymphatics producing excessive thickening of the skin, and swelling of the parts affected, usually the lower limbs. It may be due to filariasis.

elevator (*el'-e-va-tor*). An instrument used as a lever for raising bone, etc. *Tooth e.*

Used in dentistry. *Periosteal e.* To strip the periosteum in bone surgery.

elimination (*e-lim-in-a'-shun*). The removal of waste matter.

elixir (*e-liks'-er*). A sweetened spirituous liquid, used largely as a flavouring agent.

emaciation (*e-ma-she-a'-shun*). Excessive wasting of body tissues.

emanation (*em-an-a'-shun*). The act of giving out, e.g. the gamma rays from radium.

emasculation (*e-mas-ku-la'-shun*). Castration (*q.v.*).

embolectomy (*em-bol-ek'-to-me*). An operation to remove an embolus. It has been performed for pulmonary embolism, but more frequently for arterial emboli that are cutting off blood supply to the limbs.

embolism (*em'-bol-izm*). Obstruction of a blood vessel by a travelling blood clot or particle of matter. *Air e.* The presence of gas or air bubbles usually sucked into the large veins from a wound in the neck or chest. *Cerebral e.* A vessel in the brain is obstructed. *Coronary e.* A coronary vessel becomes blocked with a clot. *Fat e.* Globules of fat released into the blood from a fractured bone. *Infective e.* Detached particles of infected blood clot from an area of inflammation which, obstructing small vessels, results in abscess formation, i.e. pyaemia (*q.v.*). *Pulmonary e.* Blocking of the pulmonary artery or one of its branches by detached clot, usually due to thrombosis in the femoral or iliac veins. A complication of abdominal operations, occurring about the tenth day. Smaller clots cause infarction (*q.v.*).

embolus (*em'-bo-lus*). *Pl.* emboli. A substance carried by the blood stream till it causes obstruction by blocking a blood vessel. *See* Embolism.

embrocation (*em-bro-ka'-shun*). A liquid applied to the body by rubbing.

embryo (*em'-bre-o*). A name given to the fertilized ovum in its earliest stages until it shows human characteristics during the second month.

embryology (*em-bre-ol'-o-je*). The study of growth and development from the unicellular stage.

emesis (*em'-es-is*). Vomiting.

emetic (*em-et'-ik*). An agent which has power to induce vomiting, e.g. *salt*, or *mustard* and water by mouth; or *apomorphine* hypodermically.

emetine (*em'-et-een*). An alkaloid prepared from ipecacuanha. Used widely in amoebic dysentery, for which it is the specific cure.

emission (*e-mish'-un*). Involuntary ejection (of semen).

emmetropic (*em-me-tro'-pik*). Applied to normal vision that is neither long nor short sighted.

emollient (*e-mol'-e-ent*). Any substance used to soothe or soften the skin.

emotion (*e-mo'-shun*). A physical and psychological excitement in response to certain stimuli, e.g. happiness and sadness.

empathy (*em'-path-e*). The power of projecting oneself into the feelings of another person or situation.

emphysema (*em-fi-se'-mah*). The abnormal presence of air in tissues or cavities of the body. *Surgical e.* The presence of air, or any other gas, in the subcutaneous tissues introduced through a wound, and evidenced by crepitation on pressure. It may occur, e.g. from the lungs, owing to perforation by a fractured rib, or in tissues around a tracheostomy incision. The bacteria of gas-gangrene (*q.v.*) cause such a condition. *Pulmonary e.* A chronic disease of the lungs, in which there is abnormal distension of alveoli, so great in some cases that intervening walls are broken down and bullae form on the lung surface. An accompaniment of chronic respiratory diseases, in which narrowing of the tubes occurs so that expiration is difficult. *See also* Atelectasis.

empiric (*em-pir'-ik*). Describes treatment based on experience and not on scientific reasoning.

empyema (*em-pi-e'-mah*). A collection of pus in a cavity, most commonly referring to the pleural cavity.

emulsion (*e-mul'-shun*). A mixture in which an oil is suspended in water, by the addition of a mucilage.

enamel (*en-am'-el*). The hard outer covering of the crown of a tooth.

encanthis (*en-kan'-this*). A small fleshy growth at the inner canthus of the eye.

encapsulated (*en-kap'-su-la-ted*); **encapsuled** (*en-kap'su-ld*). Enclosed in a capsule.

encephalitis (*en-kef-al-i'-tis*). Inflammation of the brain. *E. lethargica* (epidemic e.) An inflammation of the brain due to a virus. Typical signs are increasing languor and lethargy, deepening to stupor, and accompanied by muscle weaknesses and paralyses. After-effects may be serious, and include mental deficiency paralysis agitans and deterioration of moral sense. *Post-vaccinal e.* An occasional complication of vaccination.

encephalocele (*en-kef'-al-o-seel*). Hernia of the brain, through the skull.

encephalography (*en-kef-al-og'-raf-e*). An X-ray of the ventricles of the brain following the insertion of air via a lumbar or cisternal puncture.

encephaloma (*en-kef-al-o'-mah*). Tumour of the brain.

encephalomalacia (*en-kef-al-o-mal-a'-she-ah*). Softening of the brain.

encephalomyelitis (*en-kef-al-o-mi-el-i'-tis*). Inflammation of the brain and spinal cord.

encephalomyelopathy (*en-kef-al-o-mi-el-op'-ath-e*). Any disease condition of the brain and spinal cord.

encephalon (*en-kef'-al-on*). The brain.

encephalopathy (*en-kef-al-op'-ath-e*). Cerebral dysfunction. *Hypertensive e.* A transient disturbance of function associated with hypertension. Disorientation, excitability, and abnormal behaviour that may be reversed if the pressure is reduced.

enchondroma (*en-kon-dro'-mah*). A tumour of cartilage within the shaft of the bone.

encopresis (*en-ko-pre'-sis*). Incontinence of faeces.

encysted (*en-sis'-ted*). Enclosed in a cyst.

endarterectomy (*end'-ar-ter-ek-to'-me*). The surgical removal of the lining of an artery usually for narrowing of the vessel by atheromatous plaques. *Thrombo-e.* In which a clot is removed with the lining.

endarteritis (*end-ar-ter-i'-tis*). Inflammation of the innermost coat of an artery. *E. obliterans*. A type which causes collapse and obstruction in small arteries.

endaural (*end-aw'-ral*). Within the ear, usually referring to the auditory canal.

endemic (*en-dem'-ik*). A term applied to any disease prevalent in a particular locality.

endemiology (*en-dem-e-ol'-o-je*). The study of all the factors pertaining to endemic disease.

endo- Prefix meaning 'within'.

endocarditis (*en-do-kard-i'-tis*). Inflammation of the endocardium. *Acute simple e.* This may be part of a general carditis complicating rheumatic fever. *Acute ulcerative* or *malignant e.* An acute illness resulting from infection of healthy heart valves by a blood-borne infection from another source, possibly the haemolytic streptococcus. *Subacute bacterial e.* Infection of the valves, already rendered abnormal by valvular heart disease or congenital deformity, by the *Streptococcus viridans*. Since this organism is released into the blood stream during dental extraction, prophylactic penicillin should be given to patients with valvular heart disease before extractions are undertaken.

endocardium (*en-do-kar'-de-um*). The membrane lining the heart.

endocervicitis (*en-do-ser-vis-i'-tis*). Inflammation of the membrane lining the cervix uteri.

endocrine (*en'-do-krine*). Secreting within. Applied to those glands whose secretions (*hormones*) flow directly into the blood or lymph and greatly modify bodily development. The chief endocrine glands are the thyroid, parathyroids, suprarenals and pituitary. The pancreas, stomach, liver, ovaries and testicles also produce internal secretions.

endocrinology (*en'-do-krin-ol'-o-je*). The study of the endocrine organs.

endocrinopathy (*en-do-krin-op'-ath-e*). Any disease condition of the endocrine glands.

endoderm. *See* Entoderm.

endogenous (*en-doj'-en-us*). Produced within. *E. depression*. One in which the disease derives from an innate predisposition. *E. protein*. That derived from the body tissues and not ingested.

endolymph (*en'-do-limf*). The fluid inside the membranous labyrinth of the ear.

endolysin (*en-do-li'-sin*). A factor or enzyme present in cells that can cause dissolution of the cytoplasm.

endometriosis (*en-do-me-tre-o'-sis*). Endometrium in an abnormal situation. Chocolate cyst of the ovary contains some endometrial material.

endometritis (*en-do-me-tri'-tis*). Inflammation of the endometrium.

endometrium (*en-do-me'-tre-um*). The mucous membrane lining the uterus.

end-organ An encapsulated sensory nerve ending.

endoparasite (*en-do-par'-ah-site*). One that lives within its host.

endorrhachis (*en-do-rak'-is*). The spinal dura mater.

endoscope (*en'-do-skope*). An

instrument fitted with a light, used to inspect a hollow organ or cavity.

endoscopic resection (*en-do-skop'-ik re-sek'-shun*). A method of removing part of an enlarged prostate gland by the transurethral route. Sections are excised by a cutting instrument or diathermy passed up the cystoscope.

endosteitis (*end-os-te-i'-tis*). Inflammation of endosteum.

endosteoma (*end-os-te-o'-mah*). A new growth in the medullary cavity of a bone.

endosteum (*end-os'-te-um*). The lining membrane of bone cavities, a function of which is to enlarge the medullary cavity as the bone grows by the action of osteoclasts (*q.v.*).

endothelioma (*en-do-the-le-o'-mah*). A malignant growth originating in endothelium.

endothelium (*en-do-the'-le-um*). The membranous lining of serous, synovial and other internal surfaces.

endotoxin (*en-do-toks'-in*). A poison produced and retained within the micro-organism. *See also* Exotoxin.

endotracheal (*en-do-trak-e'-al*). Within the trachea. *E. anaesthesia. See under* Anaesthesia.

enema (*en'-e-mah*). A liquid for injection into the rectum, which is either absorbed or ejected. *Evacuant e.* One to relieve constipation or to empty the bowel. 600 to 1000 ml warm tap water or soap and water. *Magnesium sulphate e.* To relieve intracranial pressure (60 g in 200 ml of water). *Retention e.* One to be retained, to increase body fluids, water or dextrose saline or as a sedative (bromide, chloral or paraldehyde).

enervation (*en-er-va'-shun*). (1) General weakness and loss of strength. (2) Removal of a nerve.

enopthalmos (*en-off-thal'-mos*). Retracted eyeball in its orbit.

enostosis (*en-os-to'-sis*). A tumour or bony growth within the medullary canal of a bone.

ensiform cartilage (*en'-se-form*). The xyphoid process at the lower end of the sternum.

Entamoeba histolytica (*en-ta-me'-bah his-to-lit'-ik-ah*). The micro-organism of amoebic dysentery.

enteralgia (*en-ter-al'-je-ah*). Pain in the intestines.

enterectomy (*en-ter-ek'-to-me*). Excision of a portion of the intestine.

enteric fever (*en-ter'-ik*). *See* Typhoid fever.

enteritis (*en-ter-i'-tis*). Inflammation of the intestine.

enterobiasis (*en-ter-o-bi'-as-is*). Infestation by threadworms (*q.v.*).

enterocele (*en'-ter-o-seel*). A hernia of the intestine. *See* Hernia.

enterococcus (*en-ter-o-kok'-us*). Any streptococcus of the human intestine. An example is *Streptococcus faecalis* only harmful out of its normal habitat when it may cause a urinary infection or endocarditis.

enterocolitis (*en-ter-o-ko'-li-tis*). Inflammation of both the large and small intestine.

enterokinase (*en'-ter-o-ki'-naze*). The activator of trypsinogen into trypsin, found in succus entericus.

enterolith (*en'-ter-o-lith*). A hard faecal concretion, sometimes found in the intestines.

enteromegaly (*en-ter-o-meg'-al-e*). An unusually large intestine. For example megaduodenum (*q.v.*).

enteron (*en'-ter-on*). The intestine.

enteropexy (*en-ter-o-peks'-e*). Fixation of a part of the intestine to the abdominal wall.

enteroptosis (*en-ter-op-to'-sis*). A prolapse of the intestines, due to weakening of the mesenteric attachments or of the abdominal wall.

enterospasm (*en'-ter-o-spasm*). Intestinal colic.

enterostomy (*en-ter-os'-to-me*). An opening into the small intestine. It may be: (1) temporary, to relieve obstruction; (2) permanent, in the form of an ileostomy in cases of total colectomy.

enterotome (*en'-ter-o-tome*). Enterotribe (*q.v.*).

enterotomy (*en-ter-ot'-o-me*). Any incision of the intestine.

enterotribe (*en'-ter-o-tribe*). A metal clamp used to destroy the spur of tissue in a double-barrelled colostomy as a preliminary to its closure.

enteroviruses (*en-ter-o-vi'rus-es*). Minute spherical particles that are normally parasitic in the intestines and include the polio, cocksackie and ECHO viruses. They tend to invade the central nervous system.

enterozoon (*en-ter-o-zo'-on*). Any intestinal parasite.

entoderm (*en'-to-derm*). The innermost of the three germ layers of the embryo. It gives rise to the lining of most of the respiratory tract, the intestinal tract and its glands.

entropion (*en-tro'-pe-on*). Inversion of an eyelid, so that the lashes rub against the globe of the eye.

enucleation (*en-u-kle-a'-shun*). The removal of a tumour or gland by shelling it out whole and free from other tissues.

enuresis (*en-u-re'-sis*). Involuntary passing of urine. *Nocturnal e.* That occurring during sleep.

environment (*en-vi'-ron-ment*). The surroundings. This may apply to objects or the habitat of living matter.

enzyme (*en'-zime*). *See* Catalyst.

enzymology (*en-zim-ol'-o-je*). The scientific study of enzymes and their action.

eosinophil (*e-o-sin'-o-fil*). Cells having an affinity for acid stains, e.g. some white blood cells.

eosinophilia (*e-o-sin-o-fil'-e-ah*). Excessive numbers of eosinophils present in the blood.

ependyma (*ep-en'-de-mah*). The membrane lining the cerebral ventricles and the central canal of the spinal cord.

ependymona (*ep-en-de-mo'-nah*). A new growth arising from the lining cells of the ventricles or central canal of the spinal cord. It gives rise to signs of hydrocephalus and is treated by surgery and radiotherapy.

ephedrine (*ef'-ed-rin*). A drug that relieves spasm of the bronchi, having a similar action to adrenaline but it can be taken orally. May be used in asthma and chronic bronchitis.

ephidrosis (*ef-id-ro'-sis*). Profuse sweating.

epi- Prefix meaning 'upon'.

epiblepharon (*ep-e-blef'-ar-on*). A congenital condition in which an excess of skin of the eyelid folds over the lid margin.

epicanthus (*ep-e-kan'-thus*). A fold of skin sometimes present over the inner canthus of the eye.

epicranium (*ep-e-kra'-ne-um*). Structures covering the cranium.

epicritic (*ep-e-krit'-ik*). Describes sensory nerve fibres in the skin which give the appreciation of touch and temperature.

epidemic (*ep-e-dem'-ik*). Any disease attacking a large number of people at the same time.

epidemiology (*ep-e-dem-e-ol'-o-je*). Scientific study of the distribution of diseases.

epidermis (*ep-e-der'-mis*). The non-vascular outer layer or cuticle of the skin. It consists of layers of cells which protect the dermis.

epidermophyton (*ep-e-der-mo-fi'-ton*). A form of ringworm in which there is a fungus infection of the nails and adjoining skin.

epidiascope (*ep-e-di'-a-skope*). A projector to throw an image on a screen from a picture or a solid body such as a pathological specimen.

epididymis (*ep-e-did'-e-mis*). The convoluted tube which lies above the testicle and receives the ducts from that gland. It is prolonged into the vas deferens and conveys the semen.

epididymitis (*ep-e-did-e-mi'-tis*). Inflammation of the epididymis.

epididymo-orchitis (*ep-e-did-e-mo-or-ki'-tis*). Inflammation of the epididymis and the testis.

epidural (*ep-e-dur'-al*). Outside the dura mater. If a spinal anaesthetic is inserted here there is less risk to the spinal cord.

epigastrium (*ep-e-gas'-tre-um*). That region of the abdomen which is situated over the stomach.

epiglottis (*ep-e-glot'-tis*). A cartilaginous structure, which covers the opening from the pharynx into the larynx, and so prevents food from passing into the windpipe in the act of swallowing.

epilation (*ep-il-a'-shun*). Removal of hairs with their roots. It may be effected by X-rays or by electrolysis.

epilepsy (*ep'-e-lep-se*). Convulsive attacks due to excessive electrical discharges by brain cells. In a major attack or '*grand mal*' the patient falls to the ground unconscious, following an aura or unpleasant sensation. There are first tonic and then clonic contractions, from which stage the patient passes into a deep sleep. A minor attack or '*petit mal*' is a momentary loss of consciousness only. *Jacksonian e.* A symptom of a cerebral lesion. The convulsive movements are often localized and close observation of the onset and course of the attack may greatly assist diagnosis.

epileptiform (*ep-e-lep'-te-form*). Resembling an epileptic fit.

epiloia (*ep-e-loy'-ah*). Tuberous sclerosis. A congenital disorder with areas of hardening in the cerebral cortex and other organs, characterized clinically by mental deficiency and epilepsy.

epimenorrhoea (*ep-e-men-or-re'-ah*). Menstruation occurring at abnormally short intervals.

epinephrine (*ep-e-nef'-rin*). Adrenaline (*q.v.*).

epineurium (*ep-e-nu'-re-um*). The sheath of tissue surrounding a nerve.

epiphora (*ep-if'-or-ah*). Persistent overflow of tears, e.g. due to obstruction in the lacrimal passages.

epiphysis (*ep-if'-is-is*). The end of a long bone developed separately but attached by cartilage to the diaphysis, with which it eventually unites. From the line of junction growth in length takes place.

epiplocele (*ep-ip'-lo-seel*). A hernia containing omentum.

epiploon (*ep-ip'-lo-on*). The greater omentum (*q.v.*).

episcleritis (*ep-e-skler-i'-tis*). Inflammation of the outer coat of the eyeball.

episiorrhaphy (*e-pis-e-or'-raf-e*). The repair of a laceration of perineum.

episiotomy (*e-pis-e-ot'-o-me*). An incision made in the perineum when it will not stretch sufficiently during the second stage of labour.

epispadias (*ep-e-spa'-de-as*). A condition in which there is an abnormal opening on the dorsal surface of the penis. *See also* Hypospadias.

epistaxis (*ep-e-staks'-is*). Bleeding from the nose.

epithelioma (*ep-e-the-le-o'-ma*). Carcinoma originating in epithelium.

epithelium (*ep-e-the'-le-um*). The surface layer of cells either of the skin or lining tissues.

epithelization (*ep-e-the-li-za'-shun*). Development of epithelium. The final stage in the healing of a surface wound.

epizoon (*ep-e-zo'-on*). Any external parasite.

eponym (*ep'-on-im*). In medicine an anatomical part, disease or structure bearing a person's name, usually that of the man who first described it.

eponymous (*ep-on'-e-mus*). Named after a particular person.

epulis (*ep-u'-lis*). A fibroid tumour of the gums.

Erb's palsy. A paralysis of the arm, often due to birth injury causing pressure on the brachial plexus or lower cervical nerve roots.

erectile (*e-rek'-tile*). Having the power of becoming erect. *E. tissue*. Vascular tissue which, under stimulus, becomes congested and swollen, causing erection of that part.

erepsin (*er-ep'-sin*). The enzyme of succus entericus which splits peptones into amino acids.

ergography (*erg-og'-raf-e*). A method of measuring the resistance to fatigue in a muscle by noting the output of effort to an electrical stimulus.

ergometrine (*er-go-met'-rin*). An alkaloid of ergot. It stimulates contraction of the uteric muscle.

ergonomics (*er-go-nom'-iks*). The scientific study of man in relation to his work and the effective use of human energy.

ergosterol (*er-gos'-ter-ol*). A substance present in subcutaneous fat which under the influence of ultra violet light forms vitamin D. Hence the use of artificial sunlight for rickets. Also found in plant and animal food-stuffs, which produce the vitamin when irradiated with ultra violet light.

ergot (*er'-got*). A drug from a fungus which grows on rye. It causes prolonged contraction of muscle fibres, especially those of blood vessels and of the uterus. Used chiefly to contract the uterus and check haemorrhage at childbirth.

ergotamine (*er-got'-a-meen*). An alkaloid of ergot used in the treatment of migraine.

ergotism (*er'-got-izm*). The effects of poisoning from ergot or of eating diseased rye, in which constriction of the arterioles may lead to gangrene.

erisiphake (*er-is'-e-fake*). A cup-shaped device attached to a suction motor used in intracapsular cataract extraction to remove the lens.

erosion (*e-ro'-zhun*). The breaking down of tissue, usually by ulceration.

eroticism (*e-rot'-is-izm*). A condition of sexual excitement.

eructation (*e-ruk-ta'-shun*). Belching. The escape of gas from the stomach, through the mouth.

erysipelas (*er-e-sip'-e-las*). An acute contagious disease, caused by the haemolytic streptococcus and characterized by localized inflammation of the skin, with pain and fever. The inflammation always commences round a wound, which is sometimes too small to be apparent, and is in the form of a raised red rash with small blebs, spreading gradually away from the centre, and having a well-defined margin. Considerable oedema occurs if near loose tissues, e.g. eyelids or scrotum. Seldom seen because the sulphonamides and penicillin have so effectively treated all forms of streptococcal infection.

erythema (*er-e-the'-mah*). A superficial redness of the skin. *E. induratum*. A manifestation of vasculitis (*q.v.*). *E. multiforme*. An acute eruption of the skin, which may be due to an allergy or to drug sensitivity. *E. nodosum*. A painful disease in which bright red, tender nodes occur below the knee or on the forearm; it may be associated with tuberculosis. *Punctate e.* is scarlatiform.

erythrasma (*er-e-thraz'-mah*). A skin disease due to a microsporon infection, attacking the armpits or groins. It causes no irritation, but is contagious.

erythroblast (*er-ith'-ro-blast*). Elementary red blood cell.

erythroblastosis fetalis (*er-ith-ro-blas-to'-sis fe-tal'-is*). Extensive production of erythroblasts in the newly born due to excessive destruction of red blood cells. Due to rhesus incompatibility between the child's and the mother's blood.

erythrocyte (*er-ith'-ro-site*). Red blood cells, which are developed in the red bone marrow found in the cancellous tissue of all bones. The *haemopoietic factor* vitamin B_{12} is essential for the change from megaloblast to normoblast, and iron, thyroxin, and vitamin C are also necessary for its perfect structure. *See* diagram. *E. sedimentation rate*. ESR. The rate at which the cells of citrated blood form a deposit in a graduated 200-mm. tube (*Westergren method*). The normal is less than 10 mm.

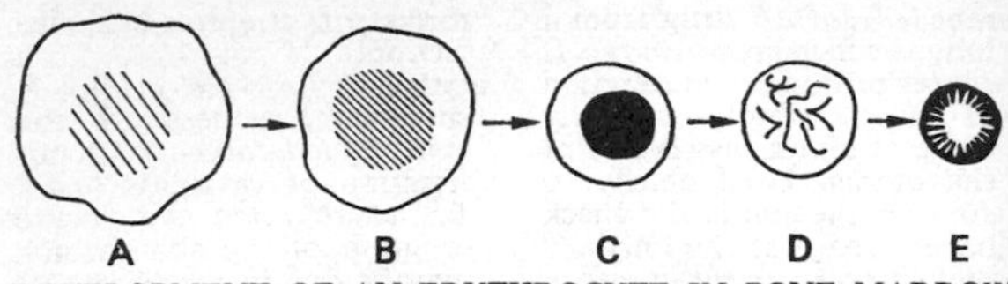

DEVELOPMENT OF AN ERYTHROCYTE IN BONE MARROW

A. Megaloblast; B. Erythroblast; C. Normoblast; D. Reticulocyte; E. Erythrocyte.

of clear plasma in 1 hr. This is much increased in severe infection, acute rheumatism and tuberculosis.

erythrocythaemia (*er-ith-ro-si-the'-me-ah*). Polycythaemia. Increase in numbers of red blood cells due to over-activity of the bone marrow. *Syn.* Vaquez's disease, poly-cythaemia vera (*q.v.*).

erythrocytopenia (*er-ith-ro-si-to-pe'-ne-ah*). Erythropenia. Deficiency in numbers of red blood cells.

erythrocytosis (*er-ith-ro-si-to'-sis*). Erythrocythaemia (*q.v.*).

erythroedema polyneuritis (*er-ith-re-de'-mah pol-e-nu-ri'-tis*). Infantile acrodynia. A rare disease of infants with redness and swelling of the hands, feet, and face; tachy-cardia, marked irritability, and photophobia. Cause un-known. 'Pink' disease.

erythromycin (*er-ith-ro-mi'-sin*). An antibiotic drug with a wide range of activity but resistance quickly develops. Best used for staphylococcal infections resistant to other antibiotics.

erythropoiesis (*er-ith-ro-poy-e'-sis*). The manufacture of red blood corpuscles.

erythropoietin (*er-ith-ro-poy-e'-tin*). A hormone produced by the kidney that stimulates the production of red blood cells in the bone marrow.

erythropsia (*er-e-throp'-se-ah*). A defect of vision, in which all objects appear red.

Esbach's albuminometer (*es'-bahks al-bu-min-om'-e-ter*). A graduated glass tube for estimating the amount of albumen in urine. *See* Ap-pendix 11.

eschar (*es'-kar*). A slough, as results from the destruction of living tissue by gangrene or burning.

Escherichia (*esh-er-ik'-e-ah*). A genus of Enterobacteriaceae. *E. coli*, an organism normally present in the intestines of man and vertebrate animals. Although not generally pathogenic it may set up infections of the gall-bladder, bile ducts and the urinary tract. It was formerly called *Bacterium coli*.

eserine (*es'-er-een*). Physostig-mine (*q.v.*).

Esmarch's tourniquet (*es'-marks toor'-ne-ka*). A rub-ber bandage used in surgery to express blood from a limb and render it less vascular.

esotropia (*es-o-tro'-pe-ah*). Convergent strabismus.

ESR. Erythrocyte sedimenta-tion rate. *See under* Erythro-cyte.

essence (*es'-ens*). A volatile oil dissolved in alcohol.

esters (*es'-ters*). A compound ether formed by the combination of an organic acid and alcohol.

ethanolamine oleate (*eth-an-ol-a-meen o-le'-ate*). An intravenous sclerosing agent used to inject varicose veins.

ether (*e'-ther*). (1) A subtle fluid said to fill all space and to penetrate all bodies; to be the medium of transmission of light, heat, X-rays, wireless rays, magnetism and electricity. *Anaesthetic e.* A volatile liquid used as a general anaesthetic agent. *E. solvens.* A skin antiseptic.

ethics (*eth'-iks*). A code of moral principles. *Nursing e.* The moral code governing a nurse's behaviour with her patients, their relatives and her colleagues.

ethmoid (*eth'-moid*). A sieve-like bone, separating the cavity of the nose from the brain. The olfactory nerves pass through its perforations.

ethmoidectomy (*eth-moid-ek'-to-me*). Surgical removal of a portion of the ethmoid bone.

ethoheptazine (*eth-o-hep'-ta-zeen*). An analgesic related to pethidine. It relieves pain and muscle spasm. A proprietary preparation is Zactirin.

ethyl biscoumacetate (*eth'il bi-coum-as'-e-tate*). An anticoagulant of the coumarin group. Tromexan is a proprietary preparation.

ethyl chloride (*eth'-il klor'-ide*). A volatile liquid used: (1) as a local anaesthetic. When sprayed on any part of the body it causes local insensitivity, through freezing. (2) A general anaesthetic by inhalation.

ethyloestrenol (*eth-il-e'-stren-ol*). An anabolic steroid that may be used to treat severe weight loss, debility and osteoporosis.

etiology (*e-te-ol'-o-je*). *See* Aetiology.

eu- Greek prefix meaning 'good'.

eugenics (*u-jen'-iks*). The study of measures which may be taken to improve future generations both physically and mentally.

eugenol (*u'-jen-ol*). A local anaesthetic and antiseptic, derived from oil of cloves and cinnamon, used in dentistry.

eunuch (*u'-nuk*). A castrated male.

eupepsia (*u-pep'-se-ah*). A good digestion with normal function of the digestive juices. It is particularly applied to the stomach.

euphoria (*u-for'-e-ah*). An exaggerated feeling of well-being often not justified by circumstances.

euplastic (*u-plas'-tik*). Capable of being transformed into healthy tissue.

eusol (*u'-sol*). A chlorine antiseptic containing hypochlorous and boric acids. The name is coined from the initials of Edinburgh University Solution of Lime.

Eustachian tube (*u-sta'-she-an*). The pharyngotympanic tube (*q.v.*). *E. valve.* A fold in the lining membrane of the right atrium of the heart.

euthanasia (*u-than-a'-ze-ah*). Painless death, by the use of drugs.

euthyroid (*u-thi'-roid*). Having a normally functioning thyroid gland. A term used following successful treatment of thyrotoxicosis (*q.v.*).

eutocia (*u-to'-se-ah*). Easy childbirth.

evacuant (*e-vak'-u-ant*). An aperient. Any drug or wash-out that empties the colon.

evacuation (*e-vak-u-a'-shun*). Emptying out. Usually referring to that of the rectum and lower bowel.

evacuator (*e-vak-u-a'-tor*). An instrument which produces evacuation. *Bigelow's e.*, *Freyer's e.* Pattern designed to wash out small particles of stone from the bladder after these have been crushed by a lithrotrite (*q.v.*).

evaporating lotion. One which, used as a compress produces local coldness and so relieves inflammation, e.g. lead lotion and eau de cologne. As these are applied in order to evaporate, they should not be covered in any way.

eventration (*e-ven-tra'-shun*). Protrusion of the intestines through the abdominal wall.

eversion (*e-ver'-shun*). Turning outwards.

evisceration (*e-vis-er-a'-shun*). Removal of internal organs. *E. of eye.* Removal of the contents of the eyeball, but not the sclera. *E. of orbit.* Removal of the eye and all structures in the orbit.

evulsion (*e-vul'-shun*). Plucking out. *See* Avulsion.

Ewing's tumour (*u'-ing*). A form of sarcoma usually affecting the shaft of a long bone.

ex- Prefix meaning 'out' or 'away from'.

exacerbation (*eks-as-er-ba'-shun*). An increase in the severity of the symptoms of a disease.

exanthematous (*eks-an-them'-at-us*). Any disease associated with a skin eruption.

excision (*eks-siz'-shun*). The cutting out of a part.

excitation (*eks-si-ta'-shun*). The act of stimulating.

excitement (*eks-site'-ment*). A physiological and emotional response to a stimulus.

excoriation (*eks-kor-e-a'-shun*). An abrasion of the skin.

excrement (*eks'-kre-ment*). Waste matter from the body.

excrescence (*eks-kres'-ense*). Abnormal overgrowth of tissue.

excreta (*eks-kre'-tah*). The natural discharges of the excretory system: faeces, urine, sweat, and sputum.

excretion (*eks-kre'-shun*). The discharge of waste from the body.

exenteration (*eks-en-ter-a'-shun*). Evisceration. The removal of an organ. *Pelvic e.* The removal of the pelvic contents. An extensive operation for malignant growth.

exfoliation (*eks-fo-le-a'-shun*). The separation of dead tissue, in thin flaky layers.

exfoliative cytology. *See* Cytology.

exhibitionism (*eks-hib-ish'-un-izm*). (1) Showing off. A desire to attract attention. (2) Exposing the genitals in order to provoke a response in one or more people.

exocrine (*eks'-o-krine*). A term applied to those glands which discharge their secretion by means of a duct, e.g. salivary glands. *See also* Endocrine.

exogenous (*eks-oj'-en-us*). Of external origin. A condition arising due to environmental factors.

exomphalos (*eks-om'-fal-os*). Umbilical hernia.

exophthalmos (*eks-off-thal'-mos*). Abnormal protrusion

of the eyeballs. *See* Goitre.

exostosis (*eks-os-to'-sis*). A bony outgrowth from the surface of a bone. May be due to chronic inflammation, constant pressure on the bone or tumour formation.

exotoxin (*eks-o-toks'-in*). Toxin secreted by micro-organisms into the surrounding media. *See also* Endotoxin.

expectorant (*eks-pek'-tor-ant*). A remedy which promotes and facilitates expectoration.

expectoration (*eks-pek-tor-a'-shun*). Sputum (*q.v.*). Secretions coughed up from the air-passages. Its characteristics are a valuable aid in diagnosis, and note should be taken of the quantity ejected, its colour, and the amount of effort required. *Frothiness* denotes that it comes from an air-containing cavity, *fluidity* indicates oedema of lung.

expiration (*eks-pi-ra'-shun*). The act of breathing out.

exploration. The operation of surgically investigating any part of the body.

expression (*eks-pres'-shun*). To press out. (1) Pressure on the uterus to facilitate the expulsion of the placenta or child. (2) Artificial extraction of milk from the breast.

exsanguination (*eks-san-gwin-a'-shun*). To make bloodless. *See* Esmarch's tourniquet.

extension (*eks-ten'-shun*). (1) The act of extending a joint as in the hip and knee when standing. (2) A weight applied at the end of a limb, in such a way that tension is exerted, which first pulls it into normal position and then keeps it thus. The apparatus used can be strips of adhesive strapping or Elastoplast, attached to the leg on either side. The ends are fixed to a wooden stirrup perforated by a cord, which passes over a pulley at the foot of the bed and the weight is attached to it. This is also known as *skin traction*. *See also* Counter extension.

extensor (*eks-ten'-sor*). A muscle which extends a part. *Quadriceps e.* That of the front of the thigh.

extirpation (*eks-ter-pa'-shun*). Complete removal.

extra (*eks'-trah*). A prefix meaning outside.

extracapsular (*eks-tra-cap-su'-lah*). Outside the capsule. May refer to a fracture occurring at the end of the bone but outside the joint capsule, or to cataract extraction.

extracellular (*eks-trah-sel'-u-lah*). Outside the cell. *E. fluid.* Tissue fluid that surrounds the cells.

extract. A preparation made by extracting the soluble principles of a drug, by steeping in water or alcohol and then evaporating the fluid.

extradural (*eks-trah-du'-ral*). Outside the dura mater. *E. haemorrhage*. *See under* Haemorrhage.

extragenital (*eks-trah-jen'-it-al*). Not related to the genitals. *E. syphilis*. Acquired but not venereal in origin; e.g. by infection of finger.

extrahepatic (*eks-trah-hep-at'-ik*). Outside the liver. Relating to a condition affecting the liver in which the cause is outside the liver.

extrapleural (*eks-trah-plu'-ral*). Between the chest wall and parietal layer of pleura. *See* Pneumothorax.

extrasystole (*eks-trah-sis'-*

tol-e). Premature contraction of atria or ventricles. *See* Systole.

extra-uterine pregnancy (*eks-trah-u'-ter-ine*). Ectopic gestation. Development of a fetus outside the uterus.

extravasation (*eks-trah-vas-a'-shun*). Effusion, or escape of fluid from its normal course into surrounding tissues. *E. of blood* is a bruise. *E. of urine* into the pelvic tissues may complicate fracture of the pelvis if the bladder is injured.

extravert (*eks'-trah-vert*). A person who is sociable, a good mixer and interested in what goes on around him. A personality type first described by Jung. *See also* Introvert.

extrinsic factor (*eks-trin'-sik*). First described by Castle, it is now considered to be vitamin B_{12}, which is necessary for the manufacture of red blood cells. The intrinsic factor produced in the stomach is necessary for the absorption of vitamin B_{12}.

extroversion (*eks-tro-ver'-shun*). Turning inside out, e.g. of the uterus, as sometimes occurs after labour.

exudation (*eks-u-da'-shun*). Oozing.

eye. The organ of sight, a globular structure with three coats. The nerve tissue of the retina receives impressions of images via the pupil and lens. From this the optic nerve conveys the impressions to the visual area of the cerebrum.

eyelids. The protective coverings of the eye, composed of muscle and dense connective tissue covered with skin, lined with conjunctiva, and fringed with eyelashes.

eye-teeth. The upper canine teeth.

F

F. Abbreviation for Fahrenheit (*q.v.*).

fabrication (*fab-re-ka'-shun*). *See* Confabulation.

face presentation. Where the face presents first during labour.

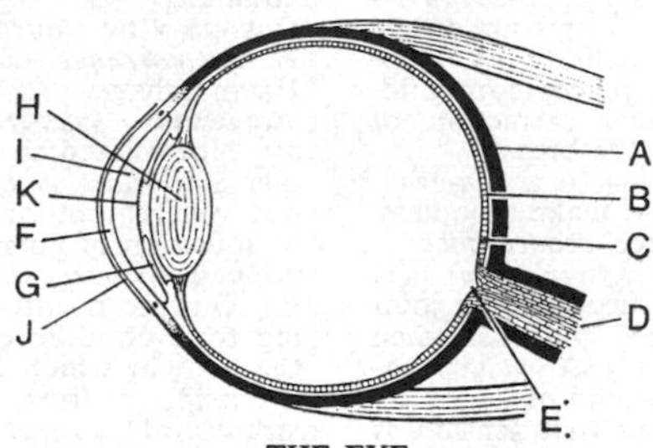

THE EYE

A. Sclerotic coat; **B.** Choroid; **C.** Retina; **D.** Optic nerve; **E.** Blind spot; **F.** Cornea; **G.** Iris; **H.** Lens; **I.** Anterior chamber; **J.** Conjunctiva; **K.** Pupil.

facet (*fas'-et*). A smooth, level surface made by movement of one part on another. Gallstones are faceted when many are present in the gall-bladder.

facet syndrome (*fas'-et sin'-drome*). A slight dislocation of the small facet joints of the vertebrae giving rise to pain and muscle spasm.

facial (*fa'-shal*). Pertaining to the face or lower anterior portion of the head. *F. paralysis*. *See* Paralysis.

facies (*fa'-she-eez*). Facial expression. *Abdominal f.* Seen in peritonitis. The face is cold and livid, eyes and cheeks sunken, and tongue and lips dry. *Adenoid f.* The open mouth and vacant expression associated with mouth breathing and nasal obstruction. *Hippocratic f.* The drawn, anxious expression seen in patients with extreme prostration; with the pinched, pointed nostrils and the cyanotic appearance of the lips and nose. *Parkinson f.* A characteristic fixed expression, due to paucity of movement of facial muscles, characteristic of paralysis agitans.

facultative (*fak'-ul-ta-tiv*). Optional. *F. bacteria* are those which, although normally *aerobes*, are also capable of being *anaerobes*.

faecalith (*fe'-ka-lith*). A hard, stony mass of faecal material which may obstruct the lumen of the appendix and be a cause of inflammation.

faeces (*fe'-sez*). Waste matter excreted by the bowel, indigestible, cellulose; food which has escaped digestion; bacteria (living and dead); and water.

Fahrenheit (*fah'-ren-hite*). A scale of heat measurement. It registers the freezing-point of water at 32°, the normal heat of the human body at 98·4°, and the boiling-point of water at 212°. *See* Appendix 15.

fainting. *See* Syncope.

falciform (*fal'-se-form*). Sickle-shaped. *F. ligament*. A fold of peritoneum which separates the two main lobes of the liver.

Fallopian tubes (*fal-o'-pe-an*). Two tubes about 10 to 14 cm (4 to 5½ in.) long, connecting the uterus with the ovaries. Their function is to conduct the ova from the ovaries to the interior of the uterus and spermatozoa from the uterus to the ovaries.

Fallot's tetralogy (*fal'-ohs tet-ral'-o-je*). A congenital heart disease with four characteris-

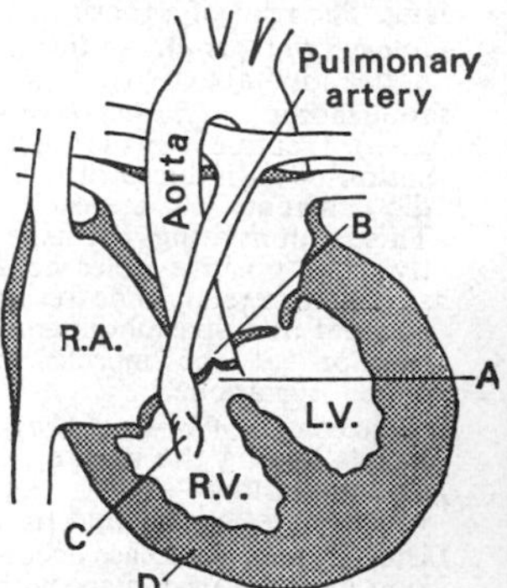

FALLOT'S TETRALOGY

A. Ventricular septal defect.
B. Dextro-position of aorta.
C. Pulmonary valvular stenosis.
D. Thickened wall of right ventricle.

tic defects: (a) pulmonary artery stenosis, (b) interventricular defects of the septum, (c) dextro-position of aorta, i.e. opening into both right and left ventricles, (d) hypertrophy of the right ventricle.

false. Not true. *F. pains.* Abdominal pains occurring in pregnancy which are not the real pains of labour. *F. pelvis.* The area between the brim of the true pelvis and the crest of the ilium. *F. joint.* Fibrous union of a fractured bone, which gives unnatural mobility. It may result from infection in an open fracture.

falx cerebi (*fal-ks ser'-e-bri*). The fold of dura mater which separates the two cerebral hemispheres.

familial (*fam-il'-e-al*). Affecting several members of one family.

fang. The root of a tooth.

fantasy (*fan'-tas-e*). An imaginative mental activity.

faradization (*far-ad-i-za'-shun*). Treatment by the application of an induced or faradic current of electricity. This is alternating, the negative and positive poles constantly reversing. The result is rapid and spasmodic contraction of the muscle to which it is applied.

farinaceous (*far-in-a'-shus*). Foods having the nature of, or containing starch, e.g. wheat, oats, barley, and rice.

farmer's lung. A disease occurring in those in contact with mouldy hay. It is thought to be due to a hypersensitivity with widespread reaction in the lung tissue and cause excessive breathlessness.

fascia (*fash'-e-ah*). A sheath of connective tissue, enclosing muscle.

fasciculation (*fas-ik-u-la'-shun*). Isolated fine muscle twitches which give a flickering appearance. It is seen in some cases of nerve impairment.

fasciculus (*fas-ik'-u-lus*). A small bundle of fibres.

fastigium (*fas-tij'-e-um*). Refers to that part of a fever when the temperature is at its height.

fat. Adipose. The white oily portion of animal tissue. *F. soluble vitamins.* Vitamins A, D, E and K. *Wool f.* Lanolin (*q.v.*).

fatigue (*fat-eeg'*). A state of weariness which may range from mental disinclination for effort to profound exhaustion following great physical and mental effort. *Muscle f.* May occur during prolonged effort due to oxygen lack and accumulation of waste products

fatty degeneration. A degenerative change in tissue cells due to the invasion of fat, and consequent weakening of the organ.

fauces (*faw'-sez*). The opening from the mouth into the pharynx. *Pillars of the f.* The two folds of muscle covered with mucous membrane which pass from the soft palate on either side of the fauces. One fold passes into the tongue, the other into the pharynx, and between them is situated the tonsil.

favus (*fa'-vus*). A contagious skin disease, with formation of scabs, in appearance like a honeycomb. It usually affects the scalp and is due to a fungus infection.

fear. A feeling of acute apprehension or anxiety. It may give rise to any of the following symptoms; tachycardia, pallor, faintness, sweating, tightness of the chest, irregular breathing, giddiness, dilated pupils, frequency of micturition and diarrhoea. *Obsessional f.* A recurring irrational fear that is not amenable to ordinary reassurance. *States of f. See* Anxiety states.

febrile (*feb'-rile*). Characterized by, or relating to fever.

fecundation (*fe-kun-da'-shun*). Fertilization.

feeblemindedness. Formerly a term for those suffering from some degree of subnormality (*q.v.*).

Felty's syndrome (*fel'-tes sin'-drome*). A variety of rheumatoid arthritis in which the spleen is enlarged and may require removal.

femoral (*fem'-or-al*). Pertaining to the femur. *F. artery.* That of the thigh, from groin to knee. *F. canal.* The opening below Poupart's ligament through which the femoral artery, etc., passes from the abdomen to the thigh. *F. hernia. See* Hernia. *F. thrombosis. See* Phlegmasia.

femur (*fe'-mer*). The thighbone.

fenestra (*fen-es'-trah*). A window-like opening. *F. ovalis.* The oval window connecting the middle and the internal ear.

fenestration (*fen-es-tra'-shun*). An operation by which a window is made in the bony labyrinth of the ear to assist hearing when deafness is due to otosclerosis.

ferment (*fer'-ment*). A substance which can produce chemical changes in other substances, without itself undergoing change. *Syn.* Enzyme.

fermentation (*fer-men-ta'-shun*). (1) A process of breaking down by an enzyme or ferment as in the production of alcohol and bread. (2) A method of bacterial identification by the production of gas during culture in a carbohydrate medium.

ferrous. An iron-containing compound. *F. fumerate*; *F. gluconate*; *F. succinate* and *F. sulphate* are all iron compounds given orally. *F. succinate* and *F. sulphate* are the most widely used.

fertilization (*fer-til-i-za'-shun*). The impregnation of the female sex cell, the ovum, by a male sex cell, a spermatozoon.

fester (*fes'-ter*). Superficial inflammation with suppuration.

festination (*fes-te-na'-shun*). The involuntary acceleration of walking which occurs when the centre of gravity is displaced in paralysis agitans.

fetishism (*fet'-ish-izm*). A superstition in which an object is regarded with an irrational fear or a strong emotional attachment.

fetus (*fe'-tus*). The developing embryo in the uterus from the second month until the time of birth.

fever. (1) A rise of body temperature above normal, accompanied by quickened pulse and respiration, dry skin, scanty highly coloured urine, vomiting, and headache. (2) Pyrexia (*q.v.*).

fiberoptics (*fi-ber-op'-tiks*). By the means of very fine glass fibres light can be transmitted along flexible tubes. Use is made of this in endoscopic instruments such as the gastroscope. Using a fiber-optic cardiac catheter pulses of light can be picked up from which the oxygen saturation can be determined.

fibre (*fi'-ber*). A thread-like structure.

fibrillation (*fib-ril-a'-shun*). A quivering, vibratory movement of muscle fibres. *Auricular* or *atrial f.* Rapid contractions of the atrium causing irregular contraction of the ventricles in both rhythm and force. *Ventricular f.* Fine rapid twitchings of the ventricles as may occur during cardiac surgery. Rapidly fatal unless it can be controlled. *See* Defibrillation.

fibrin (*fi'-brin*). A protein formed from fibrinogen in blood plasma, in the process of clotting. It is separated from the serum, and entangles the corpuscles. *F. ferment.* Thrombin. *See also* Thrombokinase.

fibrinogen (*fib-rin'-o-jen*). A soluble albuminous substance present in the blood which is converted into fibrin by the action of *thrombin* (*q.v.*) when the blood clots.

fibrinolysin (*fi-brin-o-li'-sin*). A proteolytic enzyme that dissolves fibrin.

fibrinolysis (*fi-brin-ol'-is-is*). The dissolution of a clot after healing has taken place.

fibrinopenia (*fi-brin-o-pe'-ne-ah*). Due to a lack of plasma fibrinogen there is a tendency to bleed as the coagulation time is increased.

fibro-adenoma (*fi-bro-ad-en-o'-mah*). A tumour of glandular and fibrous tissue.

fibroangioma (*fi-bro-an-je-o'-mah*). A new growth arising in both fibrous and vascular tissue.

fibroblast (*fi'-bro-blast*). Cells which form fibrous tissue.

fibrocartilage (*fi-bro-kart'-il-aj*). Cartilage with fibrous tissue in it.

fibrochondritis (*fi-bro-kon-dri'-tis*). Inflammation of fibrocartilage.

fibrocyst (*fi'-bro-sist*). Cystic degeneration in a fibroma.

fibrocystic disease of the pancreas. A disease of young children characterized by fatty stools and repeated lung infections. Treated by giving pancreatin to replace the pancreatic secretion which is missing. *Syn.* Mucoviscidosis.

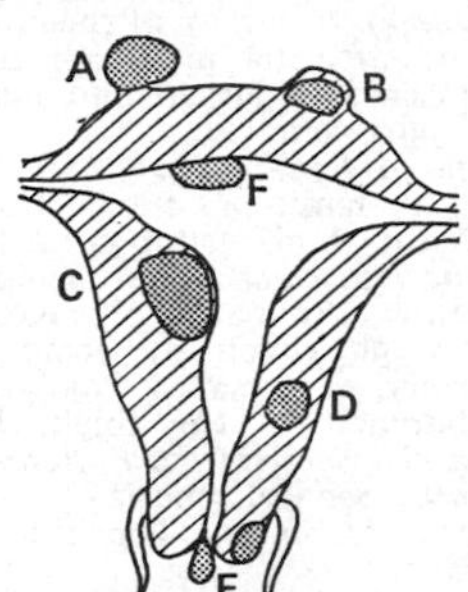

POSITIONS OF FIBROMYOMA OF UTERUS

A. Pedunculated.
B. Subserous.
C. Submural.
D. Interstitial.
E. Cervical.
F. Polypus.

fibroid (*fi'-broid*). Composed of fibrous and muscular tissue common in the uterus and more correctly a fibromyoma.

fibroma (*fi-bro'-mah*). A benign

tumour of fibrous tissue. *Cystic f.* Fibrocyst (*q.v.*).

fibromyoma (*fi-bro-mi-o'-mah*). A tumour consisting of fibrous and muscle tissue. Frequently found in or on the uterus.

fibrosarcoma (*fi-bro-sar-ko'-mah*). A malignant tumour arising in fibrous tissue.

fibrosis (*fi-bro'-sis*). Fibrous tissue formation as occurs in scar tissue, or as the result of inflammation. It is the cause of adhesions of the peritoneum or other serous membranes. *F. of lung* may precede bronchiectasis and emphysema.

fibrositis (*fi-bro-si'-tis*). A term loosely applied to pain and stiffness of sudden onset for which no other cause can be found although inflammation of fibrous tissue cannot be demonstrated. The condition is thought to arise from injury or strain to ligaments, causing muscle spasm.

fibula (*fib'-u-lah*). The slender bone from knee to ankle, on the outer side of the leg.

field of vision. That area that can be seen with the eye fixed. It can be plotted by a perimeter (*q.v.*).

filament (*fil'-a-ment*). A small thread-like structure.

Filaria (*fil-air'-e-ah*). A genus of threadworms. Found mainly in the tropics and sub-tropics.

filariasis (*fil-ar-i'-as-is*). The condition of infection by Filaria. Elephantiasis (*q.v.*).

filiform (*fil'-e-form*). Hairlike. *F. papillae.* The fine hair-like processes that cover the anterior two-thirds of the tongue.

filix mas (*fi'-liks mas*). Male fern. A drug given to destroy tapeworms.

filtrate (*fil'-trate*). The fluid which passes through a filter.

fimbria (*fim'-bre-ah*). A fringe. *Fallopian f.* The fringed ends of the Fallopian tubes in the centre of which is the abdominal ostium.

finger (*fing'-er*). A digit. *Clubbed f.* A broadening and thickening of the ends of the fingers, common in chronic diseases of the heart and lungs.

first aid. Emergency treatment carried out before medical aid is available. *See* Appendix 1.

fission (*fish'-un*). A form of asexual reproduction by dividing into two equal parts as in bacteria. *Binary f.* The splitting in two of the nucleus and the protoplasm of a cell as in protozoa. *Nuclear f.* The splitting of the nucleus of an atom with the release of a great quantity of energy.

fissure (*fish'-ur*). A cleft. (1) *F. in ano.* A painful crack in the mucous membrane of the anus, generally caused by injury from hard faeces. (2) *F. of Rolando.* A definite fold in the cortex of each cerebral hemisphere dividing the sensory from the motor area.

fistula (*fis'-tu-lah*). An abnormal passage connecting the cavity of one organ with another, or a cavity and the surface of the body. *F. in ano.* The result of an ischiorectal abscess where the channel is from the anus to the skin. *Biliary f.* Where there is leakage of bile to the exterior, following operation on the gall-bladder or ducts. *Blind f.* One which is open at only one end. *Faecal f.* Following operations on the intestines in which sepsis is present, when the channel is from the intestine through the wound. *Vesicovaginal f.* Where there is an opening from the bladder to the vagina, either from error during operation, or from ulceration as may occur in carcinoma of cervix; *recto-vaginal f.* from the rectum to the vagina may result from severe perineal tear.

fits. Paroxysmal motor discharges leading to sudden convulsive movements. These may be: (a) *local*, as the carpopedal spasms of tetany; (b) *general*, as in epilepsy, eclampsia, and hysteria. The term is sometimes applied to apoplexy (*q.v.*).

fixation (*fiks-a'-shun*). A term used to describe a failure to progress wholly or in part through the normal stages of psychological development to a fully developed personality. This is an unconscious process.

flaccid (*flak'-sid*). Soft, flabby. *F. paralysis. See* Paralysis.

flagellum (*flaj-el'-lum*). The whip-like protoplasmic filament by which some bacteria move. *Pl.* flagella.

flat-foot. *Pes planus.* A condition due to absence or sinking of the medial longitudinal arch of the foot, caused by weakening of the ligaments and tendons.

flatulence (*flat'-u-lens*). The presence of gas in the stomach which may be: (1) The result of air swallowing (*aerophagy*). Sometimes seen in nervous patients. (2) A sign of dyspepsia.

flatulent distension (*flat'-u-lent dis-ten'-shun*). This is due to gas in the intestines. It is a common complication after abdominal operations and is caused by intestinal stasis.

flatus (*fla'-tus*). Gas in the stomach or intestine.

flea (*fle*). A blood-sucking insect parasite. *Human f. Pulex irritans* does not transmit disease. *Rat f. Xenopsylla cheopis* transmits plague.

flexibilitas cerea (*fleks-e-bil'-it-as se'-re-ah*). Waxy flexibility in which a patient retains the posture of the body or of a limb in which he or someone else has placed it. A symptom of some forms of schizophrenia.

flexion (*flek'-shun*). Bending. Moving a joint so the two or more bones forming it draw towards each other. *Dorsi-f.* Drawing the foot towards the lower limb. *Plantar f.* Bending the toes downwards.

flexor (*fleks'-or*). Any muscle causing flexion of a limb or part of the body.

flexure (*fleks'-ure*). A bend or angulation.

floppy infant (*flop'-e*). Infantile hypotonia in which there is absence of tone in the muscles, often due to impaired nerve supply.

flocculent (*flok'-u-lent*). Wooly or flaky. Human milk forms a flocculent curd. Sodium citrate added to cows' milk humanizes the curd.

floaters (*flo'-ters*). Opacities in the vitreous of the eye that move about and appear as spots before the eye. Probably degenerative deposits. Muscae volitantes.

flooding. Excessive loss of blood per vaginam. It may be associated with menstruation or miscarriage.

florid (*flor'-id*). A flushed facial

appearance as seen in hypertension or after consuming alcohol.

flowmeter (*flo'-me-ter*). An instrument used to measure liquids or gas. *Oxygen f.* Measures oxygen in litres per minute. *Electro-magnetic f.* is used to measure blood flow.

fluctuation (*fluk-tew-a'-shun*). A wave-like motion felt on palpitation of the abdomen. Varying from time to time.

fludrocortisone (*flu-dro-kor'-te-zone*). A synthetic steroid used to replace aldosterone.

fluke (*flook*). A group of parasitic worms. Different varieties may affect the blood, the intestines, the liver or the lungs.

fluorescein (*flu-or-es'-in*). A dye used to detect corneal ulcer. When it is dropped on the eye the ulcer stains green.

fluorescence (*flu-or-es'-ens*). The property of reflecting back light waves, usually of a lower frequency than that absorbed, so that invisible light (e.g. ultraviolet) may becomc visible.

fluorescent screen (*flu-or-es'-ent*). A specially prepared screen in X-ray work which enables deep structures to be viewed and so more accurately examined.

fluoridation (*flu-or-id-a'-shun*). The adding of one part per million of fluorine to water in those areas where it is lacking.

fluorine (*flu'-or-in*). An element found in the water in some localities which if in excess causes a white mottled effect on the teeth but also helps to prevent dental decay. Where lacking it may be added to the water at the purification plant, making the fluoridation one part per million.

flux (*fluks*). An excessive flow of any of the body secretions.

focus (*fo'-kus*). (1) The point of meeting of rays of light. (2) The local seat of a disease. (*Pl.* foci.)

foetor (*fe'-tor*). Unpleasant smell.

folic acid (*fo'-lik*). A constituent of the vitamin B complex which influences red blood cell formation. Used in the treatment of some forms of macrocytic anaemia and sprue. Given orally. *F. a. antagonists.* Antimetabolite drugs which inhibit the action of the folic acid enzyme. This is essential for nucleoprotein synthesis.

folie à deux (*fo'-le ah der'*). The sharing of delusions by two people living in close contact.

follicle (*fol'-likl*). A very small sac or gland. *F. of tonsil.* Invagination of the covering membrane forming a depression—in which infection often occurs (*follicular tonsillitis*). *Hair f.* The sheath in which a hair grows.

folliculitis (*fol-lik-u-li'-tis*). Inflammation of a group of follicles.

folliculosis (*fol-lik-u-lo'-sis*). Hypertrophy of follicles. *Conjunctival f.* A benign non-inflammatory overgrowth of follicles of the conjunctiva of the eyelids.

fomentation (*fo-men-ta'-shun*). A hot application. *Medical f.* Several thicknesses of flannel wrung out in boiling water, applied to relieve pain. *Surgical f.* A sterile boiled foment of lint used to remove discharge and aid healing.

fomites (*fo'-mites*). Substances which have been in contact with a contagious disease and are capable of transmitting it, e.g. clothing, books and toys.

fontanelle (*fon-tan-el'*). A soft membranous space between the cranial bones of an infant. *Anterior f.* Between the parietal and frontal bones, which closes at about the age of 18 months. Rickets causes delay in this process. *Posterior f.* The junction of the occipital and parietal bones, at the sagittal suture, which closes at birth.

food-poisoning. A term commonly used to indicate an acute attack of gastro-enteritis after the consumption of unwholesome food. It may be due to chemical poisons such as antimony or arsenic or to poisonous fungi, but most frequently it is due to bacteria and their toxins, the commonest being: (1) Salmonella group, *Salmonella typhimurium* and *S. enteritidis*, infecting meat and fish preparations and duck eggs. (2) Staphylococci, often from infected milk or synthetic cream. The excreta of rats and mice, flies, or lack of care by food handlers may be the cause of an outbreak, particularly if food is allowed to stand in a warm kitchen, when the organisms can multiply. Infected food and water may also transmit dysentery and typhoid fever. *See* Botulism.

foot. The termination of the lower limb. *Athletes f.* ringworm of the feet. *F. drop.* A preventable condition in most cases, due to inability to keep the foot at the correct angle owing to lack of support or exercises, or to paralysis of the flexors of the ankle. The foot must be fixed in position at a right-angle. *F. presentation.* The presentation of one or both the legs instead of the head during labour. *Trench f.* A condition similar to frostbite occurring in soldiers and due to prolonged standing in water of trenches.

foramen (*for-a'-men*). An opening or hole, especially in a bone. *F. magnum.* The hole in the occipital bone through which the spinal cord passes. *F. ovale.* The hole between the left and right atrium in the fetus. *Obturator f.* The large hole in the os innominata.

forceps (*for'-seps*). Surgical instruments used for lifting or compressing an object: e.g. *Artery f.* (*Spencer Wells f.*) compress bleeding-points

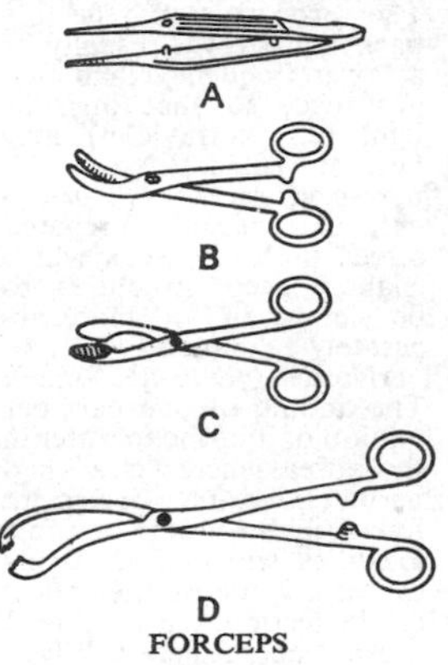

FORCEPS

A. Dissecting.
B. Pressure.
C. Dressing.
D. Volsellum.

during an operation. *Cheatle's f.* are lifting forceps. *Midwifery f.* are of various patterns, and are used in difficult labour to facilitate delivery. *Volsellum f.* have claw-like ends to grip the cervix of the uterus.

forensic (*for-en'-sik*). Applied to medicine, it is that concerned with the law and has bearing on legal problems.

foreskin (*for'-skin*). The prepuce (*q.v.*).

formaldehyde (*for-mal'-de-hide*). A gas used as a disinfectant, chiefly for rooms. A 40 per cent solution in water is known as *formalin* and is used as a spray, as a disinfectant.

formication (*form-e-ka'-shun*). A sensation as of insects creeping over the body.

formula (*form'-u-lah*). (1) A prescription. (2) A detailed statement of the ingredients of a chemical compound. (3) The presentation of the molecule of a chemical compound by chemical symbols.

formulary (*form'-u-lar-e*). A prescriber's handbook of drugs. *British National F.* One produced by the Joint Formulary Committee for easy reference for doctors and dispensers.

fornix (*for'-niks*). An arch: (1) Applied to an arched structure at the back and base of the brain; (2) The recesses at the top of the vagina in front (*anterior f.*), back (*posterior f.*), sides (*lateral f.*), of the cervix uteri. *Pl.* fornices.

fossa (*fos'-sah*). A small depression or pit. Usually applied to those in bones. *Pituitary f.* In the sphenoid bone. *See* Sella turcica. *Pl.* fossae.

Fothergill's operation (*foth'-er-gil*). Manchester operation. Amputation of the cervix, with anterior and posterior colporrhaphy for prolapse of the uterus.

fourchette (*foor-shet'*). The fold of membrane at the perineal end of the vulva.

fovea (*fo'-ve-ah*). A small depression or fossa. *F. centralis retinae.* The area of the retina which records the most distinct vision. *Syn.* Macula lutea.

fractional test meal. *See under* Test.

fracture (*frak'-chur*). A broken bone. The signs and symptoms are: Pain, swelling, deformity, shortening of the limb, loss of power, abnormal mobility, and crepitus. The cause may be direct violence, as in a blow from a heavy object, or indirect, when falling on the hand causes fracture of the clavicle or severe muscle spasm such as that of the quadriceps muscle fracturing the patella. *Closed f.* (*simple*). A clean break with no communication with the skin. *Comminuted f.* The bone is broken in several places. *Compound f.* (*open*). There is a wound from the broken bone to the skin through which infection may enter. *Depressed f.* Of the cranium in which part of the bone is driven inwards. *Greenstick f.* In children, before complete ossification of bone, a partial break or bending may occur. *F. dislocation.* Occurs near a joint and is combined with dislocation of that joint. *Impacted f.* One end of the broken bone is

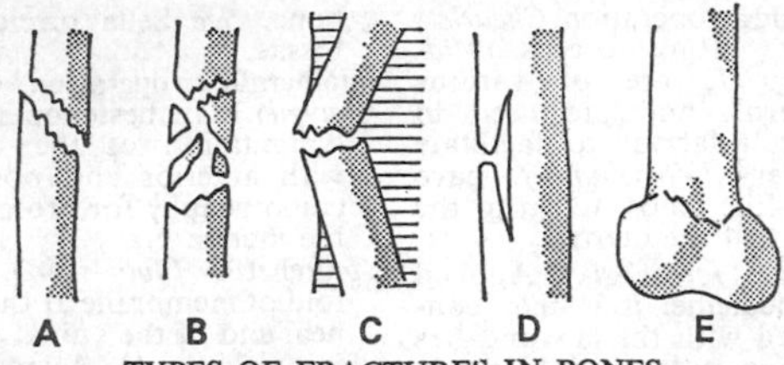

TYPES OF FRACTURES IN BONES

A. Oblique; B. Comminuted; C. Open (compound); D. Greenstick; E. Impacted.

driven into the other causing shortening. *Intracapsular f.* The break occurs within the joint capsule. *Pathological f.* Breaking occurring in diseased bones from slight injury. *Potts f.* A fracture dislocation of the ankle involving the lower end of the fibula and internal malleolus of the tibia. *Spontaneous f.* Occurs as a result of little or no violence, usually pathological. For first aid treatment, *see* Appendix 1.

fraenotomy (*fren-ot'-o-me*). The cutting of the fraenum linguae for tongue-tie.

fraenum (*fre'-num*). A fold of mucous membrane which checks or limits the movement of an organ. *F. linguae.* The fold under the tongue, which if too short causes difficulty in sucking and talking (tongue-tie) and is then partially severed.

fragilitas (*fraj-il'-it-as*). Brittleness. *F. ossium.* Abnormal fragility of bones, resulting in multiple fractures. It occurs in disorders of calcium metabolism.

framboesia (*fram-be'-ze-ah*). A tropical skin disease, known as 'yaws'. It is caused by a spirochaete susceptible to penicillin. It is not a venereal infection.

free association. *See* Association.

Frei test (*fri*). An intradermal test to aid the diagnosis of lymphogranuloma venereum.

Freiberg's disease (*fri'-berg*). Osteochondritis of the second metatarsal bone, in which there is pain on walking and standing.

fremitus (*frem'-it-us*). A thrill or vibration, e.g. that produced in the chest by speaking and felt on palpation.

Freudian (*froid'-e-an*). Relating to the doctrines of Freud on the causes of mental disorders. They are based largely on supposed unconscious sexual impressions, and of dreams as manifestations of these.

Freyer's evacuator (*fri'-ers e-vak'-u-a-tor*). *See* Evacuator.

Freyer's operation. *See* Prostatectomy.

friable (*fri'-ab-l*). Crumbling.

friar's balsam (*fri'-ars bal'-sam*). Tincture of benzoin compound. *See* Balsam.

friction (*frik'-shun*). The act of rubbing. *F. murmur.* The grating sound heard in auscultation when two rough surfaces rub together, as in dry pleurisy.

Friedländer's bacillus (*freed'-len-der*). *Klebsiella pneumoniae*, cause of a rare form of pneumonia.

Friedman's test (*freed'-mahn*). A lesser used pregnancy test. Urine from a pregnant woman, if injected into a virgin rabbit, will cause ovulation in 18 hr. It necessitates a post-mortem examination of the rabbit. *See* Aschheim–Zondik *and* Xenopus toad tests.

Friedreich's ataxia or disease (*freed'-ri-ch*). A rare form of hereditary ataxia.

frigidity (*frij-id'-it-e*). An absence of normal sexual desire, especially in women.

frog plaster. *See under* Plaster.

Fröhlich's syndrome (*fro'-lich*). A group of symptoms associated with disease of the pituitary body. These are: increased adiposity, atrophy of the genital organs, and development of feminine characteristics.

frontal (*fron'-tal*). Relating to the forehead. *F. sinus*. A pair of air sinuses situated above the nose in the frontal bone and communicating with the middle meatus of the nasal cavity.

frost-bite. Impairment of circulation chiefly affecting the fingers, the toes, the nose, and the ears, due to exposure to severe cold. The first stage is represented by chilblains, advanced cases show thrombosis and dry gangrene (*q.v.*).

frozen shoulder. A stiff and painful shoulder. The cause is unknown.

fructose (*fruk'-toze*). Fruit sugar. A monosaccharide.

frusemide (*fru'-se-mide*). An oral diuretic with a rapid and powerful action.

FSH. Follicle stimulating hormone. The hormone from the anterior pituitary that influences the production of oestrogens by the Graafian follicles.

fuchsin (*fook'-zin*). A bright red dye used in microscope work.

fugue (*fu'-g*). A period of altered awareness during which a person may wander for hours or days and perform purposive actions though his memory for the period may be lost. It may follow an epileptic fit or occur in hysteria or schizophrenia.

fulguration (*ful-gur-a'-shun*). Removal of papillomata of bladder by diathermy.

fuller's earth. Finely powdered *aluminium silicate*. A useful dusting powder which is very absorbent.

fulminating (*ful'-min-a-ting*). Sudden in onset and rapid in course.

fumigant (*fu'-mig-ant*). A substance which produces gas for fumigation.

fumigation (*fu-mig-a'-shun*). Disinfection by exposure to the fumes of a vaporized germicide.

functional disease. *See under* Disease.

fundus (*fun'-dus*). The base of an organ, or the part farthest removed from the opening. *F. of stomach*. That part above the cardiac orifice. *F. oculi*. The posterior part of the inside of the eye, as shown by the ophthalmoscope. *F. uteri*. The top of the uterus—that farthest from the cervix.

fungicide (*fun'-je-side*). A preparation that destroys fungal infection.

fungiform (*fun'-je-form*). Shaped like fungus or mushroom.

fungus (*fun'-gus*). A low form of vegetable life which includes mushrooms and moulds. Some varieties cause disease, such as actinomycosis, and ringworm.

funis (*fu'-nis*). The umbilical cord.

furor (*fu-ror'*). A state of intense excitement during which violent acts may be performed. This may occur following an epileptic fit.

furuncle (*fur-unk'-l*). A boil.

furunculosis (*fur-un-ku-lo'-sis*). A staphylococcal infection represented by many, or crops of, boils.

furunculus orientalis (*fur-un'-ku-lus or-e-en-ta'-lis*). A protozoal infection mainly of the tropics, which causes a chronic ulceration. It is known by many place names, indicating districts in which it is common, e.g. *Delhi sore*.

fusidic acid (*fu'-si-dik as'-id*). An antibiotic which is effective against staphylococci that are drug resistant or penicillin sensitive.

fusiform (*fu'-zi-form*). Shaped like a spindle.

fusion (*fu'-shun*). (1) The union between two adjacent structures. (2) The co-ordination of separate images of the same object in the two eyes into one image.

G

Gadus morrhua (*ga'-dus mor'-u-ah*). The codfish, from the liver of which oil is obtained.

Gaffky count (*gaff'-ke*). A method of sputum examination in which the tubercle bacilli present in a microscopic field are counted, e.g. G.4 indicates two to three bacilli in each field.

gag. An instrument placed between the teeth, to keep the mouth open.

gait. Manner of walking. *Ataxic g.* The foot is raised high, descends suddenly, and the whole sole strikes the ground. *Cerebellar g.* A staggering walk indicative of cerebellar disease. *Spastic g.* Stiff, shuffling walk, the legs being kept together.

galactagogue (*gal-ak'-ta-go-g*). An agent causing increased secretion of milk.

galactocele (*gal-ak'-to-seel*). A tumour containing milk, occurring in the breast.

galactorrhoea (*gal-ak-tor-re'-ah*). An excessive flow of milk.

galactosaemia (*gal-ak-to-se'-me-ah*). An inborn error of metabolism in which there is inability to convert galactose to glucose. This has proved to be one cause of retardation of mental development. If it is diagnosed early, a milk-free diet can be given with marked benefit.

galactose (*gal-ak'-toze*). Soluble sugar derived from lactose.

gall (*gawl*). Bile, a digestive fluid secreted by the liver and stored in the gall-bladder. *G.-bladder.* The sac under the lower surface of the liver, which acts as a reservoir for bile. *G.-stone.* A concretion formed in the gall-bladder. There are three varieties: (1) Cholesterol stone usually a single large ovoid one of cholesterol; (2) Pigment

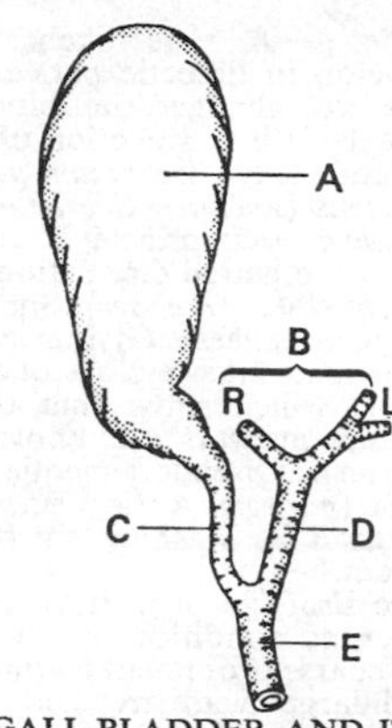

GALL-BLADDER AND ITS DUCTS

A. Gall-bladder.
B. Hepatic ducts.
C. Cystic duct.
D. Common hepatic duct.
E. Bile duct.

stones, multiple small stones occurring in haemolytic diseases; (3) Mixed stones, multiple and faceted, they contain layers of cholesterol, calcium, and pigment and are associated with infection of the gall-bladder. *G.-stone colic*. *See* Biliary colic.

gallamine (*gal'-a-meen*). A synthetic muscle relaxant, chemically related to curare but less potent and shorter acting. Flaxedil is a proprietary brand.

Gallie's operation (*gal'-le*). A living suture obtained from the fascia of a thigh muscle is used to repair the abdominal wall after reduction of a hernia.

gallipot (*gal'-le-pot*). A small receptacle for lotions.

galvanism (*gal'-van-izm*). Treatment by a continuous flow of electricity from a chemical battery. *See also* Faradism.

galvanocauterization (*gal'-van-o-kaw-ter-i-za'-shun*). Burning by means of a wire heated by galvanic current.

galvanofaradization (*gal'-van-o-far-ad-i-za'-shun*). The application of continuous and interrupted currents at the same time.

galvanometer (*gal-van-om'-e-ter*). An instrument for detecting or measuring the strength of a current of electricity.

gamete (*gam'-eet*). In reproduction, a sex cell which combines with another to form a zygote, from which a complete organism develops.

gametogenesis (*gam-et-o-jen'-e-sis*). The production of germ cells (*ova* or *sperm*) by the gonads.

gamgee tissue (*gam'-je*). Absorbent wool covered with gauze.

gamma (*gam'-mah*). The third letter in the Greek alphabet —γ.

gamma benzene hexachloride *gam'-mah-ben'-zeen heks-a-klor'-ide*). A parasitic preparation used as a shampoo to treat head lice.

gamma camera (*gam'-mah kam'-er-ah*). A large stationary detector which views the whole of an organ at once. A method of scanning that shows the radioactivity pattern.

gamma encephalography (*gam'-mah en-kef-al-og'-raf-e*). A method of localizing a brain tumour by means of a radioactive isotope and scintillating machine.

gamma globulins. Plasma proteins produced by the reticulo-endothelial cells of the spleen, bone marrow and liver. They are concerned with antibody formation. *See* Globulin.

gamma rays (*gam'-mah*). The rays given off by radioactive substances, which are used to destroy tissues in the treatment of disease.

Gammexane (*gam-meks'-ane*). A powerful proprietary insecticide used as is DDT (*q.v.*) especially for destruction of the malarial mosquito.

ganglion (*gang'-le-on*). (1) A collection of nerve cells and fibres, forming an independent nerve centre, as is found in the sympathetic nervous system. (2) A cystic swelling on a tendon *Pl.* ganglia.

ganglionectomy (*gang-le-on-ek'-to-me*). Excision of a ganglion.

gangrene (*gan'-green*). Death of tissue. Local death of bone is called *sequestrum*; of soft tissue, *slough*. *Dry g.* is due to failure of arterial blood supply, e.g. from injury or ligature of main artery, frostbite, or arterial disease. The affected part is painful, pale, and later becomes discoloured and black. There is a red line of demarcation between the living and dead tissues. *Moist g.* is caused by putrefactive changes. The part is swollen, blistered, and discoloured. There is little pain; the line of demarcation is not definite. General signs are: high fever, delirium, and all signs of blood infection. This type may result from infective thrombosis, or from pressure on veins as in strangulated hernia, etc. *Diabetic g.* A type likely to develop in diabetic patients, due to changes in blood vessels. *Gas g.* Infection of a wound with *Clostridium perfringens* (*welchii*). *See below*. *Senile g.* Seen in the aged and due to impaired circulation.

Ganser state (*Gan'-ser*). Simulated madness. Giving approximate answers to questions, which show that the correct answers are known. Hysterical pseudodementia.

gargle (*gar'-gl*). A disinfectant solution for washing out the throat.

gargoylism (*gar'-goil-izm*). An inherited condition in which the coarse prominent features and large head are said to resemble a gargoyle. The vision is defective and there is mental subnormality.

gas. Molecules of a substance very loosely combined—a vapour. *Laughing g.* Nitrous oxide. *Marsh g.* Methane. *Sternutatory g.* One which causes sneezing. *Tear g.* Is irritating to the eyes and causes excessive lacrimation.

gas–air analgesia (*an-al-je'-se-ah*). An authorized form of analgesia using nitrous oxide and air, by which the pains of labour are lessened without affecting uterine contractions.

gas-gangrene. The result of infection of a wound by anaerobic organisms, especially *Clostridium welchii*, normally found in the intestine of animals, and therefore likely to be present in cultivated soil, stable refuse, and road dirt. It has also occurred from the use of imperfectly sterilized catgut; accidental soiling of tissues if the gut has been opened during an operation;

and from perforation of the rectum in fracture of the pelvis.

gasserectomy (*gas-er-ek'-to-me*). Excision of the Gasserian ganglion.

Gasserian ganglion (*gas-se'-re-an*). The ganglion of the sensory root of the fifth cranial nerve.

gastralgia (*gas-tral'-je-ah*). Pain in the stomach of neuralgic type.

gastrectomy (*gas-trek'-to-me*). Excision of a part or whole of the stomach. *Partial g.* Commonly performed in the surgical treatment of peptic ulcer. *Bilroth g.* Most of the lesser curvature and pyloric portion are removed and the duodenum joined to the refashioned stomach. This cuts down the production of

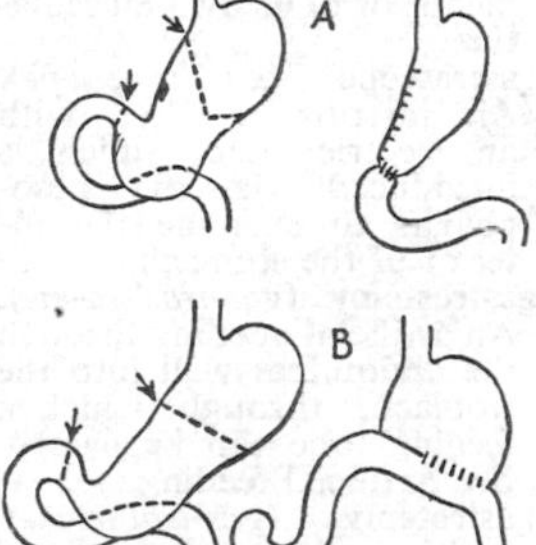

PARTIAL GASTRECTOMY
A. Bilroth type I.
B. Polya type.

secretin and of acid. *Polya g.* The first part of the duodenum and major portion of the stomach are removed and the stomach anastomosed to the jejunum. The blind portion of the duodenum supplies the bile, pancreatic and duodenal secretion. *See diagrams.*

gastric (*gas'-trik*). Pertaining to the stomach. *G. juice.* The clear fluid secreted by the glands of the stomach to assist digestion. It contains an enzyme called pepsin, which acts upon proteins in the presence of weak hydrochloric acid. *G. influenza.* A type of the infection in which vomiting, nausea, and lack of appetite are prominent signs. *G. ulcer.* Ulceration of the gastric mucosa associated with hyperacidity and often precipitated by stress.

gastrin (*gas'-trin*). A hormone secreted by the walls of the stomach, which excites continued secretion of digestive juice whilst the food is in the stomach.

gastritis (*gas-tri'-tis*). Inflammation of the stomach. *Acute g.* Severe irritation, of sudden onset, due to infected food or irritant poisons. *Chronic g.* Loss of appetite, nausea, flatulence and furred tongue, which may be due to repeated indiscretions of diet, alcohol or over-smoking. Hypochlorhydria is often present.

gastro- A prefix relating to the stomach.

gastrocele (*gas'-tro-seel*). A hernia of the stomach.

gastrocnemius (*gas-trok-ne'-me-us*). The principal muscle of the calf in the leg.

gastrocolic reflex (*gas-tro-kol'-ik*). Following a meal increased peristalsis causes the colon to empty into the rectum. This gives rise to the desire to defaecate.

gastroduodenostomy (*gas-tro-du-o-den-os'-to-me*). A surgical anastomosis between the stomach and duodenum.

gastro-enteritis (*gas-tro-en-ter-i'-tis*). Inflammation of the stomach and intestine. *Infantile g.* An acute condition of diarrhoea and vomiting producing severe dehydration. The cause may be (a) dietetic; (b) infective; (c) parenteral, when the condition is secondary to infection elsewhere in the body, e.g. otitis media or bronchitis.

gastro-enterology (*gas'-tro-en-ter-ol'-o-je*). The study of diseases of the gastro-intestinal tract.

gastro-enteropathy (*gas-tro-en-ter-op'-ath-e*). Any disease condition affecting both the stomach and the intestine.

gastro-enterostomy (*gas-tro-en-ter-os'-to-me*). A surgical anastomosis between the stomach and small intestine. Usually performed for pyloric obstruction.

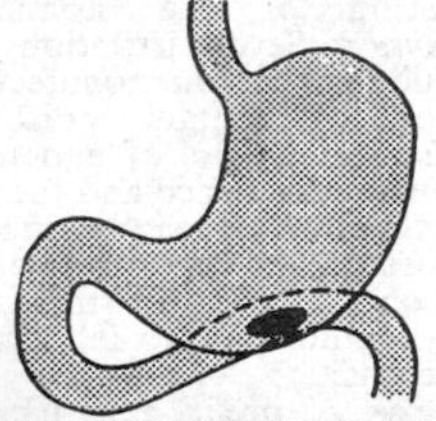

GASTRO-ENTEROSTOMY

gastrographin (*gas-tro-graf'-in*). An X-ray examination using a fluorescent screen and a fluid radio-opaque dye that may be carried out early on a patient following or suffering from haematemesis.

gastro-iliac reflex (*gas-tro-i'-le-ak*). Food entering the stomach sets up powerful peristalsis in the ileum and opening of the ileocaecal valve.

gastrojejunostomy (*gas-tro-je-ju-nos'-to-me*). A surgical anastomosis between the stomach and jejunum.

gastromalacia (*gas-tro-mal-a'-she-ah*). An abnormal softening of the walls of the stomach.

gastropathy (*gas-trop'-ath-e*). Any disease of the stomach.

gastroplasty (*gas-tro-plas'-te*). A reconstruction of the cardiac orifice of the stomach to rectify a hiatus hernia where fibrosis prevents replacement below the diaphragm.

gastroptosis (*gas-trop-to'-sis*). Downward displacement of the stomach owing to weakening of supporting ligaments, or of its own musculature.

gastroscope (*gas'-tro-skope*). An instrument fitted with an electric bulb, which is introduced via the oesophagus to examine the interior of the stomach.

gastrostomy (*gas-tros'-to-me*). An artificial opening through the abdominal wall into the stomach, through which a feeding tube can be passed. *See* Artificial feeding.

gastrotomy (*gas-trot'-o-me*). Incision of the stomach.

gastrula (*gas'-tru-lah*). One stage in the development of the fertilized ovum.

Gaucher's disease (*go-shay'*). A rare familial disease in which fat is deposited in the reticulo-endothelial cells resulting in an enlarged spleen and anaemia. No cure is known.

gauze (*gaws*). A thin open-meshed material used for

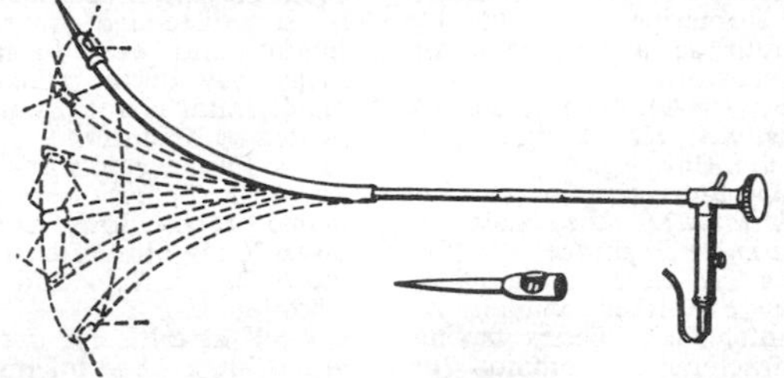

FLEXIBLE GASTROSCOPE

dressing wounds. It is sterilized by autoclave.

gavage (*gav'-arj*). Feeding by oesophageal tube.

Geiger counter (*gi'-ger*). An instrument for detecting radioactive substances. The apparatus is sensitive to the rays emitted.

gelatin (*jel'-at-in*). An albuminoid, obtained by boiling connective tissue or bones. It is used in *cooking* for the setting of jellies; in *pharmacy* for suppositories and capsules; and in *bacteriology* as a culture medium.

general paralysis of the insane. (G.P.I.). General paresis or *dementia paralytica*. A manifestation of tertiary syphilis, characterized by progressive mental and physical deterioration. The condition is uncommon now with the lessened incidence of syphilis and its early cure by penicillin.

generative (*jen'-er-a-tiv*). Referring to the reproduction of the species.

genes (*jeenz*). The hereditary factors present in the chromosomes in the germ cell which decide the physical and mental make-up of the offspring. *Dominant g.* Those that are capable of transmitting their characteristics irrespective of the genes from the other parent. *Recessive g.* Those that can pass on the characteristics only if they are present with a similar recessive gene from the other parent, and then there is only a 1 in 4 chance. *See* Mendel's law.

genetic code (*jen-et'-ik*). Term given to the arrangement of genetic material stored in the DNA molecule of the chromosome.

genetics (*jen-et'-iks*). The study of heredity and development.

genital (*jen'-it-al*). Relating to the organs of generation.

genitalia (*jen-it-a'-le-ah*). The organs of reproduction.

genito-urinary (*jen-it-o-u'-rin-are-e*). Referring to both the reproductive organs and the urinary tract.

gentian (*jen'-she-un*). A vegetable extract, which is exceedingly bitter. It is prescribed as a tonic and stomachic. *G. violet*. An aniline dye, used in 1 per cent aqueous solution: (1) for small skin lesions; (2) painting ulcers in stomatitis (*q.v.*); (3) by mouth as a treatment for threadworms.

genu (*jen′-u*). The knee. *G. valgum.* Knock-knee. *G. varum.* Bow-leg.

genupectoral position (*jen′-u-pek′-tor-al*). Knee-chest p. *See under* Position.

genus (*je′-nus*). A classification of either animals or plants, each species having characteristics common to themselves, but differing from those of others.

geriatrician (*jer-e-a-trish′-an*). A doctor who specializes in the diseases and care of the elderly.

geriatrics (*jer-e-at′-riks*). The study and treatment of the diseases of old age.

germ (*jerm*). A microbe.

German measles. *See* Rubella.

germicide (*jerm′-e-side*). An agent capable of destroying microbes and their spores.

gerontology (*jer-on-tol′-o-je*). The study of old age and the ageing processes.

gestation (*jes-ta′-shun*). Pregnancy. *Ectopic g.* Foetal development in some part other than the uterus—most usually the Fallopian tube. At about the sixth week the tube is so distended that it ruptures and severe haemorrhage may occur, which is rapidly fatal if not promptly treated by operation.

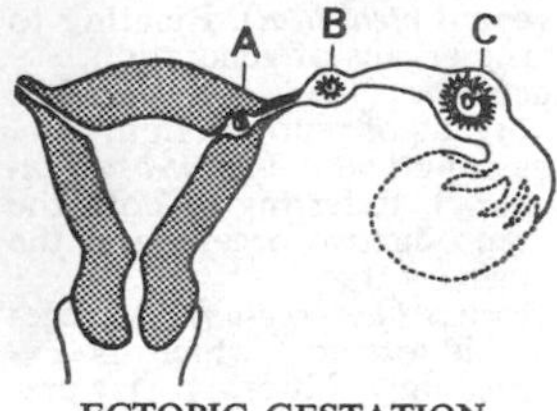

ECTOPIC GESTATION

A. Interstitial (angular).
B. Isthmic.
C. Ampullar.

Ghon's focus (*gons′ fo′-kus*). The primary lesion of pulmonary tuberculosis, as seen on an X-ray film, after it has healed by fibrosis and calcification.

giant-cell arteritis (*ji′-ant-cell ar-ter-i′-tis*). An inflammatory condition causing occlusion of arteries most often the carotid vessels and their branches. Alternative name *Temporal arteritis.*

giardiasis (*je-ar-di′-as-is*). An infection with *Giardia lamblia* that causes a persistent mild diarrhoea. Intestinal malabsorption may also be caused especially in children. A tropical condition.

gibbosity (*gib-bos′-it-e*). A humped back.

gibbus (*gib′-bus*). The name applied to the prominence caused by collapse of the vertebral body and the acute angling of the spinous processes.

gigantism (*ji-gant′-izm*). Abnormal growth of the body, due to over-activity of the anterior lobe of the pituitary gland.

Gilliam's operation (*jil′-e-am*). For correction of retroversion of the uterus by shortening the round ligaments.

ginger (*jin′-jer*). The root of a tropical plant used in dyspepsia as a carminative.

gingiva (*jin-ji′-vah*). The gums or tissues surrounding the neck of a tooth.

gingivectomy (*jin-jiv-ek′-to-me*). An operation for pyorrhoea alveolaris (*q.v.*) in which the diseased gum is removed.

gingivitis (*jin-jiv-i'-tis*). Inflammation of the gums.

ginglymus (*jin'-glim-us*). A hinge joint.

Girdlestone operation. *G. pseudoarthrosis* of hip. A false joint is made by excising

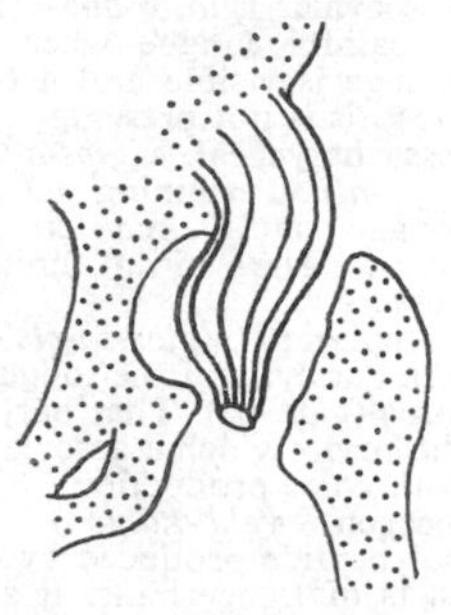

GIRDLESTONE'S OPERATION

the head and neck of femur and part of the acetabulum and suturing a muscle mass between the bones ends. A treatment for osteoarthritis.

gladiolus (*glad-e-o'-lus*). The blade-like portion of the sternum.

glanders (*glan'-ders*). A contagious disease of horses and asses, sometimes communicated to man through a crack in the skin.

glands. Special organs situated in many parts of the body. Their function is to secrete fluid prepared from the blood, either for use in the body, or for excretion as waste material. *Accessory g.* Detached glandular tissue near to one of similar structure. *Ductless g. Endocrine g.* One which produces an internal secretion but has no canal (duct) through which the secretion is carried away. An example is the thyroid gland. *Lymph g. see* Lymph nodes. *Mucous g.* One which secretes mucus. *Serous g.* One which secretes serum.

glandular fever (*gland'-u-lar*). Infective mononucleosis. A febrile condition of unknown cause, occurring chiefly in children and young adults. There is general enlargement and tenderness of lymph glands, especially those of the neck, axilla and groin, with leucocytosis. Rest during the fever but no specific treatment is known.

glans (*glanz*). An acorn-shaped body, such as the rounded end of the penis and the clitoris.

glare headache. A severe persistent headache occurring where there is strong sunlight and light reflecting surfaccs. Dark glasses are preventive.

glaucoma (*glaw-ko'-mah*). Raised intra-ocular pressure. *Primary g.* or *narrow angled g.* In which the aqueous fluid cannot drain. There is sudden onset with severe pain and blurred vision. *Chronic g.* is insidious in onset and causes progressive loss of vision by pressure on the optic nerve. *Secondary g.* Follows some pre-existing disease.

gleet. Chronic gonococcal urethritis marked by a transparent mucous discharge.

glenohumeral (*glen-o-hu'-meral*). Referring to the shoulder joint. The glenoid cavity of the scapula and the humerus.

glenoid (*glen'-oid*). Resembling a hollow. *G. cavity.* The socket of the shoulder-joint.

glia (*gli'-ah*). Neuroglia. The

connective nerve tissue of the brain and spinal cord.

glioblastoma (*gli-o-blas-to'-mah*). A malignant glioma arising in the cerebral hemispheres.

glioma (*gli-o'-mah*). A new growth of neuroglia cells and fibres affecting the brain and spinal cord. The majority are malignant but seldom metastasize. *G. retinae, see* retinoblastoma.

gliomyoma (*gli-o-mi-o'-mah*). A tumour of nerve and muscle tissue.

globin (*glo'-bin*). A protein used in the formation of haemoglobin.

globulin (*glob'-u-lin*). A protein constituent of the blood (*serum-globulin*) and cerebrospinal fluid. *Gamma g.* A blood fraction prepared from plasma containing antibodies which offers a temporary protection against measles, rubella, and sometimes poliomyelitis and other infections.

globulinuria (*glob-u-lin-u'-re-ah*). Globulin in the urine.

globus (*glo'-bus*). A ball or globe. *G. hystericus.* A symptom of hysteria when a patient feels he cannot swallow because he has a lump in his throat.

glomerulonephritis (*glo-mer-u-lo-nef-ri'-tis*). Acute nephritis following a streptococcal infection in which there is inflammation of the glomeruli of the kidneys.

glomerulosclerosis (*glo-mer-u-lo-skler-o'-sis*). Degenerative changes in the glomerular capillaries of the renal tubule leading to renal failure.

glomerulus (*glo-mer'-u-lus*). The tuft of capillaries which invaginates the kidney tubule at its commencement in the renal cortex.

glossal (*glos'-sal*). Relating to the tongue.

glossectomy (*glos-sek'-to-me*). Excision of the tongue.

glossitis (*glos-si'-tis*). Inflammation of the tongue.

glossodynia (*glos-o-din'-e-ah*). A painful tongue when no change is visible and a true glossitis is not present.

glossopharyngeal (*glos-o-far-in-je'-al*). Pertaining to the tongue and pharynx. *G. nerve.* The ninth cranial nerve.

glossoplegia (*glos-so-ple'-je-ah*). Paralysis of the tongue.

glottis (*glot'-tis*). That part of the larynx which is associated with voice production.

glucagon (*glu'-ka-gon*). A polypeptide produced by the islets of Langerhans. It aids glycogen breakdown in the liver and raising of the blood sugar level.

glucocorticoids (*glu-ko-kor'-te-koids*). The adrenal steroids that are concerned with carbohydrate metabolism. They maintain the blood sugar level and aid in storing glycogen. They are anti-inflammatory.

glucogenesis (*glu-ko-jen'-e-sis*). The production of glucose. *Hepatic g.* The liberation of glucose from glycogen in the liver.

gluconeogenesis (*glu-ko-ne-o-jen'-e-sis*). The production of new glucose from the non-nitrogen portion of the amino acids after deamination.

glucose (*glu'-koze*). Dextrose or grape-sugar found in many fruits and honey. It is the absorbable sugar to which carbohydrates are reduced by digestion, and is therefore found in the blood in considerable quantity. It is present in the urine of patients with untreated diabetes mellitus.

glucuronic acid (*glu-ku-ron'-ik*). An enzyme in the liver that acts on the bilirubin from the broken down red blood cells to form conjugated bilirubin.

gluteal (*glu'-te-al*). Relating to the buttocks. *G. muscles.* Three in number which form the fleshy part of the buttocks.

gluten (*glu'-ten*). A nitrogenous constituent of wheat and other grains.

gluten-induced enteropathy. Coeliac disease. A disease of malabsorption of the gluten in wheat or rye flour.

glutethimide (*glu-teth'-im-ide*). A non-barbiturate hypnotic. Doriden is a trade preparation.

glycerin (*glis'-er-een*). A colourless syrupy substance. obtained from fats and fixed oils. It has a hygroscopic action. As an emollient it is an ingredient of many skin preparations. *G. enema.* 3·5 to 14 ml for adults. For children and adults largely replaced by *G. suppositories,* containing 1·75 to 3·5 ml solidified with gelatin. *G. of thymol.* An antiseptic mouth wash and gargle.

glyceryl trinitrate (*glis'-er-il tri-ni'-trate*). Sublingual tablets that relieve anginal pain by dilating the coronary arteries.

glycocholate of sodium (*gli'-ko-ko'-late*). One of the salts of bile.

glycogen (*gli'-ko-jen*). The form in which carbohydrate is stored in the liver and muscles. Animal starch.

glycogenesis (*gli-ko-jen'-e-sis*). The process of glycogen formation from the blood glucose.

glycogenolysis (*gli-ko-jen-ol'-is-is*). The breakdown of glycogen in the body so that it may be utilized.

glycoside (*gli'-ko-side*). A crystalline body in plants which when acted on by acids or ferments produces sugar. If the sugar is glucose it may be termed a *glucoside. See* Digitalis.

glycosuria (*gli-ko-su'-re-ah*). Sugar in the urine, a symptom of diabetes mellitus. *Emotional g.* May arise in times of stress due to increased release of adrenaline. *Alimentary g.* The appearance of sugar in the urine after a meal rich in carbohydrate. It is transitory. *Renal g.* Sugar in the urine in an otherwise normal person, due to an unusually low renal threshold (*q.v.*).

glycyrrhiza (*glis-ir-i'-zah*). Liquorice. *Compound Powder of G.* A mild laxative.

gnathic (*na'-thik*). Pertaining to the jaw.

gnathoplasty (*na'-tho-plas-te*). A plastic operation on the jaw.

Goa powder (*go'-ah*). Derived from a tropical tree, and the source of chrysarobin (*q.v.*).

goblet cells. Special secreting cells of goblet shape found in mucous membrane.

Goeckerman régime (*ger'-ker-man*). A treatment for psoriasis which consists of warm baths, ultraviolet light and crude coal tar paste.

goitre (*goi'-ter*). Enlargement of the thyroid gland, causing a marked swelling in front of the neck, which sometimes results in pressure on the trachea. It may be endemic and give rise to no other symptoms, e.g. Derbyshire neck is of this type. *Colloid g.* An enlarged but soft thyroid gland with no signs of hyperthyroidism. *Exophthalmic g.* Hyperthyroidism with marked protrusion of eyeballs. *Lymphadenoid g.* An enlargement in which there is infiltration by lymphocytes and deposits of lymphoid tissue. *Primary toxic g.* Signs of excess of thyroxine in the blood, where the gland has not been previously enlarged. *Secondary toxic g.* In which the gland has been previously enlarged, and signs of hyperthyroidism suddenly develop. *Substernal g.* The enlargement of the gland is behind the sternum and obvious swelling in the neck may not be apparent. *Syn.* Graves's disease; thyrotoxicosis. *See also* Myxoedema.

goitrogens (*goi'-tro-jens*). Substances that block the synthesis of thyroxine and so cause goitre. The cause may be an inability to utilize iodine.

Golgi (*gol'-ge*). *G. bodies in cell.* Specialized structures seen near the nucleus of a cell during microscopic examination. *Organ of G.* The sensory end organs in muscle tendons that are sensitive to stretch.

gonad (*gon'-ad*). A sexual gland. The testicle or ovary.

gonadotrophic (*gon-ad-o-tro'-fic*). Having influence on the gonads. *G. hormones.* Those of the pituitary gland which control the ovaries and testes.

gonadotrophin (*gon-ad-o-tro'-fin*). Any hormone that stimulates either the ovaries or testes.

gonioscopy (*gon-e-os'-ko-pe*). A method of examining the iris–corneal angle by means of a contact lens, light source and magnifying device.

gonococcus (*gon-o-kok'-us*). *Neisseria gonorrhoeae.* A diplococcus which causes gonorrhoea.

gonorrhoea (*gon-or-re'-ah*). A common venereal disease caused by the *Neisseria gonorrhoeae* infecting the genital tract, causing a discharge with pain and frequency of micturition. Spread by the blood stream may give rise to iritis or arthritis. Scar tissue formation may give rise to urethral stricture or infertility owing to occlusion of the uterine tubes. Most cases can be quickly treated by penicillin but reinfection is not uncommon.

gonorrhoeal (*gon-or-re'-al*). Relating to gonorrhoea. *G. arthritis.* Intractable infection of joints causing great pain and disability. *G. ophthalmia.* In the newly born (*ophthalmia neonatorum*) a notifiable disease and a cause of blindness. Good antenatal care should prevent infection and early intensive treatment with penicillin prevent blindness.

Gordh needle (*gort'*). An intravenous needle in which there is a rubber diaphragm through which repeated injections can be given.

gorget (*gor'-jet*). A grooved instrument used in lithotomy.

gouge (*gowj*). A strong grooved

instrument, used for scooping out diseased bone, or other hard substances.

gout (*gowt*). A metabolic disease associated with an excess of uric acid in the blood. It is characterized by painful inflammation and swelling of the smaller joints, especially those of the big toe and thumb. Inflammation is accompanied by the deposit of urates around the joints. Colchium is the drug of choice in an acute attack and probenecid may be used between attacks.

Graafian follicles (*graf'-e-an fol'-ik-ls*). Small vesicles formed in the ovary, each containing an ovum. One follicle matures during each menstrual cycle.

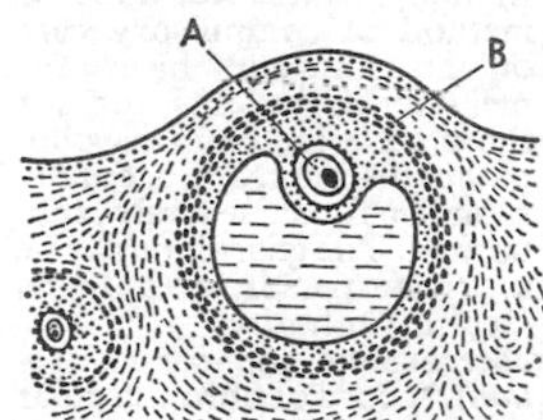

GRAAFIAN FOLLICLES

Section of ovary showing Graafian follicles with ova.

A. Ovum.

B. Mature follicle.

graft. Transplantation of healthy tissue from one part of the body to remedy a defect in a corresponding structure. *Autogenous g.* The graft is taken from and given to the same individual. *Bone g.* Transplantation of bone. *Homogenous g.* A graft is taken from one person and given to another individual of the same species. *Pedicle g.* Consists of the full thickness of the skin and subcutaneous tissue. *Pinch g.* Small pieces of skin of varying depth placed on a raw area. *Thiersch g.* Considerable pieces of partial thickness of skin are used to cover large areas.

grain. (1) A minute hard particle. (2) A unit of weight in the Apothecaries measure. *See* Appendix 14.

gram (*gramme*). The unit of weight of the metric system. In prescriptions the abbreviation G is recommended to avoid confusion with gr. *See* Appendix 14.

Gram's stain. A special stain used in bacteriology, by the taking up of which some organisms are recognized. Indicated thus:

Gram + (*positive*);
Gram − (*negative*).

grand mal (*grond mal'*). Major epilepsy. *See* Epilepsy.

granular (*gran'-u-lar*). Containing small particles. *G. cells. See* Leucocytes. *G. casts.* The degenerated cells from the lining of renal tubules excreted in the urine.

granulation (*gran-u-la'-shun*). The growth of new tissue by which wounds heal when the edges are not in apposition. It consists of new capillaries and fibroblasts which fill in the space and later form fibrous tissue. The resulting scar is liable to be hard and unsightly. A barrier of this tissue forms the walls of an abscess cavity, and the floor of an ulcer. By it inflammation is localized.

granule (*gran'-ule*). A small particle or grain.

granulocyte (*gran'-u-lo-site*). Polymorphonuclear white blood cells that may be either neutrophils, basophils, or eosinophils.

granulocytopenia (*gran-u-lo-si-to-pe'-ne-ah*). A marked reduction in the polymorphonuclear cells in the blood. The condition may precede agranulocytosis (*q.v.*).

granuloma (*gran-u-lo'-mah*). A tumour composed of granulation tissue.

granulosa cells (*gran-u-los'-ah*). Cells present in the Graafian follicle. *G. c. tumour*. A rare new growth of the ovary that produces excessive oestrogen.

grape-sugar. Dextrose.

gravel. Small calculi formed in the kidneys and bladder, and sometimes excreted with the urine.

Graves's disease. Exophthalmic goitre. Hyperthyroidism (*q.v*).

gravid (*grav'-id*). Pregnant.

gravity. Weight. *Specific g.* of any liquid is its weight compared with that of an equal volume of water, i.e. affected by the amount of solids dissolved in it.

greenstick fracture. *See under* Fracture.

Grenz rays. A source of superficial X-rays that may be used to treat skin diseases.

Griffith's types (*grif'-fith*). A method of determining varieties of streptococci by agglutination tests. Applied mainly to haemolytic streptococci of Lancefield's Group A (*q.v.*).

gripe (*gripe*). Colic.

griseofulvin (*gri-se-o-ful'-vin*). An oral antifungal antibiotic that is used in the treatment of tinea.

group psychotherapy. A method of treatment whereby patients and staff, under the guidance of a psychotherapist meet regularly to discuss the patients' problems. Insight is gained into the patients' way of meeting stress. The patient learns to understand and tries to change his behaviour as a result of the group process. He also contributes to the well-being of the other group members.

grouped breathing. Biot's respiration. *See* Biot.

guanethidine (*gwan-eth'-e-deen*). A hypotensive drug that acts by blocking the sympathetic nerve impulses to plain muscle without affecting the parasympathetic. Ismelin is a proprietary preparation.

Guardianship. Under the Mental Health Act 1959, a method of compulsory care on an informal basis for mentally ill patients and for those suffering from psychopathic disorder, the mentally subnormal, or severely subnormal. The guardian may be a private person or a Local Health Authority.

gubernaculum (*gu-ber-nak'-u-lum*). A cord of fibromuscular tissue attached to the lower pole of the testis which has the power of retracting it.

guillotine (*gil'-lo-teen*). A surgical instrument used for excising tonsils.

guinea worm. A tropical parasite which burrows into human tissues, particularly into the legs or feet.

gullet (*gul'-let*). The oesophagus.

gum-boil. An abscess at the root of a tooth.

gumma (*gum'-mah*). A soft, degenerating tumour characteristic of the tertiary stage of syphilis. It may occur in any organ or tissue.

gurgling. Caused by gas passing through liquid. *G. râle* is the sound heard on auscultation when the bronchi or lungs contain fluid.

gustatory (*gus'-ta-tor-e*). Relating to taste.

gut. The intestine.

gutta (*gut'-tah*). A drop.

gutta-percha (*gut'-tah perk'-ah*). The dried juice of a tree utilized for surgical purposes, forming a thin sheet of waterproof tissue. It cannot be sterilized by heat.

gutter splint. A plaster of Paris or plastic splint moulded to a limb in gutter shape—not encasing it.

gynaecoid (*gi'-ne-koid*). Like the female. *G. pelvis.* One with a round brim and shallow cavity suited to child bearing.

gynaecologist (*gi-ne-kol'-o-jist*). One who specializes in the diseases of women.

gynaecology (*gi-ne-kol'-o-je*). The science treating of those diseases which are peculiar to women.

gynaecomastia (*gi-ne-ko-mas'-te-ah*). Excessive growth of the male breast.

gypsum (*jip'-sum*). Plaster of Paris (*calcium sulphate*).

gyrus (*ji'-rus*). A convolution as of the brain, cochlea, etc.

H

H. Symbol for hydrogen.

habit. Automatic response to specific situations acquired as a result of repetition and learning. *Drug h.* Drug addiction. *H. training.* A method used in psychiatric nursing whereby deteriorated patients can be rehabilitated and taught personal hygiene by constant repetition and encouragement.

haema-, haemo-, haemato- (*he'-mah, he'-mo, he'-mat-o*). Prefixes, denoting or relating to blood.

haemangioma (*he-man-je-o'-mah*). A new growth arising in a blood vessel.

haemarthrosis (*he-mar-thro'-sis*). An effusion of blood into a joint.

haematemesis (*he-mat-em'-e-sis*). Vomiting of blood. If it has been in the stomach for some time and become partially digested by gastric juice, it is of a dark colour and contains particles resembling coffee-grounds.

haematin (*he'-mat-in*). The iron-containing part of blood. With globin it forms haemoglobin.

haematinic (*he-mat-tin'-ik*). An agent which increases the colouring matter in blood. *H. factors.* Those necessary for the proper formation of red blood cells. *See* Erythrocyte.

haematocele (*he'-mat-o-seel*). A swelling produced by effusion of blood; e.g. in the sheath surrounding a testicle, or a broad ligament.

haematocolpos (*he-mat-o-kol'-pos*). Collection of blood in the vagina. *See* Cryptomenorrhoea.

haematology (*he-mat-tol'-o-je*). The science dealing with the nature, functions, and diseases of blood.

haematoma (*he-mat-o'-mah*). A swelling containing blood.

haematometra (*he-mat-o-me'-trah*). Accumulation of blood in the uterus.

haematomyelia (*he-mat-o-mi-e'-le-ah*). An effusion of blood into the spinal cord.

haematomyelitis (*he-mat-o-mi-el-i'-tis*). An effusion of blood into the spinal canal with acute inflammation of the cord.

haematosalpinx (*he-mat-o-sal'-pinks*). Haemosalpinx. Accumulation of blood in the Fallopian tubes.

haematoxylin (*he-mat-toks'-il-in*). Logwood. A stain used in bacteriology.

haematozoon (*he-mat-o-zo'-on*). Any animal parasite in the blood.

haematuria (*he-mat-tu'-re-ah*). Blood in the urine, due to injury or disease of any of the urinary organs. *See* Appendix 11.

haemochromatosis (*he-mo-kro-ma-to'-sis*). A condition in which there is high absorption and deposition of iron leading to a high serum level and pigmentation of the skin. *Syn*. Bronze diabetes.

haemoconcentration (*he-mo-kon-sen-tra'-shun*). A loss of circulating fluid from the blood with a high cell volume as is common in severe burns.

haemocytometer (*he-mo-si-tom'-e-ter*). An instrument for counting the blood corpuscles. It consists of a graduated pipette into which blood can be drawn and diluted, and a glass slide and cover disc ruled into squares of 0·05 mm. This allows for counting of blood cells under a microscope.

haemodialysis (*he-mo-di-al'-is-is*). The process of removing salts and urea from the blood by means of circulating the blood through a dialyser or artificial kidney, as in certain cases of renal failure.

haemoglobin (*he-mo-glo'-bin*). The colouring matter of the red blood corpuscles. It contains globulin and haematin, and has a strong affinity for oxygen by reason of its iron content.

haemoglobinaemia (*he-mo-glo-bin-e'-me-ah*). The presence of haemoglobin in the blood plasma.

haemoglobinometer (*he-mo-glo-bin-om'-e-ter*). A simple instrument for estimating the haemoglobin level against a standard colour tube.

haemoglobinopathy (*he-mo-glo-bin-op'-ath-e*). Any one of a group of hereditary disorders in which there is an abnormality of the haemoglobin molecule. An example is sickle cell anaemia.

haemolysin (*he-mo-li'-sin*). A substance which destroys red blood cells. It may be an enzyme, an antibody or a chemical compound.

haemolysis (*he-mol'-is-is*). Disintegration of red blood cells. In excess a characteristic of some diseases, causing severe anaemia and possibly jaundice.

haemolytic (*he-mo-lit'-ik*). Having the power to destroy red blood cells. *H. jaundice*. *See* Jaundice. *H. disease of the newborn*. A condition associated with the rhesus factor (*q.v.*).

haemopericardium (*he-mo-per-e-kar'-de-um*). Blood within the pericardium either due to a penetrating injury or following surgery.

haemophilia (*hem-o-fil'-e-ah*). A familial disease transmitted by females only, to their male offspring. Characterized by delayed, or entire absence of clotting power of the blood. Due to a lack of antihaemophilic globulin (AHG) or Factor VIII. Slight injuries may be fatal, and any operation is dangerous. *Russell's viper venom* and *thrombin* will often arrest minor surface bleeding. Before operation or in an emergency an infusion of fresh frozen plasma or an injection of AHG concentrate can be given.

haemophiliac (*hem-o-fil'-e-ak*). A person afflicted with haemophilia.

Haemophilus influenza (*hem-of'-il-us in-flu-en'-zah*). A minute bacillus that may cause bronchitis and sinusitis.

haemophthalmia (*hem-of-thal'-me-ah*). Bleeding into the eye.

haemopoiesis (*he-mo-poi-e'-sis*). Manufacture of red blood cells.

haemopneumothorax (*hem-o-nu-mo-thor'-aks*). Both blood and air are present in the pleural cavity as is likely following chest surgery or trauma of the chest wall.

haemopoietic (*he-mo-poi-et'-ik*). Relating to red blood cell formation. *H. factors.* Those necessary for the development of red blood cells, e.g. vitamin B_{12} and folic acid.

haemoptysis (*he-mop'-tis-is*). Coughing up of blood. Being aerated, it is bright red and frothy if in any quantity, and if effort is used in expelling it. Blood from the lungs permeates sputum; from the upper passages a red streaked appearance is characteristic.

haemorrhage (*hem'-or-raj*). An escape of blood from its vessels. *Arterial h.* is bright red and the blood escapes in rhythmic spurts, corresponding to the beats of the heart. *Venous h.* is dark red and the blood flows evenly. *Capillary h.* is oozing of blood. Haemorrhage may also be: (a) *primary*—at the time of operation or injury; (b) *reactionary* or *recurrent*—occurring later when the blood pressure rises and a ligature slips or a vessel opens up; (c) *secondary*—as a rule about 10 days after injury, and always due to sepsis. Special types are: *Accidental h.* Bleeding from the uterus during pregnancy. It may be *revealed* or *concealed*. *Ante-partum h.* That which occurs before labour starts. *See* Placenta praevia. *Cerebral h. See* Apoplexy. *Concealed h.* The blood collects in a cavity of the body. *Contre-coup h.* That which occurs at a distance from where the force was applied, e.g. a blow on the skull may cause the brain to strike the bony casing directly opposite the site of original force, causing bruising of the nerve tissues. *Extradural h.* Bleeding inside the head, but outside the dura. The result of injury to the skull causing signs of raised intracranial pressure. The cerebrospinal fluid is not blood-stained. It is treated by trephining. removal of clot, and ligature of bleeding vessel. *Inevitable h.* That which is unavoidable, as in placenta praevia. *Intradural h.* Bleeding beneath the dura mater. It may be due to injury and causes signs of compression. The cerebrospinal fluid will be blood-stained. *Post-partum h.* That which occurs after childbirth. *Revealed h.* Bleeding which is obvious. *Subarachnoid h.* Of the cerebral vessels between the pia and arachnoid mater.

haemorrhagic (*hem-or-raj'-ik*). Pertaining to or accompanied by haemorrhage. *H. purpura.* Purpura haemorrhagica (*q.v.*).

haemorrhoidectomy (*hem-or-oid-ek'-to-me*). The surgical removal of haemorrhoids.

haemorrhoids (*hem'-or-oids*). 'Piles', or locally dilated rectal veins. They may be either external or internal to the sphincter ani. Pain is caused on defaecation, and bleeding may occur. Acute attacks of inflammation intensify the symptoms. Treatment may be by surgical removal, or by injection of phenol in almond oil which causes fibrosis of the affected veins.

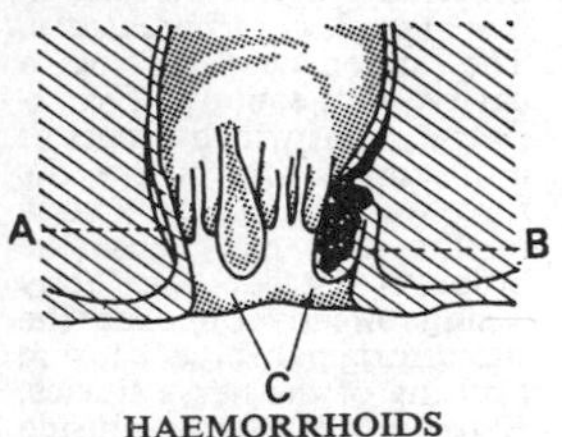

HAEMORRHOIDS
A. Venous plexus.
B. Varicosed vein.
C. Haemorrhoids.

haemosalpinx (*he-mo-sal'-pinks*). Blood in the Fallopian tube, usually caused by a tubal pregnancy. Haematosalpinx.

haemosiderosis (*he-mo-sid-er-o'-sis*). The deposition of iron in the tissues as brownish granules following excessive haemolysis of red blood cells.

haemostasis (*he-mo-sta'-sis*). The arrest of bleeding or the slowing up of blood flow in a vessel.

haemostatic (*he-mo-stat'-ik*). A drug or remedy for arresting haemorrhage.

haemothorax (*he-mo-thor'-aks*). Blood in the thoracic cavity, e.g. from injury to soft tissues as the result of fracture of rib.

hair. A delicate epidermal filament growing out of the skin. *H. follicle. See under* Follicle.

halazone (*hal'-a-zone*). A chlorine antiseptic similar to chloramine. Used for the purification of drinking water.

half-life. The term is applied to radioactive isotopes and denotes that period of time in which the element loses half activity by the process of disintegration.

halibut oil (*hal'-e-but*). Derived from the liver of halibut, and rich in vitamins A and D.

halitosis (*hal-e-to'-sis*). Foul-smelling breath.

hallucination (*hal-lu-sin-a'-shun*). A false perception in which the patient believes he sees, smells, hears, tastes or feels an object or person when there is no basis in the external environment for the belief.

hallucinogens (*hal-lu-sin'-o-jens*). Drugs, e.g. LSD, that induce in a patient false sensory impressions or cause hallucinations (*q.v.*).

hallux (*hal'-luks*). The big toe. *H. valgus.* A deformity in which the big toe is bent towards the other toes. *H. varus.* In which the big toe is bent inwards, towards the other foot.

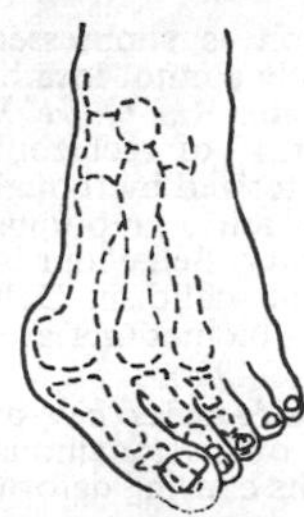
HALLUX VALGUS

halogens (*hal'-o-jens*). The chemical elements chlorine, iodine, bromine and fluorine.

halothane (*hal-o-thane'*). A volatile anaesthetic liquid derived from ether.

hamamelis (*ham-a-me'-lis*). Witch-hazel, employed as an astringent, especially in haemorrhoids.

hammer toe. A deformity in which the first phalanx is bent upwards, with plantar

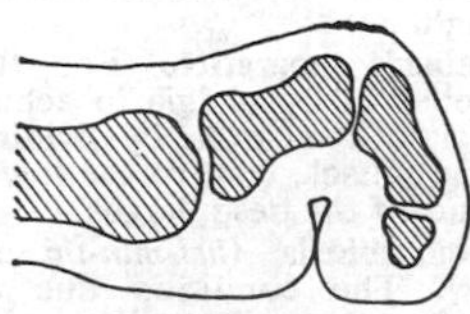
HAMMER TOE

flexion of the second and third phalanx.

hamstring muscles. The flexors of the knee joint that are situated at the back of the thigh.

handicapped (*hand'-e-kapt*). The term applied to a person with a mental or physical disability that interferes with normal living and earning capacity.

haploid (*hap'-loid*). The condition in which the cell contains one set of chromosomes after division. In man they divide into twenty-three in each gamete (*q.v.*).

hare-lip. A congenital fissure in the upper lip, often accompanied by cleft-palate. Treated by surgical repair when the child is very young.

Harris's operation. *See* Prostatectomy.

Harrison's sulcus (*sul-kus*). A depression in the chest wall above the diaphragm noticed in difficult breathing, especially in children.

Hartmann's solution (*hart'-man*). A valuable infusion fluid as it contains potassium and calcium chloride and lactic acid as well as sodium chloride. Used in the treatment of dehydration.

Hashimoto's disease (*hash-e-mo'-to*). A lymphadenoid goitre caused by the formation of antibodies to thyroglobulin. It is an autoimmune condition giving rise to hypothyroidism.

hashish (*hash'-ish*). Indian hemp. *See* Cannabis indica.

haustrations (*haws-tra'-shuns*). The pouches or sacculations of the colon.

Haversian canals (*hav-er'-se-an*). Minute canals permeating bone, containing blood and lymph vessels to maintain its nutrition. (*See also* Bone.)

hay fever. An acute catarrh affecting the nasal mucous membrane and the conjunctiva, and caused by hypersensitiveness to the pollen of grasses, etc. *See* Allergy.

healing. The process of return to normal function, after a period of disease or injury. *H. by first intention* signifies union of the edges of a clean incised wound without visible granulations, and leaving only a faint linear scar. *H. by second intention* is union of the edges of an open wound, by the formation of granulations which fill it in from the bottom and sides. These form fibrous tissue which contracts and causes an unsightly scar.

health. A state of physical, mental, and social well being.

heart. A hollow muscular organ which pumps the blood throughout the body, situated behind the sternum slightly towards the left side of the thorax. *H. block.* A form of heart disease in which the passage of impulses down the bundle of His is interrupted. It may be partial, in which every second or third beat is missed, or complete, in which there is a very slow myogenic beat uninfluenced by the nervous system. *See* Stokes-Adams syndrome. *H. failure.* May be acute, as in coronary thrombosis, or chronic. *Chronic congestive h. failure.* There is increasing congestion in the portal and pulmonary circulation and marked oedema.

heartburn. *See* Pyrosis.

heat exhaustion. Under very hot conditions there may be abdominal cramp, a rapid pulse, dizziness and dyspnoea caused by a lack of sodium chloride lost during excessive sweating.

heat stroke. A person exposed to great heat may fall unconscious, with a temperature of 40·6° to 42·2°C (105° to 108°F), because the sweat secretion is suppressed and the body cannot lose heat.

hebephrenia (*he-be-fre'-ne-ah*). A form of schizophrenia characterized by thought disorder and emotional incongruity. Behaviour is often silly and childish. Delusions and hallucinations are common.

Heberden's nodes (*heb'-er-den*). Bony or cartilaginous outgrowths causing deformity of the terminal finger joints in osteo-arthritis.

hectic (*hek'-tik*). Habitual. *H. fever. See* Fever. *H. flush.* A malar flush, seen in cases of phthisis.

Hegar's dilators (*ha'-gar*). A series of graduated dilators used to dilate the cervix uteri.

Hegar's sign. The marked softening of the cervix that takes place in early pregnancy.

heliotherapy (*he-le-o-ther'-ap-e*). Treatment of disease by exposure of the body to sunlight.

Heller's operation. For the relief of dysphagia in achalasia of the cardia, by dividing the muscle coat at the lower end of the oesophagus.

helminthiasis (*hel-min-thi'-as-is*). The condition due to infestation with worms.

hemeralopia (*hem-er-al-o'-pe-ah*). Inability to see in a bright light. *See also* Nyctalopia.

hemi- (*hem'-e*). Prefix meaning one half.

hemianopia (*hem-e-an-o'-pe-ah*). Partial blindness, in which the patient can see only one-half of the normal field of vision.

hemiballismus (*hem-e-bal-is'-mus*). Involuntary chorea like movements on one side of the body only.

hemicolectomy (*hem-e-ko-lek'-to-me*). The removal of the ascending and part of the transverse colon with an ileo-transverse colostomy.

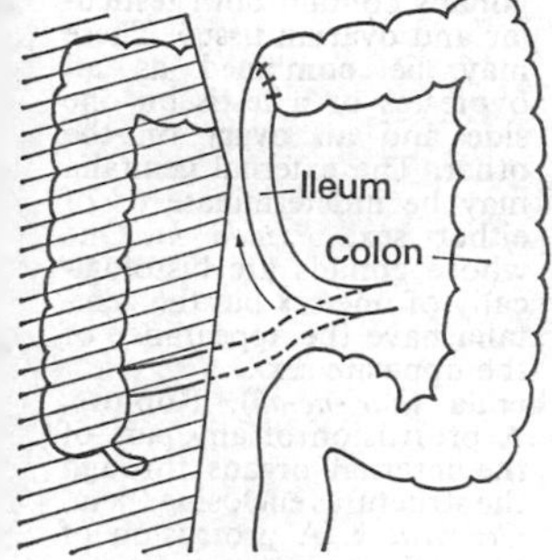

HEMICOLECTOMY AND ILEOTRANSVERSE COLOSTOMY
(shaded area is removed)

hemiglossectomy (*hem-e-glos-ek'-to-me*). Removal of approximately half the tongue.

hemiparesis (*hem-e-par-e'-sis*). A partial paralysis on one side of the body.

hemiplegia (*hem-e-ple'-je-ah*). Paralysis of one-half of the body, usually due to cerebral disease. The lesion is in the side of the brain opposite to the side paralysed, as the pyramidal fibres from each cerebral hemisphere cross in the medulla oblongata. If the right side is paralysed, speech is liable to be affected, as control of this is mainly in the left cerebrum. *Pontine h.* The cause is a lesion in the pons.

hemispheres (*hem'-is-feers*). The two halves of the cerebrum or cerebellum.

henbane (*hen'-bane*). *See* Hyoscyamus.

Henoch's purpura (*hen'-ok*). *See under* Purpura.

hepar (*he'-par*). The liver.

heparin (*hep'-ar-in*). An anticoagulant formed in the liver and circulated in the blood. Injected intravenously it prevents the conversion of prothrombin into thrombin, and is used in the treatment of thrombosis.

hepatalgia (*hep-at-al'-je-ah*). Pain in the liver.

hepatectomy (*hep-at-ek'-to-me*). Excision of a part or the whole of the liver.

hepatic (*he-pat'-ik*). Relating to the liver.

hepaticocholedochostomy (*hep'-at-ik-o-ko-le-dok-os'-to-me*). An anastomosis between the hepatic duct and the common bile duct.

hepaticojejunostomy (*hep'-at-ik-o-je-jun-os'-to-me*). The anastomosis of the hepatic duct to the jejunum usually following extensive excision for carcinoma of the pancreas.

hepaticostomy (*hep-at-ik-os'-to-me*). A surgical opening into the hepatic duct.

hepatitis (*hep-at-i'-tis*). Inflammation of the liver. *Amoebic h.* May arise during amoebic dysentery and lead to liver abscesses. *Infective h.* Caused by a virus (A or IH) spread by faecal contamination, incubation 2 to 6 weeks. *Serum h.* Occurs 6 weeks to 6 months after parenteral inoculation of the virus (B or SH) usually in blood or its products. Can be fatal.

hepatization (*hep-at-i-za'-shun*). Changing tissues into substance resembling liver.

Red h. The red solid appearance of the consolidated lung in specific pneumonia, due to the invasion of the alveoli by red blood cells and fibrin. *Grey h.* The grey appearance later in the disease before resolution occurs, when white blood cells invade the area, to destroy the infection.

hepatocele (*hep'-at-o-seel*). Hernia of the liver.

hepatocellular (*hep-at-o-sel'-u-lah*). Referring to the parenchymal cells of the liver.

hepatocirrhosis (*hep-at-o-sir-ro'-sis*). Cirrhosis of the liver.

hepatogenous (*hep-at-oj'-en-us*). Arising in the liver. Applied to jaundice where the disease arises in the parenchymal cells of the liver.

hepato-lenticular (*hep-at-o-len-tik'-u-lah*). Applied to a degenerative condition of hepatic fibrosis with neurological symptoms of Parkinsonism which is secondary to excessive copper absorption.

hepatolithiasis (*hep-at-o-lith-i'-as-is*). Calculi formation in the liver.

hepatoma (*hep-at-o'-mah*). A primary malignant tumour arising in the liver cells.

hepatomegaly (*hep-at-o-meg'-al-e*). An enlargement of the liver.

hepatosplenomegaly (*hep'-at-o-splen-o-meg'-al-e*). Enlargement of the liver and spleen as may be found in kala-azar (*q.v.*).

hepatotoxic (*hep-at-o-toks'-ik*). Applied to drugs and substances that cause destruction of liver cells.

hereditary (*her-ed'-it-ar-e*). Derived from ancestry. Inherited.

heredity (*her-ed'-it-e*). The characteristics both physical and mental derived from the parents and transmitted to the offspring. Recessive characteristics may miss one or two generations and reappear later.

hermaphrodite (*hur-maf'-ro-dite*). An individual whose gonads contain both testicular and ovarian tissue. These may be combined as an ovotestes or a testis on one side and an ovary on the other. The external genitalia may be indeterminate or of either sex. *Pseudo h.* One whose gonads are histologically of one sex but the genitalia have the appearance of the opposite sex.

hernia (*hur'-ne-ah*). Rupture. A protrusion of any part of the internal organs through the structures enclosing them. *Cerebral h.* A protrusion of brain through an opening in the skull. *Diaphragmatic h.* and *Hiatus h.* One part of the stomach through the oesophagal opening in the diaphragm. *Femoral h.* The loop of intestine protrudes through the femoral canal. More common in females. *Incisional* or *ventral h.* occurs

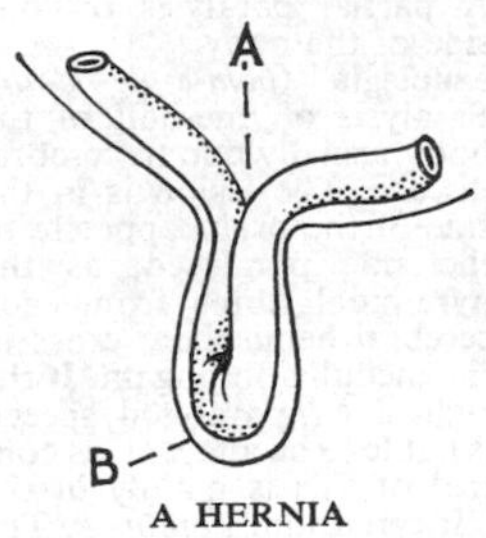

A HERNIA

A. Bowel.
B. Sac.

at the site of an old wound. *Inguinal h.* Protrusion of the intestine through the inguinal canal. This may be congenital or acquired, and is commonest in males. *Irreducible h.* One that cannot be replaced by manipulation *Reducible h.* One that can be returned to its normal position by manipulative measures. *Strangulated h.* The neck of the sac containing the bowel is so constricted that the venous circulation is impeded, and gangrene will result if not treated promptly. Constipation is complete. *Umbilical h.* Protrusion of bowel through the umbilical ring. This may be congenital or acquired. *Vaginal h.* Rectocele or cystocele (*q.v.*).

hernioplasty (*her'-ne-o-plas-te*). A plastic repair of the abdominal wall is performed after reducing the hernia. This may be by fascia, nylon or filigree wire.

herniorrhaphy (*her-ne-or'-raf-e*). Removal of the hernial sac and repair of the abdominal wall.

herniotomy (*her-ne-ot'-o-me*). An operation to remove the hernial sac.

heroin (*her'-o-in*). A diacetate of morphine used as an analgesic; it is a strong drug of addiction and its use is now discouraged.

herpes (*her'-peez*). An inflammatory skin eruption showing small vesicles. *H. simplex.* An eruption which appears around the mouth due to a virus. *H. zoster.* Shingles. In which the eruption follows the course of a cutaneous nerve; the inflammation affecting the sensory ganglion of the nerve root just as it leaves the spinal cord. Pain can be very severe.

Herxheimer reaction (*Herks'-hi-mer*). An inflammatory reaction in the tissues in cases of syphilis, which can occur on starting treatment.

hetero-. A prefix meaning other or different.

heterochromia (*het-er-o-kro'-me-ah*). A difference in colour in the two eyes. It may be congenital or secondary due to inflammation.

heterogenous (*het-er-oj'-en-us*). Composed of diverse constituents or derived from different sources.

heteroplasty (*het'-er-o-plas-te*). The plastic operation in which the graft is obtained from an animal not of the same species.

heterosexual (*het-er-o-seks'-u-al*). The attraction for, and desire to establish an emotional relationship with someone of the opposite sex.

heterotropia (*het-er-o-tro'-pe-ah*). A marked deviation of the eyes. Strabismus or squint.

heterozygous (*het-er-o-zi'-gus*). Possessing dissimilar alternative genes for a physical characteristic, that are inherited one from each parent. One gene is dominant and the other is recessive.

hexamine (*heks'-a-meen*). A urinary antiseptic which releases formaldehyde in an acid urine.

hexachlorophene (*heks-a-klor'-o-fen*). An antiseptic often added to soap, soap solutions, or dusting powder and which greatly reduces the bacteria on the skin.

Hg. Symbol for mercury (hydrargyrum).

hiatus (*hi-a'-tus*). A space or

opening. *H. hernia.* Protrusion of the fundus of the stomach through the oesophageal opening in the diaphragm.

hiccup (*hik'-kup*). Hiccough. A spasmodic contraction of the diaphragm causing an abrupt inspiratory sound.

hidrosis (*hi-dro'-sis*). Excretion of sweat.

Higginson's syringe. An india-rubber syringe with a bulb in the centre which, when compressed, forces fluid forward through the nozzle. It can be used with suitable attachments for irrigation of any cavity of the body, e.g. antra, rectum or vagina.

hilum (*hi'-lum*). A recess in an organ, by which vessels enter and leave it.

hip. The upper part of the thigh at its junction with the pelvis. *H. replacement.* An operation in which the head of the femur and cup of the acetabulum are replaced by a metal prosthesis. *See* Arthroplasty.

Hippocratic (*hip-po-krat'-ik*). Relating to Hippocrates, the Father of Medicine. *H. oath.* The still accepted standard of medical ethics, attributed to Hippocrates. *H. facies. See under* Facies.

hippuric acid test (*hip-ur'-ik*). *See under* Test.

Hirschsprung's disease (*heersh'-sprung*). *See* Megacolon.

hirsute (*hur'-sute*). Hairy.

hirudin (*hi-ru'-din*). The active principle in the secretion of the leech which prevents clotting of blood.

Hirudo (*hi-ru'-do*). The leech (*q.v.*).

histamine (*hist'-a-min*). An enzyme that causes local vasodilatation and increased permeability of the blood vessel walls. It is readily released from body tissues and is a factor in allergy response. Injected subcutaneously, it greatly increases gastric secretion of hydrochloric acid and is used to test for the same.

histiocytes (*his'-te-o-sites*). The macrophage cells of connective tissue. Derived from the reticulo-endothelial cells they act as scavengers.

histiocytoma (*his-te-o-si-to'-mah*). A benign tumour of histiocytes causing a vascular nodule.

histiocytosis (*his-te-o-si'-to-sis*). A group of diseases of bone in which granuloma appear containing histiocytes and eosinophil cells.

histocompatibility (*his-to-kom-pat-i-bil'-it-e*). The ability of cells to be accepted and to function in a new situation. Tissue typing reveals this and ensures a higher success rate in organ transplantation.

histology (*his-tol'-o-je*). The science dealing with the minute structure of tissues.

histolysis (*his-tol'-is-is*). Disintegration of tissues.

histoplasmosis (*his-to-plas-mo'-sis*). Inhalation of a yeast-like fungus causing a lung infection and rarely spreading throughout the reticulo-endothelial system.

hobnail liver. *See under* Liver.

Hodgkin's disease (*hodj'-kin*). Lymphadenoma. A progressive malignant condition of the reticulo-endothelial cells. There is progressive enlargement of lymph nodes and lymph tissue all over the body. Treated by radiotherapy and cytotoxic drugs.

Hogben test. *See* Test.

Homan's sign (*Ho'-man*). Pain elicited in the calf when the foot is dorsiflexed. Indicative of venous thrombosis.

homatropine (*ho-mat'-ro-pin*). A mydriatic (*q.v.*) derived from *atropine*, and used in ophthalmic practice. Its effect is more transitory than that of atropine, and therefore it is used to dilate the pupil for examination of the disc, and not as treatment.

homeo- (*ho'-me-o*). A prefix meaning 'similar'.

homeopathy (*ho-me-op'-athe*). A system promulgated by Hahnemann and based upon the principle that 'like cures like'. Drugs are given which produce in the patient the signs of the disease to be cured, but they are usually prescribed in very small doses.

homeostasis (*ho-me-o-sta'-sis*). Automatic self regulation of man to maintain the normal or standard state of the body under variations in the environment.

homeothermic (*ho-me-o-ther'-mik*). Warm-blooded animals, where the heat regulating mechanism maintains a constant body temperature in spite of the environment.

homicide (*hom'-e-side*). The killing of a human being, whether intentional (murder) or accidental (manslaughter).

homogenize (*ho-moj'-e-nize*). To reduce to the same consistency. A complete meal can be reduced in this way to a liquid or semi-solid state when there is difficulty in feeding.

homogenous (*hom-oj'-en-us*). Uniform in character. Similar in nature and characteristics.

homograft (*ho'-mo-graft*). A tissue or organ transplanted from one individual to another of the same species.

homolateral (*ho-mo-lat'-er-al*). On the same side.

homologous (*ho-mol'-o-gus*). Having a corresponding origin, structure and position. *H. chromosomes.* Those that pair during meiosis and contain an identical arrangement of genes in the DNA pattern.

homologue (*hom'-o-log*). A part or organ which has the same relative position or structure as another one.

homoplasty (*ho'-mo-plas-te*). Replacement by operation of a part or tissue of similar structure from another person of the same species.

homosexual (*hom-o-seks'-u-al*). Of the same sex.

homosexuality (*hom-o-seks-u-al'-it-e*). The attraction for and desire to establish an emotional relationship with a member of the same sex.

homozygous (*ho-mo-zi'-gus*). Possessing an identical pair of genes for a physical characteristic. *See also* Heterozygous.

hookworm. *See* Ankylostoma.

hordeolum (*hor-de-o'-lum*). A stye. Inflammation of sebaceous glands of eyelashes.

hormone (*hor'-mone*). A chemical substance which is generated in one organ, and carried by the blood to another in which it excites activity.

hormonotherapy (*hor'-mon-o-ther'-ap-e*). Treatment by the use of hormones.

horseshoe kidney. *See under* Kidney.

host. The animal or tissue on which a parasite lives and multiplies. *Intermediate h.* One that shelters the parasite during a non-reproductive period.

hour-glass contraction. A contraction near the middle of a hollow organ, such as the stomach or uterus, producing an outline resembling that shape. Due to muscle spasm or scar tissue formation as the result of inflammation.

housemaid's knee. Prepatellar bursitis. Inflammation of the prepatellar bursa, which becomes distended with serous fluid. It is caused by constant kneeling on hard surfaces.

humerus (*hu'-mer-us*). The bone of the upper arm.

humidity (*hu-mid'-it-e*). The amount of moisture in the air. *Relative h.* The humidity of the atmosphere compared with what it would be if the air were saturated.

humour (*hu'-mor*). Any fluid of the body, such as lymph, aqueous humour, etc.

hunger pain. Pain associated with peptic ulcer which is relieved by taking food.

Huntingdon's chorea (*Hunt'-ing-ton*). An hereditary type which may occur in adults. Choreic signs are marked and the mental powers may be affected, leading to dementia. The disease is progressive.

Hutchinson's teeth. Typical notching of the borders of the incisor teeth occurring in congenital syphilis.

hyaline (*hi'-al-een*). Resembling glass. *H. cartilage. See* Cartilage. *H. casts. See* Casts. *H. cells.* Clear white blood cells. *H. degeneration.* A form which occurs in tumours due to deficiency of blood supply. It precedes cystic degeneration. *H. membrane disease. See* Respiratory distress syndrome.

hyalitis (*hi-al-i'-tis*). Inflammation of the hyaloid membrane or vitreous humour in the eyeball.

hyaloid membrane (*hi'-al-oid*). A delicate transparent membrane surrounding the vitreous humour of the eye.

hyaluronidase (*hi-al-u-ron'-e-daze*). An enzyme which facilitates the absorption of fluids in subcutaneous tissues. Hyalase is a proprietary preparation of the enzyme.

hybrid (*hi'-brid*). The offspring of distinct but related members of a species.

hydatid (*hi-dat'-id*). A cystic swelling containing the embryo of the *Taenia echinococcus* (*q.v.*). It may be found in any organ of the body, e.g. in the liver. 'Daughter cysts' are produced from the original. Infection is from contaminated foods, e.g. salads.

hydatidiform mole (*hi-dat-id'-e-form*). *See under* Mole.

hydraemia (*hi-dre'-me-ah*). A high fluid content in the blood rendering it more dilute.

hydragogue (*hi'-drah-gog*). A purgative causing copious liquid evacuations, e.g. magnesium sulphate, jalap.

hydramnios (*hi-dram'-ne-os*). An excessive amount of amniotic fluid.

hydrargyrism (*hi-drar'-je-rizm*). Chronic mercurial poisoning.

hydrarthrosis (*hi-drar-thro'-sis*). A collection of fluid in a joint.

hydrate (*hi'-drate*). A compound of an element with water.

hydro- (*hi'-dro*). A prefix referring to either water or hydrogen.

hydroa (*hi-dro'-ah*). A hypersensitivity of the skin to light, resulting in the formation of a vesicular eruption on the exposed parts with intense irritation.

hydrocarbon (*hi-dro-kar'-bon*). A compound of hydrogen and carbon. Fats are of this type.

hydrocele (*hi'-dro-seel*). A swelling caused by accumulation of fluid, especially in the tunica vaginalis surrounding the testicle.

hydrocephalus (*hi-dro-kef'-al-us*). 'Water on the brain'. Enlargement of the skull due to an abnormal collection of cerebrospinal fluid around the brain or in the ventricles. It may be congenital or acquired from inflammation of the meninges during infancy. *See* Toxoplasmosis.

hydrochloric acid (*hi-dro-klor'-ik*). HCl. A colourless compound of hydrogen and chlorine. In 0·2 per cent solution it is present in gastric juice and aids digestion.

hydrochlorothiazide (*hi'-dro-klor-o-thi'-a-zide*). A valuable oral diuretic similar to but more potent than chlorothiazide. Proprietary preparations are Esidrex and Hydrosaluric.

hydrocortisone (*hi-dro-kor'-te-zone*). Cortisol. A hormone isolated from the secretion of the adrenal cortex. It affects carbohydrate and protein metabolism and is anti-inflammatory. Used for topical application in eye, ear and skin conditions. Also used as intra-articular injection for arthritis and intravenously in status asthmaticus and in acute adreno-cortical insufficiency.

hydrocyanic acid (*hi-dro-si-an'-ik*). A highly poisonous acid from bitter almonds. Prussic acid.

hydroflumethiazide (*hi-dro-flu-meth-i'-az-ide*). An oral thiazide diuretic. Naclex is a proprietary preparation.

hydrogen (*hi'-dro-jen*). A combustible gas, present in nearly all organic compounds which, in combination with oxygen, forms water. *H. ion concentration*. The amount of hydrogen in a liquid, which is responsible for its acidity. Expressed as the hydrogen exponent pH. The concentration in the blood is of importance in acidosis. *H. peroxide* (H_2O_2). An antiseptic. When in contact with pus the oxygen is released and causes frothing. It has also a bleaching action.

hydrolysis (*hi-drol'-is-is*). The process of splitting up into smaller molecules by uniting with water.

hydrometer (*hi-drom'-e-ter*). An instrument for estimating the specific gravity of fluids, e.g. a urinometer.

hydrometra (*hi-dro-me'-trah*). A collection of watery fluid in the uterus.

hydronephrosis (*hi-dro-nef-ro'-sis*). A collection of urine in the pelvis of the kidney, resulting in atrophy of the kidney structure, due to the constant pressure of the fluid, until finally the whole organ becomes one large cyst. The condition may be: (1) congenital, due to malformation of the kidney or ureter; (2) acquired due to any obstruction of the ureter by tumour, or stone, or to back pressure from stricture of the urethra or enlarged prostate gland.

hydropathy (*hi-drop'-ath-e*). The unscientific treatment of disease by the use of water.

hydropericarditis (*hi-dro-per-e-kard-i'-tis*). Inflammation of the pericardium resulting in serous fluid in the pericardial sac.

hydroperitoneum (*hi-dro-per-e-ton-e'-um*). *See* Ascites.

hydrophobia (*hi-dro-fo'-be-ah*). An acute infectious disease contracted by man through a bite from an animal infected with *rabies*. Caused by a virus present in the saliva. The symptoms include violent spasms of the muscles of deglutition, which are greatly aggravated by the sight of water. There are mental delusions, fever and a profuse flow of saliva. There is a long incubation period, so immediate inoculation with *anti-rabic vaccine* provides complete protection.

hydropneumothorax (*hi-dro-nu-mo-thor'-aks*). The presence of fluid and air in the pleural space.

hydrops (*hi'-drops*). Dropsy. *H. abdominis.* Ascites. *H. foetalis.* Severe form of erythroblastosis foetalis (*q.v.*). *H. tubae.* Hydrosalpinx.

hydrorachis (*hi-dror'-rak-is*). Effusion into the spinal canal.

hydrorrhoea gravidarum (*hi-dror-re'-ah grav-id-ar'-um*). An abnormal discharge of fluid during pregnancy due to excessive mucous secretion from the endometrium.

hydrosalpinx (*hi-dro-sal'-pinks*). Distension of the Fallopian tube by fluid.

Hydrosaluric (*hi-dro-sal-ur'-ik*). A proprietary preparation of hydrochlorothiazide. An oral diuretic.

hydrostatic test (*hi-dro-stat'-ik*). Determining that live birth has taken place by floating the fetal lungs in water.

hydrotherapeutics (*hi-dro-ther-ap-u'-tiks*). The treatment of disease by water.

hydrothorax (*hi-dro-thor'-aks*). Fluid in the pleural cavity due to serous effusion as in cardiac, renal and other diseases.

hygiene (*hi'-jeen*). The science of health. *Communal h.* Deals with the maintenance of the health of the community by provision of a pure water supply, efficient sanitation good housing, etc. *Industrial h.* Care of the health of workers in industry. *Mental h.* Deals with the healthy development of the mental outlook and emotional reactions. *Mouth h.* The efficient care and cleanliness of the mouth and teeth, especially important in illness. *Personal h.* Deals with measures taken by the individual to preserve his own health.

hygroma (*hi-grom'-ah*). A tumour of water. *Subdural h.* A collection of clear fluid in the subdural space.

hygrometer (*hi-grom'-et-er*). An instrument for measuring the water vapour in the air.

hygroscopic (*hi-gro-skop'-ik*). Readily absorbing moisture. *Glycerin* is used in medical treatment because it has this power, e.g. in treating chapped hands; and its use as a suppository to relieve constipation.

hymen (*hi'-men*). A fold of mucous membrane partially

closing the entrance to the vagina.

hymenectomy (*hi-men-ek'-to-me*). The surgical removal of the hymen.

hymenotomy (*hi-men-ot'-o-me*). A surgical incision of the hymen to render the orifice larger.

hyoid bone (*hi'-oid*). A U-shaped bone above the thyroid cartilage, to which the tongue is attached.

hyoscine (*hi'-os-sin*). Scopolamine. An alkaloid obtained from solanaceous plants. It is a powerful cerebral depressant and may be used in acute mania. It diminishes glandular secretions, so it is used with papaveretum pre-operatively and is a recognized preventive to sea sickness.

hyoscyamus (*hi-o-si'-am-us*). Henbane. The dried leaves have an antispasmodic action which relieves the pain of excessive peristalsis or of cystitis.

hypaemia (*hi-pe'-me-ah*). Deficiency of blood in a part.

hypaesthesia (*hip-es-the'-ze-ah*). Impairment of sensation.

hypamnios (*hip-am'-ne-os*). Lessened fluid in the amniotic sac.

hyper- Greek prefix meaning 'above'.

hyperacidity (*hi-per-as-id'-it-e*). Excessive acidity. *Gastric h.* Hyperchlorhydria (*q.v.*).

hyperaemia (*hi-per-e'-me-ah*). Excess of blood in any part.

hyperaesthesia (*hi-per-es-the'-ze-ah*). Excessively acute feeling in any part.

hyperalgesia (*hi-per-al-ge'-ze-ah*). Excessive sensibility to pain.

hyperasthenia (*hi-per-as-the'-ne-ah*). Extreme weakness.

hyperbaric (*hi-per-bar'-ik*). At greater pressure than normal. *H. oxygen. See* Appendix 4.

hypercalcaemia (*hi-per-kal-se'-me-ah*). Rise in blood calcium.

hypercarbia (*hi-per-kar'-be-ah*). An increase in the carbon dioxide content of blood.

hypercalcuria (*hi-per-kal-sur'-e-ah*). A high level of calcium in the urine leading to renal stone formation.

hypercapnia (*hi-per-kap'-ne-ah*). An increased amount of carbon dioxide in the blood causing over stimulation of the respiratory centre.

hypercatabolism (*hi-per-kat-ab'-ol-izm*). An excessive rate of catabolism. The rapid breakdown of protein or tissue.

hyperchlorhydria (*hi-per-klor-hi'-dre-ah*). Excess of hydrochloric acid in the gastric juice.

hyperchromic (*hi-per-kro'-mik*). Highly coloured or stained.

hyperdynamia (*hi-per-di-nam'-e-ah*). Excessive muscle activity. *H. uteri.* Excessive uterine contractions in labour.

hyperemesis (*hi-per-em'-es-is*). Excessive vomiting. *H. gravidarum.* A complication of pregnancy which may be serious.

hyperextension (*hi-per-eks-ten'-shun*). A form of over-extension used to correct orthopaedic deformities.

hyperflexion (*hi-per-flek'-shun*). Over-flexion of a limb.

hyperglycaemia (*hi-per-gli-se'-me-ah*). Excess of sugar in the blood (*normal* 0·08 to 0·12 per cent); a sign of diabetes mellitus.

hyperhidrosis (*hi-per-hi-dro'-sis*). Excessive perspiration.

hyperimmune gamma-globulin

(*hi-per-im-mu'-n*). *See* Immunoglobulin.

hyperkalaemia (*hi-per-kal-e'-me-ah*). A higher than normal concentration of potassium in the blood.

hyperkeratosis (*hi-per-ker-a-to'-sis*). A hyperplasia or overgrowth of the horny layers of the skin.

hyperkinesis (*hi-per-ki-ne'-sis*). A condition in which there is excessive movement.

hyperlipaemia (*hi-per-lip-e'-me-ah*). An increase in the fat content of blood. There may also be a rise in blood cholesterol.

hypermetropia (*hi-per-met-ro'-pe-ah*). Hyperopia. Far-sightedness. The light rays converge beyond the retina and a biconvex lens (*q.v.*) is required to correct it.

hypermnesia (*hi-perm-ne'-ze-ah*). Outstanding power of memory; may be found in infant prodigies or in some forms of mania.

hypermotility (*hi-per-mo-til'-it-e*). Increased movement. *Gastric h.* Increased muscle action of the stomach wall, associated with increased secretion of hydrochloric acid.

hypernatraemia (*hi-per-nat-re'-me-ah*). An increase in the sodium content of the blood plasma. The cause may be water depletion but it may arise in high protein tube feeding.

hypernephroma (*hi-per-nef-ro'-mah*). A malignant tumour of the kidney.

hyperosmolarity (*hi-per-os-mo-lar'-it-e*). A greater osmotic pressure than normal, usually applied to that exerted by salts and plasma proteins in the blood.

hyperostosis (*hi-per-os-to'-sis*). Thickening of bone: a bony outgrowth.

hyperparathyroidism (*hi-per-par-ah-thi'-roid-izm*). Excessive activity of the parathyroid glands, causing drainage of calcium from the bones, with consequent fragility and liability to spontaneous fracture.

hyperphagia (*hi-per-fa'-ge-ah*). Over-eating.

hyperpiesis (*hi-per-pi-e'-sis*). Abnormally high blood-pressure. *See* Hypertension.

hyperpituitarism (*hi-per-pit-u'-it-ar-izm*). Over-activity of the pituitary body causing acromegaly or gigantism.

hyperplasia (*hi-per-pla'-ze-ah*). Excessive formation of tissue.

hyperpnoea (*hi-perp-ne'-ah*). Deep breathing with marked use of abdominal muscles. Present in diseases in which there is acidosis (*q.v.*).

hyperpyrexia (*hi-per-pi-reks'-e-ah*). Excessively high body temperature, i.e. 40·6° to 43·3°C (105° to 110°F).

hypersecretion (*hi-per-se-kre'-shun*). Profuse secretion.

hypersensitive (*hi-per-sen'-sit-iv*). (1) Abnormally sensitive. (2) An allergic state. *See* Allergy.

hypersplenism (*hi-per-splen'-izm*). Over-activity of an enlarged spleen in the destruction of blood cells and platelets.

hypertension (*hi-per-ten'-shun*). A raised blood pressure. It is dependent on cardiac output and the resistance of the blood vessels. Systolic and diastolic readings are taken. Also termed hyperpiesis. *Essential h.* High blood pressure without demonstrable change in kidneys, blood vessels, or heart. *Malignant h.* A form of hyperpiesis which develops at a comparatively early age, and in which the prognosis is poor. *Portal h.* A raised pressure in the portal system, most often due to hepatic cirrhosis.

hyperthermia (*hi-per-ther'-me-ah*). Applied to a treatment in which a high body temperature is induced.

hyperthyroidism (*hi-per-thi'-roid-izm*). The symptoms produced by excessive thyroid secretion. This affects: (1) the metabolic process which is speeded up. The appetite is large but weight is lost. The temperature tends to be above normal, and respirations are increased; (2) the nervous system. The patient is very excitable and restless. Sleeplessness is present. Stimulation of the sympathetic nerves causes diarrhoea and excessive sweating. Exophthalmos may be present. The pulse is rapid, and auricular fibrillation is common.

hypertonic (*hi-per-ton'-ik*). (1) Excessive tone or tension as in a blood vessel or muscle. (2) Applied to solutions which are stronger than physiological saline. *H. saline.* May be used for treating infected wounds and as an enema to treat thread worms.

hypertrichiasis (*hi-per-trik-i'-as-is*). Excessive growth of hair on any part of the body.

hypertrophy (*hi-per'-tro-fe*). Excessive thickening of a part or organ by increase of its own tissues. *Compensatory h.* of cardiac muscle occurs in valvular disease of the heart to maintain the circulation by giving increased power.

hyperuricaemia (*hi-per-u-re-se'-me-ah*). A high level of uric acid in the blood as may be found in gout.

hyperventilation (*hi-per-ven-til-a'-shun*). Over breathing often associated with emotional upset. This lowers the dissolved carbon dioxide in the blood plasma which tends to alkalinity.

hyphaemia (*hi-fe'-me-ah*). Haemorrhage into the anterior chamber of the eye.

hypnosis (*hip-no'-sis*). An artificially induced state resembling sleep, in which there is increased suggestibility which may be used to abolish symptoms in hysterical states. It may also be favoured as a means of anaesthesia in childbirth and tooth extraction.

hypnotic (*hip-not'-ik*). An agent which causes sleep.

hypnotism (*hip'-not-izm*). The practice of hypnosis.

hypo- (*hi'-po*). Greek prefix meaning 'below'.

hypoalbuminaemia (*hi-po-al-bu-min-e'-me-ah*). A lack of serum albumin in the blood plasma leading to oedema in the tissues.

hypocalcaemia (*hi-po-kal-se'-me-ah*). Deficiency of blood calcium.

hypochlorhydria (*hi-po-klor-hi'-dre-ah*). A less than normal amount of hydrochloric acid in the gastric juice.

hypochlorite (*hi-po-klor'-ite*). A chlorine compound that is an effective disinfectant of clean articles but not in the presence of blood.

hypochondria (*hi-po-kon'-dre-ah*). A morbid preoccupation or anxiety about one's health.

The sufferer feels that first one part of his body and then another part is the seat of some serious disease.

hypochondriac (*hi-po-kon'-dre-ak*). One affected by hypochondria. *H. region.* The upper abdominal region situated on either side under the lower ribs and costal cartilages.

hypochondrium (*hi-po-kon'-dre-um*). The upper region of the abdomen on each side of the epigastrium.

hypochromic (*hi-po-kro'-mik*). Deficiency in pigmentation or colouring.

hypodermic (*hi-po-der'-mik*). Beneath the skin; applied to subcutaneous injections.

hypofibrinogenaemia (*hi-po-fib-rin-o-jen-e'-me-ah*). A lack of fibrinogen in the blood. This may occur in severe trauma or haemorrhage or with over-activity of fibrinolysins.

hypogammaglobulinaemia (*hi-po-gam-ma-glob-u-lin-e'-me-ah*). A deficiency of gammaglobulin in the blood rendering the person susceptible to infection.

hypogastrium (*hi-po-gas'-tre-um*). The lower middle area of the abdomen, immediately below the umbilical region.

hypoglossal (*hi-po-glos'-sal*). Under the tongue. *H. nerve.* The twelfth cranial nerve.

hypoglycaemia (*hi-po-gli-se'-me-ah*). The blood-sugar is less than normal. Usually arising in diabetic patients having insulin, due to too high a dose, delay in eating or a rapid combustion of carbohydrate. *See also* Hyperglycaemia.

hypokalaemia (*hi-po-kal-e'-me-ah*). A low potassium level in the blood plasma. This is likely to be present in dehydration and with repeated use of diuretics.

hypomania (*hi-po-ma'-ne-ah*). A degree of elation, excitement and activity higher than normal but less severe than that present in mania.

hyponatraemia (*hi-po-nat-re'-me-ah*). A deficiency of sodium in the blood. This is accompanied by an excess of water over electrolytes.

hypo-osmolarity (*hi-po-os-mo-lar'-it-e*). In medicine the term for decreased osmotic pressure in the blood.

hypoparathyroidism (*hi-po-par-ah-thi'-roid-izm*). A lack of parathyroid secretion leading to a low blood calcium and tetany.

hypophysectomy (*hi-pof-is-sek'-to-me*). Excision of the pituitary gland.

hypophysis cerebri (*hi-pof'-is-is ser'-e-bri*). The pituitary gland.

hypopiesis (*hi-po-pi-e'-sis*). Abnormally low blood pressure.

hypopituitarism (*hi-po-pit-u'-it-ar-izm*). Deficiency of secretion from the anterior lobe of the pituitary gland, causing excessive deposit of fat and infantilism in children. *See* Frohlich's syndrome. Dwarfism (Lorain type) may result. In adults asthenia, drowsiness, and increased sugar tolerance, adiposity and sometimes polyuria are present.

hypoplasia (*hi-po-pla'-ze-ah*). Imperfect development of a part or organ.

hypoproteinaemia (*hi-po-pro-tin-e'-me-ah*). A deficiency of serum proteins in the blood. The cause may be dietary or excessive loss.

hypopyon (*hi-po'-pe-on*). A collection of pus in the anterior chamber of thc eye.

hyposecretion (*hi-po-se-kre'-shun*). Under secretion from any glandular structure or secreting cells.

hypospadias (*hi-po-spa'-de-as*). A malformation in which the canal of the urethra opens upon the under surface of the penis.

hypostasis (*hi-pos'-ta-sis*). (1) A sediment or deposit. (2) Congestion of blood in a part, due to slowing of the circulation.

hypostatic (*hi-po-stat'-ik*). Relating to hypostasis. *H. pneumonia. See under* Pneumonia.

hyposthenia (*hi-pos-the'-ne-ah*). Weakness; decreased strength.

hypotension (*hi-po-ten'-shun*). A low blood pressure. *Controlled* or *induced h.* An artificially produced lowering of the blood pressure so that an operation field is rendered practically bloodless.

hypotensive (*hi-po-ten'-sif*). A reduction in tension. A drug that lowers the blood pressure.

hypothalamus (*hi-po-thal'-a-mus*). Part of the brain situated at its base and concerned with temperature control, hunger, thirst and emotional changes.

hypothermia (*hi-po-ther'-me-ah*). Cooling of the body to reduce the oxygen requirements of the tissues. *Mild h.* Reduction of the body temperature to 34°C (93°F) may be induced by surface cooling with cold air and may be used for head injuries. *Conventional h.* Reduction to 30°C (86°F) may be done by immersion in cold water and allows arrest of the circulation for 9 min, without cerebral damage. Short heart operations may be performed. *Profound h.* A reduction to 10° to 15°C (50° to 59°F) allows 1 hr for open heart surgery but the blood must still receive oxygen. This may be done by using a pump oxygenator (*heart lung machine*) and heat exchanger or by using a heat exchanger and the patient's own lungs to oxygenate the blood. The latter appears to damage the blood less and give a smoother convalescence.

hypothesis (*hi-poth'-e-sis*). A theory which attempts to explain, e.g. the cause of a disease.

hypothrombinaemia (*hi-po-throm-bin-e'-me-ah*). A diminished amount of thrombin in the blood with a consequent tendency to bleed.

hypothyroidism (*hi-po-thi'-roid-izm*). Insufficiency of thyroid secretion. *See* Myxoedema.

hypotonia (*hi-po-to'-ne-ah*). (1) Deficient muscle tone. (2) Diminished tension in the eyeball.

hypatonic (*hi-po-ton'-ik*). Describes solutions which are more diluted than normally used. Less than isotonic. *See also* Hypertonic.

hypoventilation (*hi-po-ven-til-a'-shun*). Diminished breathing or inadequate ventilation by mechanical means.

hypovolaemia (*hi-po-vol-e'-me-ah*). A reduction in the circulating blood volume due to external loss of body fluids or to loss from the blood into the tissues as in shock.

hypoxaemia (*hi-poks-e'-me-ah*).

An insufficient oxygen content in the blood.

hypoxia (*hi-poks'-e-ah*). A diminished amount of oxygen in the tissues. *Anaemic h.* Due to deficiency of haemoglobulin in the blood. *Histotoxic h.* Due to failure of the cells to extract oxygen from the blood. Occurs in cyanide poisoning. *Hypoxic h.* Due to lung disease or shortage of oxygen in inspired air so that oxygen cannot enter blood. *Stagnant h.* Due to reduction in blood flow.

hysteralgia (*his-ter-al'-je-ah*). Neuralgic pain in the uterus.

hysterectomy (*his-ter-ek'-to-me*). Removal of the uterus. *Abdominal h.* Removal via an abdominal incision. *Pan-h.* An old term for removal of uterus and adnexa. *Subtotal h.* Removal of the body of the uterus only. *Total h.* Removal of the body and the cervix. *Vaginal h.* Removal per vaginam. *Wertheim's h.* The parametrium, upper vagina, and lymph glands are excised in addition.

hysteria (*his-te'-re-ah*). A psychoneurosis manifesting itself in various disorders of the mind and body. There are mental and physical symptoms, not of organic origin, produced and maintained by motives of which the patient is unconscious, but directed at some real or fancied gain to be derived from them. *Conversion h.* The hysteria takes the form of loss of function of some part of the body. This may be loss of memory, vision or hearing or loss of muscle power or feeling in a hand or leg. The so called 'paralysis' or numbness does not correspond to the nerve distribution.

hysterical (*his-ter'-ik-l*). Relating to hysteria.

hysterocele (*his'-ter-o-seel*). A hernia containing part of the uterus.

hysteromyoma (*his-ter-o-mi-o'-mah*). A muscle tumour of the uterus.

hysteromyomectomy (*his-ter-o-mi-o-mek'-to-me*). Excision of a hysteromyoma.

hysteropathy (*his-ter-op'-ath-e*). Any uterine disease.

hysteropexy (*his'-ter-o-peks-e*). Fixation of the uterus to the abdominal wall, to remedy displacement. *See* Ventrofixation.

hysteroptosis (*his-ter-op-to'-sis*). Prolapse of the uterus.

hysterosalpingography (*his'-ter-o-sal-ping-gog'-raf-e*). An X-ray examination of the uterus and uterine tubes following the injection of a radio-opaque dye.

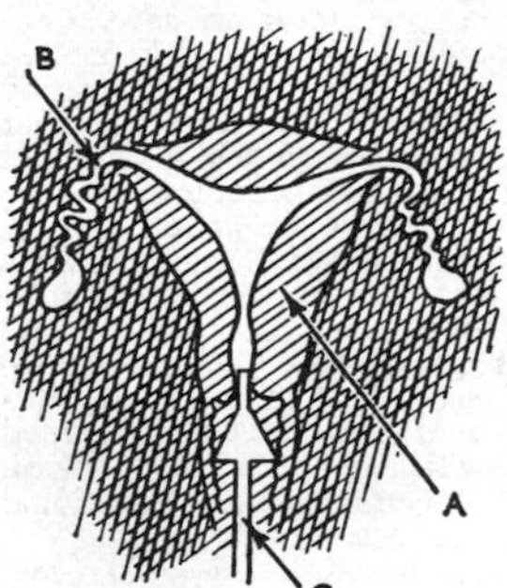

A HYSTEROSALPINGOGRAM

A. Uterus.
B. Uterine tube.
C. Cannula.

hysterosalpingostomy (*his'-ter-o-sal-ping-gos'-to-me*). Establishing an opening between the distal portion of the uterine tube and the uterus in an effort to overcome infertility when the medial portion is occluded or excised.

hysterotomy (*his-ter-ot'-o-me*). Incision of the uterus. *See* Caesarean section.

I

I. The symbol for iodine.

-iasis (*i'-as-is*). A suffix meaning 'condition of'.

iatrogenic (*i-a-tro-jen'-ik*). A condition produced when ill-advised treatments cause a worsening of a patient's condition.

ice. Water in a solid state, at or below freezing-point. *I. bag.* A rubber bag half-filled with pieces of ice and applied near or to a part. *I. compress*, is made of lint wrung out of ice-cold water. *I.-water enema.* A treatment used to reduce temperature in hyperpyrexia.

ichor (*i'-kor*). A thin colourless discharge from ulcers and raw wounds.

ichthyol (*ik'-the-ol*). A mineral preparation rich in the remains of fossilized fishes. Used for skin diseases, and as an application for erosion of the cervix.

ichthyosis (*ik-the-o'-sis*). A congenital abnormality of the skin in which there is dryness, roughness, and the horny layer is thickened and large scales appear. These patients are liable to eczema and industrial dermatitis.

icterus (*ik'-ter-us*). Jaundice. *I. gravis.* A fatal form of jaundice occurring in pregnancy. *I. gravis neonatorum.* Haemolytic disease of the newborn. *See* Rhesus factor.

id. The most primitive part of the personality, containing the instinctive drives, which lives in the unconscious.

idea (*i-de'-ah*). A mental image and the meaning attached to it. *Association of i.s.* Ideas that recall to the mind associated objects or occasions due to some similarity or contrast. *Flight of i.s.* A mode of speech in which the person passes rapidly from one idea to the next with only a slight association between them, being unable to maintain a course of thought. *I.s of reference.* Thoughts based on some external circumstances that the patient thinks refers to himself when no such thing is intended. *I.s of unreality.* The patient feels as if everything has changed and that things look different and unreal or do not exist.

ideation (*i-de-a'-shun*). The formulation of ideas.

idée fixe. A fixed idea, a delusion that impels towards some abnormal action.

identification (*i-den-te-fik-a'-shun*). A mental mechanism by which an individual adopts the attitudes and ideas of another, often admired, person. *Patient I.* The wearing of a label with the name and hospital number of the patient.

ideomotor (*i-de-o-mo'-tor*). The association of ideas and muscle action as in absent-minded acts.

ideophrenic (*i-de-o-fren'-ik*). Relating to mental disorder with perverted ideas.

idiopathic (*id-e-o-path'-ik*). Self-originated; applied to a

condition the cause of which is not known.
idiosyncrasy (*id-e-o-sin'-kras-e*). A peculiarity of constitution or temperament. It may exist in relation to drugs when e.g. small doses of iodine or quinine will cause symptoms of poisoning in some people; or foods, such as shell-fish or strawberries, give rise to urticaria in others.
idiot (*id'-e-ot*). An obsolete term. Those persons are now designated severely subnormal.
ileal (*il'-e-al*). Referring to the ileum. *I. bladder*. A section of ileum is substituted for the urinary bladder. *See* Bladder.
ileectomy (*il-e-ek'-to-me*). Excision of the ileum.
ileitis (*il'-e-i'-tis*). Inflammation of the ileum. *Regional i.* Crohn's disease. A chronic condition of the terminal portion of the ileum in which granulation and oedema may give rise to obstruction.
ileocaecal valve (*il-e-o-se'-kal*). *See under* Valve.
ileocolitis (*il-e-o-kol-i'-tis*). Inflammation of the ileum and colon.
ileocolostomy (*il-e-o-kol-os'-to-me*). Making a permanent opening between the ileum and some part of the colon.
ileoproctostomy (*il-e-o-prok-tos'-to-me*). Making an opening between the ileum and the rectum.
ileo-rectal (*il-e-o-rek'-tal*). Referring to the ileum and rectum. *I. anastomosis*. The joining of the two usually following total colectomy.
ileosigmoidostomy (*il-e-o-sig-moid-os'-to-me*). The surgical formation of an opening between the ileum and the sigmoid flexure.
ileostomy (*il-e-os'-to-me*). The operation to make an opening into the ileum. *I. bags*. Destructible or rubber bags which can be adhesive or worn on a belt and add greatly to the comfort of the patient.
ileo-ureterostomy (*il-e-o-u-re-ter-os'-to-me*). The transplantation of the ureters into a separated loop of ileum.

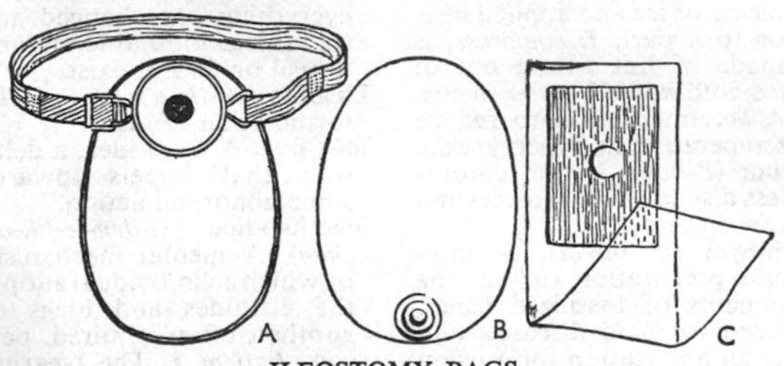

ILEOSTOMY BAGS
A. Elastic and web belt, and rubber bag.
B. Rubber bag with vulcanite outlet.
C. Disposable bag.

ileum (*il'-e-um*). The last part of the small intestine, terminating at the caecum.

ileus (*il'-e-us*). Obstruction of the bowel. *Paralytic i.* A condition resulting from local inflammation, the toxins of which affect the nerve supply to the bowel wall, and intestinal stasis results. One of the effects of peritonitis. Putrefaction takes place within the bowel, the poisons are absorbed, and the patient develops all the signs of toxaemia.

iliac (*il'-e-ak*). Pertaining to the ilium or flanks. *I. crest.* The crest of the hip-bone. *I. fossa.* The area of the abdomen over the concave surface of the iliac bone.

iliopsoas (*il-e-o-so'-as*). A name given to the flexor muscles of the hip, the iliacus and the psoas.

ilium (*il'-e-um*). The haunch-bone.

illusion (*il-lu'-zhun*). A false perception due to a misinterpretation of a sensory stimulus.

image. (1) The mental recall of a former percept. (2) The optical picture transferred to the brain cells by the optic nerve.

imagery (*im'-aj-er-e*). Abstract thought about some object. The image may be recalled by a motor or sensory stimulus.

imago (*im-a'-go*). In psychology, an idea or fanciful image of the father or some other person based on fantasy or fear.

imbalance (*im-bal'-ans*). Lack of balance, e.g. between endocrine secretions; water and electrolytes or of muscles.

imbecile (*im'-be-seel*). A term no longer used. It denoted a severe degree of subnormality.

imipramine (*im-e-pra'-meen*). A drug, chemically related to chlorpromazine, that may be effective in relieving depression. Tofranil is a proprietary preparation.

immiscible (*im-mis'-sib-l*). The inability of certain substances to mix.

immobilization (*im-mo-bil-i-za'-shun*). To make motionless. Used in the treatment of fractures and other conditions to promote healing. To immobilize a bone the joint above and below the break must be fixed.

immune (*im-mu'-n*). Protected against a disease, either by natural means or by inoculation. *I. body.* Antibody. *I. reaction.* That which causes a body to reject a transplanted organ.

immunity (*im-mu'-nit-e*). The resisting power of the body to the toxins of invading bacteria, shown by the presence in the blood of neutralizing antitoxins. *Natural i.* May be racial or familial, and is inborn. *Acquired i.* is produced by: (1) an attack of the disease; (2) repeated small infections by organisms not in themselves able to produce signs of disease, but against which the body forms antibodies which accumulate in the blood. *Artificially acquired i.* is by: (1) injection of small doses of toxins; (2) injection of vaccines (*active i.*); (3) introduction of antitoxic sera (*passive i.*).

immunization (*im-mu-ni-za'-shun*). The act of creating an active immunity.

immunology (*im-mu-nol'-o-je*). The study of the body's reactions in overcoming invasion by bacteria or viruses.

immuno-suppressive therapy. Use of drugs, e.g. actinomycin C, azothioprine and anti-lymphocyte serum (ALS) to prevent the rejection by the body of a transplanted organ.

impacted (*im-pak'-ted*). Driven into. *I. fracture. See under* Fracture.

impalpable (*im-palp'-ab-l*). Incapable of being felt by manual examination. May apply to an organ or tumour.

imperforate (*im-per'-for-ate*). Without an opening. *I. anus.* A congenital defect in which this opening is closed. *I. hymen.* Complete closure of the vaginal opening by the hymen. *See* Cryptomenorrhoea.

impetigo (*im-pet-i'-go*). An acute contagious inflammation of the skin marked by pustules and scabs; of streptococcal or staphylococcal origin. *Bullous i.* A severe form, especially if occurring in the newly born, characterized by large blebs.

implantation (*im-plant-a'-shun*). The act of planting or setting in, e.g. of the fertilized ovum in the endometrium or of malignant cells into another structure.

implants (*im'-plants*). Pellets of synthetic hormones that may be introduced under the skin for slow absorption. They may be of deoxycortone acetate, oestradiol, progesterone or testosterone.

impotence (*im'-po-tens*). Absence of sexual power.

impregnate (*im'-preg-nate*). (1) to saturate or instil. (2) To render pregnant.

impulse (*im'-puls*). A natural

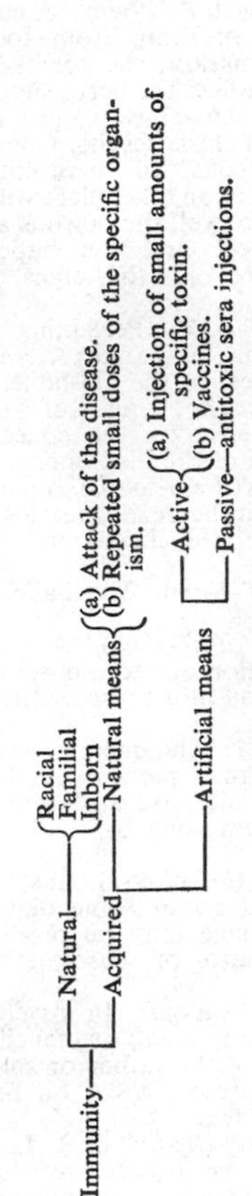

TABLE SHOWING TYPES OF IMMUNITY

or instinctive tendency to action without deliberation. *Cardiac i.* The beat of the apex of the heart as felt on the chest wall. *Morbid i.* An uncontrollable desire to act rashly. *Nerve i.* The force conveyed along nerve fibres.

inaccessibility (*in-ak-ses-ib-il'-it-e*). State of unresponsiveness characteristic of certain mental patients, e.g. schizophrenics.

inactivate (*in-ak'-tiv-ate*). To render inactive. To destroy the active principle bringing about change.

inanition (*in-an-ish'-un*). Wasting of the body from want of food.

inarticulate (*in-ar-tik'-u-late*). (1) Without joint. (2) Confused and jumbled, as applied to speech.

in articulo mortis (*ar-tik'-u-lo mor'-tis*). In the act of dying.

inborn (*in'-born*). Inherited. *I. errors of metabolism.* An increasing number of known conditions in which there is an inherited deficiency or production of toxic substances.

incarcerated (*in-kar'-ser-a-ted*). Held fast. (1) Applied to a hernia which is immovable, and therefore only curable by operation. (2) A pregnant uterus held under the sacral brim.

incest (*in-sest'*). Sexual intercourse between close relatives.

incipient (*in-sip'-e-ent*). Beginning to exist.

incision (*in-siz'-shun*). The act of cutting.

incisors (*in-si'-zors*). The cutting teeth. Four in the centre of each jaw.

inclusion bodies (*in-klu'-shun*). Any particles temporarily enclosed in the cytoplasm of a cell. For example in trachoma they are virus particles seen in the conjunctival epithelial cells.

incoherent (*in-ko-he'-rent*). Inability to be understood. Rambling speech that is disconnected.

incompatibility (*in-kom-pat-ib-il'-it-e*). The state of two or more substances being antagonistic, or destroying the efficiency of each other. Applied to mixtures of drugs, and to blood. *See* Blood grouping.

incompetence (*in-kom'-pe-tens*). Inefficiency. *Aortic i.* Failure of the aortic valves to regulate the flow of blood. *Mitral i. See under* Mitral. *Valvular i.* Describes failure of a valve of the heart to work efficiently.

incontinence (*in-kon'-tin-ens*). Inability to control natural functions or discharges. *I. of urine.* Enuresis (*q.v.*). *Paralytic i.* Loss of control of anal and urethral sphincters due to injury to nerve centres. *Stress i.* That which is due to defect in the urethral sphincters and is liable to occur when intra-abdominal pressure is increased as in coughing, lifting heavy weights, etc.

inco-ordination (*in-ko-or-din-a'-shun*). Inability to adjust harmoniously the various muscle movements.

incrustation (*in-krus-ta'-shun*). The formation of a crust or scab on a wound.

incubation (*in-ku-ba'-shun*). To maintain organisms in optimal conditions for their growth. *I. period.* The period between the date of infection and the appearance of symptoms.

incubator (*in'-ku-ba-tor*). (1)

An apparatus in which prematurely born infants can be reared. (2) An apparatus used to develop bacteria at a uniform temperature suitable to their growth.

incus (*in'-kus*). The small anvil-shaped bone of the middle ear.

Indian hemp. *See* Cannabis indica.

indicanuria (*in-de-kan-u'-re-ah*). The presence of indican in the urine—a sign of protein putrefaction in the intestine. It may be present in chronic constipation, or in intestinal obstruction.

indigenous (*in-dij'-en-us*). Occurring naturally in a certain locality.

indigestion (*in-de-jes'-chun*). *See* Dyspepsia.

indole (*in'-dol*) A product of protein decomposition in the bowel. Eliminated as indican in the urine.

indolent ulcer. One which heals slowly.

induced current (*in-duce'-d cur'-rent*). An electric current which, running through a primary coil of *thick* copper wire, induces through the air a current in a *thinner* wire which is wound round a bobbin and encircles the primary coil. The closer in proximity the stronger the current; this also makes the Faradic current.

induction (*in-duk'-shun*). Causing to occur. In obstetrics, production of labour before term. *I. coil. See* Induced current. *Stage of i.* In anaesthetic administration —the initial or first stage.

induration (*in-du-ra'-shun*). The process of becoming hardened.

industrial (*in-dus'-tre-al*). Referring to industry. *I. diseases.* Those that are caused by the nature of the work. *Prescribed i. diseases.* Those for which sickness benefit is payable and includes those that are notifiable by the Factories Act.

inertia (*in-er'-she-ah*). Sluggishness; inability to move except when stimulated by an external force. *Uterine i.* Lack of muscle contraction during the first and second stage of labour.

in extremis (*in eks-tre'-mis*). At the point of death.

infant (*in-fant'*). Educationally a child under 7 years of age.

infant feeding. Breast milk is the ideal food for the baby and if breast feeding is established satisfactorily for the first few months it can aid physical and emotional development. Where it is not possible cow's milk or a dried milk preparation can be used. A baby requires 75 ml or 420 J per 1 kg (50 calories per lb.) of body weight in 24 hours.

infantile paralysis (*in'-fan-tile par-al'-is-is*). Poliomyelitis (*q.v.*).

infantilism (*in-fan'-til-izm*). Delayed maturity. *Coeliac i.* Failure to grow in coeliac disease (*q.v.*). *Pancreatic i.* Associated with fibrocystic disease of the pancreas (*q.v.*). *Pituitary i.* The perfectly formed dwarfs associated with hyposecretion of the growth hormone. *Renal i.* Also known as *renal rickets*: associated with disease of the kidney and upset in the calcium balance in the blood. There is dwarfism with signs of rickets (*q.v.*).

infant mortality (*in-fant mor-*

tal'-it-e). Deaths of children under 1 year of age. *I. M. rate.* Deaths of children under 1 year for 12 months per 1000 live births.

infarct (*in'-farkt*). The wedge-shaped area of necrosis in an organ produced by the blocking of a blood vessel—usually due to emboli. *White i.* The area is suddenly deprived of blood and is pale in colour. *Red i.* Red blood cells infiltrate into the area.

infarction (*in-fark'-shun*). The formation of an infarct. *Pulmonary i.* A small embolism in the lungs.

infection (*in-fek'-shun*). Invasion of the body by organisms causing disease. *Cross i.* That from one person to another in immediate association, e.g. by towels, thermometers, or by the air. *Droplet i.* The organisms are spread in minute particles of moisture exhaled, especially in coughing or sneezing. *Mass i.* Invasion of the blood stream by large numbers of organisms. *Pyogenic i.* is that by pus-producing organisms. *Secondary i.* A superimposed second infection, when one is already present. *Water-borne i.* The organisms are spread by the water supply, e.g. typhoid fever.

infectious diseases. (*See* Table on p. 174).

infective (*in-fek'-tiv*). Of the nature of an infection. *I. exhaustive psychosis.* A psychosis developing during the course of another disease as in a severe infection, metabolic or glandular condition. It may subside as the disease is controlled but it may require psychiatric treatment. *I. mononucleosis.* Glandular fever (*q.v.*).

inferior. Lower, e.g. *i. vena cava*, the lower large vein.

inferiority (*in-fer-e-or'-it-e*). Of lesser rank, stature, position or ability. *Physical i.* Possessing some physical disability of which the person is sensitive, e.g. a clubfoot or squint. *I. complex. See* Complex.

infertility (*in-fer-til'-it-e*). Implies the failure of the woman to conceive a child. The cause may be in either the husband or the wife.

infestation (*in-fes-ta'-shun*). Invaded by animal parasites; applied to the presence of lice on the body or clothing, or in a house.

infiltration (*in-fil-tra'-shun*). The entrance and diffusion of some abnormal substance, either fluid or solid. *I. anaesthesia.* Injection of procaine or allied substances into the tissues for local effect.

inflammation (*in-flam-ma'-shun*). A series of changes in tissues indicating their reaction to injury, whether mechanical, chemical or bacterial, so long as the injury does not cause death of the affected part. The cardinal signs are: Heat, swelling, pain and redness. *Acute i.* The onset is sudden, the symptoms marked and progressive. *Catarrhal i.* Attacks mucous surfaces and stimulates exudation. *Caseous i.* A chronic form found in tuberculosis, in which the degenerative changes cause a cheesy material to form. *Chronic i.* Of slow development. Granulation tissue forms and tends to localize the infection. *Diffuse i.* An extensive type, as in nephritis

COMMON INFECTIOUS DISEASES

	Incubation in days	*Appearance of eruption*	*Period of isolation*
Chickenpox (*Varicella*)	14	1st day	Until all scabs have been shed.
Diphtheria	2–10	—	Not less than 3 weeks, and until three successive bacteriological examinations of throat or other swabs have been negative.
Measles (*Morbilli*)	10–16	3rd or 4th day	Not less than 2 weeks dating from appearance of rash.
Mumps (*Parotitis*)	21–28	—	Not less than 2 weeks from onset.
Rubella (*German Measles*)	17–20	1st day	Ten days from appearance of rash.
Scarlet Fever	1–7	2nd day	Until the throat swab is negative and all discharges have ceased.
Smallpox (*Variola*)	10–14	3rd or 4th day	Until all scabs have been shed.
Typhoid (*Enteric fever*)	7–21	2nd week	Until six bacteriological examinations of faeces and urine are negative.
Paratyphoid A and B	1–6	Usually earlier than in typhoid	As 'typhoid'.
Typhus	5–14	3rd to 6th day	4 weeks.
Whooping Cough (*Pertussis*)	7–14	—	2 weeks after 'whoop' has ceased.

and cellulitis. *Suppurative i.* In which the formation of pus results. *Traumatic i.* That which follows an injury, and is non-bacterial.

influenza (*in-flu-en'-zah*). An acute infectious disease caused by either Virus A, giving rise to serious epidemics, or Virus B, causing minor outbreaks. There is inflammation of the upper respiratory tract causing fever, headache, pain in the back. and limbs, anorexia and sometimes nausea and vomiting. The fever subsides in 2 to 3 days, leaving a feeling of lassitude and some mental depression. Secondary infection may lead to pneumonia and empyema.

infra (*in'-fra*). A prefix meaning below or under.

infra-red rays. Invisible rays beyond the red end of the spectrum of long wavelength. *See also* Ultra-violet rays.

infundibulum (*in-fun-dib'-u-lum*). A funnel-shaped passage or part.

infusion (*in-fu'-zhun*). (1) The process of extracting the soluble principles of substances (especially drugs) by soaking in water. (2) Treatment by the introduction of fluid into the body. *Saline i.* Subcutaneous or intravenous injection of salt and water. Dextrose may be added.

ingestion (*in-jest'-shun*). The introduction of food and drugs by the mouth.

inguinal (*in'-gwin-al*). Relating to the groin. *I. canal.* The channel through the abdominal wall, above Poupart's ligament through which the spermatic cord and vessels pass to the testis in the male, and which contains the round ligament of the uterus in the female. *I. hernia. See under* Hernia.

inhalation (*in-hal-la'-shun*). The breathing of air, vapour or volatile drugs into the lungs. *Steam i.* By: (1) Maw's inhaler; (2) a jug, with a towel arranged funnel-wise to direct the steam into the respiratory passages; (3) a steam kettle and tent. Atomizers may be used to inhale drugs, e.g. penicillin and ephedrine. *I. anaesthesia.* By general anaesthetics, as ether, chloroform etc. *Oxygen i. See* Oxygen. *Carbon dioxide i. See* Carbon dioxide.

inherent (*in-heer'-ent*). Describing a characteristic that is innate or natural and essentially a part of the person.

inhibition (*in-hib-ish'-un*). Checking or restraining. Inhibitory nerves restrain muscle action, in contrast to accelerator nerves which stimulate it. Emotionally a person may be inhibited because he has certain ideas or feelings—often unconscious—which prevent him from acting as he would wish.

injection (*in-jek'-shun*). The act of introducing a liquid into the body by means of a syringe or other instrument. *Hypodermic i.* Below the skin. *Intramuscular i.* That made into the muscles. *Intrathecal i.* Into the theca of the spinal cord. *Intravenous i.* Into the veins. *Sclerosing i.* Of drugs, as quinine and urethane, to obliterate a blood vessel, as in treatment of varicose veins. *Subcutaneous* (*hypodermic*) *i.* Below the skin. Injections of fluid, stimulants etc, can be given into the rectum.

innate (*in'-ate*). Present in the individual at birth.

innervation (*in-ner-va'-shun*). Nerve supply to a part.

innocent (*in'-no-sent*). As applied to new growth a harmless or non-malignant one.

innocuous (*in-nok'-u-ous*). Harmless.

innominate (*in-nom'-in-ate*). Unnamed. *I. artery*. A branch of the aorta now termed the brachiocephalic. *I. bone*. The united ilium, ischium and pubis.

inoculation (*in-ok-u-la'-shun*). Introduction through the skin as: (1) infection by the bites of insects; (2) injection of a vaccine to stimulate the production of antibodies against a disease.

inorganic (*in-or-gan'-ik*). Of neither animal nor vegetable origin.

inositol (*in-o'-se-tol*). A form of muscle or plant carbohydrate that has the same formula as simple sugar but not its other properties. It has been used in the treatment of dermatoses and also, combined with vitamin E, in cases of muscular dystrophy.

inotropic (*in-o-tro'-pic*). Agents which affect the force or energy of muscular contractions. The term may be applied to drugs acting on the heart muscle.

inquest (*in'-kwest*). In medicine a legal inquiry held by a coroner into the cause of sudden or unexpected death.

insanity (*in-san'-it-e*). An obsolete term for a state of severe mental disorder. Legally the person is not responsible for his actions and it is largely in this connection the term is retained. For examples, *see under* Psychosis, Mania, Schizophrenia *and* Paranoia.

insecticides (*in-sek'-te-sides*). A large group of chemical compounds that kill insect pests. Some are very toxic and can cause irritability of the nervous system and gastrointestinal upsets in man and may accumulate in the body fat.

insemination (*in-sem-in-a'-shun*). (1) Fertilization of an ovum. (2) Introduction of the semen into the vagina. *Artificial i.* By means other than sexual intercourse. *AID*. The semen used is from a donor. *AIH*. The husband's semen is used.

insensible (*in-sen'-sib-l*). Not appreciated by the senses. *I. sweat*. That of which one is not aware.

insertion. The attachment of a muscle to the bone which it moves. *I. of tendon*. Insertion of a healthy tendon into a paralysed one at the periosteum of the joint so that normal function may result. *I. of nerve*. The operation which attaches a cut nerve by insertion of it into the sheath of another.

insidious (*in-sid'-e-us*). Approaching by stealth. A term applied to any disease which develops imperceptibly.

insight (*in'-site*). Mental awareness. The capacity of an individual to estimate a situation or his own behaviour or the connection between his present attitudes and past experiences. In psychiatry, a recognition by the patient that he is ill. Insight in this connection may be complete, partial or absent and may alter during the course of the illness.

in situ (*in si'-tu*). Latin term for in the original position.

insolation (*in-sol-a'-shun*). Exposure to sun's rays.

insomnia (*in-som'-ne-ah*). Inability to sleep.

inspiration (*in-spir-a'-shun*) Drawing in the breath.

inspissated *in-spis'-a-ted*). Thickened, through evaporation or absorption. *I. serum* is a culture medium for bacteria. *I. sputum*. Occurs in pertussis and is difficult to cough up.

instillation (*in-stil-la'-shun*). Pouring a liquid into a cavity drop by drop, e.g. into the eye.

instincts. Inborn tendencies to act in a certain way without the influence of reason or previous education.

instruments, surgical. *See* Appendix 20.

insufficiency (*in-suf-fish'-en-se*). Inadequate. A term used to describe the failure of function in organs, as the heart, circulation, stomach, liver, muscles etc.

insufflation (*in'-suf-fla'-shun*). The act of blowing air or powder into a cavity.

insulate (*in'-su-late*). To surround an electrified body with a non-conducting substance, so that electricity cannot escape.

insulin (*in'-su-lin*). The endocrine secretion of the pancreas, which regulates sugar metabolism, and ensures complete fat combustion. It is extensively used in *diabetes mellitus*, controlling the blood sugar and preventing acidosis: thus enabling a less restricted diet to be taken. *Globin i., Isophane i., Protamine zinc i.* and *I. zinc suspension* are preparations in which the action is delayed and thus less frequent doses are necessary. A buffer dose of ordinary insulin may be given to tide over the period before it comes into effect. *I. coma. See under* Coma. *I. test*. One carried out to determine if all the fibres have been severed in a vagotomy operation. *See* Diabetes mellitus *and* Aceto-acetic acid.

insulinase (*in'-su-lin-aze*). An enzyme that destroys the action of insulin and when present makes the control of diabetes difficult.

insuloma (*in-sul-o'-mah*). A benign adenoma of the islet cells of the pancreas causing hypoglycaemia.

integument (*in-teg'-u-ment*). The skin.

intellect (*in'-tel-ekt*). The reasoning power, in contrast to the emotions or the will.

intelligence. General mental ability. *I. tests.* Devised to measure the level of intelligence. *I. quotient* (IQ). The ratio of the mental age (*q.v.*) to chronological age expressed as a percentage.

intention tremor (*in-ten'-shun trem'-or*). *See* Tremor.

inter- A prefix signifying 'between'.

intercellular (*in-ter-sel'-ul-ah*). Between the cells of a structure. May be applied to the connective tissue or fluid bathing the cells.

intercostal (*in-ter-kos'-tal*). Between the ribs. *I. muscles.* Those of the chest wall.

intercourse (*in-ter-kors'*). The sexual act of coitus.

intercurrent (*in-ter-kur'-ent*). Running between. *I. infection.* One which occurs during the course of another disease in the same person.

interlobar (*in-ter-lo'-bar*). Between lobes. *I. empyema.* Pus collects between the lobes. It may be difficult to diagnose and the abscess may point and rupture into an air passage—the pus being coughed up.

interlobular (*in-ter-lob'-u-lar*). Between lobules. *I. veins.* Branches of the portal vein in the liver.

intermenstrual (*in-ter-men'-stru-al*). Between the menstrual periods, when the uterus is shedding its lining.

intermittent (*in-ter-mit'-tent*). Occurring at intervals. *I. claudication. See* Claudication. *I. fever. See* Fever.

interstitial (*in-ter-stish'-al*). Between the special tissues, i.e. in the connective tissues. *I. keratitis. See* Keratitis. *I. nephritis.* Chronic nephritis associated with fibrosis and hypertension.

intertrigo (*in-ter-tri'-go*). An irritating, eczematous skin eruption, from chafing where two moist surfaces are in close apposition causing interference with evaporation.

intervertebral (*in-ter-vert'-e-bral*). Between the vertebrae. *I. disc.* The pad of fibro-cartilage between the bodies of the vertebrae. Protrusion of the contents of the disc may give rise to sciatica by pressing on the nerve roots.

intestine (*in-tes'-tin*). That part of the alimentary canal which extends from the stomach to the anus. *Small i.* The first twenty feet (6 metres), from the pylorus to the caecum, consisting of the duodenum, jejunum and ileum. *Large i.* Six feet (2 metres) in length consisting of the caecum, ascending transverse and descending colon and rectum. The canal completes the process of digestion and eliminates waste matter.

intestinal (*in-tes'-tin-al*). Referring to the intestine.

intima (*in'-tim-ah*). The innermost coat of an artery or vein.

intolerance (*in-tol'-er-ans*). Lack of power to withstand Applied to the effect of some drugs on individuals, e.g *iodine* and *quinine*. *See* Idiosyncrasy.

intoxication (*in-toks-ik-a'-shun*). (1) Poisoning by drugs or harmful substances. (2) A state of drunkenness by taking too much alcohol.

intra- A prefix signifying 'within'.

intra-abdominal (*in-trah-ab-dom'-in-al*). Within the abdomen.

intra-articular (*in-trah-ar-tik'-u-lah*). Within a joint capsule. *I-a. injections.* Those that may be injected in this way such as hydrocortizone.

intra-atrial (*in-trah-a'-tre-al*). Within the atrium. *I-a. thrombosis.* A blood clot formed in the atrium of the heart.

intracapsular (*in-trah-kap'-su-lar*). Within the capsule of a joint. *I. fracture. See under* Fracture.

intracellular (*in-trah-sel'-u-lar*). Within a cell. *I. organisms.* Those which invade cells, e.g. the gonococcus.

intracerebral (*in-trah-ser'-e-bral*). Within the brain substance. *I. haemorrhage.* Arising in the cerebrum most often from the middle cerebral artery or from an aneurysm.

intracranial (*in-trah-kra'-ne-al*). Within the skull. *I. ab-*

scess. One arising within the brain or meninges. *I. aneurysm.* Arising in one of the cerebral vessels. It may be congenital or acquired. *I. pressure.* The pressure within the cranium measured by lumbar puncture.

intradermal (*in-trah-der'-mal*). Between the layers of the skin as in tests carried out for antibody formation.

intradural (*in-trah-du'-ral*). Within the dura mater. *I. haemorrhage. See under* Haemorrhage.

intragastric (*in-trah-gas'-trik*). Within the stomach. *I. tube feeding.* Artificial feeding usually by naso-gastric tube.

intrahepatic (*in-trah-hep-at'-ik*). Within the liver. Referring to a condition of the liver cells or connective tissue.

intralobular (*in-trah-lob'-u-lar*). Within the lobule. *I. veins.* Collect blood from within the lobules of the liver.

intramedullary (*in-trah-med'-ul-lar-e*). Within the bone marrow. *I. nail.* One for fixation of a fracture.

intramuscular (*in-trah-mus'-ku-lar*). Within muscle tissue.

intranasal (*in-trah-na'-zal*). Within the nose. *I. oxygen. See* Appendix 4.

intra-ocular (*in-trah-ok'-u-lar*). Within the eyeball.

intra-osseous (*in-trah-os'-se-us*). Into a bone.

intraperitoneal (*in-trah-per-it-o-ne'-al*). Within the peritoneal cavity.

intrathecal (*in-trah-the'-kal*). Within the meninges of the spinal cord, usually in the subarachnoid space.

intratracheal (*in-trah-trak'-e-al*). Within the trachea. *I. anaesthesia.* The anaesthetic is inhaled through a tube passed into the trachea via the nose or mouth.

intra-uterine (*in-trah-u'-ter-ine*). Within the uterus. *I. device. See* IUD. *I. douche.* Irrigation of the uterine cavity; for which a special nozzle is used, having a groove in it, so that the fluid can return and is not forced into the Fallopian tubes. *I. life.* Fetal development in the uterus.

intravenous (*in-trah-ve'-nus*). Within a vein.

intraventricular (*in-tra-ven-trik'-u-lah*). Within a ventricle. It may apply to a cerebral or cardiac ventricle.

intrinsic factor (*in-trin'-sik*). An enzyme formed in gastric glands in the presence of HCl which is necessary for the absorption of the extrinsic factor (vitamin B_{12}).

introitus (*in-tro'-it-us*). An opening or entrance.

introjection (*in-tro-jek'-shun*). A mental process by which an individual takes into himself personal characteristics of another person, usually those of someone much loved or admired.

introspection (*in-tro-spek'-shun*). A subjective study of the mind and its processes, in which an individual studies his own reactions.

introversion (*in-tro-ver'-shun*). The looking inwards.

introvert (*in'-tro-vert*). A cool, thoughtful, reflective person who tends to be self-sufficient and is a poor mixer in society. *See also* Extravert.

intubation (*in-tu-ba'-shun*). The introduction of a tube into the air passages to allow air to enter the lungs. Used for administration of an anaesthetic, e.g. by Magill's catheter.

intumescence (*in-tu-mes'-ens*). A swelling or increase in bulk, like nasal mucous membrane in catarrh.

intussusception (*in-tus-sus-sep'-shun*). A condition in which one part of the intestine becomes pushed or invaginated into another part beyond.

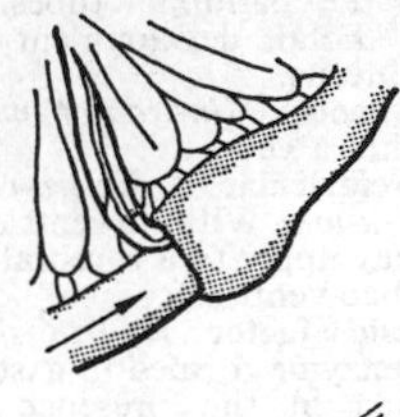

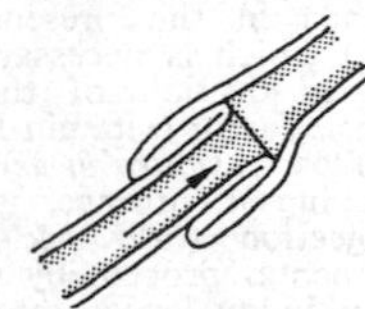

INTUSSUSCEPTION

It occurs mostly among children at the ileocaecal junction, and causes intestinal obstruction, with pain, vomiting, and small blood-stained evacuations. Prompt surgical treatment is necessary.

intussusceptum (*in-tus-sus-sep'-tum*). The invaginated part of the intestine in intussusception.

intussuscipiens (*in-tus-sus-sip'-e-ens*). The outer part of the intestine which encloses the intussusceptum.

inunction (*in-unk'-shun*) The act of rubbing an oily or fatty preparation into the skin.

invagination (*in-vaj-in-a'-shun*). Pushing of a part inwards, thus forming a pouch. The original condition of intussusception.

invasion. The onset of a disease.

inverse. Reverse of the normal. *I. temperature. See* Temperature. *I. respiration. See* Respiration. *I. uterus.* The organ is turned inside out. This occasionally occurs following labour.

invertase (*in-vert'-aze*). A ferment of intestinal juice acting on cane sugar.

in vitro (*in ve'-tro*). In a glass. As in a test tube. Refers to observations made outside the body. *See also* In vivo.

in vivo (*in ve'-vo*). Observations of processes within the living body.

involucrum (*in-vol-u'-krum*). New bone which forms a sheath around necrosed bone, as in chronic osteomyelitis.

involuntary (*in-vol'-un-ta-re*). Independent of the will.

involution (*in-vol-u'-shun*). (1) Turning inward; describes the contraction of the uterus after labour. (2) Sometimes applied to the slowing down process of aging.

involutional (*in-vol-u'-shun-al*). Relating to the changes of retrogression which occur during later life. *I. melancholia.* Depression occurring for the first time in later life and characterized by agitation and delusions of a hypochondriacal nature.

iodide (*i'-o-dide*). A compound of iodine.

iodine (*i'-o-deen*). A non-metallic element with a distinctive odour, obtained from seaweed. *Tincture of i.* A 2½ per cent spirit solution is used as a skin antiseptic. *Lugol's i.* Aqueous solution used orally in the pre- and post-operative treatment of thyrotoxicosis. *Radioactive i.* (^{131}I) is also used in the treatment and diagnosis of thyroid conditions.

iodism (*i'-o-dizm*). Poisoning from the prolonged use of iodine or iodides.

iodoform (*i-o'-do-form*). A yellow, crystalline, antiseptic powder containing iodine.

iodopsin (*i-o-dop'-sin*). A cone pigment in the retina of the eye. It is composed of a protein fraction and retinene (*q.v.*).

iodoxyl (*i-o-doks'-il*). A radio-opaque dye used in pyelography.

ion (*i'-on*). One of the components into which an electrolyte (*q.v.*) is broken up by electrolysis. *Hydrogen i. concentration.* The estimation of free hydrogen particles in the blood which govern its reaction.

ionization (*i-on-i-za'-shun*). When an electric current is passed through an electrolyte solution the molecules break up into electrically charged particles or ions. By this method, although it is not often used, substances can be introduced through the skin, e.g. copper sulphate to treat tinea pedis.

iopanoic (*i-o-pan'-oik*). A radio-opaque dye used in X-ray examination of the gall-bladder and ducts. Telepaque is a proprietary preparation.

ipecacuanha (*ip-e-kak-u-an'-ah*). The dried root of a Brazilian shrub, given in small doses as a stimulant expectorant.

iophendylate (*i-o-fen'-de-late*). A radio-opaque dye that may be used in examination of the spinal canal. Myodil is a proprietary preparation.

IPP. Intermittent positive pressure.

iproniazid (*ip-ro-ni'-az-id*). An antidepressant drug that belongs to the group of monoamine oxidase inhibitors.

ipsilateral (*ip-se-la'-ter-al*). Occurring on the same side. Applied when symptoms occur on the same side as the cerebral lesion.

iridectomy (*ir-id-ek'-to-me*). Excision of a part of the iris.

iridocele (*ir-id'-o-seel*). Hernia of a part of the iris, through a wound.

iridocyclitis (*ir-id-o-si-kli'-tis*). Inflammation of the iris and ciliary body.

iridodialysis (*ir-id-o-di-al'-is-is*). The separation of the outer border of the iris from its ciliary attachment, often a result of trauma.

iridoplegia (*ir-id-o-ple'-je-ah*). Paralysis of the iris.

iridoptosis (*ir-id-op-to'-sis*). Prolapse of iris.

iridotomy (*ir-id-ot'-o-me*). Incising the iris to make an artificial pupil.

iris (*i'-ris*). The coloured part of the eye made of two layers of muscle, the contraction of which alters the size of the pupil.

iritis (*i-ri'-tis*). Inflammation of the iris causing pain, photophobia, contraction of pupil, and discoloration of the iris.

iron. A metallic element given in tonic mixtures and for the treatment of anaemia. It causes black discoloration of the stools. *I. lung. See under* Respirator. *Radioactive* *i.* This has been used to estimate blood volume.

iron dextran. A solution of iron–dextran complex for intramuscular injection where oral iron is not successful. Trade name is Imferon.

iron sorbital (*ir-on sor'-be-tal*). A solution of iron for intramuscular injection. Jectofer is the trade preparation.

irradiation (*ir-ra-de-a'-shun*). Exposure to the action of rays, e.g. ultra-violet rays in the treatment of rickets.

irreducible (*ir-re-du'-sib-l*). Incapable of being replaced in a normal position. *I. hernia. See under* Hernia.

irrigation (*ir-re-ga'-shun*). To wash out a cavity or wound, usually with a hot lotion.

irritant (*ir'-rit-ant*). An agent causing stimulation or excitation.

irritation (*ir-rit-a'-shun*). (1) A condition of undue nervous excitement, through abnormal sensitiveness. (2) Itching of the skin. *Cerebral i.* A stage of excitement present in many brain conditions, and typical of the recovery stage of concussion.

ischaemia (*is-ke'-me-ah*). Lack of blood to a part. *Cardiac i.* Heart muscle deprived of blood as in coronary thrombosis. *See* Volkmann's ischaemic contracture.

Ishihara colour charts. Consist of a pattern of dots of the primary colours on a similar background. The patterns can be seen by a normal sighted person, but one who is colour blind will only be able to identify some of them.

ischiorectal abscess (*is-ke-o-rek'-tal*). A collection of pus in the ischiorectal connective tissue. A *fistula in ano* may result.

ischium (*is'-ke-um*). The lower posterior bone of the pelvic girdle.

islets of Langerhans (*i-lets of lan'-ger-hans*). The groups of cells in the pancreas that produce insulin.

isocarboxazid (*i-so-kar-boks'-azid*). A drug used to relieve depression. Marplan is a proprietary preparation.

iso-immunization (*i-so-im-mu-ni-za'-shun*). Development of antibodies against an antigen derived from an individual of the same species.

isolation (*i-so-la'-shun*). The separation of a person with an infectious disease from those non-infected. *I. period.* The length of time during which a patient with an infectious fever is considered capable of infecting others by contact.

isolator (*i-so-la'-tor*). A term applied to a specially constructed chamber or unit in which a patient can be nursed or undergo treatment.

isometric (*i-so-met'-rik*). Having equal proportions. *I. exercises.* Those carried out without producing movement; used to maintain muscle tone following a fracture.

isoniazid (*i-so-ni'-az-id*). A drug given orally in combination with streptomycin or sodium amino salicylate which is effective in treating tuberculosis.

isoprenaline (*i-so-pren'-a-leen*). An oral synthetic drug which has an action like adrenaline and can be used to treat asthma.

isotonic (*i-so-ton'-ik*). Having

uniform tension. *I. solution* is of the same osmotic pressure as the fluid with which it is compared. Normal saline is isotonic with blood plasma.

isotopes (*i'-so-topes*). Atoms of the same element but having different mass numbers. There are eleven isotopes of iodine. *Radioactive i.* Unstable isotopes which emit electrons (beta rays). Many also emit gamma rays. They may be used in the diagnosis and treatment of disease.

itch. (1) Scabies. (2) A skin eruption with irritation. *Baker's i.* Eczema of the hands due to the proteins of flour. *Barber's i.* Sycosis (*q.v.*) *Dhobie i.* A form of ringworm prevalent in the tropics. *Washer-woman's i.* Eczema of the hands due to the use of soda. *I. mite. Sarcoptes scabiei.*

-itis. A suffix denoting 'inflammation'.

IUD. Intra-uterine device. Contraceptive device introduced into the uterine cavity.

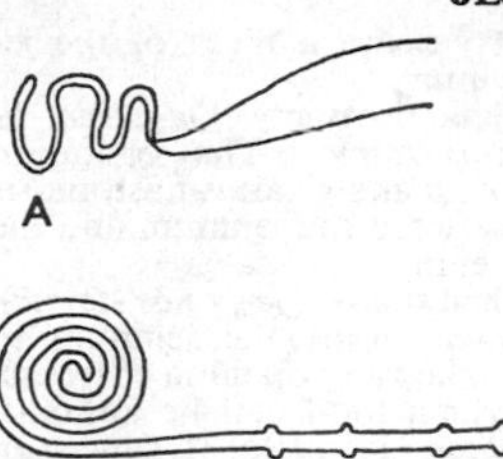

INTRA-UTERINE DEVICES
A. Lippe's loop.
B. Margulies spiral.
C. Birnberg bow.

J

Jacksonian epilepsy (*jak-so'-ne-an*). *See under* Epilepsy.

Jacquemier's sign (*zjak'-me-a*). Blueness of the lining of the vagina seen in the early weeks of pregnancy.

jactitation (*jak-tit-a'-shun*). The extreme restlessness of a patient.

jail fever. An old name for typhus fever because of its prevalence in prisons.

jaundice (*jawn'-dis*). *Syn.* Icterus. A yellow discoloration of the skin and conjunctivae, due to the presence of bile-pigment in the blood. It may be: (1) *Haemolytic j.* Due to excessive destruction of red blood cells, causing increase of bilirubin in the blood. The liver is not involved. *Acholuric j.* is of this type. It is characterized by increased fragility of red blood cells. Splenectomy effects a cure in most cases. (2) *Hepatocellular j.* In this the liver cells are damaged either by infection or drugs, most commonly the virus of *infective hepatitis*. Toxic agents may be chloroform, phosphorus, arsenic, or gold. (3) *Obstructive j.* Bile is prevented from reaching the duodenum owing to obstruction by gallstone, growth, or stricture of the common bile duct.

jejunectomy (*je-ju-nek'-to-me*).

To excise a piece of the jejunum.

jejuno-ileostomy (*je-ju'-no il-e-os'-to-me*). The operation of making an anastomosis between the jejunum and the ileum.

jejunostomy (*je-ju-nos'-to-me*). Incision of the jejunum to make an opening through which food can be administered, in cases of cancer of the duodenum, etc.

jejunotomy (*je-ju-not'-o-me*). An incision into the jejunum.

jejunum (*je-ju'-num*). The portion of the small intestine [about 8ft (2·4 m) in length], from the duodenum to the ileum.

jigger (*jig'-er*). A type of flea found in the tropics which burrows into the soles of the feet and causes severe irritation.

joint. An articulation. The point of junction of two or more bones.

judgment. The ability of an individual to estimate a situation, to arrive at reasonable conclusions, and to decide on a course of action.

jugular (*jug'-u-lar*). Relating to the neck. *J. veins.* Two large veins in the neck, which convey most of the blood from the head.

juxtaposition (*juks-ta-po-sish'-un*). Close at hand. Adjacent.

K

Kahn test (*karn*). An agglutination test for syphilis.

kala-azar (*kah-lah-ah'-zar*). A tropical disease caused by the Leishman–Donovan parasite, and marked by enlargement of the spleen and anaemia. Leishmaniasis.

kanamycin (*kan-a-mi'-sin*). An antibiotic drug for severe infections with Gram-negative organisms where penicillin ineffective. Kannasyn is a proprietary preparation.

kaolin (*ka'-o-lin*). China clay used as a dusting powder and for poultices. *Refined k.* Aluminium silicate. Given orally to treat diarrhoea.

katabolism (*kat-ab'-ol-izm*). The breaking-down process in tissue structure. Catabolism. *See* Metabolism.

kataphoresis (*kat-a-for-e'-sis*). Ionization (*q.v.*).

katonium (*kat-on-e'-um*). A diuretic in which positively charged ions are used to produce an acidosis to which the kidneys respond by an increased output of acid urine.

Keller's operation (*kel'-ler*). A bone operation for correcting hallux valgus.

keloid (*ke'-loid*). A hard, whitish tumour of the skin. A type occurs in a healed wound due to overgrowth of fibrous tissue, causing the scar to be raised above the skin level. With X-ray treatment it disappears.

keratectasia (*ker-a-tekt-a'-se-ah*). Protrusion of the cornea.

keratectomy (*ker-a-tek'-to-me*). Excision of the cornea.

keratin (*ker'-a-tin*). An albuminous substance which forms the base of all horny tissues.

keratinize (*ker'-a-tin-ise*). To become horny.

keratitis (*ker-a-ti'-tis*). Inflammation of the cornea. *Interstitial k.* A syphilitic manifestation, seen chiefly in the congenital type.

keratoconjunctivitis (*ker-a-to-kon-junk-tiv-i'-tis*). Inflammation of both the cornea and the conjunctiva of the eye.

keratoconus (*ker-a-to-ko'-nus*). A bilateral degenerative occular condition in which the cornea becomes thin and protruded into a cone-shape.

kerato-iritis (*ker-a-to-i-ri'-tis*). Inflammation of cornea and iris.

keratoma (*ker-a-to'-mah*). An overgrowth of horny tissue.

keratomalacia (*ker-a-to-mal-a'-se-ah*). Ulceration and softening of the cornea. Due to deficiency of vitamin A. *See* Appendix 10.

keratome (*ker'-a-tome*). A knife with trowel-shaped blade, for incising the cornea.

keratometer (*ker-a-tom'-e-ter*). Ophthalmometer. An instrument by which the amount of corneal astigmatism can be measured accurately.

keratoplasty (*ker'-a-to-plas-te*). Plastic operation on the cornea including that of transplantation.

keratoscope (*ker'-a-to-skope*). A battery and disc of concentric circles for examining the eye to detect keratoconus.

keratosis (*ker-a-to'-sis*). A skin disease marked by excessive growth of the epidermis or horny tissue.

keratotomy (*ker-a-tot'-o-me*). Incision of the cornea.

kerion (*ke'-re-on*). A complication of ringworm of the scalp, with formation of pustules.

kernicterus (*kern-ik'-ter-us*). A complication of haemolytic jaundice of the newly born in which there is pigmentation of, and damage to, the brain cells.

Kernig's sign (*ker'-nig*). A sign of meningitis. When the thigh is supported at right angles to the trunk, the patient is unable to straighten his leg at the knee-joint.

ketogenic diet (*ke-to-jen'-ik*). A high fat diet given to produce ketosis. Now seldom used.

ketones (*ke'-tone*). Compounds containing the carboxyl group (COOH). Products of incomplete fat metabolism in the body. *See* Aceto-acetic acid.

ketonuria (*ke-ton-ur'-e-ah*). The presence of ketones in urine.

ketosis (*ke-to'-sis*). The condition in which ketones are formed in excess in the body. *See* Acidosis.

17-ketosteroids (*ke-tos'-ter-oids*). Steroids excreted in the urine and formed from the adrenal corticosteroids, testosterone, and to a lesser extent from oestrogens.

kidney. One of two glandular, urine-secreting organs situated in the lumbar region. *Granular k.* The small fibrosed kidney of chronic nephritis. *Horseshoe k.* The congenital fusion of the two kidneys into a horseshoe shape. *Large white k.* Present in subacute, hydraemic or parenchymatous nephritis. *Polycystic k.* A congenital bilateral condition of multiple cysts replacing kidney tissue.

Killian's operation (*kil'-e-an*). Opening the frontal sinus to curette it and the ethmoid cells.

kilogram (*kil'-o-gram*). One thousand grams. *See* Appendix 14.

kinaesthesis (*kin-es-the'-sis*). The combined sensations by which position, weight, and muscular position are perceived.

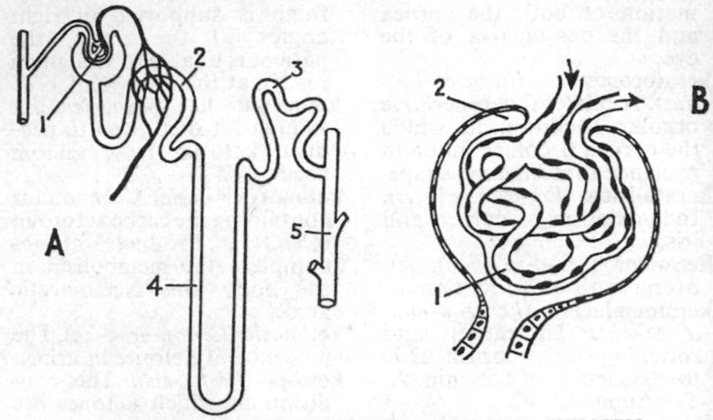

MICROSCOPICAL STRUCTURE OF THE KIDNEY

A. The nephron: (1) Bowman's capsule, (2) proximal convoluted tubule, (3) distal convoluted tubule, (4) descending and ascending loop of Henle, (5) collecting duct.

B. Bowman's capsule: (1) glomerulus, (2) invaginated end of tubule.

kinanaesthesia (*kin-an-es-the'-se-ah*). Impaired sensation. An inability to recognize position or objects not seen.

kinase (*kin'-aze*). Activator. *See* Enterokinase *and* Thrombokinase.

kinematics (*kin-e-mat'-iks*). The science of movement, in particular that of the body.

kineplastic stump (*kin-e-plas'-tik*). An amputation stump so made that the patient can control the artificial limb by the remaining muscles.

Kirschner's wire (*kirsh'-ner*). A thin wire that may be passed through a bone to exert skeletal traction.

kiss of life. The expired air method of artificial respiration, either by mouth to nose or mouth to mouth breathing. *See* Appendix 1.

Klebsiella (*kleb-se-el'-ah*). A genus of bacteria. They are short rods, Gram-negative non-spore forming, and encapsulated. They may cause infection of the lung, intestines, and urinary tract.

Klebs–Loeffler bacillus (*klebs lef'-ler*). The *Corynebacterium diphtheriae*, the cause of diphtheria.

kleptomania (*klep-to-ma'-ne-ah*). An irresistible urge to steal when there is often no need and no particular desire for the objects.

Klinefelter's syndrome. Due to a chromosome abnormality in which each cell has XXY sex chromosomes making a total of 47 (normal 46). Affected men have female breast development, small testes and are infertile.

Klumpke's paralysis (*kloomp'-ke*). Affects the hand and arm and is due usually to a birth injury to the brachial plexus.

kneading (*ne'-ding*). A method

used in massage. Pétrissage.

knee. The joint between the femur and the tibia. *K. jerk*. An upward jerk of the leg, obtained by striking the patellar tendon when the knee is passively flexed. *Housemaid's k. See* Bursitis. *Knock k.* Genu valgum.

Koch's bacillus (*kok*). The *Mycobacterium tuberculosis*, the causative organism of tuberculosis.

Köhler's disease (*ker'-ler*). A type of osteochronditis.

koilonychia (*koil-on-ik'-e-ah*). Spoon-shaped nails as present in iron deficiency anaemia.

Koplik's spots (*kop'-lik*). Small white spots in an area of hyperaemia, sometimes occurring on the cheeks inside the mouth as an early sign of measles. They appear on the second day of onset, before the general rash, and are diagnostic.

Korsakoff's syndrome or **psychosis** (*kor'-sa-kofs sin'-drome*). A chronic condition in which there is impaired memory particularly for recent events and the patient is disorientated for time and place. It may be present in psychosis of infective, toxic, or metabolic origin or in chronic alcoholism.

kraurosis vulvae (*kror-o'-sis vul'-ve*). A degenerative condition of the vagina treated by giving oestrin preparations.

Krukenberg tumour (*kru'-ken-berg*). A large secondary growth in an ovary. The primary one is usually in the stomach, and is small.

Küntscher nail (*kunt'-sch-er*) An intramedullary nail for treating fracture of long bones, especially the shaft of femur.

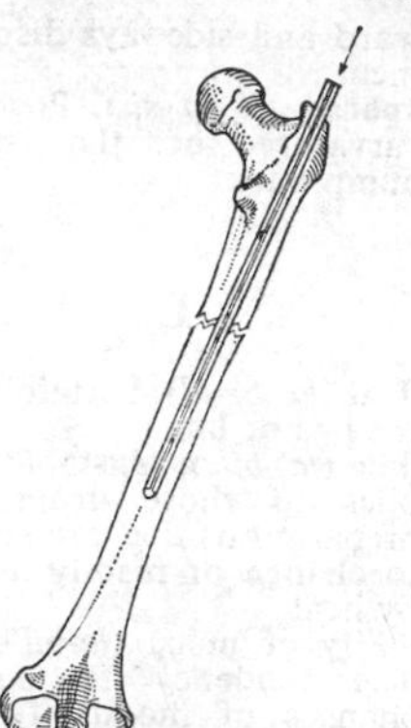

KÜNTSCHER INTRA-MEDULLARY NAIL

Kupffer's cells (*koop'-fer*). Reticulo-endothelial cells of the liver concerned in the organization of bile.

Kupperman test (*kup'-per-man*). Test for pregnancy by injecting urine into immature female rats. Results are available in 2 hr.

kwashiorkor (*kwosh-e-or'-kor*). A condition of protein malnutrition occurring in children in under-privileged populations. Fatty infiltration of the liver arises and may cause cirrhosis.

kymograph (*ki'-mo-graf*). An apparatus consisting of a rotating drum upon which graphic records can be traced of physiological or psychological processes.

kyphoscoliosis (*ki-fo-skol-e-o'-sis*). A curvature of the spine in which there is backward and sideways displacement.

kyphosis (*ki-fo'-sis*). Posterior curvature of the spine; hump-back.

L

labial (*la'-be-al*). Pertaining to the lips or labia.

labile (*la'-bile*). Unstable. Applies to those drugs and preparations that are subject to change or readily altered by heat.

lability of mood (*la-bil'-e-te*). The tendency to sudden changes of mood of short duration.

labioglossopharyngeal paralysis (*la'-be-o-glos-o-fa-rin'-je-al*). *See under* Paralysis.

labium (*la'-be-um*). A lip. *Pl.* labia, *L. majus pudendi.* The large fold of flesh surrounding the vulva. *L. minus pudendi.* The lesser fold within.

labour. Parturition or childbirth, which takes place in three stages. (1) Dilatation of the cervix uteri. (2) Passage of child through the birth canal. (3) Expulsion of placenta. *Induced l.* is brought on by artificial means before term, as in cases of contracted pelvis, or if overdue. *Obstructed l.* Due to a mechanical hindrance. *Premature l.* That which occurs before term. *Spurious l.* Pains which sometimes precede true labour pains.

labyrinth (*lab'-ir-inth*). The structures forming the internal ear, i.e. the cochlea and semicircular canals. *Bony l.* The bony canals of the internal ear. *Membranous l.* The membrane inside the bony canals.

labyrinthectomy (*lab-ir-inth-ek'-to-me*). Destruction of the membranous labyrinth of the inner ear. A possible treatment for Ménière's disease if medical treatment has failed.

labyrinthitis (*lab-ir-inth-i'-tis*). Inflammation of the labyrinth.

lac (*lak*). Milk.

laceration (*las-er-a'-shun*). A wound with torn and ragged edges—not clean cut.

lacrimal apparatus (*lak'-rim-al*). The structures secreting the tears and draining the fluid from the conjunctival sac.

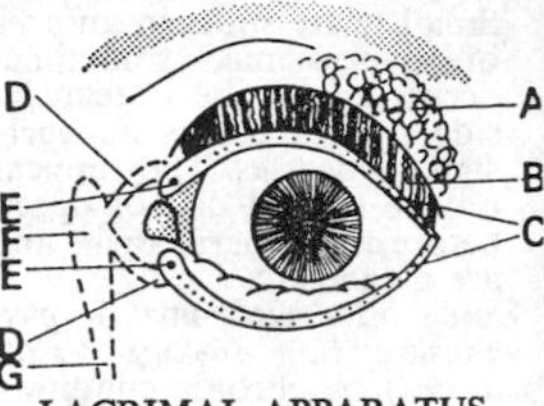

LACRIMAL APPARATUS

A. Lacrimal gland.
B. Tarsal glands.
C. Apertures of ducts.
D. Lacrimal canaliculus.
E. Punctum.
F. Lacrimal sac.
G. Naso-lacrimal duct.

lacrimation (*lak-rim-a'-shun*). An excessive secretion of tears.

lacrimators (*lak'-rim-a-tors*). Substances which cause excessive secretion of tears, e.g. tear gas.

lactagogue (*lak'-ta-gog*). *See* Galactagogue.

lactalbumin (*lakt-al'-bu-min*). An albumin of milk.

lactase (*lak'-taze*). The enzyme of succus entericus which splits lactose to glucose and galactose.

lactation (*lak-ta'-shun*). (1) The period during which the infant is nourished from the breast. (2) The process of milk secretion, carried on by the mammary glands.

lacteals (*lak'-te-als*). The lymphatics of the intestine which absorb split fats.

lactic acid (*lak'-tik*). An acid formed by the fermentation of lactose or milk sugar. It is produced naturally in the vagina before the menopause. May be used in vaginal pessaries for its antiseptic action.

lactiferous (*lak-tif'-er-us*). Conveying or secreting milk.

lactifuge (*lak'-te-fuj*). A drug or agent which retards the secretion of milk.

lactobacillus (*lak-to-bas-il'-us*). A member of a genus of micro-organisms, many of which produce fermentation.

lactoflavin (*lak'-to-flav-in*). Riboflavine (*q.v.*).

lactogenic (*lak-to-jen'-ik*). Stimulating the production of milk. *See* Luteotrophin.

lactometer (*lak-tom'-e-ter*). An instrument for measuring the specific gravity of milk.

lactose (*lak'-toze*). Milk sugar.

lactosuria (*lak-to-su'-re-ah*). Lactose in the urine.

lacuna (*lak-u'-nah*). A small cavity or depression in any part of the body. *Pl.* lacunae.

laevulose (*lev'-u-loze*). Fruit sugar.

laked. Describes blood when haemoglobin has separated from the red blood cells.

lalling (*lal'-ing*). A continuous repetitive, wordless sound as made by infants or by someone who is severely subnormal.

lambdoidal suture (*lam-doid'-al*). The junction of the occipital bone with the parietals.

lamellae (*la-mel'-le*). (1) Very thin superimposed layers of bone. (2) Minute medicated discs used in applying drugs to the eye, where they dissolve. *Sing.* lamella.

lamina (*lam'-in-ah*). A bony plate or layer.

lamina cribrosa (*lam'-in-ah krib-ro'-sah*). The portion of sclera where the fibres of the optic nerve pass through it at the optic disc.

laminectomy (*lam-in-ek'-to-me*). Excision of the posterior arch of a vertebra, sometimes performed to relieve pressure on the spinal cord or nerves.

Lancefield's groups (*lans'-feeld*). Divisions of haemolytic streptococci. Twelve groups are recognized, most human infections being due to Group A. Other groups are mainly responsible for animal infections.

lancinating (*lan'-sin-a-ting*). Sharp, cutting; it describes some pains.

Landry's disease (*lahn'-dre*). A term applied to an acute ascending paralysis from the lower limbs upwards. It may arise in polyneuritis or myelitis.

Langerhans (*lan'-ger-hans*). *Islets of L. See under* Islets. *Cells of L.* The deep cellular tissue of the chorionic villi (*q.v.*).

lanolin (*lan'-o-lin*). A fat obtained from sheep's wool, and used as a basis for ointments. *See* Adeps.

lanugo (*lan-u'-go*) A fine layer of hair seen on the body of newly born infants.
laparoscopy (*lap-ar-os'-ko-pe*). Viewing the abdominal cavity by passing a telescopic instrument through the abdominal wall.
laparotomy (*lap-ar-ot'-o-me*). Incising the abdominal wall for exploratory purposes.
lard. The fat of the pig; used as a basis for ointments.
lardaceous (*lar-da'-she-us*). The same as amyloid.
laryngeal (*la-rin'-je-al*). Pertaining to the larynx.
laryngectomy (*lar-in-jek'-to-me*). Excision of the larynx.
laryngismus stridulus (*lar-in-jiz'-mus strid'-u-lus*). A crowing sound on inspiration following a period of apnoea due to spasmodic closure of the glottis. It occurs in rickets when the calcium content of the blood is low. Treatment is as for rickets.
laryngitis (*lar-in-ji'-tis*). Inflammation of the larynx causing hoarseness or loss of voice due to acute infection or improper use (*chronic l.*). *L. stridulosa.* Spasm of the larynx, dyspnoea and stridulous inspiration at night. Occurs in nervous children with enlarged tonsils. *Tuberculous l.* A variety that responds well to anti-tuberculous drugs.
laryngologist (*lar-in-gol'-o-jist*). A specialist in diseases of the larynx.
laryngoparalysis (*lar-in'-go-par-al'-is-is*). Paralysis of the larynx.
laryngopharynx (*lar-in'-go-far'-inks*). The lower part of the pharynx.
laryngoscope (*lar-in'-go-skope*). An endoscopic instrument for

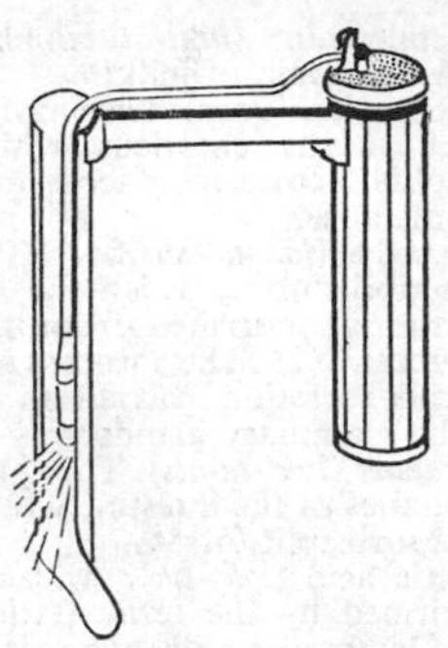

LARYNGOSCOPE

examining the larynx or for aiding the insertion of endotracheal tubes or the bronchoscope. *See diagram.*
laryngospasm (*lar-in'-go-spazm*). A reflex prolonged contraction of the laryngeal muscles that is liable to occur on insertion or withdrawal of an intratracheal tube.
laryngostenosis (*lar-in-go-sten-o'-sis*). Contraction or stricture of the larynx.
laryngostomy (*lar-in-gost'-o-me*). Incision of the larynx to provide an artificial air-passage.
laryngotracheal (*lar-in-go-trak'-e-al*). Referring to both the larynx and trachea.
laryngotracheitis (*lar-in-go-trak-e-i'-tis*). Inflammation of both the larynx and trachea.
larynx (*lar'-inks*). The organ of the voice, situated at the upper end of the trachea. It has a muscular and cartilaginous frame, lined with mucous membrane. Across it are spread the vocal cords of elastic tissue, and the vibrations and contractions of

these produce the changes in the pitch of the voice. The space between the cords is termed the *glottis*.

laser (*la'-zer*). Light Amplification by Stimulated Emission of Radiation. An extremely concentrated beam of light that can be used to cut metals. Used experimentally in surgery and in the treatment of detached retina.

Lassar's paste (*las'-ar*). A soothing paste used in skin diseases, containing salicylic acid, powdered zinc, starch and petroleum jelly.

latent (*la'-tent*). Temporarily concealed; not manifest. *L. heat*. That which brings about a change in state, i.e. from water into steam. When condensation occurs this heat is released.

lateral (*lat'-er-al*). Relating to the side.

lateroversion (*lat-er-o-ver'-shun*). Turning to one side, such as may occur of the uterus.

laudanum (*lod'-an-um*). Tincture of opium; a preparation used as a narcotic.

laughing gas. Nitrous oxide (*q.v.*).

lavage (*lav-arj'*). Washing out a cavity. *Colonic l.* Washing out the colon. Several pints of fluid are used. *Gastric l.* Of the stomach. *Rectal l.* Of the rectum.

Lawrence's line ration diet. A diabetic diet in which one line ration consisted of carbohydrates 10 g, protein 7·5 g and fat 9 g. Now superseded by the 5 g interchangeable portions diet. *See* Appendix 10.

laxative (*laks'-at-iv*). A mild aperient (*q.v.*).

lead (*led*). A metal, the salts of which are applied externally as an astringent lotion to inflamed surfaces and bruises.

leather bottle stomach. *See under* Stomach.

lecithin (*les'-ith-in*). A nitrogenous and fatty substance found in nerve tissues, blood, and bile, and also in eggs.

leech (*le'-tch*). *Hirudo medicinalis.* An aquatic worm which sucks blood and is sometimes used as a counter-irritant.

leg. The lower limb, from knee to ankle. *Barbados l.* Elephantiasis. *Bow l.* Genu valgum. *White l.* Phlegmasia alba dolens (*q.v.*). *Scissor l.* Cross legged, as occurs in Little's disease.

legumin (*leg'-u-min.*) A protein of peas, beans, and all pulses.

Leishman – Donovan bodies (*leesh'-man don'-o-van*). The intracellular forms of *Leishmania donovani*, the parasite producing kala-azar. These bodies occur in the spleen and liver of patients.

Leishmania (*leesh-ma'-ne-ah*). Parasitic protozoa having flagellae which infect the blood of man and are the cause of leishmaniasis.

leishmaniasis (*leesh-man-i'-a-sis*). Kala-azar (*q.v.*).

Lembert's suture (*lom-bair'*). For wounds of the intestine. So arranged that the edges are turned inwards and the peritoneal surfaces are in contact.

lemology (*le-mol'-o-je*). The science of epidemic diseases, especially plague.

lenitive (*len'-it-iv*). A soothing agent.

lens (*lens*). (1) The transparent, crystalline body situated behind the pupil of the eye. It serves as a refractive medium for rays of light. (2) Pieces of glass shaped to focus or scatter rays of light. They can be of varied shapes in order to improve sight. *Contact l.* A thin sheet of glass moulded to fit directly over the cornea. Worn instead of spectacles.

lentigo (*len-ti'-go*). A freckle.

leontiasis (*le-on-ti'-as-is*). A disease of the face in which osseous deformity produces a lion-like appearance. It occurs sometimes in leprosy, elephantiasis, etc.

lepidosis (*lep-id-o'-sis*). Any scaly eruption of the skin.

leprosy (*lep'-ro-se*). A chronic infectious disease affecting the skin and nerves, owing to the *Mycobacterium leprae*. There are three recognized forms: (1) Tuberculoid, in which the tissue defence is good. (2) Lepromatous, in which the tissue defence is poor or absent. (3) Dimorphous, in which there is partial tissue defence. Signs and symptoms include anaesthesia, especially of hands and feet; skin lesions (various types anywhere on the body); and the thickening of certain nerves. The last sometimes culminates in paralysis of certain muscles of the hands, feet, or face (i.e. primary deformity). Fingers and toes do *not* die and drop off, but can be 'lost' due to the fact that there is lack of sensation and therefore ulceration and sepsis ensues and the small bones of the extremities become affected (i.e. secondary deformity). Modern physiotherapeutic and operative surgical techniques can prevent much of this deformity. Sulphone preparations are used successfully in treatment.

leptazol (*lep'-ta-zol*). A respiratory stimulant used in poisoning cases where there is respiratory depression.

leptomeningitis (*lep-to-men-in-ji'-tis*). Inflammation of the pia mater and arachnoid membranes.

Leptospira (*lep-to-spi'-rah*). A class of spirochaete *L. icterohaemorrhagiae*. The cause of Weil's disease (*q.v.*).

leptospirosis (*lep-to-spi-ro'-sis*). Weil's disease (*q.v.*).

lesbianism (*les'-be-an-izm*). Sexual attraction of one woman to another.

lesion (*le'-zhun*). An injury, wound, or morbid structural change in an organ. The word is used as a general term for some local disease condition.

lethane (*leth'-ane*). A 50 per cent solution of lethane in oil may be applied to the scalp to destroy head lice. It is left on one week before washing the hair.

lethargy (*leth'-ar-je*). A condition of drowsiness or stupor which cannot be overcome by the will.

leucine (*lu'-sin*). An essential amino acid of the protein molecule; it may be excreted in the urine from excessive endogenous breakdown of protein, as in acute atrophy of the liver.

leucocyte (*lu'-ko-site*). A white blood corpuscle. There are three types: (a) *granular* (polymorphonuclear cells) formed in bone marrow, consisting of neutrophils, eosinophils and basophils; (b) lymphocytes (formed in the lymph glands), and (c) monocytes. *L. count* (normal):

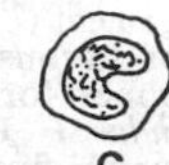

LEUCOCYTES

A. Polymorphonuclear.
B. Lymphocyte.
C. Monocyte.

	per mm^3
Neutrophils . .	5000
Lymphocytes . .	2000
Monocytes . .	350
Eosinophils . .	100
Basophils . .	50
	7500

leucocytolysis (*lu-ko-si-tol'-is-is*). Destruction of white blood cells.

leucocytosis (*lu-ko-si-to'-sis*). Increased number of leucocytes in the blood.

leucoderma (*lu-ko-der'-mah*). A congenital absence of pigment in patches or bands, producing abnormal whiteness of the skin.

leucoma (*lu-ko'-mah*). A white spot on the cornea, following an injury to the eye.

leuconychia (*lu-kon-ik'-e-ah*). White patches on the nails due to air underneath.

leucopenia (*lu-ko-pe'-ne-ah*). A decreased number of white cells, usually granulocytes, in the blood. It may be present in tuberculosis, enteric fever, influenza or undulant fever.

leucopoiesis (*lu-ko-poy-e'-sis*). The formation of white blood cells.

leucorrhoea (*lu-kor-re'-ah*). A thick whitish discharge from the vagina, which occurs when there is congestion in the pelvic organs. Blennorrhagia.

leucotomy (*lu-kot'-o-me*). Severing of white fibres. *Prefrontal l.* An operation in which the fronto-thalamic connection fibres passing into the frontal lobes of the brain are severed. It may considerably relieve symptoms of worry, tension, and fear but there may also be changes in personality, such as lack of initiative and perseverance. The process is irreversible.

leukaemia (*lu-ke'-me-ah*). A blood disease of unknown cause, in which there is great increase in the number of white cells. There are two chief forms. (1) *Lymphatic* (or *lymphocytic*) *l.* in which there is enlargement of the lymphatic glands and spleen. (2) *Myeloid l.* Associated with disease of the bone-marrow and enlargement of the spleen. Both forms may be *acute* lasting only a few weeks or months, or *chronic* lasting a number of years with long periods of remission following treatment.

leukoplakia (*lu-ko-pla'-ke-ah*). A chronic inflammation, characterized by a white thickened surface. *L. buccalis.* The condition affects the mucous membrane of the mouth. *L. vulvae.* The mucous membrane and skin of the labia become thickened and scattered white patches appear. It is a precancerous condition and the treatment is vulvectomy.

levallorphan (*lev-al-or'-fan*). A respiratory stimulant that antagonizes the action of morphine. Lorfan is a proprietary preparation.

levator (*lev-a'-tor*). A muscle which raises a part. *L. palpebrae*. Raises the eye lid.

levorphanol (*lev-or'-fan-ol*). An analgesic somewhat resembling morphine in its action and addiction potentialities. In tablet or injection form, it is subject to the Misuse of Drugs Act. Dromoran is a proprietary preparation.

libido (*lib-e'-do*). (1) The vital force or impulse which brings about purposive action. (2) Sexual drive. In Freudian psychoanalysis the motive force of all human beings.

lice. *See* Louse.

lichen (*li'-ken*). A group of inflammatory affections of the skin, in which the lesions consist of papular eruptions. *L. planus*. Raised flat patches of dull reddish-purple colour. with smooth or scaly surface. The skin is stained when they disappear.

lichenification (*li-ken-if-e-ka'-shun*). The stage of an eruption when it resembles lichen.

lichenoid (*li'-ken-oid*). A rash that resembles lichen.

lid lag. When there is an area of sclera showing between the upper lid and the iris as occurs in thyrotoxicosis.

Lieberkühn's glands (*le'-ber-koon*). Tubular glands of the small intestine.

lien (*li'-en*). The spleen.

lienculus (*li-en'-ku-lus*). An accessory spleen.

lienitis (*li-en-i'-tis*). Inflammation of the spleen (Splenitis).

lienorenal (*li-en-o-re'-nal*). Relating to the spleen and kidney. *L. anastomosis*. The joining of the splenic vein to the left renal vein. A method of reducing the blood supply to the liver in portal hypertension.

lienunculus (*li-en-un'-ku-lus*). A detached portion of spleen.

ligament (*lig'-a-ment*). A band of fibrous tissue connecting bones forming a joint. *Annular l.* The ring-like band which fixes the head of the radius to the ulna. *Crucial l.* Crossed ligaments within the knee joint. *Poupart's l.* Between the pubic bone and anterior iliac crest. *Round l.* e.g. One of the two anterior ligaments of the uterus, passing through the inguinal canal and ending in the labia majora.

ligation (*lig-a'-shun*). The application of a ligature.

ligature (*lig'-at-chur*). A thread of silk, catgut or other material used for tying vessels.

light. Electromagnetic waves which by stimulating the retina of the eye give the sensation of light. *L. baths*. Ultraviolet rays are administered by an electric arc, made by two poles (*tungsten* or *carbon rods*) or the mercury vapour lamp. These have a tonic effect and kill bacteria near the surface. Vitamin D is produced by their action on ergosterol of subcutaneous tissues. *Wood l.* That from which visible rays have been eliminated. Used in the diagnosis of skin diseases.

light coagulation. A method of treating retinal detachment by directing a beam of strong light from a carbon arc through the pupil to the affected area.

lightening. The relief experienced in the late stages of pregnancy when the uterus sinks into the pelvis and ceases to press on the diaphragm.

lightning pains. Intense, sharp, and cutting pains in the legs characteristic of locomotor ataxia.

lignocaine (*lig'-no-kane*). A local anaesthetic for infiltration or surface application. Xylocaine is a proprietary preparation.

limbus (*lim'-bus*). Applied to the eye—the border where the cornea joins the sclera.

lime. (1) The citrus fruit resembling a small lemon. (2) Calcium oxide, the salts of which help to form bone (CaO). *Chlorinated l.* Bleaching powder. *L. water.* Calcium hydrate solution. Given to counteract acidity.

linctus (*link'-tus*). A thick syrup given to soothe and allay coughing. It should not be diluted. *Opiate l. of squill* contains opium. *Codeine l.* and *methadone l.* are similar.

linea (*lin'-e-ah*). A line. *L. alba.* The tendinous area in the centre of the abdominal wall into which the transversalis and part of the oblique muscles are inserted. *L. albicantes.* White streaks that appear on the abdomen when it is distended by pregnancy or a tumour. *L. aspera.* The rough ridge on the back of the femur into which muscles are inserted. *L. nigra.* The pigmented line which often appears in pregnancy on the abdomen between the umbilicus and pubis.

lingual (*ling'-gwal*). Pertaining to the tongue.

lingula (*ling'-u-la*). A tongue-like projection of lung tissue from the left upper lobe.

liniment (*lin'-e-ment*). A liquid to be applied externally by rubbing. *Camphor l.* is of camphor and olive oil.

linseed. Seeds of the common flax, which contain an oil with a demulcent action. *L. meal* is crushed linseed used for poultices.

lint. A loosely woven cotton fabric, one side of which is fluffy, and the other smooth.

liothyronine (*li-o-thi'-ro-neen*). A preparation of thyroid hormone used in the treatment of hypothyroidism where rapid results are desired.

liothyroxine (*li-o-thi-roks'-een*). A preparation of thyroid extract for the treatment of cretinism and myxoedema.

lipaemia (*li-pe'-me-ah*). The presence of excess fat in the blood. Sometimes a feature of diabetes.

lipase (*lip'-aze*). The fat-splitting ferment of pancreatic juice. Also called *steapsin*.

Lipiodol (*lip-i'-o-dol*). A proprietary compound of iodine and oil, which being opaque to X-rays may be introduced to outline cavities; e.g. spinal canal, bronchial tubes, etc.

lipoid (*lip'-oid*). Resembling fat or oil. *L. nephrosis.* A condition of the kidney in which fat is deposited.

lipoidoses (*lip-oid-o'-ses*). A group of diseases in which there is an error in lipoid metabolism. Xanthomata (*q.v.*) are common.

lipolysis (*lip-ol'-is-is*). The breakdown of fats by the action of bile salts and enzymes to a fine emulsion and fatty acids.

lipoma (*lip-o'-mah*). A tumour composed of fatty tissue, arising in any part of the body, and developing in connective tissue. *Diffuse l.* A tumour of fat in an irregular mass without a capsule.

lipotrophic substances (*lip-o-tro'-fik*). Dietary factors which have the power to remove fat and so help to prevent fatty infiltration of the liver, e.g. choline and methionine.

lipuria (*lip-u'-re-ah*). The presence of fat in urine.

liquefaction (*lik-we-fak'-shun*). Reduction to liquid form.

liquor (*lik'-er*; Latin *li'-kwor*). A watery fluid. Drugs are administered in this form. *L. amnii.* The fluid in which the fetus floats. *L. arsenicalis.* A solution of arsenic to be taken by mouth. *L. epispasticus.* Blistering fluid. *L. sanguinis.* The plasma, or fluid part of blood.

lithagogue (*lith'-a-gog*). A drug which helps to expel calculi.

lithiasis (*lith-i'-as-is*). Formation of calculi. *Conjunctival l.* Small white chalky areas on the under surface of the eyelids.

litho- (*lith'-o*). A prefix signifying 'a stone'.

lithonephrotomy (*lith-o-nef-rot'-o-me*). Incision of the kidney to remove a stone. Nephrolithotomy.

lithopaedion (*lith-o-pe'-de-on*). A dead fetus that has been retained and become calcified.

lithosis (*lith-o'-sis*). Disease resulting from inhalation of particles of silica, etc., into the lungs. Pneumokoniosis.

lithotome (*lith'-o-tome*). A knife used in lithotomy.

lithotomy (*lith-ot'-o-me*). Incision of the bladder for the removal of calculi. *L. position. See under* Position.

lithotripsy (*lith'-o-trip-se*). Lithotrity. The crushing of calculi in the bladder.

lithotrite (*lith'-o-trite*). An instrument used for lithotripsy.

lithuresis (*lith-u-re'-sis*). Passage of small calculi or gravel in the urine.

litmus (*lit'-mus*). A blue pigment obtained from lichen and used for testing the reaction of fluids. *Blue l.* is turned red by an acid. *Red l.* is turned blue by an alkali.

litre (*le'-ter*). The unit of capacity in the metric system. One thousand millilitres. *See* Appendix 14.

Little's disease. Spastic diplegia. A congenital muscle rigidity of the lower limbs, causing 'scissor leg' deformity. The cause may be haemorrhage into, or bruising of the brain before or during birth.

liver (*liv'-er*). The large gland situated in the right upper area of the abdominal cavity. Its chief functions are: (1) the secretion of bile, (2) the maintenance of the composition of the blood, and (3) the regulation of metabolic processes. *Cirrhotic l.* Fibrotic changes which occur in the liver as the result of chronic inflammation. *Hobnail l.* The appearance of the cirrhotic liver. *Nutmeg l.* A mottled condition, typical of the effect of congestive heart failure.

livid (*liv'-id*). A bluish-grey

complexion, produced by congestion of blood.

lobar (*lo'-bar*). Relating to a lobe.

lobe. A section of an organ, separated from neighbouring parts by fissures.

lobectomy (*lo-bek'-to-me*). Removal of a lobe, e.g. of the lung. Performed, in lung abscess, or unilateral bronchiectasis.

lobotomy (*lob-ot'-o-me*). An operation in which the nerve fibres in the prefrontal area of the brain are severed to effect a change of behaviour. *Syn.* Leucotomy.

lobular (*lob'-u-lar*). Relating to a lobule.

lobule (*lob'-ule*). A small lobe.

localize (*lo'-kal-ize*). To limit the spread, e.g. of disease or infection, to a certain area.

lochia (*lo'-ke-ah*). The discharge of blood and tissue debris from the uterus following childbirth. *L. alba.* The later pale discharge. *L. rubra.* The earlier discharge first containing bright blood and later dark blood. *L. serosa.* A thin clear discharge.

lochiometra (*lo-ke-o-me'-trah*). A collection of lochia in the uterus.

locked twins. The condition of twins with their bodies so placed that neither can be born naturally.

lock-jaw. Tetanus.

locomotor ataxia (*lo-ko-mo'-tor a-taks'-e-ah*). Tabes dorsalis. *See* Ataxia.

loculated (*lok'-u-la-ted*). Divided into small locules or cavities.

loculus (*lok'-u-lus*). A small cystic cavity, one of a number.

loiasis (*lo-i'-as-is*). Infestation of the conjunctiva and eyelids with a parasitic worm, the *Loa loa.* A tropical condition.

loin. The area at the back, between the thorax and the pelvis.

long-sight. Hypermetropia (*q.v.*).

loop (1) A complete bend. (2) A platinum wire in a handle used for transferring bacteriological material. It is always flamed to red heat before and after use.

lordosis (*lor-do'-sis*). A form of spinal curvature in which there is an abnormal forward curve of the lumbar spine.

lotion (*lo'-shun*). A medicinal solution, used for bathing wounds, etc. *Calamine l.* A soothing mixture containing calamine and zinc oxide. *Evaporating l.* A dilute alcoholic solution applied to bruises. *Lead l.* A weak solution of lead acetate used for sprains and bruises where the skin is unbroken. *Red l.* Zinc oxide in solution. A stimulating lotion for sluggish tissues.

loupe (*loop*). A magnifying lens which may be used in eye examination.

louse (*lows*). A parasite which infests mammals. *Head l. Pediculus capitis. Body* or *clothes l. Pediculus corporis. Pubic* or *crab l.* Infests the hair on the body. Diseases known to be transmitted by the louse are typhus fever, relapsing fever and trench fever.

lozenge (*loz'-enj*). A medicated tablet, with sugar basis.

LSD. *See* Lysergide.

lubb-dupp. Describes the sounds heard through the stethoscope when listening to the normal heart. *Lubb* when the atrio-ventricular valves shut, and *dupp* when the semilunar valves meet each other.

lucid (*lu'-sid*). Clear, particularly of the mind. *L. interval.* May occur in cerebral injury between two periods of unconsciousness or as a sane interval in a mental disorder.

Ludwig's angina (*lood'-vig*). *See under* Angina.

Lugol's solution (*lu'-gol*). A preparation of *iodine* and *potassium iodide*. It is best given in milk, and is largely used in the treatment of toxic goitre.

lumbago (*lum-ba'-go*). A painful rheumatic affection of the muscles and fibrous tissues of the loin, usually the result of exposure to cold.

lumbar (*lum'-bar*). Pertaining to the loins. *L. puncture.* A trocar and cannula are inserted into the spinal canal, and cerebrospinal fluid is withdrawn. The manometer attached to the cannula gives a reading of the intraspinal pressure. Normally this is 120 mm.

lumbosacral (*lum-bo-sa'-kral*). Relating to both the lumbar vertebrae and the sacrum.

Lumbricus (*lum'-brik-us*). (1) A genus of worms, including the earthworm. (2) The Ascaris, which is parasitic in the intestine of man.

lumen (*lu'-men*). The space inside a tube.

lunacy (*lu'-nas-e*). A term formerly applied to insanity (*q.v.*).

lunar caustic. Nitrate of silver.

lung. One of a pair of conical organs of the respiratory system, consisting of an arrangement of air tubes terminating in air vesicles (*alveoli*) and filling almost the whole of the thorax. The right lung has three lobes and the left lung two. They are connected with the air by means of the bronchi and trachea.

lunula (*lu'-nu-lah*). The white semicircle, near the root of each nail.

lupus (*lu'-pus*). A skin disease, having many manifestations.

lupus erythematosus (*lu'-pus er-e-the-mat-o'-ses*). An urticaria which finally produces a round plaque-like area of hyperkeratosis. It is thought to be due to an autoimmune reaction to sunlight, infection, or other unknown cause. *L. vulgaris.* A tuberculous disease of the skin treated with isoniazid. *L. erythematous.* A non-tuberculous infection of the dermis characterized by red scaly patches, which on healing leave dull white scars. The cause is not known.

luteotrophin (*lu-te-o-tro'-fin*). An anterior pituitary hormone. The name now given to prolactin as it is known to influence both the secretion of milk and the corpus luteum.

luxation (*luks-a'-shun*). Dislocation.

lying. Making an untruthful statement. *Pathological l.* A disorder of conduct which may occur as a symptom in behaviour disorders of children or in certain mental disorders such as addiction or psychopathic personality.

lying in. The puerperium.

lymph (*limf*). The fluid from the blood which has transuded through capillary walls to supply nutriment to tissue cells. It is collected by lymph vessels which ultimately return it to the blood. *L.*

nodes or *glands*. Structures placed along the course of lymph vessels, through which the lymph passes and is filtered of foreign substances, e.g. bacteria. These nodes also make lymphocytes. *Plastic l.* Exuded in inflammation, which tends to cause adhesion between structures and so limit spread of infection, e.g. in peritonitis. *Vaccine l.* Used for vaccination against smallpox.

lymphadenectomy (*limf-ad-en-ek'-to-me*). Excision of a lymph gland or nodes.

lymphadenitis (*limf-ad-en-i'-tis*). Inflammation of a lymph gland.

lymphadenoma (*limf-ad-en-o'-mah*). A malignant disease of lymphoid tissue. Hodgkin's disease (*q.v.*).

lymphadenopathy (*lim-fad-en-op'-ath-e*). Any disease condition of the lymph nodes.

lymphangiectasis (*limf-an-je-ek'-tas-is*). Dilated lymph vessels due to some obstruction of the lymph current.

lymphangiogram (*limf-an'-je-o-gram*). An X-ray of lymph vessels made possible by the insertion of a dye.

lymphangioma (*limf-an-je-o'-mah*). A swelling composed of dilated lymph vessels.

lymphangioplasty (*limf-an'-ge-o-plas-te*). Any plastic operation which aims at making an artificial lymph drainage.

lymphangitis (*limf-an-ji'-tis*). Inflammation of lymph vessels, manifested by red lines on the skin over them. It occurs in cases of severe infection through the skin, usually by streptococci.

lymphatic (*limf-at'-ik*). Referring to the lymph. *L. leukaemia. See* Leukaemia. *L. system.* The system of vessels and glands through which the lymph is returned to the circulation. The vessels end in the thoracic duct (*q.v.*).

lymphoblasts (*limf'-o-blasts*). Early developmental cells that mature into lymphocytes.

lymphocyte (*limf'-o-site*). White blood cells formed in the lymphoid tissue. Their function is the production of immune bodies to overcome and protect against infection.

lymphocythaemia (*limf-o-si-the'-me-ah*). Excessive numbers of lymphocytes in the blood.

lymphocytosis (*limf-o-si-to'-sis*). Lymphocythemia (*q.v.*).

lymphoedema (*limf-o-de'-mah*). A condition in which the intercellular spaces contain an abnormal amount of lymph due to obstruction of lymph drainage.

lymphogranuloma venereum (*limf-o-gran-u-lo'-mah ven-e'-re-um*). A sexually-transmitted disease due to a virus, primarily a tropical condition.

lymphoid (*limf'-oid*). Relating to the lymph.

lymphoma (*limf-o'-mah*). A tumour of lymphoid tissue.

lymphorrhagia (*limf-o-raj'-e-ah*). The escape of lymph from a ruptured lymphatic vessel.

lymphosarcoma (*limf-o-sar-ko'-mah*). Sarcoma arising in a lymph gland.

lyophilized skin (*li'-o-fil-ized*). Skin from cadavers may be treated by lyophilization, reconstituted and used for temporary skin replacement in severe burns.

lyophilization (*li-o-fil-i-za'-shun*). A method of preserving biological substances in a stable state by freeze drying. It may be used for plasma, sera, bacteria and tissues.

lysergide (*li-serg'-ide*). Lysergic acid diethylamide. LSD. A psychotomimetic drug that may cause visual hallucination and increased auditory acuity but may prove very disrupting to the personality and affect mental ability.

lysin (*li'-sin*). A specific antibody that can destroy cells or tissues. *See* Bacteriolysin.

lysis (*li'-sis*). (1) The gradual decline of a disease, especially of a fever. The temperature falls gradually as in typhoid. (*See also* Crisis.) (2) The action of a lysin.

lysozyme (*li'-so-zime*). An enzyme present in tears, nasal mucus, and saliva that can kill most organisms coming in contact with it.

lytic mixture (*lit'-ik*). One used to assist in inducing and maintaining hypothermia (*q.v.*). It consists of chlorpromazine, pethidine and promethazine. It acts as a sedative and prevents shivering.

M

m. Abbreviation of: *misce*, mix; *metre*, a unit of length; *minim*, a unit of fluid measure.

maceration (*mas-er-a'-shun*). Softening of a solid by soaking it in liquid.

Mackenrodt's ligaments (*mak'-en-rot*). The transverse or cardinal ligaments that support the uterus in the pelvic cavity.

macrocephalus (*mak-ro-kef'-al-us*). Possessing an abnormally large head.

macrocheilia (*mak-ro-ki'-le-ah*). Excessive development of the lips caused by dilated lymphatic spaces.

macrocyte (*mak'-ro-site*). An abnormally large red corpuscle found in the blood in some forms of anaemia.

macrocythaemia (*mak-ro-si-the'-me-ah*). Abnormally large red cells in the blood.

Macrodex (*mak'-ro-deks*). A proprietary intravenous dextran solution useful as a plasma substitute in treating shock.

macroglossia (*mak-ro-glos'-se-ah*). Abnormal enlargement of the tongue.

macromastia (*mak-ro-mas'-te-ah*). Abnormal increase in the size of the breast.

macrophage (*mak'-ro-fage*). A large reticulo-endothelial cell which has the power to ingest cell debris and bacteria.

macrophthalmos (*mak-rof-thal'-mos*). A congenital condition of bilateral large eyes.

macroscopic (*mak-ro-skop'-ik*). Discernible with the naked eye.

macula (*mak'-u-lah*) or **macule.** A spot or discoloured area of the skin, not raised above the surface. *M. lutea.* The central area of the retina, where vision is clearest.

maculopapular eruption (*mak'-u-lo-pap'-u-lar*). A rash of red raised spots or papules, as in measles.

Madura foot (*ma-du'-rah*). *See* Mycetoma.

magnesium (*mag-ne'-ze-um*). A bluish-white metal. *M. sulphate* is a saline purgative. *M. trisilicate*, an antacid powder taken after food for dyspepsia and peptic ulceration. *M. carbonate* and *M. hydroxide* are neutralizing antacids used in hyperacidity.

magnet operation (*mag'-net*). *See under* Operation.

mal. Disease. *M. de mer*. Seasickness. *Grand m.*, *petit m.* Forms of epilepsy.

malabsorption (*mal-ab-sorp'-shun*). Inability to absorb. May be the cause of deficiency disease due to the lack of an essential factor.

malacia (*mal-a'-se-ah*). Softening of tissues. *Osteo-m.* Softening of bone tissue. *Kerato-m.* Softening of the cornea.

maladjustment (*mal-ad-just'-ment*). Not adjusted to society.

malaise (*mal-aze'*). A feeling of general discomfort and illness.

malar (*ma'-lar*). Relating to the cheek or cheekbone. *M. flush*. *See* Hectic.

malaria (*ma-lair'-e-ah*). A febrile disease caused by a parasite introduced into the blood by mosquitoes of the genus Anopheles. The attacks are periodic every 48 to 72 hr according to the type of plasmodium (*q.v.*). A typical malarial paroxysm consists of three stages. (1) The shivering fit. (2) High fever. (3) The sweating stage.

malarial therapy (*ma-lair'-e-al ther'-a-pe*). A hyperpyrexia is induced by infecting a patient with malaria. Sometimes used in the treatment of neurosyphilis.

malaxation (*mal-aks-a'-shun*). A kneading movement in massage.

male fern. *Filix mas.* A drug given by mouth, to expel tapeworms.

malformation (*mal-form-a'-shun*). Ill-formed, causing deformity. A structural defect.

malignant (*mal-ig'-nant*). A term applied to any disease of a virulent and fatal nature. *M. growth* or *tumour*, Cancer. *M. pustule*, Anthrax. *M. endocarditis*. *See* Endocarditis. *M. hypertension*. *See* Hypertension.

malleolus (*mal-le-o'-lus*). The projection on the tibia (*internal m.*) and on the fibula (*external m.*) at the ankle-joint.

malleus (*mal'-le-us*). The hammer-shaped bone in the middle ear.

malnutrition (*mal-nu-trish'-un*). The condition in which nutrition is defective in quantity or quality.

malocclusion (*mal-ok-klu'-shun*). Failure of the upper and lower teeth to meet together correctly on closing the jaw, thereby preventing efficient mastication.

Malpighian body (*mal-pig'-e-an*). The glomerulus and Bowman's capsule of the kidney.

malposition (*mal-po-zi'-shun*). An abnormal position of any part.

malpractice (*mal-prak'-tis*). Not maintaining the accepted ethical standards.

malpresentation (*mal-pres-en-ta'-shun*). Any abnormal position of the fetus at birth, which renders delivery difficult or impossible.

malt (*mawlt*). Grain which has been soaked, made to germinate, and dried. It is used as a nutrient in wasting diseases. *M. extract*. Aids the digestion of starches. *M. sugar*. Maltose.

Malta fever. *See* Undulant fever.

maltase (*mawl'-taze*). A sugar splitting enzyme which converts maltose to dextrose,

Present in pancreatic and intestinal juice.
maltose (*mawl'-toze*). The sugar formed by the action of digestive enzymes on starch.
malunion (*mal-u'-ne-on*). Faulty repair of a fracture.
mamilla (*mam-il'-lah*). The nipple.
mammae (*mam'-me*). The breasts or milk-secreting glands.
mammaplasty (*mam'-mah-plas-te*). A plastic operation to reduce the size of abnormally large pendulous breasts.
mammary (*mam'-mar-e*). Relating to the breasts.
mammography (*mam-og-raf'-e*). X-ray examination of the breast to try and detect early cancer.
mammothermography (*mam-o-therm-og'-raf-e*). An examination of the breast that depends on the more active cells producing heat that can be shown on a thermograph, and may indicate a precancerous stage.
Manchester operation. *See* Fothergill's operations.
mandible (*man'-dib-l*). The lower jaw-bone.
Mandl's paint (*mand'-l*). Iodine compound paint for application to an inflamed pharynx with a camel hair brush.
manganese (*man'-gan-ees*). A grey-white metal, from the salts of which the permanganates are formed.
mania (*ma'-ne-ah*). Elevation of the mood accompanied by acceleration of thought and action. *M. à potu.* Transient alcoholic excitement.
manic-depressive psychosis (*man'-ik de-pres'-iv si-ko'-sis*). A mental illness characterized by mania or endogenous depression (*q.v.*). The attacks may alternate between mania and depression or the patient may just have recurrent attacks of mania or depression.
manipulation (*man-ip-u-la'-shun*). Using the hands in a skilful manner, such as in reducing a fracture or hernia, or changing the position of the fetus.
mannerisms (*man' er-izms*). Small actions performed without thought, that are characteristic of the individual. They assume psychiatric significance when they become exaggerated or excessive and are associated with emotional stress.
Mannitol (*man'-e-tol*). A synthetic carbohydrate given intravenously to reduce intracranial pressure by its diuretic action.
mannometric (*man-o-met'-rik*). The recording of pressures applied to the body structures and so obtaining information about activity.
manometer (*man-om'-e-ter*). An instrument for measuring the volume or tension of liquids or gases. *See* Sphygmomanometer.
Mantoux reaction (*man-too'*). An intradermal injection of *old tuberculin* to determine susceptibility to tuberculosis. If positive a wheal develops in 24 to 48 hr.
manubrium (*man-u'-bre-um*). The upper part of the sternum to which the clavicle is attached.
MAOI. *See under* Monoamine oxidase.
marasmus (*mar-as'-mus*). Gradual wasting of the tissues, owing to insufficient or

unassimilated food, occurring especially in infants. It is not always possible to discover the cause.

marihuana (*mar-e-hwar'-nah*). *Cannabis indica*, Indian hemp or hashish. *See* Cannabis.

Marmite (*mar'-mite*). A proprietary extract from yeast containing vitamin B in large quantities.

Marplan (*mah'-plan*). A proprietary preparation of isocarboxazid. An antidepressive drug.

marrow (*mar'-ro*). (1) The substance contained in the middle of long bones and in the cancellous tissue of all types. *Red m.* Found in all cancellous tissue. Blood cells are made in it. *Yellow m.* The fatty substance contained in the centre of long bones. (2) *Spinal m.* The spinal cord.

Marion's tube (*mar'-e-on*). A special pattern used for suprapubic drainage.

masochism (*mas'-o-kizm*). Punishing oneself. This may be a conscious or unconscious process.

massage (*mas-sarj'*). A scientific method of rubbing, kneading, and manipulating the body to stimulate circulation, improve metabolism and break down adhesions. *External cardiac m.* Applying rhythmic pressure to the lower sternum to cause expulsion of blood from the ventricles and restart circulation in cases of sudden heart failure.

masseter (*mas'-se-ter*). The muscle of the cheek chiefly concerned in mastication.

masseur (*mas-sur'*). A man who performs massage. *Feminine.* Masseuse.

mastalgia (*mas-tal'-je-ah*). Pain in the breast.

mastatrophia (*mast-a-tro'-fe-ah*). Atrophy of the breast.

mast cells. Connective tissue cells found in many body tissues including the heart, liver, and lungs.

mastectomy (*mast-ek'-to-me*). Amputation of the breast. *Radical m.* Removal of the breast, axillary lymph glands and pectoralis muscle (*modified Halsted's operation*).

mastication (*mas-tik-a'-shun*). The act of chewing food.

mastitis (*mas-ti'-tis*). Inflammation of the breast.

mastoid (*mas'-toid*). Nipple shaped. *M. process.* The prominence on the temporal bone which projects downwards behind the ear and into which the sternocleidomastoid muscle is inserted. *M. antrum.* The cavity in this part of the temporal bone which communicates with the middle ear, and contains air. *M. cells.* Hollow spaces in the mastoid bone. *M. operation.* For drainage of these cells when infection spreads from the middle ear.

mastoidectomy (*mas-toid-ek'-to-me*). Removal of diseased bone and drainage of purulent mastoiditis.

mastoiditis (*mas-toid-i'-tis*). Inflammation of the mastoid antrum and cells.

mastoidotomy (*mas-toid-ot'-o-me*). Surgical opening of the mastoid antrum.

masturbation (*mas-ter-ba'-shun*). Production of sexual excitement by friction of the genitals.

materia medica (*mat-e'-re-ah med'-ik-ah*). The science of the source and preparation of drugs used in medicine.

matrix (*ma'-triks*). (1) That tissue in which cells are embedded. (2) The uterus or womb.

matter. Substance. *Grey m.* A collection of nerve cells or non-medullated nerve fibres. *White m.* Medullated nerve fibres massed together, as in the brain.

mattress suture (*su'-chur*). *See under* Suture.

maturation (*mat-u-ra'-shun*). Ripening or developing.

maxilla (*maks-il'-lah*). The upper or lower jawbone.

maxillary (*maks'-il-lar-e*). Pertaining to either jawbone.

McBurney's point (*mak-burn'-e*). The spot midway between the *anterior iliac spine* and the *umbilicus*, at which, on pressure, pain is felt if the appendix is inflamed.

measles (*meez'-ls*). Morbilli. An acute infectious disease of childhood caused by a virus spread by droplets. Onset is catarrhal before the rash appears at the 4th day. Koplik's spots (*q.v.*) are diagnostic earlier. Secondary infection may give rise to the serious complications of otitis media or bronchopneumonia. The severity of the attack may be lessened by giving gamma globulin between the 5th and 9th days following contact. *German m. See* Rubella.

meatus (*me-a'-tus*). An opening or passage. *Auditory m.* The opening leading into the auditory canal. *Urethral m.* Where the urethra opens to the exterior.

mecamylamine (*mek-am-il'-am-een*). A ganglion-blocking drug which given by mouth causes a marked fall in blood pressure, used in treating arterial hypertension. Inversine is a proprietary preparation.

mechanism of labour (*mek'-an-izm*). The sum of the forces which extrude the fetus through the genital passages, and the opposing resisting forces which restrain it and affect its position.

Meckel's diverticulum (*mek'-els di-ver-tik'-u-lum*). The remains of a passage which, in the embryo, connected the yolk sac and intestine, evident as an enclosed sac or tube in the region of the ileum.

meconium (*me-ko'-ne-um*). The first intestinal discharges of a newly born child. Dark green in colour consisting of epithelial cells, mucus, and bile. *M. ileus.* Intestinal obstruction due to blockage of the bowel by a plug of meconium.

median (*me'-de-an*). In the middle.

mediastinum (*me-de-as-ti'-num*). The space in the middle of the thorax, between the two pleurae.

medical (*med'-e-kal*). Pertaining to medicine. *M. jurisprudence.* Medical science as applied to aid the law, e.g. in cases of death by poisoning, violence, etc.

medical social worker. A trained hospital worker who looks after the patients' social welfare. Known formerly as Almoner.

medicated (*med'-e-ka-ted*). Impregnated with a medicinal substance.

medication (*med-e-ka'-shun*). Administration of remedies.

medicine (*med'-e-sin*). (1) A drug or preparation given for the cure of disease. (2) The science of healing by use of internal remedies. *Forensic* *m.* Medical jurisprudence (*q.v.*). *Industrial m.* That concerned with the prevention and treatment of diseases due to manufacturing processes. *Preventive m.* Medical measures taken to prevent disease, e.g. spread of infection. *Proprietary m.* A drug commercially produced and patented as suitable for use in treatment of diseases. *Psychosomatic m.* The study of the relationship of physical and mental illness. *Social m.* deals with the influences of environment and economic conditions on physical and mental ills.

medico-chirurgical (*med'-e-ko-ki-rur'-je-kal*). Applying to both medicine and surgery.

medico-social (*med-e-ko-so'-shal*). Applying to both medicine and the social factors involved.

Mediterranean fever. Undulant fever (*q.v.*).

medium (*me'-de-um*). A bacteriological preparation on which bacteria are grown.

Medresco (*me-dres'-ko*). The standard hearing aid obtainable under the National Health Act, 1948.

medulla (*me-dul'-lah*). Marrow. *M. oblongata.* That portion of the spinal cord which is contained inside the cranium. In it are the nerve centres which govern respiration and the action of the heart, etc.

medullary (*med-ul'-lar-e*). Pertaining to marrow. *M. cavity.* The hollow in the centre of long bones.

medullated (*med'-ul-la-ted*). Having a covering or sheath. *M. nerve fibre.* That with a fatty sheath, a myelin sheath.

medulloblastoma (*me-dul'-lo-blast-o'-mah*). A rapidly growing tumour of neuro-epithelial origin mostly arising in the roof of the fourth ventricle in children.

megacolon (*meg-a-ko'-lon*). Extreme dilatation of the large intestine. Hirschsprung's disease.

megaduodenum (*meg-a-du-o-de'-num*). A gross enlargement of the duodenum.

megalo- (*meg'-al-o*). A prefix meaning 'great'.

megaloblast (*meg'-al-o-blast*). A large cell from which the finished red blood cell is derived.

megalocephalic (*meg-al-o-kef-al'-ic*). Large-headed.

megalokaryocyte (*meg-al-o-kar'-e-o-site*). A large cell of the bone marrow, responsible for blood platelet formation.

megalomania (*meg-al-o-ma'-ne-ah*). Delusion of grandeur or self importance.

megrim (*me'-grim*). Migraine (*q.v.*).

Meibomian cyst. A small swelling containing the secretion of these glands. A chalazion.

Meibomian glands (*mi-bo'-me-an*). Small sebaceous glands situated beneath the conjunctiva of the eyelid.

meibomianitis (*mi-bo-me-an-i'-tis*). A bilateral chronic inflammation of the Meibomian glands.

Meigs syndrome. A fibroma or benign solid tumour of the ovary causing ascites and pleural effusion.

meiosis (*mi-o'-sis*). A stage of reduction cell division when the chromosomes are halved in number ready for union at fertilization.

Meissner's plexus (*mez'-ners*). *See* Plexus.

mel. Honey. Oxymel or purified honey is an ingredient of cough mixtures.

melaena (*mel-e'-nah*). The discharge of black faeces due to blood which has undergone change in the alimentary tract. A symptom of gastric or duodenal ulcer.

melancholia (*mel-an-ko'-le-ah*). A state of extreme depression.

melanin (*mel'-an-in*). Dark pigment found in hair, choroid coat of the eye and the skin.

melanism (*mel'-an-izm*). A condition marked by abnormal deposit of dark pigment in any organ.

melanoderma (*mel-an-o-der'-mah*). A patchy pigmentation of the skin, usually of face or neck, which may be caused by light sensitization or provoked by oil of bergamot used in the perfumery and cosmetics industry.

melanoma (*mel-an-o'-mah*). Brown pigmentation. *Simple m.* A birth mark. *Malignant m.* A tumour arising in any pigment containing tissues especially the skin and the eye.

melanosis (*mel-an-o'-sis*). *See* Melanism.

melanotic sarcoma (*mel-an-ot'-ik*). *See under* Sarcoma.

melanuria (*mel-an-u'-re-ah*). Black pigment in the urine. Present in melanotic sarcoma.

melasma (*me-laz'-mah*). Dark discoloration of the skin, e.g. in Addison's disease.

membrane (*mem'-brane*). A thin elastic tissue covering the surface of certain organs and lining the cavities of the body. *Basement m.* The delicate layer of cells beneath the surface cells of mucous membrane. *Mucous m.* Contains secreting cells and lines all cavities connected directly or indirectly with the skin. *Serous m.* Lubricating membrane lining the abdominal cavity and thorax and covering most of organs within.

menaphthone (*men-af'-thone*). A synthetic preparation of vitamin K.

menarche (*men-ar'-ke*). The first appearance of menstruation.

Mendel's law (*mend'-l*). A theory that the offspring do not inherit the characteristics of the parents in equal proportion, but that some are *dominant* while others are *recessive*.

Mendelson's syndrome. A condition in which there is severe oedema and spasm of the bronchioles due to the inhalation of acid gastric contents. *Syn.* Acid aspiration syndrome.

Ménière's disease or **syndrome** (*men-e-air'*). Attacks of vertigo and tinnitus with progressive nerve deafness. The cause is unknown.

meningeal (*men-in-je'-al*). Relating to the meninges.

meninges (*men-in'-jees*). The membranes covering the brain and spinal cord. There are three: the dura mater (outer), arachnoid (middle), and pia mater (inner).

meningioma (*men-in-je-o'-mah*). A tumour developing from the arachnoid and pia mater.

meningism (*men'-in-jizm*). Signs of cerebral irritation similar to meningitis, but no inflammation is present.

meningitis (*men-in-ji'-tis*). Inflammation of the meninges. *Meningococcal m.* or *Cerebrospinal fever.* An epidemic form with a rapid onset but quickly responds to treatment by sulphadiazine tablets, or intravenous sulphadimidine if the patient is unconscious. *Tuberculous m.* Inflammation of tuberculous origin. If diagnosed early, can now be treated successfully with streptomycin, isoniazid and sodium amino salicylate.

meningocele (*men-in'-go-seel*). A protrusion of the meninges through the skull or spinal column, appearing as a cyst filled with cerebrospinal fluid. *See also* Spina bifida.

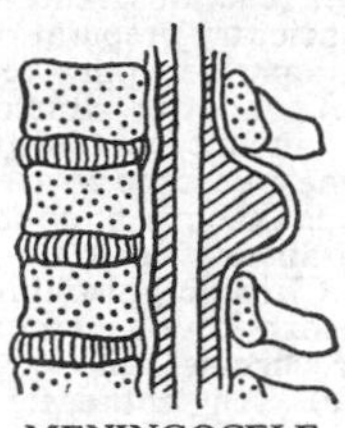

MENINGOCELE

meningococcus (*men-in'-go-kok-kus*). The *Neisseria meningitidis.* A diplococcus, the micro-organism of cerebrospinal fever.

meningo-encephalitis (*men-in-go-en-kef-al-i'-tis*). Inflammation of the brain and meninges.

meningomyelocele (*men-in-go-mi'-el-o-seel*). A protrusion of the spinal cord and meninges through a defect in the vertebral column. *Syn.* Myelomeningocele. *See also* Spina bifida.

meniscectomy (*men-is-ek'-to-me*). Removal of a semilunar cartilage.

meniscus (*men-is'-kus*). (1) The convex or concave surface of a liquid as observed in its container. (2) A semilunar cartilage.

menopause (*men'-o-paws*). The normal cessation of menstruation, usually occurring between the 45th and 50th year of life. *Artificial m.* An induced cessation by operation or treatment with radium.

menorrhagia (*men-or-raj'-e-ah*). Menorrhoea, an excessive flow of the menses.

menses (*men'-sez*). The discharge from the uterus during menstruation.

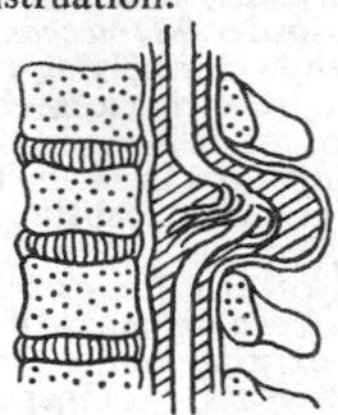

MENINGOMYELOCELE

menstrual (*men'-stru-al*). Relating to the menses. *M. cycle.* The monthly cycle commencing with the first day of menstruation, when the endometrium is shed, through a process of repair and hypertrophy till the next period. It is governed by the anterior pituitary gland and the ovarian hormones, oestrogens, and progesterone.

menstruation (*men-stru-a'-shun*). A monthly discharge of blood and endometrium from the uterus, commencing at the age of puberty and lasting until the menopause. *Vicarious m.* Discharge of blood at the time of menstruation from some other organ than the uterus, e.g.

epistaxis is not uncommon.

mental (*men'-tal*). Pertaining to the mind. *M. age.* The measurement of the intelligence level of an individual in terms of the average chronological age of children showing the same mental standard, as measured by a scale of mental tests. *M. disorder.* A term defined by the Mental Health Act, 1959 to cover all forms of mental illness and disability and include mental illness, severe subnormality and psychopathic disorder. *M. mechanisms.* A method of resolving a situation by reverting to an earlier pattern of behaviour, when the individual feels unable to reach a more realistic solution. *M. subnormality.* A condition of arrested or incomplete development of the mind existing before the age of 18 years, whether congenital or arising from disease or injury. As children they are unable to profit by the normal school education, and as adults to maintain themselves in anything but the simplest manner.

Mental Health Review Tribunal. A board to whom persons detained under compulsory admission orders or into Guardianship have the right of appeal at stated intervals.

mental welfare officer. He is appointed by the Local Health Authority and has many duties regarding the care of mentally disordered children and adults, including their compulsory admission to hospital or into Guardianship (*q.v.*).

mentha (*men'-thah*). Mint. *Aq. menth. pip.* Peppermint water.

menthol (*men'-thol*). Mint camphor. A crystalline substance derived from oil of peppermint and used in neuralgia and rhinitis, as a local anodyne and antiseptic.

mepacrine (*mep'-a-krin*). A synthetic drug used in the treatment of malaria and tapeworm infection.

mephitic (*mef-it'-ik*). Offensive or foul. Applied to gangrene with a noxious odour.

mepyramine maleate (*mep-e'-ram-een*). An antihistamine drug used in the treatment of allergic reactions. Anthisan is a proprietary preparation.

mercaptopurine (*mer-kap'-to-pur-in*). A drug which prevents nucleic acid synthesis and may be used in treating acute leukaemia in children.

mercurialism (*mer-ku'-re-al-izm*). Chronic poisoning due to absorption of mercury.

mercurochrome (*mer-ku'-ro-krome*). An antiseptic preparation of mercury with a dye. Less toxic than other forms, so is used for mucous surfaces, especially of the genito-urinary tract.

mercury (*mer'-ku-re*). Quicksilver. A heavy liquid metal, the salts of which are used occasionally as antiseptics and disinfectants. *Yellow oxide of m.* An eye ointment. *M. ointments* are used for some skin diseases. *M. vapour lamp.* Made of quartz glass which permits the ultraviolet rays to pass through. Air is exhausted from the tube and replaced by mercury vapour, through which passes a strong electric current resulting in a powerful ultraviolet light.

mersalyl (*mer'-sal-il*). A mercurial diuretic which prevents reabsorption of water in the renal tubules, so reducing oedema in heart failure and renal insufficiency.

mesarteritis (*mes-ar-ter-i'-tis*). Inflammation of the middle coat of an artery.

mesencephalon (*mes-en-kef'-al-on*). The middle brain.

mesenchyme (*mes'-en-kime*). Mesoderm (*q.v.*).

mesenteric (*mes-en-ter'-ik*). Pertaining to the mesentery.

mesentery (*mes'-en-ter-e*). A fold of the peritoneum which connects the intestine to the posterior abdominal wall.

mesmerism (*mez'-mer-izm*). Hypnotism.

mesocolon (*mes-o-ko'-lon*). A fold of the peritoneum which connects the colon with the posterior abdominal wall.

mesoderm (*mes'-o-derm*). The middle of the three primary layers of cells in the embryo from which the connective tissues develop.

mesometrium (*mes-o-me'-tre-um*). The broad ligaments connecting the uterus with the sides of the pelvis.

mesosalpinx (*mes-o-sal'-pinks*). That part of the broad ligament around the Fallopian tubes.

mesothelioma (*me-so-the-le-o'-mah*). A rapidly growing tumour of the pleura, which may be seen in patients with asbestosis.

mesovarium (*mes-o-var'-e-um*). A fold of peritoneum connecting the ovary to the broad ligament.

metabolic (*met-a-bol'-ik*). Referring to metabolism.

metabolism (*met-ab'-ol-izm*). The process of life, by which tissue cells are destroyed by combustion (*katabolism*); and renewed from chemical substances carried in the blood and derived from digested foods (*anabolism*). *Basal m.* *See* Basal metabolic rate.

metabolite (*met-ab'-o-lite*). Any product of, or taking part in metabolism. *Essential m.* A substance that is necessary for normal metabolism.

metacarpophalangeal (*met-a-kar-po-fal-an'-je-al*). Usually referring to the joint between the metacarpal bones and the phalanges.

metacarpus (*met-a-kar'-pus*). The five bones of the hand uniting the carpus with the phalanges of the fingers.

metamorphosis (*met-a-mor-fo'-sis*). A structural change or transformation.

metaphysis (*met-af'-is-is*). The junction of the epiphysis with the diaphysis in a long bone.

metastasis (*me-tas'-tas-is*). The transfer of a disease from one part of the body to another, through the blood vessels or lymph channels, e.g. (1) Secondary deposits may occur from a primary malignant growth. (2) Septic infection may arise in other organs from some original focus.

metatarsalgia (*met-a-tar-sal'-je-ah*). Neuralgia in the fore part of the foot.

metatarsus (*met-a-tar'-sus*). The five bones of the foot uniting the tarsus with the phalanges of the toes.

meteorism (*me'-te-or-izm*). Distension of the intestines with gas. Tympanites (*q.v.*).

methadone (*meth'-a-don*). A powerful analgesic with no sedative action. Amidone.

methaemoglobin (*meth-hem-o-glo'-bin*). An alteration in haemoglobin caused by the action of a drug on the red blood corpuscles. Most commonly phenacetin and other aniline derivatives.

methaemoglobinaemia (*meth-hem'-o-glo-bin-e'-me-ah*). Cyanosis and inability of the red blood cells to transport oxygen due to the presence of methaemoglobin.

methandienone (*meth-an-de'-en-one*). An anabolic steroid used to build up body tissues. Dianabol is a proprietary preparation.

methane (*me'-thane*). Marsh gas.

methicillin (*meth'-e-sil-in*). A form of penicillin that is resistant to staphylococcal penicillinase. Celbenin is a trade preparation.

methionine (*meth'-e-o-neen*). An essential amino-acid containing sulphur; it is necessary for fat metabolism.

methohexitone (*meth-o-heks'-e-tone*). A barbiturate anaesthetic agent. Given intravenously it has a quick recovery time. Brietal is a proprietary preparation.

methotrexate (*meth-o-treks'-ate*). A cytotoxic drug that antagonizes folic acid and prevents cell formation. It may be used to treat acute leukaemia in childhood.

methylamphetamine (*meth-il-am-fet'-a-meen*). A synthetic drug which stimulates the central nervous system and raises the blood pressure. Useful in the treatment of morphine and barbiturate poisoning.

methylated spirit. A preparation of methyl-alcohol, to which pyridine is now added. Also called *industrial alcohol* and *surgical spirit*.

methyldopa (*meth-il-do'-pah*). A hypotensive drug whose action is increased if used with thiazide diuretics. Used to treat hypertension. Aldomet is a proprietary preparation.

methylene blue (*meth'-il-een*). An aniline dye. Chiefly used to test renal function. If injected intravenously, it can be seen entering the bladder from the ureter within five minutes.

methylpentynol (*meth-il-pen'-tin-ol*). A sedative and tranquillizing drug which allays apprehension and may be used before operation or other procedures that might cause the patient discomfort. It is a Schedule 4 poison. Oblivon is a proprietary preparation of it.

methyl phenidate (*meth-il-fen'-e-date*). An antidepressant drug that stimulates the central nervous system. Ritalin is a proprietary preparation.

methyl salicylate (*meth'-il sal-is'-e-late*). A compound used externally for rheumatic pains, lumbago, etc. Oil of wintergreen contains it.

metra (*me'-trah*). The uterus.

metralgia (*me-tral'-je-ah*). Pain in the uterus.

metre (*me'-ter*). The unit of length in the metric system. *See* Appendix 14.

metritis (*me-tri'-tis*). Inflammation of the uterus.

metrocolpocele (*met-ro-kol'-po-seel*). The protrusion of the uterus into the vagina, the wall of the latter being pushed forward also.

metrodynia (*met-ro-din'-e-ah*). Pain in the uterus.

metronidazole (*met-ron-e-da'-zole*). A drug that is effective in overcoming Trichomonas infection of the genital tract of both sexes when taken as oral tablets. Flagyl is the proprietary preparation.

metropathia haemorrhagica (*met-ro-path'-e-ah*). A condition of excessive menstruation due to increased vascularity of the endometrium associated with follicular cysts of the ovary.

metroptosis (*met-rop-to'-sis*). Prolapse of the uterus.

metrorrhagia (*met-ror-raj'-e-ah*). Irregular bleeding from the uterus not associated with menstruation.

metrostaxis (*met-ro-staks'-is*). Persistent slight haemorrhage from the uterus.

Michel's clips (*me-shel'*). Small metal clips for suturing wounds.

micro- (*mi'-kro*). A prefix meaning 'small'.

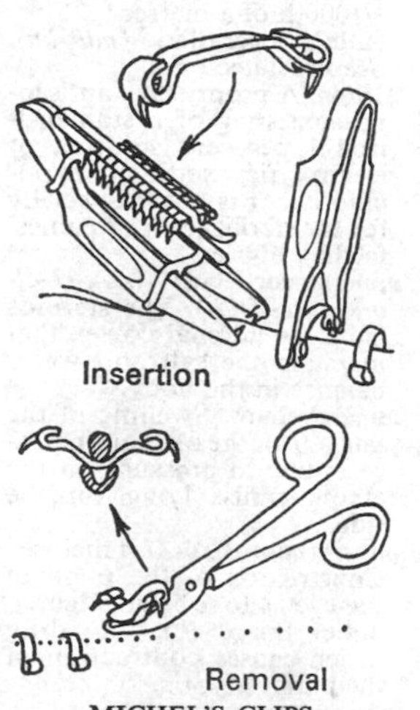

MICHEL'S CLIPS

microbe (*mi'-krobe*). A minute living organism, especially those causing disease. *See* Bacteria, Rickettsia, Virus.

microbiology (*mi-kro-bi-ol'-o-je*). The study of micro-organisms and their effect on living cells.

microcephalic (*mi-kro-kef-al'-ik*). An abnormally small head.

Micrococcus (*mi-kro-kok'-kus*). A genus of bacteria, each individual of which has a spherical shape.

microcurie (*mi-kro-ku'-re*). 1/1000 000 of a curie. A measurement of radioactivity.

microcythaemia (*mi-kro-si-the'-me-ah*). Abnormally small red cells in the blood.

microcytic (*mi-kro-sit'-ik*). Relating to small cells. As found in iron deficiency anaemia.

micrognathia (*mi-kro-nath'-e-ah*). Failure of development of the lower jaw causing a receding chin.

microgram (*mi'-kro-gram*). A unit of weight. *See* Appendix 14.

micron (*mi'-kron*). 1/1000th of a millimetre. A measurement used for bacteria, and represented by the Greek letter μ.

micro-organism (*mi-kro-or'-gan-izm*). A microbe.

microphage (*mi'-kro-fage*). A minute phagocyte.

microphthalmos (*mi-krof-thal'-mos*). An eye that is smaller than normal, its function may or may not be impaired.

microscopic (*mi-kro-skop'-ik*). Visible only by means of the microscope.

microsporon (*mi-kro-spor'-on*). A fungus; the cause of some skin diseases, especially ringworm.

micturition (*mik-tu-rish'-un*). The act of passing urine.

midbrain. The portion which connects the cerebrum with the pons and cerebellum.

midriff (*mid'-rif*). The diaphragm.

midwifery (*mid'-wif-re*). Obstetrics.

migraine (*me'-grane*). A condition in which dilatation of the cranial arteries causes episodes of severe headache, often with nausea, vomiting and visual disturbance.

miliaria (*mil-e-ar'-e-ah*). Prickly heat, an acute itching eruption common among white people in tropical and subtropical areas.

miliary (*mil'-e-ar-e*). Resembling millet seed. *M. tuberculosis*. *See* Tuberculosis.

milk. The secretion of mammary glands.

Composition of Milk

	Cow's milk	*Human milk*
Protein	3·5%	2·0%
Fats	3·5%	3·5%
Carbohydrates	4·0%	6·0%
Mineral salts	0·7%	0·2%
Water	88·0%	88·0%

Designations of m. (1) *Tuberculin tested* from herds certified free from tuberculosis. (2) *Pasteurized m.* One of several recognized methods of heat treating the milk may be used. (3) *Sterilized m.* Milk that has been heated to 100°C (212°F). *M. teeth.* The first set.

milk sugar. Lactose, a disaccharide.

Miller-Abbott tube. A double-channel intestinal tube for treating obstruction — especially that due to *paralytic ileus* of the small intestine. It has an inflatable balloon at its distal end.

milliampere (*mil-le-am'-pair*). 1/1000th of an ampere, the measurement of intensity of the electrical current.

millicurie (*mil-le-ku'-re*). The unit of radio-activity, i.e. the amount of radon which equals that of 1 mg of radium. *M. hour.* The action of one millicurie for one hour.

milliequivalent (*mil-e-e-quiv'-al-ent*). The amount of a substance that balances or is equivalent in combining power to 1 mg of hydrogen. A method of assessing the body's acid–base balance or needs during electrolyte upset.

milligram (*mil'-le-gram*). mg. 1/1000th of a gram. *See* Appendix 14.

millilitre (*mil'-le-le-ter*). ml. 1/1000th of a litre. *See* Appendix 14.

millimetre (*mil'-le-me-ter*). mm. 1/1000th of a metre.

Millin's operation (*mil'-lin*). *See* Prostatectomy.

Milton. A proprietary antiseptic consisting of a standardized 1 per cent solution of electrolytic sodium hypochlorite. It is used especially for the sterilization of babies' feeding bottles.

mineralocorticoids (*min-er-al-o-kor'-te-koids*). The steroids from the adrenal cortex that maintain the salt and water balance in the body.

miners' elbow. Swelling of the bursa over the olecranon process; due to pressure on the elbow whilst lying on the side.

miosis (*mi-o'-sis*). *Also* meiosis. Constriction of the pupil of the eye as to a bright light.

miotic (*mi-ot'-ik*). A drug which causes contraction of the pupil. Myotic.

miscarriage. Abortion (*q.v.*).

The expulsion of the fetus before the 28th week of pregnancy, i.e. before it is legally viable.

mitosis (*mi-to'-sis*). The usual method of multiplication of cells by a specific process of division.

mitral (*mi'-tral*). Shaped like a mitre. *M. incompetence*, a term applied to a defective mitral valve allowing a back flow or regurgitation when the valve is closed. *M. stenosis*. The formation of fibrous tissue causing a narrowing of the valve, usually due to rheumatic heart disease and endocarditis. *M. valve*. The bicuspid valve between the left atrium and left ventricle of the heart. *M. valvotomy*. An operation for overcoming stenosis by dividing the fibrous tissue to free the cusps.

mittelschmerz (*mit'-tel-shmer-tz*). Pain occurring in the period between the menses, accompanying ovulation.

ml. Millilitre. Approximately equivalent to 1 cm^3.

modiolus (*mo-de-o'-lus*). The central pillar of the cochlea, around which the bony labyrinth winds.

molar teeth (*mo'-lar*). The grinders, twelve in number, three on either side of each jaw.

mole. (1) A pigmented naevus or dark-coloured growth on the skin. They are of various sizes, and sometimes covered with hair. (2) A uterine tumour. *Carneous m.* The result of a missed abortion (*q.v.*). Organized blood clot surrounds a shrivelled fetus in the uterus. *Hydatidiform m.* (*vesicular m.*). A condition in pregnancy in which the chorionic villi of the placenta degenerate into clusters of cysts like hydatids (*q.v.*). Malignant growth is very likely to follow if any remnants are left in the uterus. *See* Chorion epithelioma.

molecule (*mol'-e-ku-l*). The chemical combination of two or more atoms which form a specific chemical substance, e.g. H_2O (water).

mollities ossium (*mol-lish'-e-eez os'-se-um*). Osteomalacia (*q.v.*).

molluscum (*mol-lus'-kum*). A class of skin diseases. *M. contagiosum*. A benign tumour arising in the epidermis caused by a virus, transmitted by direct contact or fomites. It is a round white elevation with a central dimple.

monarticular (*mon-ar-tik'-u-lah*). Referring to one joint only.

Mönckeberg's sclerosis (*murn'-ke-berg*). Extensive degeneration, with atrophy and calcareous deposits in the middle muscle coat of arteries, especially the small ones.

mongolism (*mon'-gol-izm*). Down's syndrome. A type of congenital mental subnormality. Associated with an extra chromosome. There is retarded mental and physical growth with characteristic facial appearance (resembling the mongolian races) and often congenital cardiac lesions are present.

Monilia (*mon-il'-e-ah*). Former name for the genus of fungi now known as Candida (*q.v.*).

monitoring (*mon'-it-or-ing*). Recording. *Patient m.* Electrodes or transducers are attached to the patient so information such as temperature, pulse, respiration, and blood pressure can be seen on a screen or automatically recorded.

Monitron (*mon'-it-ron*). An apparatus by which temperature, pulse, respiration, and systolic and diastolic blood pressures can be automatically recorded.

mono (*mon'-o*). A prefix meaning 'single'.

monoamine oxidase (*mon-o-a-meen' oks'-e-daze*). An enzyme that breaks down noradrenaline and serotonin in the body. *M. o. inhibitors* (MAOI). Drugs that prevent the breakdown of serotonin and lead to an increase in mental and physical activity. Foods containing tyramine, such as cheese, marmite, bovril and broad beans, should be avoided as severe headache and hypertension occur.

monocular (*mon-ok'-u-lar*). Pertaining to, or affecting one eye only.

monocyte (*mon'-o-site*). A white blood cell having one nucleus, derived from the reticulo cells, and having a phagocytic action.

mononucleosis (*mon-o-nu-kle-o'-sis*). *Infective m.* An infectious disease probably due to a virus, in which there is an increase of monocytes. Glandular fever.

monophasia (*mon-o-fa'-ze-ah*). Aphasia in which speech is limited to one word or phrase.

monoplegia (*mon-o-ple'-je-ah*). Paralysis of one limb or of a single muscle or group of muscles.

monorchis (*mon-or'-kis*). An individual with only one testicle.

monosaccharide (*mon-o-sak'-ar-ide*). A simple sugar. The end result of carbohydrate digestion. Examples are glucose, fructose and galactose.

monosomy (*mon-os'-o-me*). A congenital defect in the number of human chromosomes. There is one less than the normal 46.

Montgomery's glands or **tubercles** (*mont-gom'-er-e*). Sebaceous glands around the nipple, which grow larger during pregnancy.

mood. Emotional reaction. A small swing between a serious or an elated mood is natural but in certain psychiatric conditions there is severe depression in some cases and wild excitement in others, or alternations between both.

Mooren's ulcer (*moo'-ren*). A rare superficial ulcer of the cornea in elderly persons.

morbid. Diseased, or relating to an abnormal or disordered condition.

morbilli (*mor-bil'-li*). Measles (*q.v.*).

morbilliform (*mor-bil'-e-form*). A rash resembling that of measles.

moribund (*mor'-ib-und*). In a dying condition.

Morison's pouch (*mor'-e-son*). *See under* Pouch.

morning sickness. Nausea and vomiting which occurs in pregnancy during the 4th to 16th week.

moron (*mor'-on*). A former term for persons suffering from severe subnormality of the mind.

morphine (*mor'-feen*). The principal alkaloid obtained from opium, and given hypodermically as a narcotic and analgesic.

morphology (*mor-fol'-o-je*).

The study of the structure of organisms.

mortality (*mor-tal'-it-e*). Death-rate. The ratio of the number of deaths to the total population.

mortification (*mor-tif-ik-a'-shun*). Gangrene or death of tissue.

morula (*mor'-u-lah*). An early stage of development of the ovum when it is a solid mass of cells.

motile (*mo'-tile*). Capable of movement. With bacteria this may be inherent in the cell or by means of flagellae.

motions. The evacuations of the bowels.

motivate (*mo'-te-vate*). To provide an incentive or purpose for a course of action.

motivation (*mo-te-va'-shun*). The reason or reasons, conscious or unconscious behind a particular attitude or behaviour.

motive (*mo'-tiv*). The incentives that determine a course of action or its direction.

motor nerves. Those which convey an impulse from a nerve centre to a muscle or gland to promote activity.

mould (*mo-ld*). A species of fungus.

moulding (*mo'-ld-ing*). The compression of the infant's head as it is forced through the maternal passages during labour.

mountain sickness. Dyspnoea, headache, rapid pulse and vomiting, which occur on sudden change to the rarefied air of high altitudes.

movements (fetal). *See* Quickening.

mucilage (*mu'-sil-aj*). A solution of gum in water.

mucin (*mu'-sin*). The chief constituent of mucus.

mucocele (*mu'-ko-seel*). A mucous tumour. *M. of gall-bladder* occurs if a stone obstructs the cystic duct.

mucocutaneous (*mu-ko-ku-ta'-ne-us*). Pertaining to mucous membrane and skin.

mucoid (*mu'-koid*). Resembling mucus.

mucolysis (*mu-kol'-is-is*). The act of dissolving mucus.

mucolytics (*mu-ko-lit'-iks*). Drugs that have a mucus softening effect and so reduce the viscosity of the bronchial secretion.

mucopurulent (*mu-ko-pu'-ru-lent*). Containing mucus and pus.

mucosa (*mu-ko'-sah*). Mucous membrane.

mucous (*mu'-kus*). Pertaining to or secreting mucus. *M. membrane*. *See* Membrane.

mucoviscidosis (*mu-ko-vis-kid-o'-sis*). Fibrocystic disease of the pancreas. *See* Fibrocystic.

mucus (*mu'-kus*). The viscid secretion of mucous membranes.

Müllerian ducts (*mu'-ler-e-an*). A pair of ducts in the female fetus that develop into the uterine tube, uterus, and vagina.

multigravida (*mul-te-grav'-id-ah*). Multipara (*q.v.*).

multilocular (*mult-e-lok'-u-lah*). Having many locules. *M. cyst*. *See under* Cyst.

multinuclear (*mul-te-nu'-kle-ah*). A cell possessing many nuclei.

multipara (*mul-tip'-ar-ah*). A woman who has had more than one pregnancy. Multigravida.

mumps. Epidemic parotitis. A contagious disease common amongst children, and characterized by inflammation and swelling of the parotid glands. The symptoms are fever, and a painful swelling in front of the ears, making mastication difficult. *See* Infectious diseases.

muriatic acid (*mu-re-at'-ik*). Hydrochloric acid (*q.v.*).

murmur (*mer'-mer*). A blowing sound, heard on auscultation. *Aortic m.* Indicates disease of the aortic valve. *Diastolic m.* One heard after the second heart sound. *Friction m.* Present when two inflamed surfaces of serous membrane rub on each other. *Mitral m.* A sign of incompetence of the mitral valve. *Systolic m.* Heard during systole.

Musca domestica (*mus'-kah do-mes'-tik-ah*). The house fly.

muscae volitantes (*mus'-ke vol-e-tan'-tes*). Floating bodies in the vitreous humour which are visible to the patient.

muscarine (*mus'-kar-in*). A poisonous alkaloid found in certain fungi, and causing muscle paralysis.

muscle (*mus'-l*). Strong tissue composed of fibres which have the power of contraction, and thus produce movements of the body. *Cardiac m.* Partially striped interlocking cells but not under the control of the will. *Striped* or *striated m.* Voluntary muscle; transverse bands across the fibres give the characteristic appearance. It is under the control of the will. *Smooth* or *non-striated m.* Involuntary muscle of spindle shaped cells contracts independently of the will, e.g. that of the intestinal wall.

muscular dystrophies (*mus-ku-lah dis'-tro-fe*). A number of inherited diseases in which there is progressive muscle wasting.

musculocutaneous nerves (*mus'-ku-lo-ku-ta'-ne-us*). Those which supply the muscles and the skin.

musculoskeletal (*mus-ku-lo-skel'-e-tal*). Referring to both the osseus and muscular systems.

mustine hydrochloride. Nitrogen mustard. A cytotoxic drug which may be given intravenously for malignant disease of the lymph glands and reticulo-endothelial cells, e.g. Hodgkin's disease.

mutation (*mu-ta'-shun*). A chemical change in the genes of a cell causing it to show a new characteristic. Some produce evolutional changes, others disease.

myalgia (*mi-al'-je-ah*). Pain in the muscles.

myasthenia (*mi-as-the'-ne-ah*). Muscle weakness. *M. gravis.* An extreme form of muscle weakness which is progressive. A rapid onset of fatigue, thought due to the too rapid destruction of acetylcholine at the neuro-muscular junction. Commonly affected muscles are those of vision, speaking, chewing and swallowing. Neostigmine injections are useful. Thymectomy has been curative in some cases.

mycetoma (*mi-se-to'-mah*). Madura foot. A fungus infection of the foot causing ulcers; a tropical disease.

Mycobacterium (*mi-ko-bak-te'-re-um*). Rod-shaped, acid-fast bacterium. *M. leprae.* The causative organism of leprosy. *M. tuberculosis.* The cause of tuberculosis.

mycosis (*mi-ko'-sis*). Any disease which is caused by a fungus. *See* Actinomycosis.

mydriasis (*mid-ri'-as-is*). Abnormal dilatation of the pupil of the eye.

mydriatics (*mid-re-at'-iks*). Drugs which cause mydriasis.

myectomy (*mi-ek'-to-me*). Excision of a portion of muscle.

myelin (*mi'-el-in*). The fatty covering of medullated nerve fibres.

myelitis (*mi-el-i'-tis*). Inflammation of the marrow: (1) of the spinal cord; if affecting the grey matter it is called *poliomyelitis*; (2) of bone marrow. *See* Osteomyelitis.

myeloblast (*mi'-el-o-blast*). A primative cell in the bone marrow from which develop the granular leucocytes.

myelocele (*mi'-el-o-seel*). Myelomeningocele. A hernia-like protrusion of the meninges containing a portion of the spinal cord. *See* Spina bifida.

myelocyte (*mi'-el-o-site*). Cells of the bone marrow, derived from myeloblasts.

myelocytic leukaemia (*mi-el-o-sit'-ik lu-ke'-me-ah*). *See under* Leukaemia.

myelogram (*mi'-el-o-gram*). Radiograph of the spinal cord.

myelography (*mi-el-og'-raf-e*). Radiographic examination of the spinal cord following the insertion of a radio-opaque substance into the subarachnoid space by means of a lumbar puncture.

myeloid (*mi'-el-oid*). Resembling bone marrow or referring to the spinal cord. *M. leukaemia.* A malignant disease in which there is excessive production of leucocytes in the bone marrow.

myeloma (*mi-el-o'-mah*). A tumour in the medullary cavity of bone.

myelomatosis (*mi-el-o-mat-o'-sis*). Multiple myeloma.

myelomeningocele (*mi-el-o-men-in'-go-seel*). Meningomyelocele (*q.v.*).

myocarditis (*mi-o-kar-di'-tis*). Inflammation of the myocardium.

myocardium (*mi-o-kar'-de-um*). The muscle tissue of the heart.

myocele (*mi'-o-seel*). Protrusion of muscle through a rupture of its sheath.

myoclonus (*mi-o-klo'-nus*). Spasmodic contraction of muscle.

myofibrosis (*mi-o-fi-bro'-sis*). Fibrous tissue changes in a muscle. This may follow trauma where insufficient exercise impairs reabsorption of fibrin.

myogenic (*mi-o-jen'-ik*). Originating in muscle tissue. *M. contraction* of cardiac muscle is independent of nerve stimulus.

myoglobin (*mi-o-glo'-bin*). *See* Myohaemoglobin.

myohaemoglobin (*mi-o-he-mo-glo'-bin*). The haemoglobin present in muscle, having a lower molecular weight than blood haemoglobin. It colours muscle and transports oxygen.

myohaemoglobinuria (*mi-o-he-mo-glo-bin-u'-re-ah*). The presence of myohaemoglobin in the urine. It occurs in crush syndrome.

myoma (*mi-o'-mah*). A tumour of muscle tissue. *See* Fibromyoma.

myomectomy (*mi-o-mek'-to-me*). Removal of a myoma—usually referring to a uterine tumour.

myometritis (*mi-o-met-ri'-tis*). Inflammation of the myometrium.

myometrium (*mi-o-me'-tre-um*). The uterine muscle.
myoneural (*mi-o-nu'-ral*). Relating to both muscle and nerve. *M. junction*. Where nerve endings terminate in a muscle.
myopathy (*mi-op'-ath-e*). Muscular dystrophy. One of a group of hereditary degenerative diseases of muscle groups in which there is wasting and weakness.
myopia (*mi-o'-pe-ah*). Nearsightedness. The light rays focus in front of the retina and need a biconcave lens (*q.v.*) to focus them correctly.
myoplasty (*mi'-o-plas-te*). Any operation in which muscle is detached and utilized, as may be done to correct deformity.
myosarcoma (*mi-o-sar-ko'-mah*). A sarcomatous tumour in muscle.
myosin (*mi'-o-sin*). Muscle protein.
myosis (*mi-o'-sis*). Abnormal contraction of the pupil.
myositis (*mi-o-si'-tis*). Inflammation of a muscle. *M. ossificans*. A condition in which bone cells deposited in muscle continue to grow and cause hard lumps. It may occur after fractures, if passive movements are used. Active exercises only should be carried out.
myotics (*mi-ot'-iks*). Drugs which cause myosis and contract the pupil. Miotics.
myotonia (*mi-o-to'-ne-ah*). Lack of muscle tone. *M. congenita*. An hereditary disease in which the muscle action has a prolonged contraction phase and slow relaxation.
myotomy (*mi-ot'-o-me*). The division or dissection of a muscle.
myringa (*mi-rin'-gah*). The ear drum or tympanic membrane.
myringitis (*mir-in-ji'-tis*). Inflammation of the tympanic membrane.
myringoplasty (*mi-ring'-o-plas-te*). A repair of perforation of the ear drum. This may be by a skin graft taken from the anterior meatal wall.
myringotome (*mi-ring'-o-tome*). An instrument for puncturing the tympanic membrane in myringotomy.
myringotomy (*mir-in-got'-o-me*). Incision of the tympanic membrane to drain pus from the middle ear.
myxoedema (*miks-e-de'-mah*). Hypothyroidism. A disease caused by atrophy of the thyroid gland. Marked by oedematous swelling of face, limbs, and hands; dry and rough skin; loss of hair; slow pulse; subnormal temperature; slowed metabolism; and mental dullness. It is treated with preparations of thyroid gland. *Congenital m*. Cretinism (*q.v.*).
myxoma (*miks-o'-mah*). A benign tumour arising from mucous membrane.
myxosarcoma (*miks-o-sar-ko'-mah*). A sarcoma containing mucoid tissue.
myxovirus (*miks'-o-vi-rus*). The group name of a number of related viruses including the causal viruses of influenza, parainfluenza, mumps and Newcastle disease (of fowls).

N

Nabothian follicle. Cystic swelling of a cervical gland as its duct has become blocked by regenerating squamous epithelium.

naevus (*ne'-vus*). A birthmark; a circumscribed area of pigmentation of the skin due to dilated blood vessels. A haemangioma. *N. flammeus.* A flat bluish-red area usually on the neck or face; popularly known as 'port-wine stain'. *N. pilosus.* A hairy naevus. *Spider n.* A small red area surrounded by dilated capillaries. *Strawberry n.* A raised tumour-like structure of connective tissue containing spaces filled with blood.

nail. The keratinized portion of epidermis covering the dorsal extremity of the fingers and toes. *N. bed.* The area covered by a nail. *Hang n.* A strip of epidermis hanging at one side of a nail. *Ingrowing n.* Where the flesh overlaps the nail. *Spoon n.* With depression in the centre and raised edges. Sometimes present in iron deficiency anaemia.

nalorphine (*nal-or'-feen*). An antidote for morphine, pethidine and methadone overdosage. It antagonizes respiratory depression. Lethidrone is a proprietary preparation of it.

nandrolone (*nan'-dro-lone*). An anabolic steroid that promotes protein metabolism and skeletal growth and has a masculinizing effect. Durabolin is a proprietary preparation.

nape. The back of the neck.

napkin rash. An erythematous rash which may occur in infants in the napkin area. Often caused by the passage of frequent loose stools containing fatty acids which cause breakdown of urea in the urine, producing ammonia which burns the skin. Treatment is by cleanliness of the skin, and boracic acid dusting powder and exposure to the air. Alterations in the diet may be indicated.

narcissism (*nar-sis'-izm*). From the Greek legend. The stage of infant development when the child is mainly interested in himself and his own bodily needs.

narco- (*nar'-ko-*). A prefix denoting 'stupor'.

narcoanalysis (*nar-ko-an-al'-is-is*). A form of psychotherapy in which an injection of a barbiturate drug produces a drowsy relaxed state during which a patient will talk more freely, and in this way much repressed material may be brought to consciousness. This may cause emotional stress. The interview may be terminated by giving more of the drug to produce a deep sleep.

narcolepsy (*nar'-ko-lep-se*). A condition in which there is an uncontrollable desire for sleep.

narcosis (*nar-ko'-sis*). A state of unconsciousness produced by a narcotic drug. *Basal n.* A state of unconsciousness produced prior to surgical anaesthesia. The drugs that may be used are avertin, paraldehyde or a barbiturate (not so commonly used now). *Continuous n.* A less frequently used form of treatment in which the patient is kept asleep for 2 or 3 weeks at a time. It may be used in cases of extreme excitement or agitation. The patient needs to be kept quiet and under constant observation but be rousable to eat and drink, and where he does not move himself, he must be regularly turned by the nurses.

narcosynthesis (*nar-ko-sin'-thes-is*). The inducement of an hypnotic state by means of drugs. An aid to psychotherapy.

narcotic (*nar-kot'-ik*). A drug that produces narcosis or unnatural sleep.

nares (*nar'-eez*). *Sing*. naris. The nostrils. *Posterior n*. The opening of the nares into the nasopharynx.

nasal (*na'-zal*). Pertaining to the nose.

nasogastric (*na-zo-gas'-trik*). Referring to the nose and stomach. *N. tube*. One passed into the stomach via the nose.

nasolacrimal (*na-zo-lak'-re-mal*). Concerning both nose and lacrimal apparatus. *N. duct*. The duct draining the tears from the inner aspect of the eye to the inferior meatus of the nose.

nasopharynx (*na-zo-far'-inks*). The upper part of the pharynx; that above the soft palate.

nasosinusitis (*na-zo-si-nu-si'-tis*). Inflammation of the nose and adjacent sinuses.

nates (*na'-teez*). The buttocks.

nausea (*naw'-se-ah*). A sensation of sickness with inclination to vomit.

navel (*na'-vel*). The umbilicus.

navicular (*na-vik'-u-lah*). One of the tarsal bones of the foot. A former name for the scaphoid of the wrist.

nebula (*neb'-u-lah*). A slight opacity or cloudiness of the cornea.

nebulizer (*neb'-u-li-zer*). An apparatus for reducing a liquid to a fine spray.

neck. The narrow part of an organ or bone. *Anatomical n*. The constriction of the humerus just below the articulating surface. *Surgical n*. The narrowed part between the shaft and the tuberosities. *Derbyshire n*. Simple goitre. *Wry n*. Torticollis (*q.v.*).

necro- (*nek'-ro*). A prefix meaning 'dead'.

necrobiosis (*nek-ro-bi-o'-sis*). Localized death of a part as a result of degeneration.

necropsy (*nek-rop'-se*). Examination of a dead body. A post mortem.

necrosis (*nek-ro'-sis*). Death of a portion of tissue.

necrotomy (*ne-krot'-o-me*). An operation to remove a sequestrum.

needling (*need'-ling*). (1) Discission; the operation for cateract of lacerating and splitting up the lens so that it may be absorbed. (2) Capsulotomy. Tearing a hole in the remaining lens capsule after an extracapsular cataract extraction.

negative pole. The pole or cathode that attracts the positive current and repels the negative current.

negativism (*neg'-a-tiv-izm*). A symptom of mental illness in which the patient does the opposite of what is required of him and so presents an unco-operative attitude. Common in schizophrenia.

Neisseria (*ni-ser'-e-ah*). Paired Gram-negative cocci. *N. gonorrhoeae*. The causative organism of gonorrhoea. *N. meningitidis*. The cause of meningococcal meningitis.

Nematoda (*nem-at-o'-dah*). A genus of worms, including the *Ascaris* or roundworm and the *Oxyuris* or threadworm.

neo (*ne'-o*). A prefix meaning 'new'.

neoarthrosis (*ne-o-ar-thro'-sis*). A false joint.

neologism (*ne-ol'-o-jizm*). The formation of new words, either a completely new one or a contraction of two separate words. This is done particularly by schizophrenic patients.

neomycin (*ne-o-mi'-cin*). An antibiotic drug of wide range that may be used to sterilize the gut or as an ointment against skin infections.

neonatal (*ne-o-na'-tal*). Referring to the first month of life. *N. mortality*. Death rate during this period as compared with the remaining 11 months of the first year.

neonate (*ne'-o-nate*). Term applied to a baby under 1 month old.

neoplasm (*ne'-o-plazm*). A morbid new growth. It may be benign or malignant.

neostigmine (*ne-o-stig'-min*). A synthetic preparation of physostigmine used in the treatment of myasthenia gravis and as an antidote to curare.

nephralgia (*nef-ral'-je-ah*). Pain in the kidney of neuralgic type. It may be due to tuberculosis or stone.

nephralgic crises (*nef-ral'-jik kri'-ses*). Spasms of pain in the lumbar region in tabes dorsalis.

nephrectomy (*nef-rek'-to-me*). Excision of a kidney.

nephritis (*nef-ri'-tis*). Inflammation of the kidneys (Bright's disease). *Acute glomerulo-n.* or *Ellis type I.* Thought to be due to hypersensitivity to toxins from the haemolytic streptococcus; there is oliguria and haematuria. *Sub-acute n. Ellis type II* or *hydraemic n.* Characterized by excessive albuminuria and massive oedema. Cause may be unknown or it may follow acute glomerulonephritis. *Chronic n.* or *azotaemic n.* The kidneys are fibrosed and contracted. It is associated with hypertension and gradually increasing uraemia. Treatment aims at general rest, warmth and low protein diet to rest the kidneys in the acute stage. Restriction of salt and water, and a high protein diet to replace loss in the subacute case. *Acute tubular n.* May be caused by damage to tubular cells by drugs, crush syndrome or incompatible blood transfusion. Treatment is by giving glucose and restricting protein or by using renal dialysis. *Embolic n.* Small emboli in the kidney cause haematuria.

nephroblastoma (*nef-ro-blas-to'-mah*). *See* Wilms' tumour.

nephrocalcinosis (*nef-ro-kal-sin-o'-sis*). A condition in which there is deposition of calcium in the renal tubules resulting in calculi formation and renal insufficiency.

nephrocapsulectomy (*nef-ro-kap-su-lek'-to-me*). Operation for removal of the capsule of the kidney.

nephrocele (*nef'-ro-seel*). Hernia of the kidney.

nephrolith (*nef'-ro-lith*). Stone in the kidney; renal calculus.

nephrolithotomy (*nef-ro-lith-ot'-o-me*). Removal of a renal calculus.

nephroma (*nef-ro'-mah*). Tumour of the kidney.

nephron (*nef'-ron*). A uriniferous tubule, consisting of Bowman's capsule, the first and second convoluted tubule with the connecting loop of

Henle, which opens into a collecting tubule. It is the essential structure for extraction of waste materials from the blood in the form of urine.

nephropathy (*nef-rop'-ath-e*). Any disease condition of the kidney substance.

nephropexy (*nef-ro-pek'-se*). The fixation of a floating (mobile) kidney, usually by sutures to neighbouring muscle.

nephroptosis (*nef-rop-to'-sis*). Downward displacement, or undue mobility, of kidney found on palpation.

nephropyeloplasty (*nef-ro-pi'-el-o-plas-te*). A plastic operation on the pelvis of the kidney.

nephropyosis (*nef-ro-pi-o'-sis*). Suppuration in the kidney.

nephrosclerosis (*nef-ro-skler-o'-sis*). Constriction of the arterioles of the kidney. Seen in benign and malignant hypertension and in arteriosclerosis in old age.

nephrosis (*nef-ro'-sis*). Any disease of the kidney. Especially that which is characterized by oedema, albuminuria and a low plasma albumin. Caused by non-inflammatory degenerative lesions of the tubules.

nephrostomy (*nef-ros-to'-me*). Drainage of a kidney by passing a catheter at operation through the kidney substance.

nephrotic syndrome (*nef-rot'-ik*). A clinical syndrome in which there are albuminuria, low plasma protein, and gross oedema. Due to increased capillary permeability in the glomeruli. It may occur as a result of acute glomerulonephritis; in sub-acute nephritis, diabetes mellitus amyloid disease, systemic lupus erythematosus and renal vein thrombosis.

nephrotomy (*nef-rot'-o-me*). Incision of the kidney.

nephro-ureterectomy (*nef-ro-u-re-ter-ek'-to-me*). Removal of the kidney and the ureter.

nerve (*nerv*). A bundle of nerve fibres enclosed in a sheath called the epineurium. Its function is to transmit impulses between any part of the body and a nerve centre. *Sensory n.* (*afferent*) conveys sensations from an area to a nerve centre. *Motor n.* (*efferent*) conveys impulses causing activity from a nerve centre to a muscle or gland. *N. block*. A method of producing regional anaesthesia by injecting procaine into the nerves supplying the area to be operated on. *N. fibre*. The prolongation of the nerve cell, which conveys the impulse to or from the part which it controls. *Vasomotor n.* Either dilator or constrictor to blood vessels to control the muscle wall.

nervous. Pertaining to, or composed of, nerves.

nervousness. Excitability of the nervous system, characterized by a state of mental and physical unrest.

nettle-rash. An irritating rash. Urticaria.

neural (*nu'-ral*). Pertaining to the nerves. *N. arch*. The bony arch on each vertebra which encloses the spinal cord.

neuralgia (*nu-ral'-je-ah*). Sharp stabbing pain, along the course of a nerve owing to neuritis or functional disturbance.

neurapraxia (*nu-ra-praks'-e-ah*). An injury to a nerve resulting in temporary loss of function and paralysis.

neurasthenia (*nu-ras-the'-ne-ah*). An outdated term for a state of general debility, both physical and mental.

neurectasis (*nu-rek'-tas-is*). The surgical operation of stretching a nerve.

neurectomy (*nu-rek'-to-me*). Excision of part of a nerve.

neurilemma (*nu-ril-em'-mah*). The membranous sheath surrounding a nerve-fibre.

neurinoma (*nu-re-no'-mah*). An innocent tumour arising in the neurilemma of a nerve fibre. *Acoustic n.* This arises in the eighth cranial nerve.

neuritis (*nu-ri'-tis*). Inflammation of a nerve with pain, tenderness, and loss of function. *Multiple n.* That involving several nerves. Polyneuritis. *Nutritional n.* That which may be caused by alcoholism or lack of vitamin B complex. *Peripheral n.* The terminations of nerves are involved. *Sciatic n.* Sciatica (*q.v.*). *Optic n.* Of the optic nerve. Papilloedema. *Tabetic n.* A type occurring in tabes dorsalis. *Traumatic n.* That which results from an injury.

neuroblast (*nu'-ro-blast*). An embryonic nerve cell.

neuroblastoma (*nu-ro-blas-to'-mah*). A malignant tumour of immature nerve cells, most often arising in the very young.

neurodermatitis (*nu-ro-der-mat-i'-tis*). A localized prurigo of somatic and psychogenic origin. It irritates and rubbing causes thickening and pigmentation.

neuro-epithelioma (*nu-ro-ep-e-the-le-o'-mah*). A tumour of undifferentiated cells of nervous origin usually, but not always occurring in the brain.

neurofibroma (*nu-ro-fi-bro'-mah*). An innocent tumour of nerve and fibrous tissue.

neurofibromatosis (*nu-ro-fi-bro-mat-o'-is*). von Recklinghausen's disease. A generalized hereditary disease in which there are numerous tumours of the skin and nervous system.

neurogenic (*nu-ro-jen'-ik*). Derived from or caused by nerve stimulation. *N. shock. See* Shock.

neuroglia (*nu-rog'-le-ah*). The special form of connective tissue supporting nerve tissues.

neurologist (*nu-rol'-o-jist*). One who is an expert in knowledge of diseases of nerves.

neurology (*nu-rol'-o-je*). The scientific study of the nervous system.

neuroma (*nu-ro'-mah*). A tumour of nerve tissue.

neuromuscular (*nu-ro-mus'-ku-lah*). Refers to the fine nerve endings which stimulate the contraction of muscle fibres. *N. junction.* The small gap between the end of the motor nerve and the motor end-plate of the muscle fibre supplied. This gap is bridged by the release of acetylcholine whenever a nerve impulse arrives.

neuromyelitis optica (*nu-ro-mi-el-i'-tis op-tik-ah*). A disease in which there is a bilateral optic neuritis and paraplegia. It may be a form of multiple sclerosis.

neurone (*nu'-ron*). A complete nerve-cell, with its processes, including those which bring *afferent* impulses to it and those which convey *efferent* impulses from it. *Lower motor n.* In which the cell is in the grey matter of the spinal cord, and the nerve fibre passes to the skeletal muscles. *Upper motor n.* That in which the cell is in the cerebral cortex and the fibres conduct impulses to associated cells in the spinal cord.

neuropathic (*nu-ro-path'-ik*). Relating to nervous disorder.

neuropathy (*nu-rop'-ath-e*). A disease process of nerve degeneration and loss of function. *Diabetic n.* That associated with diabetes. *Ischaemic n.* That caused by a lack of blood supply.

neuroplasty (*nu'-ro-plas-te*). Operation for transplantation of nerves.

neurorrhaphy (*nu-ror'-raf-e*). The operation of suturing a divided nerve.

neurosis (*nu-ro'-sis*). A mental disorder, which does not affect the whole personality, characterized by exaggerated anxiety and tension. *Anxiety n.* There is persistent anxiety and the accompanying symptoms of fear, rapid pulse, sweating, trembling, loss of appetite and insomnia. *Obsessive–compulsive n.* This is characterized by compulsions and rumination (*q.v.*). *See* Hysteria *and* Phobia.

neurosurgery (*nu-ro-sur'-jer-e*). That branch of surgery dealing with the brain, spinal cord and nerves.

neurosyphilis (*nu-ro-sif'-il-is*). A manifestation of third stage syphilis in which the nervous system is involved. The three commonest forms are: (1) meningovascular syphilis affecting the blood vessels to the meninges, (2) tabes dorsalis, *see* Ataxia, (3) general paralysis of the insane.

neurotic (*nu-rot'-ik*). A loosely applied adjective denoting association with neurosis.

neurotmesis (*nu-rot-me'-sis*). A severing of a nerve sheath and its fibres which may be partial or complete. The usual cause is a penetrating wound.

neurotomy (*nu-rot'-o-me*). The division of a nerve.

neurotoxic (*nu-ro-toks'-ik*). Poisonous or destructive to nervous tissue.

neurotripsy (*nu-ro-trip'-se*). Bruising or crushing a nerve.

neurotropic (*nu-ro-tro'-pik*). Having an affinity for nerve tissue. *N. viruses.* Those that particularly attack the nervous system.

neutral (*nu'-tral*). Neither acid nor alkaline.

neutropenia (*nu-tro-pe'-ne-ah*). A lack of neutrophils in the blood.

neutrophils (*nu'-tro-fils*). White blood cells which stain with neutral dyes.

new growth. Abnormal growth of tissue in type or location. *Malignant n. g.* Cancer (*q.v.*).

niacin (*ni'-a-sin*). Nicotinic acid (*q.v.*).

nicotine (*nik'-o-tin*). A poisonous alkaloid in tobacco.

nicotinic acid (*nik-o-tin'-ik as-id*). A factor found in vitamin B complex. *See* Appendix 10.

nictitation (*nik-tit-a'-shun*). Uncontrollable blinking of the eyelids.

nidus (*ni'-dus*). A nest. A place in which an organism finds conditions suitable for its growth and development.

night blindness. Nyctalopia. Difficulty in seeing in the dark. This may be a congenital defect or a vitamin A deficiency.

night sweat. Profuse perspiration during sleep, especially typical of tuberculosis.

night terrors. Dreams causing acute fear.

nihilism (*ni'-hil-izm*). In psychiatry a term used to describe feelings of not existing and hopelessness, that all is lost or destroyed.

nikethamide (*nik-eth'-am-id*). A cardiac and respiratory stimulant. Coramine is a proprietary preparation.

nipple (*nip'-pl*). The small conical projection in the centre of the breast. *Depressed n.* This should be drawn out during pregnancy, so that later the infant can suck. *Retracted n.* A sign of cancer of the breast.

nit. The egg of the head louse attached to the hair near the scalp.

nitrofurantoin (*ni-tro-fur-an'-to-in*). A urinary antiseptic which is bacteriocidal and is effective against a wide range of organisms. Furadantin is a proprietary preparation of it.

nitrofurazone (*ni-tro-fur'-a-zone*). A local application used as an antibacterial agent for skin conditions. Furacin is a proprietary preparation.

nitrogen (*ni'-tro-jen*). A gaseous element of which air is largely composed, and the essential constituent of all protein foods.

nitrogen mustard hydrochloride (*ni'-tro-jen mus'-tard*). A cytotoxic drug. *See* Mustine hydrochloride.

nitroglycerin (*ni-tro-glis'-er-een*). Trinitrin, Glyceryl trinitrate. A drug which causes dilatation of the coronary arteries. In angina pectoris a tablet should be dissolved sublingually before exertion.

nitrous oxide (*ni'-trus oks'-ide*). N_2O. Laughing gas. A general anaesthetic ensuring a brief spell of unconsciousness, and used largely for dental operations. With oxygen it is extensively used as a light anaesthetic, but does not give sufficient muscle relaxation for abdominal operations unless combined with other drugs.

noci-association (*no'-se as-so-se-a'-shun*). The discharge of nervous energy which occurs unconsciously in trauma, as in surgical shock. *See also* Anoci-association.

nocturia (*nok-tu'-re-ah*). The production of large quantities of urine at night.

nocturnal (*nok-tur'-nal*). Referring to the night. *N. enuresis.* Bed wetting. Incontinence of urine during sleep.

node. A swelling or protuberance. *Atrioventricular* (*auriculoventricular*) *n.* The specialized tissue between the right atrium and ventricle, at the point where the coronary vein enters the atrium, from which is initiated the impulse of contraction down the bundle of His. *Sino-atrial* (*sino-auricular*). n. The pacemaker of the heart. The specialized neuro-muscular tissue at the junction of the superior vena cava and the right atrium, which, stimulated by the right vagus nerve, controls the rhythm of contraction in the heart. *N. of Ranvier.* A constriction occurring at intervals in a nerve fibre to enable the neurilemma with its blood supply to reach and nourish the axon of the nerve.

nodule (*nod'-ule*). A small

swelling or protuberance.

noma (*no'-mah*). Cancrum oris (*q.v.*).

nomenclature (*no-men'-kla-ture*). The terminology of a science; a classified system of names.

non compos mentis (*non kom'-pos men'tis*). A person whose mental state is such that he is unable to manage his own affairs.

noradrenaline (*nor-ad-ren'-a-lin*). A hormone present in extracts of the suprarenal medulla. It causes vasoconstriction and raises both the systolic and diastolic blood pressure but does not stimulate general metabolism.

norethandrolone (*nor-eth-an'-dro-lone*). An anabolic steroid that aids in the utilization of protein. May be used to treat severe wasting and in osteoporosis.

norethisterone (*nor-eth-is'-ter-one*). An anabolic steroid. *See above*. Primolut N. is a proprietary preparation.

normal (*nor'-mal*). Conforming to a standard; regular or usual. *N. saline*. Isotonic (*q.v.*) solution of sodium chloride. *Syn*. Physiological (*q.v.*) solution.

normoblast (*nor'-mo-blast*). A nucleated red blood cell in bone marrow. *See* Erythrocyte.

normochromic (*nor-mo-kro'-mik*). When the haemoglobin level in the red blood corpuscle is within normal limits.

normoglycaemia (*nor-mo-gli-se'-me-ah*). When the blood sugar level is within the normal range.

normotension (*nor-mo-ten'-shun*). Normal tone, tension or pressure. Usually used in relation to blood pressure.

normovolaemic shock. A state of shock in which the blood volume is normal. Coronary thrombosis is an example.

nose. The organ of smell and of respiration.

nosology (*nos-ol'-o-je*). The scientific classification of diseases.

nostalgia (*nos-tal'-je-ah*). Home-sickness.

nostril (*nos'-tril*). One of the anterior orifices of the nose.

notifiable (*no-te-fi'-ab-l*). A term applied to such diseases as must be reported to the Medical Officer of Health. These include measles, scarlet fever, typhus and typhoid fever, cholera, smallpox, diphtheria, and tuberculosis.

novobiocin (*nov-o-bi'-o-sin*). A wide-range oral antibiotic that is effective against *Proteus* organisms.

noxious (*nok'-she-us*). A harmful substance. The term may be applied to drugs or other substances liable to cause injury.

nucha (*nu'-kah*). The nape of the neck.

nucleoproteins (*nu'-kle-o-pro'-teens*). Constituents of cell nuclei from which purins are derived.

nucleus (*nu'-kle-us*). (1) The essential part of a cell, governing nutrition and reproduction, its division being essential for the formation of new cells. (2) A group of nerve cells in the central nervous system. *Caudate n.*, *lenticular n.* are part of the basal ganglia (*q.v.*). *N. pulposus.* The jelly-like centre of an intervertebral (*q.v.*) disc, which may prolapse and cause pressure upon one of the spinal nerve roots; most commonly the sciatic.

nullipara (*nul-ip'-ar-ah*). A woman who has never given birth to a child.

nutation (*nu-ta'-shun*). Uncontrollable nodding of the head.

nutmeg liver. *See under* Liver.

nutrition (*nu-trish'-un*). The process by which food is assimilated into the body in order to nourish it.

nutritional disease (*nu-trish'-un-al*). One that is due to the continued absence of a necessary food factor.

nux vomica (*nuks vom'-ik-ah*). The seed of an East Indian tree, from which strychnine is derived. In small doses it is a tonic. *See* Strychnine.

nyctalgia (*nik-tal'-je-ah*). Pain occurring during the night.

nyctalopia (*nik-tal-o'-pe-ah*). Night blindness. Defective vision in a dim light especially due to deficiency of vitamin A. *See* Appendix 10.

nycturia (*nik-tu'-re-ah*). Incontinence of urine at night or excessive production of urine.

nymphae (*nim'-fe*). The labia minora. *See* Labia.

nymphomania (*nim-fo-ma'-ne-ah*). Excessive sexual desire in a woman.

nystagmus (*ni-stag'-mus*). An involuntary, rapid movement of the eyeball. It may be hereditary; result from disease of the semicircular canals; or of the central nervous system. It can occur from visual defect or be associated with other muscle spasms. *Miner's n.* An occupational form.

nystatin (*ni'-stat-in*). An antibiotic drug particularly useful in treating thrush and moniliasis of the vagina.

O

O. Chemical symbol for oxygen.

obesity (*o-be'-sit-e*). Corpulence; excessive development of fat throughout the body.

objective signs. Those which the observer notes, as distinct from symptoms of which the patient complains (*subjective*).

obsession (*ob-ses'-shun*). An idea which persistently recurs to an individual although he resists it and regards it as being senseless. A compulsive thought. *See* Compulsion.

obsessive neurosis. *See* Neurosis.

obstetrician (*ob-stet-rish'-un*). One who is trained and specializes in obstetrics.

obstetrics (*ob-stet'-riks*). The branch of medicine dealing with pregnancy and labour.

obturator (*ob'-tur-a-tor*). That which closes an opening. *O. foramen*. The large hole in the os innominatum closed by fascia and muscle.

obtusion (*ob-tu'-shun*). Weakening or blunting of normal sensations, a condition produced by certain diseases.

occipital (*ok-sip'-it-al*). Relating to the occiput.

occipito-anterior (*ok-sip'-it-o an-te'-re-or*). When the back of the head is to the front of the pelvis as the child's head comes through the birth canal. *Occipito-posterior* is the reverse position.

occiput (*ok'-sip-ut*). The back of the head.

occlusion (*ok-klu'-shun*). Closed, applied particularly to alignment of the teeth in the jaws, or the lumen of a blood vessel.

occlusive therapy (*ok-klu'-siv ther'-ap-e*). In ophthalmology covering the good eye to encourage the use of a lazy or deviated eye.

occult blood. A term applied to blood excreted in the stools in such small quantity as to require chemical tests to detect.

occupational disease (*ok-ku-pa'-shun-al dis-eez'*). One due to the nature of one's work. Industrial diseases.

occupational therapy (*ok-ku-pa'-shun-al ther'-ap-e*). *See under* Therapy.

Ochsner-Sherran treatment (*oks'-ner sher'-an*). A conservative method of treating acute appendicitis if conditions are unfavourable or in late cases with generalized peritonitis when localization is aimed at before operation.

ocular (*ok'-u-lar*). Relating to the eye.

oculogyric (*ok-u-lo-ji'-rik*). Causing movements of the eye-balls.

oculentum (*ok-u-len'-tum*). An eye ointment.

oculomotor (*ok-u-lo-mo'-tor*). Relating to movements of the eye. *O. nerves.* The 3rd pair of cranial nerves which control the eye muscles.

odontalgia (*o-don-tal'-je-ah*). Toothache.

odontoid (*o-don'-toid*). Resembling a tooth. *O. process.* A projection from the axis vertebra upon which the head rotates.

odontolith (*o-don'-to-lith*). Tartar, the calcareous matter deposited upon teeth.

odontology (*o-don-tol'-o-je*). The science of treating teeth. Dentistry.

odontoma (*o-don-to'-mah*). A tumour of tooth structures.

odontoprisis (*o-don-to-pri'-sis*). Grinding of the teeth.

-odynia (*o-din'-e-ah*). Suffix meaning 'pain'.

oedema (*e-de'-mah*). Dropsy. An effusion of fluid into the tissues. If the finger is pressed upon an affected part, the surface pits and regains slowly its original contour. *Cardiac oe.* That due to heart failure. *Famine oe.* Due to diet deficiency. *Lymphatic oe.* That due to blockage of the lymph vessels. *Pulmonary oe.* Effusion of fluid into the alveoli and tissues between them. A serious cause of cyanosis. *Renal oe.* That occurring in nephritis. *Venous oe.* Fluid due to obstruction in veins.

Oedipus complex (*e'-dip-us*). From Greek mythology. The exaggerated affection of a son for his mother, with hostility towards the father. It is a normal stage in the early development of the child, but may become fixed or a complex if the child cannot solve the conflict during the early years or during adolescence.

oesophageal (*e-sof-aj'-e-al*). Pertaining to the oesophagus.

oesophagectasis (*e-sof-aj-ekt'-as-is*). Dilatation of the oesophagus.

oesophagitis (*e-sof-aj-i'-tis*). Inflammation of the oesophagus. *Reflux oe.* That caused by regurgitation of acid stomach contents through the cardiac sphincter.

oesophagojejunostomy (*e-sof'-ag-o-je-ju-nos'-to-me*). An anastomosis of the jejunum with the oesophagus following a total gastrectomy.

oesophagoscope (*e-sof'-ag-os-kope*). An instrument for

viewing the inside of the oesophagus.

oesophagoscopy (*e-sof-ag-os'-ko-pe*). An examination carried out with an oesophagoscope.

oesophagotomy (*e-sof-ag-ot'-o-me*). Incision of the oesophagus.

oesophagus (*e-sof'-ag-us*). The canal which extends from the pharynx to the stomach. It is about 9 in. (23 cm) long.

oestradiol (*e-stra'-di-ol*). The chief naturally occurring oestrogen in the ovary and can be chemically prepared and is marketed in different forms, *e.g. O. benzoate* or *ethinyl o.*

oestrin (*e'-strin*). A general term to describe the endocrine secretion of the Graafian follicle. *See* Oestrogens.

oestrogens (*e'-stro-jens*). Hormones that have the same action as oestradiol, and though largely produced in the ovary, can also be extracted from the placenta, adrenal cortex, and the testis.

Oidium albicans (*o-id'-e-um al'-be-kans*). The former term for *Candida albicans* which causes thrush or moniliasis.

ointment (*oint'-ment*). An external application with a base of lard, lanolin or petroleum jelly in which the remedy is incorporated.

olecranon (*o-lek'-ran-on*). The curved process of the ulna which forms the point of the elbow.

oleum (*o'-le-um*). Oil. *O. morrhuae*. Cod-liver oil. *O. ricini*. Castor oil.

olfactory (*ol-fak'-tor-e*). Relating to the sense of smell. *O. nerves*. The first pair of cranial nerves; those of smell.

oligaemia (*ol-ig-e'-me-ah*). Deficient quantity of blood.

oligocythaemia (*ol-ig-o-si-the'-me-ah*). Blood cell deficiency.

oligohydramnios (*ol-ig-o-hi-dram'-ne-os*). Deficiency in the amount of amniotic fluid.

oligomenorrhoea (*ol-ig-o-men-or-e'-ah*). A diminished flow at the menstrual period. Scanty menstruation.

oligophrenia (*ol-ig-o-fre'-ne-ah*). Mental subnormality. The condition may be congenital or due to disease or injury. *Phenylpyruvic o.* An hereditary abnormality associated with an excessive excretion of phenylpyruvic acid (*q.v.*).

oligo-spermia (*ol-ig-o-sper'-me-ah*). A diminished output of sperm. Production may be stimulated by testosterone.

oliguria (*ol-ig-u'-re-ah*). Deficient secretion of urine.

olive oil. A vegetable oil used as a food and intestinal lubricant. *O. enema*. Given to soften faeces after rectal or perineal operations, or for obstinate constipation.

omentopexy (*o-men'-to-peks-e*). Fixation of the omentum. *Cardio-o*. The omentum may be attached to the heart to establish a collateral circulation when there is coronary occlusion.

omentum (*o-men'-tum*). A fold of peritoneum. *Greater o.* Reflected from the greater curvature of the stomach and lying in front of the intestines. *Lesser o.* Reflected from the lesser curvature and attaching the stomach to the under surface of the liver.

omphalitis (*om-fal-i'-tis*). Inflammation of the umbilicus.

omphalocele (*om'-fal-o-seel*). Umbilical hernia.

omphaloproptosis (*om-fal-o-prop-to'-sis*). Excessive protrusion of the umbilicus.

omphalus (*om'-phal-us*). The umbilicus.

Onchocerca volvulus (*on-ko-ser'-ka vol'-vu-lus*). A filarial worm that may give rise to skin and subcutaneous lesions and attack the eye.

onchocerciasis (*on-ko-ser-ki'-as-is*). A filariasis caused by the Onchocerca volvulus.

oncogenic (*on-ko-jen'-ik*). Giving rise to tumour formation.

oncology (*on-kol'-o-je*). The scientific study of tumours.

oncometer (*on-kom'-e-ter*). An instrument for measuring the blood volume in a limb. *See* Plethysmography.

onychia (*on-ik'-e-ah*). Inflammation of the matrix of a nail, with suppuration, which may cause the nail to fall off.

onychomycosis (*on-ik-o-mi-ko'-sis*). Infection of the nails by fungi. Ringworm of the nails.

onychosis (*on-ik-o'-sis*). Deformity of the nails or of a nail.

oocyte (*o'-o-site*). The immature egg cell or ovum in the ovary.

oogenesis (*o-o-jen'-e-sis*). The development and production of the ovum.

oophoralgia (*o-off-or-al'-je-ah*). Pain in the ovary.

oophorectomy (*o-off-or-ek'-to-me*). Excision of an ovary.

oophoritis (*o-off-or-i'-tis*). Inflammation of an ovary.

oophoron (*o-off'-or-on*). The ovary (*q.v.*).

oophorosalpingectomy (*o-off'-or-o-sal-pin-jek'-to-me*). Removal of the ovary and its associated Fallopian tube.

opacity (*o-pas'-it-e*). Cloudiness, lack of transparency.

open fracture. *See under* Fracture.

operation (*op-er-a'-shun*). A surgical procedure in which instruments or hands are used by the operator. *Avascular o.* One in which there is little or no bleeding achieved by applying an Esmarch's bandage from the extremity upwards on an elevated limb or by the use of drugs causing hypotension. *Magnet o.* The removal of a foreign body from the eye by means of a magnet. *Palliative o.* Relieves symptoms, but does not cure, e.g. gastro-enterostomy in carcinoma of the pylorus.

ophthalmia (*off-thal'-me-ah*). Inflammation of the eye, involving especially the conjunctiva. *Gonorrhoeal o.* or *o. neonatorum.* A serious infection caused by *Neisseria gonorrhoea*. *Granular o.* An acute and purulent form when there is a gritty feeling on moving the eyelids. *Phlyctenular o. See* Conjunctivitis. *Purulent o.* When the discharge is pus. *See also* Trachoma.

ophthalmic (*off-thal'-mik*). Relating to the eye.

ophthalmitis (*off-thal-mi'-tis*). Inflammation of the eyeball. *Sympathetic o.* A serious complication in the sound eye following a perforating wound in the opposite eye.

ophthalmologist (*off-thal-mol'-o-jist*). A specialist in diseases of the eye.

ophthalmology (*off-thal-mol'-o-je*). The study of the eye and its diseases.

ophthalmometer (*off-thal-mom'-e-ter*). An instrument for accurately measuring corneal astigmatism.

ophthalmometry (*off-thal-mom'-e-tre*). The use of the ophthalmometer.

ophthalmoplegia (*off-thal-mo-ple'-je-ah*). Paralysis of the muscles of the eye.

ophthalmoscope (*off-thal'-mo-skope*). An instrument fitted with a battery, light, and lenses by which the retina of the eye can be illuminated and examined.

OPHTHALMOSCOPE

ophthalmoscopy (*off-thal-mos'-ko-pe*). The examination of the eye by the aid of an ophthalmoscope.

ophthalmotomy (*off-thal-mot'-o-me*). Incision into the eye.

ophthalmotonometer (*off-thal'-mo-ton-om'-e-ter*). An instrument for measuring the intra-ocular tension of the eye.

opiate (*o'-pe-ate*). Any medicine containing opium.

opisthotonos (*op-is-thot'-on-os*). A muscle spasm causing the back to be arched and the head retracted, with great rigidity of the muscles of the neck and back. This condition may be present in acute cases of meningitis, tetanus, and strychnine poisoning.

opium (*o'-pe-um*). A drug derived from dried poppy-juice and used as a narcotic. It produces deep sleep, slows the pulse and respiration, contracts the pupils and checks all secretions of the body except sweat. *Alkaloids of o.* Morphine, codeine, papaverine, etc. *Tincture of o.* Laudanum.

opponens (*op-po'-nens*). Opposing. Adductor muscles of the fingers and toes. *O. pollicis.* Adducts the thumb, so that it and the little finger can be brought together.

opsonic index (*op-son'-ik*). A measurement of the bactericidal power of phagocytes.

opsonins (*op'-son-ins*). Substances present in the blood which render bacteria more easily destroyed by the phagocytes. Each kind of bacteria has its specific opsonin.

optic (*op'-tik*). Relating to vision. *O. chiasma.* The crossing of the fibres of the optic nerves at the base of the brain. *O. disc.* Where the optic nerve enters the eyeball.

optical density (*op'-tik-al den'-se-te*). The refractive power of the transparent tissues through which light rays pass, changing the direction of the ray.

optician (*op-tish'-an*). One who makes and fits spectacles.

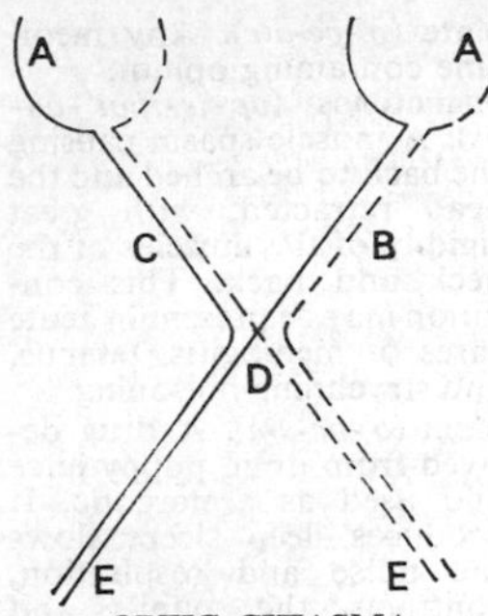

OPTIC CHIASMA

A. Retina.
B. Right optic nerve.
C. Left optic nerve.
D. Optic chiasma.
E. To the occipital lobes.

optimum (*op'-te-mum*). Most favourable conditions.

optometry (*op-tom'-e-tre*). The measuring of visual acuity and the fitting of glasses to correct visual defects.

oral (*or'-al*). Relating to the mouth.

oral eroticism (*or'-al e-rot'-is-izm*). Oral gratification which the infant gains from sucking and exploring objects with his mouth. It is still in evidence in later life in the pleasure derived from eating, gum-chewing, smoking and kissing.

orbicular (*or-bik'-u-lar*). Circular.

orbit (*or'-bit*). The bony cavity containing the eyeball.

orchidectomy (*or-kid-ek'-to-me*). Excision of a testicle.

orchidopexy (*or'-kid-o-pek'-se*). An operation to free an undescended testicle and place it in the scrotum.

orchiepididymitis (*or-ke-ep-e-did-e-mi'-tis*). Inflammation of testicle and epididymis.

orchis (*or'-kis*). The testicle.

orchitis (*or-ki'-tis*). Inflammation of a testicle.

orf (*orf*). A virus infection transmitted from sheep to man. It may give rise to a boil-like lesion on the hands of meat handlers.

organ. A part of the body designed to perform a particular function. *End o.* The termination of nerve-fibres. *O. of Corti.* The sensitive nerve terminals in the internal ear.

organic (*or-gan'-ik*). Pertaining to the organs. *O. disease* is of an organ and accompanied by structural changes.

organism (*or'-gan-izm*). An individual living being, animal or vegetable.

orgasm (*org'-azm*). The climax in sexual intercourse.

oriental sore (*or-e-en'-tal*). *See* Furunculus.

orientation (*or-e-en-ta'-shun*). A sense of direction. The ability of a person to estimate his position in regard to time, place and persons. Imparting relevant information at the onset of a course or conference so that its content and objects may be understood.

orifice (*or'-e-fis*). Any opening in the body.

ornithosis (*or-ne-tho'-sis*). A newer term for psittacosis (*q.v.*) as it has been found the virus may be transmitted by a wider group of birds.

oropharynx (*or-o-far'-inks*). The lower portion of the pharynx behind the mouth and above the oesophagus and larynx.

ortho (*or'-tho*). A prefix meaning 'straight'.

orthodontia (*or-tho-don'-she'-ah*). Dentistry which deals with the prevention and correction of irregularities of the teeth.

orthopaedic (*or-tho-pe'-dik*). Relating to the correction of deformities.

orthopnoea (*or-thop-ne'-ah*). Difficulty in breathing unless in an upright position, i.e. sitting up in bed.

orthoptic (*or-thop'-tik*). Relating to correction of oblique vision (squint).

orthostatic (*or-tho-stat'-ik*). Standing erect. *O. albuminuria*. *See* Albuminuria.

os. (1) A bone. *O. calcis*. The heel-bone or calcaneum. (2) A mouth or opening. *External o*. The opening of the cervix into the vagina. *Internal o*. The junction of the cervical canal and body of the uterus.

oscheocele (*os'-ke-o-seel*). Scrotal hernia or swelling.

oscillation (*os-sil-a'-shun*). A swinging or tremulous motion.

Ortolani's sign. A test performed soon after birth to detect possible congenital dislocation of the hip. A 'click' is felt on reversing the movements of abduction and rotation of the hip while the child is lying with knees flexed.

oscilloscope (*os'-sil-o-skope*). An instrument that indicates when an electrical current is passed through it.

Osler's nodes (*o'-zler*). Small painful swellings which occur in or beneath the skin, especially of the extremities in subacute bacterial endocarditis, caused by minute emboli. They usually disappear in 1 to 3 days.

osmosis (*oz-mo'-sis*). The diffusion of fluids through a semi-permeable membrane. *Osmotic pressure*. A pressure exerted by large molecules in the blood, e.g. albumen and globulin proteins, which draws fluid into the bloodstream from the surrounding tissues.

osseous (*os'-se-us*). Bony.

ossicle (*os'-sik-l*). A small bone. *Auditory o's*. Those of the middle ear: the malleus, incus, and stapes.

ossification (*os-sif-ik-a'-shun*). The formation of bone.

ostalgia (*os-tal'-je-ah*). Pain in a bone.

osteectomy (*os-te-ek'-to-me*). Excision of bone.

osteitis (*os-te-i'-tis*). Inflammation of bone. *O. deformans*. *See* Paget's disease. *O. fibrosa cystica* or *parathyroid o*. Defects of ossification, with fibrous tissue production, leading to weakening and deformity. It affects children chiefly, and is associated with parathyroid tumour, removal of which checks it. *See* von Recklinghausen's disease.

osteo-arthritis (*os-te-o-ar-thri'-tis*). A form of arthritis in which there is destruction of articular cartilage and bony outgrowths at the edges of joints. A painful disease of the elderly, occurring in the larger joints where most weight is carried.

osteo-arthrotomy (*os-te-o-ar-throt'-o-me*). Excision of the jointed end of a bone.

osteoblasts (*os'-te-o-blasts*). Bone-forming cells that aid in growth and repair and the deposition of calcium.

osteochondritis (*os-te-o-kon-dri'-tis*). A non-inflammatory disease of the epiphysis causing pain and deformity. When occurring in the hip it is termed *Perthes's disease*; in the tarsal scaphoid bone—*Köhler's d.*; in the tibial tubercle—*Schlatter's d.*

osteochondroma (*os-te-o-kon-dro'-mah*). A new growth arising from both bone and cartilage.

osteoclasis (*os-te-ok'-la-sis*). The manual fracture of bones to correct a deformity such as bow-legs.

osteoclasts (*os'-te-o-klasts*). (1) Large bone cells that absorb and remove bone tissue and callus. (2) Instruments designed for surgical fracture of bone.

osteocyte (*os'-te-o-site*). A bone cell.

osteogenesis (*os-te-o-jen'-e-sis*). The formation of bone. *O. imperfecta cystica.* In which X-ray examination shows cystic spaces in the bone. Due to over-secretion of the parathyroids causing decalcification of the bones and a high blood calcium.

osteogenic (*os-te-o-jen'-ik*). Originating or derived from bone. *O. sarcoma.* A malignant growth of bone.

osteoma (*os-te-o'-mah*). An innocent new growth arising in a bone-forming cell or osteoblast.

osteomalacia (*os-te-o-mal-a'-se-ah*). A disease characterized by painful softening of bones. Due to vitamin D deficiency.

osteomyelitis (*os-te-o-mi-el-i'-tis*). Inflammation of the bone and marrow. *Acute o.* Commonly occurs in children due to a blood-borne staphylococcal infection. The vascular edge of the epiphyseal cartilage is first attacked. *Chronic o.* can result from an acute attack or from an open fracture.

osteopath (*os'-te-o-path*). One who practises bone manipulation and treats bone conditions. Often medically unqualified.

osteopathic back (*os-te-o-path'-ik*). A term used to describe acute pain and muscle spasm following displacement of one of the small facet type joints of the spine.

osteopathy (*os-te-op'-ath-e*). Any bone disease. Also commonly used for the treatment of disease by manipulation of bones.

osteoperiostitis (*os'-te-o-per-e-os-ti'-tis*). Inflammation of bone and periosteum.

osteophony (*os-te-off'-on-e*). Conduction of sound by bone.

osteophyte (*os'-te-o-fite*). A small outgrowth of bone.

osteoplasty (*os'-te-o-plas-te*). Plastic operations on bone.

osteoporosis (*os-te-o-por-o'-sis*). The bones are lacking in mineral salts due to deficiency of bony matrix. This may be due to protein or hormone insufficiency.

osteosarcoma (*os-te-o-sar-ko'-mah*). A sarcoma in bone.

osteotome (*os'-te-o-tome*). A surgical instrument for cutting bone.

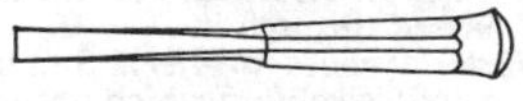

OSTEOTOME

osteotomy (*os-te-ot'-o-me*). The cutting of bone, usually performed to correct deformity. *O. of hip.* A method of treating osteo-arthritis by cutting the bone and altering the line of weight bearing. *See* diagram.

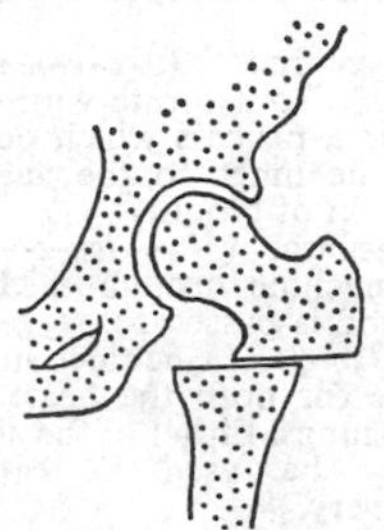

OSTEOTOMY OF THE HIP

ostium (*os'-te-um*). A mouth. *Abdominal o.* The opening at the end of the Fallopian tube into the peritoneal cavity.

otalgia (*o-tal'-je-ah*). Ear-ache.

otic (*o'-tik*). Relating to the ear.

otitis (*o-ti'-tis*). Inflammation of the ear. *O. media.* Middle-ear disease.

otolaryngology (*o-to-lar-in-gol'-o-je*). The scientific study of the ear and the larynx and the diseases concerned with them.

otoliths (*o'-to-lith*). Ear stones. Calcareous concretions of the inner ear, at the base of the semicircular canals.

otologist (*o-tol'-o-jist*). A specialist in diseases of the ear.

otomycosis (*o-to-mi-ko'-sis*). A fungal infection of the auditory canal.

otophone (*o'-to-fone*). Ear trumpet.

otorrhoea (*o-tor-re'-ah*). Discharge from the ear—especially of pus.

otosclerosis (*o-to-skle-ro'-sis*). A thickening and ossification of the tissues and ligaments that convey the sound waves to the internal ear. The stapes becoming fixed in the oval window.

otoscope (*o'-to-skope*). Auriscope. An instrument for examining the ear.

otoscopy (*o-tos'-ko-pe*). An examination of the tympanic membrane and auditory canal by means of an otoscope.

ounce (*ounse*). An Imperial measurement of weight and of volume. *See* Appendix 14.

ovarian (*o-va'-re-an*). Relating to an ovary. *O. cyst.* A tumour of the ovary containing fluid.

ovariectomy (*o-va-re-ek'-to-me*). Excision of an ovary. Oophorectomy.

ovariotomy (*o-va-re-ot'-o-me*). Usually taken to mean removal of an ovary, but literally, incision of an ovary.

ovaritis (*o-var-i'-tis*). Oophoritis (*q.v.*).

ovary (*o'-var-e*). One of a pair of glandular organs in the female pelvis, associated with the uterus. Its function is the production of ova.

over-compensation (*o-ver-kom-pen-sa'-shun*). A mental mechanism by which a person tries to assert himself by aggressive behaviour or by talking or acting 'big' to compensate for a feeling of inadequacy.

overdosage (*o-ver-do'-saj*). Denotes the toxic effects resulting from too high a blood level of a drug. This may be from too large or repeated doses or from the cumulative effect.

overhydration (*o-ver-hi-dra'-shun*). The administration of too much intravenous fluid.

oviducts (*o'-ve-dukts*). The Fallopian tubes (*q.v.*).

ovotestis (*o-vo-tes'-tis*). A gonad containing both ovarian and testicular tissue.

ovulation (*ov-u-la'-shun*). The process of rupture of the mature Graafian follicle when the ovum is shed from the ovary.

ovum (*o'-vum*). An egg. The reproductive cell of the female. *Pl.* ova.

oxalic acid (*oks'-al-ik as'-id*). Salts of lemon. A corrosive poison that can be precipitated by lime water, milk, or a suspension of chalk.

oxaluria (*oks-al-u'-re-ah*). Oxalates in urine.

Oxford inflator. A simple hand pump with facemask for applying emergency artificial respiration.

oxidization (*oks-e-di-za'-shun*). Oxidation. The process of oxidizing by which combustion occurs and breaking up of matter takes place; e.g. oxidation of carbohydrates gives carbon dioxide and water.

$$C_6H_{12}O_6 + 6O_2 = 6CO_2 + 6H_2O.$$

oximeter (*oks-im'-e-ter*). A photoelectric cell used to determine the oxygen saturation of blood. *Ear o.* One attached to the ear by which the oxygen content of blood flowing through the ear can be measured.

oxycyanide of mercury (*oks-e-si'-an-ide of mer-ku'-re*). A mercurial antiseptic that may be used for urethral or bladder irrigation.

oxygen (*oks'-e-jen*). O_2. A colourless, odourless gas constituting one-fifth of the atmosphere. It is stored in cylinders at high pressure or as liquid oxygen and released for inhalation in cases of dyspnoea. For methods of administration, *see* Appendix 4.

oxygenation (*oks-e-jen-a'-shun*). To saturate with oxygen; a process which occurs in the lungs to the haemoglobin of blood.

oxygenator (*oks-e-jen-a-'-tor*). A machine through which the blood is passed to oxygenate it. *Pump o.* Machines substitute for both the heart and the lungs. Either of the above may be used in cardiac surgery.

oxyhaemoglobin (*oks-e-he-mo-glo'-bin*). Haemoglobin oxygenated, as in arterial blood.

oxyntic cells (*oks-in'-tik*). Those which secrete acid, e.g. HCl in the stomach is made by these cells of the gastric glands.

oxytetracycline (*oks-e-tet-ra-si'-kleen*). An antibiotic drug produced from a mould. Terramycin is a proprietary preparation of it.

oxytocic (*oks-e-to'-sik*). Any drug which stimulates uterine contractions and may be used to hasten delivery.

oxytocin (*oks-e-to'-sin*). That part of pituitrin which contracts the uterus. Pitocin is a proprietary form.

oxyuriasis (*oks-e-u-ri'-a-sis*). Infestation by thread worms.

Oxyuris (*oks'-e-u'-ris*). A genus of nematode worms found in the intestines. Family Ascaridae.

ozaena (*o-ze'-nah*). Atrophic rhinitis. A condition of the nose in which there is loss and shrinkage of the ciliated mucous membrane and of the turbinate bones.

ozone (*o'-zone*). An intensified

form of oxygen containing three O atoms to the molecule, O_3, and often discharged by electrical machines such as X-ray apparatus. In medicine it is employed as an antiseptic and oxidizing agent.

P

Pacchionian bodies (*pak-e-o'-ne-an*). Arachnoid granulations by which the cerebrospinal fluid drains into the venous channels in the dura mater.

pace-maker. The sino-atrial node. *See* Node. *Artificial p.* An instrument that takes over the function of the sino-atrial node by sending small electrical impulses to the heart. An electrode may be sewn on to the epicardium and attached either to an external p. or to one that is implanted in the rectus abdominis muscle. Alternatively an electrode may be passed through a vein (in the elbow or neck) into the apex of the right ventricle and attached either to an external p. or to one that is implanted under the skin in the axilla.

pachy- (*pak'-e*). A prefix meaning 'thick'.

pachydermatous (*pak-e-der'-mat-us*). Thick-skinned.

pachydermia (*pak-e-der'-me-ah*). A thick skin. *P. laryngis.* A chronic hypertrophy of the vocal cords.

pachymeningitis (*pak-e-men-in-ji'-tis*) Inflammation—with thickening—of the dura mater.

pachysomia (*pak-e-so'-me-ah*). Much thickening of soft parts as in acromegaly.

Pacini's corpuscles (*pah-che'-ne*). Specialized end-organs, situated in the subcutaneous tissue of the extremities and near joints, that respond to firm pressure.

pack. Ribbon or folded gauze for placing in a cavity. *Abdominal p.* One used in the theatre to protect or seal off a part. *Cold p.* A little used method of reducing temperature. *Hot p.* May be applied to a limb or part to relieve pain or reduce muscle spasm as in poliomyelitis.

paediatrician (*pe-de-a-trish'-an*). A specialist in the diseases of children.

paediatrics (*pe-de-at'-riks*). The branch of medicine dealing with diseases of children.

Paget's disease (*paj'-et*). (1) Of bone in which over-activity of the osteoblasts and osteoclasts leads to dense bone formation with areas of rarefaction. Osteitis deformans. (2) Carcinoma of the nipple.

painter's colic. *See* Colic.

palate (*pal'-ate*). The roof of the mouth. *Hard p.* in front, is of bone. *Soft p.* continues from it, and is of muscle which forms the pillars of the fauces and the uvula. *Artificial p.* A plate made to close a cleft palate. *Cleft p.* A congenital deformity where there is lack of fusion of the two bones forming the palate.

palatine (*pal'-at-ine*). Two bones forming most of the hard palate. *P. processes.* The horizontal portions of the superior maxillae forming the anterior portion of the hard palate.

palatoplegia (*pal-at-o-ple'-je-

ah). Paralysis of the soft palate.

palliative (*pal'-le-a-tiv*). An agent which relieves, but does not cure disease.

pallidectomy (*pal-le-dek'-to-me*). An operation performed to decrease the activity of the globus pallidum, the medial part of the lentiform nucleus in the base of the cerebrum. It has brought about a marked improvement in severely agitated cases of paralysis agitans.

pallor (*pal'-or*). Lack of colour.

palmar (*pal'-mar*). Relating to the palm of the hand. *P. fascia*. The arrangement of tendons in the palm of the hand. *Deep* and *superficial p. arches*. The chief arterial blood supply to the hand formed by anastomosis of ulnar and radial arteries.

palpation (*pal-pa'-shun*). Examination of the organs by touch, or pressure of the hand over the part.

palpebra (*pal'-pe-brah*). The eyelid.

palpebral (*pal'-pe-bral*). Referring to the eyelids. *P. ligaments*. Stretch from the junction of the upper and lower lid to the orbital bones both medially and laterally.

palpitation (*pal-pit-a'-shun*). Rapid and forceful contraction of the heart of which the patient is conscious.

palsy (*pawl'-ze*). Paralysis. *Bell's p*. Paralysis of the facial muscles on one side, supplied by the seventh cranial nerve. *Creeping p*. Progressive muscular atrophy. *Crutch p*. Due to pressure of the crutch on the radial nerve and a cause of 'dropped wrist'. *Erb's p*. Paralysis of one arm due to a birth injury to the brachial plexus. *Shaking p*. Paralysis agitans.

panacea (*pan-a-se'-ah*). A cure-all.

panarthritis (*pan-ar-thri'-tis*). Inflammation of all the structures of a joint.

pancarditis (*pan-kar-di'-tis*). Inflammation of all the structures of the heart—as may occur in rheumatic infection.

pancreas (*pan'-kre-as*). An elongated, racemose gland about 6 in. (15 cm) long, lying behind the stomach, with its head in the curve of the duodenum, and its tail in contact with the spleen. It secretes a digestive fluid (*pancreatic juice*) containing ferments, which act on all classes of foods. The fluid enters the duodenum by the pancreatic duct which joins the common bile duct. The pancreas also secretes the hormone *insulin* (*q.v.*).

pancreatectomy (*pan-kre-a-tek'-to-me*). Excision of the head and body of the pancreas for carcinoma.

pancreatico-duodenal (*pan-kre-at'-ik-o du-o-de'-nal*). Relating to the pancreas and duodenum. *P. artery*. That to the head of the pancreas and duodenum.

pancreatin (*pan'-kre-at-in*). An extract from the pancreas containing the digestive enzymes. Used to treat deficiency as in fibrocystic disease of the pancreas.

pancreatitis (*pan-kre-at-i'-tis*). Inflammation of the pancreas. *Acute p*. A severe condition in which the pancreatic enzymes can cause self-digestion. *Subacute p*. May follow mumps or influenza infections. A usually chronic form.

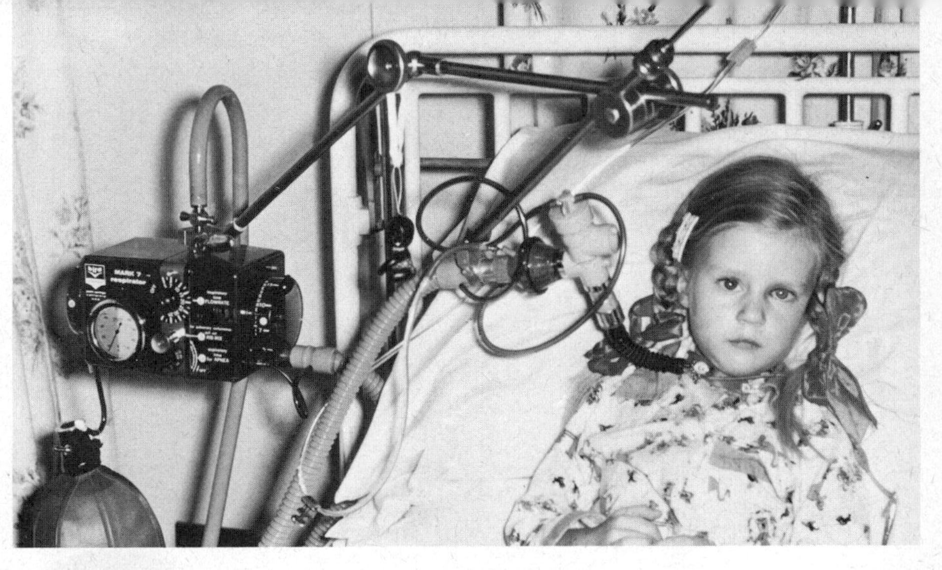

PLATE I. BIRD RESPIRATOR (Appendix 1)
A respirator that responds to the patient's own rhythm giving added inspiratory effort to maintain adequate lung ventilation (*Saint Bartholomew's Hospital*)

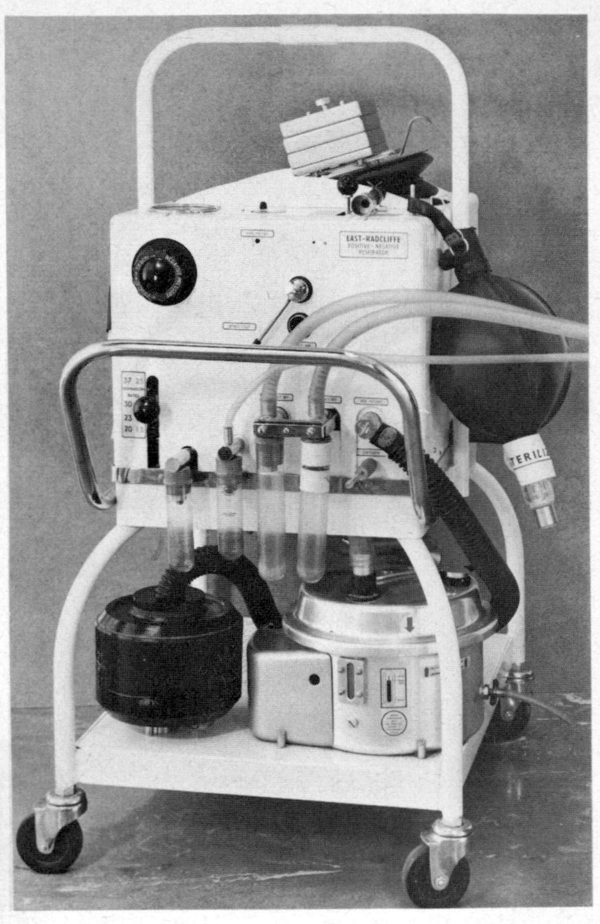

PLATE II. EAST RADCLIFFE RESPIRATOR (Appendix 1)
An intermittent positive-pressure machine used to maintain respiration. Tracheal intubation or a tracheostomy is performed first (*Saint Bartholomew's Hospital*)

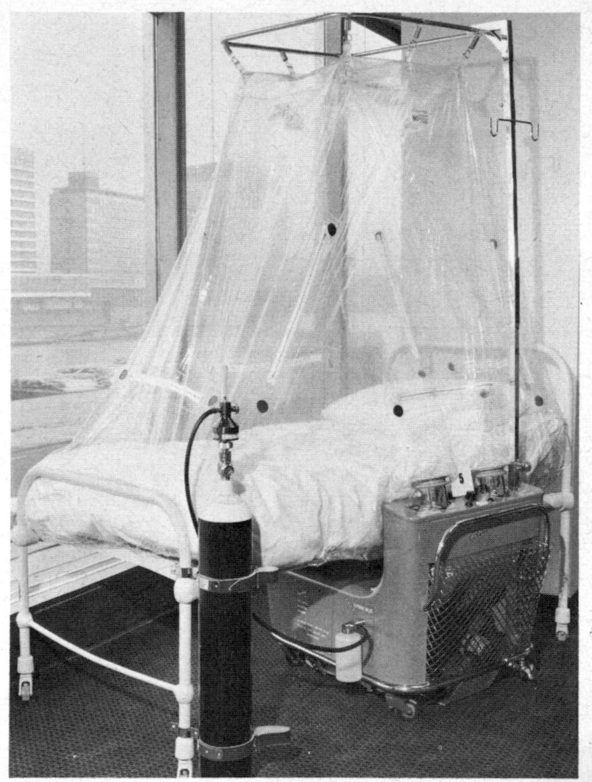

PLATE III. OXYGEN TENT (Appendix 4)

The tent is fully transparent and completely covers the bed. The electrically controlled refrigeration unit fits under the bed and is mounted on anti-static castors. The oxygen concentration, the washing out of carbon dioxide, the temperature and the humidity can all be readily controlled (*Vickers*)

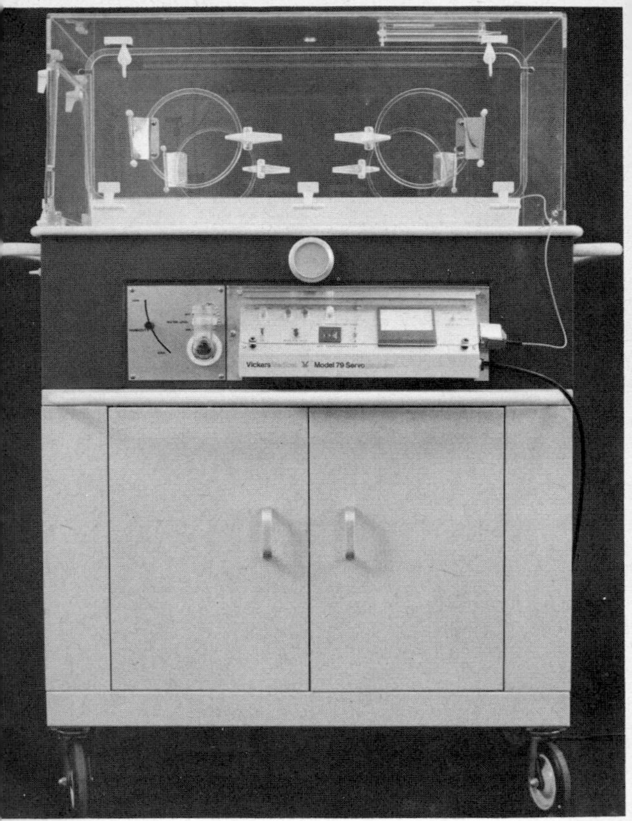

PLATE IV. INFANT INCUBATOR

The incubator provides continuous monitoring of the temperature of sick or premature babies and automatically alters the environmental temperature of the infant. The baby's temperature is therefore maintained within finely controlled limits (*Vickers*)

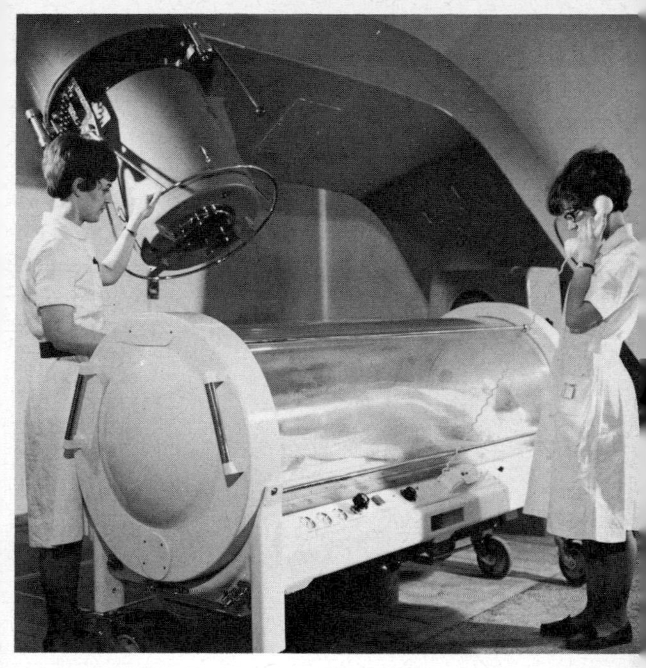

PLATE V. HYPERBARIC OXYGEN CHAMBER
(Appendix 4) (*Vickers*)

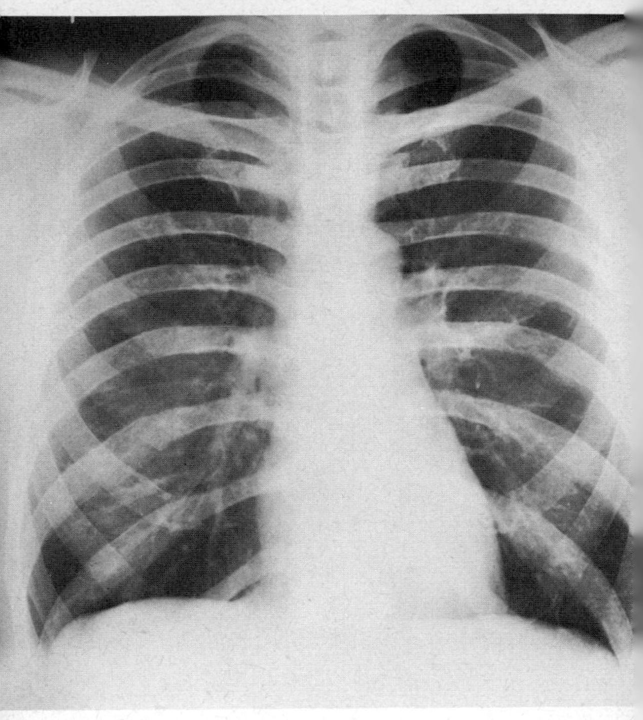

PLATE VI. CHEST ON INSPIRATION
Expansion of the chest in all three dimensions, i.e. fall of the diaphragm and upward and outward swing of the ribs

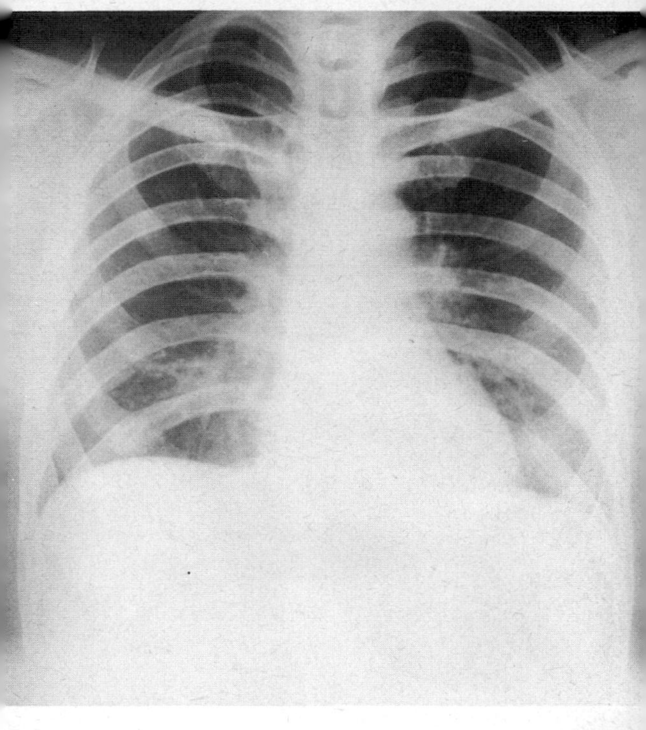

PLATE VII. CHEST ON EXPIRATION

Rise of the diaphragm regaining domed shape, return of ribs to original position

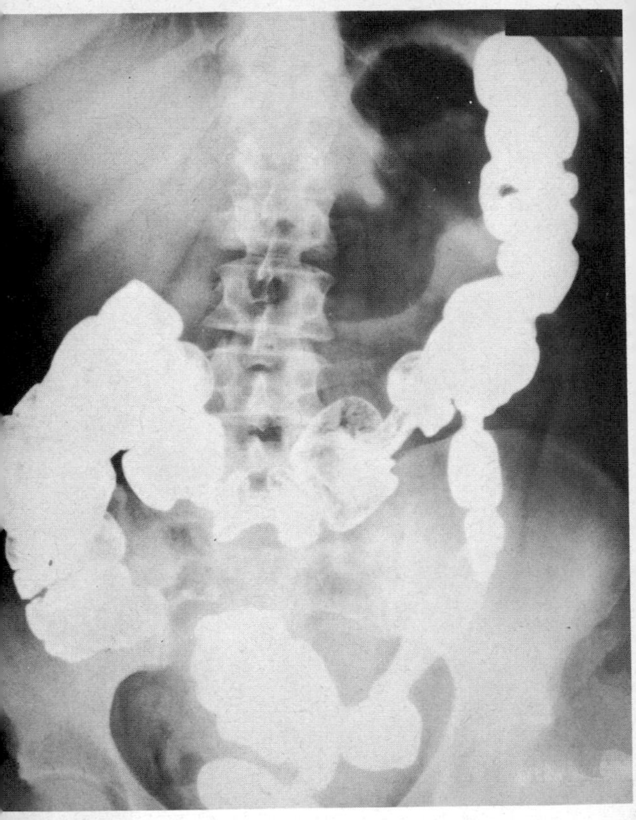

PLATE VIII. THE LARGE INTESTINE
Leading from the caecum (left side of X-ray) to the ascending colon, across the transverse colon and up to the splenic flexure, then down the descending colon to the sigmoid flexure and finally to the rectum

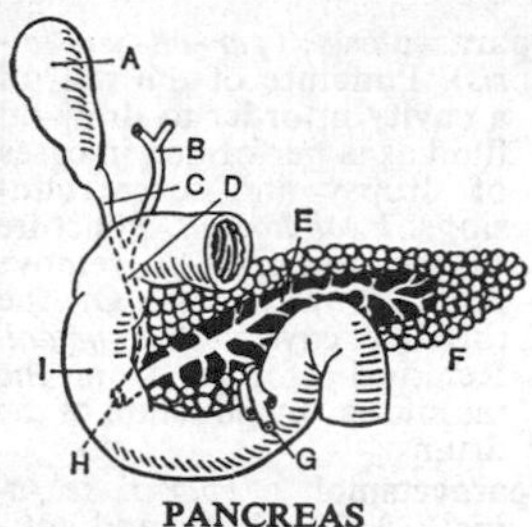

PANCREAS

A. Gall-bladder.
B. Hepatic ducts.
C. Cystic duct.
D. Common bile duct.
E. Pancreatic duct.
F. Pancreas.
G. Superior mesenteric artery.
H. Opening of bile and pancreatic duct.
I. Duodenum.

pancreozymin (*pan-kre-o-zi'-men*). A hormone secreted in the small intestine that stimulates the secretion of pancreatic enzymes.

pancytopenia (*pan-si-to-pe'-ne-ah*). A lack of all the blood cells due to failure of bone marrow formation.

pandemic (*pan-dem'-ik*). An epidemic spreading over a wide area.

panhysterectomy (*pan-his-ter-ek'-to-me*). *See* Hysterectomy.

panic-state. A feeling of overwhelming fear or terror. It may occur in anxiety states, war neurosis, or acute schizophrenia.

panicula (*pan-ik'-u-lah*). A little swelling.

panleucopenia (*pan-lu-ko-pe'-ne-ah*). A lack of all the white blood cells.

panmyelopathy (*pan-my-el-op'-ath-e*). Disease affecting all the cells formed in the bone.

panniculitis (*pan-ik-ul-i'-tis*). A disease in which tender nodules appear in the subcutaneous fat accompanied by periods of fever.

panniculis (*pan-ik'-u-lus*). A sheet of membranous tissue.

pannus (*pan'-nus*). Increased vascularity of the cornea leading to granulation tissue formation and impaired vision.

panophthalmia (*pan-off-thal'-me-ah*). Panophthalmitis. Inflammation of all the tissues of the eyeball.

panophthalmitis (*pan-off-thal-mi'-tis*). Inflammation of the eye involving all three coats, the retina, choroid, and sclera.

panosteitis (*pan-os-te-i'-tis*). Inflammation of all the structures of a bone.

panotitis (*pan-o-ti'-tis*). Inflammation of the internal, as well as of the middle ear.

pantropic (*pan'-tro-pik*). An adjective applied to organisms that attack a wide range of structures.

Papanicolaou test (*pa-pa-nik'-o-lou*). *See* Test.

papaveretum (*pa-pa-ver'-e-tum*). A preparation of the alkaloids of opium. Omnopon is a proprietary preparation.

papaverine (*pa-pav'-er-een*). An alkaloid of opium.

papilla (*pap-il'-lah*). A small nipple-like eminence. *Pl.* papillae. *Circumvallate p.* At the back of the tongue arranged in a V shape, and containing taste buds. *Filiform p.* Fine, slender filaments on the main part of the tongue which give it its velvety appearance. *Fungi-*

form p. Mushroom-shaped papillae of the tongue. *Optic p.* The optic disc where the optic nerve leaves the eyeball. *Tactile p.* The projections on the true skin containing touch corpuscles.

papillary (*pap'-il-lar-e*). Composed of or pertaining to papillae.

papilliferous cyst (*pap-il-lif'-er-us*). *See under* Cyst.

papillitis (*pap-il-li'-tis*). Inflammation of the optic disc. It may also be termed optic neuritis.

papilloedema (*pap-il-e-de'-mah*). Oedematous swelling of the optic disc indicating increase of intracranial pressure.

papilloma (*pap-il-lo'-mah*). An innocent growth of epithelial tissue, e.g. a wart.

papillomatosis (*pap-il-lo-mat-o'-sis*). The occurrence of multiple papilloma.

papular (*pap'-u-lah*). Referring to papules.

papule (*pap'-ule*). A pimple, or small solid elevation of the skin.

papulopustular (*pap'-u-lo-pus'-tu-lar*). Showing both papules and pustules.

papulosquamous (*pap-u-lo-skwa'-mus*). Eruptions of the skin involving the epidermis including such conditions as psoariasis and lichen planus.

para-aminobenzoic acid (*par-ah-am-in-o-ben-zo'-ik*). Filters the ultraviolet rays of the sun and in a cream protects against sunburn.

para-aminosalicylic acid (*par-ah-am-in-o-sal-is-il'-ic*). In the form of a calcium or sodium salt this is an antituberculous drug used with streptomycin and/or isoniazid. PAS.

paracentesis (*par-ah-sen-te'-sis*). Puncture of the wall of a cavity in order to draw off fluid as is performed in cases of dropsy and severe effusions. *P. abdominis.* Puncture of the abdomen to remove fluid. *P. thoracisis.* Of the thoracic cavity. *P. tympani.* Removal of fluid from the middle ear by puncture of the drum.

paracetamol (*par-ah-set'-a-mol*). An analgesic and antipyretic. Panadol is a proprietary preparation.

parachlorometacresol (*par-ah-klor-o-met-ah-kre'-sol*). Chlorocresol (*q.v.*). A coal tar antiseptic preparation.

parachlorometaxylenol (*par'-ah-klor-o-met-aks-i'-le-nol*). Chloroxylenol (*q.v.*). A group of antiseptics of which Dettol and Roxenol are examples.

paracusis (*par-ah-ku'-sis*). A perverted sense of hearing. *P. willisiana.* Hearing better in a noise, as in a railway train.

paradoxical breathing (*par-ah-doks'-ic-al*). This occurs when the two lungs are not working in unison as may occur in pneumothorax.

paraesthesia (*par-es-the'-ze-ah*). Disorder of sensation, e.g. a feeling of tingling or as of 'pins and needles'.

paraffin (*par'-af-in*). Any saturated hydrocarbon obtained from coal-tar. *P. molle.* Petroleum jelly. *P. wax.* A hard paraffin that can be used for wax treatment for chronic inflammation of joints. *Liquid p.* An intestinal lubricant, extensively used as a fine emulsion. Also applied to wounds to prevent the injury of new granulations when dressings are removed, e.g. flavine emulsion.

paraform (*par'-ah-form*). Paraformaldehyde. A preparation of formaldehyde used as an antiseptic, and also for fumigating rooms.

paraldehyde (*par-al'-de-hide*). A drug with a most pungent taste. It is hypnotic and anaesthetic.

paralysis (*par-al'-is-is*). Loss of sensation and the power of movement of any part, as the result of interference with the nerve supply. *P. agitans*

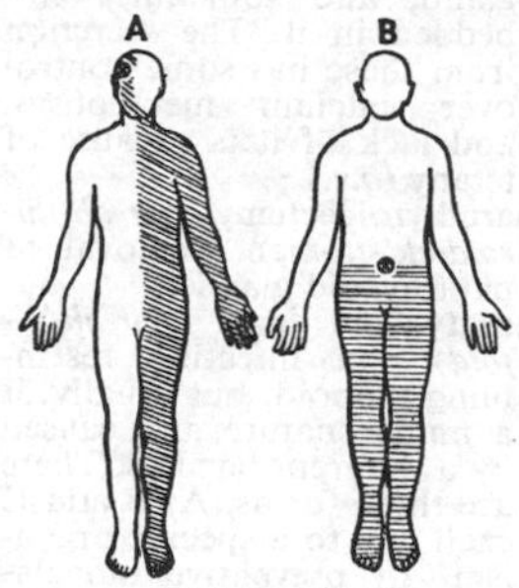

PARALYSIS

Diagram to show cerebral or spinal origin.
A. Hemiplegia (cortical lesion).
B. Paraplegia (spinal cord lesion).
Shaded areas show extent of paralysis.

('shaking palsy') is a disease occurring in people of middle age, slow in development and characterized by rigidity of the muscles of the face, producing a mask-like expression, typical tremors of the limbs, great muscle weakness and a peculiar gait. Also known as Parkinson's disease *Bulbar p.* (*labioglossopharyngeal p.*). Due to changes in the motor centres of the medulla oblongata. It affects the muscle of the mouth, tongue, and pharynx. *Diphtheritic p.* A complication of diphtheria, the soft palate being first affected. *Facial p.* (*Bell's palsy*). Affects the muscles of the face, and is due to injury to or inflammation of the facial nerve. *Flaccid p.* in which there is loss of tone and absence of reflexes in the paralysed muscles. *Infantile p.* A former term for acute anterior poliomyelitis. (*See* Poliomyelitis.) *Spastic p.* is characterized by rigidity of affected muscles.

paralytic (*par-ah-lit'-ik*). Affected by or relating to paralysis. *P. ileus.* Absence of peristalsis in a portion of the intestine associated with peritonitis.

paramedian incision (*par-ah-me'-de-an*). One to the side of the midline.

paramedical (*par-ah-med'-e-kal*). Having some association with the science or practice of medicine. The paramedical services include occupational, speech and physical therapy; and medical social work.

parametric (*par-ah-met'-rik*). Concerning the tissue surrounding the uterus.

parametritis (*par-ah-met-ri'-tis*). Inflammation of the parametrium; pelvic cellulitis.

parametrium (*par-ah-me'-tre-um*). The connective tissue around the uterus.

paramnesia (*par-am-ne'-ze-ah*). A defect of memory in which there is a false recollection. The patient may fill in the forgotten period with imaginary events which he describes in great detail.

paramyotonia congenita (*par-ah-mi-o-to'-ne-ah con-jen'-it-a*). Congenital muscle weakness and lack of muscle tone only when the patient is exposed to cold.

paranoia (*par-ah-noi'-ah*). A mental disorder characterized by delusions of grandeur or persecution which may be fully systematized in logical form, with the personality remaining fairly well preserved.

paranoid (*par'-ah-noid*). Resembling paranoia. A condition that can occur in many forms of mental disease. Delusions of persecution are a marked feature. *P. schizophrenia*. *See* Schizophrenia.

paraparesis (*par-ah-par-e'-sis*). An incomplete paralysis, especially of the lower limbs.

paraphimosis (*par-ah-fi-mo'-sis*). Retraction of the prepuce behind the glans penis, with inability to replace it.

paraphrenia (*par-ah-fre'-ne-ah*). Schizophrenia occurring for the first time in later life and not accompanied by deterioration of the personality.

paraplegia (*par-ah-ple'-je-ah*). Paralysis of the lower extremities and lower trunk. All parts below the point of lesion in the spinal cord are affected. It may be of sudden onset from injury to the cord, or develop slowly as the result of disease as in *locomotor ataxia*, *transverse myelitis*, etc.

parasite (*par'-ah-site*). Any animal or vegetable organism living upon or within another, from which it derives its nourishment.

parasiticide (*par-ah-sit'-is-ide*). A drug which kills parasites.

parasympathetic system (*par-ah-sim-path-et'-ik*). Part of the autonomic nervous system (*q.v.*).

parasympatholytic (*para-sim'-path-o-lit'-ik*). Drugs that neutralize the effect of the parasympathetic nerves.

parathormone (*par-ah-thor'-mone*). The endocrine secretion of the parathyroid glands.

parathyroid glands (*par-ah-thi'-roid*). Four small endocrine glands—two associated with each lobe of the thyroid gland, and sometimes embedded in it. The secretion from these has some control over calcium metabolism, and lack of it is a cause of tetany (*q.v.*).

parathyroidectomy (*par-ah-thi-roid-ek'-to-me*). Removal of parathyroid glands.

paratyphoid fever (*par-ah-ti'-foid*). An infection resembling typhoid, but usually of a milder nature and caused by a different bacillus. There are three forms, A, B and C each due to a specific organism. In preventive inoculation, TAB vaccine, prepared from typhoid and paratyphoid A and B bacilli, may be given, or a vaccine to which paratyphoid C has been added.

paravertebral (*par-ah-ver'-te-bral*). Near or at the side of the vertebrae.

parencephalous (*par-en-kef'-al-us*). Having a congenital malformation of the brain.

parenchyma (*par-eng'-ke-ma*). The essential active cells of an organ as distinguished from its vascular and connective tissue.

parenteral (*par-en'-ter-al*). Apart from the alimentary canal. Applied to the introduction into the body of drugs or fluids by routes other than the mouth or rectum, e.g. intravenously or subcutaneously.

paresis (*par'-e-sis*). Partial paralysis.

parietal (*par-i'-et-al*). Relating to the walls of any cavity; e.g. *p. pleura*, the pleura attached to the chest wall. *P. bones*. The two bones forming part of the roof and sides of the skull.

parietal cells (*par-i'-et-al*). Alternative name for the oxyntic cells in the gastric mucosa that secrete hydrochloric acid.

parietes (*par-i'-et-ez*). The walls of any cavity.

Paris technique. A method of treating carcinoma of the cervix of the uterus by irradiation with radium in large doses.

Parkinson's disease (*park'-in-son*). Paralysis agitans. *See* Paralysis.

paronychia (*par-on-ik'-e-ah*). An abscess near the fingernail; a whitlow or felon. *P. tendinosa*. When the infection spreads and involves the tendon sheath.

parosmia (*par-os'-me-ah*). A disordered sense of smell.

parotid (*par-ot'-id*). Situated near the ear. *P. glands*. Two salivary glands, one in front of each ear.

parotitis (*par-o-ti'-tis*). Inflammation of the parotid gland. Caused usually by ascending infection via its duct, e.g. when hygiene of the mouth is neglected or when the natural secretions are lessened, especially in severe illness or following operation. *Epidemic p*. Mumps (*q.v.*).

parous (*par'-us*). A woman who has borne one or more children.

paroxysm (*par'-oks-izm*). A sudden attack, or recurrence of a symptom of a disease.

paroxysmal (*par-oks-iz'-mal*). Occurring in paroxysms. *P. cardiac dyspnoea*. Cardiac asthma. Recurrent attacks of dyspnoea associated with pulmonary oedema and left sided heart failure. *P. tachycardia*. Recurrent attacks of rapid heart beats that may occur without heart disease.

parrot disease. *See* Psittacosis.

parthenogenesis (*par-then-o-jen'-es-is*). A sexual reproduction by means of an egg without fertilization by the male.

parturient (*par-tu'-re-ent*). Giving birth; relating to childbirth.

parturition (*par-tu-rish'-un*). The act of giving birth to a child.

Paschen bodies (*pah'-shen*). Small granules demonstrable in the fluid of the vesicles of smallpox.

passive. Not active. *P. immunity*. *See* Immunity. *P. movements*. In massage, manipulations without the help of the patient.

passivity feelings (*pas-iv'-e-te*). Psychiatric term for a delusional feeling that a person is under some outside control.

Pasteurella (*pas-tur-el'-lah*). A genus of short rod-shaped bacilli. *P. pestis*. The causative organism of plague transmitted by rat fleas to man.

Pasteur treatment (*pahs-tur'*). To prevent hydrophobia (*q.v.*) by injecting a very weak form of the virus of rabies and gradually producing immunity.

pasteurization (*pas-tur-i-za'-*

shun). The process of checking fermentation in milk and other fluids, by heating them to a temperature between 63° to 68°C (145° to 150°F) for 30 min and then rapidly cooling. This kills all pathogenic bacteria and has safeguarded the nation's milk supply. Variations of the above time and temperatures may be used.

patella (*pat-el'-lah*). The small, circular, sesamoid bone forming the knee-cap.

patellectomy (*pat-el-ek'-to-me*). Excision of the patella.

patent (*pa'-tent*). Open. *P. ductus arteriosus.* When the ductus arteriosus (*q.v.*) fails to close at birth, so that deoxygenated blood enters the systemic circulation. One cause of a 'blue baby' (*q.v.*).

patho- (*path'-o*). A prefix denoting 'disease'.

pathogenic (*path-o-jen'-ik*). Causing disease. *P. bacteria.* Disease-causing organisms.

pathognomonic (*path-og-no-mon'-ik*). Specifically characteristic of a disease sign or symptom by which a pathological condition can be identified.

pathological (*path-o-loj'-ik-al*). Pertaining to the study of disease.

pathology (*path-ol'-o-je*). The branch of medicine treating of disease, and the changes in structure and function which it causes.

pathophobia (*path-o-fo'-be-ah*). Exaggerated dread of disease.

Paul-Bragg respirator. An apparatus fitted around the chest by which artificial respiration may be carried out.

Paul-Bunnell test (*pawl-bun'-nel*). An agglutination test which, if positive, confirms the diagnosis of glandular fever.

Paul's tube. A bent glass tube, used chiefly for colonic drainage.

peau d'orange (*po-dor-ahn'-je*). The appearance of the overlying skin in advanced carcinoma of the breast. Blockage of the skin lymphatics causes dimpling of the hair follicle openings which resembles orange skin.

pecten (*pek'-ten*). The middle third of the anal canal.

pectin (*pek'-tin*). A setting agent used in cookery, formed from pectose, a carbohydrate found in fruit.

pectoral (*pek'-tor-al*). Relating to the chest. *P. muscles.* The pectoralis major and minor.

pectus (*pek'-tus*). The chest.

pedicle (*ped'-ik-l*). The stem or neck of a tumour. *P. graft.* A tissue graft that is partially

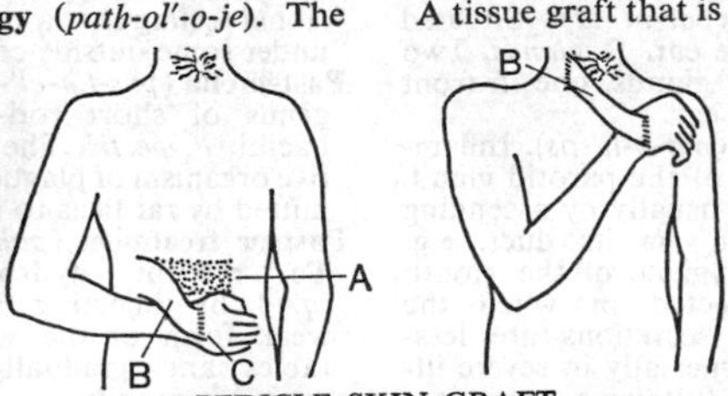

PEDICLE SKIN GRAFT
A. Donor area; B. Pedicle; C. First attachment.

detached and inserted in its new position while temporarily still obtaining its blood supply from the original source.

pediculosis (*ped-ik-u-lo'-sis*). The condition of being infested with lice.

Pediculus (*ped-ik'-u-lus*). The louse, a small parasite infesting the skin and hairy parts of the body. *See* Louse.

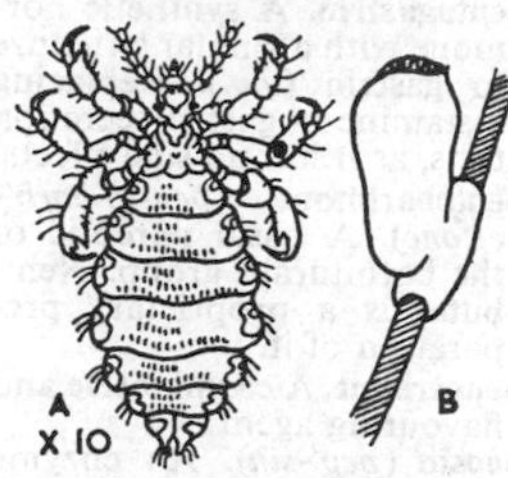

PEDICULUS

A. Pediculus capitis.
B. Egg or 'nit' attached to hair.

peduncle (*ped-un'-kl*). A narrow part of a structure acting as a support. *P. of cerebellum*. One of the collections of nerve-fibres connecting the cerebellum with the medulla oblongata.

peeling. Desquamation (*q.v.*).

Pel-Ebstein's fever (*pel-eb'-stine*). A recurrent pyrexia having a span of 15 to 21 days seen especially in cases of lymphadenoma.

pellagra (*pel-lag'-grah*). A deficiency disease due to lack of vitamin B (*nicotinic acid*). It is characterized by debility, spinal pains, digestive disorders, and erythema with exfoliation of the skin. *See* Appendix 10.

pellicle (*pel'-lik-l*). (1) A scum on the surface of a liquid. (2) A thin skin or membrane.

pelvic (*pel'-vik*). Pertaining to the pelvis. *P. girdle*. The ossa innominata and sacrum. *P. peritonitis*. *See* Peritonitis.

pelvimeter (*pel-vim'-e-ter*). Calipers for measuring the diameter of the pelvis.

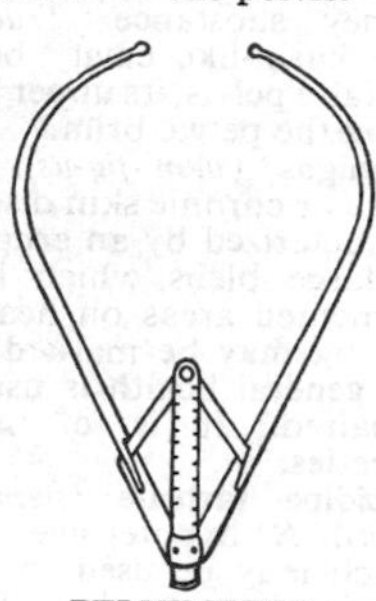

PELVIMETER

pelvimetry (*pel-vim'-et-re*). Measuring of the pelvis. *X-ray p.* Can be used to measure the internal pelvic diameters and late in pregnancy this can be assessed in relation to the fetal head. *Cephalopelvimetry*.

pelvirectal (*pel-ve-rek'-tal*). The term applied to the flexure where the pelvic colon joins the rectum at an acute angle.

pelvis (*pel'-vis*). A basin-shaped cavity. *Bony p.* The pelvic girdle formed of the innominate bones and the sacrum. *Contracted p.* Narrowing of the diameter of the pelvis. *See* Conjugate. It may be of the *true* conjugate or the *diagonal*. Effective antenatal care will recognize this condition, and Caesarean section is often necessary to ensure live birth. The deformity may be the result of rickets. *False p.* The part formed by the concavity of the iliac bones above the ileopectineal line. *Renal p.* The dilatation of the ureter, which by enclosing the hilus surrounds the pyramids of the kidney substance. *True p.* The basin-like cavity below the false pelvis, its upper limit being the pelvic brim.

pemphigus (*pem'-fig-us*). An acute or chronic skin disease, characterized by an eruption of large blebs which leave pigmented areas on healing. Itching may be marked and the general health is usually impaired. It is of many varieties.

pempidine tartrate (*pem'-pe-deen*). A hypotensive drug which may be used to treat arterial hypertension. Perolysen and Tenormal are proprietary preparations.

pendulous (*pen'-du-lus*). Hanging down. *P. abdomen.* Due to weakness and laxity of abdominal muscles. In pregnancy it causes the uterus to fall forwards.

penicillamine (*pen-is-il'-a-meen*). A chelating agent that is used in copper and lead poisoning to aid excretion of the metal.

penicillin (*pen-is-il'-in*). A group of antibiotics that are bacteriocidal for those organisms that are sensitive to the drug used. *Benzyl p.* A soluble form quickly absorbed giving high blood levels but rapidly excreted. *Procaine p.* A less soluble form, so there is slow release and absorption from the intramuscular site. Effective for 24 hr. Other preparations are: *ampicillin*, *cloxacillin*, *methicillin* and *phenoxymethylpenicillin* (*q.v.*).

penicillinase (*pen-is-il'-in-aze*). An enzyme that destroys penicillin. Many staphylococci produce this enzyme.

Penicillium notatum (*pen-is-il'-e-um no-ta'-tum*). A mould from which penicillin first derived.

penis (*pe'-nis*). The male organ of copulation.

pentagastrin. A synthetic hormone with a similar structure to gastrin (*q.v.*). Replacing histamine in gastric secretion tests, as it has no side effects.

pentobarbitone (*pen-to-barb'-e-tone*). A basal narcotic of the barbiturate group. Nembutal is a proprietary preparation of it.

peppermint. A carminative and flavouring agent.

pepsin (*pep'-sin*). An enzyme found in gastric juice. It partially digests proteins in an acid solution.

pepsinogen (*pep-sin'-o-jen*). The precursor of pepsin, activated by HCl.

peptic (*pep'-tik*). Applied to the gastric secretions and areas affected by them. *P. glands.* The gastric glands. *P. ulcer.* One arising in the stomach or duodenum associated with hyperacidity.

peptone (*pep'-tone*). The result of the action of pepsin on protein.

peptonized foods (*pep'-ton-ized*). Foods partially digested by artificial methods.

peptonuria (*pep-ton-u'-re-ah*). Peptones in the urine.

percept or **perception** (*per'-sept*, *per-sep'-shun*). An awareness and understanding of an impression that has been presented to the senses.

The mental process by which we perceive.

perchloride of mercury (*per-klor'-ide*). Corrosive sublimate.

percussion (*per-kush'-un*). A method of diagnosis by tapping with the fingers upon any part of the body. By the sounds produced, information can be gained as to the condition of organs below the skin.

perflation (*per-fla'-shun*). Ventilation by forcing air into a room.

perforation (*per-for-a'-shun*). A hole through the whole thickness of a wall of a cavity or organ. It may be caused by ulceration or trauma.

perfusion (*per-fu'-shun*). Pouring fluid over. *P. fluid.* One used to bathe a tissue usually to maintain its health, often by allowing a chemical exchange of necessary and waste products.

peri- (*per'-e*). Prefix meaning 'around'.

peri-anal (*per-e-a'-nal*). Surrounding or located around the anus. *P. abscess.* A small subcutaneous pocket of pus near the anal margin.

periarteritis (*per-e-ar-ter-i'-tis*). Inflammation of the outer coat of an artery.

periarthritis (*per-e-ar-thri'-tis*). Inflammation of the tissues surrounding a joint.

pericardiectomy (*per-e-kar-de-ek'-to-me*). Excision of a large part of the pericardium. Sometimes performed to check impaired cardiac action in constrictive pericarditis.

pericarditis (*per-e-kar-di'-tis*). Inflammation of the pericardium secondary to other disease such as rheumatic fever, tuberculosis or myocardial infarction. *Adhesive p.* Adhesions occur between the two layers of pericardium owing to a thick fibrinous exudate. *Constrictive p.* Progressive fibrosis causing constriction of heart movement. *Purulent p.* Is due to pyogenic infection. *Serous p.* Excessive serous exudate impairing heart function.

pericardium (*per-e-kar'-de-um*). The smooth membranous sac enveloping the heart, consisting of an outer fibrous and an inner serous coat. *Adherent p.* Fibrous tissue formation between the layers, the result of acute pericarditis.

pericardotomy (*per-e-kard-ot'-o-me*). An operation to open the pericardium, sometimes performed to break down adhesions following pericarditis.

perichondrium (*per-e-kon'-dre-um*). The membrane covering cartilaginous surfaces.

pericolpitis (*per-e-kol-pi'-tis*). Inflammation of the tissues around the vagina.

pericranium (*per-e-kra'-ne-um*). The periosteum of cranial bones.

pericystitis (*per-e-sis-ti'-tis*). Inflammation of the tissues surrounding the bladder.

perihepatitis (*per-e-hep-at-ti'-tis*). Inflammation of the peritoneum covering the liver.

perilymph (*per'-e-limf*). Lymph separating bone and membrane in the bony labyrinth of the ear.

perimeter (*per-rim'-e-ter*). (1) The line marking the boundary of any area or geometrical figure; the circumference. (2) An instrument for measuring the field of vision.

perimetritis (*per-e-me-tri'-tis*). Inflammation of the perimetrium.

perimetrium (*per-e-me'-tre-um*). The peritoneal covering of the uterus.

perimetry (*per-im'-et-re*). The process of mapping the visual fields.

perineal (*per-e-ne'-al*). Relating to the perineum.

perineorrhaphy (*per-e-ne-or'-raf-e*). Suture of the perineum to repair a laceration caused during childbirth.

perinephric (*per-e-nef'-rik*). Around the kidney.

perinephritis (*per-e-nef-ri'-tis*). Inflammation of the tissues enveloping the kidney.

perineum (*per-e-ne'-um*). The tissues between the anus and external genitals. *Lacerated p.* May result from childbirth but is often forestalled by performing an episiotomy (*q.v.*). Treatment is by perineorrhaphy.

periodontitis (*per-e-o-don-ti'-tis*). Inflammation of the tissues surrounding a tooth.

periodontium (*per-e-o-don'-te-um*). The connective tissue between the teeth and their bony sockets.

periosteal (*per-e-os'-te-al*). Pertaining to or composed of periosteum. *P. elevator*. An instrument for separating the periosteum from bone.

periosteotome (*per-e-os'-te-o-tome*). An instrument for incising the periosteum and separating it from the bone.

periosteum (*per-e-os'-te-um*). The fibrous membrane covering the surface of bone. It consists of two layers, the inner or *osteogenetic*, which is closely adherent, and which forms new cells, by which the bone grows in girth; and in close contact with it the *fibrous* layer richly supplied with blood vessels.

periostitis (*per-e-os-ti'-tis*). Inflammation of the periosteum.

peripheral (*per-if'-er-al*). Relating to the periphery. *P. neuritis*. Inflammation of terminal nerves. *See* Neuritis.

periphery (*per-if'-er-e*). The outer surface or circumference.

perisalpingitis (*per-e-sal-pin-ji'-tis*). Inflammation of the peritoneal covering of the Fallopian tube.

perisplenitis (*per-e-splen-i'-tis*). Inflammation of the peritoneum over the spleen.

peristalsis (*per-e-stal'-sis*). A wave-like contraction, preceded by a wave of dilatation, which travels along the walls of a tubular organ, tending to press its contents onwards. It occurs in the muscle coat of the alimentary canal. *Reversed p.* The wave of contraction passes the reverse way towards the mouth.

peritomy (*per-it'-o-me*). Excision of a portion of the conjunctiva at the edge of the cornea, for the cure of pannus.

peritoneal (*per-it-o'-ne-al*). Referring to the peritoneum. *P. cavity*. The abdominal cavity lined by peritoneum. *P. dialysis*. A method of removing waste products from the blood by passing a cannula into the peritoneal cavity, running in a fluid, and after an interval, draining it off.

peritoneoscope (*per-it-o'-ne-o-skope*). An endoscopic instrument for viewing the peritoneal cavity through the abdominal wall.

peritoneoscopy (*per-it-o-ne-os'-ko-pe*). Visual examination of the peritoneum by means of a peritoneoscope.

peritoneum (*per-it-o-ne'-um*). The serous membrane lining the abdominal cavity and forming a covering for the abdominal organs. *Parietal p.* That which lines the abdominal cavity. *Visceral p.* The inner layer which closely covers the organs, and includes the mesenteries. *Pelvic p.* That which covers the pelvic organs.

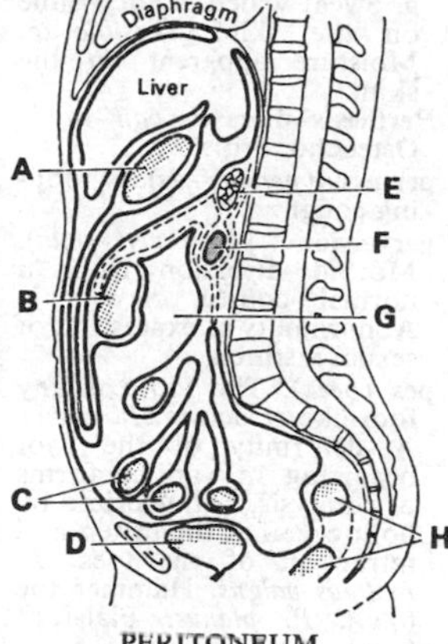

PERITONEUM

A. Stomach.
B. Transverse colon.
C. Small intestine.
D. Bladder.
E. Pancreas.
F. Duodenum.
G. Peritoneal cavity.
H. Rectum.

peritonitis (*per-it-on-i'-tis*). Inflammation of the peritoneum due to infection. This may occur from: (1) Perforation of a viscus, e.g. the stomach. (2) Infection of an organ, e.g. the appendix. (3) Intestinal obstruction, as in strangulated hernia. (4) Injury, as a stab wound. (5) Blood-borne infection, e.g. Streptococcus or pneumococcus. *Pelvic p.* That confined to the peritoneum of pelvic organs. *Septic p.* Due to a pyogenic organism. *Tuberculous p.* A chronic form due to the tubercle bacillus affecting chiefly mesenteric glands.

peritonsillar (*per-e-ton'-sil-lar*). Around the tonsil. *P. abscess. See* Quinsy.

perityphlitis (*per-e-tif-li'-tis*). Inflammation of peritoneum around the caecum and appendix.

perlèche (*pair-lash'*). A superficial fissuring at the angles of the mouth often due to vitamin B deficiency.

permeability (*per-me-a-bil'-it-e*). The degree to which a fluid can pass from one structure through a wall or membrane to another.

pernicious (*per-nish'-us*). Highly destructive; fatal. *P. anaemia.* An anaemia due to lack of absorption of vitamin B_{12} for the formation of red blood cells. At one time a fatal condition.

perniosis (*per-ne-o'-sis*). Chilblains. A result of vascular spasm in the superficial arterioles of the hands and feet, causing thrombosis and necrosis.

peromelia (*per-o-me'-le-ah*). A defect of a limb which resembles an amputation though bud-like remnants of the peripheral segments may exist.

peroneal (*per-o-ne′-al*). Relating to the fibula. *P. muscles.* Of the leg.

peroral (*per-or′-al*). By the mouth.

per os. By the mouth.

peroxide (*per-oks′-ide*). A compound of any element with more than the normal quantity of oxygen required to form an oxide. *P. of hydrogen. See* Hydrogen peroxide.

perphenazine (*per-fen′-a-zeen*). An antiemetic and tranquillizing drug similar to chlorpromazine. Fentazin is a proprietary preparation.

persecution (*per-se-ku′-shun*). In psychiatry a fear of being harmed when there is no just cause for fear. A symptom of schizophrenia and paranoia.

perseveration (*per-sev-er-a′-shun*). The constant recurrence of an idea, or the tendency to keep repeating the same words or actions.

personality (*per-son-al′-it-e*). The sum total of heredity and inborn tendencies, with influences from environment and education, which goes to form the mental make-up of a person and influence his attitude to life. *Cycloid p.* An unstable person who has periods of great activity and elation followed by periods of depression. *Dual p.* The patient suffers from such a degree of dissociation that he leads two lives, one personality not knowing what the other is doing. *Hysterical p.* An emotionally unstable person whose behaviour is designed to attract attention. Such people are very open to suggestion, are self-centred and long for sympathy. *Schizoid p.* An introverted person who is shy and retiring. A poor mixer in society, given to day dreaming.

Perspex (*per′-speks*). A plastic material used for splinting. It can be moulded to individual requirements, is semitransparent, light, washable, and is not affected by immersion in water.

perspiration. The secretion of the sweat glands. *Insensible p.* Sweat which is not visible on the skin. *Sensible p.* Moisture apparent on the skin.

Perthes's disease (*pair′-tays*). Osteochondritis.

pertussis (*per-tus′-sis*). Whooping cough.

perversion (*per-ver′-shun*). Morbid diversion from a normal course. *Sexual p.* Abnormality of expression of sexual instinct.

pes (*peez*). The foot, or any foot-like structure. *P. cavus.* A deformity of the foot occurring in various forms of paralysis, characterized by hollowness of the instep and retraction of the toes. *P. malleus valgus.* Hammer toe (*q.v.*). *P. planus.* Flat-foot (*q.v.*).

pessary (*pes′-sar-e*). (a) An instrument for supporting a displaced uterus, by insertion into the vagina. (1) *Ring p.* Made of rubber or plastic material. (2) *Hodge p.* Of vulcanite or plastic. (b) A medicated suppository inserted into the vagina, for antiseptic purposes. *See* Vaginitis. (c) *Diaphragm p.* A contraceptive.

pesticides (*pes′-te-sides*). Chemical agents that destroy

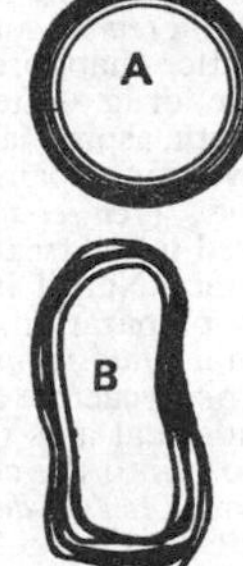

PESSARIES
A. Ring pessary.
B. Hodge pessary.

pests. They may give rise to poisoning.

pestilence (*pest'-il-ense*). Any deadly epidemic disease; a term commonly applied to plague.

pestis (*pes'-tis*). Plague (*q.v.*).

petechia (*pe-te'-ke-ah*). A small spot due to effusion of blood under the skin, e.g. the spots of purpura and typhus fever. *Pl.* petechiae.

pethidine (*peth'-e-dine*). A synthetic drug which relieves pain and has an antispasmodic action on plain muscle. In obstetrics it may be combined with hyoscine. Given by mouth or by hypodermic injection.

petit mal (*pet'-e mal*). A form of epilepsy (*q.v.*).

petri dishes (*pet'-re*). Shallow glass dishes in which organisms are grown on a culture medium.

pétrissage (*pa-tris-sahj'*). A kneading action used in massage.

petroleum (*pet-ro'-le-um*). An oily liquid found in the earth in various parts of the world. In medicine, it is used as an antiseptic, a laxative, and for skin diseases.

petrositis (*pe-tro-si'-tis*). Inflammation of the petrous portion of the temporal bone usually spread from a middle ear infection.

petrous (*pet'-rus*). Stony. *P. bone*. Part of the temporal bone, containing the organ of hearing.

Peyer's glands or **patches** (*pi'-er*). Small lymph nodules situated in the mucous membrane of the lower part of the small intestine. In typhoid fever they become infected and ulcerated.

pH. A measure of the hydrogen ion concentration and so the acidity or alkalinity of a fluid. Expressed numerically 1 to 14; 7 is neutral, below this is acid and above alkaline.

phaeochromocytoma (*fe-o-kro-mo-si-to'-mah*). A tumour of the adrenal medulla which gives rise to paroxysmal hypertension.

phagocytes (*fag'-o-sites*). Polymorphonuclear leucocytes and large lymphocytes which have the power of destroying harmful micro-organisms in the blood. *See* Leucocyte.

phagocytosis (*fag-o-si-to'-sis*). The action of phagocytes.

phalanges (*fal-an'-jez*). The bones of the fingers or toes. *Sing.*: Phalanx.

phallitis (*fal-i'-tis*). Inflammation of the penis.

phallus (*fal'-lus*). The penis.

phantasy (*fan'-tas-e*). A mental activity in which imagination weaves thoughts and feelings which bear little relation to reality.

phantom limb (*fan'-tom*). Following amputation when the patient can still feel the limb.

phantom tumour or **cyst.** A tumour-like swelling of the abdomen caused by contraction of the muscles, or to localized gas.

pharmaceutical (*far-mah-su'-tik-l*). Relating to drugs.

pharmacogenetics (*far-mah-ko-jen-et'-iks*). The study of genetically determined variations in drug metabolism and the response of the individual.

pharmacology (*far-mah-kol'-o-je*). The science of the nature and preparation of drugs.

pharmacopoeia (*far-mah-ko-pe'-ah*). An authoritative publication which gives the standard formulae and preparation of drugs as used in a given country. *British P.* That authorized for use in Great Britain.

pharmacy (*far'-mas-e*). The art of preparing, compounding, and dispensing medicines.

pharyngeal (*far-in'-je-al*). Relating to the pharynx.

pharyngectomy (*far-in-jek'-to-me*). Excision of a section of the pharynx.

pharyngitis (*far-in-ji'-tis*). Inflammation of the pharynx.

pharyngolaryngeal (*far'-in-go-lar-in-je'-al*). Referring to both the pharynx and larynx.

pharyngotympanic tube (*far-in-go-tim-pan'-ik*). Eustachian tube leading from the pharynx to the middle ear.

pharynx (*far'-inks*). The muscular pouch lined with mucous membrane situated at the back of the mouth. It leads into the oesophagus, and also communicates with the nose through the posterior nares, with the ears through the Eustachian tubes, and with the larynx.

phenacetin (*fen-as'-e-tin*). An antipyretic, diaphoretic and analgesic drug. Often combined with aspirin and used to relieve minor pain.

phenelzine (*fen'-el-zeen*). A drug used in the treatment of depression. Nardil is a proprietary preparation.

phenformin (*fen'-for-min*). An oral hypoglycaemic agent. A biguanide that aids the entry of glucose into the cells.

phenindione (*fen'-in-de-one*). A synthetic anticoagulant for oral administration given for the prevention and treatment of thrombosis, the dose depending on the prothrombin level in the blood. Dindevan is a proprietary preparation.

pheniodol (*fen-i'-o-dol*). A dye which is opaque to X-ray used for testing gall-bladder efficiency.

phenobarbitone (*fe-no-bar'-bit-one*). A barbiturate drug which depresses the cerebral cortex and is useful in small oral doses for mild sedation or in larger doses intramuscularly for violent states due to cerebral irritation.

phenol (*fen'-ol*). Carbolic acid. A disinfectant derived from coal tar.

phenoxybenzamine (*fen-oks-e-benz'-a-meen*). A vasodilator drug useful in treating peripheral conditions such as Raynaud's disease. Dibenyline is a proprietary preparation.

phenoxymethylpenicillin (*fen'-oks-e-meth'-il-pen-is-il'-in*). An acid resistant penicillin that can be administered orally. Penicillin V.

phenylalanine (*fen-il-al'-a-neen*). An essential amino

acid that cannot be properly metabolized in persons suffering from phenylketonuria (*q.v.*).

phenylbutazone (*fen-il-boo'-ta-zone*). An analgesic and antiseptic drug used in the treatment of gout and rheumatic disorders. Butazolidin is a proprietary preparation of it.

phenylketonuria (*fen-il-ke-ton-u'-re-ah*). The presence in the urine of phenylpyruvic acid due to the incomplete breakdown of phenylalanine, an amino acid. It is a hereditary abnormality leading to severe mental deficiency which if detected early can be treated by a diet that is very low in protein.

phenylpyruvic acid (*fen-il-pi-ru'-vik*). An abnormality of the urine present in phenylketonuria (*q.v.*) which can be detected by the use of Phenistix. *See* Appendix 11

phenytoin sodium (*fen'-e-toin so'-de-um*). A drug with anticonvulsant properties particularly useful in controlling major epilepsy. Epanutin is a proprietary preparation of it.

phial (*fi'-al*). A small glass container or bottle for drugs.

phimosis (*fi-mo'-sis*). Constriction of the prepuce so that it cannot be drawn back over the glans penis. The usual treatment is circumcision.

phlebectomy (*fleb-ek'-to-me*). Excision of a portion of a vein.

phlebitis (*fleb-i'-tis*). Inflammation of a vein which tends to formation of a thrombus. The symptoms are: pain and swelling of the affected part, and redness along the course of the vein, which is felt later as a hard, tender cord.

phlebolith (*fleb'-o-lith*). A calculus occasionally formed in a vein.

phlebothrombosis (*fleb-o-throm-bo'-sis*). Simple clotting of blood within a vein without local inflammation, so the clot does not become firmly attached and is likely to break away as an embolus.

Phlebotomus (*fleb-ot'-o-mus*). A genus of sandflies that transmits the protozoa Leishmania causing leishmaniasis.

phlebotomy (*fleb-ot'-o-me*). Venesection.

phlegm (*flem*). Mucus secreted by the lining of the air-passages and expectorated.

phlegmasia (*fleg-ma'-ze-ah*). Inflammation. *P. alba dolens* or '*white leg*' is due to lymphatic blockage and deep femoral thrombosis sometimes occurring after labour.

phlegmatic (*fleg-mat'-ik*). Dull and apathetic.

phlegmon (*fleg'-mon*). A brawny swelling resulting from inflammation of connective tissue. It may lead to suppuration or ulceration.

phlyctenules (*flik'-ten-ules*). Small vesicles on the conjunctiva. *See* Conjunctivitis.

phobia (*fo'-be-ah*). An irrational fear produced by a specific situation which the patient attempts to avoid.

phocomelia (*fo-ko-me'-le-ah*). A congenital deformity in which the long bones of the limbs are minimal or absent and the individual has 'seal' hands or feet or stump-like limbs of various lengths.

pholcodine (*fol'-ko-deen*). A linctus for the suppression of a non-productive or irritating cough.

phonetic (*fo-net'-ik*). Representing sounds or pertaining to the voice.

phonic spasm (*fo'-nik spazm*). An affliction of singers and public speakers when they are unable to perform in public but can talk normally.

phonocardiogram (*fo-no-kar'-de-o-gram*). A record of the heart sounds made by a phonocardiograph.

phonocardiograph (*fo-no-kar'-de-o-graf*). An instrument that records heart sounds and murmurs.

phosgene (*fos'-jeen*). A lung-irritant gas.

phosphatase(s) (*fos'-fat-ase*). Enzymes involved in the metabolism of phosphate. *Alkaline p.* One formed by osteoblasts in the bone and by liver cells and excreted in the bile. A high blood level denotes obstructive jaundice or excessive bone activity. A moderate increase occurs in disease of the liver cells.

phosphates (*fos'-fates*). Salts of phosphoric acid, sometimes prescribed as tonics.

phosphaturia (*fos-fa-tu'-re-ah*). Excess of phosphates in the urine.

phospholipids (*fos-fo-li'-pids*). Esters of glycerol fats that are found in cells especially of the nervous system.

phosphorus (*fos'-for-us*). A non-metallic highly inflammable element. Not used in medicine except as phosphoric acid or its salts. It is poisonous, causing fatty degeneration of organs, especially the liver.

photalgia (*fo-tal'-je-ah*). Painful eyes from exposure to too much light.

photocoagulation (*fo'-to-ko-ag-ul-a'-shun*). The use of a powerful light source to induce inflammation of the retina and choroid to treat retinal detachment.

photophobia (*fo-to-fo'-be-ah*). Intolerance of light.

photosensitive (*fo-to-sens'-e-tiv*). Reacting to light rays.

phrenectomy (*fren-ek'-to-me*). The removal of a phrenic nerve. *See* Avulsion.

phrenemphraxis (*fren-em-fraks'-is*). The operation in which the phrenic nerve is crushed, not removed. The resulting paralysis is then likely to be only temporary. *See also* Phrenectomy.

phrenic (*fren'-ik*). (1) Relating to the mind. (2) Pertaining to the diaphragm. *P. avulsion. See* Avulsion.

phrenicotomy (*fren-e-kot'-o-me*). Division of a phrenic nerve to paralyse one-half of the diaphragm. *See* Avulsion.

phthalylsulphathiazole (*thal-il-sul-fa-thi'-a-zol*). An insoluble sulphonamide, poorly absorbed in the intestine so used to kill intestinal bacteria prior to surgery.

Phthirus pubis (*thi'-rus pu'-bis*). The crab louse.

phthisis (*thi'-sis*). Advanced or chronic tuberculosis of the lungs, in which wasting is marked. Previously termed consumption, it is less often seen with the advance in the treatment of early cases.

physical (*fiz'-ik-al*). In medicine, relating to the body as opposed to the mental processes. *P. signs.* Those observed by inspection, percussion, etc.

physician (*fiz-ish'-an*). One who practises medicine as opposed to surgery.

physics (*fiz'-iks*). The study of

the laws and phenomena of nature.

physiological solutions (*fiz-e-o-loj'-ik-al*). Those of the same salt composition and same osmotic pressure as blood plasma.

physiology (*fiz-e-ol'-o-je*). The science of the functions of living bodies.

physiotherapy (*fiz-e-o-ther'-ap-e*). Treatment by natural forces, e.g. heat, light, electricity, massage, etc.

physique (*fiz-eek'*). The structure of the body.

physostigmine (*fi-so-stig'-min*). *Eserine*. An alkaloid from the Calabar bean. It is an antidote to curare; it constricts the pupils and is used in the treatment of myasthenia gravis. Neostigmine is a similar synthetic drug.

phytomenadione (*fi'-to-men-a-de'-one*). An intravenous preparation of vitamin K, effective in treating haemorrhage occurring during anticoagulant therapy. Konakion is a proprietary preparation. Mephyton is an emulsion for oral administration.

pia mater (*pe'-ah ma'-ter*). The innermost membrane enveloping the brain and spinal cord consisting of a network of small blood-vessels connected by areolar tissue. This dips down into all the folds of the nerve substance.

pica (*pi'-kah*). Unnatural craving for strange foods. It may occur in pregnancy, and sometimes in mental diseases.

Pick's disease. (1) Hepatic enlargement with ascites and pleural effusion, associated with constrictive pericarditis. (2) A form of presenile dementia with atrophy of the frontal lobes of the cerebrum.

picric acid (*pik'-rik*). A derivative of phenol. It is used chiefly as the reagent in Esbach's test for albuminuria. *See* Appendix 11.

pigeon breast. A deformity in which the sternum is unduly prominent. A result of rickets.

pigment (*pig'-ment*). Colouring matter. *Bile p.* Bilirubin and biliverdin. *Blood p.* Haematin. *Melanotic p.* Melanin (*q.v.*).

pigmentation (*pig-ment-a'-shun*). The deposition in the tissues of an abnormal amount of pigment.

piles. Haemorrhoids.

pill. A rounded mass of one or more drugs in powder form held together by glycerin and sometimes coated with sugar.

pilocarpine (*pi-lo-kar'-pin*). An alkaloid prepared from jaborandi leaves. It is used to constrict the pupils.

pilomotor nerves (*pi-lo-mo'-tor*). Those supplying plain muscle connected with hair follicles. Stimulation causes the hair to be erected, and also the condition of 'goose-flesh' of the skin.

pilonidal cyst (*pi-lo-ni'-dal*). A congenital infolding of hair-bearing skin over the coccyx. It may become infected and lead to sinus formation.

pilosebaceous (*pi-lo-se-ba'-shus*). Applied to sebaceous glands that open into the hair follicles.

pilosis (*pi-lo'-sis*). Abnormal growth of hair.

pilula (*pil'-u-lah*). Latin for pill.

pimple. A small papule or pustule.

pineal (*pin'-e-al*). Shaped like a pine cone. *P. body*. A small cone-shaped structure on the base of the brain and composed of glandular substance. It is supposed to have an endocrine secretion but this is not definitely established.

pine oil. A volatile oil from pine prescribed for inhalation in cases of laryngitis and bronchitis.

pinguecula (*pin-gwek'-u-lah*). Nodules of hyaline and yellow elastic tissue that occur on the cornea. A degenerative condition in which inflammation is common.

pink disease. Erythroedema polyneuritis (*q.v.*).

pink eye. Infective conjunctivitis.

pinna (*pin'-nah*). The projecting part of the external ear; the auricle.

pinocytosis (*pin-o-si-to'-sis*). A process similar to phagocytosis by which molecules of protein enter or are absorbed by cells.

pint. Twenty fluid ounces. *See* Appendix 14.

pinta (*pin'-tah*). A non-venereal skin infection caused by the *Treponema pinta* prevalent in the West Indies and Central America.

piperazine (*pi-per'-az-een*). An anthelmintic in tablet or elixir form given in the treatment of threadworms and roundworms.

pipette (*pip-et'*). A glass tube for conveying small quantities of liquid.

piriform fossae (*pir'-e-form foss-e*). Spaces between the larynx and pharyngeal walls that may be viewed with a laryngeal mirror.

pisiform (*pi'-se-form*). Pea-shaped; one of the carpal bones.

pitchblende (*pitch'-blend*). Uranium oxide, a black mineral from which radium is obtained.

pituitary gland (*pit-tu'-it-ar-e*). An endocrine gland suspended from the base of the brain and protected by the sella turcica in the sphenoid bone. It consists of two lobes. (1) *Anterior*, which has some influence in regulating growth and metabolism and influences the other endocrine glands. (2) *Posterior*, which secretes oxytocin and vasopressin (*q.v.*).

pityriasis (*pit-e-ri'-as-is*). A skin disease characterized by fine scaly desquamation. *P. rosea.* An inflammatory form, in which the affected areas are macular and ring-shaped.

placebo (*plas-e'-bo*). Any inactive substance resembling medicine given during controlled experiments or to satisfy a patient.

placenta (*plas-en'-tah*). The after-birth. A vascular structure inside the pregnant uterus supplying the fetus with nourishment through the connecting umbilical cord. The placenta develops about the third month of pregnancy, and is expelled after the birth of the child. *Battledore p.* In which the cord is attached to the margin and not the centre. *P. praevia* is one attached to the lower part of the uterine wall. As labour advances, it may be a cause of severe antepartum haemorrhage.

placidity (*plas-id'-e-te*). A placid state the opposite of rage in which it takes a strong stimulus to evoke a response.

plague (*plaig*). An acute fever endemic in Asia and Africa.

The causative organism is *Pasteurella pestis* transmitted by the bites of fleas who have derived the infection from diseased rats. *Bubonic p.* Characterized by buboes. *Pneumonic p.* In which the infection attacks chiefly the lung tissues. A very fatal form.

plantar (*plan'-tar*). Relating to the sole of the foot. *P. arch.* The arch made by anastomosis of the plantar arteries. *P. flexion.* Bending of the toes downward and so arching the foot. *P. reflex.* Contraction of the toes on stroking the sole of the foot.

plasma (*plaz'-mah*). The fluid part of blood. *Reconstituted p.* Dried plasma when again made liquid by addition of distilled water.

plasmaphoresis (*plaz-mah-for-e'-sis*). A method of removing a portion of the plasma from circulation. Venesection is performed, the blood allowed to settle, then the cellular part returned to circulation.

plasma proteins. Those present in the blood plasma: albumin, globulin, and fibrinogen.

plasma values. The salt and chemical content of blood plasma. *See* List of normal values, Appendix 12.

plasminogen (*plas-min'-o-jen*). The inactive precursor of plasmin. Plasmin has the property of dissolving fibrin and so aid in the dispersal of blood clots.

Plasmodium (*plas-mo'-de-um*). The parasite which causes malaria. *P. falciparum.* The cause of malignant tertian malaria. *P. vivax* causes the benign tertian form.

plaster (*plah'-ster*). A substance for application to the surface of the body. It is prepared in various forms. *Adhesive p.* Used for (a) drawing together the edges of wounds; (b) holding in position small dressings; (c) for support, e.g. of a sprained ankle. *P. bandage. See* Plaster of Paris. *Bivalve p.* A plaster of Paris splint cut into two pieces. *See* Croft's splint. *Bohler's p.* for Pott's fracture. A leg splint of plaster of Paris, in which is embedded an iron stirrup extending below the foot, which enables the patient to walk without putting weight on the joint. *Corn p.* One impregnated with salicylic acid. *Frog p.* A plaster of Paris splint used to maintain the position after correction of the deformity due to congenital dislocation

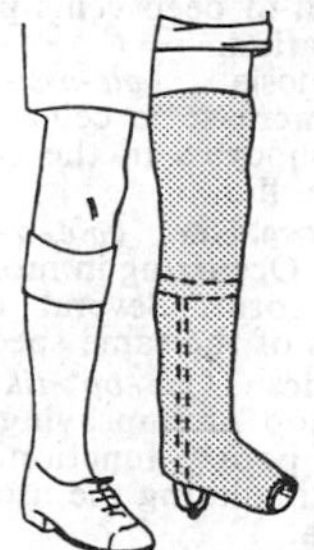

BOHLER'S PLASTER

of the hip. *P. jacket.* One of plaster of Paris applied to support the spine. *P. of Paris.* Calcium sulphate or gypsum with which book muslin is impregnated and used to form a plaster caste to immobilize a part.

plastic (*plas'-tik*). Constructive. Tissue-forming. *P. surgery.* The grafting of tissue from a healthy area of the body, to restore an injured or deformed part. *P. lymph.* The exudate which in wounds and inflamed serous tissues is organized into fibrous tissue and promotes healing.

plasticity (*plas-tis'-e-te*). A stiffness as present in the limbs following a cerebral lesion.

platelets (*plate'-lets*). Thrombocytes. *See* Blood.

platinum (*plat'-in-um*). A metal. Used to encase radium (1 mm thick), as it prevents penetration of the *alpha* and *beta* rays which cause burning, but does not hold back the *gamma* rays.

plebogram (*pleb'-o-gram*). An X-ray examination after dye insertion, to see the condition of deep veins prior to operation.

pleocytosis (*ple-o-si-to'-sis*). An increase in cells, usually lymphocytes in the cerebrospinal fluid.

pleomorphism (*ple-o-morf'-izm*). Occurring in more than one form. Several distinct types of the same species.

pleoptics (*ple-op'-tiks*). A method of improving vision in a poorly functioning eye by stimulating the use of the fovea.

plethora (*pleth'-or-ah*). Fulness. Excess of blood in the vessels, characterized by florid complexion, full pulse, and tendency for the nose to bleed.

plethysmography (*pleth-is-mog'-raf-e*). The study of the circulation in the extremity by enclosing the limb in an oncometer and noting by means of an amplifier the changes in volume.

pleura (*plu'-rah*). The serous membrane, lining the thorax and enveloping each lung. *Parietal p.* The layer which lines the chest wall. *Visceral p.* The inner layer which is in close contact with the lung.

pleurisy (*plu'-ris-e*). Inflammation of the pleura. *Diaphragmatic p.* When that part covering the diaphragm is affected most. *Dry p.* (*fibrinous*). In which the membrane is inflamed and roughened, but no fluid is formed. This causes a purposeless cough and a sharp stabbing pain on inspiration. *P. with effusion* (*wet pleurisy*). Characterized by inflammation and exudation of serous fluid into the pleural cavity. Pain is less, but cardiac and respiratory function may be impeded to such an extent that the fluid has to be aspirated. This may result from infection or irritation of the pleura. *Purulent p.* or *empyema.* When pus is formed in the pleural cavity. An operation for drainage is necessary.

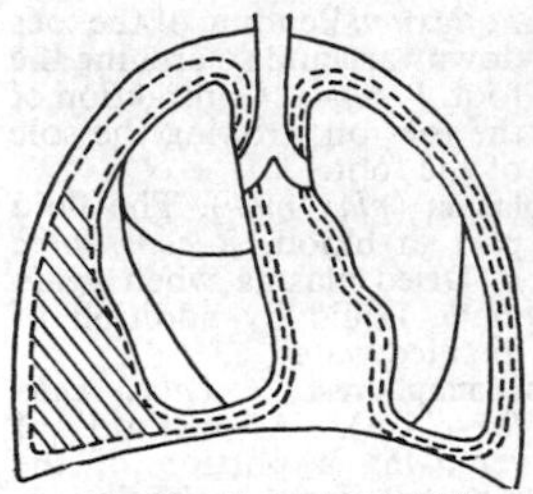

PLEURAL EFFUSION
Longitudinal section

pleurocele (*plu'-ro-seel*). Hernia of the lung or pleural tissue.

pleurodesis (*plu-ro-de'-sis*). Occluding the pleural space by the insertion of silver nitrate to cause adhesions in cases of chronic or recurrent pneumothorax.

pleurodynia (*plu-ro-din'-e-ah*). Pain in the intercostal muscles, probably rheumatic in origin.

pleurolysis (*plu-rol'-is-is*). Pneumolysis (*q.v.*).

plexor (*pleks'-or*). An instrument resembling a hammer, used in percussion.

plexus (*pleks'-us*). A network of veins or nerves. *Auerbach's p.* The nerve ganglion situated between the longitudinal and circular muscle fibres of the intestine. They are motor nerves. *Brachial p.* The network of nerves of the neck and axilla. *Choroid p.* A capillary network situated in the ventricles of the brain which forms the cerebrospinal fluid. *Meissner's p.* The sensory nerve ganglion situated in the submucous layer of the intestinal wall. *Solar* or *coeliac p.* The network of nerves and ganglia at the back of the stomach, which supply the abdominal viscera. *Haemorrhoidal* or *rectal p.* The network of veins which surrounds the rectum and forms a direct communication between the systemic and portal circulations.

plicate (*pli'-kate*). Folded or plaited.

plumbism (*plum'-bizm*). Lead poisoning.

plumbum (*plum'-bum*). Lead.

Plummer-Vinson syndrome. Difficulty in swallowing, associated with glossitis and iron deficiency anaemia.

pneumatocele (*nu-mat'-o-seel*). (1) A swelling, containing a collection of gas. (2) Hernia of the lung.

pneumaturia (*nu-mat-tu'-re-ah*). Flatus is passed with the urine owing to a vesico-colic fistula and air from the bowel entering the bladder.

pneumocephalus (*nu-mo-kef'-al-us*). Aerocele. Air entering the brain as from an anterior fracture of the base of the skull.

pneumococci (*nu-mo-kok'-i*). (*Diplococcus pneumoniae*). Bacteria that may cause lobar or bronchopneumonia, meningitis or otitis media. They can be divided into over thirty serological types by agglutination tests.

pneumoconiosis (*nu-mo-ko-ne-o'-sis*). *See* Pneumokoniosis.

pneumodynamics (*nu-mo-di-nam'-iks*). The mechanism of respiration. *See* Appendix 4.

pneumo-encephalography (*nu'-mo-en-kef-al-og'-raf-e*). *See* Encephalography.

pneumogastric (*nu-mo-gas'-trik*). Pertaining to lungs and stomach. *P. nerve.* The 10th cranial nerve to the lungs, stomach, etc. The vagus nerve.

pneumokoniosis (*nu-mo-ko-ne-o'-sis*). Referring to any fibrosis of lung due to inhalation of dust particles. *See* Anthracosis, Asbestosis *and* Silicosis.

pneumolysis (*nu-mol'-is-is*). The operation of detaching the pleura from the chest wall in order to collapse the lung when the two pleural layers are adherent.

pneumomycosis (*nu-mo-mi-*

ko'-sis). Infection of the lung by microfungi. *See* Bronchomycosis *and* Mycosis.

pneumonectomy (*nu-mon-ek'-to-me*). Removal of a lung. A treatment for disease when only one lung is affected, such as by bronchiectasis or new growth.

pneumonia (*nu-mo'-ne-ah*). Inflammation of the lung. *Aspiration p.* One arising from inhaled material from another infected lesion or, following operation, of vomitus. *Broncho-p.* A descending infection of the bronchi. Widespread and patchy in distribution. *Pneumococcal p.* A specific p. caused by the *Klebsiella pneumoniae*. *Specific p.* One caused by a particular organism, affecting one or more lobes. *Virus p.* The causative organism is a virus.

pneumonitis (*nu-mon-i'-tis*). An imprecise term denoting any inflammatory condition of the lung.

pneumoperitoneum (*nu-mo-per-it-o-ne'-um*). Air in the peritoneal cavity. It can be introduced into the upper part of the cavity to limit movement of the diaphragm, and was a treatment for pulmonary tuberculosis affecting the base of the lung. It may be performed prior to peritoneal dialysis or peritoneoscopy.

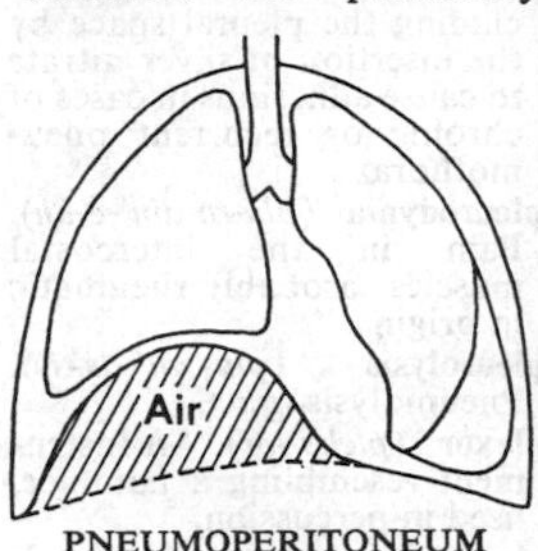

PNEUMOPERITONEUM

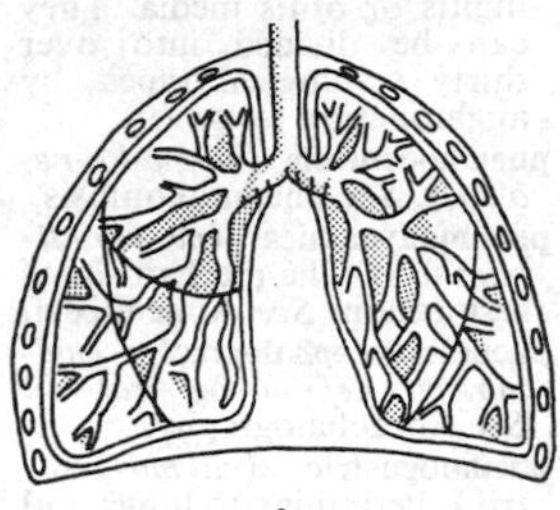

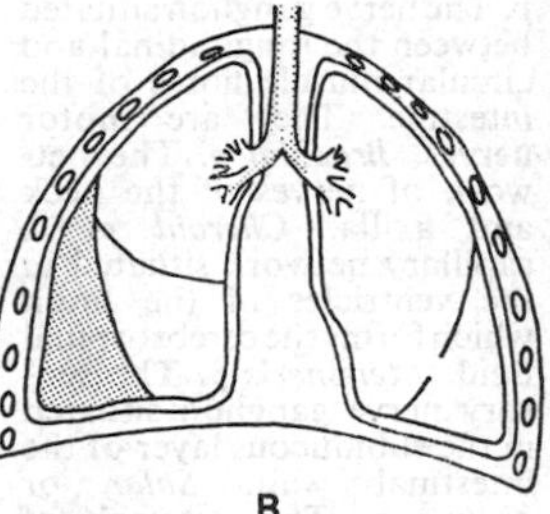

PNEUMONIA
A. Broncho-pneumonia.
B. Specific pneumonia.

pneumopyothorax (*nu-mo-pi-o-thor'-aks*). *See* Pyopneumothorax.

pneumoradiography (*nu-mo-ra-de-og'-raf-e*). X-ray of a cavity or part after air has been injected into it.

pneumotaxic centre (*nu-mo-

taks'-ik). The centre in the pons (*q.v.*) that influences inspiratory effort during respiration.

pneumothorax (*nu-mo-thor'-aks*). Air in the pleural cavity, caused by perforation of the chest wall, or of the lung pleura in which case air enters via the bronchi. Both cause the lung to collapse. The signs may be slight or of a rapidly increasing dyspnoea as the intrapleural pressure rises. Immediate steps must be taken to relieve the pressure by aspirating the air or by a 'water seal' drainage. If due to trauma a petroleum jelly pad will seal the air inlet. *Artificial p.* The introduction of air into the pleural space. A seldom used treatment of collapsing the lung tissue. *Extrapleural p.* The parietal pleura is stripped from the chest wall to enable air to be placed outside the pleura when adhesions are present. *Spontaneous p.* Due to rupture of an over-dilated air-sac as in emphysema which causes the air passages to communicate with the pleura.

pneumoventriculography (*nu-mo-ven-trik-u-log'-raf-e*). *See* Ventriculography.

pock. The pustule of smallpox, or other eruptive fever.

podagra (*pod-ag'-rah*). Gout, particularly of the foot's joint or the big toe.

podarthritis (*pod-ar-thri'-tis*). Inflammation of joints of the foot.

podopompholyx (*pod-o-pom'-fol-iks*). Eczema of the feet, between the toes and mid-sole where the sweat glands are most prolific.

poikilocyte(*poi'-kil-o-site*). An irregularly shaped red blood cell.

poikilocythaemia (*poi-kil-o-si-the'-me-ah*). *Poikilocytosis.* The presence in the blood of red cells irregular in shape and size. The condition indicates excessive activity of the bone marrow.

poikilothermic (*poi-kil-o-ther'-mik*). Any cold blooded animal. Their temperature varies widely with the environment.

poison. Any substance which applied to the body externally or taken internally causes injury to any part or the whole. *Carbon monoxide p. See* Carbon monoxide. *Corrosive p.* One which corrodes or destroys tissues with which it comes in contact. *Irritant p.* One which causes inflammation, as caustic alkalis and mineral acids. *Narcotic p.* One which causes extreme narcosis. *See* Appendix 1.

polar body (*po'-lah*). The small body containing half the chromosomes when the ovum undergoes reduction division (*q.v.*) as it matures.

polio-encephalitis (*pol'-e-o en-kef-al-i'-tis*). Inflammation of the cortex of the brain.

poliomyelitis (*pol-e-o-mi-el-i'-tis*). Inflammation of the grey matter of the spinal cord. *Acute anterior p.* An acute specific fever, due to a virus. It mainly attacks young adults and children, and the inflammation of the anterior horn cells of the spinal cord may result in paralysis and wasting of muscle groups. *Bulbar p.* may only affect the swallowing reflex, requiring great care in feeding the patient. *Bulbospinal p.* A severe form in which the medulla and spinal cord are affected; the respiratory and swallowing reflexes are lost and artificial respiration is essential.

Politzer's bag (*pol'-it-zer*). A rubber bag attached to a Eustachian catheter for forcing air into the Eustachian tube to clear it.

politzerization (*pol-it-zer-i-za'-shun*). Insufflation of the pharyngo-tympanic (Eustachian) tube to restore patency.

pollen antigen (*pol'-en ant'-e-jen*). *See* Antigen.

pollution (*pol-u'-shun*). To destroy the purity of or to contaminate. *Air p.* The discharge of smoke containing impurities into the atmosphere. *Water p.* The discharge of untreated sewage or factory waste into rivers or streams.

poly- (*pol'-e*). Prefix meaning 'many'.

polyarteritis (*pol-e-ar-ter-i'-tis*). Inflammatory changes in the walls of the small arteries likely to lead to hypertension or renal disease.

polyarthralgia (*pol-e-ar-thral'-je-ah*). Pain of a neuralgic type in several joints at a time.

polyarthritis (*pol-e-ar-thri'-tis*). Inflammation of several joints at the same time, as seen in rheumatoid arthritis and Still's disease.

polycystic (*pol-e-sist'-ik*). Many cysts. *P. disease of the kidneys.* A congenital disease. The kidneys are much enlarged with many cysts. There is a slowly developing renal failure and hypertension.

polycythaemia (*pol-e-si-the'-me-ah*). Erythrocythaemia. *P. vera.* A rare disease in which there is a greatly increased production of red blood cells. Many cases have been satisfactorily treated by injections of radioactive phosphorus.

polydactylism (*pol-e-dak'-til-izm*). The condition of having more than the normal number of fingers or toes.

polydipsia (*pol-e-dip'-se-ah*). Abnormal thirst.

polymorphonuclear (*pol-e-morf-o-nu'-kle-ar*). (1) Having nuclei of many different shapes. (2) Phagocytic blood cells. *See* Leucocyte.

polymorphous (*pol-e-morf'-us*). Occurring in several or many different forms.

polymyalgia rheumatica (*pol-e-mi-al'-je-ah ru-mat'-ik-ah*). Persistent aching pain in the muscles often involving the shoulder or pelvic girdle.

polymyositis (*pol-e-mi-o-si'-tis*). Insiduous wasting and weakness of muscles.

polyneuritis (*pol-e-nu-ri'-tis*). Multiple neuritis.

polyneuropathy (*pol-e-nur-op'-ath-e*). A number of disease conditions of the nervous system. There may be polyneuritis, abdominal pain, and mental disturbance.

polypeptides (*pol-e-pep'-tides*). Proteins.

polyposis (*pol-e-po'-sis*). The condition of many polypi in an organ. *P. coli.* Familial polyposis. A hereditary condition in which there are thousands of polypi in the large bowel. Develops in childhood and eventually leads to carcinoma of colon if not excised.

polypus (*pol'-e-pus*). Polyp. A small pedunculated tumour arising from any mucous surface. *Cervical p.* In the cervical canal. *Fibroid p.*

Occurs in the uterus and contains fibrous tissue. *Nasal p.* A very vascular one arising in the nose.

polysaccharides (*pol-e-sak'-ar-ides*). Starches.

polyserositis (*pol-e-ser-o-si'-tis*). General inflammation of serous membranes. *See* Pick's disease.

polythene (*pol'-e-theen*). A general term for synthetic resins forming plastic material that can be used for many different purposes. In medicine, largely replacing rubber and mackintosh and used for many utensils.

polyuria (*pol-e-u'-re-ah*). An excessive increase in the discharge of urine, due, e.g. (1) to diuretics, (2) to diabetes.

pompholyx (*pom'-fo-liks*). An eczematous condition involving the sweat glands.

pons. A bridge of tissue connecting two parts of an organ. *P. varolii.* The part of the brain which connects the cerebrum, cerebellum and medulla oblongata.

pontine hemiplegia (*pon'-tin*). The lesion is in the pons. *See* Hemiplegia.

popliteal (*pop-lit'-e-al*). Relating to the posterior part of the knee.

pore (*por*). A minute circular opening on a surface, such as of a sweat gland.

porphyria (*por-fe'-re-ah*). An inherited abnormality in red blood cell formation. *Acute p.* That precipitated by taking barbiturates or alcohol. *Congenital p.* There is photosensitivity and the child cannot be exposed to sunlight.

porphyrins (*por'-fe-rins*). Substances used in the production of the haem portion of haemoglobin.

porphyrinuria (*por-fe-rin-u'-re-ah*). A minor metabolic disorder when urinary porphyrins are present. They are present in lead intoxication in lead workers.

portacaval anastomosis (*por-tah-ka'-val an-as-tom-o'-sis*). The joining of the portal vein to the inferior vena cava so that much of the blood by-passes the liver. A successful operation in selected cases of Banti's syndrome.

portal circulation. *See under* Circulation.

portal hypertension. *See* Hypertension.

position. Attitude or posture. *Dorsal p.* Lying flat on the back. *Genupectoral* or *knee-chest p.* Resting on the knees and chest with arms crossed above the head. *Left lateral p.* On the left side. *Lithotomy p.* Lying on the back with thighs raised and knees supported and held widely apart. *Prone p.* On the face, with pillows under the head and chest or abdomen, and to prevent pressure on the toes. *Recumbent p.* Lying on the back. *Sims's p. or semi-prone p.* An exaggerated *left lateral p.* with the right knee well flexed and the left arm drawn back over the edge of the bed. *Trendelenburg p.* Lying down. on a tilted plane (usually an operating table at an angle of 45 degrees to the floor), with the head lowermost and the legs hanging over the raised end of the table. *See diagram.*

posology (*pos-ol'-o-je*). The science of the dosage of drugs.

posseting (*pos'-et-ing*). Re-

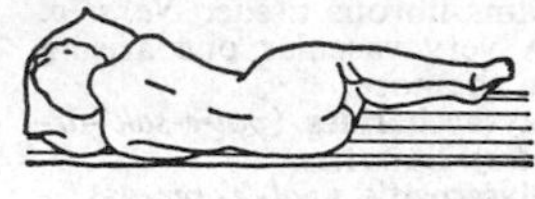

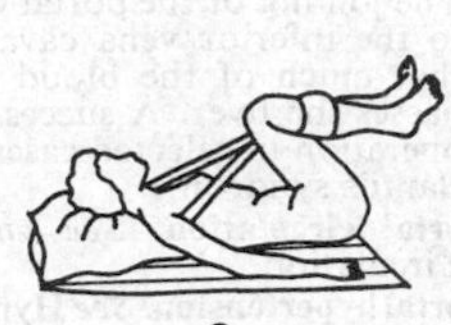

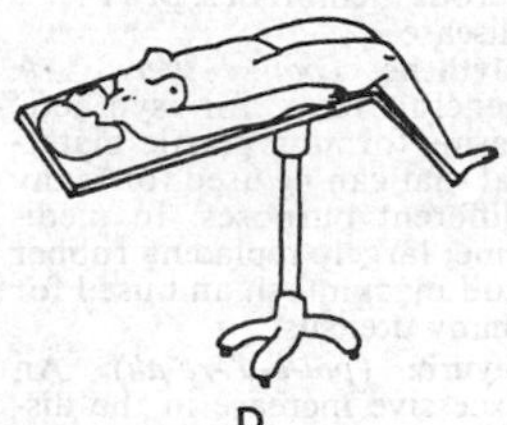

GYNAECOLOGICAL POSITIONS

A. Genupectoral } for examination.
B. Left lateral }
C. Lithotomy } for operation.
D. Trendelenburg }

gurgitation of foods in infants.

Possum. Patient-Operated Selector Mechanism. A machine that can be operated with a very slight degree of pressure or suction, using the mouth, if no other muscle movement possible. It may transmit messages from a lighted panel or be adapted for typing, telephoning, or working certain machinery.

post- A prefix meaning 'after' or 'behind'.

post-anaesthetic (*post-an-es-thet'-ik*). Occurring after anaesthesia. *P.-a. pneumonia. See* Pneumonia.

post-concussional syndrome. Constant headaches with mental fatigue, difficulty in concentration and insomnia that may persist after head injury.

post-epileptic (*post-ep-e-lep'-tik*). Occurring after an epileptic fit. *P.-e. automatism.* A period sometimes following epileptic attacks, of which the patient has no memory, and during which he cannot be held responsible for his behaviour.

postganglionic (*post-gang-le-on'-ik*). Situated posterior or distal to a ganglion (a collection of nerve cells). *P. fibre.* Nerve fibre posterior to a ganglion of the autonomic nervous system.

post-gastrectomy syndrome. *See* 'Dumping syndrome'.

posterior (*pos-te'-re-or*). Placed at the back.

posthitis (*pos-thi'-tis*). Inflammation of the prepuce.

posthumous (*pos'-tu-mus*). Occurring after death. *P. birth.* One occurring after the death of the father, or by Caesarean section after the death of the mother.

postmature (*post'-mat-ure*). Applied to a fetus before or a baby after birth when it has remained in the uterus longer then 280 days.

post mortem (*post mor'-tem*). After death. *P.-m. examination.* Autopsy.

post partum (*post par'-tum*). Following labour.

potassium (*pot-as'-se-um*). An alkaline substance the salts of which are largely used in medicine.

potential (*po-ten'-shal*). Ready for action. *P. energy.* That stored up but not in actual use. The opposite of kinetic.

Pott's disease. Caries of the vertebrae, usually due to tuberculosis of one or more

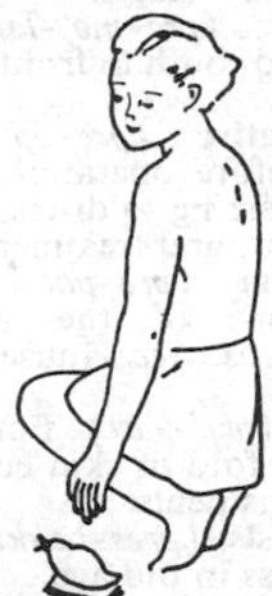

POTT'S DISEASE

A child picking up a toy from the floor keeps the spine rigid but flexes the knees.

of the vertebrae. The resultant necrosis causes kyphosis of the spine.

Pott's fracture. A fracture-dislocation of the ankle, involving the fibula, internal malleolus of the tibia and displacement of the talus.

pouch. A pocket-like space or cavity. *P. of Douglas.* The lowest fold of the peritoneum between the uterus and rectum. *Morison's p.* A fold of peritoneum below the liver. *Uterovesical p.* The fold of peritoneum between the uterus and bladder.

poultice (*pole'-tis*). Cataplasm. A local application used to improve circulation and relieve pain as in the use of kaolin or linseed. *Starch p.* A cold gelatinous mass to soften and remove crusts from skin lesions.

Poupart's ligament (*poo'-part*). The inguinal ligament. The tendinous lower border of the external oblique muscle of the abdominal wall, which passes from the anterior spine of the ilium to the os pubis.

poverty of movement. When the natural movements of facial expression and of the limbs are few or absent as in Parkinson's disease.

powder. Finely powdered drugs.

pox (*poks*). Any disease characterized by an eruption on the skin.

pre- A prefix meaning 'before'.

precancerous (*pre-kan'-ser-us*). Applied to conditions or histological changes that may precede cancer.

precipitins (*pre-sip'-e-tins*). Substances present in blood, causing precipitation. Produced by antigens.

precocious (*pre-ko'-shus*). Medically applied to premature development so that puberty arises at an early age.

precognition (*pre-kog-nish'-*

un). A direct perception of a future event which is beyond the reach of inference and which is not brought about to fulfil the prediction.

precordial (*pre-kor'-de-al*). Relating to the area over the heart.

precursor (*pre-kurs'-or*). A forerunner, e.g. prothrombin (*q.v.*).

predigestion (*pre-di-jest'-shun*). Partial digestion of food by artificial means before it is taken into the body.

predisposition (*pre-dis-pos-ish'-un*). Implies susceptibility to a specific disease.

prednisolone (*pred'-ni-so-lone*). A synthetic compound that is similar in structure and action to hydrocortisone. It can be given orally and is effective in smaller doses and is less likely to result in salt and water retention.

prednisone (*pred'-ni-sone*). A synthetic cortisone-like drug that is five times as potent and may be given in preference to cortisone (*q.v.*).

pre-eclamptic (*pre-e-klam'-tik*). The symptoms that precede eclampsia: albuminuria, hypertension, and oedema.

prefrontal leucotomy. *See* Leucotomy.

pregnancy (*preg'-nan-se*). Being with child; the condition from conception to the expulsion of the fetus. The normal period is 280 days, or nine calendar months. *Ectopic* or *extra-uterine p.* Occurs in the uterine tube (*tubal p.*) or very rarely in the abdominal cavity. *P. tests.* These are possible because the pregnant woman secretes chorionic gonadotrophic hormones which not only stimulate the human gonads but also those of mice, rabbits, and toads. *See* Aschheim-Zondek, Friedman, *and* Hogben.

premature (*prem'-at-ure*). Occurring before the anticipated time. *P. infant.* A child weighing 2500 g (5½ lb.) or less at birth is considered premature. *P. contraction.* A form of cardiac irregularity in which the ventricle contracts before its anticipated time. *See* Systole.

premedication (*pre-med-ik-a'-shun*). Narcotic drugs given prior to a general anaesthetic. Basal narcosis.

premenstrual (*pre-men'-stru-al*). Preceding menstruation. *P. endometrium.* The hypertrophied and vascular mucous lining of the uterus immediately before the menstrual flow starts.

premolar (*pre-mo'-lar*). A bicuspid tooth in front of the molars.

pre-operative (*pre-op'-er-a-tiv*). Before operation. Usually referring to drugs, investigations, and treatment.

prepatellar (*pre-pat-el'-lar*). In front of the patella. *P. bursitis. See* Housemaid's knee.

prepuce (*pre'-puse*). Foreskin; a loose fold of skin covering the glans penis.

presbycusis (*pres-be-ku'-sis*). Deafness in old age.

presbyopia (*pres-be-o'-pe-ah*). Impairment of vision with long sight occurring in old age, due to loss of accommodating power of the lens, so that the near point of distinct vision is removed farther from the eye.

prescription (*pre-skrip'-shun*). A formula written by a physician, directing the pharmacists to prepare a remedy.

presentation. That portion of the fetus felt at the os uteri by the examining finger in the vagina. The presenting parts may be: *vertex*, *face*, *brow*, *breech*, or *shoulder*.

surface skin due to pressure, which causes interference with the blood supply to the area. Formerly termed *bed-sores*.

presystolic (*pre-sis-tol'-ik*). Occurring just before systole.

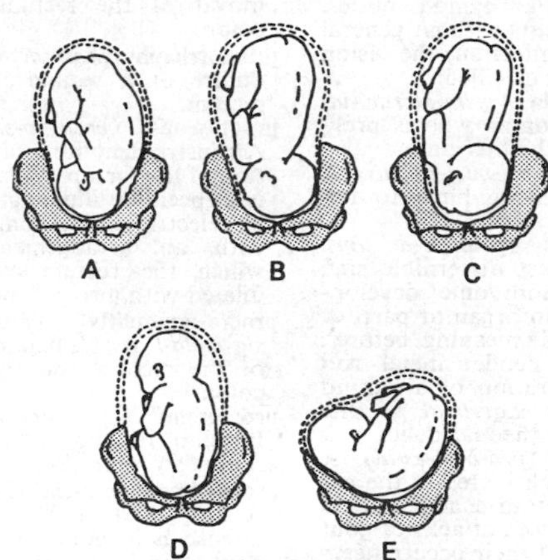

PRESENTATION

A. Vertex; B. Brow; C. Face; D. Breech; E. Shoulder.

pressor (*pres'-or*). A substance that stimulates the vasomotor centre causing vasoconstriction and a rise in the blood pressure.

pressure areas. Areas of the body where the tissues may be compressed between the bed and the underlying bone, especially the sacrum, greater trochanters and heels; so that the tissues become ischaemic.

pressure point. The point at which an artery can be compressed against a bone in order to stop bleeding.

pressure sore. A break in the

prevesical (*pre-ves'-ik-al*). In front of the bladder.

priapism (*pri'-ap-izm*). Persistent erection of the penis usually without sexual desire. It may be caused by local or spinal cord injury.

Price precipitation reaction (PPR). A serological test for syphilis.

prickle cell. One possessing delicate rod-shaped processes, by which it is connected to other cells. *Prickle layer*. The lowest stratum of the epidermis, formed of prickle cells.

prickly heat A skin eruption

characterized by minute red spots with central vesicles. *See* Miliaria.

primary complex. The combination of Ghon's focus (*q.v.*) in lung tissue with caseous infection of the associated hilar lymph nodes. Often occurs without general signs of infection, the lesion becoming calcified.

primigravida (*prim-e-grav'-id-ah*). A woman who is pregnant for the first time.

primipara (*pri-mip'-ar-ah*). A woman giving birth to her first child.

primordium (*prim-or-de'-um*). The earliest discernible sign during embryonic development of an organ or part.

pro- A prefix meaning 'before'.

probe. A slender metal rod for exploration of a wound or cavity. *Lacrimal p.* One for use in the tear ducts.

probenecid (*pro-ben'-es-id*). A drug which increases the excretion of uric acid and is used between attacks of gout to prevent their occurrence.

procainamide (*pro-kane'-a-mide*). A cardiac depressant drug that may be used in ventricular tachycardia.

procaine (*pro'-kane*). A local anaesthetic.

process (*pro'-ses*). A prominence or outgrowth of any part.

procidentia (*pro-se-den'-she-ah*). Complete prolapse of the uterus so that it extrudes through the vagina.

proctalgia (*prok-tal'-je-ah*). Pain in the rectum.

proctatresia (*prok-ta-tre'-se-ah*). Imperforate anus.

proctectomy (*prok-tek'-to-me*). Excision of the rectum.

proctitis (*prok-ti'-tis*). Inflammation of the anus or rectum.

proctocele (*prok'-to-seel*). Hernia or prolapse of the rectum.

proctoclysis (*prok-tok'-lis-is*). Irrigation of the rectum.

proctocolectomy (*prok-to-kol-ek'-to-me*). The surgical removal of the rectum and colon.

proctorrhaphy (*prok-tor'-raf-e*). Suture of a wound in the rectum.

proctoscope (*prok'-to-skope*). An instrument for examination of the rectum. *Tuttle's p.* is a speculum illuminated by an electric bulb, combined with an arrangement by which the rectum can be dilated with air.

proctosigmoiditis (*prok-to-sig-moid-i'-tis*). Inflammation of the rectum and sigmoid colon.

proctotomy (*prok-tot'-o-me*). Incision of the rectum to relieve stricture.

procyclidine (*pro-sik'-le-deen*). A drug used in Parkinson's disease as it reduces rigidity. Kemadrin is the proprietary preparation.

prodromal (*pro-dro'-mal*). Preceding. *P. rash.* One which comes out before the true rash, e.g. in measles. *P. period.* That between the onset of symptoms until the diagnostic signs appear.

proflavine (*pro-fla'-vin*). An antiseptic effective against the *Staphylococcus aureus* and non-harmful to body tissues.

progeria (*pro-je'-re-ah*). Premature senility.

progesterone (*pro-jes'-ter-one*). Formerly known as progestin. A hormone of the corpus luteum, which plays an important part in the regulation of the menstrual

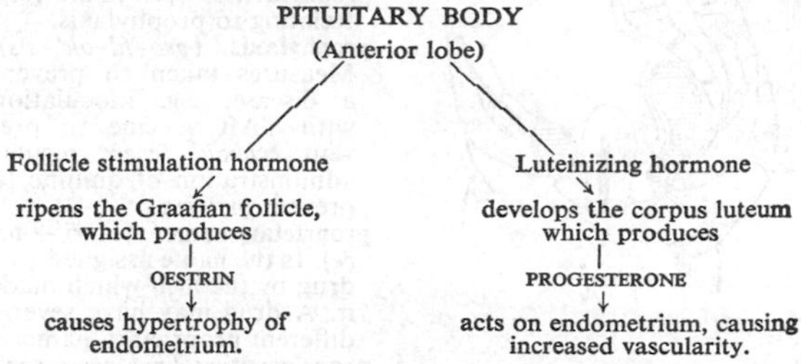

PITUITARY BODY
(Anterior lobe)

Follicle stimulation hormone	Luteinizing hormone
↓	↓
ripens the Graafian follicle, which produces	develops the corpus luteum which produces
OESTRIN	PROGESTERONE
↓	↓
causes hypertrophy of endometrium.	acts on endometrium, causing increased vascularity.

SHOWING HORMONE INFLUENCE ON OVARIAN FUNCTION

cycle and in pregnancy (*see table*).

progestogens (*pro-jes'-to-jens*). Steroids or chemical substances that have an action like progesterone.

proglottis (*pro-glot'-tis*). A mature segment of a tapeworm.

prognathism (*prog'-nath-izm*). Enlargement and protrusion of the lower jaw.

prognathous (*prog-na'-thus*). Having projecting jaws.

prognosis (*prog-no'-sis*). A forecast of the course and duration of a disease.

projectile vomiting. *See under* Vomiting.

projection (*pro-jek'-shun*). An unconscious process by which painful thoughts or impulses are made acceptable by transferring them on to another person or object in the environment.

prolactin (*pro-lak'-tin*). A milk-producing hormone of the anterior lobe of the pituitary body, that stimulates the mammary gland. Now termed luteotrophin as it also stimulates the continued secretion of the corpus luteum.

prolapse (*pro'-laps*). Sinking, or falling down. *P. of the cord.* When the umbilical cord is expelled first during labour. *P. of iris.* Protrusion of a part of the iris through a wound in the cornea. *P. of rectum.* Protrusion of the mucous membrane, and sometimes of the muscle coat also, through the anal canal to the exterior. Normally due to general weakness, or straining. *P. of uterus.* In which it protrudes into the vagina, as the result of weakening of its supports.

proliferation (*pro-lif-er-a'-shun*). Rapid multiplication of cells, as may occur in a malignant growth.

promazine (*pro-ma'-zeen*). A tranquillizing drug used in psychiatry. Sparine is the proprietary preparation.

promethazine (*pro-meth'-a-zeen*). An antihistamine drug used in conditions of hypersensitivity, e.g. *hay fever, contact dermatitis, drug rashes* etc. Phenergan is a pro-

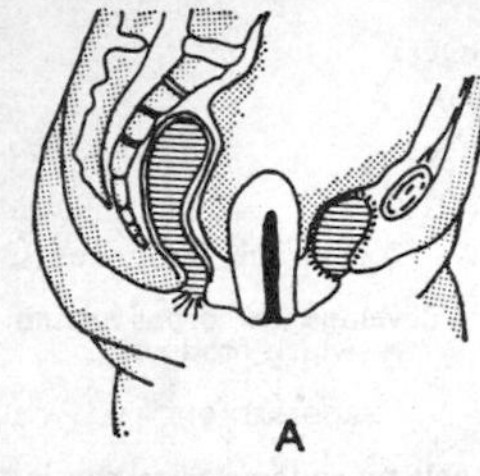

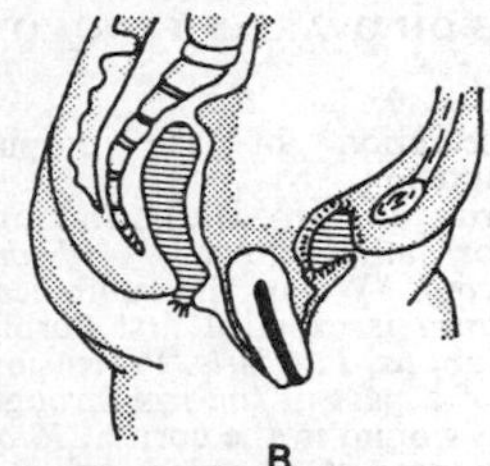

PROLAPSE OF THE UTERUS
A. Early stage.
B. Complete procidentia.

prietary preparation of it. *P. theoclate*. Avomine, a similar preparation.

pronation (*pro-na'-shun*). Turning the palm of the hand downward.

prone (*pro-n*). Lying face downward.

proof puncture. An exploratory puncture of the maxillary sinus to assess the necessity for further treatment.

propantheline (*pro-pan'-the-leen*). An antispasmodic drug that blocks the impulses from the vagus nerve to the stomach and may be used to inhibit gastric secretion and motility in peptic ulceration.

prophylactic (*pro-fil-ak'-tik*). Relating to prophylaxis.

prophylaxis (*pro-fil-ak'-sis*). Measures taken to prevent a disease, e.g. inoculation with TAB vaccine to prevent *typhoid fever*; regular administration of quinine to prevent *malaria*.

proprietary name (*pro-pri'-e-ta-re*). Is the name assigned to a drug by the firm which made it. A drug may have several different proprietary names.

proprioception (*pro-pre-o-sep'-shun*). Awareness of the position of parts of the body in space without looking at them.

proprioceptors (*pro-pre-o-sep'-tors*). The sensory end-organs that provide information about movements and position of the body. They occur chiefly in the muscles, tendons, joint capsules and labyrinth.

proptosis (*prop-to'-sis*). Projecting forward, e.g. of the eyeball.

prostate (*pros'-tate*). The gland surrounding the male urethra at its junction with the bladder and associated with the genital organs. It often becomes enlarged after middle age and may require removal, if it causes obstruction to the outflow of urine.

prostatectomy (*pros-tat-ek'-to-me*). Excision of the prostate gland. *Harris p.* and *Freyer's p.* are both suprapubic operations in which the gland is removed after the bladder has been incised. *Millin's p.* or *retropubic p.* The bladder is not opened and the gland is enucleated from around the bladder neck. *Transurethral p.* Removal of the gland via the urethra, by means of a diathermy knife and a cystoscope.

prostatitis (*pros-tat-i'-tis*). Inflammation of the prostate gland.

prostatocystitis (*pros-tat-o-sis'-ti'-tis*). Inflammation of the prostate and urinary bladder.

prostatorrhoea (*pros-tat-or-re'-ah*). A thin urethral discharge from the prostate gland in prostatitis.

prosthesis (*pros-the'-sis*). The fitting of artificial parts to the body; e.g. dentures.

prostration (*pros-tra'-shun*). A condition of extreme exhaustion.

protamine sulphate (*pro-ta-min sulf'-ate*). A sterile solution of protein from fish sperm that neutralizes circulating heparin should haemorrhage arise during anticoagulant therapy.

protamine zinc insulin (*pro'-ta-min-zink*). *See under* Insulin.

protanopia (*pro-tan-o'-pe-ah*). Colour blindness (*q.v.*) for red hues.

protein (*pro'-teen*). A complex compound of varying combinations of amino acids (*q.v.*). *P.* is man's only source of nitrogen which is necessary for body cells. *First class p.* Provides the essential amino acids. Sources are meat, poultry, fish, cheese, eggs, and milk. *Second class p.* The source is vegetable; peas, beans, and whole cereal but these cannot supply all the body's needs.

proteinuria (*pro-teen-u'-re-ah*). When plasma proteins are present in the urine often due to increased permeability of the tubules.

proteolysis (*pro-te-ol'-is-is*). The processes by which proteins are reduced to an absorbable form.

proteoses (*pro'-te-o-ses*). The first products in the breakdown of proteins.

Proteus vulgaris (*pro-te-us vul-gar'-is*). A bacillus that commonly occurs in secondary infections of wounds and the urinary tract.

prothrombin (*pro-throm'-bin*). Thrombogen. The precursor of thrombin which is formed in the presence of calcium salts and thrombokinase when blood is shed.

protoplasm (*pro'-to-plazm*). The essential chemical compound of which living cells are made.

Protozoa (*pro-to-zo'-ah*). The most primitive class of animal organisms, some of which are pathogenic, e.g. *Entamoeba histolytica* of amoebic dysentery, and *Plasmodium vivax* of malaria

provitamin (*pro-vi'-ta-min*). A precursor of a vitamin. *P.* '*A*' is carotene. *P.* '*D*' is said to be ergosterol.

proximal (*proks'-im-al*). Nearest that point which is considered the centre of a system. The opposite to distal.

prurigo (*pru-ri'-go*). A chronic skin disease with an irritating papular eruption.

pruritis (*pru-ri'-tus*). Great irritation of the skin. It may affect the whole surface of the body, as in certain skin diseases and nervous disorders, or it may be limited in area.

prussic acid (*prus'-sik*). Hydrocyanic acid (*q.v.*).

pseudo- (*su'-do-*). A prefix meaning 'false'.

pseudo-angina (*su-do-an-ji'-nah*). False angina. Precordial pain occurring in anxious individuals without evidence of organic heart disease. May be part of effort syndrome (*q.v.*).

pseudo-arthrosis (*su-do-arth-ro'-sis*). A false joint.

pseudocrisis (*su-do-kri'-sis*). A false crisis which is sometimes accompanied by the symptoms of true crisis, but the temperature rises again almost at once, and there is continuation of the disease.

pseudocroup (*su-do-kroop'*). False croup. Laryngismus stridulus.

pseudocyesis (*su-do-si-e'-sis*). A false pregnancy in which subjective signs may be present; amenorrhoea, enlarged abdomen, and breast changes but no fetus.

pseudogynaecomastia (*su-do-gi-ne-ko-mas'-te-ah*). The deposition of adipose tissue in the male breast that may give the appearance of enlarged mammary glands.

pseudohermaphroditism (*su-do-hur-maf'-ro-di-tizm*). Due to a hormone imbalance some of the characteristics of the opposite sex are present and confusion may arise as to the true sex of the individual.

pseudoisochromatic charts (*su-do-i-so-kro-mat'-ik*). Charts of coloured dots for testing colour blindness.

pseudomeningitis (*su-do-men-in-ji'-tis*). *See* Meningism.

Pseudomonas pyocyanea (*su-do-mon-as pi-o-si-an'-e-ah*). A motile, rod-shaped bacillus normally present in the colon that may infect the urinary tract or wounds.

pseudomucinous (*su-do-mu'-sin-us*). Allied to mucin. *P. cyst. See under* Cyst.

pseudomyopia (*su-do-mi-o'-pe-ah*). Spasm of the ciliary muscle causing the same focusing defect as in myopia (*q.v.*).

pseudoplegia (*su-do-ple'-je-ah*). Apparent loss of muscle power but not true paralysis. It may be hysterical in origin.

psittacosis (*sit-a-ko'-sis*). A virus disease of parrots communicable to man. Conveyed by the budgerigar variety. The symptoms resemble paratyphoid fever with bronchopneumonia.

psoas (*so'-as*). A long strap muscle originating from the lumbar spine with insertion into the lesser trochanter of the femur. It flexes the thigh on the abdomen. *P. abscess.* Arises in the lumbar region and is due to spinal caries as a result of tuberculous infection. It may track down the muscle and point in the region of its insertion in the groin.

psoriasis (*sor-i'-as-is*). A chronic skin disease characterized by reddish marginated patches with profuse silvery scaling on extensor surfaces like the knees and elbows, but may be widespread. It is non-infectious and the cause is unknown. *See* Goeckerman régime.

psyche (*si'-ke*). The mind, both conscious and unconscious.

psychiatrist (*si-ki'-at-rist*). A doctor who has devoted himself to the study of illness of mental disorders and their treatment.

psychiatry (*si-ki'-at-re*). The branch of medicine which deals with mental disorders and their treatment.

psychoanalysis (*si'-ko-an-al'-is-is*). A prolonged and intensive method of psychotherapy (*q.v.*) developed by Freud in which the patient is encouraged to speak freely concerning anything on his mind. Repressed material may be brought into consciousness. This may be helpful in partially or completely solving emotional problems and thus helping patients with neurotic traits or symptoms. *See* Association *and* Transference.

psychoanalyst (*si-ko-an'-al-ist*). One who specializes in psychoanalysis. He may or may not be medically qualified.

psychodrama (*si-ko-drah'-mah*). A form of group psychotherapy in which the patient with other group members acts out past incidents in his life. This is followed by group discussion, and under guidance of the psychiatrist an effort is made to give the patient a greater awareness of his behaviour and to try to solve the problem or conflict presented.

psychodynamic (*si-ko-di-nam'-ik*). The understanding and interpretation of psychiatric symptoms or abnormal behaviour in terms of unconscious mental mechanisms.

psychogenic (*si-ko-jen'-ik*). Originating in the mind. *P. illness.* A disorder having a psychological origin as opposed to an organic basis.

psychogeriatrics (*si-ko-jer-e-at'-riks*). The study and treatment of the psychological and psychiatric problems of the aged.

psychologist (*si-kol'-o-jist*). One who studies normal and abnormal mental processes, development and behaviour.

psychology (*si-kol'-o-je*). The study of mental life and behaviour.

psychometric (*si-ko-met'-rik*). Related to the measurement of mental characteristics.

psychomimetics (*si-ko-mi-met'-iks*). A group of drugs that produce an abnormal mental state that may resemble schizophrenia.

psychomotor (*si-ko-mo'-tor*). Related to the motor effects of mental activity.

psychoneurosis (*si-ko-nu-ro'-sis*). *See* Neurosis.

psychopath (*si'-ko-path*). A term used to describe a person with a defect in his personality. His actions will vary, he may be asocial, withdrawn, inadequate, and unable to take responsibility for himself or others. He may be anti-social, a criminal psychopath, or he may have long-standing sexual perversions.

psychopathic disorder (*si-ko-path'-ik*). Mental Health Act 1959. A persistent disorder or disability of the mind which results in abnormally aggressive or seriously irresponsible conduct on the part of the patient, and requires or is susceptible to medical treatment.

psychopathology (*si-ko-path-ol'-o-je*). The study of the nature and disease of mental diseases.

psychosexual development (*si-ko-seks'-u-al*). The stages through which an individual passes from birth to full maturity, especially in regard to sexual urges, in the total development of the person.

psychosis (*si-ko'-sis*). A severe mental illness affecting the whole personality. *Manic-depressive p.* There may be mild or severe attacks of elation or depression or both alternating. *Organic p.* May be due to trauma, new growth or degenerative changes. *Senile p.* That occurring in the aged. *Syphilitic p.* A manifestation of 3rd stage syphilis. *Toxic p.* May be due to alcohol or metallic poisoning.

psychosomatic (*si-ko-so-mat'-ik*). A condition relating to the mind and the body. *P. disorders.* Those illnesses in which emotional factors have a profound influence. Some better known examples are migraine, asthma, and ulcerative colitis.

psychotherapy (*si-ko-ther'-ap-e*). The treatment of disease by psychological methods. This may be by suggestion, persuasion, hypnosis, or by psychoanalytical methods. *See* Group psychotherapy.

psychotomimetics (*si-ko-to-mi-met'-iks*). Hallucinatory drugs that produce an abnormal mental state, mood changes, and delusions.

psychotropic drugs (*si-ko-tro'-pik*). Drugs that have an effect on the psyche. These include anti-depressants and tranquillizers.

pterygium (*te-rij'-e-um*). A patch of thickened conjunctiva which may develop over part of the cornea.

pterylglutamic acid (*ter-il-glu-tam'-ik*). Folic acid (*q.v.*).

ptomaines (*to'-manes*). Alkaloid compounds formed by putrefaction of animal or vegetable tissue.

ptosis (*to'-sis*). (1) Dropping of the upper eyelid due to loss of control by the 3rd cranial nerve. (2) Prolapse of an organ; e.g. *gastroptosis*.

ptyalin (*ti'-al-in*). The enzyme (amylase) in saliva which splits starches.

ptyalism (*ti'-al-izm*). Salivation.

ptyalolith (*ti'-al-o-lith*). Salivary calculus.

puberty (*pu'-ber-te*). The age at which the reproductive organs become functionally active. Generally between the 12th and 17th year.

pubes (*pu'-beez*). The region over the os pubis.

pudenda (*pu-den'-dah*). The external genitals.

pudendal block (*pu-den'-dal*). Infiltration of the sacral nerves that supply the perineum and clitoris, with a local anaesthetic.

puerperal (*pu-er'-per-al*). Pertaining to childbirth. *P. fever* or *sepsis.* Infection of the genital tract following childbirth.

puerperium (*pu-er-pe'-re-um*). A period of about six weeks following childbirth when the reproductive organs are returning to their normal state.

puking (*pu'-king*). Vomiting.

Pulex (*pu'-leks*). The flea. *P. irritans.* That parasitic on man. *Pasteurella pestis*, a type which infests rats may transmit plague to man.

pulmonary (*pul'-mon-ar-e*). Pertaining to or affecting the lungs. *P. circulation. See* Circulation. *P. embolism. See* Embolism. *P. infarction* is due to the occlusion of a small blood vessel in the lung by a clot, which causes death of the tissue supplied by that vessel. *P. tuberculosis. See* Tuberculosis.

pulp. Any soft, juicy animal or vegetable tissue. *P. cavity.*

The centre of a tooth containing blood tissue and nerves. *Digital p.* The soft pads at the ends of the digits. *Splenic p.* The reddish-brown tissue of the spleen.

pulsation (*pul-sa'-shun*). A beating or throbbing.

pulse (*puls*). The local rhythmic expansion of an artery, which can be felt with the finger, corresponding to each contraction of the left ventricle of the heart. It may be felt in any artery sufficiently near the surface of the body, and the normal adult rate is about 72 per minute. In childhood it is more rapid, varying from 130 in infants to 80 in older children. *P. deficit.* When the pulse rate is slower than the apex beat. A sign of atrial fibrillation. *Dicrotic p. See* Dicrotic. *High-tension p.* In which the duration of the impulse in the artery is long, and the artery feels firm and like a cord between the beats. *Low-tension p.* One easily obliterated by pressure. *P. pressure.* The difference between diastolic and systolic blood pressures, as measured by the sphygmomanometer. *Running p.* When there is little distinction between the beats. It occurs in haemorrhage. *Thready p.* is thin and almost imperceptible. *Venous p.* That felt in a vein—it is usually taken in the right jugular vein. *Water-hammer p.* (Corrigan's pulse). A full volume, but rapidly collapsing pulse occurring in aortic regurgitation.

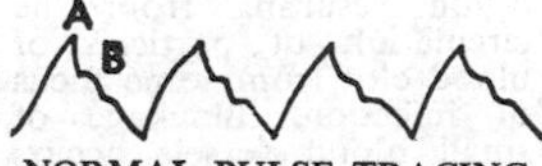

NORMAL PULSE TRACING
A. Ventricular wave.
B. Dicrotic notch.

pulsus alternans (*pul'-sus al'-ter-nans*). Strong and weak pulse beats alternate.

pulsus paradoxus (*pul'-sus par-ah-doks'-us*). The pulse rate slows on inspiration and quickens on expiration. It may occur in pericarditis.

pulvis (*pul'-vis*). A powder (Latin).

pump oxygenator. A heart-lung machine in which the blood bypasses the heart and lungs. The blood is removed from both venae cavae, oxygenated and returned into the femoral artery so that it runs into the aorta and so to the rest of the body, e.g. Melrose machine.

puncta (*punk'-tah*). Openings of the lacrimal ducts at the inner canthus of the eye.

punctate (*punk'-tate*). Dotted. *P. erythema.* A rash of very fine spots.

puncture (*punk'-chur*). To pierce. *Cisternal p.* To withdraw fluid from the cisterna magna (*q.v.*). *Exploratory p.* To pierce where fluid is suspected, and withdraw it for examination. *Lumbar p.* To remove cerebrospinal fluid by puncture between the 3rd and 4th lumbar vertebra. *Sternal p.* Into the manubrium of the sternum to withdraw bone marrow for examination. *Ventricular p.* Into a cerebral ventricle to withdraw fluid.

pupil (*pu'-pil*). The circular aperture in the centre of the iris, through which light passes into the eye. *Argyll Robertson p.* There is absence of response to light but not to accommodation, characteristic of locomotor ataxia, *Artificial p.* One made by cutting a piece out of the iris.

pupillary (*pu'-pil-lar-re*). Referring to the pupil.

purgative (*pur'-gat-iv*). A drug which produces evacuation of the bowels. They may be: (1) Irritants like cascara, senna, rhubarb, and castor oil. (2) Lubricants like paraffin emulsion. (3) Mechanical agents that increase bulk like saline aperients and agar preparations.

purins (*pu'-rins*). Nucleoproteins, metabolism of which produces uric acid. The blood level of uric acid is high in gout.

Purkinje cells (*pur-kin'-je*). A layer of cells with an extensive dendritic network that are connector neurones in the cerebellar cortex.

purpura (*pur'-pu-rah*). A condition characterized by extravasation of blood in the skin and mucous membranes, causing purple spots and patches. It may be a *primary* disease, most probably an auto-immune process, or a *secondary* sign in other diseases where there is failure of platelet production. (1) *P. haemorrhagica* or *thrombocytopenic p.* A severe form with profuse haemorrhage, especially from the mucous membranes, any of which may be involved. (2) *Non-thrombocytopenic p. Henoch's p.* Occurs in children and is characterized by purpura within the intestinal canal and the passage of blood and mucus in the stools. *Schonlein's p.* Occurs in young adults. Crops of purpuric spots, haemorrhages into joints causing painful swellings.

purulent (*pu'-ru-lent*). Containing or resembling pus.

pus. A thick, yellow semiliquid substance consisting of dead leucocytes and bacteria, debris of cells, and tissue fluids. It results from inflammation caused by invading bacteria which have destroyed the phagocytes and set up local suppuration. The chief of these pus-forming bacteria are *Streptococcus pyogenes* and *Staphylococcus pyogenes*. *Blue p.* Produced by infection with *Bacillus pyocyaneus*.

pustule (*pus'-tule*). A small pimple or elevation of the skin, containing pus. *Malignant p. See* Anthrax.

putrefaction (*pu-tre-fak'-shun*). Decomposition of animal or vegetable matter under the influence of micro-organisms, usually accompanied by an offensive odour due to gas formation.

Putti's splint (*put'-te*). *See* Divaricator.

pyaemia (*pi-e'-me-ah*). A condition resulting from the circulation of particles of blood clot from some focus of infection. Blockage of small blood vessels occurs with resultant formation of abscesses, the development of which cause rigor and high fever. *Portal p.* Pylephlebitis (*q.v.*). *See also* Embolism *and* Thrombophlebitis.

pyarthrosis (*pi-ar-thro'-sis*). Suppuration in a joint.

pyelitis (*pi-el-i'-tis*). A seldom used term as infection affects not only the pelvis of the kidney but also the renal substance. *See* Pyelonephritis.

pyelography (*pi-el-og'-raf-e*). A method of X-ray examination of the kidney. (1) *Intravenous p*. The dye is inserted into a vein and within 10 min is being excreted by the renal tubules. *Retro-grade p*. The dye is inserted via cytoscope and ureteric catheters.

pyelolithotomy (*pi-el-o-lith-ot'-o-me*). Removal of a stone from the renal pelvis.

pyelonephritis (*pi-el-o-nef-ri'-tis*). Inflammation of the renal pelvis and renal substance characterized by fever, acute loin pain, frequency of micturition with pus and albumin in the urine. Due to an ascending infection from the ureters and below (urinary stasis or urinary obstruction being important contributory factors) or from the blood stream. Treatment is according to the causative organism, either sulphonamides or penicillin are used. Recurrent acute attacks may lead to chronic infection and eventual renal failure.

pyknic (*pik'-nik*). A type of physique, a stocky rounded figure with a good chest and abdominal capacity and a tendency to put on fat, that is said to go with the cheerful extraverted type of personality.

pyknolepsy (*pik'-no-lep-se*). Slight and frequent fits which may occur in children. A form of minor epilepsy which ceases as the child grows up.

pylephlebitis (*pi-le-fleb-i'-tis*). Inflammation of the portal vein which gives rise to severe symptoms of septicaemia or pyaemia.

pylethrombosis (*pi-le-throm-bo'-sis*). Thrombosis of the portal vein.

pyloric stenosis (*pi-lor'-ik*). Stricture of the pyloric orifice. It may be: (1) Hypertrophic, when there is thickening of normal tissue. This is congenital and occurs in infants from 4 to 7 weeks old, usually males and first babies. (2) Due to scarring from ulceration. (3) Due to carcinoma.

pyloromyotomy (*pi-lor-o-mi-ot'-o-me*). Rammstedt's operation. An incision of the pylorus.

pyloroplasty (*pi-lor'-o-plas-te*). Plastic operation on the pylorus to enlarge the outlet. A longitudinal incision is made and it is resutured transversely.

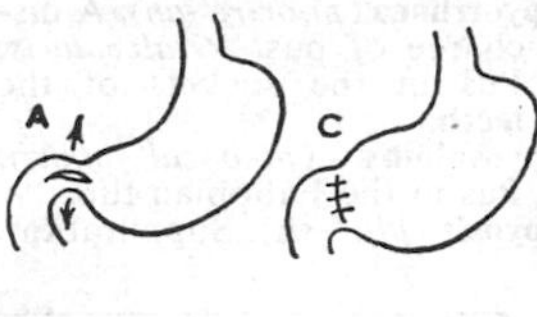

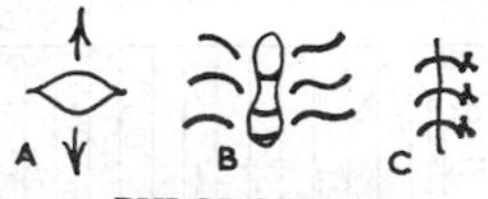

PYLOROPLASTY

A. Longitudinal incision.
B and C. Resutured transversely.

pylorospasm (*pi-lor-o-spazm'*). Forceful muscle contraction of the pylorus that delays emptying of the stomach.

pylorus (*pi-lor'-us*). The sphincter muscle which guards the opening of the stomach into the duodenum.

pyocolpos (*pi-o-kol'-pos*). Accumulated pus in the vagina.

pyocyanic (*pi-o-si-an'-ik*). Relating to blue pus produced by infection with the *Pseudomonas pyocyaneus.*

pyogenic (*pi-o-jen'-ik*). Producing pus.

pyometra (*pi-o-me'-trah*). Pus in the uterus.

pyonephrosis (*pi-o-nef-ro'-sis*). There is obstruction and infection of the pelvis of the kidney. The calyces and pelvis are dilated, contain pus and usually calculi.

pyopericarditis (*pi-o-per-e-kard-i'-tis*). Suppurative infection of the pericardium.

pyopneumothorax (*pi-o-nu-mo-thor'-aks*). Air and pus in the pleural cavity, as may result from rupture of an abscess on the surface of the lung.

pyorrhoea (*pi-or-re'-ah*). A discharge of pus. *P. alveolaris.* Pus in the sockets of the teeth.

pyosalpinx (*pi-o-sal'-pinks*). Pus in the Fallopian tube.

pyosis (*pi-o'-sis*). Suppuration.

pyothorax (*pi-o-thor'-aks*). Pus in the pleural cavity. Empyema (*q.v.*).

pyramidal (*pi-ram'-id-al*). Of pyramid shape. *P. cells.* Cortical cells from which originate nerve impulses to voluntary muscle. *P. tract.* The nerve fibres which transmit impulses from pyramidal cells through the brain and spinal cord.

pyretic (*pi-ret'-ik*). Pertaining to fever.

pyrexia (*pi-rek'-se-ah*). Fever; a rise of body temperature to any point between 99° and 104°F; above this is hyperpyrexia. *Continuous p.* The temperature is high and does not vary more than one degree in 24 hr. *Intermittent p.* Rising very high and falling below normal each day. *Remittent p.* The temperature varies more than one degree but never reaches normal.

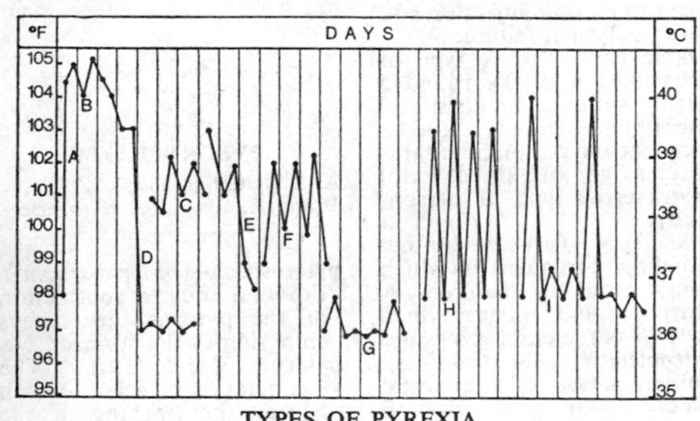

TYPES OF PYREXIA

A. Rigor.
B. Hyperpyrexia } continuous.
C. Pyrexia }
D. Crisis.
E. Lysis.
F. Remittent.
G. Apyrexia (subnormal).
H. Intermittent (hectic).
I. Intermittent (periodic).

pyridostigmine (*pi-re-do-stig'-meen*). A drug that prevents destruction of acetylcholine at the neuromuscular junctions and is used in treating myasthenia gravis. It is less powerful than neostigmine but has a more prolonged action. Mestinon is a proprietary preparation.

pyridoxine (*pi-re-doks'-een*). Vitamin B_6. This vitamin is concerned with protein metabolism and blood formation.

pyrogen (*pi'-ro-jen*). A substance that can produce fever.

pyrogenic (*pi-ro-jen'-ik*). Producing fever.

pyromania (*pi-ro-ma'-ne-ah*). An irresistible desire to set things on fire.

pyrosis (*pi-ro'-sis*). Heartburn, a symptom of dyspepsia, marked by a burning sensation in the stomach and oesophagus with eructation of acid fluid.

pyuria (*pi-u'-re-ah*). Pus in the urine. It is visible as a whitish sediment, which becomes thick and ropy, on the addition of liquor potassae or pus cells can be seen on microscopic examination. *See* Appendix 11.

Q

quadrant (*kwod'-rant*). A quarter of a circle or a fourth part.

quadriceps (*kwod'-re-seps*). Four-headed. *Q. extensor muscle*. The principal extensor of the thigh.

quadriplegia (*kwod-re-ple'-je-ah*). Paralysis in which all four limbs are affected.

quadruple vaccine (*kwod'-ru-pl vak'-seen*). A vaccine to immunize against diphtheria, pertussis, poliomyelitis, and tetanus.

qualitative (*kwal-e-ta'-tif*). Referring to or concerned with quality.

quantitative (*kwan-te-ta'-tif*). Referring to the amount or quantity.

quarantine (*kwor'-an-teen*). The period of isolation of an infectious or suspected case, to prevent the spread of disease. For contacts, this is the longest incubation period known for the specific disease.

quartan (*kwor'-tan*). An intermittent fever recurring every third day, i.e. 1st, 4th, 7th, etc. In malaria each attack corresponds with a fresh invasion of red corpuscles by the malarial parasites.

quartz (*kwor'-tz*). Rock crystal. Ultraviolet rays can penetrate it. *Q. lamp*. That used for treatment by artificial sunlight.

quarternary ammonium compounds (*kwa-ter'-na-re*). A group of bactericidal agents. Examples are cetramide (Cetavlon), benzalkonium (Roccal), and domiphen (Bradosol).

Queckenstedt's test (*kwek'-en-sted*). A test carried out during lumbar puncture by compression of the jugular veins. When normal there is a sharp rise in pressure, followed by a fall as the compression is released. Blockage of the spinal canal or thrombosis of the jugular vein will result in an absence of rise, or only a sluggish rise and fall.

'quickening'. The first perceptible fetal movements, felt by the mother between the fourth and fifth months of pregnancy.

quicklime. Calcium oxide.

quiescent (*kwi-es'-ent*). Inactive or at rest. Periods when the symptoms of a disease are not evident.

quinalbarbitone (*kwin-al-bar'-be-tone*). A short-acting, quickly absorbed analgesic. Seconal is a proprietary preparation.

quinidine (*kwin'-i-deen*). An alkaloid from cinchona. It restores normal rhythm in cases of atrial fibrillation, for which purpose it is given in selected cases.

quinine (*kwin-een'*). An alkaloid obtained from cinchona bark. In small doses it is tonic and antipyretic. In larger doses it is used in the treatment of malaria as a prophylactic and curative. It is also stimulative to uterine contractions. *Q. urethane* is used for injection treatment of varicose veins to cause sclerosis of the vessels.

quinism (*kwin'-izm*). Cinchonism (*q.v.*).

quinsy (*kwin'-ze*). Peritonsillar abscess. Acute inflammation of the tonsil and surrounding cellular tissue with suppuration. It is characterized by fever, abscess formation, and great pain and difficulty in swallowing. Antibiotic treatment may abort the attack but if suppuration occurs incision is necessary.

quotient (*kwo'-shent*). A number obtained by division. *Intelligence q.* The degree of intelligence estimated by dividing the mental age reckoned from standard tests by the age in years. *Respiratory q.* The ratio between the CO_2 expired and the O_2 inspired during a specified time.

R

rabid (*rab'-id*). Infected with rabies.

rabies (*ra'-beez*). An acute infectious disease of animals, especially of the dog, cat, and wolf. The virus is found in the saliva of infected animals, and if transmitted to man produces hydrophobia.

racemose (*race'-moze*). Grape-like. *R. glands* are compound lobulated in structure, e.g. salivary glands.

rachis (*rak'-is*). The vertebral column.

rad. A unit for measuring radiation dosage. It is a measure of the amount of energy absorbed from a radioactive source.

radial (*ra'-de-al*). Relating to the radius. *R. artery.* The artery at the wrist.

radiant (*ra'-de-ant*). Emitting rays. *R. heat bath.* Exposure of the whole or part of the body to heat rays generated by electricity.

radiation pneumonitis (*ra-de-a'-shun nu-mon-i'-tis*). Inflammatory changes in the alveoli and interstitial tissue due to radiation which may lead to fibrosis later.

radiation sickness (*ra-de-a'-shun*). The reaction of the body to radiation. Any or all of the following may be present; anorexia, nausea, vomiting, and diarrhoea.

radical (*rad'-ik-al*). Dealing with the root or cause of a disease. *R. cure.* One which cures by complete removal of the cause.

radioactive (*ra-de-o-ak'-tiv*). Having the power of radioactivity. *See* Isotope. *R. gold* has been used in treating malignant disease. *R. iodine. See* Iodine. *R. phosphorus.* Used to check polycythaemia.

radioactivity (*ra-de-o-ak-tiv'-e-te*). Some elements of high atomic weight have the power of emitting α and β particles and some γ-rays. This results in disintegration of the element to one of lower atomic weight. *Induced r.* Can be produced in certain elements as in an atomic pile by bombarding the nuclei with neutrons.

radio-autography (*ra-de-o-aw-tog'-raf-e*). A form of photography in which molecules labelled with radioactive atoms reveal themselves in photographic emulsion.

radiobiology (*ra-de-o-bi-ol'-o-je*). The branch of medical science that studies the effect of radiation on live animal and human tissues.

radiodermatitis (*ra-de-o-der-mat-i'-tis*). A late skin complication of radiotherapy in which there is atrophy, scarring, pigmentation and telangiectases of the skin.

radiograph (*ra'-de-o-graf*). Skiagram. The picture obtained on a sensitive plate by X-rays passing through the body.

radiographer (*ra-de-og'-raf-er*). One who is trained to take X-ray pictures.

radiography (*ra-de-og'-raf-e*). The method of examination by means of the Röntgen or X-rays. Some substances are less easily penetrated than others, and therefore throw a shadow on the film. Bone and many diseased tissues are semi-opaque. X-rays will not penetrate metal and some types of adhesive plaster, which must be remembered when fractured bones are photographed. For diagnosis, drugs opaque to the rays are introduced into the body. *See* Barium, Bismuth.

radiologist (*ra-de-ol'-o-gist*). One who is skilled in the science of radiology.

radiology (*ra-de-ol'-o-je*). The science of radiant energy. In medicine the term refers to its use in the diagnosis and treatment of disease.

radio-sensitive (*ra-de-o-sen'-se-tif*). Those structures that respond well to radiotherapy.

radiotherapy (*ra-de-o-ther'-ap-e*). Treatment of disease by radium, X-rays and radioactive isotopes.

radium (*ra'-de-um*). A radioactive element obtained from pitchblende and other uranium ores, which gives off emanations of great radioactive power. Usually used in the form of radium bromide, a yellow crystalline powder. It emits three distinct rays:—*alpha* (α); *beta* (β); *gamma* (γ). The last are similar to X-rays but shorter, and it is these which are destructive to malignant cells. Used in the treatment of malignant growth, for rodent ulcer, and to induce artificial menopause.

radius (*ra'-de-us*). The smaller bone of the forearm.

radon seeds (*ra'-don*). A method of treatment by which the emanations from radium are collected, sealed in a container, and inserted into places from which it would be inconvenient to remove radium itself. These emanations lose their effect after a few days; the containers remain harmlessly in the tissues.

râle (*rahl*). An abnormal rattling sound, heard on auscultation of the chest during respiration in cases of bronchitis.

rami (*ra'-mi*). Branches, as of arteries, veins and nerves. *R. communicantes*. The nerve fibres which connect the sympathetic ganglia with the spinal cord.

Rammstedt's operation (*ram'-stet*). For congenital stricture of the pylorus in which the fibres of the sphincter muscle are divided but the canal is not opened.

ranula (*ran'-u-lah*). A retention cyst usually under the tongue when blockage occurs in a submaxillary or sublingual duct, or in a mucous gland.

raphe (*raf'-e*). A seam or ridge of tissue indicating the juncture of two parts.

rapport (*rap-port'*). A psychiatric term used to describe a satisfactory relationship between two persons, either the doctor and patient or nurse and patient, or the patient with any other person significant to him.

rarefaction (*rair-e-fak'-shun*). Thinning. *R. of bone*. Thinning as occurs in tuberculous infection of bone.

rash. A superficial eruption on the skin, frequently characteristic of some specific fever. Desquamation follows it. *Nettle r.* Urticaria (*q.v.*). *Serum r.* An irritating urticaria which may appear 8 to 10 days after an injection of serum. *See* Anaphylaxis.

raspatory (*ras'-pat-or-e*). An instrument used to strip the periosteum from bone.

rat-bite fever. *See* Weil's disease.

rationalization (*rash-un-al-i-za'-shun*). The mental process by which an individual explains his behaviour, giving reasons that are advantageous to himself or are socially acceptable. It may be a conscious or an unconscious act.

ray-fungus (*ra'-fun-gus*). A genus of fungi which cause actinomycosis.

Raynaud's disease (*ra'-no*). Spasm of the arterioles of the extremities causing numbness, tingling and discoloration. The treatment is protection from cold and vasodilator drugs. Sympathectomy may prove beneficial, but the condition is progressive.

Raynaud's phenomenon. Spasm of the digital arteries in response to cold. *Secondary R's p.* May arise as an occupational hazard in those who work with vibrating tools—pneumatic drills, etc.

rays. Lines of light or heat. Various ones are used in medical treatment. Light from the sun when divided up has colours ranging from red, through orange, yellow, green, blue and indigo, to violet: this is the *visible spectrum*. It extends much farther at each end, and these rays can be made apparent by photography or fluorescence. Those below the red rays (*infra-red*) include the Hertzian or wireless waves; while the invisible ones beyond the violet are extremely short, i.e. the *X-ray* and *ultra-*

violet ray. According to their intensity these cause ordinary sunburn, the burns of ultraviolet light, or destruction of malignant growths.

re- A prefix meaning 'back' or 'again'.

reaction (*re - ak' - shun*). Counteraction; a response to the application of a stimulus. *Acid r.* A test for the presence of acids; blue litmus paper turns red. *Alkaline r.* An indication of the presence of alkalis; red litmus paper turns blue.

reactive (*re-ak'-tiv*). In psychiatry, the response of an individual to adverse external circumstances causing an exogenous depression.

reagent (*re-a'-jent*). A substance employed to produce a chemical reaction. *Esbach's r.* A solution of picric acid used in Esbach's albuminometer. *See* Appendix 11.

reamer (*re'-mur*). An instrument to reshape the head of the femur during arthroplasty.

rebore (*re'-bor*). Coring out or recanalizing. *See* Disobliteration.

recall (*re'-kawl*). To bring back to consciousness. Memory consists of registering, retaining, and recall.

receptaculum chyli (*re-sep-tak'-u-lum ki'-li*). The pouch-like lower end of the thoracic duct, into which the fat passes when absorbed from the intestine.

receptors (*re-sep'-tors*). The sensory nerve endings that receive stimuli for transmission.

recessive (*re-cess'-if*). The opposite to dominant. *R. genes.* A gene which will produce its characteristics only when present in a homozygous state, that is when both parents possess this gene. Then the child has only a 1 in 4 chance of inheriting it.

recipient (*re-sip'-e-ent*). (1) One who receives blood from another by transfusion. (2) One who receives an organ or tissue from another by transplantation. *Universal r.* A person who can receive blood from all groups of donors without harmful effect. *See* Blood grouping.

Recklinghausen's disease. *See* Neurofibromatosis.

recrudescence (*re-kru-des'-sense*). Renewed aggravation of symptoms following an interval of abatement.

rectal (*rek'-tal*). Relating to the rectum. *R. anaesthesia. See* Anaesthesia. *R. examination.* By insertion of a glove-covered finger, or with the aid of a proctoscope.

rectified spirit (*rek'-te-fide*). Alcohol having 10 per cent of water in it.

rectocele (*rek'-to-seel*). Hernia of the rectum, caused by

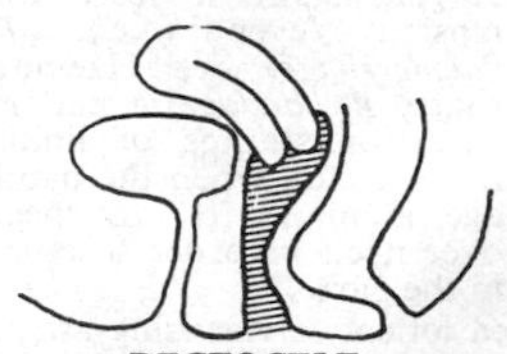

RECTOCELE

overstretching of the vaginal wall at childbirth. Treated by posterior colporrhaphy.

rectoperineorrhaphy (*rek-to-per-in-e-or'-raf-e*). The operation for repair of the perineum and rectal wall.

rectopexy (*rek'-to-peks-e*). The

operation for fixation of a prolapsed rectum.

rectoscope (*rek'-to-skope*). *See* Proctoscope.

rectovaginal (*rek-to-vaj-i'-nal*). Concerning the rectum and vagina. *R. fistula. See* Fistula.

rectovesical (*rek-to-ves'-ik-al*). Concerning the rectum and bladder. *R. fistula. See* Fistula.

rectum (*rek'-tum*). The lower end of the large intestine from the sigmoid flexure to the anus.

rectus (*rek'-tus*). Straight. *R. abdominis.* The straight muscle passing up the front of the abdomen from the pubis to the ribs. *R. femoris.* The straight muscle of the thigh; part of the quadriceps extensor. *R. muscles of the eye.* The four straight muscles which move the eyeball.

recumbent (*re-kum'-bent*). Lying down in the dorsal position.

recuperation (*re-ku-per-a'-shun*). Convalescence.

recurrent (*re-kur'-rent*). Occurring again. *R. fever.* Relapsing fever (*q.v.*). *R. haemorrhage. See* Haemorrhage. *R. bandage.* A pattern used for stumps of limbs, fingers, etc., when the bandage is made to turn back over itself in order to cover in the part.

red lotion. A cleansing astringent lotion containing zinc sulphate.

reduce. To restore to normal position; a term applied, e.g. to a hernia or dislocation.

reduction division. Type of multiplication of sex cells in which the chromosomes separate into two duplicate strands, instead of splitting into two as they do in other cells.

reduction en masse (*re-duk'-shun on mass*). Describes an attempt to reduce a strangulated hernia, but the sac is pushed back intact, so that the bowel remains strangulated and the condition is not relieved.

re-education (*re-ed-u-ka'-shun*). The training of the physically disabled or mentally disordered person; so that he may completely, or in some degree, regain his former powers.

reef knot. A knot used in surgery which does not slip. *See also* 'granny' knot.

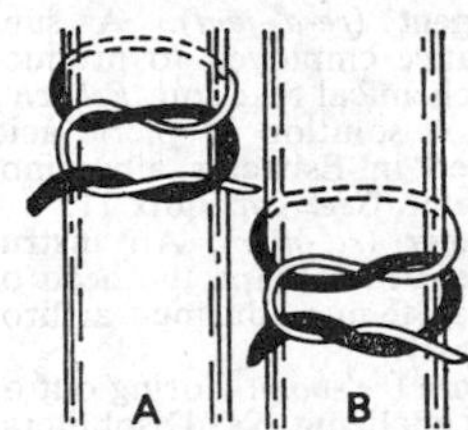

A. GRANNY KNOT
B. REEF KNOT

referred pain. That which occurs at a distance from the place of origin due to the sensory nerves entering the cord at the same level, i.e. the phrenic nerve supplying the diaphragm enters the cord in the cervical region as do the nerves from the shoulder.

reflex (*re'-fleks*). Reflected or thrown back. *R. action.* An involuntary action following immediately upon some stimulus, e.g. the knee jerk, or the withdrawal of a limb

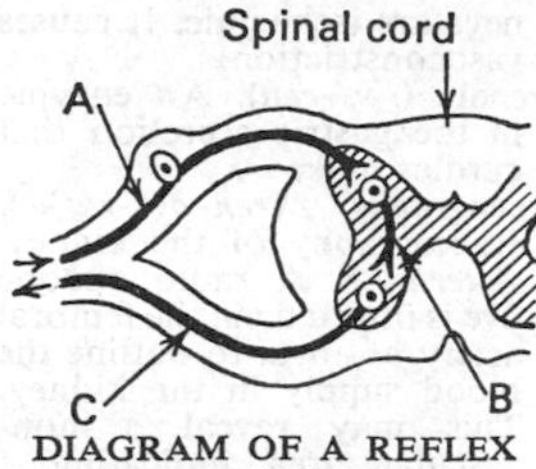

DIAGRAM OF A REFLEX ARC

A. Sensory neurone.
B. Connector neurone.
C. Motor neurone.

from a pinprick. *R. arc*. The sensory and motor neurones together with the connector neurone which carry out a reflex action. *R. of accommodation*. When the size of the pupil alters according to the distance of the image viewed. *Conditioned r*. That which is not natural, but is developed by association and frequent repetition until it appears natural. *Corneal r*. Light pressure on the cornea causes the eyelids to close. This is a test for unconsciousness which is absolute when there is no response. *Deep r*. A muscle reflex elicited by tapping the tendon or bone of attachment. *R. to light*. Alteration of the size of the pupil in response to exposure to light. *Spinal r*. That which takes place through centres in the spinal cord. *Swallowing r*. Initiated by stimulation of the palate. *R. vomiting*. *See* Vomiting.

reflux (*re'-fluks*). A backward flow.

refraction (*re-frak'-shun*). The bending or deviation of rays of light, as they pass obliquely through one medium and penetrate another of different density.

refractive (*re-frak'-tiv*). Relating to refraction. *R. error*. A defect that prevents light rays from converging on a single focus on the retina.

refractory (*re-frak'-to-re*). Not yielding to, or resistant to, treatment.

refrigeration (*re-frig-er-a'-shun*). The cooling of a part to reduce the metabolic requirements. May be used to aid the formation of a collateral circulation or as a form of anaesthesia.

regeneration (*re-jen-er-a'-shun*). To renew again, e.g. new growth of tissue in its specific form after injury.

regional ileitis (*re'-jun-al il-e-i'-tis*). Crohn's disease. A localized area of inflammation of the small intestine. The cause is unknown.

regression (*re-gresh'-un*). A tendency to return to primitive or child-like modes of behaviour. This may be done as a means of solving a problem when under emotional stress.

regurgitation (*re-gur-jit-a'-shun*). Backward flow, e.g. of food into the mouth from the stomach. Fluids regurgitate through the nose in paralysis affecting the soft palate. *Aortic r*. Backward flow of blood into the left ventricle when the aortic valve is incompetent. *Mitral r*. *See under* Mitral.

rehabilitation (*re-hab-il-e-ta'-shun*). Re-education. *R. centre* is one which provides for organized employment within the capacity of the patient, and with especial regard to the psychical influence of the work.

Reiter protein complement fixation (*ri'-ter*). RPCF. A serological test used to aid the diagnosis of syphilis.

Reiter's syndrome (*ri'-ters sindrome*). A non-specific urethritis in which there is also arthritis and conjunctivitis.

relapse (*re-laps'*). The return of a disease, after an interval of convalescence.

relapsing fevers. Certain louse- or tick-borne tropical fevers. The fever lasts a few days, but relapses are common. Tetracycline has proved successful in treatment.

relaxant (*re-laks'-ant*). A drug or other agent that brings about muscle relaxation or relieves tension.

relaxin (*re-laks'-in*). Polypeptides that are produced by the ovary and soften the cervix and loosen the ligaments of the symphasis pubis to aid the birth of the baby.

remission (*re-mish'-un*). Subsidence of the symptoms of a disease for a time.

remittent (*re-mit'-tent*). Returning at intervals. *R. fever. See* Fever *and* Pyrexia.

renal (*re'-nal*). Relating to the kidney. *R. asthma. See* Asthma. *R. calculus.* Stone in the kidney. *R. threshold.* The level of the blood sugar, beyond which it is excreted in the urine. Normally 0·18 per cent. *R. rickets, dwarfism,* or *infantilism.* A form of interstitial nephritis, sometimes occurring in children, associated with delayed growth and marked rickets.

renin (*ren'-in*). A proteolytic enzyme released into the blood stream when the kidneys are ischaemic. It causes vasoconstriction.

rennin (*ren'-een*). An enzyme in the gastric secretion that curdles milk.

renography (*ren-og'-raf-e*). Radiography of the kidney. *Arterial r.* A radio opaque dye is inserted via the femoral artery or aorta to outline the blood supply in the kidney. This may reveal a non-vascular area indicating a tumour.

reorganization (*re-or-gan-i-za'-shun*). Healing by formation of new tissue, or by operative reconstruction. *See* Arthroplasty.

repolarization (*re-po-lar-i-za'-shun*). The reforming of an electric charge at the neuromuscular junction (*q.v.*) after its dispersal by the passage of a nerve impulse.

repositor (*re-pos'-it-or*). An instrument for replacing a prolapsed organ. *Iris r.* An instrument for replacing the iris following an intra-ocular operation.

repression (*re-presh'-un*). The inability of an individual to recognize motives and feelings which are unacceptable to him. It is a defence mechanism by which painful experiences are forced out into and kept in the unconscious.

resection (*re-sek'-shun*). Removal of a part. *Submucous r.* Removal of part of a deflected nasal septum, from beneath a flap of mucous membrane which is then replaced. *Transurethral r.* A method of removing portions of an enlarged prostate gland via the urethra.

resectoscope (*re-sek'-to-skope*). A telescopic instrument by which pieces of tissue can also be removed. Used for transurethral prostatectomy.

reserpine (*re-ser'-pen*). An alkaloid from *Rauwolfia*, a drug used to reduce the blood pressure by hypertension. It may be used in conjunction with mecamylamine (*q.v.*) or with the diuretic hydrochlorothiazide K in the trade preparation of Salupres.

residual (*re-zid'-u-al*). Remaining. *R. air. See under* Air. *R. juice*. Gastric juice withdrawn from the stomach by a syringe and through a Ryle's tube, before a test meal is given.

resilient (*re-zil'-e-ent*). The power to return to normal shape after stretching or compressing.

resistance. (1) In *electricity*, the opposition made by a non-conducting substance to the passage of a current. (2) In *psychology*, the opposition, stemming from the unconscious, to repressed ideas being brought to consciousness. *R. to infection.* The natural power of the body to withstand the toxins of disease. It can be maintained and increased by conserving the patient's strength by good diet, fresh air, rest, and freedom from mental worries. Artificially, it is increased by injection of vaccines and antitoxic sera. *Peripheral r.* is that offered to the passage of blood through small vessels and capillaries.

resolution (*rez-o-lu'-shun*). The process of returning to normal. It sometimes occurs in inflammatory conditions without the formation of pus.

resonance (*rez'-on-ans*). The reverberating sound obtained on percussing over a cavity or hollow organ, such as the lung.

resorcinol (*re-sor'-sin-ol*). Resorcin. A phenol compound used as an ointment in skin diseases, and sometimes as an antiseptic.

resorption (*re-sorp'-shun*). (1) The absorption of morbid deposits, such as the products of inflammation. (2) The absorption of excreted materials.

respiration (*res-pir-a'-shun*). The gaseous interchange between the tissue cells and the atmosphere. *External r.* In man consists of *inspiration*, when the external intercostal muscles and the diaphragm contract and air is drawn into the lungs, and *expiration* or breathing out. *Artificial r.* is the production of respiratory movements by external effort. *See* Appendix 1. *Internal* or *tissue r.* The interchange of gases which occurs between tissues and blood through the walls of capillaries. *Inverse r.* Causes a grunting sound and the sequence is *expiration*, *inspiration*, *pause*. Noticeably present in bronchopneumonia, especially in young children. *Laboured r.* That which is difficult and distressed. *Stertorous r.* Snoring. A noisy breathing. *See also* Cheyne-Stokes respiration.

respirator (*res'-pir-a-tor*). A device to aid respiration. (1) *A face mask* for giving oxygen or a drug or for removing impurities or poison gases. (2) *Tank r.* The iron lung into which the patient is put except for the head and respiration is brought about by intermittent negative pressure, drawing air into the lungs. (3) *Cuirass r.* The negative pressure is created by an appliance strapped to the chest leaving the limbs free. (4) A *positive pressure r.* The patient is attached to a machine which blows air into the lungs via an intratracheal tube or tracheostomy. *Pump r.* The heart lung machine, by which the blood can be removed from the body, oxygenated, and returned into circulation.

respiratory distress syndrome. Dyspnoea occurring between soon after birth and the third day of life. Associated with prematurity it is characterized by severe retraction of the chest wall with expiratory grunting and cyanosis. *Syn.* Hyaline membrane disease.

resuscitation (*re-sus-sit-a'-shun*). Bringing back to life one who is apparently dead. *See* Appendix 1.

retardation (*re-tard-a'-shun*). Late or delayed activity. *Mental r.* A state of arrested development of the mind, that has existed from birth or from an early age. *Syn.* Subnormality (*q.v.*). *Psychomotor r.* A slowing down of mental processes and of bodily movement.

retching (*ret'-ching*). An involuntary, spasmodic, but ineffectual effort to vomit.

retention (*re-ten'-shun*). Holding back. *R. of urine.* Inability to pass urine from the bladder, which may be due to obstruction or of nervous origin. *R. cyst. See under* Cyst. *R. enema. See under* Enema. *R. defect.* A term used in psychiatry to describe a defect of memory. Inability to retain material in the mind so that it can be recalled when required.

reticular (*re-tik'-u-lar*). Resembling a net.

reticulocyte (*re-tik'-u-lo-site*). A red blood cell that is not fully mature, it still retains strands of nucleus material.

reticulocytosis (*re-tik'-u-lo-si-to'-sis*). The presence of an increased number of immature red cells in the blood, indicating over-activity of the bone marrow.

reticulo-endothelial system (*re-tik'-u-lo en-do-the'-le-al*). Consists of endothelial cells in the liver, spleen, bone marrow, and lymph glands that produce large mononuclear cells or macrophages. These are phagocytic, they destroy red blood cells and have the power of making some antibodies.

reticuloses (*re-tik-u-lo'-seez*). A group of rare malignant diseases of the reticulo-endothelial system. These include Hodgkin's disease, lymphosarcoma and reticulum-cell sarcoma.

reticulosarcoma (*re-tik-u-lo-sar-ko'-mah*). A malignant disease of the blood in which the liver and spleen are involved. It is one of the reticuloses.

retina (*ret'-in-ah*). The innermost coat of the eyeball, formed of nerve cells and fibres, and from which the optic nerve leaves the eyeball and passes to the visual area of the cerebrum. The impression of the image is focused upon it.

retinal (*ret'-in-al*). Relating to the retina. *R. detachment.* When the retina becomes partially detached from the underlying choroid layer, resulting in loss of vision.

retinene (*ret'-in-een*). The component of rhodopsin which can be converted into vitamin A in the light and resynthesized into rhodopsin in the dark, allowing maximum vision in a dim light.

retinitis (*ret-in-i'-tis*). Inflammation of the retina.

retinoblastoma (*ret-in-o-blasto'-mah*). A malignant growth of nerve cells of the retina that have failed to develop normally. It is congenital and may affect several members of one family.

retinopathy (*ret-in-op'-ath-e*). Degenerative changes occurring in the retinal blood vessels leading to loss of vision. *Diabetic r.* A complication occurring in diabetes.

retinotoxic (*ret-in-o-toks'-ik*). Drugs which may result in damage to the retina in susceptible persons.

retractile (*re-trak'-tile*). Capable of being drawn back.

retraction (*re-trak'-shun*). Drawing back. (1) The process of retraction of the uterus during labour to expel the fetus. (2) Drawing back of the ends of a cut blood vessel before a clot forms in the lumen. *R. ring.* A ridge sometimes felt above the pubes between the upper contracting part of the uterus and the lower dilatable part.

retractor (*re-trak'-tor*). A surgical instrument for drawing apart the edges of a wound to allow the deeper structures to be more accessible.

retro- (*ret'-ro*). A prefix meaning 'backward'.

retrobulbar neuritis (*ret-ro-bul'-bar nu-ri'-tis*). Dimness of vision due to inflammation of the optic nerve. This may be temporary or permanent in some cases of disseminated sclerosis.

retroflexion (*ret-ro-flek'-shun*). Bent backward; applied to the uterus when it is bent backward at an acute angle, the cervix being in its normal position.

retrograde (*ret'-ro-grade*). Going backwards. *R. pyelography.* X-ray of the kidney by injecting an opaque substance into the renal pelvis via the urethra and ureteric catheters.

retrogression (*ret-ro-gres'-shun*). Going backwards. Reverting to primitive type.

retrolental fibroplasia (*ret-ro-len'-tal fi-bro-pla'-ze-ah*). A fibrous condition of the anterior vitreous body which develops when a premature infant is kept in too high an oxygen saturation for too long. Both eyes are affected and it may cause blindness.

retro-ocular (*ret-ro-ok'-u-lar*). Behind the eyeball.

retroperitoneal (*ret-ro-per-it-o-ne'-al*). Behind the peritoneum.

retropharyngeal abscess (*ret-ro-far-in-je'-al*). One between the pharynx and the spine. It may occur in caries of the cervical vertebrae, or in glandular affections.

retropubic (*ret-ro-pu'-bik*). Behind the pubic bone.

retrospection (*ret-ro-spek'-shun*). Morbid dwelling on memories.

retrosternal (*ret-ro-ster'-nal*). Behind the sternum.

retroversion (*ret-ro-ver'-shun*). A turning back; applied to the uterus when the whole organ is tilted backward. *See also* Retroflexion.

Reverdin's graft (*rev'-er-din*).

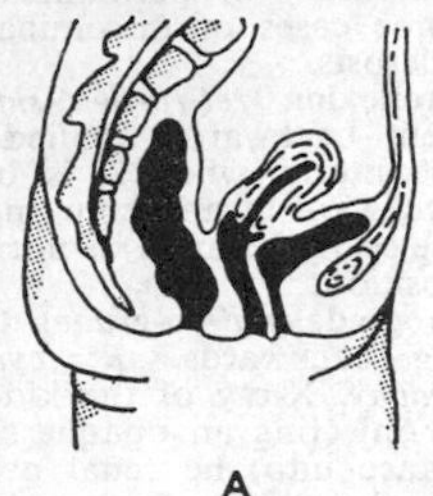

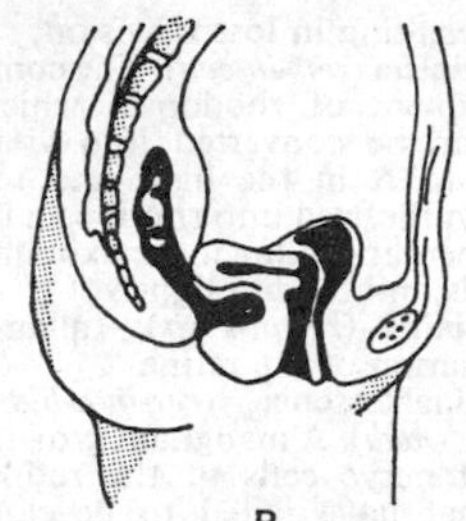

RETROVERSION OF UTERUS

A. Normal position.
B. Acute retroversion.

A form of skin graft in which pieces of skin are placed as islands over the area. *See also* Thiersch's graft.

rhabdomyosarcoma (*rab-do-mi-o-sar-ko'-mah*). A rare malignant growth of skeletal muscle. It grows rapidly and metastasizes early.

rhagades (*rag'-ad-ez*). Cracks or fissures in the skin.

rheostat (*re'-o-stat*). An instrument for regulating the force of resistance against an electric current.

rhesus factor (*re'-sus fak'-tor*). Rh factor. The red blood cells of most humans contain the rhesus factor. Those that do not are said to be rhesus-negative. This is of importance as a probable cause of anaemia and jaundice in the newly born when the infant is rhesus-positive and the mother rhesus-negative. The result of this incompatibility is the formation of an antibody which causes excessive haemolysis in the child's blood. Treatment is by blood transfusion, but not with the mother's blood. *See* Anti-rhesus serum.

rheum (*room*). Any watery discharge.

rheumatic (*ru-mat'-ik*). Relating to rheumatism. *R. fever*. *See* Rheumatism. *R. gout*. The same as rheumatoid arthritis. *R. nodules*. Specific lesions of acute rheumatism appearing as small fibrous swellings under the skin, especially over bony ridges, e.g. elbow, spine, occiput, etc. Their presence is a strong indication of active endocarditis.

rheumatism (*ru'-mat-izm*). (1) *Acute r.* or *rheumatic fever*. An acute fever associated with previous streptococcal infection and occurring most commonly in children. The onset is usually sudden with pain, swelling, and stiffness in one or more joints. There is fever, sweating, and tachycardia, and carditis is present in most cases. Recurrences are likely and this disease is the commonest cause of mitral stenosis in later life as scar tissue results from the inflammation. In a subacute attack there may be no fever but fatigue, malaise, and loss of weight. (2) The term may be loosely applied to any pain of unknown cause in the joints or muscles.

rheumatoid (*ru'-mat-oid*). Resembling rheumatism. *R. arthritis. See under* Arthritis.

rheumatology (*ru-mat-ol'-o-je*). The study of rheumatic disease.

rh factor. *See* Rhesus factor.

rhinitis (*ri-ni'-tis*). Inflammation of the mucous membrane of the nose. *Allergic r.* Hay fever. *Atrophic r.* Ozaena. A degenerative condition of the nasal mucous membrane and inferior turbinate bones.

rhino- (*ri'-no-*). A prefix meaning 'nose'.

rhinoplasty (*ri'-no-plas-te*). Plastic operation on the nose; repairing a part or forming an entirely new nose.

rhinorrhoea (*ri-nor-re'-ah*). Nasal discharge.

rhinoscope (*ri'-no-skope*). A speculum used to examine nasal cavities.

rhinoscopy (*ri-nos'-kop-e*). Examination of the nose anteriorly by means of a head mirror and speculum. *Posterior r.* Examination of the nasopharynx by means of a post-nasal mirror.

rhinoviruses (*ri-no-vi'-rus-ez*). One of several groups of viruses that can cause the common cold.

rhizodontropy (*ri-zo-don'-tro-pe*). Fixing an artificial crown on to a natural tooth root.

rhizoid (*ri'-zoid*). Like a root.

rhizotomy (*ri-zot'-o-me*). Division of a spinal nerve root for the relief of pain.

rhodopsin (*rod-op'-sin*). The visual purple of the retina, the formation of which is dependent upon vitamin A in the diet.

rhonchus (*rong'-kus*). A wheezing sound produced in the bronchial tubes and heard on auscultation.

rhubarb (*ru'-barb*). The root of the rheum plant. In small doses it is highly stimulative to the stomach and liver, in large ones it acts as a purgative.

rhythm (*rithm*). A regular recurring action. *Cardiac r.* The smooth action of the heart when systole is followed by diastole.

riboflavine (*rib-o-flav'-in*). A chemical factor in vitamin B complex. *See* Appendix 10.

ribonuclease (*ri-bo-nu'-kle-aze*). An enzyme from the pancreas which is responsible for the breakdown of nucleic acid.

ribonucleic acid (*ri-bo-nu'-kle-ik*). RNA. A complex chemical found in the cytoplasm of animal cells and thought to be concerned with protein synthesis.

ribs. The twelve pairs of long, flat curved bones of the thorax, each united by cartilage to the spinal vertebrae at the back, and to the sternum in front. *Cervical r.* Elongation of the cervical processes towards the front of the chest. Pressure of this may cause impairment of nerve or vascular function. *See* Scalenus syndrome. *False r.* The last five pairs, the upper three of which are attached by cartilage to each other. *Floating r.* The last two pairs connected only to the vertebra. *True r.* The seven pairs attached directly to the sternum.

Richter's hernia (*rikh'-ter*). One in which only a portion of the circumference of the intestine is contained within the hernial sac.

rickets (*rik'-ets*). A deficiency disease of young children from 6 months to 2 years of age. It is caused by a lack of vitamin D which results in a failure of calcium and phosphorus absorption from the diet. This leads to softening and irregular growth of the bones resulting in deformity, such as bowing of the long bones and enlargement of the epiphyses. The disease is preventable, and can be treated by giving adequate vitamin D (*see* Appendix 10) and by exposure to sunlight or ultraviolet light.

Rickettsia (*rik-et'-se-ah*). A group of micro-organisms which are parasitic in lice and similar insects. The bite of the host is thus the means of transmitting the organism, some of which are disease producing. *R. prowazeki*. Inhabits the digestive tract of lice and is the cause of epidemic typhus fever. *R. tsutsugamushi*. The cause of scrub typhus.

rigor (*ri'-gor*). An attack of intense shivering occurring when the heat regulation is disturbed. The temperature rises rapidly and may either stay elevated or fall rapidly as profuse sweating occurs. *R. mortis* is a name given to the stiffening of the body, occurring soon after death owing to coagulation of the muscle plasma. It begins in the muscles of the neck and jaw, then proceeds to those of the chest and upper extremities, finally reaching those of the lower limbs. The time of its appearance varies (1 to 24 hr after death) and its duration may be from a few minutes to several days.

rima (*ri'-mah*). A narrow fissure or crack. *R. glottidis*. The chink between the vocal cords.

Ringer's solution. A physiological solution of salt to which small amounts of calcium and potassium salts have been added.

ringworm. A contagious skin disease, characterized by circular patches, pinkish in colour, with a desquamating surface, and due to a parasitic fungus. When affecting the scalp it is called *tinea capitis* or *tinea tonsurans*. *See* Tinea.

Rinne's test (*rin'-e*). For hearing, in which the degree of conductivity through bone is tested, by holding a vibrating tuning fork alternately in front of the ear and over the mastoid bone.

risus sardonicus (*ri'-sus sar-don'-ik-us*). A peculiar grin caused by muscle spasm around the mouth, seen in tetanus and strychnine poisoning.

RNA. Ribonucleic acid (*q.v.*).

rocking. A repetitive action the child of 10 months starts when in its cot. It may only last a few weeks but may become habitual and be difficult to stop.

rodent ulcer (*ro'-dent*). *See under* Ulcer.

rods. Receptor end-organs in the retina that are sensitive to light and responsible for night vision.

Romberg's sign (*rom'-berg*).

Inability to stand erect without swaying if the eyes are closed. A sign of tabes dorsalis.

Röntgen (*ront'-gen*). A unit of measure for X and gamma radiation but it is a measure of exposure to the beam. For dosage received, *see* Rad.

Rorschach test. An intelligence test that consists of ten ink blot designs, some in colours and some in black and white. The patient is asked to look at the cards and tell what he sees. This test also measures some aspects of personality.

rosacea (*ro-za'-se-ah*). *See* Acne rosacea.

rose bengal (*rose ben'-gal*). A staining agent used in the eye to detect mucous threads in kerato-conjunctivitis.

roseola (*ro-ze-o'-lah*). A rose-coloured rash.

Rose-Waaler test. Performed on the blood serum of a patient to aid in the diagnosis of rheumatoid arthritis.

rotator (*ro-ta'-tor*). A muscle which causes rotation of any part.

Roth spots. Small white spots in the retina which may be surrounded by haemorrhages. Seen in bacterial endocarditis.

Rothera's test (*roth'-er-ah*). One for the presence of acetone bodies in urine. *See* Appendix 11.

roughage (*ruf'-faj*). Coarse vegetable fibres and cellulose that give bulk to the diet and stimulate peristalsis.

round ligament. *See under* Ligament.

roundworm. *See* Ascaris.

Rovsing's sign (*ro'-v-sing*). A test for acute appendicitis in which pressure in the left iliac fossa causes pain in the right iliac fossa.

RPCF. *See* Reiter.

rubefacient (*ru-be-fa'-shent*). An agent causing redness of the skin.

rubella (*ru-bel'-lah*). German measles. A mild contagious disease of short duration in which there is slight pyrexia, enlarged cervical lymph glands and a rash. The greatest risk from this disease is to the offspring of mothers who contract it during the early weeks of pregnancy. The child may be born blind, a deaf mute, or have other congenital defects.

rugae (*ru'-ge*). Ridges or creases, e.g. of the mucosa of the stomach.

rumination (*ru-min-a'-shun*).

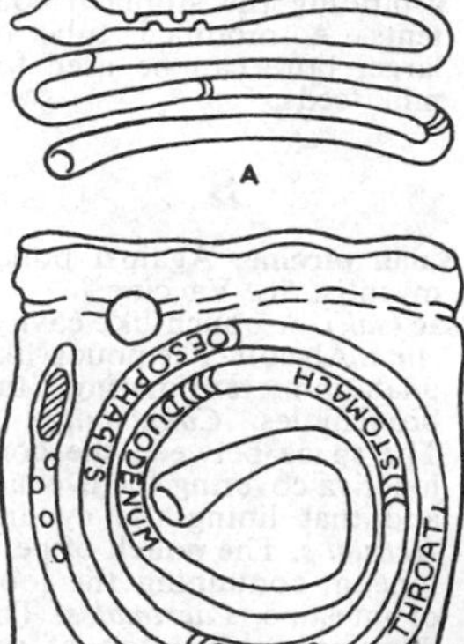

RYLE'S TUBE

A. Original (rubber) pattern.

B. Plastic tube sterilized by gamma radiation.

Recurring thoughts. *Obsessional r.* Thoughts which persistently recur against the patient's will and from which he cannot rid himself.

rupture (*rup'-chur*). (1) Tearing or bursting of a part, as in rupture of an aneurysm; of the membranes during labour; or of a tubal pregnancy. (2) A term commonly applied to hernia.

Russell traction. A form of extension by use of skin traction and sling supports without the use of a splint. Suitable for some cases of fractured femur. *See* Traction.

Ryle's tube. A thin, weighted rubber or plastic tube used for giving a test meal or for aspirating the stomach contents. A modified tube of larger bore can be used for milk feeds.

S

Sabin vaccine. Against poliomyelitis. *See* Vaccine.

sac (*sak*). A pouch-like cavity. *Air s.* Alveoli. The pouch-like dilatation terminating the bronchioles. *Conjunctival s.* The space between the conjunctiva covering the eyeball, and that lining the eye-lid. *Hernial s.* The pouch of peritoneum containing the loop of intestine. *Lacrimal s.* The dilatation at the top of the lacrimal duct.

saccharides (*sak'-ar-ides*). A series of carbohydrates, including the sugars.

saccharin (*sak'-ar-in*). Gluside. A crystalline substance used as a substitute for sugar.

Saccharomyces (*sak-ar-o-mi'-sez*). A genus of fungi, of which yeast is an example.

sacculated (*sak'-u-la-ted*). Divided into small sacs.

sacral (*sa'-kral*). Relating to the sacrum.

sacro-iliac (*sa-kro-il'-e-ak*). Relating to the sacrum and the ilium.

sacrum (*sa'-krum*). A triangular bone composed of five united vertebrae, situated between the lowest lumbar vertebra and the coccyx. It forms the back of the pelvis.

saddle-nose. Flattening of the bridge of the nose, which may occur in congenital syphilis from infection of the nasal bones.

sadism (*sa'-dizm*). A form of sexual perversion in which the individual takes pleasure in inflicting mental and physical pain.

sagittal (*saj-it'-tal*). Arrow-shaped. *S. suture.* The junction of the parietal bones.

St Anthony's fire. A term applied to erysipelas (*q.v.*) or to gangrene resulting from ergotism.

St Vitus's dance. Chorea (*q.v.*).

sal. Salt. *S. volatile.* Aromatic ammonium carbonate. Diluted with water it may be given in cases of syncope.

salicylate (*sal-is'-il-ate*). A salt of salicylic acid. *Methyl s.* is the active ingredient in ointments and lotions for joint pains and sprains. *Sodium s.* is the specific drug used for rheumatic fever. It reduces the pyrexia and relieves the pain but does not prevent cardiac complications. Where there is intolerance aspirin or calcium aspirin may be substituted.

saline (*sa'-line*). (1) A solution of sodium chloride and water. *Hypertonic s.* A stronger than normal strength. *Hypotonic s.* A weaker than normal, usually $\frac{1}{5}$ strength is used. *Normal* or *physiological s.* An 0·9 per cent solution which is isotonic with blood. *See* Appendix 2. (2) Salts of alkalis which are aperient, owing to their hygroscopic action, e.g. magnesium sulphate.

saliva (*sal-i'-vah*). The secretion of the salivary glands which is poured into the mouth when food is taken. It moistens and dissolves certain substances, and partially digests carbohydrates by the action of its enzyme, *ptyalin.*

salivary (*sal'-iv-ar-e*). Relating to saliva. *S. glands.* The parotid, submaxillary and sublingual glands. *S. calculus.* A stony concretion in a salivary duct. *S. fistula.* An unnatural opening into a salivary duct or gland.

salivation (*sal-iv-a'-shun*). Ptyalism, an excessive flow of saliva. A symptom of overdose of mercury.

Salk vaccine. *See* Vaccine.

Salmonella (*sal-mon-el'-lah*). A genus of bacteria that are parasites of the intestinal tract of man and animals. *S. typhi and S. paratyphi.* Are exclusively human pathogens which cause typhoid and paratyphoid fevers (*q.v.*). Other strains, e.g *S. typhimurium* can give rise to acute gastro-enteritis (food poisoning).

salmonellosis (*sal-mon-el-lo'-sis*). Infection with salmonellae, especially paratyphoid fever and food poisoning; caused by the ingestion of food containing the organisms or their products.

salpingectomy (*sal-pin-jek'-to-me*). Excision of one or both of the Fallopian tubes.

salpingemphraxis (*sal-pin-jem-fraks'-is*). Closure of a Fallopian tube.

salpingitis (*sal-pin-ji'-tis*). (1) Inflammation of the Fallopian tubes. *Acute s.* Most often a bilateral ascending infection due to the streptococcus or gonococcus. One tube may be infected from adjacent structure like the appendix. *Chronic s.* A less acute form that may be blood borne and may be due to the tubercle bacillus. (2) Inflammation of the pharyngotympanic (Eustachian) tube.

salpingography (*sal-pin-gog'-raf-e*). Radiography of Fallopian tubes after injection of a radio-opaque substance to determine their patency.

salpingo-oophorectomy (*sal-pin'-go-o-off-or-ek'-to-me*). Removal of a Fallopian tube and ovary.

salpingostomy (*sal-pin-gos'-to-me*). Making a surgical opening in the tube near the uterus to restore patency.

salpinx (*sal'-pinks*). A tube—applied to the Fallopian or pharyngotympanic (Eustachian) tubes.

salt. (1) Sodium chloride, common salt, used in solution as a cleansing lotion, a stimulating bath, or for fusion into the blood, etc. (2) Any compound of an acid with an alkali or base. (3) A saline purgative such as Epsom salts. *Smelling s.* Aromatic ammonium carbonate. A restorative in fainting.

salt depletion (*salt de-ple'-shun*). A loss of salt from the body without water depletion. Only likely to arise where there is profuse sweating and replacement by water only.

salve (*salv*). An ointment.

sanatorium (*san-at-or′-e-um*). A building used for restoring to health, usually used for the treatment of long term illness like tuberculosis.

sandfly fever. A fever transmitted by the bites of sandflies, and common in Mediterranean countries. Similar to *dengue* (*q.v.*) and sometimes known as *three-day fever*.

sanguineous (*san-gwin′-e-us*). Pertaining to or containing blood.

sanguis (*san′-gwis*). The blood.

sanies (*sa′-ne-eez*). A fetid discharge from a wound consisting of serum, pus and blood.

sanitary (*san′-it-ar-e*). Relating to or promoting health.

Santé manner (*san-ta′*). Rocking or rolling the patient from side to side to help free the bronchi from blockage.

saphena (*saf-e′-nah*). Several veins, chiefly superficial, that carry blood from the toes upwards.

saphenous (*saf-e′-nus*). Relating to the saphena.

sapo (*sap′-o*). Soap.

saponaceous (*sap-on-a′-she-us*). Soapy; having the nature of soap.

saponify (*sap-on′-if-i*). To make into soap by combining a fat and an alkali.

sapraemia (*sap-re′-me-ah*). Similar to toxaemia. The toxins are produced by saphrophytes and circulate in the blood.

sapro- (*sap′-ro*). A prefix signifying putrefaction.

saprophyte (*sap′-ro-fite*). An organism bred in and living on putrefying matter.

sarco- (*sar′-ko-*). A prefix denoting 'flesh'.

sarcocele (*sar′-ko-seel*). A tumour of the testicle.

sarcoidosis (*sar-koi-do′-sis*). A rare disease in some ways similar to tuberculosis. It chiefly affects the skin, the lymphatic glands and the lungs.

sarcolemma (*sar-ko-lem′-mah*). A delicate membrane enveloping each striated muscle fibre.

sarcoma (*sar-ko′-mah*). A malignant tumour developed from connective tissue cells, and their stroma. The cells may be round, spindle-shaped, or large like those of bone marrow. *Chondrosarcoma.* One arising in cartilage. *Fibrosarcoma.* One containing much fibrous tissue; this may arise in the fibrous sheath of a muscle. *Melanotic s.* A very malignant type, pigmented with melanin. *Round-celled s.* A very malignant growth, composed of a primitive type of cell. *See also* Carcinoma.

sarcomatosis (*sar-ko-ma-to′-sis*). Multiple sarcomatous growths in various parts of the body.

Sarcoptes (*sar-kop′-tes*). A class of acarids. *S. scabiei.* The cause of scabies (*q.v.*).

sardonic grin. *See* Risus sardonicus.

sartorius (*sar-tor′-e-us*). A long muscle of the thigh, which flexes the leg and bends it inwards.

saturated solution (*sat′-u-rated*). A liquid containing the largest amount of a solid which can be dissolved in it without forming a precipitate.

Sayre's jacket (*sa-er*). A jacket

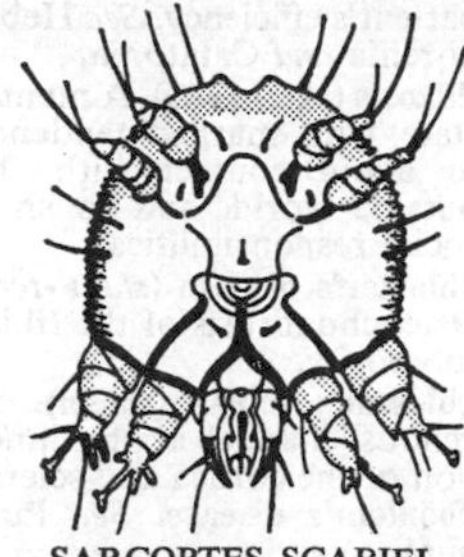

SARCOPTES SCABIEI

made of plaster of Paris used to support the back in cases of spinal caries. *S. sling*. A suspension apparatus for the head, for the correction of torticollis.

scab. The crust on a superficial wound consisting of dried lymph, etc. *See also* Scale.

scabies (*ska'-beez*). 'The itch'. A contagious skin disease caused by the itch mite (*Sarcoptes scabiei*), the female of which burrows beneath the skin and deposits eggs at intervals. It is intensely irritating, and the rash is aggravated by scratching. The sites affected are chiefly between the fingers and toes, the axillae, and groins. It is treated with benzyl benzoate emulsion.

scald (*skawld*). A burn caused by hot liquid or vapour.

scale. Compact layers of epithelial tissue shed from the skin.

scalenus syndrome (*skal-e'-nus sin'-drome*). Symptoms of pain and tenderness in the shoulder, with sensory loss and wasting of the medial aspect of the arm. It may be caused by pressure on the brachial plexus by spasm of the scalenus anticus muscle or by a cervical rib.

scalp (*skalp*). The hairy skin which covers the cranium.

scalpel (*skal'-pel*). A small pointed surgical knife.

scanning speech (*skan'-ing*). The syllables are separated from each other. A speech disorder that may be present in cerebellar disease.

scaphoid (*skaf'-oid*). Boat-shaped. A term applied to the sunken abdomen seen in cases of meningitis and severe emaciation. *S. bone*. A boat-shaped bone of the carpus and the tarsus.

scapula (*skap'-u-lah*). The large flat triangular bone forming the shoulder-blade.

scar. The fibrous tissue by which a wound heals. *Contracted s.* results if much tissue has been lost, e.g. in a burn. *Keloid s.* An overgrowth of scar tissue. *See* Keloid.

scarfskin. The epidermis.

scarlet fever (*skar'-let*). Scarlatina. An acute infectious disease which of latter years has much decreased in severity. It is caused by a haemolytic streptococcus. There is sore throat, high fever, and a punctate rash. Now it is readily treated by penicillin or the sulpha drugs, and the complications of nephritis and middle ear infection are less common.

Scarpa's triangle (*skar'-pah*). The triangular area on the inner side of the thigh, bounded above by Poupart's ligament, and on one side by the sartorius and on the other the adductor longus muscle. The femoral artery and vein, with nerves of the thigh, are superficial in this position.

schematic eye (*ske'-mat-ik*). A model of an eye that enables a student to practise examination of the retina and fundus by an ophthalmoscope (*q.v.*).

Schick test (*shik*). To test susceptibility to diphtheria. *See under* Test.

Schilling test. One used to confirm the diagnosis of pernicious anaemia by estimating the absorption of ingested radioactive vitamin B_{12}.

Schistosoma (*skis-to-so'-mah*). A genus of minute leaf-shaped worms or flukes, some of which are parasitic in man.

schistosomiasis (*skis-to-so-mi'-as-is*). A parasitic infection of the intestinal or urinary tract, common in Egypt. The parasite enters the skin from contaminated water, and causes diarrhoea, haematuria, and anaemia. The treatment is by the administration of antimony or lucanthone. Bilharziasis.

Schizomycetes (*skiz-o-mi-se'-tes*). A class of minute vegetable organisms that reproduce themselves by fission; bacteria and yeasts are of this type.

schizophrenia (*skiz-o-fre'-ne-ah*). A psychosis of unknown cause but showing hereditary links. Characteristically the patient feels himself to be influenced in a strange way by external forces and suffers delusions and hallucinations; his thought processes are disordered. *Paranoid s.* Shows predominance of delusions of a persecutory nature. *Simple s.* There is a progressive deterioration of the patient's efficiency. *See* Hebephrenia *and* Catatonia.

schizosis (*skiz-o'-sis*). A mental state with marked tendency to avoid contact with the outside world, and to shun social responsibilities.

Schlatter's disease (*shlat'-ter*). Osteochondrosis of the tibial tuberosity.

Schlemm's canal (*shlem*). A venous channel at the junction of the cornea and sclera.

Schönlein's disease. *See* Purpura.

Schonlein–Henoch syndrome. *See* Purpura.

Schultz-Charlton blanching test (*shults' charl'-ton*). By this an intradermal injection of scarlet fever antitoxin is made into an area of rash. An area of blanching will arise and persist if the patient has scarlet fever.

Schwartz's operation (*shvart'-ses*). Opening the mastoid cells, without involvement of the middle ear, in order to drain a mastoid abscess.

sciatic (*si-at'-ik*). Relating to the sciatic nerve which runs down the back of the thigh.

sciatica (*si-at'-ik-ah*). Pain down the back of the leg in the area supplied by the sciatic nerve. It may be owing to pressure on the nerve roots; by a protrusion of intervertebral disc; by a spinal tumour; by tuberculosis of the spine or by malignant disease of the pelvis.

scilla (*sil'-lah*). Squill, an extract from the root of a plant. In large doses it is irritant; in small ones expectorant and diuretic.

scintillography (*sin-til-og'-raf-e*). The method of examination by means of α-rays on a fluorescent screen.

scirrhous (*skir'-rus*). Hard; resembling a scirrhus.

scirrhus (*skir'-rus*). A hard cancer, containing much connective tissue.

scissor leg deformity. The legs are crossed in walking, as sometimes occurs in disease of both hip joints. *See also* Little's disease.

sclera (*skleer'-ah*). The fibrous coat of the eyeball—the white of the eye, which covers the posterior part and in front becomes the cornea.

scleritis (*skler-i'-tis*). Inflammation of the sclerotic coat.

scleroderma (*skler-o-der'-mah*). A disease marked by progressive hardening of the skin in patches or diffusely, with rigidity of the underlying tissues. It is often a chronic condition.

scleroma (*skler-o'-mah*). A patch of hardened tissue.

sclerosis (*skler-o'-sis*). The hardening of any part from an overgrowth of fibrous and connective tissue, often due to chronic inflammation. *Amyotrophic lateral s.* Rapid degeneration of the pyramidal (motor nerves) tract and anterior horn cells in the spinal cord. Characterized by weakness and spasm of limb muscles with wasting of the muscle, difficulty with talking and swallowing. *Arterio-s.* The changes occurring in walls of arteries which cause hardening and loss of elasticity. *Athero-s.* The deposition of fatty plaques and hardening and fibrosis of the artery lining. *Disseminated s. See* Multiple s. *Mönckeberg's s.* Extensive degeneration with atrophy and calcareous deposits in the middle muscle coat of arteries, expecially of the small ones. *Multiple s.* Scattered (disseminated) patches of degeneration in the nerve sheaths in the brain and spinal cord. Characterized by relapses and remissions. Symptoms include disturbances of speech, vision and micturition, and muscular weakness of a limb or limbs.

sclerotherapy (*skler-o-ther'-ap-e*). Treatment by the artificial production of fibrosis. *Compression s.* Permanent fibrous occlusion of incompetent perforating veins of the leg by inserting a sclerosing agent while the vein is compressed either side of the injection.

sclerotic (*skler-ot'-ik*). Hard. *S. coat.* The tough membrane forming the outer covering of the eyeball, excepting in front of the iris, where it becomes the clear horny cornea.

sclerotomy (*skler-ot'-o-me*). Incision of the sclerotic coat, usually for the relief of glaucoma.

scolex (*sko'-leks*). The head of a tapeworm.

scoliosis (*skol-e-o'-sis*). Abnormal curvature of the spine, but most commonly applied to a lateral deviation. *See* Lordosis *and* Kyphosis.

scopolamine (*sko-pol'-am-in*). Hyoscine (*q.v.*).

scorbutus (*skor-bu'-tus*). Scurvy (*q.v.*).

scotoma (*sko-to'-mah*). A blind area in the field of vision, due to some lesion of the retina.

scrotum (*skro'-tum*). The pouch of skin and soft tissues containing the testicles.

scurf (*skerf*). Dandruff (*q.v.*).

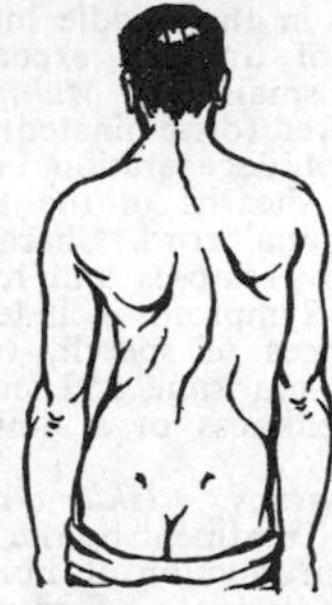
SCOLIOSIS

scurvy (*sker'-ve*). A deficiency disease due to incorrect diet, i.e. one lacking in raw fruits and vegetables and therefore in vitamin C. It rapidly improves with adequate diet. *Infantile s.* may occur in artificially fed infants as milk is a poor source of vitamin C. To prevent it such children should be given orange, tomato, or rose hip juice daily. *See* Appendix 10.

scybalum (*sib'-al-um*). A mass of abnormally hard faecal matter. *Pl.* Scybala.

sebaceous (*se-ba'-shus*). Fatty, or pertaining to the sebum. *S. glands* are found in the skin, communicating with the hair follicles and secreting sebum. *S. cyst. See under* Cyst.

seborrhoea (*se-bor-re'-ah*). A disease of the sebaceous glands, marked by an excessive secretion of sebum which collects on the skin in oily scales. It is usually associated with itching and burning.

sebum (*se'-bum*). The fatty secretion of the sebaceous glands.

secondary (*sek'-on-dar-e*). Second in order of time or importance. *S. disease. See under* Disease. *S. haemorrhage. See* Haemorrhage. *S. deposits. See* Metastases.

secretagogue (*se-kre'-ta-gog*). Any agent that stimulates the secretion of a gland.

secrete (*se-kreet'*). The action of cells in producing a new substance which either passes into the blood stream or by ducts to where it is required.

secretin (*se-kre'-tin*). The hormone originating in the duodenum which, in the presence of bile salts, is absorbed into the blood stream and stimulates the secretion of pancreatic juice.

secretin test (*se-kre'-tin*). A complicated test, both qualitative and quantitative carried out to estimate external pancreatic secretion.

secretions (*se-kre'-shuns*). Various substances separated from the blood by glands. They are: (a) used for special purposes in the body, as the digestive juices, or hormones made by endocrine glands, (b) excreted as urine and sweat.

section (*sek'-shun*). (1) The act of cutting. (2) A portion which has been cut through. *See* Caesarian. *Frozen s.* A thin slice that has been cut from frozen tissue for examination under a microscope.

sedative (*sed'-at-iv*). An agent which lessens excitement or functional activity.

sedentary (*sed'-en-ter-e*). Pertaining to sitting, physically inactive.

sedimentation (*sed-e-men-ta'-shun*). Deposition of solids in a fluid to form a sediment.

Erythrocyte s. rate (ESR). *See* Erythrocyte.

segment (*seg'-ment*). A small piece separated from any part by an actual or imaginary line.

segregation (*seg-re-ga'-shun*). Separation of a number of people from others, e.g. infectious patients in a fever hospital; or those mentally affected, tuberculous, etc., in special communities.

Seidlitz powder (*sed'-lits*). A saline purgative.

sella turcica (*sel-lah turs'-ik-ah*). The fossa in the sphenoid body which protects the pituitary gland.

semen (*se'-men*). The secretion of the testicles containing spermatozoa.

semi- (*sem'-e*). A prefix meaning 'half'.

semicircular canals (*sem-e-ser'-ku-lar*). Part of the labyrinth of the internal ear, consisting of three canals in the form of arches which contain fluid, and by their nerve supply are connected with the cerebellum. Impressions of change of position of the body are registered in these canals by oscillation of the fluid, and are conveyed by the nerves to the cerebellum—the balancing organ of the brain.

semicomatose (*sem-e-ko'-ma-tose*). A condition of unconsciousness from which one can be roused by painful stimuli.

semilunar (*sem-e-lu'-nar*). Shaped like a half-moon. *S. cartilages.* Two crescent-shaped cartilages in the knee-joint. *S. valves. See* Valve.

seminal (*sem'-in-al*). Relating to the semen. *S. vesicles. See* Vesicle.

seminoma (*se-me-no'-mah*). A malignant tumour of the testis.

semipermeable (*sem-e-per'-me-a-bl*). Used to describe a membrane that permits the passage of some substances in solution and hinders that of others.

semiprone (*sem-e-pro'-n*). Partly prone. *See Sims's p. under* Position.

senega (*sen'-e-gah*). An expectorant vegetable drug. In large doses it is emetic.

senescence (*sen-es'-ense*). The process of growing old.

Sengstaken tube (*sen'-stak-en*). An oesophageal compression tube for the treatment of bleeding oesophageal varices.

senile (*se'-nile*). Related to the involutional changes associated with old age. *S. delirium.* The patient is disorientated, restless and unable to sleep and often there are visual or auditory hallucinations. *S. dementia.* Deterioration of mental activity in the elderly associated with impaired blood supply to the brain.

senility (*sen-il'-it-e*). The condition of being senile.

senna (*sen'-nah*). A laxative derived from the cassia plant, given in the form of an infusion of the pods in water. Proprietary standardized preparations, e.g. Senokot, are available as tablets or granules.

sense. The power by which conditions and properties of things are perceived, e.g. hunger, or pain. *Special s.* Any one of the faculties of sight, hearing, touch, smell, taste, and muscle sense, through which the consciousness receives impressions from the external world. *S. organ.* One which receives a sensory stimulus.

sensible. Perceptible to the senses. *S. perspiration.* That obvious on the skin as moisture.

sensitive (*sens'-it-iv*). Reacting to a stimulus. *See also* Hypersensitive.

sensitization (*sen-si-ti-za'-shun*). Rendering susceptible. *Protein s.* The condition occurring in an individual when a foreign protein is absorbed into the body, e.g. shell fish causing urticaria when eaten. *See also* Desensitization.

sensitized. Rendered sensitive.

sensory (*sen'-sor-e*). Relating to sensation. *S. nerve.* A nerve conveying impressions from the periphery to the brain or spinal cord.

sentiment (*sen'-te-ment*). An organized system of tendencies directed towards some object or person. Sentiments are acquired and profoundly influence a person's actions.

sepsis (*sep'-sis*). Describes the condition of infection of the body by pus-forming bacteria. *Oral s.* Infection of the mouth which causes general ill-health by absorption of toxins. *Puerperal s.* That occurring during the puerperium. *See also* Asepsis.

septal (*sep'-tal*). Relating to a septum. *S. defect.* Usually refers to a congenital defect when there is either an opening between the two atria or two ventricles of the heart.

septic (*sep'-tik*). Relating to sepsis. (1) *S. wound.* One infected by pus-forming bacteria. (2) *S. tank.* One in which sewage is liquefied and purified by anaerobic organisms.

septicaemia (*sep-tis-e'-me-ah*). The presence in the blood of bacteria and their toxins. The symptoms are: a rapid rise of temperature, which is later intermittent, rigors, sweating, and all signs of acute fever. It is treated by antibiotic drugs which have to a great extent reduced the development of this condition.

septum (*sep'-tum*). A division or partition. (1) That between the right and left ventricles of the heart. (2) The structure made of bone and cartilage which separates the nasal cavities.

sequelae (*se-kwe'-le*). Morbid conditions following a disease and resulting from it.

sequestrectomy (*se-kwes-trek'-to-me*). The removal of a sequestrum.

sequestrum (*se-kwes'-trum*). *Pl.* Sequestra. A piece of dead bone. Inflammation in bone leads to pressure and thrombosis of blood vessels resulting in necrosis of the affected part, which separates from the living structure.

serological (*se-ro-loj'-ik-al*). Relating to serum. *S. tests.* Those that are dependent on the formation of antibodies in the blood as a response to specific organisms or proteins.

serology (*se-rol'-o-je*). The scientific study of sera, their actions and reactions. A branch of medicine particularly concerned with diagnosis and immunity.

serosa (*se-ro'-sah*). A serous membrane. It consists of two layers—the *visceral*, in close contact with the organ, and the *parietal*, lining the cavity. The serum exudes, and lubricates between the layers giving a smooth movement without friction.

serotonin (*ser-ro-ton'-in*). An amine present in blood platelets, the intestine and the brain. It is derived from the amino acid tryptophan and inactivated by monoamine oxidase.

serous (*se'-rus*). Related to serum. *S. effusion.* Increase of serous exudate. *S. inflammation.* Inflammation of a serous membrane. *See* Serosa.

serpiginous (*ser-pij'-in-us*). Creeping from one place to another.

serrated (*ser-a'-ted*). With saw-like edge.

serum (*se'-rum*). The clear, fluid residue of blood, from which the corpuscles and fibrin have been removed. *Antidiphtheritic s.* Contains antibodies to neutralize the toxins of diphtheria. *Antitetanic s.* That which contains antibodics to neutralize toxins of tetanus. *Antitoxic s.* One which contains the antibodies to some specific infection. *S. sickness.* An allergic reaction usually 8 to 10 days after a serum injection. It may be manifest by an irritating urticaria, pyrexia and painful joints. It readily responds to adrenaline and antihistaminic drugs. *See* Anaphylaxis. *S. therapy.* The treatment of infectious diseases by injection of antitoxic serum made by inoculation of animals (usually the horse) with the virus of the disease. It produces passive immunity (*q.v.*).

serum alkaline phosphatase. The level of this in the blood plasma is a measure of osteoblastic activity. It is raised in hyperparathyroidism.

sesamoid (*ses'-a-moid*). Resembling a sesame seed. *S. bone.* One roughly this shape and developed in a tendon, e.g. the patella and pisiform.

sessile tumour (*ses'-ile*). A tumour without a peduncle. *See* Tumour.

sex. The fundamental differences between men and women. Often taken to mean the emotions and pleasures associated with a relationship between the two.

sex chromatin (*seks kro'-ma-tin*). An extra bit of *c.* found in the nuclei of cells in women who possess two X chromosomes and not in men.

sex chromosomes (*seks kro'-mo-somes*). The chromosomes in the human cell that decide the sex. Women have two X *c.* and men one X and one Y *c.*

sex-linked (*seks linkt'*). Transmitted by genes that are located on the sex chromosomes, e.g. haemophilia.

SGOT. Serum glutamic oxalacetic transaminase, an enzyme excreted by damaged heart muscle. A raised serum level occurs in cardiac infarction.

SGPT. Serum glutamic pyruvic transaminase. An enzyme excreted by the parenchymal cells of the liver. There is a raised blood level in infectious hepatitis.

shelf operation. A type of arthroplasty in which the acetabulum is deepened by splitting the ilium and drawing the split portion down.

Shigella (*she-gel'-ah*). A genus of bacilli containing a number of species that cause dysentery. *S. sonnei*. Commonest in the West. *S. flexneri* and *S. shigae*. Common in the East.

shingles (*shing'-gls*). Herpes zoster (*q.v.*).

Shirodkar's operation (*Shirod'-kars*). A suture is placed round an incompetent cervix during pregnancy to prevent abortion. It is removed at the thirty-eighth week.

shock. A condition in which there is a sudden fall in blood pressure; this, untreated, will lead to lack of oxygen in the tissues and greater permeability of the capillary walls, so increasing the degree of shock, by greater loss of fluid. *Primary s.*, *neurogenic s.* or *vasovagal s.* Arises at the time from pain, fear or unpleasant sight as in a faint. *Hypovolaemic state*. A state of shock in which there is loss of fluid from circulation as in haemorrhage or burns. *Normovolaemic s.* Shock arising when there is no reduction in blood volume, as in coronary thrombosis. *Anaphylactic s.* The severe reaction produced by the injection of a protein to which the person is sensitive. *Electric s.* Caused by the passage of an electric current through the body. *See* Appendix 1. *Protein s.* A little-used method of producing a severe reaction with fever by introducing a foreign protein, e.g. boiled milk.

short-circuit. A term applied to intestinal anastomosis.

short sight. Myopia (*q.v.*).

'show'. A term used to denote the blood-stained discharge at the onset of labour.

shunt. Bypassing the normal channel. It may be a congenital defect as between the two atria in the heart or a surgical anastomosis such as joining the portal vein to the inferior vena cava in treating portal hypertension.

sialogogue (*si-al'-o-gog*). A drug increasing the flow of saliva.

sialogram (*si-al'-o-gram*). An X-ray of the salivary ducts following the insertion of a radio-opaque dye.

sialolith (*si-al'-o-lith*). A salivary calculus.

sibilus (*sib'-il-us*). A high-pitched sound heard on auscultation.

sibling (*sib'-ling*). One of a family of children having the same parents. Applied in psychology to one of two or more children of the same parent or substitute parent figure. *S. rivalry*. Jealousy, compounded of love and hate of one child for its sibling.

sick headache. Migraine (*q.v.*).

sickle-cell anaemia (*sik'-l-sell an-e'-me-ah*). An inherited disease of Negro races in which the red blood cells are cresent-shaped and very friable.

siderosis (*sid-er-o'-sis*). Chronic inflammation of the lung due to inhalation of particles of iron.

sigmoid (*sig'-moid*). Shaped like the Greek letter Σ. *S. flexure*. That part of the colon in the left iliac fossa just above the rectum.

sigmoidoscope (*sig-moid'-o-skope*). An instrument, by which the interior of the rectum and sigmoid flexure can be seen.

sigmoidostomy (*sig-moid-os'-to-me*). An artificial opening into the sigmoid flexure.

sign. The presence of disease that can be seen or elicited.

silicones (*sil'-ik-cones*). A group of organic compounds which have silica as part of their molecule and when used on the skin, on glass, or on metals, are repellent to water.

silicosis (*sil-ik-o'-sis*). A fibrosis of lung due to the inhalation of silica dust particles. It occurs in miners, stone masons and quarry workers and is often complicated by tuberculosis.

silk ligature. Thread silk used for deep sutures. Non-absorbable.

silver nitrate (*ni'-trate*). $AgNO_3$. A crystalline salt. In solid form it is used as a caustic for reducing excessive granulation tissue. In solution it is antiseptic and astringent.

Simmond's disease. A condition of anterior pituitary deficiency, causing arrest of growth and premature senility.

Sim's position. *See under* Position.

sinapis (*sin-a'-pis*). Mustard.

sinew (*sin'-u*). A tendon.

sino-atrial node (*si'-no a'-tre-al*). *See under* Node.

sinogram (*si'-no-gram*). Outlining the extent of a sinus by means of a radio-opaque dye.

sinus (*si'-nus*). (1) A cavity in a bone. (2) A venous channel, especially within the cranium. (3) An unhealed passage leading from an abscess or internal lesion to the surface. *Air s.* A cavity in a bone containing air. *Cavernous s.* A venous sinus which lies along the body of the sphenoid bone. *Coronary s.* The vein which returns the blood from the heart muscle into the right atrium. *Ethnoid s.* Air spaces in the ethmoid bone. *Frontal s.* Air spaces in the frontal bone. *Sphenoid s.* Air spaces in the sphenoid bone. *S. arrhythmia. See* Arrhythmia. *S. thrombosis.* Clotting of blood in a cranial venous channel. In the lateral sinus it is a complication of mastoiditis.

sinusitis (*si-nu-si'-tis*). Inflammation of a sinus, especially applied to the bony cavities of the face.

sinusoid (*si'-nu-soid*). Like a sinus. Used to describe the irregular channels by which blood vessels anastomose in certain organs, as the liver, suprarenal glands, heart, etc.

siphonage (*si'-fon-aj*). A method of drawing a liquid from one vessel into another.

sitz-bath (*sits*). A hip bath.

skatole (*ska'-tol*). A product of protein decomposition in the intestine.

skeleton (*skel'-e-ton*). The bony framework of the body, supporting and protecting the organs and soft tissues.

skiagram (*ski'-a-gram*). An X-ray photograph.

skiagraphy (*ski-ag'-raf-e*). Photography by X-rays.

skin. The outer protective covering of the body. It consists of the *epidermis* or cuticle, and the *dermis* or corium, which is known as 'true skin'. The skin and nervous system are developed from the same primitive layer of cells in the embryo, and keep this deep-rooted relation through life, as is often seen in disease. *Scarf s.* The cuticle. *S. grafting.* Transplantation of pieces of healthy skin to an area where loss of surface tissue has occurred.

skull. The bony framework of the head, consisting of the cranium and facial bones.

sleeping sickness. Trypanosomiasis. A tropical fever occurring in parts of Africa, caused by a protozoal parasite (Trypanosoma) which is conveyed by the tsetse fly.

sling. A bandage for support of the upper limb.

slit lamp. A special light source so arranged with a microscope that examination of the eyelids and eye can be carried out at the level of each layer. Such an examination is also termed biomicroscopy.

slough (*sluf*). Local death of soft tissues due to injury or thrombosis in small veins of the part. It is ultimately washed away by exuded serum, leaving a granulating surface.

smallpox. *See* Variola.

smear. A specimen for microscopic examination that has been prepared by spreading a thin film of the material across a glass slide.

smegma (*smeg'-mah*). The secretion of sebaceous glands of the clitoris and prepuce.

Smith-Petersen nail. A metal nail used to fix the fragments of bone in intracapsular fracture of the head of the femur.

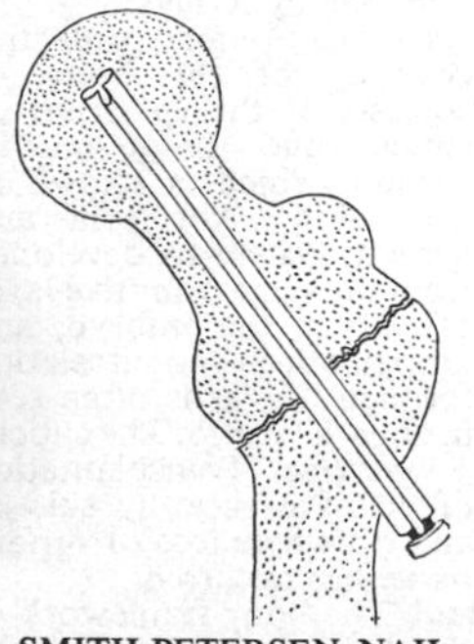

SMITH-PETERSEN NAIL

snake venom antitoxin (*ven'-om*). Made from a horse serum, it is specific against cobra bites but may be given in all cases of snake bite since individual antitoxins are not available.

Snellen's test types (*snel'-len*). Square-shaped letters on a chart, used for sight testing.

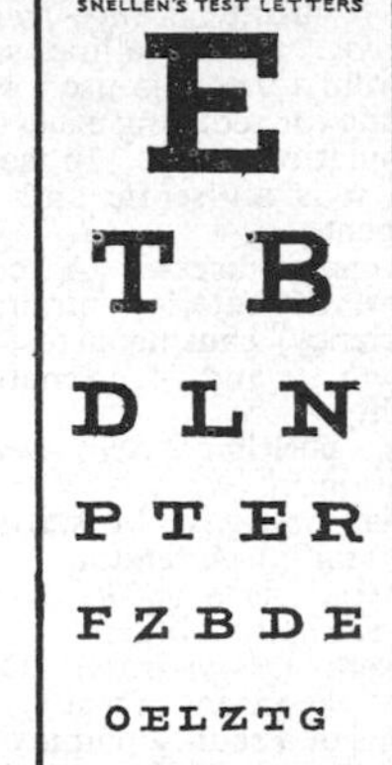

SNELLEN'S TEST TYPES

snow. Frozen water vapour. *Carbon dioxide s.* Solidified frozen carbon dioxide, used in the treatment of warts and naevi.

snow blindness. Photophobia due to the glare of snow.

snuffles (*snuf'-fls*). A chronic discharge from the nose occurring in congenital syphilis, due to infection of the nasal mucous membrane.

sociology (*so-si-ol'-o-je*). The scientific study of the development of man's social relationships and organization, i.e. interpersonal and intergroup behaviour as distinct from the behaviour of an individual.

sodium (*so'-de-um*). A metallic alkaline element widely distributed in nature, and forming an important constituent of animal tissues. *S. aminosalicylate*. An antituberculous drug used in conjunction with streptomycin and isoniazid (*q.v.*). *S. bicarbonate* is an antacid but its use is inadvisable as it stimulates the gastric mucosa and later increases acidity. Repeated use can cause alkalosis. *S. chloride* (common salt) is widely used for the cleansing of wounds, irrigation of body cavities and for intravenous therapy. *S. citrate* is used to prevent clotting of blood during blood transfusions. *S. morrhuate*. Used for injection in the treatment of varicose veins to sclerose the veins. *S. phosphate* and *S. sulphate* are purgatives.

soft chancre (*shan'-ker*). *See* Chancroid.

soft soap. A mixture of oil and potash.

solapsone (*sol-ap'-zone*). A sulphone drug used in the treatment of leprosy.

solar plexus (*so'-lar pleks'-us*). A network of sympathetic nerve ganglia in the abdomen; the nerve supply to abdominal organs under the diaphragm.

solarium (*sol-ar'-e-um*). A room designed to admit as much sunlight as possible.

solution (*so-lu'-shun*). (1) A liquid in which a substance has been dissolved. (2) A break in continuity, e.g. a fracture.

solvent (*sol'-vent*). A liquid which dissolves, or has power to dissolve.

somatic (*so-mat'-ik*). Relating to the body as opposed to the mind.

somnambulism (*som-nam'-bu-lizm*). Walking and carrying out other complex activities during a state of sleep. It is a state of dissociation and may occur in hysteria, in epilepsy and in a condition of low blood sugar.

sonograph (*so'-no-graf*). A tracing of sounds heard by use of a sonometer (*q.v.*).

sonometer (*so-nom'-e-ter*). An instrument for measuring the acuity of hearing or the frequency and pitch of sound waves.

Sonne dysentery (*son'-ne*). *See under* Dysentery.

sopor (*so'-por*). Profound sleep.

soporific (*sop-or-if'-ik*). Causing sleep.

sorbitol (*sor'-bit-ol*). A sweetening agent which is converted into sugar in the body though it is slowly absorbed from the intestine. It is used in some diabetic foods but as it has the same calorific value as sugar it should not be used in reducing diets.

sorbo (*sor'-bo*). A foam or aerated rubber used for the manufacture of air rings mattresses, and pillows.

sordes (*sor'-dez*). Brown crusts which form on the teeth and lips of unconscious patients, or those suffering from acute or prolonged fevers. The result of neglect of mouth hygiene.

sore. A general term for any ulcer or open skin lesion. *Cold s.* Herpes (*q.v.*). *Pressure s.* One due to impaired blood supply due to pressure.

souffle (*soo'-fl*). A blowing sound heard on auscultation.

sound. An instrument shaped like a probe for exploring cavities and detecting the presence of foreign bodies. Also for dilatation of a canal.

Sourdille's operation (*soor'-deele*). *See* Fenestration.

Southey's tubes (*south'-e*). Small perforated metal tubes with trocar, for drainage of fluid from subcutaneous tissues, and from the peritoneal cavity.

Spanish fly. A species of beetle from which cantharidin, a blistering agent, is derived.

spansule (*span'-sule*). A drug made up in a capsule in such a way that there is slow release of its contents.

spasm (*spazm*). A sudden involuntary muscle contraction. *Carpopedal s.* Of the hands and feet. A sign of tetany. *Clonic s.* Alternate muscle rigidity and relaxation. *Habit s.* A tic. *Nictitating s.* Spasmodic twitching of the eyelid. *Tetanic s.* Violent muscle spasms, including opisthotonos. *Tonic s.* Muscle rigidity.

spasmolytic (*spaz-mo-lit'-ik*). A drug which reduces spasm, such as propantheline.

spastic (*spas'-tik*). Characterized by spasm. *S. paralysis.* One associated with lesions of the upper motor neurone as in cerebral vascular accidents and characterized by increased muscle tone and rigidity.

spasticity (*spas-tis'-it-e*). Marked rigidity of muscle.

spastics (*spas'-tiks*). A term applied to persons suffering from congenital paralysis due to some cerebral lesion or impairment.

spatial (*spa'-shal*). Pertaining to space.

spatula (*spat'-u-lah*). (1) A flexible blunt blade used for spreading ointment. (2) A rigid blade-shaped instrument for depressing the tongue in throat examination, etc.

spatulated (*spat'-u-la-ted*). Flattened like a spatula.

Special Hospitals. Under the Mental Health Act, 1959, those for the detention of mentally disordered persons who in the opinion of the Minister require treatment under conditions of special security on account of their dangerous, violent, or criminal propensities.

species (*spe'-sheez*). A subdivision of genus.

specific (*spes-if'-ik*). (1) Relating to a species. (2) The special remedy for a particular disease. *S. medicine.* A remedy which has a distinct curative influence on a particular disease, e.g. quinine in malaria. *S. disease.* A disease produced by a specified micro-organism and running a definite course. *S. gravity.* The density of fluid compared with that of an equal volume of water.

spectacles (*spek'-tak-ls*). A frame containing lenses worn in front of the eyes to correct errors of vision.

spectrum. The division of light into its component colours by a prism which separates the colours. *See* Rays.

speculum (*spek' - u - lum*). Specula (*pl.*). An instrument for dilating and holding open the orifice of a body cavity to assist examination of the interior.

speech. The utterance of vocal sounds. *Clipped s.* The words are incomplete. It may be a sign of general paresis. *Incoherent s.* Due to disturbance of the sequence of thought. *Staccato's s.* Each syllable is separately pronounced. It may occur in disseminated sclerosis.

Spencer-Wells forceps. *See under* Forceps.

sperm. Abbreviation for spermatozoon, the male sex cell.

spermatic (*sper-mat'-ik*). Pertaining to the semen. *S. cord. See under* Cord.

spermatorrhoea (*sper-mat-or-re'-ah*). Involuntary discharge of semen.

spermatozoa (*sper-mat-o-zo'-ah*). *Pl.* The generative cells which form the essential part of semen. *Sing.* Spermatozoon.

spermicide (*sper'-mis-ide*). Any agent which will destroy the reproductive cell.

sphenoid (*sfen'-oid*). Wedge-shaped. *S. bone.* Forms part of the base of the skull. Its shape resembles that of a bat.

spherocytosis (*sfer - o - si - to' - sis*). When the erythrocytes are more nearly spherical than biconcave. A feature of acholuric jaundice also known as *hereditary s.*

sphincter (*sfink'-ter*). A ring-shaped muscle, contraction of which closes a natural orifice.

sphincterotomy (*sfink-ter-ot'-o-me*). Cutting a sphincter to relieve constriction.

sphygmic (*sfig'-mik*). Relating to the pulse.

sphygmocardiograph (*sfig-mo-kard'-e-o-graf*). An instrument that records both the pulse and heart-beat.

sphygmograph (*sfig'-mo-graf*). An instrument which, when applied to the wrist, registers graphically the force and character of the pulse-beats.

sphygmomanometer (*sfig-mo-man-om'-e-ter*). An instrument for measuring the force of the arterial blood pressure.

spica (*spi'-kah*). A bandage applied to a joint in a series of 'figures of eight'.

spicule (*spi'-kul*). A splinter-like fragment of bone.

Spigelius's lobe (*Spi-jel'-e-us*). The small lobe on the under surface of the liver.

spigot (*spig'-ot*). A small wooden or plastic peg to close the opening of a tube.

spina (*spi'-nah*). Any sharp projection. *S. bifida.* A congenital defect of non-union

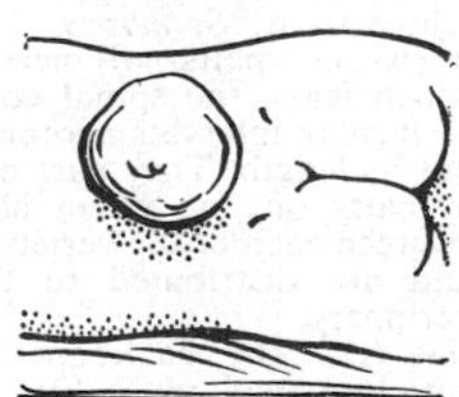

SPINA BIFIDA

of one or more vertebral arches, allowing protrusion of the meninges and possibly their contents. *See* Meningocele and Meningomyelocele.

spinal (*spi'-nal*). Relating to the spine. *S. anaesthesia. See* Anaesthesia. *S. bed* is made of plaster of Paris. It is a cast of the back of the head and trunk of the patient, and is so designed that he may rest in it and maintain complete immobility of the spine. Used in spinal caries, or following operation on the vertebrae. *S. canal.* The hollow in the spine formed by the neural arches of the vertebrae. It contains the spinal cord, meninges, and cerebrospinal fluid. *S. caries.* Disease of the vertebra, usually tuberculous. *See* Pott's disease. *S. column.* The backbone, composed of thirty-three vertebrae, separated by pads of cartilage, and enclosing the spinal canal. *S. cord. See* Cord. *S. curvature.* Abnormal curving of the spine. If associated with caries, it is known as Pott's disease. (*See also* Kyphosis, Lordosis, *and* Scoliosis.) *S. jacket.* A support for the spine, made of plaster of Paris, or other material, and used to give rest in caries of spine, or after injury to it. *S. nerves.* The thirty-one pairs of nerves which leave the spinal cord at regular intervals throughout its length. They pass out in pairs one on either side between each of the vertebra, and are distributed to the periphery.

spine. (1) The backbone or vertebral column. (2) A sharp process of bone.

spiral (*spi'-ral*). Winding, as the method of applying a roller bandage. *S. fracture.* One that is usually due to a rotational strain.

Spirillum (*spi-ril'-lum*). A genus of spiral-shaped bacteria.

spirit. An alcoholic solution of a volatile substance. *See Rectified s.*

spiritus (*spir'-it-us*). Latin for spirit. *S. frumenti.* Whisky. *S. vini gallici.* Brandy.

spirochaete (*spi'-ro-ket*). Micro-organisms in the form of a spiral. They are motile. An example is the *Treponema pallidum*, the causative organism of syphilis.

spirograph (*spi'-ro-graf*). An instrument for registering respiratory movements.

spirometer (*spi-rom'-e-ter*). An instrument for measuring the air capacity of the lungs.

spironolactone (*spir-on-o-lak'-tone*). A diuretic drug used when there is excess secretion of aldosterone. It promotes the excretion of sodium and water but retention of potassium.

Spitz-Holter valve. This is used in the treatment of hydrocephalus to drain the cerebrospinal fluid from the ventricles

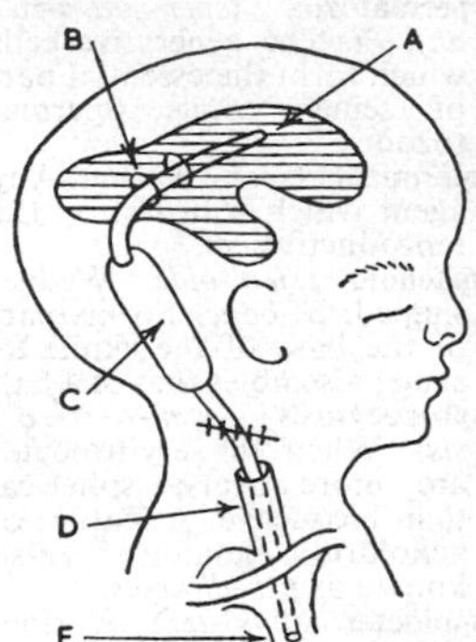

SPITZ-HOLTER VALVE

A. Lateral ventricle.
B. Trephine of skull.
C. Valve pump.
D. Jugular vein.
E. Superior vena cava.

into the superior vena cava or right atrium.

splanchnic (*splank'-nik*). Pertaining to the viscera. *S. nerves*. Sympathetic nerves to the viscera. *S. sympathectomy*. An operation performed with the object of giving relief in some cases of high blood pressure. *See* Sympathectomy.

spleen (*splee-n*). A very vascular lymphoid organ, situated in the left hypochondrium under the border of the stomach. It manufactures lymphocytes and breaks down red blood corpuscles.

splenectomy (*splen-ek'-to-me*). Excision of the spleen.

spleneolus (*splen-e-o'-lus*). An accessory spleen.

splenic anaemia (*splen'-ik an-e'-me-ah*). *See under* Anaemia.

splenitis (*splen-i'-tis*). Inflammation of the spleen.

splenomegaly (*splen-o-meg'-al-e*). Enlargement of the spleen.

splenorenal (*splen-o-re'-nal*). Applied to the spleen and the kidney. *S. anastomosis*. The spleen is excised and the splenic vein is inserted into the renal vein.

splenovenography (*splen-o-ven-og'-raf-e*). An X-ray of the spleen and its blood vessels following the insertion of a radio-opaque dye.

splint. An appliance used to support or immobilize a part while healing takes place or to correct or prevent deformity.

spondylitis (*spon-dil-i'-tis*). Inflammation of a vertebra. *Ankylosing s.* A disease chiefly of young males in which there is abnormal ossification with pain and rigidity of the intervertebral, hip and sacroiliac joints.

spondylolisthesis (*spon-di-lo-lis-the'-sis*). A sliding forwards or displacement of one vertebra over another. Usually the fifth lumbar over the sacrum, causing symptoms such as low back pain due to pressure on the nerve roots.

spondylosis (*spon-dil-o'-sis*). Ankylosis of vertebral joints.

sponging. A method of reducing high temperature by encouraging evaporation from the skin. The temperatures suggested are approximate, but suitable ones are: *Cold s.* 20°C (65°F), *Tepid s.* 30°C (85°F), *Hot s.* 40°C (105°F).

spongioblastoma multiforme (*spon-je-o-blas-to'-mah mult'-e-form*). A rapidly growing brain tumour that is highly malignant.

spontaneous (*spon-ta'-ne-us*). Occurring suddenly and without force. Applies to certain cases of fracture or pneumothorax (*q.v.*).

sporadic (*spor-ad'-ik*). A term applied to isolated cases of a disease which occurs in various and scattered places.

spore (*spor*). (1) A reproductive stage of some of the lowest forms of vegetable life, e.g. moulds. (2) A protective state which some of the bacilli are able to assume in adverse conditions, such as lack of moisture, food, or heat. In this form the organism can remain alive, but inert, for years.

spotted fever. A name given both to cerebrospinal fever and typhus on account of the purpuric rash which may be present in either disease.

sprain. Wrenching of a joint, producing laceration of the capsule or stretching of the ligaments, with consequent swelling, which is due to effusion of fluid into the affected part. Firm bandaging at once will prevent swelling and lessen disability. If there is effusion, applications of heat or cold can be made and support by a firm bandage or splint will be needed to ensure rest. Exercises are started early.

Sprengel's shoulder deformity (*spren'-gel*). A congenital condition in which one scapula is higher than the other, causing some limitation of abduction power.

sprue (*sproo*). A disease of malabsorption in the intestine, associated with the tropics; there is steatorrhoea, diarrhoea, glossitis, and anaemia. Lack of absorption of vitamin K leads to easy bleeding. Treatment is by giving vitamin B, particularly B_{12} and folic acid, vitamin K, iron and calcium. A gluten-free diet does not usually help these patients.

spurious labour (*spu'-re-us*). *See under* Labour.

sputum (*spu'-tum*). Excess of secretions from the air-passages. It consists chiefly of mucus and saliva, but in diseased conditions of the air-passages it may be purulent, blood-stained, frothy, and contain many bacteria. *Rusty s.* Having altered blood permeating the mucus. Characteristic of acute lobar pneumonia. Sputum should always be regarded as highly infectious and should be expectorated wherever possible into disposable containers and incinerated.

squamous (*skwa'-mus*). Scaly. *S. bone.* The thin part of the temporal bone which articulates with the parietal and frontal bones.

squill (*skwill*). *Scilla* (*q.v.*).

squint (*skwint*). *See* Strabismus.

Stacke's operation (*stah'-ke*). Removal of bony structures between the mastoid cells and middle ear so that one cavity is made. An operation for chronic infection in this area.

stadium (*sta'-de-um*). The stage of a disease. *S. decrementii.* The period of decline in severity. Defervescence (*q.v.*). *S. incrementi.* The stage of advance when symptoms are developing.

stammering (*stam'-mer-ing*). A speech disturbance with repetition of syllables.

stapedectomy (*sta-pe-dek'-to-me*). Removal of the stapes and insertion of a vein graft or other device to re-establish conduction of sound waves in otosclerosis.

stapediolysis (*sta-pe-di-ol'-is-is*). An operation of mobilizing the footpiece of the stapes to aid conduction deafness from otosclerosis.

stapes (*sta'-pez*). The stirrup-shaped bone of the middle ear.

staphylectomy (*staf-il-ek'-to-me*). Removal of the uvula.

Staphylococcus (*staf-il-o-kok'-kus*). A species of pyogenic bacteria which, under the microscope, appear grouped together in small masses like bunches of grapes. This organism is especially responsible for the formation of boils and carbuncles. *S. pyogenes* or *S. aureus.* A type which grows as yellow colonies on artificial media, and is pus-producing.

staphyloma (*staf-il-o'-mah*). A protrusion of the cornea or sclerotic coat of the eyeball as the result of inflammation or wound.

staphyloptosis (*staf-il-op-to'-sis*). Elongation of the uvula.

staphylorrhaphy (*staf-il-or'-raf-e*). The operation for suture of a cleft soft palate or the uvula.

starch. A carbohydrate occurring in many vegetable tissues. *S. bath.* An emollient bath for skin diseases. 1 kg (2 lb.) of starch tied in a muslin bag is fixed to the hot water tap, and the water allowed to run through it into the bath. *S. powder* is often used with zinc powder as a soothing external application. *S. poultice* is a stiff mucilage of starch spread on old linen and applied cool to remove scabs; e.g. in skin diseases.

starve. To deprive of or to suffer from a lack of food.

stasis (*sta'-sis*). Stagnation or stoppage. *Intestinal s.* Sluggish movement of the muscles of the bowel wall, which may be due to simple causes as unsuitable dietary or lack of exercise. More seriously it may be caused by paralysis of the muscle wall or to obstruction. *See* Ileus. *Venous s.* Congestion of blood in the veins.

static (*stat'-ik*). Stationary, at rest. *S. electricity.* The term applied to a build up of an electrical charge which may cause an explosion. *See* Appendix 5.

stationary air. *See under* Air.

status (*stat'-us*). Condition. *S. asthmaticus.* A severe and prolonged attack of asthma. *S. epilepticus.* A condition in which there is rapid succession of epileptic fits. *S. lymphaticus.* A condition in which all lymphatic tissues are hypertrophied, especially the thymus gland. This may be found at post-mortem following sudden death.

steapsin (*ste-ap'-sin*). *See* Lipase.

steatoma (*ste-at-o'-mah*) A sebaceous cyst or a fatty tumour.

steatopygia (*ste-at-o-pi'-je-ah*). Excessive deposit of fat in the buttocks.

steatorrhoea (*ste-at-or-re'-ah*). The presence of undigested fat in the stools. A sign of pancreatic deficiency and occurring in coeliac disease.

steatosis (*ste-at-o'-sis*). (1) Fatty degeneration. (2) Disease of sebaceous glands.

Steinmann's pin (*sti'-n-man*). A fine metal rod passed through bone, by which extension is applied to overcome muscle contraction in certain fractures. *See also* Kirschner's wire.

stellate (*stel'-ate*). Starlike. *S. ganglion.* The sympathetic ganglion of the first dorsal region. *S. fracture.* A radiating fracture of the patella.

Stellwag's sign (*stel-vags*). Infrequent blinking as may occur in exophthalmos.

stenocardia (*sten-o-kar'-de-ah*). Angina pectoris.

stenosis (*sten-o'-sis*). Narrowing or contraction of a channel or opening. *Aortic s.* Narrowing of the aortic valve as the aorta leaves the heart, due to scar tissue formation, as the result of inflammation. *Mitral s.* Of the mitral orifice from the same cause. *Pyloric s.* Of the stomach due to scar tissue, new growth, or congenital hypertrophy.

Stenson's duct (*sten'-son*). The duct of the parotid gland, opening into the mouth at the level of the first upper molar.

stent (*stent*). An impression of the shape of the jaws taken on a plastic material which sets very hard. Used in dentistry when an artificial denture has to be made.

stercobilin (*ster-ko-bil'-in*). The colouring matter of the faeces; derived from bile.

stercolith (*ster'-ko-lith*). A faecal concretion which sometimes blocks the lumen of the vermiform appendix. Faecalith (*q.v.*).

stercoraceous (*ster-kor-a'-shus*). Faecal, or resembling faeces. *S. vomit.* Faecal vomit. *See under* Vomiting.

stereognosis (*ster-e-og-no'-sis*). The identification of objects through the sense of touch.

stereostatics (*ster-e-o-stat'-iks*). The science relating to weight and its mechanical effects.

stereotaxy (*ster-e-o-taks'-e*). A manipulative operation for replacing displaced parts as in hernia reduction. The precise direction of an instrument into the brain tissue.

stereotypy (*ster'-e-o-ti-pe*). Term used to describe repetitive actions carried out or maintained for long periods in a monotonous fashion.

sterile (*ster'-ile*). (1) Barren; incapable of producing young. (2) Aseptic; free from micro-organisms.

sterility (*ster-il'-it-e*). The inability of a woman to become pregnant or of a man to produce sperm.

sterilization (*ster-il-i-za'-shun*). (1) To render incapable of reproduction by any means, e.g. removal of ovaries in the female, or bilateral severing of the vas deferens in the male. (2) Rendering dressings, instruments, etc., aseptic—usually by heat. *See* Appendix 7. *High pressure steam s. See* Autoclave.

sterilizer (*ster'-il-i-zer*). An apparatus in which objects can be sterilized. A term previously applied to a water boiler.

sternal (*ster'-nal*). Relating to the sternum. *S. puncture. See under* Puncture. *S. transfusion.* A method of introducing blood into the circulation via the bone marrow.

sternocleidomastoid (*ster-no-kli-do-mas'-toid*). A muscle group stretching from the mastoid process to the sternum and clavicle.

sternotomy (*ster-not'-o-me*). The operation in which the sternum is cut through.

sternum (*ster'-num*). The breast-bone; the flat narrow bone in the centre of the anterior wall of the thorax.

sternutator (*stern'-u-ta-tor*). A substance which causes sneezing. Nose gas.

steroids (*ster'-oids*). Hormones whose chemical structure is closely related to sterols. They include oestrogens, progestins, androgens, and hormones of the adrenal cortex. They may be naturally occurring or they may be synthetized.

sterol (*ster'-ol*). Non-saponifiable fats. Cholesterol is one.

stertorous (*ster'-tor-us*). Snoring; applied to a snoring sound produced in breathing in cases of cerebral compression, apoplexy, etc.

stethometer (*steth-om'-e-ter*). An instrument for measuring the expansion of the chest.

stethoscope (*steth'-o-skope*). The instrument used in mediate auscultation. It consists of a hollow tube, one end of which is placed over the part to be examined and the other at the ear of the examiner. *Binaural s.* branches into two flexible tubes, one for each ear of the examiner.

sthenic (*sthen'-ik*). Strong, active. *S. fever* is marked by high temperature, rapid strong pulse, and highly coloured urine.

stibophen (*stib'-o-fen*). A preparation of antimony given intramuscularly. Used in the treatment of schistosomiasis.

stigma (*stig'-mah*). (1) A small haemorrhagic spot or mark on the skin. (2) Any mark or sign characteristic of a condition or defect, or of a disease, e.g. the *stigmata* of congenital syphilis—the depressed bridge of nose, radiating scars round the mouth, Hutchinson's teeth, etc. It refers to visible signs rather than symptoms.

stilboestrol (*stil-be'-strol*). A synthetic oestrogen preparation.

stilette (*stil-et'*). A wire or rod for keeping the lumen of tubes clear, e.g. of catheters, hollow needles, and cannulae.

stillbirth. As defined by the Central Midwives Board; a fetus, born after the twenty-eighth week of pregnancy, which, after complete expulsion, has not breathed or shown any sign of life.

Still's disease. A form of rheumatoid arthritis in children, associated with enlargement of lymph glands. The cause is unknown.

stimulant (*stim'-u-lant*). An agent which causes temporary increased energy or functional activity of any organ. *Alcoholic s.* Wines, brandy, whisky and malt liquors. *Cardiac s.* One which increases the action of the heart, as nikethamide.

stimulus (*stim'-u-lus*). An impulse causing stimulation. *Chemical s.* One which produces chemical change in a tissue. *Electric s.* Galvanic or other form of electric current applied to muscle tissue. *Thermal s.* Application of heat to produce a response.

stirrup bone (*stir'-rup*). *See* Stapes.

stitch. (1) A sudden sharp pain. (2) A suture. *S. abscess.* Pus formation where a stitch is inserted.

stock culture. A growth of specific organisms on culture media from which fresh growths can be made. *Stock vaccines* are made from such a culture.

Stockholm technique (*stok'-ho-lm tek-neek'*). A treatment of carcinoma of the uterine cervix by radium. Radium applicators are inserted in the cervical canal and fornices for 22h. The treatment is repeated 1 week later and again after 2 weeks.

Stokes-Adams syndrome. Attacks of syncope or fainting due to cerebral anaemia in some cases of complete heart block. The heart stops, but breathing continues. Convulsions or death occur if the heart does not establish its own ventricular beat. *See* Myogenic.

stoma (*sto'-mah*). An orifice or opening to a free surface.

stomach (*stum'-ak*). The dilated portion of the alimentary canal between the oesophagus and the duodenum, just below the diaphragm. *Hourglass s.* Describes the shape of the organ in a type of deformity resulting from scar-tissue formation. *Leather bottle s.* Induration and thickening of the gastric wall, usually the result of cancer. *Senoran's s. pump.* Removes the contents of the stomach by suction. *S. tube* is a tube used for washing out the stomach, or for the administration of liquid food.

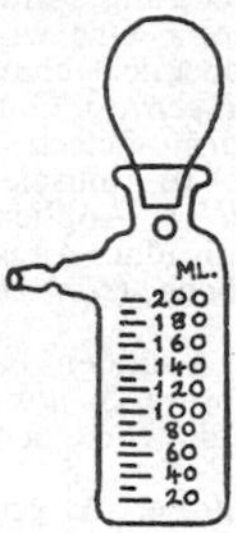

SENORAN'S STOMACH PUMP

stomachic (*sto-mak'-ik*). (1) Pertaining to the stomach. (2) A gastric tonic. A drug which stimulates and improves gastric function.

stomatitis (*sto-ma-ti'-tis*). Inflammation of the mouth, either simple or with ulceration. The latter condition is accompanied by copious salivation, fetid breath, slight fever, and at times great prostration. Disinfectant mouthwashes, gentian violet and nystatin, are used in treatment. It occurs in scurvy, acute leukaemia, and in infections of the mouth, as in thrush. *Aphthous s.* Characterized by small, white, superficial ulcers on the mucous membrane. *Ulcerative s.* shows painful shallow ulcers on the tongue, cheeks and lips. A severe type having serious constitutional effects.

stomatonoma (*sto-mat-o-no'-mah*). Gangrene of the mouth. Noma.

-stomy (*sto'-me*). A suffix meaning to make an opening or mouth. *See also* '-ectomy'.

stool. A motion or discharge from the bowels. *Fatty s.* That which contains undigested fat.

stop-needle. A needle with an enlargement on the shank to prevent deep penetration, e.g. Sternal marrow puncture needle.

strabismus (*strab-iz'-mus*). Squint. A fixed deviation of either eye from its normal direction. It is called *convergent* when the eye turns in toward the nose, and *divergent* when it turns outward.

strain. (1) Over-use or stretching of a part, e.g. muscle or tendon. (2) To pass a liquid through a filter.

stramonium (*stra-mo'-ne-um*). A vegetable drug containing the alkaloid hyoscyamine, which in its action resembles belladonna. It may be used in paralysis agitans.

strangulated (*strang'-gu-la-ted*). Compressed or constricted, e.g. so that the circulation of the blood is arrested. *S. hernia. See* Hernia.

strangulation (*strang-gu-la'-shun*). (1) Choking caused by compression of the air passages. (2) Arrested circulation to a part, which will result in gangrene.

strangury (*strang'-gu-re*). A frequent desire to micturate, but only a few drops of urine are passed with difficulty and pain. It results from local inflammatory conditions and muscle spasm. It may also occur in fracture of the pelvis, when it indicates rupture of the bladder or urethra.

stratified (*strat'-e-fide*). A covering tissue in which the cells are arranged in layers. The germinating cells are the lowest and as surface cells are shed there is continual replacement.

stratum (*strah'-tum*). A layer; applied to structures such as the skin and mucous membranes. *S. corneum.* The outer, horny layer of epidermis.

Streptococcus (*strep-to-kok'-kus*). A genus of bacteria occurring in chain-like formation. *S. faecalis.* A type which inhabits the intestines. *S. haemolyticus.* This may be the cause of acute tonsillitis, cellulitis, otitis media, scarlet fever, septicaemia, and puerperal fever. Its toxins cause haemolysis of red blood cells. It may be divided into Lancefield Groups of which A is most important to man and this can be further divided into serological Griffith types, by which the source of infection can be more easily traced. *S. viridans* is commonly found in the mouth and may enter the blood stream during dental extraction. It is the possible cause of bacterial endocarditis, and some forms of non-suppurative arthritis which sometimes follow teeth extraction.

streptokinase (*strep-to-kin'-aze*). An enzyme derived from a streptococcal culture and used to liquefy clotted blood and pus. Vasidase contains it.

streptomycin (*strep-to-mi'-sin*). An antibiotic drug derived from a mould used particularly in the treatment of tuberculosis, and then usually given in conjunction with calcium or sodium aminosalicylate or isoniazid.

Streptothrix (*strep'-to-thrix*). A genus of micro-organisms which grow in long, branching filaments. One of its forms causes actinomycosis.

stress. The reaction, both physical and mental, to the demands made upon a person. *S. disorders.* Are those associated with the individual's inability to meet these demands.

striae gravidarum (*stri'-e grav-id-ar'-um*). The lines which appear on the abdomen of pregnant women. They are red in first pregnancy, but white subsequently and are due to stretching and rupture of the elastic fibres.

stricture (*strik'-chur*). A narrowing or local contraction of a canal. It may be caused by muscle spasm, new growth, or scar tissue formation following inflammation.

stridor (*stri'-dor*) A harsh, vibrating, shrill sound, produced during respiration.

stridulous (*strid'-u-lus*). Accompanied by stridor. *See* Laryngismus.

stroke. A popular term to describe the sudden onset of symptoms especially those of cerebral origin. *Apoplectic s.* Cerebral haemorrhage. *Heat s.* A hyperpyrexia accompanied by cerebral symptoms. It may occur in someone newly arrived in a very hot climate.

stroma (*stro'-mah*). The tissue forming the foundation and framework of an organ which supports the functioning cells. Disease may attack either the stroma or the specialized cells.

strontium 90 (*stron'-te-um*). A radioactive isotope with a half-life of 28 years, it is a fission product of atomic explosions. The danger lies in its power to replace calcium in the skeleton, especially in young growing bones.

strychnine (*strik'-neen*). A highly poisonous alkaloid, the active principle of *Strychnos nux vomica*. In small doses it may be given as a nerve and muscle stimulant.

stupor (*stu'-por*). A state occurring in the course of many varieties of mental illness where the patient does not move, speak, and makes no response to stimuli, but consciousness is intact. *Depressive s.* Stupor occurring in the course of endogenous depression. *See* Catatonia.

stuporous (*stu'-por-us*). In a drowsy or semi-conscious state.

stye. *See* Hordeolum.

styloid (*sti'-loid*). Like a pen. *S. process.* A sharp point on the temporal and ulna bones.

styptic (*stip'-tik*). An astringent which, applied locally, arrests haemorrhage, e.g. alum and tannic acid.

sub- A prefix denoting 'under' or 'near'.

subacute (*sub'-a-kute*). Moderately acute. *S. combined degeneration of the spinal cord. See* Degeneration.

subarachnoid (*sub-ar-ak'-noid*). Below the arachnoid. *S. space.* Between the arachnoid and pia mater of the brain and spinal cord, and containing cerebrospinal fluid.

subclavian (*sub-kla'-ve-an*). Beneath the clavicle. *S. artery.* The main vessel of supply to the upper limb.

subclinical (*sub-klin'-ik-al*). An infection in which the signs are so mild that a diagnosis is not made.

subconjunctival (*sub-kon-junk-ti'-val*). Occurring below the conjunctiva as in a haemorrhage.

subconscious (*sub-kon'-shus*). The condition in which memories are not within the consciousness, but can be recalled to it with greater or less effort, sometimes called the preconscious.

subcutaneous (*sub-ku-ta'-ne-us*). Beneath the skin. *S. injection.* One given hypodermically.

subdural (*sub-du'-ral*). Below the dura mater. *S. haematoma.* A blood clot between the arachnoid and dura mater It may be acute or arise slowly from a minor injury.

subinvolution (*sub-in-vo-lu'-shun*). Incomplete contraction of the uterus after labour.

subjective (*sub-jek'-tiv*). Related to the individual. *S. symptoms.* Those of which the patient is aware by sensory stimulation, but cannot easily be seen by others. *Cf.* Objective.

sublimate (*sub'-lim-ate*). A substance obtained by vaporization of a solid and condensation of the vapour.

sublimation (*sub-lim-a'-shun*). A redirecting of energy at an unconscious level. The transference into socially acceptable channels of tendencies that cannot be expressed. An important aspect of maturity.

subliminal (*sub-lim'-in-al*). Below the threshold of perception.

sublingual (*sub-lin'-gwal*). Beneath the tongue. *S. glands.* Two salivary glands in the floor of the mouth.

sublobular (*sub-lob'-u-lar*). Beneath the lobules. *S. veins.* Convey the blood from the liver lobules.

subluxation (*sub-luks-a'-shun*). Partial dislocation.

submaxillary (*sub-maks'-il-lar-e*). Beneath the lower jaw. *S. glands.* Two salivary glands on the floor of the mouth.

submucous (*sub-mu'-kus*). Beneath mucous membrane. *S. resection.* An operation to correct a deflated nasal septum.

subnormality (*sub-nor-mal'-it-e*). Mental Health Act 1959. A state of arrested or incomplete development of the mind and is of a nature or degree which requires or is susceptible to medical treatment or other special care or training. *Severe s.* The degree of arrested or incomplete development is of such a nature that the patient is incapable of living an independent life or of guarding himself against serious exploitation.

subperiosteal (*sub-per-e-os'-te-al*). Beneath the periosteum.

subphrenic (*sub-fren'-ik*). Beneath the diaphragm. *S. abscess.* One which develops below the diaphragm and may point into the pleural cavity.

substitution (*sub-ste-tu'-shun*). The acceptance of an alternative. In psychology this may be the nurse or foster mother for the child's own mother. In psychotherapy the nurse or therapist may be substituted for someone in the patient's background.

subtertian (*sub-ter'-shun*). The term applied to the more continuous fever present in malaria due to infection by *Plasmodium falciparum.*

subtotal hysterectomy (*sub-to'-tal his-ter-ek'-to-me*). *See under* Hysterectomy.

succinylsulphathiazole (*suk-sin-il-sul-fa-thi'-az-ol*). A sulphonamide preparation used for intestinal infections. It is not absorbed from the tract. Especially successful in infantile epidemic diarrhoea.

succus (*suk'-kus*). A juice. *S. citri.* Lime juice. *S. entericus.* A clear alkaline digestive fluid secreted by intestinal glands.

succussion splash (*suk-kush'-un*). The sound made by shaking the patient when free fluid is present in a cavity in the body.

sucrose (*su'-krose*). Cane or beet sugar.

suction (*suk'-shun*). The removal of air or fluid from a container by decreasing the pressure. *Hydraulic s.* Removing fluid from a body cavity by an attachment to a water tap or by the three bottle method as illustrated.

sudamina (*su-dam'-in-ah*). An eruption of whitish vesicles

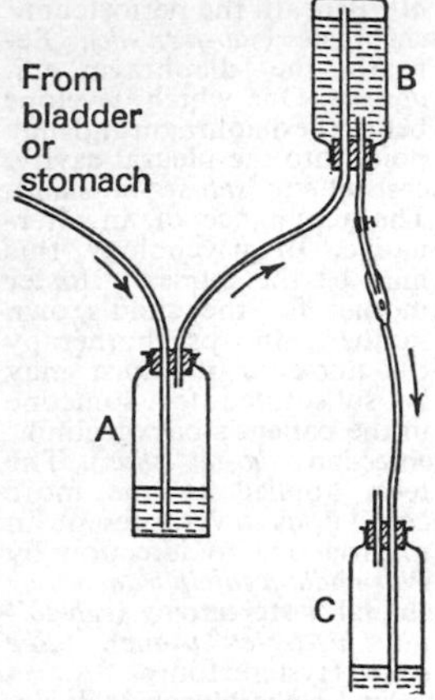

SUCTION

As water passes from B to C, air is drawn from A to B. This creates a negative pressure in A which draws fluid from a body cavity.

associated with retention of sweat, and sometimes occurring in febrile conditions.

sudor (*su'-dor*). Sweat.

sudorific (*su-dor-if'-ik*). Diaphoretic; an agent causing sweating.

suffusion (*suf-fu'-zhun*). A sudden flushing of the skin, as in blushing.

sugar. A class of carbohydrates which include the following: (1) *Fermentable s.* (a) *Cane s.*, from the sugar-cane; (b) *Glucose* or *grape-s.*, from fruits, honey, etc. (2) *Lactose*, a non-fermentable sugar of milk. (3) *Muscle s.*: *Inositol*. Found in muscle and other tissues, and in the juice of asparagus and various vegetables.

suggestibility (*suj-es-ti-bil'-it-e*). A condition in which there is a greater susceptibility to suggestion.

suggestion (*suj-est'-shun*). A tool of psychotherapy in which an idea is presented to a patient and accepted by him. *Post-hypnotic s.* This influence lasts after his return to normal condition.

sulcus (*sul'-kus*). A furrow or fissure; applied especially to those of the brain.

sulphacetamide (*sul-fa-set'-a-mide*). A soluble sulphonamide useful for treating urinary infection and as drops or ointment for eye infections.

sulphadiazine (*sul-fa-di'-az-in*). A useful sulphonamide drug which is relatively non-toxic.

sulphadimidine (*sul-fa-di'-mid-in*). A sulphonamide in which a high blood level can be obtained but toxic effects are rare.

sulphaemoglobinaemia (*sulf-heem-o-glob-in-e'-me-ah*). A condition of cyanosis that used to arise during the administration of the earlier sulphonamides. Now rarely seen but should it arise it can be treated by giving methylene blue.

sulphafurazole (*sul-fa-fur'-a-zole*). A soluble, rapidly excreted sulphonamide useful in treating renal tract infections.

sulphaguanidine (*sul-fa-gwan'-id-in*). A sulphonamide preparation having specific action on organisms causing bacillary dysentery.

sulphamethizole (*sul-fa-meth'-e-zole*). A sulphonamide used in urinary infection as it is rapidly excreted in an active form.

sulphanilamide (*sul-fan-il'-am-ide*). A simple sulphonamide compound, less active than sulphadimidine.

sulphasalazine (*sul-fa-sal'-az-een*). A sulphonamide that has been used with some success in treating ulcerative colitis.

sulphate (*sul'-fate*). A salt of sulphuric acid.

sulphathiazole (*sul-fa-thi'-a-zol*). A very active but less used preparation; liable to give rise to rashes and drug fever; very rapidly excreted from the body.

sulphmethaemoglobin (*sulf-met-hem-o-glo'-bin*). The substance produced in the blood by excess of sulphur which gives rise to sulphaemoglobinaemia (*q.v.*).

sulphonamide (*sul-fon'-am-ide*). The generic term for all *aminobenzine - sulphonamide* preparations.

sulphones (*sul'-fones*). A group of drugs which with prolonged use have been successful in treating leprosy.

sulphonylureas (*sul-fon-il-ur-e'-ahs*). Oral hypoglycaemic drugs that may be used in milder forms of diabetes. Examples are tolbutamide and chlorpropamide.

sulphuric acid (*sul-fu'-rik*). Oil of vitriol. A heavy colourless liquid and corrosive poison, which burns any organic substance with which it comes into contact.

sunburn. A dermatitis due to exposure to the sun's rays, causing burning and redness.

sunstroke. Overwhelming prostration caused by exposure to excessive heat from the sun. *See* Heat stroke.

super- (*su'-per*). A prefix meaning 'over'.

superciliary (*su-per-sil'-e-ar-e*). Relating to the eye-brow.

supercillium (*su-per-sil'-e-um*). The eye-brow.

superego (*su-per-e'-go*). That part of the personality that is concerned with moral standards and ideals that are derived unconsciously from the parents, teachers and environment, and influence the person's whole mental make-up acting as a control on impulses of the ego.

superfatted (*su-per-fat'-ted*). Having in it more fat than can combine with the alkali present.

superficial (*su-per-fish'-al*). On or near the surface. Often applied to those blood vessels near the skin.

superior (*su-per'-e-or*). Above; the upper of two parts.

superstition (*su - per - sti' - shun*). A belief or practice which is unnatural and not based on reason. *See* Fetishism.

supination (*su-pi-na'-shun*). Turning upwards. *S. of hand.* The palm is upward. *Cf.* Pronation.

supine (*su'-pine*). Lying on the back, with the face upward.

suppository (*sup-pos'-it-or-e*). A method of introducing a drug in solid form into a body cavity so that it will dissolve at body temperature. *Rectal s.* May be used to evacuate the bowels (*glycerin* or *Dulcolax*) or to relieve muscle spasm (*aminophyllin*). *Vaginal s.*, *see* pessary.

suppressant (*sup-pres'-ant*). A drug the administration of which, will prevent a disease from developing, e.g. quinine suppresses malaria.

suppression (*sup-presh'-un*). (1) Complete cessation of a secretion. *S. of urine.* No secretion of urine by the kidneys. (2) In psychology, *conscious* inhibition as distinct from *repression* which is *unconscious.*

suppuration (*sup-pu-ra'-shun*). The formation of pus.

supra- (*su'-pra*). A prefix meaning 'above'.

suprapubic (*su-pra-pu'-bik*). Above the pubic bone. *S. catheters.* Those used for drainage following cystostomy. *S. cystotomy.* Opening the bladder above the pubis. *S. drainage.* A method of draining the bladder after cystotomy, with or without prostactectomy.

supracondylar (*su-pra-kon'-de-lah*). Above the condyles. *S. fracture.* Usually refers to one above the lower end of the humerus.

suprarenal (*su'-pra-re'-nal*). Above the kidney. *S. capsule.* A small triangular, endocrine gland, one above each kidney. *See* Adrenal *and* Cortin.

surdity (*sur'-dit-e*). Deafness.

surgery (*sur'-je-re*). The branch of medicine that treats disease by operative measures.

surgical (*sur'-jik-al*). Pertaining to surgery. *S. neck.* The narrower part of the humerus, just below the tuberosities.

surrogate (*sur'-o-gate*). In psychology, an imagined person by which the patient conceals the real individual from his consciousness.

susceptibility (to disease) (*sus-sep-tib-il'-it-e*). The lack of resistance to infection of the individual.

suspensory bandage (*sus-pen'-sor-e*). A bandage worn to support the scrotum.

suture (*su'-chur*). (1) A stitch or series of stitches used to close a wound. (2) The jagged line of junction of the bones of the cranium. *Atraumatic s.* The suture is fused to the needle, for delicate structures there is less trauma. *Continuous s.* A form of oversewing with one length of suture. *Blanket s.* A continuous blanket stitch. *Everting s.* A form of mattress s. that turns the edges outwards to give a closer approximation. *Fascial s.* A strip of fascia from the patient is used. *Interrupted s.* A series of separate sutures. *Mattress s.* Each is taken twice through the wound

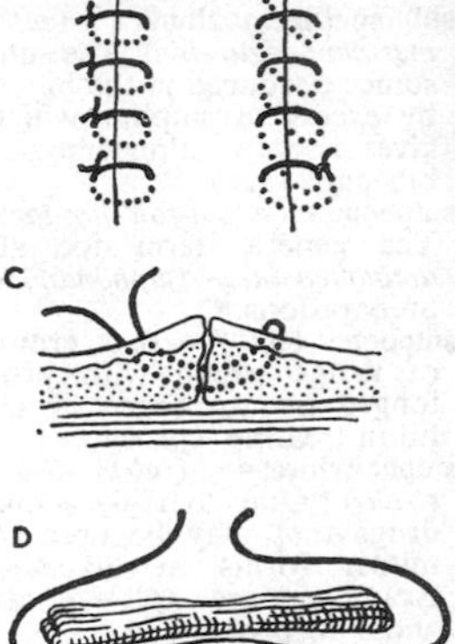

SUTURES

A. Interrupted.
B. Continuous.
C. Mattress.
D. Subcuticular.

giving a loop one side and a knot the other. *Purse strings s.* A circular continuous one round a small wound or appendix stump. *Subcuticular s.* A continuous one just below the skin. *Tension s.* One taking a large bite and relieving the tension on the true stitch line.

suxamethonium chloride (*suks-a-meth-on'-e-um*). A short-acting muscle-relaxant drug that may be used to get good muscle relaxation during operation. Scoline is a proprietary preparation.

swab. (1) A small piece of wool or gauze. (2) In pathology a dressed stick used in taking bacteriological specimens.

swallowing (*swal'-lo-ing*). The act of deglutition in which food is passed from the mouth to the oesophagus.

sweat (*swet*). A clear watery fluid secreted by the sudoriferous glands. *S. test.* Pilocarpine is passed through the epidermis by means of an electrode and stimulates the sweat glands. The sweat is collected and tested for sodium chloride, of which there is an excessive secretion in fibrocystic disease of the pancreas.

sweetbread. The pancreas.

sycosis (*si-ko'-sis*). Staphylococcal inflammation of the hair-follicles, especially those of the beard. It is characterized by pustules which form into scabs. *S. barbae.* That affecting the beard. Barber's itch.

symbiosis (*sim-bi-o'-sis*). When a parasite and its host are of mutual benefit to each other.

symblepharon (*sim-blef'-ar-on*). Adhesion of an eyelid to the eyeball.

symbolism (*sim'-bol-izm*). An abnormal mental condition in which events or objects are interpreted as symbols of the patient's own thoughts. In psychiatry, when repressed material re-enters consciousness in another form though it was previously unacceptable. A child's play may be symbolic or the painting of an emotionally disturbed patient.

symbols (*sim'-bols*). (1) Letters or marks used by convention to denote a substance or process. (2) Objects or activities representing and substituting for something else.

Syme's amputation (*sime*). Amputation of the foot, at the ankle-joint.

sympathectomy (*sim-path-ek'-to-me*). Division of the pre- or post-ganglionic fibres which control specific involuntary muscles. An operation performed for many conditions, e.g. Raynaud's disease; severe spasmodic dysmenorrhoea; or megacolon.

sympathetic (*sim-path-et-ik*). (1) Exhibiting sympathy. (2) A division of the autonomic nervous system. *S. anuria.* Suppression of urine, which may occur in the remaining kidney if the other has been removed, or is temporarily out of action. *S. ganglionectomy.* An operation performed for the same reasons as sympathectomy, but with removal of the ganglion concerned. *S. nervous system.* A branch of the automatic nervous system which supplies involuntary muscle and glands. It stimulates the ductless glands and the circulatory and respiratory systems but inhibits the digestive system. *S. ophthalmia*. Inflammation leading to loss of sight in the opposite eye following a perforating injury in the ciliary region.

sympathin (*sim'-path-in*). A substance released into the blood stream when sympathetic nerve fibres are stimulated. It is similar to adrenaline in action.

sympathomimetic (*sim-path-o-mim-et'-ik*). Drugs that mimic or act in the same way as the sympathetic nerves.

symphysis (*sim'-fis-is*). The line of union of two bones which originally were separate. *S. pubis*. The cartilaginous junction of the two pubic bones.

symptom (*simp'-tum*). Any evidence as to the nature and location of a disease. It is *subjective*, i.e. noted by the patient; *signs* are noted by the observer and are therefore *objective*. Thus the phrase 'signs and symptoms'. *Withdrawal s.* Those arising when a drug or alcohol is withheld from an individual who is dependent on it.

symptomatology (*simp-to-mat-ol'-o-je*). The study of the symptoms of disease.

syn- A prefix meaning 'together'.

synalgia (*sin-al'-je-ah*). Pain felt in one part of the body but caused by inflammation of or injury to another part.

synapse (*sin'-aps*). The termination of an axon with the dendrites of another nerve cell. Chemical transmitters pass the impulse across the space.

synarthrosis (*sin-ar-thro'-sis*). A form of articulation, in which the bones are wedged immovably together with no intervening synovial membrane, e.g. crania sutures.

synchondrosis (*sin-kon-dro'-sis*). The junction of bones by means of cartilage.

syncope (*sin'-ko-pe*). A simple faint or temporary loss of consciousness due to cerebral anaemia; often caused by dilatation of the peripheral blood vessels and a sudden fall in blood pressure. Cardiac S. *See* Stokes-Adams syndrome.

syncytium (*sin-sit'-e-um*). The superficial layer of cells covering the chorionic villi.

syndactylism (*sin-dak'-til-izm*). Webbed fingers or toes.

syndrome (*sin'-drome*). A group of symptoms typical of a distinctive disease or frequently occur together and so are labelled collectively. *See* Stokes-Adams *s. and* Fröhlich's *s.*

synechia (*sin-ek'-e-ah*). Adhesion of the iris to the cornea in front (*anterior s.*) or capsule of the lens behind (*posterior s.*).

synergy (*sin'-er-je*). The harmonious action of two agents or muscles working together.

synovectomy (*si-no-vek'-to-me*). Excision of a diseased synovial membrane to restore movement.

synovial membrane (*si-no'-ve-al*). A serous membrane lining the articular capsule of a movable joint, and terminating at the edge of the articular cartilage. It secretes a lubricating fluid—*synovia*.

synovitis (*si-no-vi'-tis*). Inflammation of a synovial membrane. It may be suppurative and result in ankylosis.

synthesis (*sin'-thes-is*). The building up of a more complex structure from simple components. This may apply to drugs or to plant or animal tissues.

synthetic (*sin-thet'-ik*). Artificial. Made by synthesis.

syphilide (*sif'-il-id*). Any disease of the skin due to syphilis. It may be erythematous, vesicular, pustular, etc.

syphilis (*sif'-il-is*). A specific, contagious venereal disease, caused by the *Treponema pallidum*. *Acquired s.* Commonly transmitted by sexual intercourse; there is an early infectious stage, followed by a latent period of many years before the non-infectious late stage when serious disorders of the nervous and vascular systems arise. *Congenital s.* This is transmitted by the mother to her child but is preventable if the mother receives a full course of penicillin during her pregnancy.

syringe. An instrument for injecting fluids or for aspirating or irrigating body cavities. *Aural s.* one for ear irrigation. *Bladder s.* for bladder irrigation or for aspiration of blood clots. *Eccentric s.* The needle mount is placed on the circumference, making intravenous injection easier. *Luer Lok s.* A syringe used for chest aspiration that is fitted with a simple locking device so that the needle will not be accidentally displaced.

syringing (*sir'-in-jing*). The act of using a syringe to wash out a cavity.

syringobulbia (*sir-in-go-bul'-be-ah*). The formation of cavities in the brain stem.

syringomyelia (*sir-in-go-mi-e'-le-ah*). A disease of the nervous system causing the formation of cavities filled with fluid, inside the spinal cord. Impairment of muscle function and sensation result. Painless injury may be the first symptom.

syringomyelitis (*sir-in-go-mi-el-i'-tis*). Inflammation of the spinal cord, as the result of which cavities are formed in it.

syringomyelocele (*sir-in-go-mi'-el-o-seel*). A type of spina bifida in which the protruded sac of fluid communicates with the central canal of the spinal cord.

syrup (*sir'-up*). An aqueous solution of refined sugar to which drugs may be added. *Easton's s.* A tonic containing iron, quinine, strychnine, and phosphates. *S. of figs* or *senna*. Pleasant-tasting aperients for children. *S. of codeine*. Soothing for cough.

system (*sis'-tem*). A combination of organs in the performance of a common function, e.g. the organs of digestion = the digestive system.

systemic (*sis-tem'-ik*). Pertaining to a whole system or collection of systems. *S. circulation*. Circulation of the blood throughout the whole body.

systole (*sis'-to-le*). The contraction of the heart. *See also* Diastole. *Extra-s.* A premature contraction of the atrium or ventricle, without alteration of the fundamental rhythm of the pacemaker. *Ventricular s.* The contraction of the heart by which the blood is pumped into the aorta and pulmonary artery.

systolic murmur (*sis-tol'-ik*). An abnormal sound produced during systole, in heart affections.

T

TAB. A vaccine of the killed organisms that cause typhoid fever and paratyphoid A and B. Used as a preventive against these diseases giving an active immunity.

tabes (*ta'-beez*). Wasting away. *T. dorsalis.* Locomotor ataxia. A slowly progressive disease of the nervous system affecting the posterior nerve roots and spinal cord. It is a late manifestation of syphilis (*q.v.*).

tabetic (*ta-bet'-ik*). Affected with tabes.

taboparesis (*ta-bo-par-e'-sis*). When the symptoms of both tabes dorsalis and general paralysis of the insane are present in a patient suffering from late syphilis.

tabloid (*tab'-loid*). A medicinal tablet or lozenge.

tachy- A prefix meaning 'rapid'.

tachycardia (*tak-e-kar'-de-ah*). Abnormally rapid action of the heart and consequent increase in pulse rate. (*See also* Bradycardia.) *Paroxysmal t.* Spasmodic increase in cardiac contractions of sudden onset lasting a variable time from a few seconds to hours. Sometimes a sign of ailing heart muscle, but in young people especially it may be of nervous origin.

tachylalia (*tak-e-la'-le-ah*). Extreme rapidity of speech.

tachyphrasia (*tak-e-fra'-ze-ah*). Tachyphemia. Extreme volubility of speech. It may be a sign of mental disorder.

tachypnoea (*tak-e-pne'-ah*). Rapid, shallow respirations; a reflex response to stimulation of the vagus nerve endings in the pulmonary vessels.

tachyphrenia (*tak-e-fre'-ne-ah*). Hyperactivity of the mental processes.

tactile (*tak'-tile*). Relating to the sense of touch.

T-bandage. Used to retain a perineal dressing in position.

Taenia. A tapeworm. *T. echinococcus.* The form parasitic in dogs, which may accidentally infect man, and give rise to hydatid cysts. *T. saginata.* The common type of tapeworm found in the human intestine. *T. solium.* The pork tapeworm; can also be parasitic in man.

taeniafuge (*te'-ne-ah-fuj*). Drugs which expel tapeworms, e.g. filix mas.

TAF. Toxoid-antitoxin floccules. A preparation used for diphtheria immunization. *See* Toxoid.

talcum (*tal'-kum*). A preparation of magnesium silicate, used as a dusting powder.

talipes (*tal'-ip-eez*). Clubfoot. Deformity caused by congenital or acquired contraction of muscles or tendons of the foot. *T. calcaneous.* The heel alone touches the ground on standing. *T. equinus.* Walking on the toes only. *T. valgus.* The inner edge of the foot only is in contact with the ground. *T. varus.* The person walks on the outer edge of the foot.

talus (*ta'-lus*). The astragalus or ankle bone.

tampon (*tam'-pon*). An absorbent wool plug with long thread attached by which it can be anchored. Used to restrain haemorrhage or absorb secretion.

tamponade (*tam-pon-ade'*). The surgical use of tampons.

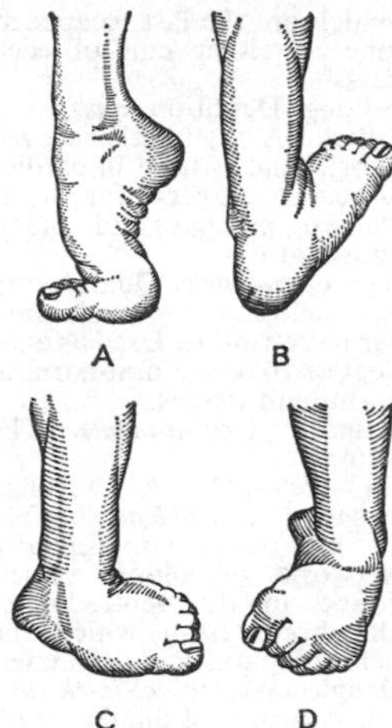

TALIPES

A. Talipes equinus.
B. Talipes calcaneous.
C. Talipes valgus.
D. Talipes varus.

Cardiac t. Impairment of heart action by haemorrhage into the pericardium. This may be owing to a stab wound or following surgery.

tannin (*tan'-nin*). Tannic acid. A yellowish powder prepared from vegetable substances, e.g. from tea. A powerful astringent and haemostatic, which on contact with any mucous membrane causes contraction and diminishes secretions.

tantalum (*tan'-ta-lum*). A metal used for prosthesis and wire sutures. *Radioactive t.* (^{182}Ta) emits γ- and β-rays. It is a flexible wire and can be used to treat carcinoma in difficult situations such as the mouth and the bladder.

tantrum (*tan'-trum*). An outburst of ill-temper. *Temper t.* A behaviour disorder of childhood. A display of bad temper in which the child performs uncontrolled actions in a state of emotional stress.

tap water. Water direct from the main supply. It is sometimes given as a rectal injection in dehydration in preference to saline solution as it is more readily absorbed. *See* Enema.

tapeworm. Taenia (*q.v.*). A species of cestode worms parasitic in the intestines of man and lower animals. The adult consists of a round head with suckers or hooklets for attachment. From this numerous segments arise, each of which produces ova capable of independent existence for a considerable length of time. Treatment is by drugs to expel the parasite, and cure is not complete until the *head* is discharged or destroyed as from this growth takes place.

tapotement (*tap-ote-mon'*). A tapping movement used in massage.

tapping (*tap'-ping*). *See* Paracentesis.

tar. A dark brown or black viscid fluid, derived from the bark of various species of pine. Used externally in certain skin diseases. *Coal t.* Obtained from coal or petroleum. The source of phenol, creosol, xylene, benzene, etc.

tarsal (*tar'-sal*). Relating to the tarsus. *T. bones.* The seven irregular bones of the foot. *T. cyst.* Chalazion (*q.v.*). *T. plates.* Small cartilages in the upper eyelids.

tarsalgia (*tar-sal'-je-ah*). Pain in the foot, with flattening of the arch.

tarsoplasty (*tar'-so-plas-te*). Plastic surgery of the eyelid.

tarsorrhaphy (*tar-sor'-raf-e*). Stitching the eyelids together to protect the cornea or to allow healing of an abrasion.

tarsus (*tar'-sus*). (1) The seven small bones of the instep. (2) The connective tissue which forms the firm supporting tissue of the eyelid.

tartar (*tar'-tar*). (1) Potassium bitartrate (*cream of t.*). (2) A hard incrustation deposited on neglected teeth.

taurocholate of sodium (*tor-o-ko'-late*). One of the bile salts.

Taussig's operation (*tow'-sig*). Block dissection of the pelvic lymphatic glands for carcinoma of the uterus.

Tawara's node (*tah-wah'-rah*). The atrioventricular node. *See* Node.

taxis (*taks'-is*). Manipulation by hand to restore any part to its normal position. It can be used to reduce a hernia.

Tay-Sachs disease. *See* Amaurotic familial idiocy.

technetium (*tek-ne'-te-um*). A metallic element. *Radioactive t.* (^{99}Tc) is used in a number of diagnostic tracer tests.

technique (*tek-neek'*). The details of a method of procedure. *Aseptic t.* That by which a wound is kept surgically clean. *T. for ward dressings*. *See* Appendix 6.

teeth. Structures designed for mastication of food. *Deciduous t.* The milk set. *Eye t.* The canines. *Hutchinson's t.* Having notched and irregular edges. *Wisdom t.* Molars which are the last to appear, one at either end of each jaw.

teething. Dentition (*q.v.*).

Teflon. A synthetic woven fabric that is used in cardiovascular surgery for heart valves, patches and blood vessel grafts.

Tego compounds. Quarternary ammonium compounds similar to cetrimide. Used as antiseptics they are non-harmful to human tissues.

tegument (*teg'-u-ment*). The skin.

tela (*te'-lah*). A web-like tissue. *T. choroidea.* The fold of pia mater containing a network of blood vessels found in the ventricles of the brain from which the cerebrospinal fluid originates.

telangiectasis (*tel-an-je-ek'-tas-is*). A group of dilated capillaries, web-like or radiating in form, seen chiefly on the face in certain disorders of the circulation.

telangioma (*tel-an-je-o'-mah*). A tumour of dilated blood capillaries.

teleceptors (*tel-e-sep'-tors*). Nerve receptors concerned with events at a distance.

telecurietherapy (*tel-e-ku-re-ther'-a-pe*). A γ-ray beam unit in which the source of radiation is housed in a well-protected chamber and only brought to the aperture head when the patient is in position and the personnel have left the area. Radium, cobalt and caesium may be used.

teleradium (*tel-e-ra'-de-um*). The treatment of disease by gamma radiation from a large source of radium. Radium beam therapy.

telophase (*te'-lo-faze*). The stage in the division of cells when the chromosomes have been reconstituted in the nuclei at either end of the cell and the cell cytoplasm divides forming two new cells.

temperature (*tem'-per-at-chur*). The degree of heat of a substance or body as measured by a thermometer. *Inverse t.* One which is lower in the evening than the morning. *Normal t.* of the human body is 36·9°C (98·4°F) with a slight decrease in the early morning, and a slight increase at night. It indicates the balance between heat production and heat loss. A thermometer inserted under the tongue or into the rectum will register slightly higher than when placed in the axilla or groin. *Subnormal t.* is below the normal. A sign of shock. *See also* Pyrexia *and* Fever.

temporal (*tem'-por-al*). Pertaining to the side of the head. *T. bone.* That at the side of the skull and containing the organ of hearing.

temporal arteritis (*tem'-por-al ar-ter-i'-tis*). Giant cell arteritis. An inflammatory condition of the carotid arteries and their branches.

temporomandibular (*tem-por-o-man-dib'-u-lar*). Relating to the temporal region or bone and the mandible.

tenacious (*ten-a'-shus*). Thick and viscid, a term applied to sputum or other body fluids.

tenaculum (*ten-ak'-u-lum*). A hook-shaped instrument.

tendinous (*ten'-din-us*). Having the nature of a tendon.

tendon (*ten'-don*). A band of fibrous tissue, forming the termination of a muscle and attaching it to a bone. *T. of Achilles.* That inserted into the calcaneum. *T. grafting.* An operation which repairs a defect in one tendon by a graft from another. *T. of insertion.* The attachment of a muscle to a bone which it moves. *Kangaroo t.* A form of suture derived from the tail of a kangaroo. *T. of origin.* The beginning of a muscle at its attachment to the more fixed bone. *T. reflex.* The muscle action produced on percussing a tendon.

tenesmus (*ten-ez'-mus*). A painful ineffectual straining to empty the bowel or bladder.

Tenon's capsule (*te'-nons cap'-sul*). The fibrous tissue in which the eyeball is situated.

tenoplasty (*ten'-o-plas-te*). Plastic operation on a tendon.

tenorrhaphy (*ten-or'-raf-e*). The suturing together of the ends of a divided tendon.

tenosynovitis (*te-no-si-no-vi'-tis*). Inflammation of a tendon and its synovial sheath.

tenotomy (*ten-ot'-o-me*). Cutting a tendon.

tension (*ten'-shun*). The act of stretching or the state of being stretched. *Arterial t.* The pressure of blood on the vessel wall during cardiac contraction. *Intra-ocular t.* Pressure of the contents of the eye on its walls, measured by a tonometer. *Premenstrual t.* Symptoms of abdominal distension, headache, emotional lability and depression occurring a few days before the onset of menstruation. *See also* Cyclical syndrome. *Surface t.* The resistance offered by a liquid to another substance in contact with it. *See* Bile tests, Appendix 11.

T. suture. See under Suture.

tensor (*ten'-sor*). A muscle which stretches a part.

tent. (1) A small cone-shaped plug of compressed seaweed which swells considerably on the absorption of moisture. It may be used to dilate the cervix. *See* Laminaria. (2) *Steam t.* A contrivance by which the head of the bed is surrounded by screens and the top covered over to form a tent. A long-spouted kettle projects steam into this enclosure to moisten and warm the air. Used with benefit for upper respiratory diseases such as laryngitis.

tentorium (*ten-tor'-e-um*). The dividing wall of dura mater between the cerebrum and the cerebellum.

tepid (*tep'-id*). Slightly warm; 32·2°–36·7°C (90°–98°F).

teratogenesis (*ter-at-o-jen'-e-sis*). The development and birth of a monster or a child with gross congenital abnormalities.

teratoma (*ter-at-o'-mah*). A solid tumour of the ovary containing tissues similar to those of a dermoid cyst. 80 per cent of these tumours are malignant.

teres (*ter'-ez*). Round. *Ligamentum t.* Round ligament.

terminal (*ter'-min-al*). Placed at, or forming the extremity. The ends of the conducting wires of an electric battery. *T. infection.* An added infection which is fatal.

terminology (*ter-min-ol'-o-je*). The science of nomenclature (*q.v.*) of scientific and technical subjects.

tertian (*ter'-she-an*). Recurring every 48 hr. *See* Malaria.

tertiary (*ter'-she-ar-e*). Third. *T. syphilis.* The non-infectious stage of neurosyphilis.

test. (1) A trial. (2) Analysis of the composition of a substance, by the use of chemical reagents. *Colloidal gold t.* Carried out on the cerebrospinal fluid, it aids in the diagnosis of neurosyphilis. *Hippuric acid t.* One for liver efficiency, when sodium benzolate given by mouth is excreted in the urine. *Hogben t.* A test for pregnancy in which urine of the patient is injected into the Xenopus toad; if positive, eggs are voided by the toad 8 hr later. *Papanicolaou t.* A cervical smear is examined for cell changes indicating a precancerous phase of the cervix. *Schick t.* An intradermal test for susceptibility to diphtheria which has proved invaluable in preventing the disease, as those without resistance can be immunized. *T. meal.* A procedure used to test the digestive powers of the gastric juice. *Fractional test meal.* Designed to estimate the activity of the gastric glands in producing hydrochloric acid. Alcohol, histamine or pentagastrin may be used and successive specimens taken to estimate the acid content. *T. tube.* A thin glass tube closed at one end, used for carrying out chemical tests on fluids. *T. type.* A card of letters of varying size for testing the acuity of sight. For *renal function*, and *urine t.s, see* Appendix 11.

testamentary capacity (*tes-ta-ment'-a-re ka-pas'-e-te*). The ability of a person to understand fully what he is doing when he wishes to make a will.

testicles or **testes** (*test'-ik-kls,*

tes'-teez). The two glands in the scrotum which produce spermatozoa. *Undescended t.* When the organ remains in the pelvis or inguinal canal.

testosterone (*tes-tos'-ter-one*). The hormone produced by the test which stimulates the development of sex characteristics. Now made synthetically. It is used medicinally in cases of failure of sex function and in some cases of female cancer.

tetanic (*tet-an'-ik*). Relating to tetanus. *T. spasms* occur also in strychnine poisoning.

tetanus (*tet'-an-us*). A disease due to *Clostridium tetani*, an anaerobe found in cultivated soil and manure, and therefore likely to infect accidental wounds. The incubation period is 3 to 10 days but may be much longer. *Signs.* Stiffness of muscles around the wound, followed by rigidity of face and neck muscles, hence '*lockjaw*'. All muscles are then affected and opisthotonos may occur. *T. vaccine* or *toxoid* will give an active immunity. *T. antitoxin.* A serum that gives a short-term passive immunity or used for treatment for a case of tetanus.

tetany (*tet'-an-e*). An increased excitability of the nerves due to a lack of available calcium, accompanied by painful muscle spasm (*carpopedal spasm*). The cause may be hypothyroidism or alkalosis owing to excessive vomiting or hypoventilation (*q.v.*).

tetracycline (*tet-ra-si'-kleen*). An antibiotic drug belonging to the group known as the tetracyclines which are used to combat organisms that are resistant to penicillin. Achromycin is a proprietary preparation.

tetradactylous (*tet-ra-dak'-til-us*). Having four digits on each limb.

tetralogy of Fallot (*tet'-ral'-o-je*). Congenital heart lesions. *See* Fallot.

tetraparalysis (*tet-ra-par-al'-e-sis*). Paralysis of all four limbs. Quadriplegia.

tetraparesis (*tet-ra-par-e'-sis*). Partial paralysis of all four limbs.

thalamotomy (*thal-am-ot'-o-me*). The destruction of the nucleus in the thalamus by diathermy. The area needs to be carefully localized first.

thalamus (*thal'-am-us*). A mass of nerve cells at the base of the cerebrum. Most sensory impulses from the body pass to this area and are transmitted to the cortex.

thalassaemia (*thal-a-se'-me-ah*). A disease mostly found in the Mediterranean region, caused by the inheritance of an abnormal haemoglobin. *T. minor.* Moderate to mild anaemia. *T. major.* There is severe anaemia and physical and mental retardation, with death usually occurring before adolescence.

theca (*the'-kah*). A sheath, such as the covering of a tendon. *T. vertebralis.* The membranes enclosing the spinal cord.

theine (*the'-een*). The alkaloid found in tea.

theinism (*the'-in-izm*). The effect on the health of excessive tea drinking.

thenar (*the'-nar*). The palm of the hand or sole of the foot.

Theobroma (*the-o-bro'-mah*). A genus of plants, the oil of which is cacao butter used as a base for suppositories and ointments.

theobromine (*the-o-bro'-min*). An alkaloid from Theobroma whose action is similar to that of caffeine.

theophylline (*the-o-fil'-een*). An alkaloid from tea leaves. Used as a diuretic as is aminophylline.

therapeutics (*ther-a-pu'-tiks*). The science and art of healing and the treatment of disease.

therapy (*ther'-ap-e*). Treatment. *Curie t.* Treatment with radium. *Group t.* A form of psychotherapy. *See* Group. *Occupational t.* Treatment by providing interesting and congenial work within the limitations of the patient in mental diseases, and in order to re-educate and co-ordinate muscles in physical defects. *See* Rehabilitation. *Oxygen t.* Treatment by inhalations of oxygen. *Rôle t.* A method of psychiatric treatment in which the patient casts the nurse or psychotherapist into the rôle of someone who has had a great influence on his past. The nurse, under guidance of the psychiatrist, assists by behaving in the manner of the object of the patient's emotion. *Solar t.* Heliotherapy (*q.v.*).

therm (*ther'-m*). A unit of heat. *See under* Unit.

thermal (*ther'-mal*). Relating to heat.

thermocautery (*ther-mo-kaw'-ter-e*). The 'actual' cautery. *See Cautery.*

thermodilution (*ther-mo-di-lu'-shun*). A method of measuring the volume of blood in the ventricles. A temperature recording head is inserted in a cardiac catheter and ice cold water, which causes a drop in temperature, is introduced. The result is obtained by mathematical formula.

thermogenesis (*ther-mo-jen'-e-sis*). The production of heat.

thermography (*therm-og'-ra-fe*). A photographic method of early detection of cancer by means of infrared rays. It depends on the greater blood supply of a cancerous growth to that of the surrounding tissue.

thermolysis (*ther-mol'-is-is*). The loss of body heat.

thermometer (*ther-mom'-e-ter*). An instrument for measuring temperature. *Centigrade t.* One graduated to the Centigrade (Celsius) scale. Internationally used in industry and increasingly in medicine. *Clinical t.* One used to measure the body temperature. *Fahrenheit t.* One marked in the Fahrenheit scale. *See* Appendix 15.

thermostat (*ther'-mo-stat*). An apparatus which automatically regulates the temperature by cutting out the source of heat.

thermotaxis (*ther-mo-taks'-is*). The regulation of body temperature by maintaining the balance between heat production and heat loss.

thermotherapy (*ther-mo-ther'-ap-e*). The treatment of disease by application of heat.

thiamine (*thi'-a-min*). Vitamin B_1, or aneurine. Necessary for healthy nerves and mucous membranes. The source is liver and unrefined cereals.

Thiersch's skin graft (*teersh*). The transplantation of areas of partial thickness skin. *See* Graft.

thigh (*thi*). The lower limb, from the pelvis to the knee.

thiopentone sodium (*thi-o-pen'-*

ton). A basal narcotic of the barbiturate group given intravenously. Pentothal is a proprietary preparation of it.

thiotepa (*thi-o-te'-pa*). An intravenous cytotoxic drug used in the treatment of leukaemia.

thiouracil (*thi-o-u'-ras-il*). A synthetic drug used in the medical treatment of hyperthyroidism or to stabilize a patient before operation. *Methyl-t.* and *prophyl-t.* are the forms used and are unlikely to give rise to the toxic effects of fever, rash and agranulocytosis.

thirst. An uncomfortable sensation of dryness of the mouth and throat with a desire for oral fluids.

Thomas's frame. A metal frame used in the treatment of tuberculosis of the spine.

Thomas's splint. A useful splint. The limb is supported by cross-pieces of material slung between side rods. It is used for fractured femur, and for injuries to the lower limb.

thoracentesis (*thor-a-sen-te'-sis*). Aspiration of the pleural cavity.

thoracic (*thor-as'-ik*). Relating to the thorax. *T. duct.* The large lymphatic vessel, situated in the thorax along the spine. It opens into the left subclavian vein.

thoracoplasty (*thor'-ak-o-plas-te*). An operation on the chest, e.g. to produce collapse of the lung or to obliterate an empyema cavity by removing a number of ribs.

thoracoscopy (*thor-ak-os'-ko-pe*). Examination of the pleural cavity by means of an endoscopic instrument.

thoracotomy (*thor-ak-ot'-o-me*). An incision into the thorax, e.g. to break down adhesions or for drainage purposes.

thorax (*thor'-aks*). The chest; a cavity containing the heart, lungs, bronchi and oesophagus. It is bounded by the diaphragm, the sternum, the dorsal vertebrae, and the ribs. *Barrel-shaped t.* A development in emphysema, when the chest is malformed like a barrel.

threadworm. A species of Oxyuris, parasitic in the colon of children.

thrill. A tremor discerned by palpation.

throat. (1) The anterior surface of the neck. (2) The pharynx. *Sore t.* Pharyngitis. *Clergyman's sore t.* Laryngitis.

thrombectomy (*throm-bek'-to-me*). Excision of a thrombus.

thrombin (*throm'-bin*). An enzyme released in the clotting process from the precursor prothrombin.

thrombo-angeitis (*throm-bo-an-je-i'-tis*). Inflammation of blood vessels with clot formation. *T-a. obliterans.* Obstruction of the circulation, causing gangrene. Usually, but not invariably, occurs in the lower limb. Buerger's disease.

thrombocytes (*throm'-bo-sites*). Blood platelets (*q.v.*).

thrombocytopenia (*throm-bo-si-to-pee'-ne-ah*). A disease in the platelets in the blood. Spontaneous bleeding may occur.

thrombocytopenic purpura (*throm-bo-si-to-pe'-nik pur'-pu-rah*). A severe disease in which there are too few platelets and haemorrhages arise from all mucous surfaces. Purpura haemorrhagica.

PROCESS IN CLOTTING OF BLOOD

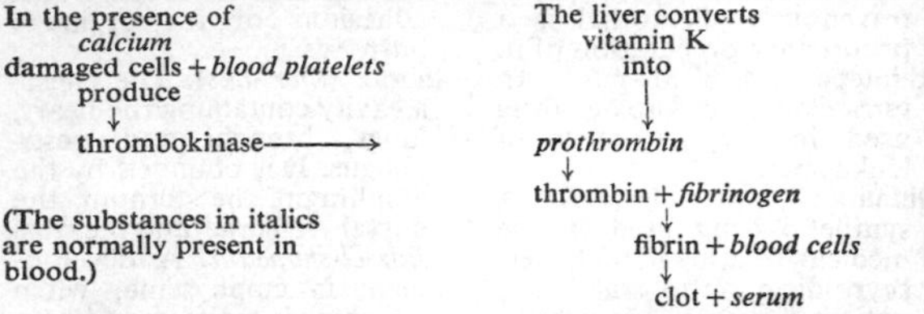

In the presence of
calcium
damaged cells + *blood platelets*
produce
↓
thrombokinase ——→

The liver converts
vitamin K
into
↓
prothrombin
↓
thrombin + *fibrinogen*
↓
fibrin + *blood cells*
↓
clot + *serum*

(The substances in italics are normally present in blood.)

thrombocytosis (*throm-bo-si-to'-sis*). Increase in the number of platelets in blood.

thrombo-endarterectomy (*throm'-bo end-art-er-ek'-to-me*). Removal of a clot from a thrombosed vessel.

thrombo-endarteritis (*throm'-bo end-art-er-i'-tis*). Inflammation in small arteries with clot formation as a result.

thrombogen (*throm'-bo-jen*). Prothrombin. The precursor of thrombin.

thrombokinase (*throm-bo-kin'-aze*). Thromboplastin. A lipid containing protein activated by blood platelets and injured tissues, which is capable of activating prothrombin to form thrombin.

thrombolysis (*throm-bol'-is-is*). The disintegration or dissolving of a clot.

thromboplastin (*throm-bo-plas'-tin*). *See* Thrombokinase.

thrombophlebitis (*throm-bo-fle-bi'-tis*). A term applied to blood clot formation in a vein with inflammation of the vessel lining.

thrombosis (*throm-bo'-sis*). The formation of a thrombus. *Cavernous sinus t.* This may be a result of infection of the face, when the veins in the sinus are affected via ophthalmic vessels. *Coronary t.* The occlusion of a coronary vessel, by which the heart muscle is deprived of blood according to the size of the vessel blocked. *Lateral sinus t.* A complication of mastoiditis when infection of the sinus occurs and there is clot formation.

thrombotest (*throm'-bo-test*). A test used to measure factors IX and X in the blood, which may be affected by anticoagulants, and where deficiency may lead to bleeding.

thrombus (*throm'-bus*). A stationary blood clot caused by coagulation of the blood, usually in a vein, and often the result of stasis.

thrush. An infection of the mucous membrane of the mouth by a fungus, the *Candida albicans*. It arises in under-nourished infants when unclean teats and bottles are used, also in older persons suffering from debilitating disease where there is lack of oral hygiene. Thus it is a preventable disease. It can be treated by application of nystatin. *See* Stomatitis.

thymectomy (*thi-mek'-to-me*). Removal of the thymus gland.

A treatment for myasthenia gravis.

thymokesis (*thi-mo-ke'-sis*). Persistence of the thymus gland in an adult.

thymol (*thi'-mol*). An aromatic antiseptic used in solution as a mouth wash.

thymoma (*thi-mo'-mah*). A benign new growth that originates in thymus tissue and is found to be present in a number of patients suffering from myasthenia gravis.

thymus (*thi'-mus*). A gland-like structure situated in the upper thorax and neck. Present in early life, it reaches its maximum size at 10 to 12 years and then slowly regresses. Its only known function is the formation of lymphocytes. The gland is often enlarged in myasthenia gravis and its removal has benefited a number of patients.

thyrocricotomy (*thi-ro-kri-kot'-o-me*). An opening made between the thyroid and cricoid cartilages.

thyroglobin (*thi-ro-glo'-bin*). The protein in thyroxine, the endocrine secretion of the thyroid.

thyroglossal (*thi-ro-glos'-al*). Relating to the thyroid and the tongue. *T. cyst*. *See under* Cyst.

thyroid (*thi'-roid*). Shaped like a shield. *T. crisis*. A serious complication of partial thyroidectomy in which there is hyperpyrexia, tachycardia and extreme restlessness. Now less common because it is possible to stabilize the patient before operation by the use of an antithyroid drug. *T. cartilage* is the largest of the laryngeal cartilages. *T. extract* is a preparation from the thyroid gland of animals, used to treat cretinism and myxoedema (*q.v.*). *T. gland* is a bilobed endocrine gland situated in front of the trachea. *Retrosternal t.* when the gland is wholly or in part behind the sternum.

thyroidectomy (*thi-roid-ek'-to-me*). Partial or complete removal of the thyroid gland.

thyroparathyroidectomy (*thi'-ro-par-ah-thi-roid-ek'-to-me*). Removal of the thyroid and parathyroid glands.

thyrotomy (*thi-rot'-o-me*). Division of the thyroid cartilage.

thyrotoxicosis (*thi-ro-toks-e-ko'-sis*). Hyperthyroidism. The symptoms arising when there is overactivity of the thyroid gland. The metabolism is speeded up and there is enlargement of the gland and exophthalmos.

thyrotrophic (*thi-ro-tro'-fik*). The hormone secreted by the pituitary that stimulates the thyroid gland.

thyroxine (*thi-roks'-in*). The iodine-containing hormone secreted by the thyroid gland. Now prepared synthetically.

tibia (*tib'-e-ah*). The shin bone. The larger of the two bones of the leg, extending from knee to ankle.

tic. Spasmodic twitching of certain muscles, usually of the face or neck. *T. douloureux*. Spasmodic facial neuralgia.

tick. A blood-sucking parasite, which may transmit the organisms of disease.

tidal air. *See under* Air.

tincture (*tink'-chur*). An alcoholic solution of a drug.

tinea (*tin'-e-ah*). A skin disease caused by parasitic fungi of the genus Trichophyton. Named after the area of the body affected; *T. barbae*—the beard; *T. capitis*—the head; *T. circinata* or *T. corporis*—the body and *T. cruris*, the groin. *See* Ringworm.

tinnitus (*tin'-it-us*). A ringing or roaring sound in the ears.

tintometer (*tin-tom'-e-ter*). An instrument by which changes in colour can be measured.

tissue (*tis'-u*). A mass of cells or fibres forming one of the structures of which the body is composed. *Adipose t.* Fatty tissue. *Areolar t.* Connective tissue of bundles of white fibres, elastic fibres, and connective tissue cells. *Cancellous t.* The honeycomb arrangement of bone cells beneath the compact layer, especially at the ends of long bones, and in the centre of such bones as the clavicle, sternum, ribs, cranium and vertebra. It contains red bone marrow. *Compact t.* The close arrangement of bone cells which forms the outer layer of all bones and is especially thick in the shafts. *Connective t.* A general term for all those tissues of the body which support and connect the various organs and other structures. *Fibrous t.* Connective tissue composed of bundles of white fibres. *Elastic t.* Connective tissue chiefly composed of yellow elastic fibres. *Gamgee t.* A layer of wool completely enclosed in gauze. Used as a surgical dressing. *Interstitial t.* The stroma (*q.v.*). *Homologous t.* One similar in structure to another. *Parenchymatous t.* The essential functioning cells of an organ, as distinct from its supporting tissues. *Trophoblastic t.* The lining cells of the chorionic villi.

tissue culture. The ability to grow animal and human tissues in a test-tube. Tissues have been used as a medium for cultivating the virus of poliomyelitis.

titrate (*ti'-trate*). To estimate by titration.

titration (*ti-tra'-shun*). A method of estimating the weight of a solute in solution by dropping a measured amount of a reagent into a measured quantity of solution and the expected colour change or reaction occurs.

tocopherol (*tok-of'-er-ol*). Vitamin E present in wheat germ, green leaves and milk.

tolazoline (*tol-az'-ol-in*). A vaso-dilator drug of the peripheral blood vessels. It may be used in treating Raynaud's disease. Priscol is a proprietary preparation.

tolbutamide (*tol-bu'-ta-mide*). An oral drug that appears to stimulate the release of insulin from the pancreas and may be used in some cases of diabetes.

tolerance (*tol'-er-anse*). The capacity for assimilating large amounts of a drug or food without harmful effects. *Sugar t.* The amount of sugar which a diabetic can metabolize as shown by the blood sugar curve, or by the appearance of sugar in the urine.

tolu (*tol-oo'*). An aromatic balsam. An ingredient in linctus preparations.

tomograph (*to'-mo-graf*). An X-ray apparatus so designed that a photograph can be taken at any depth of tissue. A clear picture is thus obtained.

-tomy (*to'-me*). A suffix meaning 'to cut'.

tone. The normal degree of tension, e.g. in a muscle.

tongue (*tung*). The movable muscular organ attached to the floor of the mouth and concerned in taste, mastication and speech. It is covered by mucous membrane from which project numerous papillae. *Strawberry t.* Typical of scarlet fever. It is at first thickly furred but dotted with protruding red papillae. In a day or two the fur peels off leaving the characteristic bright red appearance.

tonic (*ton'-ik*). To restore to normal tone. A term popularly applied to drugs supposed to brace or tone up the body, or any particular part or organ. *T. spasm.* A prolonged contraction of one or several muscles. *See also* Clonic.

tonicity (*ton-is'-it-e*). A term applied to the effective osmotic pressure of a fluid in relation to plasma.

tonography (*ton-og'-raf-e*). A tracing made by an electric tonometer recording the intra-ocular pressure and so indirectly the drainage of aqueous humour from the eye.

tonometer (*ton-om'-e-ter*). An instrument for measuring intra-ocular pressure.

tonsil (*ton'-sil*). One of two small almond-shaped bodies, situated one on each side between the pillars of the fauces. It is composed of lymphoid tissue covered by mucous membrane, and its surface is pitted with follicles. *Pharyngeal t.* The lymphadenoid tissue of the pharynx between the Eustachian tubes.

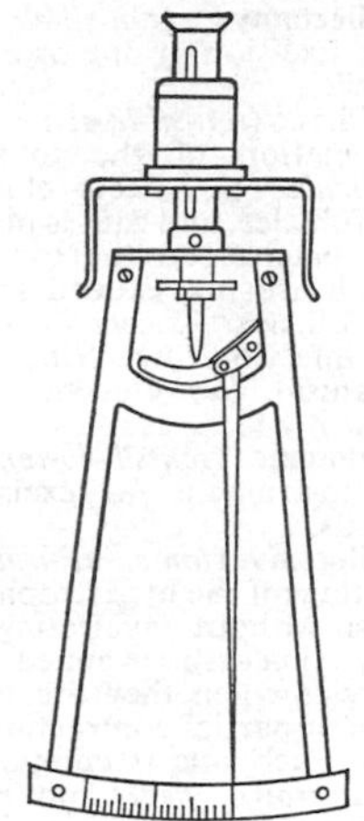

TONOMETER

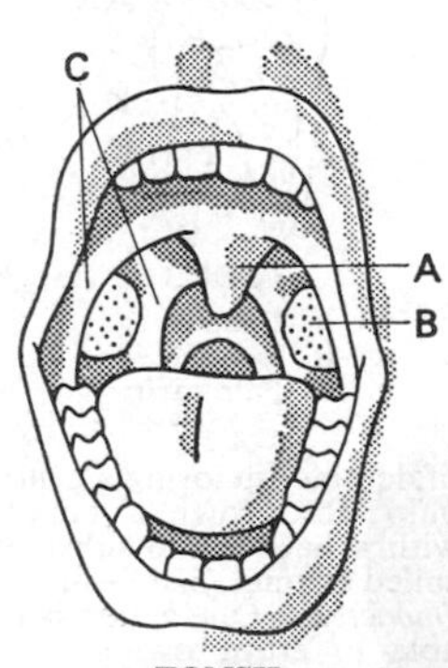

TONSIL

A. Uvula.
B. Tonsil.
C. Pillars of the fauces.

tonsillectomy (*ton-sil-ek'-to-me*). Excision of one or both tonsils.

tonsillitis (*ton-sil-li'-tis*). Inflammation of the tonsils. *Follicular t.* Affects chiefly the follicles, and causes purulent patches on the tonsils, which are pus exuded from the follicles. *Vincent's t.* Due to infection by Vincent's organism. *See* Vincent's angina.

tonsillotome (*ton-sil'-lo-tome*). An instrument for excising tonsils.

tonsillotomy (*ton-sil-ot'-o-me*). Cutting off the hypertrophied tonsil without enucleating it.

tonus (*ton'-us*). Applied to muscles when they are in a state of partial contraction.

tooth. Each one is composed of a *crown*, *neck* and *root* with one or more fangs. The main bulk of the tooth is

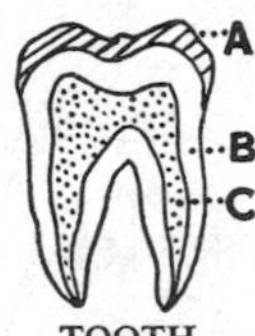

TOOTH

A. Enamel.
B. Dentine.
C. Pulp cavity.

of dentine enclosing a central pulp; the crown is covered with a hard white substance called enamel. *See* Dentition. *Impacted t.* One which is unable to erupt owing to its position in the jaw.

topectomy (*to-pek'-to-me*). Gyrectomy. The cutting of part of the frontal lobe of the cerebral cortex. A method of cerebral surgery in mental illness.

tophus (*to'-fus*). A small, hard, chalky deposit occurring in gout, and sometimes appearing on the auricle of the ear It is composed of urate of sodium.

topical (*top'-ik-al*). Relating to a particular spot; local. *T. fluid.* One for local or external application.

topography (*to-pog'-raf-e*). Mapping out the surface of the body in reference to the underlying structures.

torpor (*tor'-por*). A sluggish condition, in which response to stimuli is absent or very slow.

torsion (*tor'-shun*). Twisting. (1) Of an artery to arrest haemorrhage; (2) of the pedicle of a cyst which produces venous congestion in the cyst and consequent gangrene—a possible complication of ovarian cyst.

torso (*tor'-so*). The trunk.

torticollis (*tor-te-kol'-lis*). Wry-neck, a contraction of one or more of the cervical muscles on one side only, resulting in an abnormal position of the head. *Congenital t.* Is due to injury to the sternocleidomastoid muscle at birth. It becomes a fibrous cord. *Spasmodic t.* May occur due to spasmodic contraction of the sterno-mastoid muscle.

tourniquet (*toor'-ne-ket*). Any constrictive band applied to a limb to arrest arterial haemorrhage. When available an inflated sphygmomanometer cuff is the safest type to apply. If in an emergency an improvised or rubber tourniquet is applied there is a grave risk of permanent damage to muscles or nerve supply.

tow (*to*). The coarse part of flax used for padding splints.

toxaemia (*toks-e'-me-ah*). Poisoning of the blood by the absorption of toxins. *T. of pregnancy*. Characterized by albuminuria, hypertension and oedema, with the possibility of eclampsia developing if untreated.

toxic (*toks'-ik*). Poisonous, relating to a poison. May refer to substances produced in the body by infection or metabolic disturbance.

toxicity (*toks-is'-it-e*). The degree of virulence of a poison.

toxicology (*toks-e-kol'-o-je*). The science dealing with poisons.

toxicosis (*toks-e-ko'-sis*). The state of poisoning by toxins.

toxin (*toks'-in*). Any poisonous nitrogenous compound, usually referring to that produced by bacteria.

toxoid (*toks'-oid*). A toxin which has been deprived of some of its harmful properties but is still capable of producing immunity. *Diphtheria t.* Toxin which has been treated with formaldehyde. Used for immunization against diphtheria. *See* TAF *and* APT.

toxoid-antitoxin (*toks'-oid an-te-toks'-in*). A mixture of a toxoid and its antitoxin.

toxoplasmosis (*toks-o-plaz-mo'-sis*). A condition of enlarged glands and fever caused by a protozoon, the Toxoplasma. May cause hydrocephalus and other disorders in infants born of infected mothers.

trabecula (*trab-ek'-u-lah*). A dividing band or septum, extending from the capsule of an organ into its interior and holding the functioning cells in position.

tracer. A substance or instrument that can be used to gain information, e.g. *t.* doses of radioactive iodine are used to investigate disease of the thyroid gland.

trachea (*trak-e'-ah*). The windpipe: a cartilaginous tube lined with ciliated mucous membrane, extending from the lower part of the larynx to the commencement of the bronchi.

tracheitis (*trak-e-i'-tis*). Inflammation of the trachea.

trachelorrhaphy (*trak-el-or'-raf-e*). Operation for suturing lacerations of the cervix of the uterus.

tracheostomy (*trak-e-os'-to-me*). Making an opening or stoma into the trachea. *T. tubes*. Those used to maintain an airway following this operation until the normal use of the air-passages is regained. The tube must be kept clear, the inner one being removed frequently and cleaned in bicarbonate of soda solution. The operation is used to maintain respiration and to treat excessive bronchial secretions in many surgical and medical conditions. It is usually a temporary measure. *Inferior t.* The opening is made below the thyroid isthmus. *Superior t.* The opening is made above the thyroid isthmus.

tracheotomy (*trak-e-ot'-o-me*). Cutting into the trachea.

trachoma (*trak-o'-mah*). A contagious conjunctivitis marked by granulations on the membrane and contractions of the lids to scar tissue formation.

traction (*trak'-shun*). The act of pulling or drawing. *Skeletal t.* A method of keeping the fractured ends of bone in position by actual pull on the bone. A metal pin or wire is passed through the distal

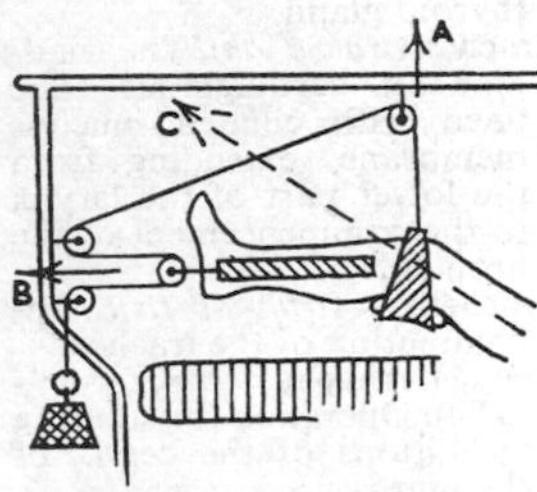

RUSSELL TRACTION
Traction at A and B.
C. Resultant force exerted here.

fragment or adjacent bone to overcome muscle contraction. *Russell t.* A form of movable traction in which there is an upward pull over a beam and the cord is continuous with a series of three pulleys attached to the limb by skin traction horizontally. The combined direction of pull on the femur is between the two at 45°. *Skin t. See* Extension.

tragacanth (*trag'-a-kanth*). A substance resembling *gum arabic*. Used in pharmacy for suspending insoluble powders. A demulcent. *T. powder*. A useful skin application around an ileostomy.

tragi (*tra'-gi*). Pl. of tragus. The hairs at the external auditory meatus.

tragus (*tra'-gus*). (1) The small prominence of cartilage at the external meatus of the ear. (2) One of the hairs at the external auditory meatus.

trait (*tra*). An inherited physical or mental characteristic.

trance (*trahnse*). A condition of unnatural sleep of hysterical, cataleptic or hypnotic origin. It is not due to organic disease.

tranquillizers (*tran'-kwil-i-zers*). Drugs that allay anxiety and have a calming effect on the patient, and appear to render them indifferent to pain, e.g. chlorpromazine and promethazine.

trans- A prefix meaning 'through' or 'across'.

transaminase test (*trans-am'-in-ase*). A diagnostic test for cardiac infarction and infective hepatitis. The *serum glutamic oxalacetic t.* (SGOT) is raised in cardiac infarction; it is an enzyme excreted by damaged heart muscle. The *serum glutamic pyruvic t.* (SGPT) is raised in infective hepatitis as it is excreted by damaged parenchymal cells of the liver.

transducers (*trans-du'-cers*). The data sources or electrodes attached to the patient to enable recordings to be made. *See* Monitoring.

transection (*trans-sek'-shun*). Section across the long axis of a part, e.g. *t. of stomach*, which is performed in partial gastrectomy.

transference (*trans'-fer-ense*). A term used in psychiatry whereby the patient unconsciously transfers on to the psychiatrist feelings which belong to other people significant to him, both past and present.

transfusion (*trans-fu'-zhun*). The introduction of whole blood or plasma into a vein, performed in cases of severe loss of blood, shock, septicaemia, etc. It is used to supply actual volume of blood, or to introduce constituents as clotting factors, or antibodies, which are deficient in the patient. *Exchange* or *Exsanguination t.* Performed on newly born infants for complete replacement of the baby's blood. *See* Rhesus factor. *Intra-arterial t.* Blood is passed into an artery under positive pressure in cases where large quantities are required rapidly as in cardiovascular surgery. *Intramedullary t.* The needle or special cannula is passed into the bone marrow either of the sternum or tibia. *Plasma t.* The fluid is transfused after the cell content has been removed.

transillumination (*trans-il-lu-min-a'-shun*). The illumination of a cavity by means of an electric light, as an aid to diagnosis.

translocation (*trans-lo-ka'-shun*). In morphology the transfer of a segment of a chromosome to a different site on the same chromosome or to a different chromosome. It can be a cause of congenital abnormality.

translumbar (*trans-lum'-bar*). Via the lumbar area, often used in aortography.

transmigration (*trans-mi-gra'-shun*). Wandering. The passage of blood cells through the walls of the capillaries. Diapedesis. *External t.* The passage of an ovum from its ovary to the Fallopian tube on the opposite side.

transplacental (*trans-plas-ent'-al*). The ability of antibodies, drugs or toxins to pass through the placenta from mother to fetus during pregnancy or in reverse from fetus to mother.

transplantation (*trans-plant-a'-shun*). The removal of a section of tissue from one part to another, or to another body. *Tendon t.* The transfer of a strip of tendon from a healthy muscle to a paralysed one. *T. of ureters.* A necessary accompaniment to excision of the bladder. The ureters are usually implanted in the colon or loop of ileum.

transposition (*trans-po-sish'-un*). (1) Displacement of any of the viscera to the opposite side of the body. (2) The operation which partially removes a piece of tissue from one part of the body to another, the complete severance being delayed until it has become established in its new position.

transudate (*trans'-u-date*). Any fluid which passes through a membrane. *T. pleurisy.* When fluid oozes into the pleural sac, as may occur in oedematous conditions, e.g. chronic nephritis or congestive heart failure.

transurethral (*trans-u-re'-thral*). Via the urethra. *T. prostatectomy. See* Prostatectomy.

transverse (*trans-verse'*). Oblique, cross-wise. *T. presentation.* The child lies across the pelvis, which position must be corrected before normal birth can take place. *T. ligaments.* Those stretching from the pelvis to the cervix and supporting the uterus.

tranylcypromine (*tra-nil-si-pro'-meen*). A drug used in psychiatry for the treatment of depression. Parnate is a proprietary preparation.

trapezium (*trap-e'-ze-um*). A bone in the distal row of the carpus.

trapezius (*trap-e'-ze-us*). One of two large muscles situated between the shoulders; its action is to draw the head backward.

Trasylol (*tra'-se-lol*). A non-toxic inhibitor of proteolytic enzymes that may be given intravenously in acute pancreatitis.

trauma (*traw'-mah*). A wound or injury. *Psychic t.* A mental or physical injury which can lead to mental illness.

traumatic (*traw-mat'-ik*). Caused by injury. *T. automatism.* As the result of injury, the patient responds normally to his environment, but has no memory of such actions. *T. fever.* That following an operation or injury when no bacterial infection is present. It is due to absorption of injured tissues, especially blood. Also known as *aseptic* fever.

treatment. Mode of dealing with a patient or disease. *Active t.* is vigorously applied. *Ante-natal t.* Deals with the care of the mother during pregnancy to maintain her health and ensure normal delivery of the child. *Conservative t.* That which aims at preserving and restoring injured parts by natural means, e.g. rest, fluid replacement, etc., as opposed to radical or surgical methods. *Empirical t.* is based on observation of symptoms and not on science. *Expectant t.* In which symptoms only are treated, leaving nature to cure. *Palliative t.* Relieves symptoms but does not cure disease. *Prophylactic t.* Aims at the prevention of disease.

Trematoda (*trem-a-to'-dah*). Fluke-worms.

tremor (*trem'-or*). An involuntary, muscular quivering which may be due to fatigue, emotion, or disease. *Fine t.* One which occurs with 10 to 12 vibrations per second. *Intention t.* One which occurs on attempting a movement, as in disseminated sclerosis.

Trendelenburg's operation. Section and ligature of the long saphenous vein in the treatment of varicose veins.

Trendelenburg position (*tren'-del-en-berg*). *See under* Position.

Trendelenburg's sign. An aid in diagnosis of congenital dislocation of the hip. The patient stands on the affected leg and flexes the other knee and hip. If there is dislocation the pelvis is lower on the side of the flexed leg which is the reverse of normal.

trephine (*tre-fine'*). An instrument for cutting out a circular piece of bone, usually from the skull; employed in certain cases of cerebral compression.

Treponema pallidum (*tre-po-ne'-mah pal'-id-um*). The parasite of syphilis. Formerly known as the *Spirochaeta pallida*. *T. p. immobilization.* A complement fixation test for syphilis.

Treponema pertenue (*tre-po-me'-mah per-ten'-u*). The spirochaete causing yaws (*q.v.*).

Treponema pinta (*tre-po-ne' mah pin'-ta*). The spirochaete causing pinta (*q.v.*).

tretamine (*tre-ta'-meen*). T.E.M. A cytotoxic drug

that is related to nitrogen mustard and interferes with division of the cell nucleus. The drug can be administered orally or intravenously.

triamcinolone (*tri-am-sin-o'-lone*). A glucocorticoid steroid which is less likely to cause salt and water retention.

triamterine (*tri-am'-ter-een*). A diuretic that acts by antagonizing aldosterone and does not cause potassium loss.

triangular bandage. A triangle of unbleached calico, useful for various emergencies. A large folded scarf or handkerchief is a substitute.

triceps (*tri'-seps*). Having three heads. The muscle which extends the forearm.

trichiasis (*trik-i'-as-is*). Friction and irritation of the cornea due to abnormal position of the eyelashes.

trichinosis (*trik-in-o'-sis*). A disease caused by eating underdone pork containing a parasite—the *Trichinella spiralis*. This becomes deposited in muscle, and causes stiffness and painful swelling. There may also be nausea, diarrhoea, fever, and in severe cases, prostration.

trichloroethylene (*tri-klor-o-eth'-e-leen*). An anaesthetic, the fumes of which are inhaled to produce a light anaesthesia with freedom from pain. Useful in midwifery, for painful dressings and in general anaesthesia as it is non-explosive.

Trichomonas (*trik-o-mo'-nas*). A ciliated protozoon which normally inhabits the bowel and may give rise to vaginitis.

trichomoniasis (*trik-o-mon-i'-as-is*). Infestation of the genital tract with a parasite of the genus Trichomonas.

trichophytosis (*trik-o-fi-to'-sis*). Disease of the hair produced by a fungus, the Trichophyton. It may attack many areas of the body. Griseofulvin is an effective treatment. *See* Tinea.

trichorrhoea (*trik-o-re'-ah*). Premature loss of hair.

trichosis (*trik-o'-sis*). Any abnormal growth of hair.

Trichuris (*trik-u'-ris*). A genus of whipworms, which sometimes infects the colon of man and causes diarrhoea.

trichuriasis (*trik-ur-i'-as-is*). Infestation by the whipworm.

tricuspid (*tri-kus'-pid*). Having three flaps or cusps. *T. valve*. That at the opening between the right auricle and the right ventricle of the heart.

trifluoperazine (*tri-flu-o-per'-a-zeen*). A potent tranquillizing drug that is used in psychiatry. Stelazine is the proprietary preparation.

trigeminal nerve (*tri-jem'-in-al*). The fifth pair of cranial nerves, each of which is divided into three main branches and supplies one side of the face.

trigeminus (*tri-jem'-in-us*). Triple. *Pulsus t.* The type of pulse in which there are three beats and then a missed beat. A regular irregularity. *See also* Bigeminus.

trigger finger. A stenosing of the tendon sheath at the metacarpophalangeal joint allowing flexion of the finger but not extension without assistance when it 'clicks' into position.

trigone (*tri'-gone*). A triangular area. *T. of the bladder*. The triangular space on the floor of the bladder, between the ureteric openings and the urethral orifice.

triglycerides (*tri-glis'-er-ides*). Esters of glycerol and the fatty acids; palmitic, oleic and stearic.

Trilene (*tri'-leen*). A proprietary preparation of trichloroethylene (*q.v.*).

trimeprazine (*tri-mep'-ra-zeen*). An antihistamine drug with a sedative action. It is supplied in syrup or tablet form and may be used for premedication. Vallergan is a proprietary preparation.

trimester (*tre-mes'-ter*). A third part. *First t. of pregnancy*. The first 3 months during which rapid development is taking place.

trinitrin (*tri-ni'-trin*). Nitroglycerin. A vasodilatant drug used in the treatment of angina pectoris.

trismus (*triz'-mus*). Lock-jaw. A tonic spasm of the muscles of the jaw caused either by tetanus, or it may result from caries of the jaw.

trisomy (*tri'-som-e*). The cause of mongolism, namely the presence of three chromosomes 21, an abnormality of chromosome division.

tritium (*trit'-e-um*). An isotope of hydrogen (H_3) that is used as a tracer in studies of metabolism.

trocar (*tro'-kar*). A pointed instrument used with a cannula for performing paracentesis.

trochanter (*tro-kan'-ter*). Two prominences, below the neck of the femur. *Large* or *Great t.* That on the outer side forming the bony prominence of the hip. *Minor* or *Lesser t.* On the inner side at the neck of the femur.

troche (*tro'-ke*). A medicated tablet.

trochlea (*trok'-le-ah*). Any pulley-shaped structure; but particularly the fibrocartilage near the inner angular process of the frontal bone through which passes the tendon of the superior oblique muscle of the eye.

trochlear nerves. The fourth pair of cranial nerves.

trophic (*trof'-ik*). Relating to nutrition. *T. nerves*. Those which control the nutrition of a part. *T. ulcer*. *See* Ulcer.

trophic hormones (*trof-ik hor'-mones*). The hormones of the anterior pituitary that stimulate the secretion of other endocrine glands.

trophoblast (*trof'-o-blast*). The layer of cells surrounding the embryo at the time of and responsible for implantation.

trophoneurosis (*trof-o-nu-ro'-sis*). Malnutrition of a part, due to disturbance of the trophic nerves.

tropical (*trop'-ik-al*). Relating to the areas north and south of the equator termed the tropics. *T. medicine*. That concerned with diseases that are more prevalent in hot climates.

truancy (*tru'-an-se*). When a child stays away from school without leave. A disorder of conduct which may result from emotional insecurity or a feeling of unfairness.

truncus arteriosus (*trunk'-us ar-ter-e-o'-sus*). The arterial trunk connected to the fetal heart which develops into the aortic and pulmonary arteries. *Persistent t.a.* A rare congenital deformity in which this persists causing a mixing of the systemic and pulmonary circulation

truss (*trus*). An apparatus in the form of a belt with a pressure pad, for retaining a hernia in place after reduction.

Trypanosoma (*trip-an-o-so'-mah*). A genus of parasites, which may pass one half of their life cycle in the blood of man. *T. gambiense* and *T. rhodensiense*. Transmitted by the bite of the tsetse fly, and the cause of sleeping sickness.

trypanosomiasis (*trip-an-o-so-mi'-as-is*). *See* Sleeping sickness.

trypsin (*trip'-sin*). A digestive enzyme converting protein into amino acids.

trypsinogen (*trip-sin'-o-jen*). The precursor of trypsin. It is secreted in the pancreatic juice, and activated by the enterokinase of the succus entericus into trypsin.

tryptophan (*trip'-to-fan*). One of the essential amino acids.

tsetse fly (*tset'-se*). The insect which transmits the parasite *Trypanosoma* to man.

tsutsugamushi disease (*tsu-tsu-ga-mu'-shi*). Scrub typhus that occurs in Japan and is transmitted by the bite of a mite.

tubal. Relating to a tube. *T. pregnancy*. Extra-uterine pregnancy where the embryo develops in the Fallopian tube.

tubectomy (*tu-bek'-to-me*). Excision of a portion of a Fallopian tube.

tubercle (*tu'-ber-kl*). (1) A small nodule or a rounded prominence on a bone. (2) The specific lesion—a small nodule—produced by the tubercle bacillus.

tuberculides (*tu-ber'-ku-lids*). Eruptions on the skin of tuberculous origin.

tuberculin (*tu-ber'-ku-lin*). The filtrate from a fluid medium in which the *Mycobacterium tuberculosis* has been grown and which contains its toxins. *Old t.* or *tuberculin T.* is prepared from the human bacillus. It is used in skin tests in diagnosing tuberculosis. *See* Mantoux test.

tuberculosis (*tu-ber-ku-lo'-sis*). A specific infectious disease produced by the *Mycobacterium tuberculosis*, discovered by Koch. *Bovine t.* A form found in cattle and spread by infected milk. *Miliary t.* A severe form with small tuberculous lesions spread throughout the body with severe toxaemia. *Open t.* Pulmonary tuberculosis in which the organisms are being excreted in the sputum. *Pulmonary t.* That affecting the lungs; also termed phthisis.

tuberculous (*tu-ber'-ku-lus*). Infected with or relating to tuberculosis.

tuberosity (*tu-ber-os'-it-e*). A flat protuberance on a bone. *Radial t.* The surface into which the tendon of the biceps muscle is inserted. *T. of tibia.* A raised and roughened surface on the tibia.

tuberous sclerosis (*tu'-ber-us skle-ro'-sis*). *See* Epiloia.

tubocurarine (*tu-bo-ku-rar'-ine*). A preparation of curare (*q.v.*) used to secure muscle relaxation during abdominal surgery or to relieve muscle spasm in tetanus or to prevent convulsions during electro-convulsive therapy.

tubular (*tu'-bu-lar*). Relating to or resembling a tube.

tubules (*tu'-bule*). Small tubes. *Renal* or *Uriniferous t.* The essential secreting tubes of the kidney.

Tudor Edwards spectacles (*tu'-dor ed'-wards*). A spectacle frame with attachments by which oxygen may be introduced into each nostril.

tularaemia (*tu-lar-e'-me-ah*). An undulant fever, the cause of which (*Pasteurella tularensis*) may be transmitted to man by various insects or by rats. The lymph glands are involved and they may suppurate.

tulle gras (*tule grah'*). A French preparation of gauze impregnated with petroleum jelly. Other drugs may be added. Most useful on a granulating surface to stop a dressing adhering.

tumefaction (*tu-me-fak'-shun*). A swelling.

tumour (*tu'-mor*). A swelling due to morbid growth of tissue, not resulting from inflammation. *Cystic t.* One which contains fluid. *Innocent*, *simple*, or *benign t.* is encapsulated, does not infiltrate or cause metastases, and is unlikely to recur if removed. *Malignant t.* One which is not encapsulated and causes metastatic deposits. *Phantom t.* An abdominal swelling, usually of gas. A form of neurosis. *Sessile t.* One with a broad base, not pedunculated.

tunica (*tu'-nik-ah*). A coat. *T. adventitia*, *t. media*, *t. intima*. The outer, middle, and inner coats of an artery.

tuning fork. A metal instrument used for testing hearing by means of the sounds produced by its vibration. *See* Rinne's *and* Weber Tests.

turbinate (*tur'-bin-ate*). Scroll-shaped. *T. bones.* Those in the nose which increase the surface area for warming and moistening the inspired air.

turbinectomy (*tur-bin-ek'-to-me*). Excision of a turbinate bone.

turgescence (*tur-jes'-sense*). Swelling due to congestion of blood as in catarrh.

turgid (*tur'-jed*). Swollen and congested with blood.

turgor (*tur'-jor*). The state of being swollen or distended.

Turner's syndrome (*turn'-ers sin'-drome*). A condition in which there is absence of one X chromosome. Congenital abnormalities result, commonly ovarian agenesis, infantile sex characteristics and webbing of the neck.

tussis (*tus'-sis*). A cough.

twilight states. Periods of dissociation in which a patient may perform acts of which he is not conscious later on. Though rare, they may follow an epileptic fit. *Hysterical t.s.* The patient shows mild clouding of consciousness giving rise to irrelevant speech or clumsy actions.

twin. One of a pair of individuals who have developed in the uterus together. *Binovular t.* Each has developed from a separate ovum. *Uniovular t.* Both have developed from the same cell. Identical twins.

tylosis (*ti-lo'-sis*). The formation of hard patches of skin. A callosity.

tympanectomy (*tim-pan-ek'-to-me*). Excision of the tympanum of the ear.

tympanic (*tim-pan'-ik*). Relating to the tympanum. *T. membrane.* The drum of the ear.

tympanites (*tim-pan-i'-tez*). Distension of the abdomen by accumulation of gas in the intestines.

tympanitis (*tim-pan-i'-tis*). Inflammation of the middle ear. Otitis media.

tympanoplasty (*tim-pan-o-plas'-te*). An operation to restore conductivity to the middle ear.

tympanosclerosis (*tim-pan-o-skler-o'-sis*). Fibrosis and the formation of calcified deposits in the middle ear that lead to deafness.

tympanum (*tim'-pan-um*). (1) The middle ear. (2) The ear drum or tympanic membrane.

typhlitis (*tif-li'-tis*). Inflammation of the caecum.

typhlon (*tif'-lon*). The caecum.

typhlosis (*tif-lo'-sis*). Blindness.

typhoid fever (*ti'-foid*). Enteric fever. An acute specific infectious disease caused by the *Salmonella typhi*; the incidence of which is rare in Britain although it occurs in areas where the sanitation is poor and the water supplies are contaminated. *T. carrier*. One who harbours the infection, and discharges the organisms in the faeces. The gall-bladder is usually the seat of infection.

typhus (*ti'-fus*). An acute infectious fever lasting about 14 days, and then terminating abruptly. It is likely to occur where there is overcrowding, lack of personal cleanliness, and bad hygienic conditions, as the infection is spread solely by bites of infected lice or by rat fleas. The causative organism is *Rickettsia prowazekii*. It is treated by chloramphenicol or the tetracyclines. *Scrub t.* A form spread by mites, and widespread in the Far East.

tyramine (*ti'-ra-meen*). An enzyme present in cheese, game, broad bean pods, yeast extracts, wine, and strong beer. All these should be avoided when monoamine oxidase inhibitors are used to treat depression.

tyrosine (*ti'-ro-sin*). An amino acid. In some diseases especially of the liver, it is present in the urine.

tyrosinosis (*ti-ro-sin-o'-sis*). An alternative name for phenylketonuria in which there is an error of metabolism and phenylalanin cannot be reduced to tyrosine.

U

ulcer (*ul'-ser*). An erosion or loss of continuity of the skin or of a mucous membrane, often accompanied by suppuration. *Duodenal u.* Occurs in the mucous lining of the first inch of the small intestine. *Gastric u.* One in the

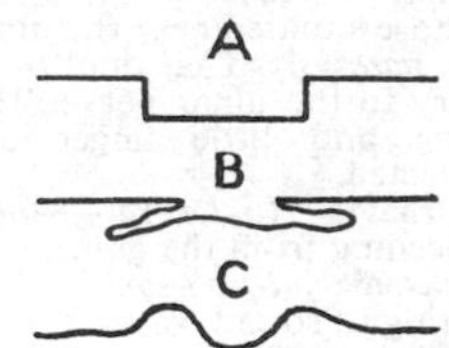

TYPES OF ULCER IN SECTION(DIAGRAMMATIC)

A. Gummatous.
B. Tuberculous.
C. Malignant.

lining of the stomach. *Gravitational u.* A varicose ulcer of the leg which is difficult to heal because of its dependent position and the poor venous return. *Gummatous u.* One arising in late non-infective syphilis; they are slow to heal. *Indolent u.* One which heals slowly. *Intractable u.* One which does not respond to treatment. *Peptic u.* Occurs on the mucous membrane of either the stomach or duodenum. *Perforated u.* Erodes through the thickness of the wall of an organ. *Rodent u.* A slow-growing epithelioma of the face which may cause much local destruction and ulceration, but does not give rise to metastases. *Trophic u.* One due to failure of nutrition. *Varicose u.* Gravitational ulcer. *See above.*

ulcerative (*ul'-ser-a-tiv*). Characterized by ulceration—the formation of ulcers. *U. colitis.* A condition of inflammation and ulceration of the colon of unknown cause.

ulna (*ul'-nah*). The bone on the inner side of the forearm from elbow to wrist.

ulnar (*ul'-nar*). Relating to the ulna. *U. artery, U. nerve.* Those situated near the ulna. *U. paralysis.* That due to injury to the ulnar nerve. The ring and little finger are affected.

ulorrhagia (*u-lor-ra'-je-ah*). Bleeding from the gums.

ultrasonic (*ul-trah-son'ik*). Relating to sound waves having a frequency range beyond the upper limit perceived by the human ear. *U. echo sounding.* Reflected sound waves are used to localize the placental site. This is valuable in the diagnosis of placenta praevia or before amniocentosis (*q.v.*) *U. echo tests.* An aid to the detection of brain tumours by the transmission of very high frequency vibrations that reflect back changes in tissue density.

ultraviolet rays (*ul'-trah vi'-o-let*). Those beyond the violet end of the spectrum. *U.-v. light* is used to promote vitamin D formation and for skin conditions.

umbilical (*um-bil-i'-kal*). Relating to the umbilicus. *U. cord. See under* Cord. *U. hernia. See under* Hernia.

umbilicated (*um-bil'-ik-a-ted*). Having a depression like that of the navel, as on a smallpox vesicle.

umbilicus (*um-bil-i'-kus*). The navel; the circular depressed scar in the centre of the abdomen.

unciform (*un'-se-form*). Hook-shaped. *U. bone* (*hamate*). A bone of the carpus. *U. process.* A hook-shaped projection on the unciform bones.

uncinate process (*un'-se-nate*). A part of the ethmoid bone.

unconscious (*un-kon'-shus*). Receiving no sensory impulses. Insensible. *U. mind.* A term used in psychology for that part of the mind containing the urges, feelings, and experiences of which the individual is unaware and which he cannot normally recall although they influence his actions.

unconsciousness (*un-kon'-shus-nes*). The state of being in coma (*q.v.*). This may vary in depth. (1) *Deep u.* When no response can be obtained. (2) Lesser degrees of *u.* are seen when the patient can be roused by painful stimuli and (3) when the patient can be roused by speech or non-painful stimuli.

undine irrigator (*un'-dine*). A

form of glass flask with long spout used for irrigation of the eye.

undulant fever (*un-'du-lant*). Recurring attacks of fever with enlargement of spleen, swelling of joints, neuralgic pains, and profuse sweating. Repeated attacks cause weakness and anaemia. The cause is *Brucella abortus* transmitted in cow's milk or *Brucella melitensis* from goat's milk (*Malta fever*). *Syn.* Brucellosis.

unguentum (*ung-gwen'-tum*). An ointment.

unguis (*ung'-gwis*). A finger- or toe-nail.

uni- A prefix meaning 'one'.

unicellular (*u-ne-sel'-u-lar*). Consisting of one cell.

unilateral (*u-ne-lat'-er-al*). On one side only.

union (*u'-ne-on*). The repair of tissue after separation by incision or fracture. *See* Callus *and* Healing.

uniovular (*u-ne-o'-vu-lar*). From one ovum. *U. twins* are of the same sex.

unipara (*u-nip'-ar-ah*). A woman who has had only one child.

unit. A standard of measurement. *British Thermal u.* The amount of heat which will raise 1 lb. of water through one degree Fahrenheit. *U. of heat.* A calorie (*q.v.*). *U. of insulin.* An international measurement of the pure crystalline insulin arrived at by biological assay. *See also* Electromotive force *and* Angström unit.

Unna's zinc gelatin (*oon'-ner*). A useful paste for treating skin conditions and in which other drugs can be incorporated.

unsealed sources. The term applied to radioactive isotopes that are not enclosed in metal containers but used in liquid form either orally or by injection.

urachal (*u'-rak-al*). Referring to the urachus. *U. cyst.* A congenital abnormality when a small cyst persists along the course of the urachus. *U. fistula.* When the urachus fails to close and urine may leak from the umbilicus.

urachus (*u'-rak-us*). A tubular canal existing in the fetus, connecting the bladder with the umbilicus. In the adult it persists in the form of a solid fibrous cord.

uraemia (*u-re'-me-ah*). A condition of high blood urea, muscle weakness and increasing drowsiness. Renal function is impaired. *Renal u.* The cause lies in disease of kidney structure. *Extrarenal u.* The cause is outside the kidney such as circulatory failure due to shock or haemorrhage.

uraniscorrhaphy (*u-ran-is-kor'-raf-e*). Suture of a cleft palate.

uranium (*u-ra'-ne-um*). The metal from which radium is derived.

urate (*u'-rate*). A salt of uric acid. *Sodium u.* is generally found in concentration around joints in cases of gout.

uraturia (*u-rat-u'-re-ah*). Excess of urates in the urine. Lithuria.

urea (*u-re'-ah*). Carbamide. A white crystalline substance which is the chief nitrogenous constituent of urine. The normal daily output is about 33 g. *Blood u.* That which is present in the blood. Normal 20 to 40 mg per 100 ml. For *U. clearance test, see* Appendix 11.

urecchysis (*u-rek'-is-is*). The extravasation of urine into cellular tissue, e.g. in rupture of the bladder as a complication of fractured pelvis.

uresis (*u-re'-sis*). Urination.

ureter (*u-re'-ter*). One of the two long narrow tubes which convey the urine from the kidney to the bladder.

ureteric (*u-re-ter'-ik*). Relating to the ureter. *U. catheter*. A fine catheter for insertion via the ureter into the pelvis of the kidney, either for drainage or for retrograde pyelography. *See* Renal function tests—Appendix 11.

ureteric transplantation. The ureters are divided from the bladder and implanted in the colon or loop of ileum. Congenital defects or malignant growth may make this necessary.

ureteritis (*u-re-ter-i'-tis*). Inflammation of the ureter.

ureterocolostomy (*u-re-ter-o-kol-os'-to-me*). *See* Ureterosigmoidoscopy.

ureterolith (*u-re'-ter-o-lith*). Calculus in a ureter.

ureterolithotomy (*u-re-ter-o-lith-ot'-o-me*). Removal of a stone from the ureter.

ureterosigmoidostomy (*u-re-ter-o-sig-moid-os'-to-me*). Implantation of the ureters into the sigmoid colon.

ureterostomy (*u-re-ter-os'-to-me*). Making a permanent opening through which the ureter discharges urine. *Cutaneous u.* When the ureters are transplanted to open onto the abdominal wall.

ureterovaginal (*u-re'-ter-o-vaj-i'-nal*). Relating to the ureter and vagina. *U. fistula*. An opening into the ureter by which urine escapes via the vagina. It may be congenital due to erosion, as in carcinoma of the cervix, or to an error in operative technique.

urethane (*u'-re-thane*). Ethyl carbamate used in the treatment of myeloid leukaemia. Also, with quinine, in the injection treatment of varicose veins.

urethra (*u-re'-thrah*). The canal through which the urine is discharged from the bladder. In a man it measures 20 or 23 cm (8 or 9 in.) in length; in a woman 4 cm ($1\frac{1}{2}$ in.).

urethral (*u-re'-thral*). Relating to the urethra. *U. caruncle*. *See* Caruncle.

urethritis (*u-re-thri'-tis*). Inflammation ot the urethra.

urethrocele (*u-re-thro'-seel*). A prolapse of the urethral wall which may result from damage to the pelvic floor during childbirth.

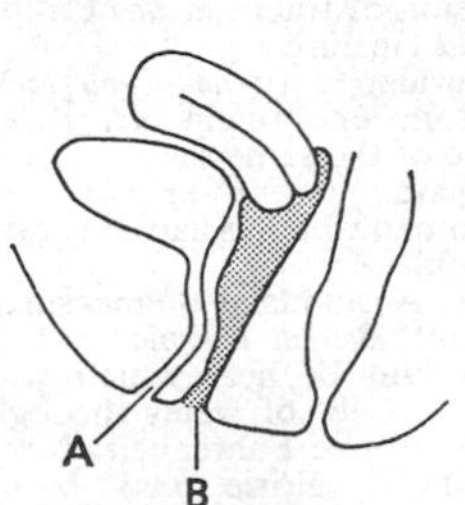

URETHROCELE
A. Urethra.
B. Vagina.

urethrogram (*u-re'-thro-gram*). An X-ray examination of the urethra. The dye may be inserted by catheter which is then removed and X-ray films taken as the urine is voided.

urethroplasty (*u-re'-thro-plas-te*). Operation for repair of the urethra.

urethroscope (*u-re'-thro-skope*). An instrument for examining the interior of the urethra.

urethrostenosis (*u-re-thro-sten-o'-sis*). Stricture of the urethra.

urethrotomy (*u-re-throt'-o-me*). Incision of the urethra, to remedy stricture.

uric acid (*u'-rik*). Lithic acid, a normal constituent of urine. Its accumulation in the blood produces uricaemia. Renal calculi are frequently formed of it.

uricosuric (*ur-ik-o-sur'-ik*). A drug that promotes the excretion of uric acid in the urine. Useful in treating gout.

uridrosis (*u-rid-ro'-sis*). The presence of urinary constituents, such as urea and uric acid in the perspiration. They may become deposited as crystals upon the skin.

urinalysis (*u-rin-al'-e-sis*). Examination of the urine. *See* Appendix 11.

urinary (*u'-rin-ar-e*). Relating to urine. *U. diversion.* When the ureters are transplanted into either the colon, the ileum (see ileal bladder) or onto the abdominal wall (*see* ureterostomy).

urination (*u - rin - a' - shun*). Micturition.

urine (*u'-rin*). The fluid secreted by the kidneys and excreted through the bladder and urethra. It is 96 per cent water and 4 per cent solid constituents, the most important being urea and uric acid. *Examination of the u. See* Appendix 11. *Residual u.* That which remains in the bladder after micturition, as in cases of cystocele or enlargement of the prostate gland. *U. tests. See* Appendix 11.

urinalysis (*u-rin-al'-e-sis*). Examination of the urine for normal and abnormal contents.

uriniferous (*u-rin-if'-er-us*). Conveying urine. *U. tubule. See* Tubule.

urinometer (*u-rin-om'-e-ter*). A glass instrument consisting of a graduated stem weighted

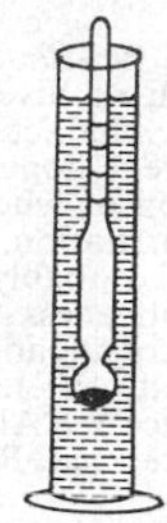

URINOMETER

with a mercury bulb, used for measuring the specific gravity of urine.

urobilin (*u-ro-bi'-lin*). The main pigment of urine, derived from urobilinogen.

urobilinogen (*u-ro-bi-lin'-o-jen*). A pigment derived from bilirubin which on oxidation forms urobilin.

urochrome (*u'-ro-krome*). Colouring matter of urine.

urogenital (*u-ro-jen'-it-al*). Relating to urinary and genital organs.

urography (*u-rog'-raf-e*). Radiography of any part of the urinary tract.

urokinase (*u-ro-kin'-aze*). An enzyme in urine which may be activated by trauma or disease and so retard the normal clotting mechanism and cause bleeding from the kidney.

urolith (*u'-ro-lith*). A calculus passed with the urine.

urologist (*u-rol'-o-jist*). A specialist in urology.

urology (*u-rol'-o-je*). The study of diseases of the urinary tract.

uropathy (*u-rop'-ath-e*). Any disease condition affecting the excretory power of the kidneys.

urticaria (*ur-tik-a'-re-ah*). Nettle-rash or hives. A skin condition characterized by the recurrent appearance of an eruption of wheals, causing great irritation. The condition is probably due to hypersensitiveness to some form of protein, and is therefore allied to hay fever, asthma, etc. *See* Allergy.

uterine (*u'-ter-ine*). Relating to the uterus.

uterogestation (*u-ter-o-jes-ta'-shun*). Development of a fetus within the uterus. *See also* Extra-uterine gestation.

uterovesical (*u-ter-o-ves'-ik-al*). Referring to the uterus and bladder. *U. pouch*. The fold of peritoneum between the two organs.

uterus (*u'-ter-us*). The womb; a triangular, hollow, muscle organ situated in the pelvic cavity between the bladder and the rectum. Its function is the nourishment and protection of the fetus during pregnancy and its expulsion at term. *Bicornate u.* One having two horns. A congenital malformation. *U. didelphys.* A double uterus owing to the failure of union of the two Müllerian ducts from which it is formed.

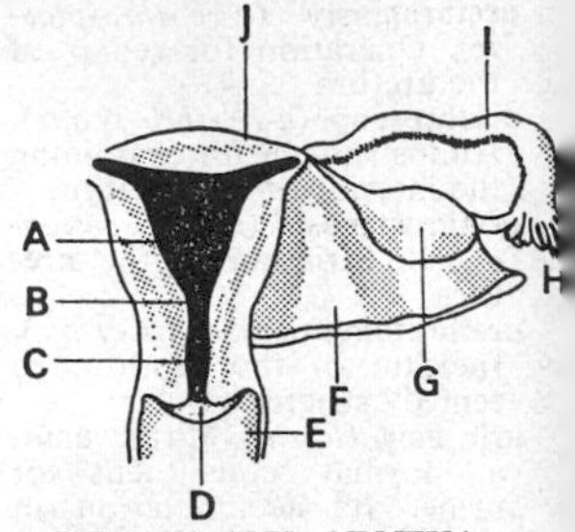

UTERUS AND ADNEXA

A. Cavity of uterus.
B. Internal os.
C. Cervical canal.
D. External os.
E. Fornix of vagina.
F. Broad ligament.
G. Ovary.
H. Fimbriae.
I. Fallopian tube.
J. Fundus.

Gravid u. The pregnant uterus.

utricle (*u'-trik-l*). The delicate membranous sac in the bony vestibule of the ear.

uvea (*u'-ve-ah*). Uveal tract. The pigmented layer of the eye, consisting of the iris, ciliary body and choroid.

uveitis (*u-ve-i'-tis*). Inflammation of the iris, ciliary body and choroid coat of the eye.

uvula (*u'-vu-lah*). The small fleshy appendage which is the free edge of the soft palate, hanging from the roof of the mouth.

uvulitis (*u-vu-li'-tis*). Inflammation of the uvula.

uvulotomy (*u-vu-lot'-o-me*). The operation of cutting off a part or the whole of the uvula.

V

vaccinate (*vak'-sin-ate*). To inoculate with a vaccine to produce an active immunity to a disease.

vaccination (*vak-sin-a'-shun*). (1) Inoculation with the virus of cowpox in order to protect against smallpox. It is recommended that it should first be done during the 2nd year and again between 8 and 12 years and every 3 to 5 years afterwards. (2) The injection of a vaccine in order to produce artificial active immunity.

vaccine (*vak'-seen*). A suspension of killed or attenuated organisms in normal saline designed to protect the body against a specific disease by stimulating the formation of antibodies. *Attenuated v.* One prepared from living organisms which through long cultivation have lost their virulence. *Bacille Calmette Guérin v.* An attenuated bovine bacillus to give immunity from tuberculosis. *Quadruple v.* Protects against whooping cough, diphtheria, poliomyelitis, and tetanus. *Triple v.* Protects against diphtheria, tetanus, and whooping cough. *V. lymph.* Used to prevent smallpox and prepared from healthy calves inoculated with smallpox. *Sabin v.* An attenuated poliovirus *v.* that can be administered by mouth, in a syrup or on sugar. *Salk v.* One prepared from an inactivated strain of poliomyelitis virus. *TAB v.* A sterile solution of the organisms that cause typhoid and paratyphoid A and B. Paratyphoid C may now be included.

vaccinia (*vak-sin'-e-ah*). Cowpox, a disease resembling smallpox, affecting animals and human beings.

vaccinotherapy (*vak-sin-o-ther'-ap-e*). Treatment by means of bacterial vaccines.

vacuole (*vak'-u-ol*). A clear space in a cell substance.

vacuum (*vak'-u-um*). A space from which air has been extracted. *V. extractor.* An instrument to assist delivery of the fetus. A suction cup is attached to the head and a vacuum created slowly. Traction is applied during uterine contractions.

vagal (*va'-gal*). Relating to the vagus nerve.

vagina (*vaj-i'-nah*). The canal, lined with mucous membrane, which leads from the vulva to the cervix uteri.

vaginismus (*vaj-in-iz'-mus*). Muscular spasm of the vagina on being touched.

vaginitis (*vaj-in-i'-tis*). Inflammation of the vagina. *Gonococcal v. See* Gonorrhoea. *Senile v.* That occurring in the aged, causing discharge, and adhesions which may obliterate the canal. *Trichomonas v.* Infection owing to the *Trichomonas*, a protozoan which causes a thin, yellowish discharge, giving rise to local tenderness and pruritis.

vagotomy (*va-got'-o-me*). To cut the vagus nerve. A treatment for peptic ulcer.

vagus (*va'-gus*). *Pl.* vagi. The tenth cranial nerve arising in the medulla and providing the parasympathetic nerve supply to the organs in the thorax and abdomen. *V. resection.* Operation on the vagus nerve. *See* Vagotomy.

valgus (*val'-gus*). Turned inwards. *Genu v.* Knock-kneed. *Hallux v.* Big toe displaced towards other toes.

Valsalva's auto-inflation (*val-sal'-vahs au-to-in-fla'-shun*). Insufflation of the Eustachian tubes by closing the nostrils and mouth and blowing out the cheeks to force air back into the nasopharynx.

valve. A fold of membrane in a passage or tube, so placed as to permit passage of fluid in one direction only. They are important structures in veins and lymph vessels, to help the ascent of fluid against gravity. *Auriculoventricular v's.* The bicuspid and tricuspid valves of the heart. *Houston's v's.* Folds of mucous membrane in the rectum. *Ileocaecal v.* Membranous folds at the junction of the ileum and caecum. *Pyloric v.* A fold of mucous membrane at the junction of the stomach and duodenum. *Semilunar v.s.* At the junction of the pulmonary artery and aorta respectively, with the heart.

valve replacement. A cardiac

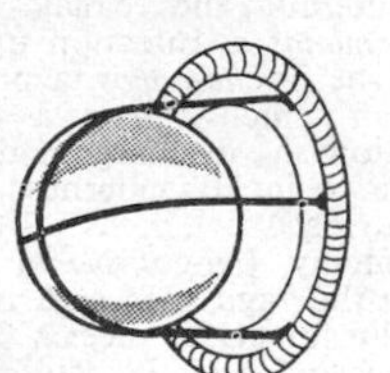

PROSTHETIC HEART VALVE

operation to replace a diseased aortic or mitral valve.

valvotomy (*val-vot'-o-me*). A surgical operation to increase the lumen of a fibrosed valve, e.g. mitral valvotomy to relieve mitral stenosis.

valvulae (*val'-vu-le*). Small valves. *V. conniventes.* Transverse folds of mucous membrane in the lining of the small intestine.

valvulitis (*val-vu-li'-tis*). Inflammation of a valve, particularly of the heart.

van den Bergh's test (*van-den-berg'*). For jaundice. A chemical test to aid the diagnosis.

Vaquez's disease (*vak'-a*). Polycythaemia vera (*q.v.*).

varicella (*var-e-sel'-lah*). Chickenpox. An infectious disease of childhood having an incubation period of 14 days. There is slight fever, and an eruption of transparent vesicles on the chest on the first day of disease, which come out in successive crops all over the body. The vesicles soon dry up, sometimes leaving shallow pits in the skin. The isolation period is until all scabs have been shed and complications are rare.

varicelliform (*var-e-sel'-e-form*). With vesicles similar to those of varicella.

varices (*var'-e-seez*). Plural of varix. Dilated veins. *Oesophageal v.* Those at the lower end of the oesophagus due to portal hypertension. *Rectal v.* Haemorrhoids (*q.v.*).

varicocele (*var'-ik-o-seel*). A dilatation of the veins of the spermatic cord.

varicocelectomy (*var-ik-o-se-lek'-to-me*). Operation for removal of dilated veins from the scrotum.

varicose (*var'-ik-oze*). Swollen or dilated. *V. veins.* A dilated and twisted condition of the veins (usually those of the leg), due to structural changes in the walls or valves of the vessels. *V. ulcer*. *See* Ulcer.

varicotomy (*var-ik-ot'-o-me*). Excision of a varicose vein.

variola (*var-e-o'-lah*). Smallpox. A highly contagious virus infection spread by droplets or contaminated articles. Its incidence is controlled by widespread vaccination. It is occasionally introduced into Great Britain from abroad. There is a high mortality in unvaccinated cases. *V. minor*. A modified form of smallpox may arise in a partially immune person who has previously been vaccinated but the rash is sparser and the fever milder. The danger is that a non-immune contact may develop a major attack.

varioloid (*var'-e-o-loid*). Variola minor (*q.v.*).

varix (*var'-iks*). An enlarged or varicose vein.

varus (*va'-rus*). A bending outwards. *Genu v.* Bow legged. *Talipes v.* The foot is inverted and weight is carried on the outer aspect.

vasa vasorum (*va'-zah vaz-or'-um*). The minute nutrient vessels that supply the walls of the arteries and veins.

vascular (*vas'-ku-lar*). Relating to, or consisting largely of vessels.

vascularization (*vas-ku-lar-i-za'-shun*). The process of becoming vascular.

vasculitis (*vas-ku-li'-tis*). A severe allergic response to drugs or to cold. Arising in small arteries or veins with fibrosis and thrombi formation.

vas deferens (*vas def'-er-ens*). The duct conveying the semen from the epididymis up the spermatic cord to its opening in the prostatic part of the urethra.

vasectomy (*vas-ek'-to-me*). Removal of a part of the vas deferens.

vasoconstrictor (*va-zo-kon-strik'-tor*). A nerve or a drug that causes contraction of a blood vessel wall. Applies to nerves or drugs that decrease the size of the lumen of a blood vessel.

vasodilator (*va-zo-di-la'-tor*). A drug or motor nerve that causes an increase in the lumen of blood vessels.

vasomotor (*va-zo-mo'-tor*). Controlling the muscles of blood vessels, both dilator and constrictor. *V. nerves*. Sympathetic nerves regulating the tension of the blood vessels. *V. centre*. Nerve cells in the medulla oblongata controlling the vasomotor nerves.

vasopressin (*va-zo-press'-in*). A hormone from the posterior lobe of the pituitary gland which causes constriction of plain muscle fibres and reabsorption of water in the renal tubules. It is used to relieve symptoms in diabetes insipidus.

vasovagal attack (*va-zo-va'-gal*). Fainting or syncope from psychogenic causes such as fear or witnessing an unpleasant sight. There is postural hypotension.

vasovesiculitis (*va-so-ves-ik-u-li'-tis*). Inflammation of the vas deferens and seminal vesicles.

vectis (*vek'-tis*). An instrument used to hasten delivery of the fetal head in parturition.

vector (*vek'-tor*). An animal that carries organisms or parasites from one host to another, either of the same species or to one of another species.

vegetation (*vej-e-ta'-shun*). An overgrowth. *Adenoid v.* Overgrowth of lymphoid tissue in the nasopharynx.

vehicle (*ve'-e-kul*). A substance or medium in which a drug is administered.

vein (*vane*). A vessel carrying blood from the capillaries back to the heart. It has thin walls and a lining endothelium from which the venous valves are formed.

Velactin (*vel-ak'-tin*). A complete milk substitute when a milk free diet is required. The protein is from soya beans, the fat arachis oil and the carbohydrate is starch, dextrose dextrin and sucrose.

vena cava (*ve'-nah ka'-vah*). *Pl.* venae cavae. *Superior* and *inferior v. c.* are the two large veins which return the venous blood to the right atrium of the heart.

venepuncture (*ve-ne-punk'-ture*). The insertion of a needle into a vein usually to obtain a blood specimen.

venereal (*ven-e'-re-al*). Pertaining to or caused by sexual intercourse. *V. diseases.* Syphilis, gonorrhoea, and soft chancre.

venereology (*ven-er'-e-ol-o-je*). The study and treatment of venereal disease.

venesection (*ve-ne-sek'-shun*). Surgical blood-letting by opening a vein or introducing a wide bore needle. Commonly performed on blood donors and occasionally to relieve venous congestion.

venoclysis (*ve-nok'-lis-is*). Introduction of fluids directly into veins.

venofibrosis (*ve-no-fi-bro'-sis*). Sclerosis of veins.

venogram (*ven'-o-gram*). The skiagram or X-ray taken at venography.

venography (*ven-og'-rafe*). The insertion of a dye to trace the pathway of veins.

venom antiserum. A serum containing antibodies against the bites of poisonous snakes.

venous (*ve'-nus*). Pertaining to the veins. *V. sinus.* A channel in the cranium by which blood leaves the brain.

ventilation (*ven-til-a'-shun*). The process of removing vitiated air (the products of respiration, combustion, or putrefaction), and replacing it with fresh air. *Natural v.* By natural diffusion of gases, controlled by windows, doors, and ventilating devices. *Artificial v.* By propulsion and extraction methods. as is used for large buildings, mines, underground railways, etc.

ventilator (*ven-til-la'-tor*). A machine which inflates the lungs by positive pressure through an endotracheal or tracheostomy tube, in a rhythmic manner.

ventral (*ven'-tral*). Pertaining to a hollow structure or belly. *V. aspect.* That of the belly.

ventricle (*ven'-trik-l*). A small pouch or cavity; applied especially to the lower chambers of the heart, and to the four cavities of the brain.

ventricular folds (*ven-trik'-u-lah*). Are the outer folds of mucous membrane forming the false vocal cords.

ventriculography (*ven-trik-u-log'-raf-e*). An aid to diagnosis, by which the ventricles of the brain are filled with air, and an X-ray photograph taken. Used to help locate a cerebral tumour.

ventriculoscope (*ven-trik'-u-lo-skope*). An instrument for viewing the inside of the ventricles of the brain. It may also be used for coagulating blood vessels.

ventrofixation (*ven-tro-fiks-a'-shun*). Stitching a displaced uterus or other abdominal organ to the abdominal wall.

ventrosuspension (*ven-tro-sus-pen'-shun*). An abdominal operation performed to remedy displacement of uterus.

venule (*ven'-ule*). (1) A minute vein. (2) A special type of syringe or evacuated glass phial for collecting blood from a vein.

verbigeration (*ver-be-jer-a'-shun*). The monotonous repetition of phrases. A disturbance of behaviour that may be present in schizophrenia.

veress needle (*ver'-ess*). One consisting of a sharp needle with a blunt ended trochar with a lateral hole used to perform a pneumoperitoneum. When the trochar projects from the needle the gut is pushed safely away from the needle point.

vermicide (*ver'-mis-ide*). An agent which destroys intestinal worms.

vermiform (*ver'-me-form*). Worm-shaped. *V. appendix*. The worm-like structure attached to the caecum.

vermifuge (*ver'-me-fuj*). An agent which expels intestinal worms; an anthelmintic.

verminous (*ver'-min-us*). Infested with worms or other animal parasites, such as lice.

vermix (*ver'-miks*). The vermiform appendix.

vernix caseosa (*ver'-nix ka-se-o'-sah*). The fatty covering on the skin of the fetus during the last months of pregnancy. It consists of cells and sebaceous material.

verruca (*ver-ru'-kah*). A wart. A localized hypertrophy of the prickle cell layer of the epidermis and thickening of the horny layer. A virus is the causative organism. *V. acuminata*. A venereal wart that appears on the external genitalia and may be associated with gonorrhoea.

version (*ver'-shun*). Turning a part; applied particularly to the turning of a fetus in order to facilitate delivery. *External v.* Manipulation of the uterus through the abdominal wall in order to change the position of the child. *Internal v.* Rotation of the fetus by means of manipulation with one hand in the vagina. *Podalic v.* Turning of the fetus so that the head is uppermost and the feet presenting.

vertebrae (*ver'-te-bre*). The thirty-three irregular bones forming the spinal column. They are divided into: 7 *cervical*, 12 *dorsal*, 5 *lumbar*, 5 *sacral* (sacrum), and 4 *coccygeal* (coccyx). *Sing*. vertebra.

vertebrate (*ver'-te-brate*). Possessing a vertebral column.

vertex (*ver'-teks*). The crown of the head. *V. presentation*. The fetus is so placed that the crown of the head appears in the vagina first.

vertigo (*ver'-tig-o*). A feeling of rotation or of going round, either oneself or one's surroundings and is particularly associated with disease of the cerebellum and vestibular nerve of the ear. It may occur in diplopia or Ménière's syndrome.

vesica (*ves-i'-kah*). A bladder; usually referring to the urinary bladder. *See* Ectopia vesicae.

vesical (*ves'-ik-al*). Relating to the bladder.

vesicant (*ves'-ik-ant*). A blistering agent.

vesicle (*ves'-ik-l*). A blister or small sac usually containing fluid. *Air v.* An alveolus of the lung. *Seminal v.* The sac which arises from the vas deferens near the bladder and contains semen.

vesico-ureteric (*ves-i-ko-u-re-ter'-ik*). Relating to the urinary bladder and the ureters. *V. reflux.* When urine is also passed backwards up the ureter during micturition. A cause of pyelonephritis especially in children.

vesicovaginal (*ves'-ik-o-vaj-i'-nal*). Relating to the bladder and vagina. *See* Fistula.

vesicular (*ves-ik'-u-lar*). Relating to, or containing vesicles. *V. breathing.* The soft murmur of normal respiration, as heard on auscultation. *V. mole.* Hydatidiform mole (*q.v.*).

vesiculitis (*ves-ik-u-li'-tis*). Inflammation of the seminal vesicles.

vesiculopapular (*ves-ik'-u-lo-pap'-u-lar*). An eruption of both vesicles and papules.

vessel (*ves'-sel*). A tube or canal for conveying fluid, usually blood or lymph.

vestibular (*ves-tib'-u-lar*). Relating to a vestibule. *V. glands.* Those in the vestibule of the vagina, including Bartholin's glands. *V. nerve.* A branch of the 8th cranial nerve supplying the semicircular canals and concerned with balance and equilibrium.

vestibule (*ves'-tib-ule*). An entrance, e.g. the cavity at the entrance to the cochlea of the ear.

vestigial (*ves-tij'-e-al*). Referring to the remains of an anatomical structure, which being of no further use has atrophied. Rudimentary.

viable (*vi'-ab-l*). Capable of independent life. A term applied to the fetus after 7 months of intra-uterine life.

Vibrio (*vib'-re-o*). A micro-organism short, curved, and motile by having flagellae. *Vibrio cholerae*, or *V. comma*, is that which causes cholera.

vicarious (*vik-a'-re-us*). Substituted for another; a term used when one organ functions instead of another.

villi (*vil'-li*). Finger-like processes from a surface. *Intestinal v.* Those of the mucous membrane of the small intestine, each of which contains a blood capillary and lacteal. *Chorionic v.* The essential structure of the placenta by which the fetus is nourished. *Sing.* villus.

Vincent's angina (*vin'-sentz an-ji'-nah*). *See under* Angina.

vinyl (*vi'-nil*). A plastic material now used extensively for medical equipment.

viraemia (*vi-re'-me-ah*). The presence of viruses in the blood.

virilism (*vir'-il-izm*). Masculine traits exhibited by the female owing to the production of excessive amounts of androgenic hormone either in the adrenal cortex or from an ovarian tumour. *See* Arrhenoblastoma.

virology (*vi-rol'-o-je*). The scientific study of viruses, their growth and diseases caused by them.

virulence (*vir'-u-lense*). The power to produce toxins or poisons. In infection this depends on: (1) the number and power of the bacteria invading; (2) the resistance of the patient.

virulent (*vir'-u-lent*). Malignant; dangerously poisonous. *V. infection.* One which is abnormally severe and dangerous.

virus (*vi'-rus*). A minute living organism smaller than bacteria. Only the largest viruses can be seen with the ordinary microscope. An electron microscope is required to 'see' the majority. Viruses can be grown only in living cells, e.g. chick embryos, tissue cultures (*q.v.*). They cause many diseases such as influenza, measles and poliomyelitis.

viscera (*vis'-er-a*). Plural of viscus (*q.v.*).

visceroptosis (*vis-ser-op-to'-sis*). A general tendency to prolapse of the abdominal organs.

viscid (*vis'-id*). Sticky and glutinous.

viscosity (*vis-kos'-it-e*). Having a sticky and glutinous quality.

viscus (*vis'-kus*). A term applied to any one of the organs contained in the body—especially in the abdomen. *Pl.* viscera.

visual (*viz'-u-al*). Relating to sight. *V. acuity.* Acuteness of vision. *V. cells.* The rods and cones of the retina. *V. field.* The area within which objects can be seen. *V. purple.* The pigment in the outer layers of the retina.

vita glass (*ve'-tah*). Quartz glass which is capable of transmitting ultraviolet rays of light.

vital (*vi'-tal*). Relating to life. *V. capacity.* The amount of air which can be expelled from the lungs after a full inspiration. *V. statistics.* The records kept of births and deaths among the population; including the causes of death, and the factors which seem to influence their rise and fall.

vitallium (*vi-tal'-e-um*). A metal alloy used in dentistry and for screws and plates in bone surgery.

vitamins (*vi'-tam-ins*). Accessory food factors. Substances contained in foodstuffs which are essential to life, growth, and reproduction. *See* Appendix 10.

vitamin B_{12}. This substance was first isolated from liver and is now extracted from the mould of streptomycin. It was found to be the missing anti-anaemic factor in pernicious anaemia. Cyanocobalamin.

vitamin K. Encourages the coagulation of blood. It is found in alfalfa, spinach, egg yolk, hemp seed, etc., and is also prepared synthetically. Used pre-operatively and post-operatively in those cases where bleeding is likely to be excessive, as in obstructive jaundice.

vitellin (*vi-tel'-in*). The chief protein of egg yolk.

vitellus (*vi-tel'-us*). The yolk of an ovum, or egg.

vitiation (*vish-e-a'-shun*). Lessening of efficiency.

vitiligo (*vit-il-i'-go*). A skin disease marked by an absence of pigment, producing white patches on the face and body. Leucoderma.

vitreous (*vit'-re-us*). Glassy. *V. humour*. The transparent jelly-like substance filling the posterior of the eye, from lens to retina.

vivisection (*viv-e-sek'-shun*). Experiment on or dissection of an animal while still alive but anaesthetized. It is most carefully controlled by law.

vocal (*vo'-kal*). Pertaining to the organs which produce the voice. *V. cords*. Vocal folds in the larynx formed of fibrous tissue covered with squamous epithelium.

volatile (*vol'-at-ile*). Having a tendency to evaporate readily.

volition (*vo-lish'-on*). The conscious adoption by the individual of a line of action and maintaining it.

volitional (*vo-lish'-on-al*). Being impelled by will power.

Volkmann's ischaemic contracture (*volk'-mans is-kee-'mik*). Atrophy and fibrosis occurring in the muscles owing to an impaired blood supply. Usually applied to the upper-limb when the brachial artery is compressed by a fracture of the lower end of the humerus.

volt. The unit of electromotive force (*q.v.*).

volume (*vol'-ume*). The space occupied by a substance; usually expressed in cubic measure. *Minute v*. The total volume of air breathed in or out in 1 min. *Packed cell v*. That occupied by the blood cells after centrifuging, about 45 per cent of the blood sample.

voluntary (*vol'-un-ta-re*). Under the control of the will. *See also* Involuntary.

volvulus (*vol'-vu-lus*). Twisting of a part of the intestine, causing obstruction. Most common in the sigmoid colon.

vomer (*vo'-mer*). A thin plate of bone forming the posterior septum of the nose.

vomit (*vom'-it*). Material vomited. *Bilious v*. Bile is mixed with the matter ejected. *Coffee-ground v*. Small quantities of altered blood ejected, which have this appearance. *Faecal* or *stercoraceous v*. Arises in intestinal obstruction when the contents of the upper intestine regurgitate back into the stomach. It is dark brown with an unpleasant odour. To vomit. *See* Vomiting.

vomiting (*vom'-it-ing*). Is a reflex act of expulsion of the stomach contents via the oesophagus and mouth. It may be preceded by nausea and excess salivation if the cause is local irritation in the stomach. *Cyclical v*. Recurrent attacks of vomiting often occurring in children and associated with acidosis. *Morning v*. Occurs on rising as in pregnancy and chronic gastritis. *Projectile v*. The gastric contents are forcibly ejected, usually without warning. Present in hypertrophic pyloric stenosis, and in cerebral diseases. *Psychogenic v*. That without organic cause.

von Recklinghausen's disease (*rek'-ling-how-sen*). (1) *Neurofibromatosis*. A rare disease of skin pigmentation and multiple painless fibromata along the course of the peripheral nerves. (2) *Osteitis fibrosa cystica* or hyperparathyroidism of the bones in which the blood calcium is raised but there is decalcification of bone tissue.

vulnerability (*vul-ner-ab-il'-*

i-te). Susceptibility to injury or infection.

vulva (*vul'-vah*). The external female genital organs.

vulvectomy (*vul-vek'-to-me*). Excision of the vulva.

vulvitis (*vul-vi'-tis*). Inflammation of the vulva.

vulvovaginitis (*vul-vo-vaj-in-i'-tis*). Inflammation of the vulva and vagina.

W

wafer (*wa'-fer*). A thin double layer of flour paste used to enclose a dose of medicinal powder. A cachet.

Waldeyer's ring (*val'-di-er*). The circle of lymphoid tissue in the pharynx formed by the *lingual*, *faucial*, and *pharyngeal* tonsils. *W. fascia*. A portion of the pelvic fascia that sheaths the lower part of the ureter. It contains some plain muscle fibres and kinking may occur here when the bladder is over distended.

Wangensteen tube (*wan'-gen-steen*). A gastro-intestinal aspiration tube with a tip that is opaque to X-rays.

warfarin (*war'-farin*). An anticoagulant drug that depresses the prothrombin level.

wart (*wawt*). An elevation of the skin, which is often of a brownish colour, caused by hypertrophy of papillae in the dermis. *See* Verruca *and* Condyloma.

Wassermann reaction (*vas'-ser-man*). A method of testing the blood serum of a patient to aid in the diagnosis of syphilis. It can also show the progress whilst under treatment.

water balance or fluid balance. That between the fluid intake by all routes (oral, intravenous and rectal) and the fluid lost by all routes (urine, vomit or drainage from any body cavity).

water-borne. Diseases spread by contaminated water.

water-brash. The eructation of dilute acid from the stomach to the pharynx, giving a burning sensation. Pyrosis (*q.v.*).

water-hammer pulse. *See* Pulse.

Waterston's operation (*war'-ter-stones*). A palliative operation of anastomosis of the right pulmonary artery to the ascending aorta. Used in the treatment of Fallot's tetralogy in the young child.

water seal drainage. A closed method of drainage from the pleural space allowing the escape of fluid and air but preventing air entering

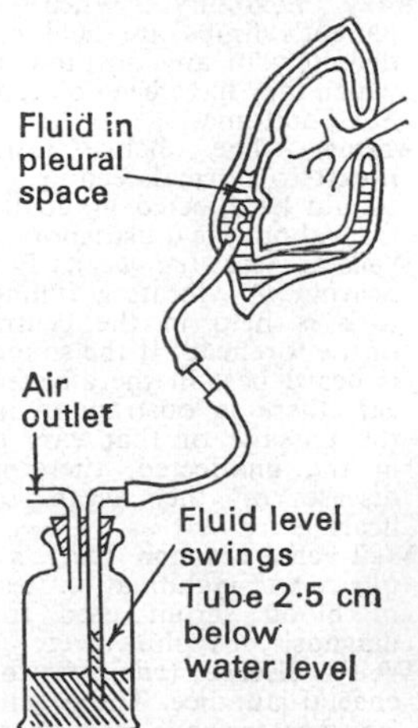

WATER SEAL DRAINAGE

as the drainage tube discharges under water.

watt. A unit of electric power.

wave length. Is the measurement from the crest of one wave to the crest of the next one. Applied to the electromagnetic spectrum the longest are wireless waves and the shortest are X-rays and γ-rays.

waves. Uniform advancing undulation. *Electromagnetic w.* The entire range of waves including light waves in the ether.

wax. In pharmacy, *beeswax*, used for making ointments. *Ear w. See* Cerumen. *Bone w.* An antiseptic form for stopping bleeding from bone, especially whilst performing operations on the skull. *Paraffin w.* Hard paraffin prepared from petroleum.

waxy flexibility. When a patient's limbs are held indefinitely in any position in which they have been placed. *See* Catatonia.

weaning. The change from breast to normal feeding. It should be effected gradually from about the fourth month.

Weber's test (*va'-ber*). For hearing. A vibrating tuning fork is held in the centre of the forehead. If the sound is heard best in the affected ear, there is obstruction in the passage of that ear; if in the unaffected, there is disease of the organ of hearing.

Weil-Felix reaction (*vile fa'-liks*). An agglutination test of blood serum used for diagnosis of typhus fever.

Weil's disease (*vile*). Spirochaetal jaundice. The organism, *Leptospira icterohaemorrhagiae*, is harboured and excreted by rats and enters through a bite or skin abrasion and infected water.

Welch's bacillus (*welsh*). *Clostridium welchii* or *perfringens*, the organism most usually found in gas gangrene.

wen. A small sebaceous cyst.

Wernicke's encephalopathy (*ver'-nik-es en-kef-al-op'-ath-e*). A congenital neurological condition due to vitamin B_1 deficiency. Untreated it progresses from double vision to lethargy and coma.

Wertheim's operation (*ver'-time*). *See* Hysterectomy.

Wharton's duct (*hwor'-tun*). The duct of the submaxillary gland. *W. jelly.* Connective tissue of the umbilical cord.

wheal (*hweel*). A raised stripe on the skin, as is caused by the lash of a whip. Typical of urticaria (*q.v.*).

Wheelhouse's operation (*hweel-house*). Perineal incision for the relief of urethral obstruction,

wheeze (*hweez*). To breathe with difficulty, producing a hoarse whistling sound.

Whipple's operation. One performed for carcinoma of the head of the pancreas in which most of the pancreas, the pylorus, duodenum and the common bile duct are excised. Gastrojejunostomy is performed with anastomosis of the tail of the pancreas and gall-bladder to the jejunum.

whipworm. *See* Trichuris.

Whitehead's varnish (*hwite'-hed*). A preparation containing *benzoin*, *iodoform*, and ether. It may be used as a protective covering to a wound.

white leg. *See* Phlegmasia.

'white fluids'. Coal tar disinfectants which are suitable

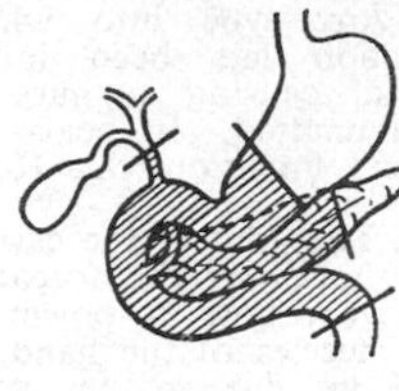

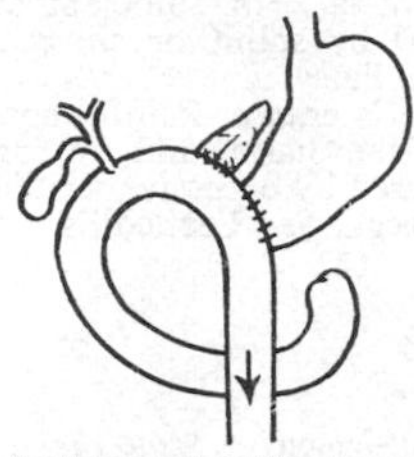

WHIPPLE'S OPERATION
(shaded area is removed)

for linen and unstained wood as they do not cause discoloration.

'whites'. A popular term for leucorrhoea.

White's tar paste. A paste of zinc and starch containing crude coal tar used in the treatment of psoriasis.

Whitfield's ointment (*hwit'-fee-ld*). Used for skin diseases. It consists of: *Salicyclic acid*, 3 per cent and *benzoic acid*, 6 per cent, in a petroleum jelly base. Benzoic acid compound ointment.

whitlow (*hwit'-lo*). A suppurating inflammation of a finger near the nail. *Subperiosteal w.* The infection involves the bone covering. *Superficial w.* A pustule between the true skin and cuticle. *See* Paronychia.

whooping cough. Pertussis. An infectious disease usually occurring in children, characterized by acute respiratory catarrh, with paroxysms of coughing. These terminate with a long-drawn noisy inspiration giving the typical *whoop*. Aureomycin and chloramphenicol have shortened the course and severity of the disease.

Widal reaction (*vee'-dal*). A blood agglutination test for typhoid fever. Sufficient antibodies are usually present from the second week to confirm diagnosis.

Wilms's tumour (*vilm*). A highly malignant congenital tumour of the kidney. An embryoma of kidney. Treated by radiotherapy and nephrectomy.

Wilson's disease (*wil'-sons*). Hepatolenticular degeneration. A congenital abnormality in the metabolism of copper leading to neurological degeneration.

wintergreen oil. *See* Methyl salicylate.

wiring (*wi'-ring*). The fixing together of a broken or split bone by the use of a wire. Commonly used for the jaw, the patella, and the sternum.

wisdom teeth. The back molar teeth, the appearance of which is often delayed until maturity.

wish fulfilment. A desire, not always acknowledged consciously by the person, which is fulfilled through dreams or by day-dreaming.

witch hazel. *See* Hamamelis.

withdrawal. In psychiatry a defence mechanism in which an individual turns into himself and away from the world.

withdrawal bleeding. Bleeding

that occurs from the uterus following the cessation of giving oestrogens for therapeutic reasons.

Wolffian bodies (*wool'-fe-an*). Two small organs in the embryo, representing the primitive kidneys.

Wood's glass. Glass containing *nickel oxide*. It produces fluorescence of infected hairs when placed over a scalp affected with ringworm.

woolsorter's disease. Anthrax (*q.v.*).

word salad. Rapid speech in which the words are strung together without meaning.

worms. A group of invertebrate animals. *See* Ascaris; Bilharziasis; Echinococcus; Tapeworm; *and* Oxyuris.

wound. A cut or break in continuity of any tissue, caused by injury or operation. It is classified according to its nature: *Abrased w.* The skin is scraped off, but there is no deeper injury. *Aseptic w.* A non-infected one. *Contused w.* With bruising of the surrounding tissue. *Incised w.* Usually the result of operation, and produced by a knife or similar instrument. The edges of the wound can remain in apposition, and it should heal by first intention. *Lacerated w.* One with torn edges and tissues, usually the result of accident or injury. It is often septic, and heals by second intention. *Open w.* One which is draining freely. *Penetrating w.* is often made by gunshot, shrapnel, etc. There may be an inlet and outlet hole and vital organs are often penetrated by the missile. *Punctured w.* Made by a pointed or spiked instrument. *Septic w.* Any type into which infection has been introduced, causing suppurative inflammation. It heals by second intention. *See* Healing.

wrist. The joint of the carpus and bones of the forearm. *W. drop.* Loss of power in the muscles of the hand. It may be due to nerve or tendon injury, but can result from lack of sufficient support by splint or sling. *See also* Palsy.

writer's cramp. Painful spasm of the hand and forearm, caused by excessive writing.

wryneck. *See* Torticollis.

X

xanthelasma (*zan-thel-az'-mah*). A disease marked by the formation of flat or slightly raised yellow patches on the eyelids.

xanthine (*zan'-thin*). A nucleoprotein. Sometimes found in renal calculi. *X. diuretics.* Those that increase the glomerular filtration rate, such as caffeine.

xanthoma (*zan-tho'-mah*). *Pl.* xanthomata. The presence in the skin of flat areas of yellowish pigmentation due to deposits of lipoids. There are several varieties. *X. palpebrarum*, Xanthelasma.

xanthopsia (*zan-thop'-se-ah*). Yellow vision, a condition in which all objects appear yellow. It sometimes results from taking santonin.

xanthosis (*zan-tho'-sis*). A yellow skin pigmentation, seen in some cases of cancer.

X-chromosome (*eks kro'-mo-some*). The sex chromosome

present in all female gametes and only half the male gametes, the rest having a *Y-c*. When union takes place two *X-c*. result in a female child (*XX*) but one of each results in a male child (*XY*).

xenon (*zen'-on*). An inert gaseous element. *Radioactive X* (^{133}Xe) is used in blood flow clearance tests as it dissolves in the blood but does not form a chemical combination and the gas is excreted as the blood flows through the lungs.

Xenopsylla cheopis (*zen-op-sil'-ah che-op'-is*). Rat flea that transmits bubonic plague.

Xenopus toad (*zen'-op-us*). An animal used for early diagnosis of pregnancy. Similar to the Aschheim-Zondek test but more economical as if positive the toad sheds its eggs, and it is thus unnecessary to kill it.

xeroderma (*zer-o-der'-mah*). A disease in which there is excessive dryness of the skin. A mild form of ichthyosis (*q.v.*).

xerophthalmia (*zer-off-thal'-me-ah*). A condition in which the cornea becomes horny and necrosed. It is due to the dietary deficiency of vitamin A. A symptom is night blindness.

xerosis (*zer-o'-sis*). A condition in which the conjunctiva appears dry and lustreless. Small white patches of horny epithelium appear on the cornea (*Bitôt's spots*). Mild cases may appear in children during the summer months.

xerostomia (*zer-os-to'-me-ah*). Dryness of the mouth.

xiphoid (*zif'-oid*). Sword-shaped. *X. cartilage*. That at the lower end of the sternum.

X-rays. Röntgen-rays. Electromagnetic waves of short length which are capable of penetrating many substances and of producing chemical changes and reactions in living matter. They are used to aid diagnosis and to treat disease.

xylose (*zi'-lose*). A pentose sugar not metabolized in the body. *X. absorption*. An oral dose is given and the urine collected for five hours. The amount of xylose present is proportional to that absorbed through the intestinal wall. It is a test for malabsorption.

Y

yawning (*yaw'-ning*). A respiratory act the physiology of which is not understood. It may accompany tiredness and is infectious.

yaws (*yaws*). A skin infection common in tropical countries caused by the *Treponema pertenue*. Associated with dirt and poverty it is not a venereal disease though the Wassermann and Kahn tests are positive. *See* Framboesia.

Y-chromosome (*wi kro'-mo-some*). The chromosome present in some male gametes which determines the sex of the offspring. *See* X-chromosome.

yeast (*yee-st*). Saccharomyses. A species of vegetable micro-organisms. They produce fermentation in malt, and in sweetened fruit juices, resulting in the formation of alcoholic solutions such as beer and wines. Thrush (*q.v.*) is due to infection by a species of yeast.

yellow fever. An acute, specific,

infectious disease of the tropics, spread through the bite of a mosquito (*Aedes aegypti*). The incubation period varies from a few hours to several days, and the onset is marked by rigor, headache, pain in the back and limbs, high fever and black vomit. Haemorrhage from the intestinal mucous membrane may occur. There is a high mortality rate but vaccination with 17D virus vaccine gives active immunity for 7 years.

yellow ointment. *See* Ointment.

yellow spot. Macula lutea (*q.v.*).

Young's rule. To determine the dose of a drug suitable for a child from the adult dose.

yttrium (*it'-tre-um*). An element used as radioactive yttrium (^{90}Y) in the treatment of malignant effusions or to destroy remnants of the pituitary gland that cannot be removed by surgery.

Z

zactirin (*zak'-tir-in*). An analgesic. A proprietary preparation of ethoheptazine.

Ziehl-Neelsen's stain (*tseel'-neel'-sen*). A method of staining tubercle bacilli for microscopic study.

zein (*tse'-in*). Maize protein.

zinc (*zink*). A bluish-white metallic element. *Z. chloride* is used as disinfectant for the treatment of ulcers, and as an astringent. *Z. acetate* is used in ophthalmia. *Z. sulphate* is given as an emetic. *Z. ointment* is an emollient dressing.

zingiber (*zin'-jib-er*). Ginger.

zona (*zo'-nah*). Encircling. *Herpes zoster* (*q.v.*). Shingles. *Z. facialis*. Herpes of the face. *Z. ophthalmica*. Herpes over the ophthalmic nerve.

zonular fibres (*zon'-u-lar*). The suspensory ligament that suspends the lens behind the iris. Zonules.

zonulolysis (*zon-u-lol'-is-is*). Dissolving the zonular fibres by zonulysin to aid cataract extraction.

zonulysin (*zon-u-li'-sin*). A proteolytic enzyme that may be used in eye surgery to dissolve the suspensory ligament.

zoogloea layer (*zo-og-le'-ah*). A gelatinous layer of algae and protozoa that forms on the surface of a sand filter bed and aids the purification of water.

zoology (*zo-ol'-o-je*). The science of animal life.

zoster (*zos'-ter*). *See* Herpes.

zygoma (*zi-go'-mah*). The arch formed by the union of the temporal with the malar bone in front of the ear.

zygote (*zi'-got*). A single fertilized cell formed from two gametes. *Dizygote* twins developed from two fertilized cells termed fraternal twins. *Monozygote* twins developed from the same cell termed identical twins.

zymosis (*zi-mo'-sis*). (1) Fermentation. (2) The development of infectious diseases.

zymotic (*zi-mot'-ik*). Relating to zymosis. *Z. disease*. A general term including all epidemic, contagious, and endemic diseases due to the action of micro-organisms.

Z-plasty. A plastic operation for removing and repairing deformity resulting from a contraction scar.

APPENDICES

APPENDIX 1

EMERGENCY TREATMENT

In an emergency much valuable time can be saved and further injury to the patient prevented by the nurse or the helper quickly assessing the situation and having an informed knowledge of priorities and of the best treatment.

Medical assistance should be sent for as soon as possible, for preference through an onlooker being given clear, possibly written instructions. An ambulance may be required.

THE MAINTENANCE OF RESPIRATION AND OF CARDIAC ACTION

In all conditions of unconsciousness, from whatever cause, the first consideration is maintenance of the airway. In hospital the commonest form of unconsciousness, apart from sleep, is that induced at operation, and every student is instructed at an early stage of her training in the care of these patients. The necessary equipment should always be at hand. This should include a mouth gag, an angled spatula, sponge-holding forceps and swabs and a tongue clip. Equipment for oxygen administration, for suction and for artificial respiration should also be available.

For the sake of safety, unconscious patients are best transported and placed in bed in the lateral or semi-prone position. This enables the tongue to fall forward, preventing blockage of the larynx, and allows the secretions to collect in the lower cheek or run out of the mouth. If, owing to the patient's condition, this position is not possible, the angle of the jaw should be drawn forward and supported. The patient must be breathing quietly and adequately and no cyanosis should be present.

Obstructed Airway

Should the breathing appear laboured, the nostrils dilated or the soft tissues of the neck and upper thorax be sucked inwards, obstruction of the airway must be suspected. The jaw and tongue should be drawn forward, but if this does not relieve the obstruction, a gag must be inserted, the tongue drawn forward and the back of the throat cleared using swabs and sponge-holding forceps. This emergency is unlikely to arise with good positioning of the patient, but it may occur owing to inhalation of food or foreign bodies and if immediate steps are not taken to dislodge the obstruction either by sweeping the finger across the back of the throat or, in the case of a child, holding his head down and giving him a few taps on the back of the chest, asphyxia may easily result.

Cessation of Breathing

If breathing has ceased, artificial respiration must be started at once to supply oxygen to the blood and the blood must reach the brain within 3 min or irreparable damage will be done.

Expired Air Artificial Respiration

Mouth-to-Nose Respiration

(1) Sweep the finger round the back of the patient's mouth to remove any obstructing matter.

(2) Grasp the patient's head with one hand and extend his neck by pressing his head backwards and at the same time lifting his jaw upwards and forwards with the other hand. Close his mouth with the thumb.

(3) Take a deep breath, place the mouth over the patient's nostrils and exhale forcibly into his lungs. Chest expansion should be observed.

(4) Withdraw the mouth and take another deep breath while the patient exhales. Repeat the cycle 10 to 12 times a minute. The first six breaths should be given as rapidly as possible.

(5) In a child both his mouth and nose may be covered by the lips and the breaths should be gentler.

Mouth-to-Mouth Respiration

This method may be preferred, in which case the patient's nostrils should be closed by pressing with the finger and thumb and the breath exhaled into his mouth. Apart from this the procedure is the same as for mouth-to-nose respiration.

An *artificial mouthpiece and airway*, if available, may be used. Draw the patient's jaw forward, open his mouth and insert the airway, directing it first towards the roof of the mouth and then rotating it downwards behind his tongue.

The stomach may become blown up with air, especially if the head is not properly extended. If this occurs, apply pressure over the upper part of the abdomen.

Holger Nielsen Method of Artificial Respiration

This method may be suitably used when, because the face is smashed, it is impossible to use the expired air method of artificial respiration.

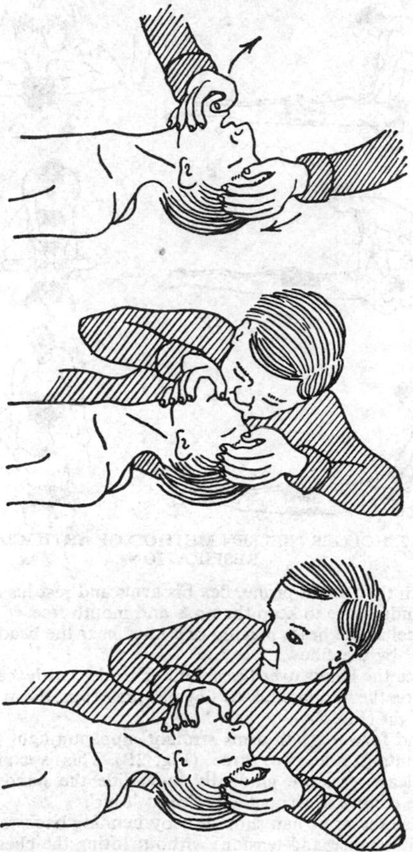

Fig. 1. EXPIRED AIR ARTIFICIAL RESPIRATION
Mouth-to-nose method

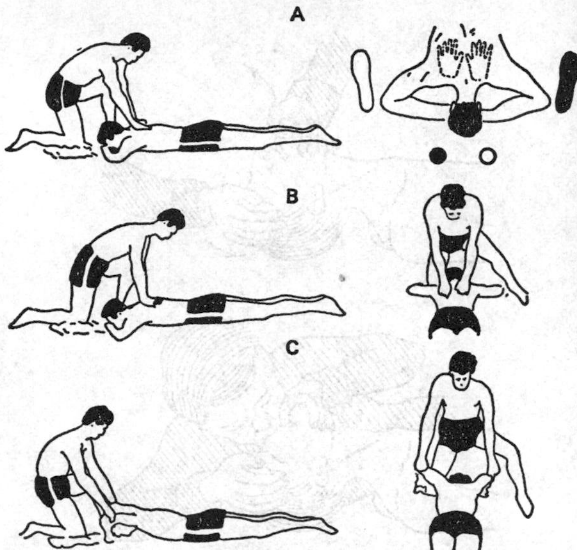

Fig. 2. HOLGER NIELSEN METHOD OF ARTIFICIAL RESPIRATION

(1) With the patient prone, flex his arms and rest his forehead on his hands, so as to keep the nose and mouth free.

(2) Kneel at the head, placing one knee near the head and the other foot by the elbow.

(3) Place the hands over the shoulder blades, with the thumbs touching on the midline and the fingers spread out, the arms being kept straight (Fig. 2A).

(4) Bend forward with arms straight, applying light pressure, while counting 'one, two, three' (Fig. 2B). This is expiration.

(5) Release pressure gradually and slide the hands to just above the elbows of the patient. Count 'four'.

(6) Raise the arms and shoulders by bending backwards until you feel resistance and tension, without lifting the chest off the ground, while counting 'five, six, seven' (Fig. 2C). This is inspiration.

(7) Lay the arms down and replace your hands on the patient's back while counting 'eight'.

(8) Repeat (3) to (7) with a rhythmic movement at the rate of 9 times a minute.

(9) When breathing is re-established, carry out arm raising and lowering (6 and 7 above) alone, 12 times a minute. Arm-raising—one, two, three (inspiration). Arm-lowering—four, five, six (expiration).

External Cardiac Massage

Once the lungs have been inflated several times, the operator must feel for the patient's pulse in the carotid artery, or on the radial or femoral pressure point. Should no pulse be present cardiac arrest has occurred and another helper must start external cardiac massage. If no assistant is present the operator must carry out artificial respiration and cardiac massage alternately.

(1) Place the patient on a firm surface, e.g. the floor, a trolley, or a board placed on a bed.

(2) Place the heel of one hand on the lower third of the patient's sternum and superimpose the other hand upon it.

(3) Depress the sternum rhythmically 3 to 4 cm towards the spine and repeat 50 to 60 times per minute until the patient's circulation becomes re-established.

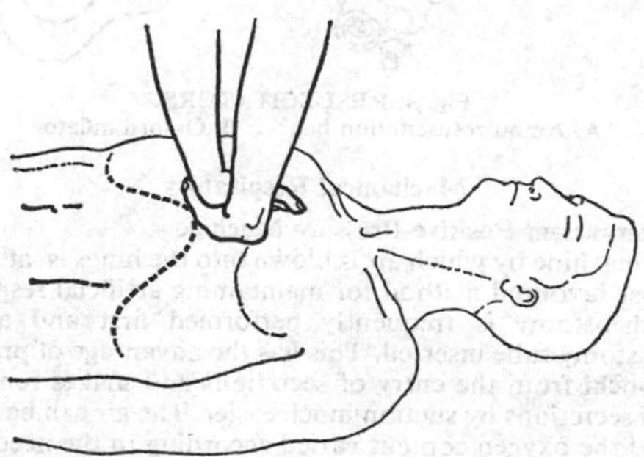

Fig. 3. EXTERNAL CARDIAC MASSAGE

This procedure entails the risk of fracturing the ribs and should not be carried out unless necessary, a factor which makes practice difficult. However, models are available and the operator can check the success of his efforts, as blood pressure readings can be taken and the lungs can be seen to inflate.

Manual Resuscitators

There are several simple devices that can be manually operated to maintain respiration by blowing air into the lungs. Two examples are the Ambu Resuscitator and Oxford Inflator.

Where artificial respiration has to be maintained for a prolonged period the above methods are inadequate and a power-driven mechanical respirator is required.

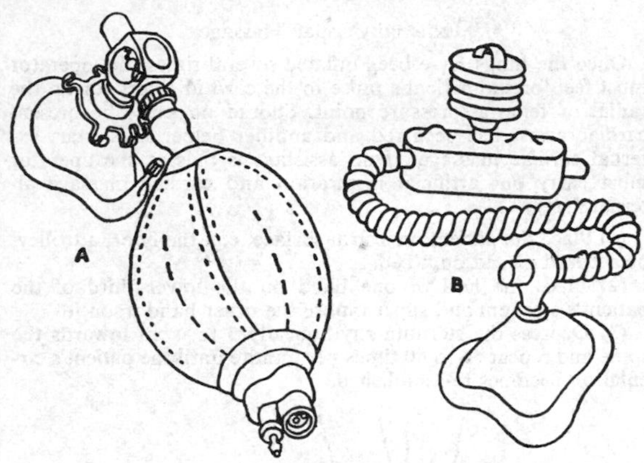

Fig. 4. RESUSCITATORS
A. Ambu resuscitation bag B. Oxford inflator

Mechanical Respirators

The Intermittent Positive-Pressure Machine

This machine by which air is blown into the lungs is, at present, the most favoured method for maintaining artificial respiration. A tracheostomy is frequently performed first and a cuffed tracheostomy tube inserted. This has the advantage of protecting the bronchi from the entry of secretions and makes removal of normal secretions by suction much easier. The air can be humidified and the oxygen content varied according to the needs of the individual patient. The nurse can then attend to all the patient's other bodily requirements quite easily and there is no restriction of movement of the limbs (see Plate II).

This type of artificial respiration is used for a great variety of conditions where the patient cannot adequately maintain normal breathing or where the nerve supply to the pharyngeal muscles is impaired and the protective mechanisms of the larynx are lost.

Suction of the Airway via a Tracheostomy Tube

No patient with a newly performed tracheostomy should be left unattended; and to keep the airway clear the nurse requires a suction machine, a plentiful supply of sterile suction catheters (No. 10 E. G. rectal tubes are ideal for this purpose) and forceps for holding and inserting the catheter. To suck out the airway a sterile catheter is picked up by the forceps and attached to the suction machine, which is then switched on. The catheter is occluded and passed down the tracheostomy tube using the forceps, as far as the carina; it is then released and slowly withdrawn sucking all the time. Should secretion be aspirated, pause at this level so that all secretion may be withdrawn and then continue to remove the tube. A fresh sterile catheter must be used each time suction is carried out.

UNCONSCIOUSNESS

Unconsciousness may be due to many different causes such as asphyxia, trauma, shock, or poisoning, but in all cases the first two conditions to be treated are cessation of breathing and cessation of heart beat. The helper should note if there is continuing danger from fire, fumes, electric current, or traffic and eliminate the source or remove the patient from it.

Next make sure the airway is clear by loosening constrictive clothing, clearing the mouth with the fingers; tilt the head backwards, and draw the jaw forward. If breathing is established, place the patient in the semi-prone position and continue to

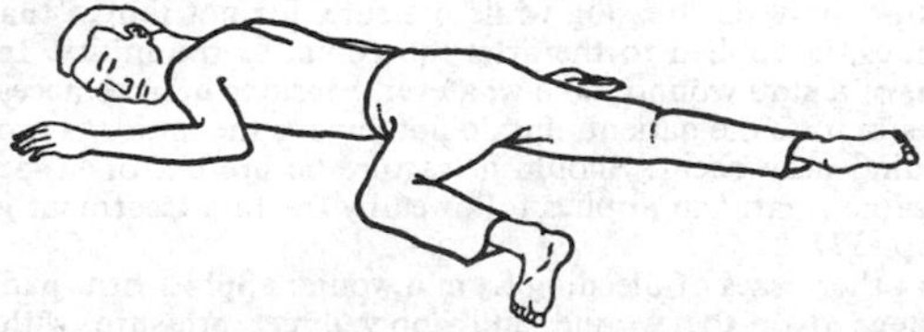

Fig. 5. SEMI-PRONE POSITION
Note: the head is tilted slightly backward and no cushion is used.

observe closely. Should breathing not resume immediately, expired air artificial respiration must be started without delay. Full details are given and illustrated on pp. 370–3.

After breathing into the patient's lungs three times, the pulse must be felt in order to establish whether the heart is beating and if it is not, external cardiac massage must be begun. Full details of this are given on p. 373.

Once the heart is beating and respiration established other measures can be taken.

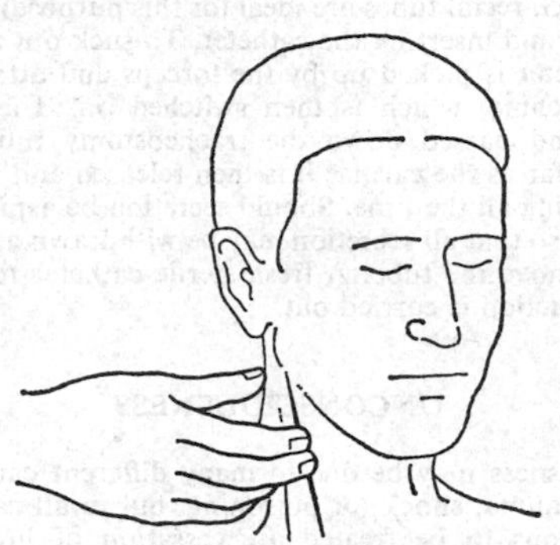

Fig. 6. TAKING THE CAROTID PULSE

HAEMORRHAGE

External bleeding. When the bleeding is visible, examine the wound to see whether any cause such as projecting metal or glass can be seen. When there is danger that either may still be present in the wound, the area should be lightly covered with a clean cloth or first aid dressing while pressure, for not longer than 15 minutes, is applied to the artery proximal to the injury. In the event of a stab wound, take whatever measures may be necessary to resuscitate the patient, but do not remove the knife, as profuse bleeding may occur. Should a fracture be present or suspected the same treatment applies followed by fracture treatment given on pp. 377–8.

In other cases of bleeding from a wound apply a firm pad and bandage over the wound and apply direct pressure with the fingers for 5 to 15 min. With a large wound area press the sides of the wound firmly but gently together. If a limb is involved elevate the part. If the bleeding has been severe or shock is present treat as below.

Internal bleeding. The signs of haemorrhage are an increasing pulse rate, pallor and deep sighing respirations. The patient will be restless and anxious and may complain of thirst, a feeling of

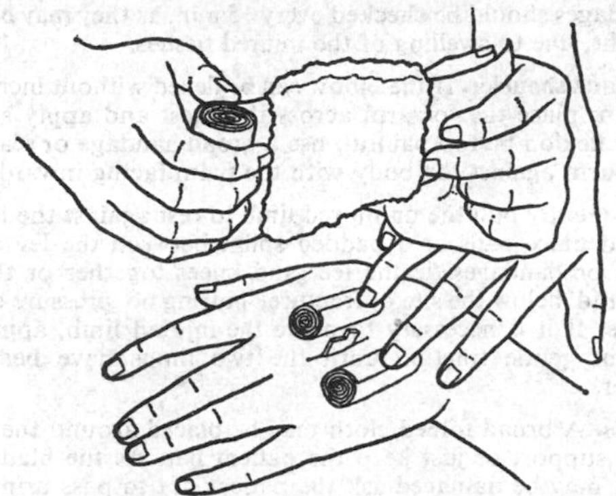

Fig. 7. APPLYING AN IMPROVISED DRESSING TO THE WOUND TO PREVENT FURTHER DAMAGE FROM THE EMBEDDED FRAGMENT

faintness and blurred vision. This patient is in a state of shock and the helper must treat this and at the same time send for a doctor.

Shock. To treat the shock reassure and calm the patient, lay him flat with the head low. Cover him but do not apply heat and give nothing by mouth. Record the pulse and respiration every 15 min.

FRACTURES

Fractures may be either closed, simple fractures or compound fractures in which there is communication between the site of the fracture and the air through either the skin or a mucous surface. In the latter case the risk of infection entering the wound must be minimized and in treating any fractures the first aid worker must handle the injured part with great care in order that further damage may not be done.

Suspected fractures should be treated as fractures without trying to elicit signs of fracture such as unnatural mobility and crepitus. Cover any wound with as clean a dressing as is available and if there is much bleeding apply pressure to the arterial pressure point proximal to the wound. Give the treatment for shock as above.

Immobilize the fracture by moving the injured part as little as is necessary. Untrained workers are advised to use the body and slings for immobilizing the part.

Bandages should be checked every 15 min, as they may become too tight, due to swelling of the injured tissues.

Arm and shoulder. If the elbow can be flexed without increasing the pain, place the forearm across the chest and apply a sling. Should flexion be too painful, use a broad bandage or scarf and tie the arm against the body with the palm facing inwards.

Leg. Gently pull the uninjured limb to rest against the injured one and place pads or a padded splint between the legs. With scarves or bandages tie the feet and knees together or the legs above and below the site of fracture, putting no pressure on the fracture. If it is necessary to move the injured limb, apply and maintain gentle traction until the two limbs have been tied together.

Pelvis. A broad folded cloth may be placed around the pelvis to give support or just keep the patient flat. As the bladder or urethra may be damaged ask the patient not to pass urine.

Spine. When there is a suspected injury to the spine do not move the patient until there is a stretcher available and a sufficient number of helpers. The whole body must be lifted or turned in unison with two of the team exerting slight traction on the head and feet. Place pads on the stretcher for the neck, lumbar curve, and ankles, and transport the patient in the dorsal position.

Skull. Lay the patient down and record the pulse every 15 min. Observe the condition of the eyes and pupils and note whether there is any bleeding or fluid discharge from the ears or nose. If the patient is unconscious treat as described on page 375. Facial injuries may necessitate the Holger Nielsen method of artificial respiration (p. 372).

All patients suffering from fractures should be removed to hospital as quickly and gently as possible. Rough handling will greatly increase the degree of shock.

ROAD ACCIDENTS

Carry out the following as required in descending order:

Remove the injured person immediately (whether in a vehicle or on the roadway) only if he is in danger, e.g. from fire or oncoming traffic. Unnecessary movement may worsen the injuries.

Treat asphyxia (p. 370)
Treat cardiac arrest (373)
Arrest haemorrhage (p. 376)
Treat for shock (p. 377)

Immobilize fractures (p. 377)
Cleanse and cover wounds
Send for help as soon as possible

POISONING

Take a quick note of the surroundings to establish the cause if possible and send for medical aid, stating the drug if known. If the patient is unconscious, notice whether he is breathing and whether his pulse can be felt. Should these be absent, follow the instructions on pp. 370–3. If respiration and circulation are present or restored but the patient is unconscious no attempt must be made to make him vomit and no stomach washout should be carried out until medical aid is present.

Corrosive poisoning. The lips may be stained grey or yellowish and the patient have a burning pain in the mouth and throat denoting that a corrosive has been taken. Do not make the patient vomit, but give demulcent drinks such as milk or egg white to sooth and dilute the poison. If an acid has been taken it can be neutralized by magnesium oxide or other alkali and an alkaline poison by giving diluted vinegar 100 ml to 0·5 litre of water (3 to 4 oz. to 1 pint).

Non-corrosive poisoning. When the poison taken is non-corrosive and the patient is conscious he may be made to vomit by giving him copious amounts of salt and water and placing a finger or spoon handle at the back of the mouth. This may be followed by a stomach washout when the equipment is available.

Aspirin. Should the cause be aspirin or iron tablets the stomach should be washed out with sodium bicarbonate solution and a small quantity left in the stomach.

Barbiturates. Barbiturates and tranquillizers are commonly consumed poisons and the danger of overdosage is greatly increased if taken at the same time as alcohol. In a drowsy state an accidental overdosage may be taken if the container is by the bedside.

Hospital care. Patients suffering from poisoning need the facilities available in hospital for their treatment and there should be no delay in transporting them there, guarding against shock and respiratory failure in transit.

National Poisons Information Centres have been set up from which a doctor may obtain advice in a case where he is in doubt about the correct treatment for a particular drug.

Inhalation of Poisonous Gas

Where possible turn off the gas and remove the patient to the fresh air or an open window. Loosen tight clothing and begin artificial respiration and cardiac massage if required (p. 373).

BURNS

Extinguish burning clothing by smothering the flames with a rug or coat. Reassure and calm the patient and relatives while immersing the burnt part in cold water if feasible. Do not remove adherent burnt clothing but cover the area with a freshly laundered cotton article. Treat the patient for shock and transfer him to hospital as quickly as possible.

Chemical Burns

To remove the chemical wash the burnt area by flooding the part thoroughly with gallons of water to which a neutralizing agent may be added. Use slowly running water, ensuring that it drains away freely and safely. Remove contaminated clothing if possible at the same time. Treat an acid burn with a solution of sodium bicarbonate and a corrosive alkali with weak vinegar or lemon juice. Speed in treatment is essential and if obtaining the correct antidote would entail loss of time the use of plain water is to be preferred; this particularly applies to splash injuries to the eye.

APPENDIX 2

FLUID AND ELECTROLYTE BALANCE

Fluid

An average-sized man has some 40 litres of water in his body, and this water accounts for approximately 60 per cent of his weight. The quantity present remains relatively constant and the balance between the quantities of water and of electrolytes present in the body fluids is controlled by a most delicate mechanism. To understand how this balance can be upset during disease or surgical procedures it is necessary to have some knowledge of the normal functioning of the salt and water balance in the body.

Fluid is normally lost from the body by:

(1) Excretion from the kidneys and colon
(2) Evaporation of sweat from the skin
(3) Expiration of moist air.

The body normally obtains its fluid from:

(1) The fluids taken in in liquid form
(2) The high fluid content of most foods eaten
(3) The metabolism of food and cell activity. Much cell activity is a process of oxidation in which water is released.

This can be illustrated by an example:

1 molecule glucose + 6 molecules oxygen
= 6 molecules carbon dioxide + 6 molecules water + energy

$$C_6H_{12}O_6 + 6O_2 = 6CO_2 + 6H_2O + \text{energy}$$

In health the balance between fluid intake and fluid output depends mainly on the kidneys, which are able to excrete large amounts of dilute urine when the fluid intake is high and excrete only small quantities of concentrated urine when less fluid is available. The latter condition may be the result of a lessened fluid intake or of an increased fluid loss from the body.

The skin is primarily concerned with the regulation of body temperature, and the amount of fluid evaporated from the skin depends on the body's need either to lose or to conserve heat. If the body is warm or the atmospheric temperature is high, much sweat will be excreted and evaporated in an attempt to cool the body. Under cool conditions the sweat glands will be less active in an endeavour to retain more heat within the body.

The fluid in the body is present in three different compartments:

(1) The smallest quantity is the circulating fluid or blood plasma. This is about 7 per cent of the total.

(2) The tissue fluid which bathes all the cells forms about 23 per cent.

These two together are termed the extracellular fluid.

(3) The fluid within the cell walls forms the greatest proportion of the body fluid, amounting to 70 per cent. This is termed intracellular fluid.

Different factors help in maintaining the level of fluid in these three compartments. The plasma proteins, serum albumin, serum globulin, and fibrinogen are the chief factors that maintain the osmotic pressure within the capillaries and so keep the circulating fluid within the vessels. The salt content chiefly influences the tissue fluid and intracellular fluid.

Salts and Electrolytes

Electrolytes are inorganic elements in solution in the body fluid. These elements are either basic (or alkaline) when they are positive ions (cations), or acid when they are negative ions (anions). A salt is made up of a base combined with an acid and when in solution the elements separate, forming electrolytes. Sodium chloride (NaCl), the chief salt of blood plasma and tissue fluid, can be split up into the two electrolytes sodium (Na) and chloride (Cl). The sodium is basic and provides positive ions while the chloride is acid and supplies negative ions. In intracellular fluid potassium (K) is the main positive ion and phosphate (PO_3) and sulphate (SO_4) provide the negative ions.

In each of the fluid compartments of the body there has to be a balance between the positive ions and the negative ions. In other words the acid–base equilibrium has to be maintained. The kidneys also play a part here as they have the ability to excrete either acid or alkaline salts to maintain the blood plasma in its correct reaction, which is slightly alkaline.

Hormones

The pituitary and adrenal glands both have an influence on the salt and water balance in the body. The antidiuretic hormone from the posterior lobe of the pituitary gland controls the final reabsorption of water in the renal tubules. If the hormone is lacking there is excessive diuresis. Aldosterone from the adrenal cortex increases the reabsorption of sodium by the renal tubules and reduces the sodium content of sweat.

Disturbance of the Fluid and Electrolyte Balance

Upset of the fluid and electrolyte balance may occur in many different ways:

Water Depletion

(1) When there is lack of intake.

(2) When there is excessive loss from vomiting, diarrhoea, sweating, or haemorrhage.

There is loss of fluid from the subcutaneous tissues and the skin becomes hot and dry and loses its elasticity. The circulating fluid becomes less, the capillary walls suffer from lack of oxygen and become more permeable, and further leakage from the vessels occurs, giving rise to the condition of shock.

Sodium Depletion

(1) In excessive sweating.

(2) In diarrhoea or where there is much faecal loss from a fistula or ileostomy.

(3) In pathological conditions, such as Addison's disease or hypopituitarism, where the kidneys are unable to conserve sodium.

Chloride Depletion

(1) Persistent vomiting where there is heavy loss of chlorides from the hydrochloric acid will lead to the condition of alkalosis.

(2) Prolonged gastic aspiration.

Potassium Depletion

This may arise whenever there is prolonged diarrhoea, vomiting, condition of shock, or lack of intake, and where there is excessive diuresis or continued use of diuretics such as chlorothiazide.

In prolonged loss of sodium and chloride, potassium ...tes from the cells to replace extracellular salt. Potass... slow to leave the cells but also is slow to permeate b... the cells when replacement is being carried out. Its la... muscular weakness, apathy, and mental conf... kidneys still excrete potassium, making the con...

Protein Depletion

(1) Where there ...ake, malnutrition, or starvation.

(2) Where there is excessive protein loss in nephritis or severe burns.
There is loss of osmotic pressure in the blood and great loss of fluid into the tissues.

(3) In severe haemorrhage where the only satisfactory replacement is by blood of the correct group. *See* Appendix 3.

It is seldom that any one of these depletions occurs alone. Fluid, sodium, and chloride are all lost together, but in severe diarrhoea more sodium is lost and in persistent vomiting it is the heavy loss of chlorides which upsets the acid–base balance.

Normally a diet containing an adequate protein and fluid content will also supply the necessary sodium, chloride, and potassium.

REPLACEMENT OF FLUID LOSS

Oral fluids. Where there is a fluid lack, replacement is best by the oral route. It is unlikely there will be a lack of water only, and for excessive sweating a ⅕ strength normal saline may be taken by mouth. Most of the other conditions will not benefit from oral fluids and another route will have to be chosen.

Rectal fluids. These may be given for temporary relief of dehydration but their administration cannot be maintained over a period of days. Tap water is commonly used.

Subcutaneous infusion. Normal saline (a 0·9 per cent solution of sodium chloride) may be given to replace salt and water loss. The use of hyaluronidase, the spreading factor, aids absorption.

Intravenous infusion. This is the commonest way of combating water and salt depletion and if due regard is paid to the electrolyte balance it can be maintained over long periods. It is most usual to give a 4 per cent dextrose solution in ⅕ strength normal saline (0·18 per cent solution). Into every third or fourth bottle 1 g of potassium may be put. This should be diluted in the full so[illegible] or every third or fourth bottle may be of Hartmann's solu[illegible] as this will supply the necessary potassium. Hartmann's [illegible] an isotonic solution containing salts of sodium, potass[illegible] calcium with lactic acid.

In any [illegible] in which there is likely to be a depletion of water, sal[illegible], or whenever parenteral fluids are given, there must [illegible] observation of the patient with careful measurement [illegible] of all sources of fluid loss and fluid intake. Analysis [illegible] chemistry will be carried out in all severe or prolon[illegible]

cortex increases the reabsorption of sodium by the renal tubules and reduces the sodium content of sweat.

Disturbance of the Fluid and Electrolyte Balance

Upset of the fluid and electrolyte balance may occur in many different ways:

Water Depletion

(1) When there is lack of intake.
(2) When there is excessive loss from vomiting, diarrhoea, sweating, or haemorrhage.

There is loss of fluid from the subcutaneous tissues and the skin becomes hot and dry and loses its elasticity. The circulating fluid becomes less, the capillary walls suffer from lack of oxygen and become more permeable, and further leakage from the vessels occurs, giving rise to the condition of shock.

Sodium Depletion

(1) In excessive sweating.
(2) In diarrhoea or where there is much faecal loss from a fistula or ileostomy.
(3) In pathological conditions, such as Addison's disease or hypopituitarism, where the kidneys are unable to conserve sodium.

Chloride Depletion

(1) Persistent vomiting where there is heavy loss of chlorides from the hydrochloric acid will lead to the condition of alkalosis.
(2) Prolonged gastic aspiration.

Potassium Depletion

This may arise whenever there is prolonged diarrhoea, vomiting, condition of shock, or lack of intake, and where there is excessive diuresis or continued use of diuretics such as chlorothiazide.

In prolonged loss of sodium and chloride, potassium migrates from the cells to replace extracellular salt. Potassium is slow to leave the cells but also is slow to permeate back into the cells when replacement is being carried out. Its lack leads to muscular weakness, apathy, and mental confusion. The kidneys still excrete potassium, making the condition worse.

Protein Depletion

(1) Where there is inadequate intake, malnutrition, or starvation.

(2) Where there is excessive protein loss in nephritis or severe burns.
There is loss of osmotic pressure in the blood and great loss of fluid into the tissues.

(3) In severe haemorrhage where the only satisfactory replacement is by blood of the correct group. *See* Appendix 3.

It is seldom that any one of these depletions occurs alone. Fluid, sodium, and chloride are all lost together, but in severe diarrhoea more sodium is lost and in persistent vomiting it is the heavy loss of chlorides which upsets the acid–base balance.

Normally a diet containing an adequate protein and fluid content will also supply the necessary sodium, chloride, and potassium.

REPLACEMENT OF FLUID LOSS

Oral fluids. Where there is a fluid lack, replacement is best by the oral route. It is unlikely there will be a lack of water only, and for excessive sweating a $\frac{1}{5}$ strength normal saline may be taken by mouth. Most of the other conditions will not benefit from oral fluids and another route will have to be chosen.

Rectal fluids. These may be given for temporary relief of dehydration but their administration cannot be maintained over a period of days. Tap water is commonly used.

Subcutaneous infusion. Normal saline (a 0·9 per cent solution of sodium chloride) may be given to replace salt and water loss. The use of hyaluronidase, the spreading factor, aids absorption.

Intravenous infusion. This is the commonest way of combating water and salt depletion and if due regard is paid to the electrolyte balance it can be maintained over long periods. It is most usual to give a 4 per cent dextrose solution in $\frac{1}{5}$ strength normal saline (0·18 per cent solution). Into every third or fourth bottle 1 g of potassium may be put. This should be diluted in the full bottle or every third or fourth bottle may be of Hartmann's solution as this will supply the necessary potassium. Hartmann's solution is an isotonic solution containing salts of sodium, potassium and calcium with lactic acid.

In any condition in which there is likely to be a depletion of water, salts, or protein, or whenever parenteral fluids are given, there must be close observation of the patient with careful measurement and recording of all sources of fluid loss and fluid intake. Analysis of the blood chemistry will be carried out in all severe or prolonged cases.

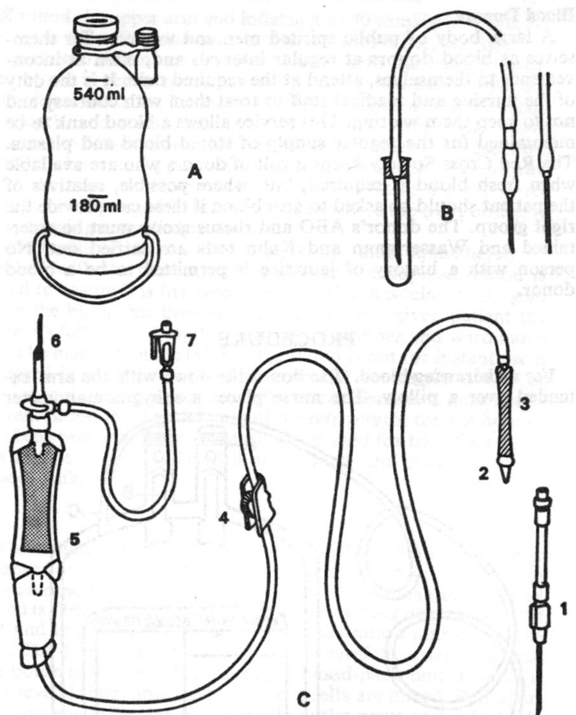

Fig. 8. A BLOOD TRANSFUSION OUTFIT

A, Blood transfusion bottle; B, Taking set; C, Disposable giving set.

(1) Needle with Luer fitting. (2) Luer fitting mount. (3) 5 cm (2 in.) of latex rubber tubing for drugs to be added. (4) Clip or control clamp for regulating rate of flow through polythene tubing. (5) Filter and drip. (6) Connector with needle to pierce bung of sterile infusion container. (7) Air inlet filter to be hooked above fluid level in the container.

sterility. A small section of latex tubing allows for the introduction of intravenous drugs. The giving needle if supplied is enclosed in a separate sealed tube. The instructions for use are printed on each packet.

check the apparatus to see that the blood is still flowing at the required rate and that the needle is in position. Kinking of the tube must be avoided and the limb should be kept warm.

Sometimes needles other than those supplied with the giving set may be used for insertion. A favourite one is a Guest cannula (disposable) in which there is an outer blunt cannula and inner sharp needle with a stilette. The sharp needle aids insertion and once inserted it is withdrawn leaving the blunt cannula in position which is less likely to damage the vein wall.

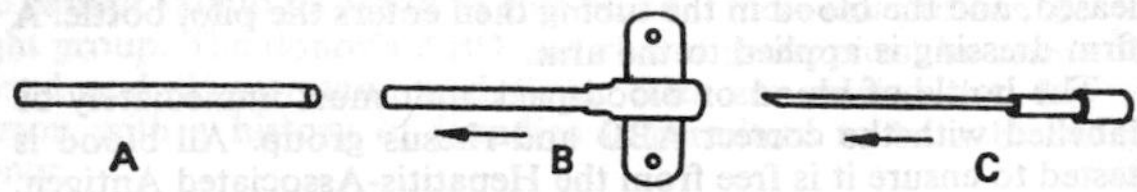

Fig. 10. DISPOSABLE GUEST CANNULA

A, Protective sheath; B, Cannula; C, Needle.

A polythene cannula may be supplied pre-sterilized and can be passed quite a distance up the vein, so providing the advantage of a quick dilution of fluid in the blood stream and a lessened risk of local trauma.

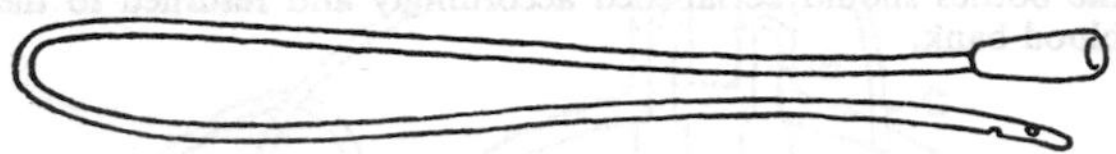

Fig. 11. POLYTHENE INTRAVENOUS CANNULA

Exchange Transfusion

An exchange or replacement transfusion may be carried out on a newly born Rh+ infant born to a Rh− mother. In this case a syringe with two three-way adaptors may be used. A fine polythene cannula is passed up the umbilical vein into the inferior vena cava and blood can be alternately withdrawn and inserted. This procedure is repeated until one litre of blood has been used, and most of the baby's Rh+ cells that have been damaged by the mother's antibodies have been replaced by Rh− cells.

TRANSFUSION FLUIDS

1. Fresh blood. This is particularly useful in cases of active sepsis or haemolytic disease because the cells will not have undergone change.

2. Stored blood. This is stored at 4°C and may be kept for up to 3 weeks. A slight reaction is likely if the blood has been

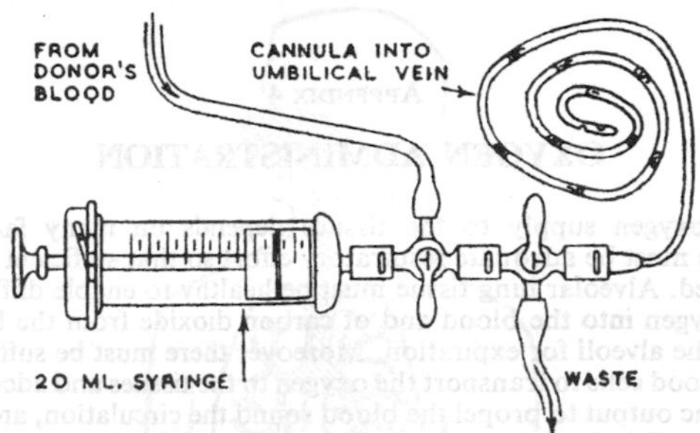

Fig. 12. APPARATUS FOR EXCHANGE TRANSFUSION

kept for 3 weeks. It is particularly useful for all emergency cases of haemorrhage, and as a pre- or post-operative measure or during operation when special hazards are encountered.

3. **Frozen blood.** Liquid nitrogen held at a temperature of −79°C. enables blood to be stored indefinitely. Several hours are needed to prepare it for use, by a process of washing and centrifugation.

4. **Packed red cells.** Part of the plasma is removed from whole blood. Using the closed sterile system (transfer unit attached to blood-pack unit) the packed red cells can be stored for 21 days; whereas bottled red cells must be used within 12 to 24 hr. It is used when it is desired to increase the number of cells without overloading the circulation with fluid, as in some cases of anaemia.

5. **Platelet rich blood.** This may be collected with silicone-treated equipment or into a disposable bag in which there is 50 ml of EDTA solution (a di-sodium salt of ethylene diamine tetra-acetic acid), an anticoagulant which is preferable to acid citrate dextrose solution in preserving the platelet content of blood. Platelets are required in controlling haemorrhage in haemolytic disease.

For details of other infusion fluids that may be administered by the same equipment see Appendix 2.

no rebreathing. The thin stream of oxygen draws in a good volume of air, which helps to flush out the dead space air. It is the best type of face mask for use where there is serious impairment of lung ventilation. There are three models giving a controlled intake of 24 or 28 per cent at 4 litres of oxygen per minute, or 35 per cent oxygen at a flow rate of 8 litres per minute.

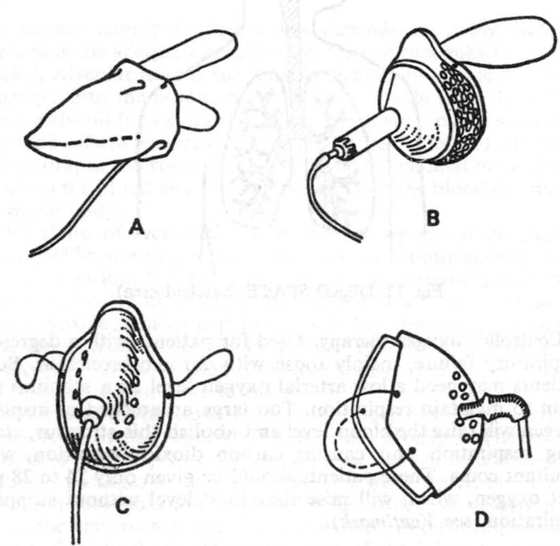

Fig. 14. OXYGEN MASKS
A, Polymask; B, Ventimask; C, Harris mask; D, M.C. mask.

Harris mask. The Harris mask is a stiff transparent plastic disposable mask with good air entry holes. It does not cause rebreathing or increase the dead space air. Where a controlled intake is not necessary it is a cheaper model than the Ventimask.

M.C. and Edinburgh masks. These are transparent semi-rigid plastic masks, comfortable to wear and very useful if no controlled oxygen percentage is required as the concentration does vary with the lung ventilation. There is some rebreathing but less than with soft plastic masks.

Nasal catheters. Nasal catheters used with a humidifier have the advantage that there is no rebreathing and oxygen administration can be continued during meals. The percentage of oxygen

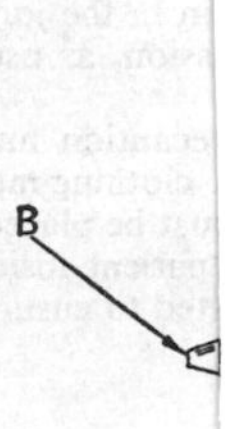

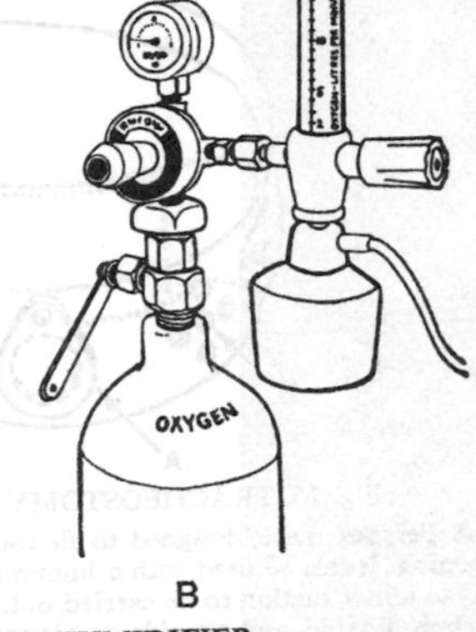

Fig. 15. OXYGEN HUMIDIFIER

A, Attached to wall supply; B, Attached to oxygen cylinder.

received is considerably higher if the patient breathes through the nose than through the mouth. The catheters need to be cleaned and lubricated regularly.

Oxygen by tracheostomy or endotracheal tubes. If oxygen is administered by these methods humidification of oxygen is required to prevent the mucous membrane from drying. This can be done by attaching a humidifier to the flowmeter on the oxygen cylinder or to a wall supply. The humidifier can also be used as a nebulizer to administer drugs.

Oxygen tents. In modern oxygen tents every effort has been made to control the oxygen concentration, the carbon dioxide content, the humidity, and the temperature. The control of oxygen concentration is not easy since the patient treated in a tent is the very person who requires repeated physiotherapy and nursing attention which necessitates opening the tent. With improved tracheostomy and endotracheal care the tents are used less often than formerly but are still useful for young children, or adults who cannot tolerate a face mask or nasal catheters.

Nursing Observations

During oxygen administration the nurse should observe the rate and depth of respiration, the rate and strength of the pulse and the colour of the skin. A patient who becomes pink, who is

type of chamber and it can also be used for operating on congenital heart lesions.

If more than 2 atm of pressure are used there is serious risk on decompression of the release of nitrogen bubbles in the blood giving rise to decompression sickness. This is characterized by abdominal pain, cramp and vomiting, and pain in the joints. It may, however, be avoided by slow decompression, as used for deep-sea divers.

The fire risk is high and every possible precaution must be taken against a spark discharge. All towels and clothing must be fire-resistant and the monitoring equipment must be placed outside the chamber with only the leads to the patient inside the chamber. All equipment necessary must be tested to ensure that it is suitable for use at high pressures.

Fig. 16. Tr

A Perspex mask opening. It can be u (A) to allow suction carbon dioxide, and supply of oxygen.

difficult to rouse infrequent is likely dioxide retention.

The apparatus that it is working risk of fire. No sn antistatic precauti

This is oxygen u to be carried in th blood cells is full amount of oxygen number of red blo then oxygen is diss tissues. Raised atr sures of the indivi their percentage of nitrogen. Hyperba

(1) The patient i with a transparent raised. He can how periods since nursi enclosed. This typ

Appendix 5

STATIC ELECTRICITY AND ANTISTATIC PRECAUTIONS

Static electricity is produced by two different surfaces being in close association or rubbing against each other, so that the objects become electrically charged. This charge may be built up so that a spark discharge of electricity may occur. This may give rise to an unpleasant sensation, or cause minor accidents such as the spilling of hot fluids; if it happens in the vicinity of oxygen or other explosive anaesthetic vapours it may cause a serious explosion. Thus the question of static electricity is an important one in the anaesthetic room and operating theatre or where oxygen is being administered.

If the substances charged are good conductors of electricity or are in contact with good conductors the charge will drain away and not be built up. Water is a good conductor so that in a humid atmosphere sparks of static electricity are less likely to occur and an electric charge is unlikely to be built up on a moist surface. Conversely, a dry atmosphere (particularly where there is central heating), dry blankets, mackintoshes and rubber surfaces are poor conductors and an electric spark may easily occur.

When a patient is conveyed to the theatre on a metal trolley with ordinary rubber tyres and rubber sheeting and is covered by blankets, and the attendants also are wearing rubber shoes or where the floor is of non-conducting material, a powerful charge of static electricity can be built up.

Similarly, nylon in contact with the skin can build up an electric charge, and this can occur also when garments are of different materials, e.g. wool next to nylon or nylon next to artificial silk. Most nurses will have experienced the crackling that occurs on removing garments that have become electrically charged.

Precautions. To minimize the risks attached to a spark discharge, special precautions should be taken:

(1) An antistatic rubber has been manufactured in which carbon particles are impregnated in the rubber and these particles drain away the electric charge. Owing to the presence of the carbon particles this rubber is always black and in Great Britain is identified by a bright yellow disc or patch. This yellow may be seen on the wheels of trolleys fitted with antistatic tyres, or on the

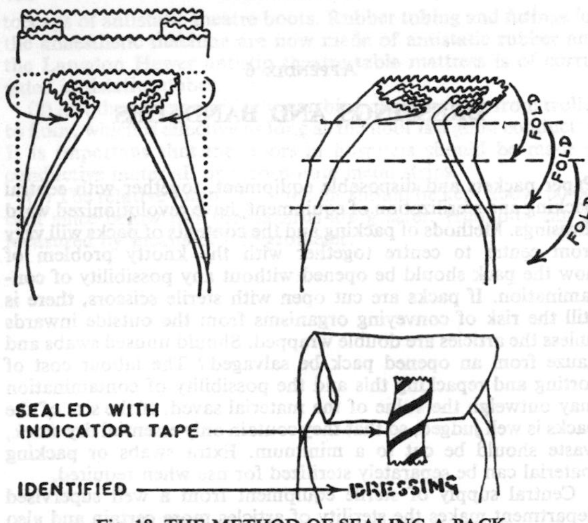

Fig. 18. THE METHOD OF SEALING A PACK

a pair of scissors kept solely for cutting the fixatives, a 15-cm metal bowl on the lower shelf and a clip attached to the side of the trolley.

The nurse about to do a dressing washes her hands, dries them and with a folded paper towel swabs systematically the top of the trolley with a minimum of Sudol 1 per cent that has been sprayed on. This is allowed a few seconds to dry while she adds to the bottom of the trolley the required lotions and any additional packs required.

Contents of a Large Dressing Pack

A sheet of bonded fibre (wrapping paper)
1 wool pad 225 × 225 mm
5 absorbent squares 100 × 100 mm } all bought prepared
10 cotton wool balls—large }
1 gallipot (disposable) × 60 ml
1 pair Vigo scissors
2 pairs dissecting forceps
1 paper tissue as a handling surface
1 paper dressing towel.

The above are folded in the wrapping paper leaving the corners uppermost. On top of this are placed two pairs of French's dressing forceps in a separate paper bag.

All the above are now placed in a paper bag and sealed (see Fig. 18).

The small and medium dressing packs are similar but contain fewer absorbent squares and cotton wool balls and no wool pads and are suitable for many minor dressings, for removal of stitches and clips and for procedures like sternal marrow puncture or an aspiration where it is necessary to clean the skin and to provide a sterile field. Many articles that might be required for a dressing are separately packed, among which are the following: clip-removing forceps, wool pads for packing, cotton wool balls and absorbent squares, safety pins, irrigating equipment, 60 ml gallipots and small measures for diluting lotions.

Fig. 19. TROLLEY BEFORE OPENING PACK

Preparing the Patient

The dressing may be carried out at the bedside or in a treatment room; in the former case the bed curtains should be drawn 20 min before to allow dust to settle and the nurse should ensure there is sufficient room for the trolley at the appropriate side of the bed. For most dressings extra pillows, backrest or air-ring are removed leaving the patient comfortably recumbent. The bedclothes are neatly turned back to the necessary level and the nightwear is adjusted. Where the patient's condition permits this may all be done before the trolley is prepared. (Should the patient be very ill two nurses should be available, one to prepare the trolley and the other to prepare the patient.) The nurse washes her hands, prepares the trolley and brings it to the bedside.

Rayon elastic (Rayolast) has more elasticity than the plain crepe and is advocated for application to amputation stumps to aid healing with the formation of a good firm stump by preventing oedema.

Cling. This is a very light bandage of fine cotton mesh and is particularly useful when a dressing requires supporting with the minimum of material and the avoidance of even slight pressure or the use of adhesive. This applies to the extremities when the blood supply to the area is much reduced.

Tubular Bandages

Tubular gauze. This is a light-weight cotton woven bandage in tubular form that can be applied to any part of the body. In many cases a special applicator is required. The bandages can be applied with varying degrees of tension and they are cool and comfortable to wear. Tubular gauze is particularly recommended for finger and head dressings and where extensive covering is required in the treatment of skin diseases.

Further details of tubular gauze bandaging may be obtained from the Scholl Manufacturing Company Limited, 182–204 St John Street, London, EC1.

Netelast. This is a tubular mesh bandage of cotton and elastic fibres. It is strongly elastic and supporting but stretches widely and is not constrictive. It is a more expensive bandage but this is offset by the comfort to the patient in securing a dressing in an area that is awkward to bandage by the older methods. It can be applied to most areas of the body.

Further details of Netelast bandaging can be obtained from the manufacturers: Roussel Laboratories Limited, Columbus House, Wembley Park, Middlesex.

Appendix 7

METHODS OF STERILIZATION

Autoclave

Autoclaving, or sterilization by steam under pressure, is a very effective way of destroying organisms and spores, and is the method of choice for all linen or cotton articles, surgeons' and nurses' gowns and towels. Dressing packs, or any pack incorporating absorbent wool dressing, or absorbent gauze or cotton wool balls, should be sterilized by this method. It is also suitable for glass, metal and rubber articles. Polyproparine, a plastic from which measures, kidney dishes and bowls may be made, can be sterilized in this way but many other plastics will be damaged by autoclaving.

The temperature reached inside the autoclave will depend on the efficiency of the vacuum created and the pressure of the steam. The greater the vacuum and the higher the pressure, the higher will be the temperature reached and the shorter the time necessary for sterilization. The nature of the load must be considered so that there is complete penetration by the steam. High vacuum high pressure autoclaves are machines in which a high vacuum is rapidly created by an electric pump. For sterilizing dressings, gowns and towels in such a machine, after loading a vacuum of 75 cm (30 in.) is created and steam under pressure is introduced for a preliminary warming, then a second vacuum is drawn and steam at 13·5 kg (30 lb.) pressure is let in. This will raise the temperature to 135°C (275°F) where it is held for 3½ mins. A third vacuum draws off the steam and the articles are left to dry. The whole cycle is fully automatic and takes between 20 and 28 min.

Small machines can be installed in ward or theatre units to sterilize smooth articles such as instruments. Penetration is not required, so no preliminary warming or drying time is necessary and the whole cycle takes 6 min.

Hot Air Oven

Dry heat in a hot air oven may be used for sterilization. Dry heat requires a higher temperature for efficient sterilization than moist heat, and that commonly used is 160°C for 1 hr. This method is suitable for delicate eye instruments and for syringes. The instru-

solution suitable for disinfecting purposes, but Milton 1:80 is to be preferred for sterilizing glassware and babies' feeding bottles. Milton may also be used for the irrigation of wounds.

Chlorhexidine (Hibitane)

Chlorhexidine is an antiseptic which is bacteriostatic and bactericidal and is non-injurious to tissues. It may be used for skin cleansing or disinfection in a 1 per cent solution or for bladder irrigation 0·02 per cent (1:5000). It is supplied as a bactericidal cream or added to other disinfectants to enhance their effect. Savlon consists of cetrimide 0·5 per cent and chlorhexidine 0·05 per cent and is popular in midwifery practice.

Cetrimide (Cetavlon)

Cetrimide is a good skin cleansing agent effective against many organisms but not the tubercle bacilli or spores. It should not be stored in bottles with corks which in themselves may be a source of contamination.

Hexachlorophene

Hexachlorophene 1·0 per cent in soap causes a great reduction in bacteria recovered from the skin and is being widely used in skin preparation before operation, for the patient, the surgeon and the nurse. pHisoHex solution and Ster-Zac powder both contain hexachlorophene.

Proflavine Hemisulphate

Proflavine is slowly bactericidal and may be used with effect for wound cleansing to prevent sepsis arising.

Alcohol

A 70 per cent solution with water is the most effective strength in killing bacteria but it does not kill spores. Isopropanol is 70 per cent isopropyl alcohol and is the alcohol of choice for skin cleansing. Industrial methylated spirit is a 95 per cent solution and is much less effective since without the water it cannot penetrate the surface to kill the organisms. Though this preparation may be used for individual syringes it is not recommended for ward storage of either instruments or syringes.

Sudol

Sudol is a coal tar derivative which is less likely to cause burn injuries than Lysol, which it resembles. It is an efficient disinfectant where crude disinfection is required. As a 1·0 per cent solution it can be mixed with infected excreta for one hour before disposal or for disinfecting bedpans or lavatory brush jars.

Ethylene Oxide Gas

Effective sterilization may be achieved when this vapour is used in rigidly controlled conditions of humidity and pressure. Some substances such as rubber absorb the ethylene oxide, so time must be allowed for the gas to disperse. Articles that may be sterilized by this method include embolectomy catheters, cardiac pacemakers, cryothermy electrodes and probes and heart valve prostheses.

Disinfection of bulky equipment such as respirators, incubators and suction machines can be achieved by allowing them to cycle for 24 hr in an atmosphere of 10 per cent ethylene oxide.

CENTRAL SUPPLY STERILIZING DEPARTMENT

From the foregoing it will be seen that the most efficient methods of sterilization are those employing heat and where the most expensive equipment is required. If this equipment is assembled in a central department under the supervision of a senior member of the staff there should be a more uniform efficiency in the sterilization and the cost of the equipment is more economic. At the same time great advances have been made in the manufacture of disposable equipment to cut down the labour costs and laundry.

In planning a department considerable thought must go into the arrangement of the production line. The non-disposable equipment is received into the dirty area, where it is sorted and mechanically washed either in a washing machine or in an ultrasonic washer where vibrations loosen the dirt and then it is rinsed off. From the washers the articles are placed on trays in a drying cabinet before they are packed. The packing area should be so arranged that the articles are readily to hand at a comfortable height for the packers, who must be well drilled in the packing procedure. This must be uniform and reliable so that the user of the pack may know the contents and be able to open it without contaminating the articles it contains.

Some departments favour the method where each article is separately wrapped while others favour standard basic packs with separate packing of additional articles that may be required. Most packs are double-wrapped, first in bonded fibre (strong paper) and then in paper bags. Theatre packs have a third dust wrapping that is removed when the pack is taken from the theatre pack store before it is conveyed to the theatre. The packs are sealed with indicator tape that will indicate that the pack has been through the autoclave. The prepared packs should be placed directly in perforated containers that will fit into the autoclave.

although minor variations in details may occur in individual institutions.*

(1) A special cupboard is used for storing such drugs, and this should be marked 'C.D.'
(2) The cupboard is kept locked, and the key carried on the person of the state registered nurse in charge.
(3) Renewal of supplies can only be obtained by an order signed by a medical officer; and they can only be given under the written instructions of such.
(4) Each dose of these drugs administered must be entered into a special Register provided for the purpose, with the date, patient's name and time of giving. The persons giving and checking the drug must sign this entry.

In most hospitals it is a rule that each dose given is checked by two persons, one of whom should be a state registered nurse. This person should see the bottle from which the drug is taken, and check the dose with the written prescription.

All bottles containing controlled drugs should be marked conspicuously with a special label.

The hospital pharmacist usually checks at intervals the contents of the C.D. cupboard and compares its contents with the records of the Register.

The Poisons Act. Many substances are covered by this act and these are divided into 'Schedules,' of which 1 and 4 are concerned with medicine.

In hospitals such drugs are kept under lock and key and they should be distinctively labelled and stored in bottles of special shape.

SCHEDULE 1 lists all the preparations to which special restrictions apply under the Poisons Rules. These drugs may be sold only to persons known to the chemist, on a medical prescription, or on a police order. The poisons book must be signed. The commoner ones, including their alkaloids or salts, which are used in hospitals are the following:

Apomorphine	Digitalis
Arsenic	Emetine
Atropine	Ergot
Belladonna	Hyoscine
Carbachol	Methylpentynol (*Oblivon*)
	Strychnine

* *See* Department of Health and Social Security report of joint subcommittee on the Control of Dangerous Drugs and Poisons in Hospital.

SCHEDULE 4 lists those substances to be sold by retailers only upon a prescription given by a duly qualified medical practitioner. These drugs are also included in Schedule 1. The group of drugs can be divided into Schedule 4A and 4B, the prescriptions for which must fulfil different requirements, Schedule 4A having rules similar to the Misuse of Drugs Act. This applies chiefly to pharmacists and doctors, but for nurses the same rules apply to all poisons.

Examples of Schedule 4A drugs:

Most barbiturate drugs	Cyclophosphamide
Gallamine injections	Mercaptopurine
Mustine injections	

Examples of Schedule 4B drugs:

Chlorpromazine	Sulphonamide drugs
Milder sedatives	Thiazide diuretics
Tranquilizers	Thyroid preparations

The Therapeutic Substances Act. This act controls the manufacture, supply and sale of certain drugs and preparations. The provisions of the Act are similar to those controlling the Poisons Schedules. The preparations controlled are:

Antibiotics	Heparin
Corticosteroids and corticotrophin	Insulin
Curare	Surgical ligatures
Blood	Vaccines and sera

The Misuse of Drugs (Notification of and Supply to Addicts) Regulations 1973. Medical practitioners may not prescribe, administer or supply cocaine or diamorphine, or their salts, to addicted persons, except for the purpose of treating organic disease or injury, unless they have obtained a special licence and work in a specially licensed NHS hospital or similar institution. Addicts will have to undergo treatment in such a hospital or clinic. For further information apply to the Department of Health and Social Security, Alexander Fleming House, London SE1.

ABBREVIATIONS USED IN PRESCRIPTIONS

Abbreviations of Latin terms are being replaced by English versions which are considered safer. The nurse may still meet these terms.

Term	*Latin*	*English*
a.c.	ante cibum	before food
ad lib.	ad libitum	to the desired amount
b.d. or b.i.d.	bis in die	twice a day
c.	cum	with
o.m.	omnimane	every morning
o.n.	omni nocte	every night
p.c.	post cibum	after food
p.r.n.	pro re nata	whenever necessary
q.d. or q.i.d.	quater in die	four times a day
℞	recipe	take
s.o.s.	si opus sit	if necessary
stat.	statim	at once
t.d.s.	ter die sumendus	three times a day
t.i.d.	ter in die	three times a day

APPENDIX 10

DIETETICS

ENERGY REQUIREMENTS

A Calorie (*kilocalorie*) is the unit used for the measurement of the heat-producing power of foods.

Definition of a Calorie

A Calorie is the amount of heat required to raise one kilogram of water 1°C.

The only food materials producing heat are carbohydrates, proteins, fats, and alcohol.

1 g of carbohydrate gives	4 calories
1 g of protein gives	4 calories
1 g of fat gives	9 calories
1 g of alcohol gives	7 calories

The new unit of energy in nutrition is the joule. 1 Calorie (*kilocalorie*) = 4·186 kilojoules.

Basal Metabolism

Basal metabolism is the rate of energy metabolism of the body when at complete rest in a room of comfortable temperature 12 to 18 hr after the last intake of food.

Fever increases basal metabolism about 7 per cent for every degree Fahrenheit rise in temperature.

Everyone requires the calories for basal metabolism (men 1700 cal, women 1450 cal) added to those for all the activities and work undertaken during the 24 hr.

Approximate Calories Required for Various Occupations each Day*

Men		
18–35 years	No work (lying in bed)	1750
	Sedentary (clerical)	2700
	Moderately active (light industry)	3000
	Very active (wood cutter)	3600
35–65 years	Classified as above, 100 Calories less	
65–75 years	Assuming a sedentary life	2350
75 and over	Assuming a sedentary life	2100

*Based on Report No. 120 of the Department of Health and Social Security 1969 (HMSO).

Women		
18–55 years	No work (lying in bed)	1500
	Most occupations	2200
	Very active	2500
55–75 years	Assuming a sedentary life	2050
75 and over	Assuming a sedentary life	1900

The calories required vary with the age, sex and build of the individual. In everyday practice it is best to ensure that the essential foods are supplied and then allow the appetitite to decide the remaining calories in carbohydrate foods provided the person does not become overweight, when it is the carbohydrate foods that should first be reduced.

Approximate Calories Required by Children each Day*

					Boys	*Girls*
Age, years:	0–1	1–2	2–3	3–9	9–18	9–18
Calories:	800	1200	1400	1600–2100	2500–3000	2300

The components of a normal diet are carbohydrates, proteins, fats, mineral salts and vitamins. Water is an essential to life, and 1½ pints should be taken daily, but it supplies no calorie or nutrient value.

Carbohydrate is utilized by the body for energy. If excess to immediate needs is taken in, some can be stored in the liver and muscles as glycogen and the surplus converted into fat and stored in the fat depots. Sugar is an easily absorbed carbohydrate but the body's main requirements are consumed in the form of starch, a more complex carbohydrate which is found in bread and potatoes.

Protein is used in the body for growth and repair of tissue and must be taken in regularly as it cannot be stored for use later. Excess protein can be utilized only in the same way as carbohydrate and fat after the nitrogen portion of the molecule has been removed by the liver. The waste products are then excreted by the kidneys. Protein is made up of numerous amino acids, many of which can be converted from one kind to another in the body, but ten cannot be manufactured and are termed essential amino acids. Animal sources of protein are rich in essential amino acids but in vegetable sources some of them are lacking. In a vegetarian diet a greater variety of different vegetable pro-

*Based on Report No. 120 of the Department of Health and Social Security 1969 (HMSO).

teins must be taken than if the body's requirements are supplied from animal and vegetable sources combined.

Fats are the richest heat-producing foods.

MINERAL REQUIREMENTS

The following are the principal minerals essential to health in adults and children, and for growth in children: calcium, phosphorus, iron, sodium, potassium, iodine, copper, magnesium, sulphur, and manganese. In a varied diet the only two which may not be supplied in sufficient quantities are calcium and iron.

Approximate Daily Requirements

	Adults	*Children*
Calcium	0·5 g	0·5–1·4 g
Iron	10–15 mg	6–15 mg

The richest sources of *calcium* are milk, cheese, sardines, herrings, watercress, bread and flour.

0·57 litres (1 pint) milk supplies 0·68 g

The richest sources of *iron* are liver, kidney, meat, particularly beef, egg yolk, baked beans, wholemeal bread, raisins, and watercress.

30 g (1 oz.) of beef supplies 1·1 mg of iron and 30 g (1 oz.) of wholemeal bread supplies 0·6 mg.

FOOD VALUES

100 Calorie Portions

Protein foods	g	oz	*Fat foods*	g	oz	*Carbohydrate foods*	g	oz
Streaky			Olive oil	10	$\frac{1}{3}$	Sugar	30	1
bacon	20	$\frac{2}{3}$	Butter	15	$\frac{1}{2}$	Cream crackers	20	$\frac{2}{3}$
Cheese	22	$\frac{3}{4}$	Margarine	15	$\frac{1}{2}$	Syrup	30	1
Beef (lean)	30	1	Dripping	10	$\frac{1}{3}$	Shredded		
Ham	45	$1\frac{1}{2}$	Cream	30	1	wheat (1)	30	1
Mutton	30	1				Bread	45	$1\frac{1}{2}$
1 Egg						Potatoes	120	4
Corned beef	45	$1\frac{1}{2}$				Apples	270	9
Liver	45	$1\frac{1}{2}$				Oranges	300	10
Chicken	60	2				Carrots	600	20
Herring	60	2				Milk	150	5
Kipper	60	2						
Rabbit	60	2						
Tinned salmon	75	$2\frac{1}{2}$						
Tripe	105	$3\frac{1}{2}$						
White fish	120	4						

Protein Foods—7 Gram Portions

Animal sources	g	oz.	*Vegetable sources*	g	oz.
Meat	30	1	Soya flour	15	½
Cheese	30	1	Bread (Hovis)	90	3
Poultry	30	1	Bread (white)	90	3
Bacon	30	1	Chocolate (milk)	90	3
Fish	45	1½	Beans (baked)	120	4
Milk (dried, skimmed)	22	¾	Beans (dry boiled)	105	3½
Milk (evaporated)	90	3	Peas (boiled)	150	5
Milk (fresh)	210	7	Lentils (boiled)	120	4

SPECIAL DIETS

1000 Calorie Diet. A reducing diet for those who are overweight and particularly those suffering from heart failure, hypertension and osteo-arthritis.

This diet is achieved by allowing the patient in each 24 hr:

five 100-calorie portions of protein foods	500 cal
60 g (2 oz.) only of bread	150
15 g (½ oz.) of butter	100
150 g (5 oz.) of milk	100
3 helpings of fruit (except those listed below)	150

Green vegetables and salad can be taken as much as desired.

Avoid:

Potatoes, peas, beans or beetroot
Bananas, grapes, prunes, figs or dried fruits
Sugar, pastry, cake or confectionery

Saccharin must be used for sweetening.

Unsugared fruit drinks, Marmite, Oxo and Bovril may be taken as desired.

High Calorie Diet. Designed for those who are underweight or have had a debilitating illness. A full general diet can be taken with the addition of extra milk, and milk reinforced by the addition of dried milk powder. Reinforced milk can be used in the cooking for milk puddings, creamed soup and porridge. Glucose and lactose may be added. Biscuits should be served with the mid-morning and late night drink, and mayonnaise with a sardine, salmon or cheese salad at teatime.

Low Protein Diet. Various levels of protein restriction may be ordered for patients with renal or hepatic disorders. The following constitutes 40 g of protein.

Bread is limited to 180 g (6 oz.) a day, or 150 g (5 oz.) and 1 helping of cereal.

Milk is limited to 300 g (10 oz.) a day.

One 7-g portion of protein is allowed at breakfast, lunch, and supper (see p. 422).

Fruit and vegetables may be taken freely except peas, beans, and lentils.

Butter, sugar, jam, boiled sweets, and treacle should be taken liberally to prevent breakdown of body protein for energy purposes.

High Protein Diet. Over 100 g of protein a day should be taken by patients suffering from burns, subacute nephritis and where much repair of body tissue is required. The diet should include 1 litre (2 pints) of milk and eight 7-g portions (see p. 422) of protein divided throughout the day's meals, e.g.

Breakfast	1 egg and 30 g (1 oz.) bacon
Lunch	60 g (2 oz.) meat
Tea	30 g (1 oz.) cheese or sardine
Supper	135 g (4½ oz.) fish

No restriction on the amount of bread, cake, fruit, and vegetables consumed, from all of which a portion of the day's protein requirements will be obtained. Where there is a still greater requirement of protein or where a patient is not eating well, protein supplements can be added to the milk or in the cooking. Casilan contains 90 per cent, Complan 31 per cent and skimmed milk powder 34·5 per cent of protein.

Low Fat Diet. Useful in cases of jaundice or cholecystitis and in certain malabsorption syndromes.

Skimmed milk should be used. Give white fish, lean meat, and a plentiful supply of fruit, vegetables, and green salad; honey, jam, syrup or Marmite spread on the bread. Boiled sweets and barley sugar may be taken.

Avoid the following:

- Butter, margarine, and dripping
- Fat meats, salmon, herrings, and sardines
- All fried foods
- Nuts, egg yolk, salad cream and olive oil
- Pastries, puddings, and cakes in the making of which suet, cooking fat or margarine has been used.

Low Residue or Gastric Diet. The diet for patients with ulceration or inflammation of the gastrointestinal tract is much less restrictive than formerly. The diet should consist of small helpings taken at regular intervals with a short rest before and after meals. The meal should be eaten slowly and the food well chewed. These points are considered more important than the content of the diet and within certain limits the patient can have the food he enjoys but should avoid those foods he finds disagree with him.

Fried foods are best avoided and those containing tough fibres, skins and pips, also highly seasoned foods and pickles. In the acute stages alcohol and smoking should be avoided and even later these should not be indulged in when the stomach is empty.

High Residue Diet. Suitable for those suffering from atonic constipation. The aim is to increase the bulk of the diet to stimulate peristalsis. It is recommended that a plentiful supply of the following be included in the normal diet and more refined cereals be avoided.

Wholemeal or brown bread
Wholemeal biscuits
Wholemeal flour in cooking
Oatmeal, Ryvita, and All Bran
All fruits including the peel of apples and pears
Vegetables, particularly green vegetables, salads, peas, and beans.

Low Salt Diet. This may be ordered for patients with congestive heart failure and severe hypertension where there is much tissue oedema.

(1) A moderate restriction of sodium (5 g of sodium chloride giving 1·5 g of sodium (66 mEq a day) can be achieved by:

Using no table salt, or salt in the cooking.
Avoiding all foods containing bicarbonate of soda or baking powder.
Avoiding salty foods like bacon, smoked haddock, and kippers, tinned, and frozen meat, fish and vegetables.

No chocolate or syrup allowed.

(2) A greater restriction (1·5 g of sodium chloride containing 0·5 g of sodium 22 mEq) can be achieved only by obtaining low salt bread and butter and restricting the milk and protein foods.

Gluten-free Diet. This diet is essential for all patients with coeliac disease and dermatitis herpetiformes. Medical opinion at the present time favours total exclusion of gluten throughout life. Coeliac patients are unable to absorb gluten, which is the protein present in wheat, rye, barley and possibly oats. Therefore a major dietary change is necessary; that of excluding ordinary flour from the diet.

In the initial stages of severe coeliac disease it is usual to give 2- to 3-hourly feeds of skimmed milk, Prosol (Trufood Ltd) and glucose, gradually increasing the diet by adding gluten-free cereals, fruit, animal protein and fat. When a full gluten-free diet is given Prosol can be omitted.

Certain foods are prescribed on form EC10 for coeliac patients. These are (*a*) gluten-free flour, (*b*) gluten-free bread, (*c*) gluten-free biscuits, and (*d*) gluten-free pasta. There are several manufacturers of these products. Further information may be obtained from *The Coeliac Society*, P.O. Box No. 181, London NW2 2Q7. The aim of the Society is to promote the welfare of coeliacs and to help them in as many ways as possible. Cooking with gluten-free flour is different from ordinary flour. Manufacturers of the above products supply recipes for use with their products. Further details from the *Coeliac Handbook*, edited by Bee Nilson (The Coeliac Society); also *Diets for Sick Children* by Francis and Dixon (Oxford: Blackwell Scientific).

The following is a brief guide to foods to be excluded because they contain gluten:

If there is doubt about any food it should not be eaten.

Baking powder—unless certified gluten-free.

Bread made from wheat or rye flour.

Biscuits, cakes and pastry.

Breakfast cereals—puffed wheat, Weetabix, Grapenuts, Bemax, Farex, Farley's rusks, oatmeal.

'Compound' condiments (pure pepper and pure mustard only permitted).

Drinks—Bengers, Horlicks, malted milks, Ovaltine.

Flour—wheat and rye and products made from flour such as pasta, semolina. Barley.

Meats containing 'cereal binder' or rusk, e.g. sausages, certain cooked meats.

Preserves such as mincemeat and lemon curd unless known to be gluten-free.

Sauces and soups unless guaranteed gluten-free.

Sweets—Caution with all sweets, especially unwrapped sweets and filled chocolates.

Vegetables, e.g. frozen potato croquettes.

Many manufactured foods contain gluten and the Coeliac Society's current list of cluten-free manufactured foods gives more detail. Nevertheless always check the ingredients panel.

Some foods carry this symbol which is the manufacturer's guarantee of a gluten-free food:

Cereals which do not contain gluten are:

Pure cornflour and custard powder—if guaranteed gluten-free.
Potato starch—potato flour or farina.
Rice flour.
Soya flour.
Rice Krispies, cornflakes.
Rice, sago, tapioca.

DIABETIC DIET

Protein Foods

Average helpings of the following foods may be eaten; but if the patient has to lose weight care must be taken with the foods in the left-hand column.

Cheese (not cream cheese)	Eggs	Crab meat
Grilled lean bacon	Corned beef	Bloaters
Lean ham	Boiled beef	Fish roes
Lean mutton chop	Liver	Salmon
Duck (small portion)	Chicken	Rabbit
Goose (small portion)	Grouse	Tripe
Lean roast beef	Kidneys	White fish
Lean roast lamb	Herring	Kipper
Lean roast mutton		Smoked haddock
Lean roast pork		
Sardines (drain off the oil)		

Fat Foods

Those patients who require to lose weight should avoid fried foods and take only very little, and certainly no more than the stated amount, of the following:

Butter	Dripping
Margarine	Olive oil
Cooking fat	Cream

Many mild diabetics are overweight and for them a 1000 Calorie reducing diet will be suitable, since this automatically restricts carbohydrates.

Carbohydrate (CHO) includes sugar, glucose, sweets, chocolate, jams, marmalade, syrup, sweet biscuits, cakes and pastries, sweetened minerals. In general all these should be avoided by all diabetics since they are concentrated sources of CHO. In addition, bread, potatoes, plain biscuits are moderate sources of carbohydrate and may be taken in controlled amounts.

For this purpose carbohydrate-containing foods are classified according to the amount of that food which yield one 10-g carbohydrate exchange, e.g. a diet of 150 g CHO = 15 × 10 g Carbohydrate exchanges from the following list:

Carbohydrate Foods in 10-g Portions

Cereals, etc.	g	oz.			oz.
Biscuits, plain	15	½	Milk, fresh	200 ml	7
Bread	20	⅔	Milk, evaporated	90 ml	3
Breakfast cereal	15	½	Bournvita, etc.	15 g	½
Oatmeal, dry	15	½	Cocoa powder (unsweetened)	30 g	1
Rice, semolina, tapioca, cornflour, etc.	15	½			

Vegetables

	g	oz.		g	oz.
Beans, baked	60	2	Parsnips	90	3
Beans, broad	150	5	Peas, fresh or frozen	120	4
Beans, haricot	60	2	Peas, dried	60	2
Beetroot	120	4	Potatoes	60	2
			Potato, chips	30	1

Fruits (weighed with stones and juice, but no peel)

	g	oz.		g	oz.
Apple, raw	120	4	Greengages, raw	120	4
Apple, stewed	150	5	Greengages, stewed	120	4
Apricots, fresh	180	6	Melon	210	7
Apricots, dried, stewed	60	2	Orange	120	4
			Peaches, fresh	120	4
Banana, raw	60	2	Pears, raw	120	4
Cherries, raw	120	4	Pears, stewed	150	5
Cherries, stewed	120	4	Plums, stewed	240	8
Damsons, stewed	180	6	Prunes, stewed	60	2
Gooseberries, raw, ripe	120	4	Raspberries, raw	180	6
			Strawberries, raw	180	6
Grapes	80	2⅔			

The following contain little or no carbohydrate and need not be weighed.

Vegetables	*Salads*	*Fruits*
Artichokes, green	Cucumber	Blackcurrants
Asparagus	Lettuce	Gooseberries, stewed
Beans, french	Mustard and cress	Grapefruit
Beans, runner	Radishes	Loganberries
Broccoli	Watercress	Rhubarb

Vegetables	*Beverages*	*Condiments*
Brussels sprouts	Tea	Salt
Cabbage	Coffee	Pepper
Cauliflower	Soda water	Mustard
Celery	Clear meat or chicken soup	Vinegar
Marrow	Marmite	Saccharine
Mushrooms	Oxo, Bovril	Vanilla
Onions	Diabetic squash	Lemon juice
Spinach		Salad oil
Tomatoes		

Supplements

One tablespoon of the following may be given once a day.

Artichokes (Jerusalem), cooked
Carrots, raw or cooked
Leeks, boiled
Swedes, boiled
Turnips, boiled

Emergencies

Diabetics on insulin must never stop their insulin. In sickness it may be necessary to take CHO in a simple form:

10 g ($\frac{1}{3}$oz.) 2 tsp Sugar or glucose or 3 small sugar lumps	= 10 g CHO
120 ml Fresh fruit juice	
15 ml Ribena	
60 ml Lucozade	
198 g (7oz.) Milk	

Sample of a 150-g carbohydrate diet when the patient is having soluble insulin morning and evening.

		CHO g	Exchanges
Milk for tea throughout day = ⅓ pint over and above this as indicated.		10	1
EARLY MORNING	Tea—milk from allowance		
BREAKFAST	Tea or coffee		
	Milk for cereal 100 ml (3½ oz.)	5	½
45 g or	15 g (½ oz.) cereal or porridge oats	10	1
4½ exchanges	Protein as required		
	56 g (2 oz.) bread	30	3
	Butter as required		
MID-MORNING	Milk for coffee 100 ml (3½ oz.)	5	½
10 g or	1 plain biscuit		
1 exchange			
LUNCH	56 g (2 oz.) bread for sandwich	30	3
30 g or	Meat, fish, cheese, egg as required		
3 exchanges	Tea—milk from allowance		
TEA	Tea—milk from allowance	5	½
5 g or	1 plain biscuit		
½ exchange			
EVENING MEAL	Meat, fish, egg		
	Vegetables, salad as required		
40 g or	113 g (4 oz.) potato	20	2
4 exchanges	Fruit—1 exchange	10	1
	2 cream crackers	10	1
	cheese, butter as required		
BEDTIME	Tea—milk from allowance		
10 g or	2 plain biscuits	10	1
1 exchange			
		150	15

VITAMINS

	Vitamins	Functions	Deficiency	Chemical Properties	Sources	Average Daily Requirements*
Fat-Soluble	A	For normal growth in children. To maintain a healthy condition of the skin and mucous membranes, particularly of the respiratory tract and conjunctiva. Aids night vision.	Roughened and dry skin. More liable to infection where mucous membranes in poor condition. Inability to see in dim light. Xerophthalmia leading to blindness.	Can be synthesized in the body from carotene present in coloured fruits and vegetables. May be stored in the liver.	Halibut- and cod-liver oil, liver, butter, margarine, cheese and egg yolk. Carrots, spinach, water-cress, dried apricots and tomatoes.	750 μg (Retinol equivalents) Retinol.
	D Calciferol	Necessary for the absorption and metabolism of calcium and phosphorus in the body.	Rickets. Osteomalacia. Defective deposition of enamel leading to dental caries.	Can be formed by the action of ultra-violet light on the ergosterol in the skin.	Halibut- and cod-liver oil. Fat fish. Egg yolk. Butter, margarine, cheese and milk.	2·5 μg cholecalciferol.
	E Tocopherol	Related to reproduction in rats but no conclusive evidence that it plays any part in fertility in human beings.	—	—	Wheat germ, lettuce, green leaves and milk.	—

FAT-SOLUBLE	K	Essential for the proper clotting of blood.	Deficiency only temporary due to jaundice or sterilization of the gut by chemotherapy.	Not absorbed from the gut if bile missing. Can be synthesized in the bowel.	Green plants, cabbage and green peas.	—
WATER-SOLUBLE	B COMPLEX B_1 Thiamine	To obtain a steady and continuous release of energy from carbohydrate.	Check in growth of children. Neuritis. Beri-beri.	Easily destroyed by high temperatures and baking soda.	Brewers' yeast, bacon, liver. Wholemeal and national bread. Vegetables.	1·2 mg
	B_2 Riboflavine		Checks growth. Cracks and soreness at corner of the mouth and of the tongue. Opacity of the cornea. Skin becomes rough and red. Diarrhoea and digestive upsets. Mental symptoms. Pellagra.	Little lost during normal cooking.	Yeast, dairy produce, eggs, and liver.	1·7 mg
	Nicotinic acid or niacin				Yeast, meat extracts, meat, offal. Wholemeal bread.	18 mg

*For a moderately active man (excludes infants, pregnancy, lactation). Based on Report No. 120 of the Department of Health and Social Security 1969 (HMSO).

Chemical Urine Tests

Test	Reagent	Method	Reaction +
FOR ALBUMIN			
(1) Albustix	Reagent strips	Dip the strip in urine and remove it immediately. Compare it with colour scale.	Turns green at once.
(2) Hot	Acetic acid	Heat over a methylated lamp the top of a test tube three parts full of urine, turning the tube in the fingers at the same time. When boiling add a few drops of the acid.	Urates will disappear on heating, phosphates when the acid is added. Any cloud left is due to the presence of coagulated albumin.
(3) Salicyl-sulphonic acid	Salicyl-sulphonic acid (saturated solution)	To 2 cm of the urine in a test tube add a few drops of the reagent.	An opalescent cloud.
(4) Quantitative (Esbach's)	Esbach's solution of picric acid	In the special graduated tube place urine up to the marking 'U'. Add solution to 'R'. Cork and shake thoroughly. Allow to stand in special holder for 24 hours.	The albumin will be seen as a sediment at the bottom of the tube. The graduations at the bottom give the amount of albumin in grammes per 1000 ml of urine. This divided by 10 gives the percentage.

N.B. The specific gravity must be 1008. Dilute if necessary

Test	Reagent	Method	Reaction +
FOR PROTEIN AND GLUCOSE			
Uristix	Reagent strip	Dip in urine and remove.	Protein portion turns green. Glucose portion turns purple, within 10 seconds.

Test	Reagent	Method	Reaction +
FOR BLOOD			
Hemastix	Reagent strips	Dip in urine and remove. Compare with colour chart.	Turns blue in 30 sec.
Microscopic examination			
FOR GLUCOSE			
(1) Clinistix	Reagent strips	Dip the test end of Clinistix in urine and remove.	Turns purple in 10 seconds.
N.B. If positive, use Clinitest to determine concentration of glucose.			
(2) Clinitest	Reagent tablets. These deteriorate with moisture and must not be used if blue in colour	1. With dropper provided, place 5 drops of urine in test tube. Rinse dropper, add 10 drops of water. 2. Drop in 1 tablet and watch reaction. 3. Do not shake till 15 sec after reaction ceases.	Colour change from blue green to orange. Compare with colour chart provided. If, during the test, a bright orange colour appears and then changes to brown, more than 2 per cent of sugar is present.
(3) Benedict's	Benedict's solution (copper sulphate)	Place 5 ml of the solution in a test tube. Add 8 to 10 drops of urine with a pipette and boil for 2 min. at least.	Any change of colour within 15 minutes. This varies from a greenish - yellow to a deep orange precipitate.

APPENDIX 12

LIST OF NORMAL VALUES

Blood

Blood Count

Red cells: men 4 500 000–6 500 000 per mm^3
women 3 900 000–5 600 000 per mm^3

White cells 4000–10 000 per mm^3

Differential white count (adults)

Neutrophils	3000–6000 per mm^3 or 50–70 per cent
Eosinophils	50–300 per mm^3 or 0·5–3 per cent
Basophils	0–75 per mm^3 or 0–1 per cent
Lymphocytes	1000–3000 per mm^3 or 20–30 per cent
Monocytes	300–600 per mm^3 or 3–10 per cent

Platelets: 250 000–500 000 per mm^3

Reticulocytes: 0·5 to 1·5 per cent of red blood cells

Haemoglobin: men 14 to 17 g per 100 ml (95–115 per cent Haldane)
women 12 to 15·5 g per 100 ml (82–105 per cent Haldane)

Colour index: 0·9 to 1·1

Bleeding time: 2 to 5 min

Clotting or coagulation time: 3 min (Dale & Laidlaw method)
4 to 10 min (White method)

Packed cell volume (haematocrit value)
men 40 to 54 per cent
women 36 to 47 per cent

Sedimentation rate (Westergren):
men 2 to 5 mm in 1 hr
women and children 4 to 7 mm in 1 hr

Blood Chemistry

	per unit of plasma or serum	milliequivalents per litre (mEq/l)
Amylase	3 to 10 Wohlgemuth units/ml	

	per unit of plasma of serum	milliequivalents per litre (mEq/l)
Bicarbonate (alkali reserve)	53–77mg/100 ml	24–34
Bilirubin	0·1–0·5 mg/100 ml	
Calcium	9–11 mg/100 ml	4·5–5·5
Chloride	560–620 mg/100 ml	96–106
Cholesterol	200–300 mg/100 ml	
Fibrinogen	200–400 mg/100 ml	
Glucose (fasting)	80–120 mg/100 ml	
Phosphatase acid	1–3 King Armstrong units/100 ml	
Phosphatase alkaline	3–13 King Armstrong units/100 ml	
Potassium	15–22 mg/100 ml	3·9–5·6
Proteins, total	5·6–8·5 g/100 ml	
albumin	4–6·7 g/100 ml	
globulin	1·2–2·9 g/100 ml	
Protein-bound iodine	4·0–7·5 μg/100 ml	
Sodium	315–350 mg/100 ml	137–152
Transaminase		
glutamic oxaloacetic	< 40 units/ml	
glutamic pyruvic	< 30 units/ml	
Urea	15–40 mg/100 ml	
Uric acid	1–5 mg/100 ml	

Cerebrospinal Fluid

Pressure	60–150 mm (in horizontal position)
Cells	1–3 lymphocytes/mm
Chlorides (as sodium chloride)	700–760 mg/100 ml
Protein (total)	20–40 mg/100 ml
Sugar	45–100 mg/100 ml
Urea	10–40 mg/100 ml

Urine

Volume	1000–1800 ml in 24 hours
Specific gravity	1010–1025
Total solids	4–7 g in 100 ml (55–70 g in 24 hr)
Urea	1·0–2·5 g in 100 ml (15–35 g in 24 hr)
Chlorides	0·3–1·5 g in 100 ml (5–15 g in 24 hr)

Appendix 13

AVERAGE HEIGHTS AND WEIGHTS

Children from Birth to Eighteen Years

Boys Height (in.)	Boys Weight kg	Boys Weight lb.	Age (years)	Girls Height (in.)	Girls Weight kg	Girls Weight lb.
20	3·4	7½	Birth	19½	3·2	7¼
29½	9·9	22	1	29	9·5	21
34	12·2	27	2	34	11·7	26
37	14·0	31	3	36	13·1	29
39	15·4	34	4	40	15·8	35
42	17·6	39	5	43	18·5	41
44	19·9	44	6	65	20·4	45
46	21·7	48	7	47	22·6	50
48	24·0	53	8	49	24·9	55
50	27·6	61	9	51	27·6	61
52	30·3	67	10	53	30·8	68
55	33·1	73	11	55	33·5	74
56	34·9	77	12	57	37·1	82
58	38·5	85	13	60	43·9	97
62	43·9	97	14	62	45·8	101
64	50·8	112	15	63	50·8	112
67	56·6	125	16	63½	53·0	117
68	59·8	132	17	63¾	54·4	120
69	67·1	148	18	64	54·8	121

The above figures are only a guide, and nurses and parents should realize that for each age group there may be variations. The normal range of variations is 3 in. above and below the figure given for 2-year-olds and as much as 7 in. for 12-year-olds. Weight may vary by 2 kg (4 lb.) at 2 years and 12·5 kg (28 lb.) at 12 years. Provided that the child who is above average weight is also above average height there is no cause for anxiety.

Men				Women	
Weight		Height		Weight	
kg	lb.	(ft.	in.)	kg	lb.
		4	11	45–50	98–110
		5	0	46–51	101–113
		5	1	47–53	104–116
54–59	118–129	5	2	48–54	107–119
55–60	121–133	5	3	50–55	110–122
56–62	124–136	5	4	51–57	113–126
58–63	127–139	5	5	53–59	116–130
59–65	130–143	5	6	54–61	120–135
61–67	134–147	5	7	56–63	124–139
63–69	138–152	5	8	58–65	128–143
64–70	142–156	5	9	60–67	132–147
66–72	146–160	5	10	62–68	136–151
68–75	150–165	5	11	63–70	140–155
70–77	154–170	6	0	65–72	144–159
72–79	158–175	6	1		
73–81	162–180	6	2		

The above figures are of the ideal weight for men and women of 25 years and over according to height (in ordinary clothes and shoes). The figures are for men and women of medium frame. A large-framed person may add 3·5 to 4·5 kg (8 to 10 lb.) to the above figures.

A person who is overweight and reducing is advised to aim at the figure for a large-framed person.

Between 25 and 55 years the average increase in weight for men in Great Britain is 3·5 to 4·05 kg (8 to 9 lb.) and for women 6·5 to 8 kg (14 to 18 lb.). Ideally this weight gain should not occur.

APPENDIX 14

COMPARATIVE WEIGHTS AND MEASURES

Measures of Length

1 kilometre (km)	=	1000 metres	=	1093·63 yards
1 metre (m)	=	1000 millimetres	=	39·37 inches
1 millimetre (mm)	=	1000 micrometres (μm)	=	0·0394 inch
1 mile	=	1·6 kilometres	=	1760 yards
1 yard	=	36 inches	=	914 millimetres
1 inch	=	25·4 millimetres		

Measure of Capacity

1 litre (l)	=	1000 millimetres	=	1·76 pints
1 millilitre (ml)	=		=	16·89 minims
1 gallon	=	8 pints	=	4·55 litres
1 pint	=	20 fluid ounces	=	568·37 millilitres
1 fluid ounce	=	8 fluid drachms	=	28·42 millilitres
1 fluid drachm	=	60 minims	=	3·55 millilitres
1 minim			=	0·059 millilitre

Measures of Weight

1 kilogram (kg)	=	1000 grams	=	35·27 ounces (2·2 pounds)
1 gram (g)*	=	1000 milligrams	=	15·43 grains
1 milligram (mg)	=	1000 micrograms	=	0·015 grains
1 ton	=	20 hundredweight	=	1016 kilograms
1 hundredweight	=	112 pounds	=	51 kilograms
1 pound	=	16 ounces	=	453·6 grams
1 ounce	=	437 grains	=	28·35 grams
1 grain			=	64·8 milligrams

* In prescriptions the abbreviation G for gram should be used to avoid confusion with grain (gr.).

Appendix 15

COMPARATIVE TEMPERATURES

Degrees

Celsius °C		*Fahrenheit* °F	*Celsius* °C		*Fahrenheit* °F
100	Boiling	212	38·5		101·3
	point		38		100·4
95		203	37·5		99·5
90		194	37		98·6
85		185	36·5		97·7
80		176	36		96·8
75		167	35·5		95·9
70		158	35		95
65		149	34		93·2
60		140	33		91·4
55		131	32		89·6
50		122	31		87·8
45		113	30		86
44		112·2	25		77
43		109·4	20		68
42		107·6	15		59
41		105·8	10		50
40		104	5		41
39·15		103·1	0	Freezing	32
39		102·2		point	

To convert readings of the Fahrenheit scale into Celsius degrees subtract 32, multiply by 5, and divide by 9, as follows: $98-32=66\times 5=330\div 9=36{\cdot}6$. Therefore 98° F=36·6°C.

To convert readings of the Celsius scale into Fahrenheit degrees multiply by 9, divide by 5, and add 32, as follows: $36{\cdot}6\times 9=330\div 5=66+32=98$. Therefore 36·6°C=98°F.

The term 'Celsius' (from the name of the Swede who invented the scale in 1742) is now being internationally used instead of 'Centigrade', which term is employed in some countries to denote fractions of an angle.

Appendix 16

LEGAL ASPECTS OF NURSING

The aim of this short appendix is to bring to the awareness of the nurse some legal aspects of nursing. Every student and nurse will do well to think seriously about the following points and to exert the utmost care both in carrying out all nursing procedures and in dealing with patients and their relatives since neglect may cause great distress to her patients and their families and damage the good name of the hospital. Carelessness or negligence may lead to an action in court and heavy damages could be awarded against the nurse or the hospital authority. A student nurse having a particular legal problem is advised to consult her matron or the senior administrative officer of the hospital. A trained nurse who is a member of her professional organization, the Royal College of Nursing and National Council of Nurses of the United Kingdom (the Rcn), should without delay consult its legal department whether she is working in a hospital or in the community. Fully paid membership entitles her to free advice and representation at any inquiry or inquest, and the indemnity insurance will protect her should costs or damages be awarded against her.

Consent for Operation

A patient coming into hospital still retains his rights as a citizen and his entry only denotes his willingness to undergo an investigation or a course of treatment. Any investigation or treatment of a serious nature, or an operation in which an anaesthetic is used requires the written consent of the patient. A patient may give his own consent if he is of full age, i.e. has attained the age of 18 years, or is a minor who has attained the age of 16 years.

No one should be asked to sign an operation consent form before the nurse has ascertained that the patient fully understands the nature of the procedures likely to be involved. The proposed operation is described on the consent form in general terms only, leaving the exact extent of the surgery to the discretion of the surgeon, but a patient has the right to refuse surgery going beyond the extent to which he has agreed to submit. If he does so, or wishes further explanation, the nurse should refer the question to the surgeon before getting the form signed.

If a patient makes any reservations or conditions—even by word of mouth—when signing, the surgeon must be informed.

For patients under 16 years of age in England and Wales and for minors in Scotland (12 years for a girl and 14 years for a boy) the consent of the parent or guardian is normally obtained. In the event of any difficulty, the ward sister should inform the surgeon and the senior administrative officer. This also applies in those cases where the patient is unfit to give consent and no relative is available.

Correct Identity

The nurse or the midwife has the grave responsibility to make sure that all babies born in hospital are correctly labelled at birth and to ensure that at no time are they placed in the wrong cot or handed to the wrong patient.

An unconscious patient admitted as a casualty must be labelled as soon as his identity is known. In busy departments labelling may apply to all cases.

Every patient, before being given premedication for an operation, should be labelled in the manner approved by the hospital. The label will state the patient's name and hospital number. Moreover, a written request stating the same details should be brought to the ward by the theatre porters to ensure that the correct patient is taken to the right theatre. In the theatre it is the anaesthetist and surgeon's responsibility to see that they have received the proper patient and that the correct operation is carried out. It is not the nurses' duty to indicate the exact area of operation, which digit or whether the left or right side is to be operated on. But the ward sister or her deputy may be responsible for making sure that, before the patient is sent to the theatre, the medical staff have indicated clearly the site of operation, and for reporting to the surgeon if this has not been done.

In the Theatre

During operations the 'scrubbed' nurse must check the number of all instruments, needles, swabs and packs on her trolleys and as the operation proceeds, check that each item used is returned to her. She will then have to carry out a final check before the body cavity is closed. If any doubt arises she must inform the surgeon, who should delay his final closure until a recount has taken place. At the conclusion the theatre nurse in charge and the surgeon sign the operation register stating that a final count was obtained.

Drugs

The legal requirements for the nurse in regard to the storage and administration of drugs are set out in Appendix 8.

Accidents or Injury

Should a patient sustain an injury while in hospital he may bring an action against the hospital authority or against the person to whom he attributes the injury—this may be a member of the medical, nursing, or ancillary staff. The hospital has a certain degree of responsibility for the actions of its staff, but a member of the staff who has been negligent or incompetent and has so caused loss or injury to a patient may be found guilty of culpable negligence and damages will then be awarded against her personally. In the case of a student nurse it may have to be shown that she has received proper instruction in the procedure undertaken, for example, where a burn has been received from an unprotected hot water bottle.

Accidents could arise to visitors or employees of the hospital through negligence in such matters as cleaning equipment placed on stairways, polish or grease left on the floor, faulty electrical equipment, or torn furnishings. Hospital staff should constantly be alert to the risks entailed and bring them to the notice of the persons concerned or the proper authority. In the case of a pure accident where no negligence or incompetence is involved there is no liability at law.

An action may be brought against the hospital several years after the accident has occurred. It is therefore necessary that at the time of the incident an accurate and full record should be made on the special form provided. This form will contain a complete factual statement of how the accident occurred, of the kind of steps taken, e.g. whether or not X-rays were made, and will list the names of witnesses and of the medical officer called to carry out an examination.

Self-discharge of Patient

When a patient demands to discharge himself the nurse on duty should try to dissuade him and inform the medical officer concerned with his care. If the patient is adamant, each hospital will follow its own procedure. It is probable that a senior administrative officer will see the patient and ask him to sign a written statement to the effect that he is discharging himself against medical advice. Should he refuse to sign, a note to this effect will have to be made and signed by two witnesses, one of whom is usually the administrative officer concerned and the other the nurse in charge at the time. The patient must be allowed to leave except in the case of a mentally disordered patient who is subject to a restriction order, or where it is felt he may be a danger to himself or others, when he may be detained for three days to enable an order to be obtained.

Mentally Disordered Patients

The proper care and treatment of these patients which includes those with *mental illness, subnormality, severe subnormality* and *psychopathic disorder*, and the safeguarding of their property and affairs is laid down in the *Mental Health Act, 1959*, and the rules made thereunder. Most of these patients are now admitted without legal formality (*informal admission*) provided that they are not unwilling to enter hospital. They may leave when they wish unless detained for three days.

A person may only be liable to detention in hospital or guardianship under the Act if he is suffering from one of the *named* forms of disorder and if, for his own health or safety or for the protection of others, he needs restraint or control.

Unless subject to a Court Order, subnormal or psychopathic patients can only first be made subject to detention or guardianship before 21 years. This ceases at 25 years unless a report has been furnished by the responsible medical officer that they would be likely to act in a manner dangerous to themselves or others. Except in criminal cases and subject to the aforesaid, detention in hospital or guardianship is for two consecutive periods of 1 year and then for 2 yearly periods. Renewal of authority in each instance is on report by the responsible medical officer that continuance of the detention or guardianship is necessary for the patient's own health or safety or for the protection of others.

Professional Confidence

Guarding the confidences of the patient is an ethical duty of the medical and nursing professions and nurses must take care never to discuss personal information received by nature of their position, except with senior members of the staff when the knowledge may help in the patient's treatment. Even then it will in many cases be wise to ask the patient's permission to pass on the relevant information. No confidential information should be divulged to relatives or friends, nor should details of the patient's condition be passed on to his employer as this may cause loss to the patient for which the nurse may be legally liable. This does not mean that near relatives should not be informed of the patient's progress; but discretion must be exercised.

Patient's Property

The Department of Health and Social Security requires all hospitals under its care to inform patients that the hospital cannot accept responsibility for valuables or money unless these have been handed over for safe keeping. Where it is known that a patient has an excess of money he should be invited to hand it

APPENDIX 17

PROFESSIONAL ORGANIZATIONS AND STATUTORY BODIES

The Royal College of Nursing and National Council of Nurses of the United Kingdom

Known as the Rcn, this is the professional organization for all registered nurses in Great Britain and Northern Ireland. It was formed in 1963 by the amalgamation of the Royal College of Nursing with the National Council of Nurses. The headquarters are in London with the National Board for Scotland in Edinburgh, for Northern Ireland in Belfast and for Wales in Cardiff. There are over 200 branches throughout the country. The Rcn Council consisting of forty elected members is the governing body.

The Rcn Institute of Advanced Nursing Education (in London and Birmingham) prepares trained nurses for positions particularly in nurse administration and teaching. It is recognized by the Department of Education and Science as a major establishment for further education and as an examining and certificate-granting body. Also, it administers an extensive research programme sponsored by the Department of Health and Social Security.

The Professional Nursing Department includes the work of the specialist groups and the professional sections; Ward and Departmental, Tutor, Student, Psychiatric, Nurse Administrators, Enrolled Nurses, Private Nurses, Occupational Health and Community Health. Help with personal problems is given to nurses, whether or not they are Rcn members, by the Rcn Welfare Advisory Service for Nurses.

The International Department deals with work at the international level as a result of the Rcn membership of the International Council of Nurses (ICN) and the Western European Group of National Nurses Associations (GNOE). It advises and arranges programmes for overseas visitors to this country and for Rcn members visiting overseas countries to work or study.

The Labour Relations Department is concerned with salaries and conditions of service (the Rcn is a nationally recognized negotiating body). It advises members with regard to employment problems, represents members at enquiries and appeals and handles cases covered by the Indemnity Insurance Schemes.

The Library of Nursing is a professional library of over 20 000 volumes, from which books may be borrowed in person or by post. It can always obtain any book, not in its own stock, that may be required. Also, it takes 200 periodicals from Britain and overseas, the main articles from these being indexed.

Rcn Student Section

The Student Nurses' Association (S.N.A.) has been reformed as the Student Section within the Rcn with an annually elected student committee of twenty-four members. The section includes nurses in training for the Register and the Roll from general, psychiatric, paediatric, ophthalmic and the Forces Training Schools. The Rcn allows special subscription rates for the first 3 years of full membership upon qualification.

Rcn Student Units are formed within hospitals and these organize professional and social meetings and arrange interchange visits with other local units. Student nurses are welcome and have their own programme at the International Council of Nurses Congress held every four years.

Student members are affiliated to the National Union of Students (N.U.S.) which is a federation of student unions from over 300 universities and colleges. This affiliation gives opportunities for contact with students from other disciplines. All members receive an N.U.S. identity card which entitles them to financial concessions including cheaper travel and holidays, full details of which can be obtained from the Unit Secretary or Student Section of the Rcn.

Society of Registered Male Nurses

The Society was formed to provide a professional organization for registered male nurses, and associate membership is granted to student male nurses. The aim of the society is the improvement of conditions of service and protection of the interests of male nurses. It aims also at promoting good will amongst colleagues and co-operation with allied associations. It encourages the educational and social activities of its members.

General Nursing Council for England and Wales

Usually referred to as the General Nursing Council (G.N.C.), it is the statutory body set up following the Nurses Registration Act of 1919. It is concerned with the training and registration of nurses. The same functions are fulfilled in Scotland by the General Nursing Council for Scotland and in Northern Ireland by the Joint Nursing and Midwives Council for Northern Ireland.

The General Nursing Council inspects and approves nurse

forms the Educational Division, aimed at improving nursing service by the furthering of nursing education. It has established a centre of information on educational opportunities in nursing in all countries. The Foundation arranges study programmes, research projects and advises individual nurses on nursing education.

King Edward's Hospital Fund for London

This fund was founded by King Edward VII for the support, benefit or extension of the hospitals of London. It makes grants to hospitals and convalescent homes serving the London area. It maintains the Hospital Centre for the dissemination of knowledge and improvements in design of hospital equipment. It has an extensive information and advisory service. The premises include a large reference library, a lecture hall, discussion rooms and a display area for hospital equipment.

The King Edward's Hospital Fund provides staff colleges for residential courses in preparation for senior positions in hospital. It also provides the Emergency Bed Service which in the London metropolitan regions aids doctors seeking a hospital bed for an acute case.

Nuffield Foundation

The aim of the Nuffield Foundation is the advancement of health and the prevention and relief of disease by means of research and education. It provides research grants and scholarships and supports research projects.

The aim of the Nuffield Provincial Hospitals Trust is to improve the organization and the efficiency of hospital, medical and health services in the provinces. It finances the Nuffield Centre for Hospital and Health Service Studies of the University of Leeds. The centre provides residential courses in hospital administration and supports research.

Whitley Councils for the Health Services (Great Britain)

The Whitley Councils are the national organizations set up to negotiate salaries and conditions of service for persons engaged in the National Health Service. It consists of a General Council that deals with matters common to all personnel, such as travelling and subsistence allowance, and of nine functional councils which deal with remuneration and conditions of service applying to a particular group. These comprise:

The Administrative and Clerical Staffs Council
The Ancillary Staffs Council
The Dental Whitley Council (Local Authorities)

SURGICAL I

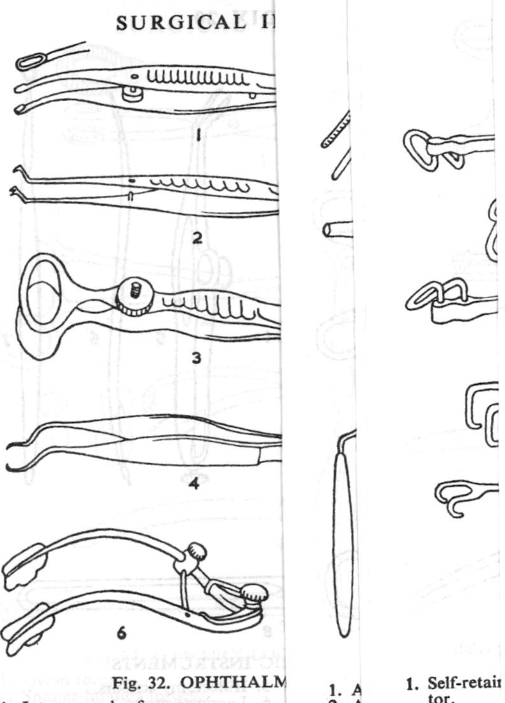

Fig. 32. OPHTHALM

1. Intra-capsular forceps.
2. Corneo-scleral disc forceps.
3. Entropium forceps.
4. Iridectomy forceps.

1. A
2. A
3. H
4. N

1. Self-retai tor.
2. Abdomin

DE

St.A.A
St.J.A
St.J.A
S.C.M
S.E.N
S.N.A
S.R.N
S.S.St

W.H.
W.P.I
W.R.
V.A.I

A

DEGREES, DIPLOM

A.D.M.S.	Assistan
A.M.I.A.	Associat Social
A.R.R.C.	Associat
A.S.H.M.	Associat
A.S.M.	Associat
B.A.	Bachelo
B.A.O.	Bachelo
B.C., B.Ch., B.Chir.	Bachelo
B.Ch.D., B.D.S.	Bachelo
B.D.A.	British
B.M.	Bachelo
B.M.A.	British
B.P.	British
B.R.C.S.	British
B.S.	Bachelo
B.Sc.	Bachelo
Ch.B.	Bachel
C.C.D.	Central
C.C.H.E.	Central
C.M., Ch.M.	Master
C.M.B.	Centra
C.N.N.	Certific
C.P.H.	Certific
C.S.P.	Charte
C.U.	Casual
D.A.	Diplor
D.Ch.	Docto
D.C.H.	Diplor
D.C.P.	Diplor
D.D.A.	Dange
D.D.M.S.	Deput
D.D.S.	Docto
D.Hyg.	Docto
D.I.H.	Diplo
D.M.	Docto
D.N.	Diplo

The Medical and (Hospital) Dental Whitley Council
The Nurses and Midwives Council
The Optical Council
The Pharmaceutical Council
The Professional and Technical Staffs Council A and Council B.

Each council has a management side and a staff side. In the case of the Nurses and Midwives Council the members of the management side are appointed by the Ministry of Health, regional boards and employing authorities. The staff side represents the employees, and the members are appointed by the participating organizations such as the Royal College of Nursing, Royal College of Midwives and National Unions of which nurses and midwives are members.

458 A

The Welsh Board, Ty
Cardiff CF4 4XZ.
Royal National Institute f
London W1. Tel.
Royal National Institute
WC1. Tel. 01-437
Royal National Pension
Buckingham Stree
01-839 6785
Society for Registered M
ham, Lancs. Tel.
United Nursing Services
Secretary 01-470 1
Women's Royal Volunta
W1. Tel. 01-499 6

462

M.S.
M.S.
M.S.
M.S.
M.Sc.
M.T.
N.A.
N.A.
N.A.
N.H.
N.H.
N.N.
O.N.
P.M.
P.S.V
Ph.D
Q.A.
Q.A.
Q.H.
Q.H.
Q.H.
Q.I.
R.A.
R.A.
R.C.
Rcn
R.F.
R.G.
R.H.
R.M
R.M
R.N
R.N
R.N
R.N
R.R
R.S.

466

1. Aneurys
2. Probe.
3. Towel cl
4. Suture p

47

1.
2.
3.

474 APPE

3

4

6

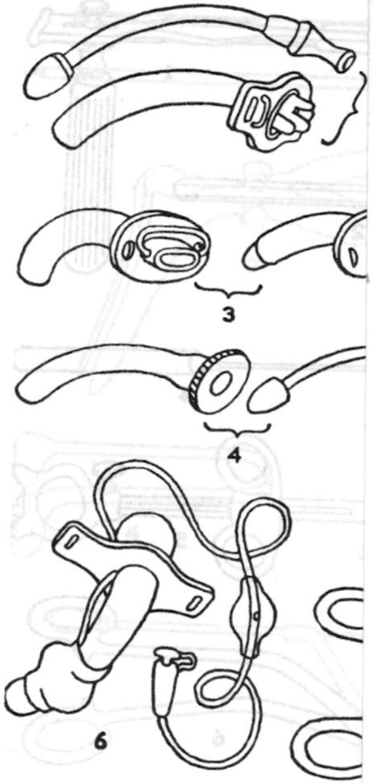

Fig. 31. TRACHE

1. Chevalier Jackson tube and introducer.
2. Rubber or plastic tube.
3. Laryngostomy tube and introducer.
4. Negus tube and introducer.

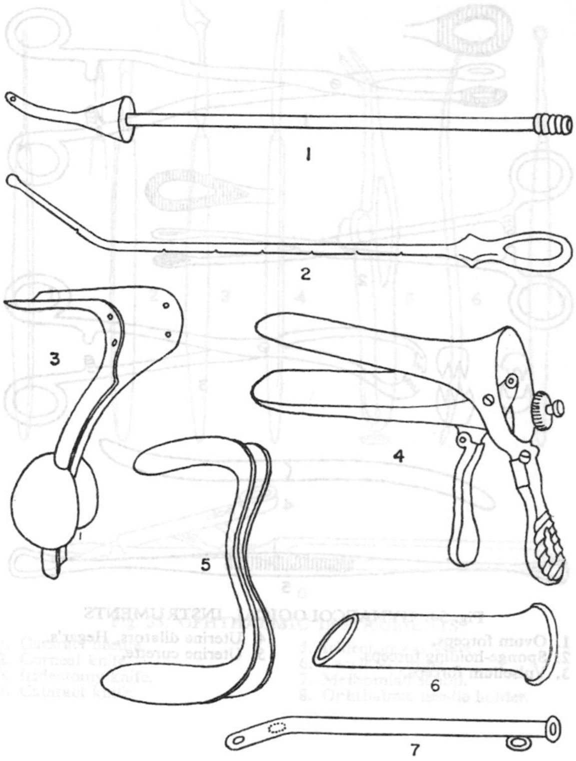

478 APPENDIX 20

Fig. 35. GYNAECOLOGICAL INSTRUMENTS

1. Intrauterine cannula.
2. Uterine sound.
3. Vaginal speculum, Auvard's.
4. Vaginal speculum, Cusco's.
5. Vaginal speculum, Sims's.
6. Vaginal speculum, Fergusson's.
7. Female silver catheter.

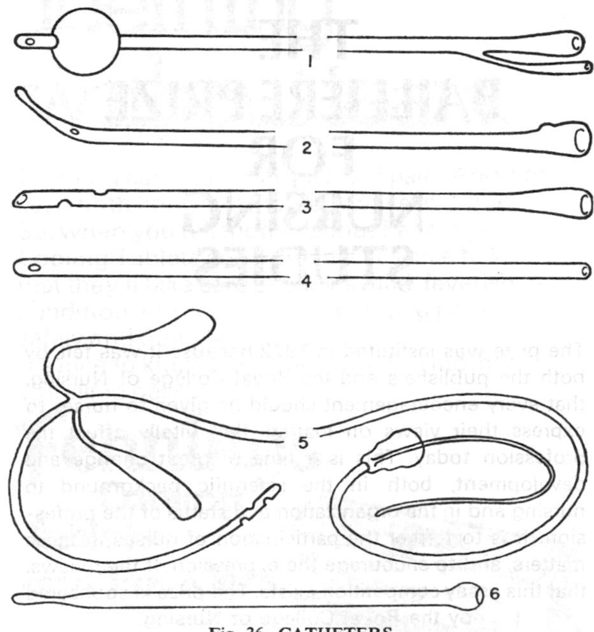

Fig. 36. CATHETERS

1. Foley's.
2. Tiemann's.
3. Whistle tip.
4. Straight.
5. Gibbon's.
6. Bougie.

See over

For the Advanced Student

NURSES' AIDS SERIES SPECIAL INTEREST TEXTS

Special Interest Texts will enable the student nurse to study a particular subject in greater detail during training or after basic studies have been completed.

Gastroenterological Nursing/ Gribble *1977 • 1st edn.*

Neuromedical & Neurosurgical Nursing/Purchese *1977 • 1st edn.*

Baillière's Medical Transparencies

* A visual reference library for lecturers and students.

*Of special interest to Nurses and Nurse Tutors are 'BMT 1', on the Anatomy of the Head, Neck and Limbs and 'BMT 2', on the Anatomy of the Thorax and Abdomen. Each set illustrates the major anatomical features of the regions with 21 and 18 slides in full colour. Other sets of interest to nurses specializing in these topics are **Paediatrics** 'BMT 17' and **Venereal Diseases** 'BMT 9' together with **Other Sexually Transmitted Diseases** 'BMT 19'. 24 slides in each set.